SOCIOLOGY
Concepts and Characteristics
FOURTH EDITION

Judson R. Landis
California State University, Sacramento

Wadsworth Publishing Company
Belmont, California

A Division of Wadsworth, Inc.

Sociology Editor: Curt Peoples
Editorial/Production Services: Phoenix Publishing Services

Printed in the United States of America
1 2 3 4 5 6 7 8 9 10—84 83 82 81 80

Photo Credits

Chapter 1   © Bernard Pierre Wolff / Magnum Photos, Inc.
Chapter 2   © Abigail Heyman / Magnum Photos, Inc.
Chapter 3   © Richard Kalvar / Magnum Photos, Inc.
Chapter 4   © Cary Wolinsky / Stock, Boston
Chapter 5   © Robert Eckert / EKM-Nepenthe
Chapter 6   Richard Kalvar / © Magnum Photos, Inc.
Chapter 7   Earl Dotter / Magnum Photos, Inc.
Chapter 8   Charles Harbutt / © Magnum Photos, Inc.
Chapter 9   Jean-Claude Lejeune / Stock, Boston
Chapter 10   Elliott Erwitt / © Magnum Photos, Inc.
Chapter 11   Gilles Peress / © Magnum Photos, Inc.
Chapter 12   © Alex Webb / Magnum Photos, Inc.

Library of Congress Cataloging in Publication Data
   Landis, Judson R
      Sociology: concepts and characteristics.

      Bibliography: p.
      Includes index.
      1. Sociology. I. Title
      HM51.L255   1980   301   79–23485
      ISBN 0–534–00784–8

Contents

3   Norms, Roles, Culture   59

PART II   Social Organization   91

4   Groups   93

Preface

The purposes of a first course in a discipline usually are several—to introduce an area of study, to communicate its unique perspective or way of looking at the world, and to offer the promise of secrets yet to be discovered—all in the hope that interested students will come back for more (maybe even thirty units more). That there are many different views of the best way to achieve these ambitions is apparent in sociology from some of the introductory textbooks available.

Many books provide an encyclopedic analysis of what a discipline is and does—all its tools, techniques, and substantive areas. I have decided not to try to do that in this book. It seems to me that a feeling for an area of study and its unique perspective may be gained by sampling the concepts of that field. Concepts are the building blocks—the language—of most disciplines. Once one has this language, the rest comes more easily and makes more sense. This book approaches the task of helping students develop a general understanding of the sociological perspective by focusing on the basic concepts of sociology. Through examining several substantive areas and the research connected with them, students can begin to see how the concepts contribute to sociological analysis.

At the end of most of the chapters I have included readings to further illustrate the chapter's concepts. These readings are drawn from a variety of sources. Included are descriptions of research and excerpts from novels, autobiographies, and nonfiction works. Some of the selections were written by professional social scientists; some were not. For example, writings of both Helen Keller and Malcolm X are used to illustrate socialization and development of self. In addition, there are selections by David Halberstam on the workings of power, Alvin Toffler on social change, Stanley Milgram on the conditions of obedience to authority, Dee Brown on the history of the American Indian, and Jerzy Kosinski on reactions to deviants. The readings, I think, illustrate the concepts and ideas in an interesting and unusual way.

A number of changes have been made in this edition. All the chapters have been revised, some slightly, some much more so. All statistical information has been updated to the most recent available. New sections have been added on poverty and social welfare (Chapter 5) and on the elderly (Chapter 6). The discussion of social theory now appears in Chapter 1. A number of illustrative boxes and introductions to topics have been added. Five of the thirty-three readings are new to this edition.

Many people have helped me with ideas and criticism (although they may now refuse to admit it): colleagues Louise Kanter, Carole Barnes, Pat McGillivray, Dean Dorn, David Lee, Worth Summers, Ivy Lee, Andres Rendon, Ayad Al-Qazzaz, Robi Chakravorti, Frank Darknell, Linda Fritschner, and Rodney Kingsnorth. Reviewers Elaine Lindgren, Joan Newcomb, Julia Petry, William Powers, Kathy Schomaker, and Dale Strick were also most helpful. I'd also like to thank secretary Lois Hill; the people at Wadsworth—Curt Peoples, Peggy Meehan, and Sandy Craig; and especially Judy Chaffin at Phoenix Publishing Services, who badgered and wheedled at me to get it right. They *all* deserve a share of the royalties (but won't get it).

This is dedicated to Sheron, who criticized and encouraged, and to young Jeffrey, Brian, and Kevin who hindered constantly (but were patient with me).

1 Introduction: Knowledge, Science, and Sociology

The purpose of this book is to acquaint you with a field of study called *sociology.* Generally speaking, sociology is the study of human society; it is the study of social behavior and the interaction of people in groups. Sociologists study various aspects of social life, including behavior in large organizations and small groups, deviant behavior, the characteristics of political and religious institutions and social movements, social psychological explanations for behavior, and so on. It would be tempting at this point to leap straight into a discussion of such topics as prostitutes working for big business; parents seeing differences in behavior and temperament between newborn babies when no differences exist; who really runs the country—elected officials or a wealthy elite that has never been elected to anything; and whether, if you were told to, you would give a painful and perhaps fatal electric shock to someone.

But perhaps we should delay these topics for a few pages while we approach a more basic question: Why is there such a thing as sociology anyway? For ages people have been fascinated about their own existence, and they have persistently tried to find out more about themselves and the world in which they live. Their attempts have occasionally been bumbling and crude, but this has not discouraged them. Slowly but surely a body of knowledge has accumulated. This knowledge has come through several means, one of which is science. Science has developed to the extent that we speak now of categories of science: the physical sciences, the biological sciences, and the social sciences. The common denominator of these various areas of study is their commitment to the scientific method as the appropriate way to gain knowledge. Sociology, as one of the social sciences, has its own particular perspectives, techniques, and theories, that it uses to gain knowledge about human behavior. In this chapter, I want to expand on the relationship among these three concepts: knowledge, science, and sociology.

Knowledge

Early attempts at gaining knowledge were sometimes very primitive, sometimes amazingly sophisticated. In the late Neolithic period (around 1900 B.C.) the Beaker people began building Stonehenge, a structure of posts, mounds, holes, and stones on the Salisbury plain southwest of London. Some of the stones they used were huge, up to thirty feet long and fifty tons in weight. The stones were placed in holes on end in an intricate pattern of circles and alleys. It took the Beaker people and the Wessex people who continued the work some 300 years to complete what amounted to a giant calendar, a sort of Stone Age computer. The stones were set up so that sighting through cracks between stones would show sunrise, sunset, moonrise, and moonset on certain important days (for example, midsummer day, midwinter day, first day of summer, first day of winter). Other sightings allowed the Wessex people to predict eclipses of the moon.

Why was this elaborate structure built? As a calendar it was useful to tell the proper time for planting and harvesting of crops. It probably also proved helpful to the priest or chief. He could amaze and impress others with his apparent power to make the sun and moon rise and set where he wanted them to. And possibly Stonehenge was built just because the Beaker and Wessex people were curious and wanted to see if it could be done.

Aside from the enormous physical work involved, the builders of Stonehenge had to collect and correlate information on numerous factors—harvest and planting times, times of sunrise and sunset, phases of the moon. They also had to pass this information on from generation to generation. Archeologists who have studied Stonehenge tell us that what looks like a single monument is actually several. The first structure didn't work as well as the builders wanted, and a second model was built over the first. It likewise needed improvement, and a third was constructed.

Unlike most primitive structures, Stonehenge lasted to modern times. The stones weathered and some fell from their positions. Others were taken by farmers for stone fences. But much of the structure remains intact. Its presence and purpose have confounded people for years, although some who have studied it are convinced that its purpose had something to do with positions of the sun and moon. Ironically, the true complexity of Stonehenge did not come to light until 1961 when an astronomy professor named Hawkins fed the positions and relationships of the stones, posts, and holes into a computer for analysis. Then modern people learned what it was that the Beaker and Wessex people learned 3,500 years earlier.[1]

In the late 1600s some chemists, faced with perplexing problems in explaining what happens when substances are heated or burned, came up with the theory of phlogiston. The theory stated that phlogiston is an invisible substance that exists in all combustible bodies and is released during combustion (burning). Substances rich in phlogiston burned easily. Perhaps fire was a manifestation of phlogiston. The theory was immediately accepted. It helped explain things, and the famous scientists of the day were guided by the new theory. The problem, of course, was that it was totally wrong. It is interesting that even when confronted with evidence in the 1780s that discredited the phlogiston theory, scientists were very slow to give up on it. Joseph Priestley, a famous scientist of the time, died in 1804 still believing in phlogiston.[2]

These are just two from countless examples of people's attempts to describe and understand their world, to gain knowledge about their existence. Regardless of how it is collected and sometimes even regardless of its accuracy, knowledge tends to accumulate. Explanations seem to last if they work. That is, they are believed as long as they seem to explain a part of human experience. If the explanations leave elements out or don't explain something they should, then they tend to be modified or abandoned to be replaced by something better.

The change from inaccurate to better explanations, however, isn't always easy. Some explanations that eventually proved clearly wrong were held as true for amazingly long times. They worked at a certain time in history given the state of knowledge at the time. Later, from a better vantage point, people looked back with amusement at the primitive beliefs of their ancestors. The phlogiston theory worked well for a while—fifty years. When factors came up that it couldn't explain, it was modified so that it did explain them.

There is another problem with the assumption that good ideas always replace bad and knowledge thereby accumulates. Some explanations or theories are very dearly held. They have backers (even fans) who believe in them so fiercely that the ideas remain prominent even when other theories work better. Scientists become advocates competing with and concealing findings from each other in order to arrive at a discovery first and to make certain the discovery stands. This situation hinders the growth of knowledge.

Let us examine the question, How do we know what we know? How do we gain knowledge? As we have already seen, the Wessex people and the phlogiston chemists approached the task of describing parts of their universe in rather different ways. From among the numerous ways people have used to gain knowledge some general categories appear. Three such categories are mysticism, rationalism, and empiricism. **Mysticism** refers to knowledge gained by intuition, revelation,

---

[1]For more detail on the fascinating story of Stonehenge, see Gerald Hawkins, *Stonehenge Decoded* (New York: Dell, 1965).

[2]There is a short discussion of phlogiston in *On Understanding Science*, by James Conant (New York: New American Library-Mentor, 1951), Chapter 3.

inspiration, magic, visions, or spells. Societies often hold special places for those among them who know in special ways—the magician, the spiritualist, the priest, or the witch doctor. Ceremonial use of drugs to produce vision is also highly valued among some peoples. In the seventeenth century, the Puritans of Massachusetts Bay Colony were heartily convinced of the presence of witchcraft in their midst. Their evidence came from several young girls who, in between dramatic seizures brought on by angry witches, were able to point out fellow villagers who were aiding the devil in his dirty work. The girls became so energetic in their attempts to cast out evil that shortly 350 people were in custody or accused as witches.[3]

Knowledge derived through mysticism tends to be private knowledge. Only the person experiencing the revelation or vision has it, and others must take the mystic's word for it. While this tends to enhance the importance of the mystic, it tends to compromise the quality of the product. If no one else saw it or felt it, can it really be true? Public knowledge will probably have a greater impact than private knowledge.

Rationalism refers to knowledge gained through common sense, logic, and reason. The writings of Aristotle and the dialogues of Plato in ancient times, and the ideas of Descartes, Spinoza, Voltaire, and Thomas Paine in the seventeenth and eighteenth centuries provide examples of knowledge emerging through the careful use of logic and reason. In the twentieth century many continue to find the use of common sense, logic, and reason the most appropriate way to arrive at knowledge. As with mysticism, however, there are limitations. For example, at one time knowledge emerging from a common-sense analysis told us that the earth is flat ("Couldn't be round, people on the other side would fall off. . . . "), and that if two metal objects—a heavy one and a light one—were dropped from a height, the heavy object would fall much faster. The major criterion for judgment in common sense, as the English philosopher Alfred North Whitehead (1861–1947) pointed out, is that new ideas shall look like old ones. The lessons of history are important, of course, but not to the extent that they blind us to the present.

Empiricism refers to knowledge that is gained by sense observation—by observing or experiencing phenomena with the senses of touch, sight, hearing, smell, or taste. This is the basis of science. Instead of armchair reasoning about the heavy and light objects, we drop them from a tall building and observe whether the heavy one falls faster. Public knowledge (as opposed to private) becomes possible as we invite a crowd of observers to help us watch the fall of the objects, or we suggest that the experiment be tried by others in other places.

Science

A one-sentence definition of what scientists are up to could run something like this: *science* is *understanding* through *description* by means of *measurement* and makes possible *prediction* and thus *adjustment* to or *control* of the environment. The essential points of this definition are *description*, *prediction*, and *control*.

[3]For a more detailed discussion of the Puritans and their problems, see Kai Erikson, *Wayward Puritans* (New York: Wiley, 1966).

Violent windstorms occasionally spring out of the Caribbean and the western North Atlantic. Huge waves caused by the storms are hazardous to shipping, and tremendous damage often results if a storm crosses land. Some years ago scientists began trying to understand these storms. They began by collecting information on numerous storms. They listed the traits that were common to most such storms until a fairly consistent description emerged: Certain conditions of wind and atmospheric pressure lead to a situation in which a low pressure cell is surrounded by circular moving winds traveling counterclockwise at speeds in excess of seventy-three miles per hour. Then predictions about these storms (called hurricanes) became possible. The conditions that would produce them, the time of year when they were most likely to occur (June to November, most frequent in September), their direction (west, then north, finally east), speed (ten to thirty miles per hour), and destructive power could all be predicted. This allowed societies to control their impact. Seeding clouds with chemicals may reduce the force of the hurricane, and advance knowledge of the hurricane's arrival means that measures can be taken to move people and material out of its way.

In a similar way, medical researchers observe a disease. Careful description of its characteristics allows predictions about its future occurrence and suggestions for control—antibiotics, isolation, rest, and so on.

Science (empiricism) as a way of gaining knowledge involves certain characteristics and assumptions. One such assumption is that the best way to know about the world is through the senses, aided when possible by microscopes, scales, telescopes, and other such extensions of the senses. Scientists assume that knowledge obtained in this way is better than that of rationalists or mystics before them. If we pressed the scientists on what they meant by *better,* they would probably admit that science doesn't remove all doubt and that absolute truth is impossible, but they would add that the knowledge gained through science seems to explain and predict phenomena more adequately than does that obtained by other methods.

Another basic assumption of most scientific endeavors is that phenomena are related causally. Science maintains that a *cause-effect relationship* exists in that each event has a prior cause or causes that theoretically can be discovered. Gravity causes the objects to fall from the building (effect). If the heavy one falls faster or if they fall at the same speed, these effects are also caused by something that we can try to discover.

However, there are usually many causes of an event rather than a single cause. This is referred to as *multiple causation*. A person dies. Why? His heart stopped. Why? He had lung cancer that had spread to the sac enclosing his heart and affected the heart's function. Shallow, rapid breathing resulting from inefficient lungs changed his blood chemistry and worsened his condition. Hardening of the arteries related to advanced age (he was seventy-five years old) reduced the circulation of his blood. Finally, since he was in much pain, he decided he had lived long enough —he had no more will to live. Again, what caused his death?

Because isolating a single cause or even several causes becomes enormously difficult when working on a complex problem, scientists search for relationships and correlations. One such complex problem is that of juvenile delinquency. Why does a young person commit crime? The factors involved are very complicated. Instead of searching for a single cause, therefore, criminologists try to isolate factors associated or correlated with becoming delinquent. Family background, living conditions, social class, number of delinquent friends, and criminal opportunities are among the factors that seem to be related to becoming delinquent. The point is that by itself a certain family background doesn't cause delinquent behavior. Some young people from unhappy families become delinquent, but some do not. Obviously other factors affect the situation. The best explanation is that delinquent behavior is the outcome of a complex relationship of factors. Some of these factors we know about—others we don't.

The idea of *control* is essential to science. Control has several meanings. I used it above to describe a *product* of knowledge. If we know certain things (when a hurricane will hit), then we can regulate or control events to a certain extent (get people out of the way). As we learn about disease we can often control its effects with antibiotics. The second meaning of control refers to its use as an aid in the process of gaining knowledge. Scientists attempt to control those factors in the environment that they are not studying but that might have an effect on what they are studying. Our friends who are dropping objects from tall buildings may decide to perform their experiment only on calm, clear days. They are not studying wind and rain, but these might affect how the objects drop, and so they would want to control for them. (Ideally, they would probably want to perform the experiment in a vacuum if that were possible.)

As problems become more complicated, controlling for all the relevant variables becomes more difficult. Important control variables may be left out, either because they are overlooked or because they are too difficult to control. Two psychologists decided to test the idea that hospitalization for serious mental illness (psychosis) had increased over a century (between 1845 and 1945). They found that it *had* increased substantially, and they had many good reasons to offer in explanation—increased stress, shift from farm to city, breakdown of family and religion, more complex life, and so on. The information and conclusion make sense. But they are *wrong*. The results and interpretation changed completely when the psychologists controlled for *age*. When they looked at hospitalization for each age group, instead of an increase in hospitalization they found virtually no change over the century-long period. People lived longer in 1945 than in 1845. That fact meant that the population contained more old people, who are more susceptible to the senility psychoses related to physiological degeneration of the brain and central nervous system. Conclusion: (1) same percentage of hospitalization by age; (2) more total hospitalization only because of more older (over fifty years old) people in the population; (3) variations have nothing or very little to do with societal stress.[4]

Careful *definitions of terms* is part of science. These are often called operational or working definitions. They allow others to know precisely what the scientists studied and how they carried out their experiments. The object-dropping experiment would include at least the following information: the size and weight of the

---

[4]This and other examples of control failures are discussed in *The Logic of Survey Analysis*, by Morris Rosenberg (New York: Basic Books, 1968), pp. 29–33.

objects being dropped, how far they are to be dropped, method of observation of the drop, and pressure and temperature at the time of the drop.

Scientists are assumed to be *objective*. They are expected to note what they actually see, not what they hope to see or wish they had seen. They don't select or choose only those data that will fit or prove the hypothesis on which they are working while ignoring contrary evidence. (One doesn't test the idea that sociology professors are absent-minded by looking for a sociology professor who is so afflicted and then saying, "I told you so.") If the light object falls faster, or if both objects *rise* when dropped, then that is what the scientist reports.

Of course absolute objectivity is impossible, and the scientists who suggest that they are totally objective are misleading themselves and us. Scientists are human after all and as such have beliefs and values that are bound to enter into their work. The suggestion that when scientists put on their white coats they leave behind all nonscientific human emotions and biases is unreasonable. It's just not that way. Objectivity asks rather that scientists try to be aware of their biases and make them public so that they may be considered when their work is evaluated.

Finally, *replication* is an essential characteristic of science. Studies are repeated by others in similar and in unique circumstances to see if the results are consistent. The objects would be dropped numerous times from the same height. Then the experimenters might change the height from thirty feet to sixty feet, then to ninety feet. Then the weight of the objects might be varied, and so on. It is through replication that one develops confidence in the results.

Types of Science

Generally when the word *scientist* is mentioned one imagines a white-coated figure bending over a microscope and surrounded by forty test tubes and a Bunsen burner or an astronomer peering through a telescope discovering the secrets of the universe. In fact, the range of matters in which scientists are involved is probably far wider than most people think.. There are numerous types or categories of science, and they involve widely differing methods. Pure and applied science represent two complementary approaches. *Pure* science attempts to discover facts and principles about the universe without regard for possible uses the knowledge may have. *Applied* science concerns itself with making knowledge useful to people. The applied scientist devises practical and utilitarian uses of knowledge obtained through pure scientific endeavors. Splitting the atom was for the most part a product of pure science. Harnessing the atom to make bombs, power submarines, and fuel power plants is a product of applied science. The two—pure and applied —are closely linked, and the distinction between them is sometimes more artificial than real.

Science is also categorized by subject matter. The physical sciences—astronomy, chemistry, physics, geology—are concerned with the nature of the physical universe. The biological sciences—botany, zoology, biology, paleontology—are concerned with the study of living organisms, plants, and animals. The social sciences—anthropology, economics, history, political science, geography, psychology, sociology—are concerned with the study of people, groups, and societies. The natural sciences (physical and biological) are older and more exact, and hence, more respected than the social sciences. Whether the scientific method and especially the controlled experiment can work as well in the study of human behavior as they have in the natural sciences remains to be seen.

Social Science

Social science in general and sociology in particular have developed from certain characteristics observed in human beings. For example, humans tend to group together and cooperate. People discovered long ago that they could accomplish much more working together than they could separately. Cooperation had obvious rewards. But we also know that not all human behavior is cooperative. Conflict is also an important part of the human condition. One of those first cooperative group efforts probably involved a battle or conflict with another group. Conflict arises when people compete for scarce resources such as wealth or power. Very often when one party or group benefits, another party or group is deprived, and a major school of thought in social science now focuses on the conflict involved in human interaction.

Another basic characteristic of human beings is that they tend in similar situations to behave in the same ways time after time. Their behavior is predictable. We all know this. When a car comes toward us, we have a pretty good idea of which side of the road it will be on. Students can correctly predict the behavior of their instructor on the first day of class, just as the instructor can usually anticipate the questions and concerns that the students will have about the class. I can tell you how the people on almost any elevator will behave. Generally they will get in, push the button for their floor, stand as far as possible from others, face the front, stare at the numbers flashing, and be quiet and subdued. Amazing? Not really, for human behavior in its simpler aspects is not difficult to predict.

The more complex aspects of behavior, however, present another problem. As people get together in groups, organizations, and societies, factors multiply, behavior becomes more complicated, and prediction becomes more difficult. Consider these questions. Many young people in high-crime areas of the city are involved in crime, but some aren't. What insulates these few from delinquency? Do large organizations—General Motors, The CIA, your school—have similar characteristics? If so, what are they and why do they occur? Are these beneficial or detrimental to the organization's performance? How do people behave in a disaster—a flood, earthquake, or bombing? Is their behavior consistent, or is it different in every disaster situation? Do they panic? Do they become immobilized?

To be sure, these questions are far more difficult than guessing which side of the road that car approaching us will be on. But the answers to these complex questions can be found. Social scientists, guided by the general principles of science, study these and similar questions about human behavior. They describe regularities and attempt to find consistent patterns in human activities. As regularities are described, prediction of future events becomes possible. If description and prediction are achieved, control may become possible. Let's say that we're worried about airplane hijacking. We first try to describe the condition. What sort of people are involved—first offenders or people with prior criminal histories? What motivates them—psychological problems, financial needs, a political viewpoint? Adequate description of the event may allow us to predict its occurrence. Careful screening of passengers in order to select out the hijacker type may, if we're very good at it, allow us to control the occurrence of the event. The experts aren't that good at it yet, as you know. There are fewer airplane hijackings than there used to be, but they still occur. Maybe we'll get better at controlling them. But the point is that knowledge can be gained about human behavior using the general principles of science, and it is this study that social scientists are involved in.

The different social sciences approach this difficult task of studying and recording human behavior in a variety of ways. Anthropologists traditionally have gone about the task by examining artifacts and remains of long-extinct communities, or by living with and studying preliterate tribes and societies. The study of culture is of central importance in anthropological analysis. Historians record an accurate chronology of past events. As events are placed in perspective, analysis of emerging trends may lead historians to make predictions about the future. Political scientists study the characteristics and patterns of political systems, the principles and conduct of government. Their topics include political parties, elections, systems of government, foreign policy, and the comparative structure of governments. Economists are interested in patterns of production, distribution, and consumption of goods and services. They study such topics as price and market theories; consumer behavior; merchandising and selling practices; money, banking, and credit; economic growth and development. Psychologists deal with individuals, their adjustment and personalities, their patterns of learning, motivation, and perception. Sociologists focus on groups, on patterns of interaction, on descriptions of the institutions and social organization of society.

The techniques used by social scientists are as varied as their subject matter. Historians study documents, archives, and other records for evidence about the past. Psychologists gain knowledge by using projective tests such as the Rorschach ink-blot test, by using sensitive laboratory equipment to conduct experiments on perception, by running rats through mazes, and by using interview rooms with one-way mirrors. Anthropologists use the technique of participant observation to study primitive societies, delinquent gangs, and community, ethnic, and class stratification. Sociologists are much involved in survey research using large numbers of questionnaires and interviews analyzed by computers.

And yet distinguishing between the social sciences is difficult, for they are much more similar than different. In some areas, anthropologists and sociologists approach their tasks in the same way. Sociologists frequently make use of cross-cultural analysis and participant observation, techniques anthropologists use. Likewise, many anthropologists are studying aspects of contemporary industrialized societies, which are usually the province of sociologists. In other areas, it is difficult to distinguish between sociological and psychological approaches. A relatively new science—social psychology—has developed, formally combining aspects of sociology and psychology. Many sociologists use historical analysis, and many historians conduct their research in ways that we are convinced are sociological. In his book *Wayward Puritans*, sociologist Kai Erikson applied current theories of deviant behavior to the seventeenth-century century Puritans of Massachusetts Bay (see footnote 3). His study involved extensive analysis of historical documents and represented a coordination of historical and sociological analyses. In summary, we find some slight differences among respective social sciences in matters of emphasis and perspective rather than marked differences in approach.

Sociology

A sociologist is a person who goes to a football game and watches the crowd.

This book is about a particular social science called sociology. The dictionary tells us that sociology is the "science or study of the origin, development, organization, and functioning of human society." Sociologists study human society and social behavior, and they focus on groups, institutions, and social organization. There are several areas of study within the discipline of sociology. For example, sociologists specialize in such areas as small groups, large-scale organizations, race relations, religion, marriage and the family, social problems, collective behavior, criminology and delinquency, social class, urban and rural sociology, population and demography, age and sex roles, political sociology, and the sociology of medicine and law.

In sociology as in other disciplines, the process of discovery centers around the interplay of two elements: research methods and theory. A theory or theoretical approach provides a framework for understanding phenomena. The theory suggests certain hypotheses or predictions that one might make. Then by employing appropriate research methods one can test the hypotheses empirically through controlled sense observation. The research findings often suggest modifications of the theory that in turn will make it more complete. This is the interplay of research and theory. For example, Einstein's theory of relativity provides a framework for making predictions about the speed of light under various conditions. Physicists and astronomers test these predictions using sophisticated research methods involving laser beams, high-speed aircraft, and complicated mathematics.

In the next few pages we will examine more closely these two elements—research method and theory—that sociologists use in their search for understanding of the human condition. First, let's look at research methods in sociology.

Types of Research

Like other social sciences, sociology attempts to understand human behavior from the scientific point of view. This means that the sociologist is guided by the principles and assumptions of science that were outlined earlier in this chapter. To get some idea of what this means, let's consider some of the ways in which sociological research has been done. First, we must distinguish between two categories of research, reactive and nonreactive.[5] **Reactive research** refers to situations in which the observer or researcher is a part of the research situation. Much of social science research is based on questionnaires and interviews. The researcher creates a questionnaire or interview, administers it to a group of people—the subjects—and measures the attitudes or behaviors of the subjects responding to the questionnaire or interview. These reactive measures are widely used because they are relatively inexpensive, easy to administer, can be done on a group basis, and are less complicated than other methods. Also, in some cases they require less time to develop and administer than other methods.

The problem is that this type of research also *creates* attitudes and behavior. Something new (a questionnaire or interview) is injected into the situation, and the subjects react—they react to the researcher and to the study. Here's a simple illustration: If you *know* you're being observed and your behavior is being recorded, what happens? Well, you behave *differently*—you are uneasy, on guard, tentative. The situation is not normal, and you don't behave the way you usually would. The researcher may be liked or disliked, the subjects may cooperate or not, they may be ignorant of the subject matter of the questionnaire or knowledgeable —any of a number of things may happen. This is the issue with reactive research —by introducing a foreign element into a situation we create attitudes as well as measure them.

Nonreactive research has no intruding observer and doesn't use questionnaires or interviews. Instead, nonreactive research focuses on physical traces and signs left behind by people, on records and archives (hospital records, census data, government records, etc.), and on simple observation in which the researcher observes but does not intrude. Some simple comparisons between reactive and nonreactive studies may help at this point.

1. Suppose you want to know which radio station is most listened to in your city.
   Reactive study: Go door to door and ask the people who answer what their favorite radio station is.
   Nonreactive study (using physical traces): Go to a busy gas station and as each car comes in, look in and note the spot on the dial the car radio is tuned to.
2. Suppose you want to determine who are the most liberal and most conservative members of Congress in your state.
   Reactive study: Devise an in-depth interview or questionnaire measuring liberalism-conservatism; and give it to each member of Congress.
   Nonreactive study (using records): Choose several issues that came up during the last legislative session that divided people along liberal and conservative lines; and see how the members of Congress actually voted on these issues.
3. Suppose you want to find out who uses more profanity in everyday conversation, males or females.
   Reactive study: Design a questionnaire or interview that asks people about their language patterns (including how often they swear), and administer it to a group of males and a group of females.
   Nonreactive study (using simple observation): Gather several observers and have each

[5]This distinction is best made in *Unobtrusive Measures: Nonreactive Research in the Social Sciences,* by Eugene Webb, Donald Campbell, Richard Schwartz, and Lee Sechrest (Chicago: Rand McNally, 1966). Also see a good summary in *The Research Act,* by Norman Denzin (Chicago: Aldine, 1970), Chapter 11.

of them listen in on several casual conversations of people in all-male or all-female groups. The observers could jot notes, though tape recording the conversations would be better. It is important that the observers *not* affect the group's behavior (the observers could appear to be part of the groups, or totally removed from them —sitting across the room apparently reading).

The strength of the nonreactive study is that it is hidden. Traces or records of behavior are examined after the people have left them, or the observation is hidden in that the people don't know they are being observed. If people don't know they are being studied, it seems that we should get a more accurate measurement of whatever it is that we are studying. On the other hand, nonreactive studies tend to lack depth and flexibility. We may know about *what* but be curious about *why*, and nonreactive studies won't provide us with that answer. The interview is more flexible, however, and can probe at some of the answers that escape the nonreactive study. In summary, these contrasting approaches—reactive and nonreactive—each have strengths and weaknesses. Probably the most effective study is one that combines elements of each approach. Keep these two categories in mind as we look further at sociological research.

Research Techniques

To get a better idea of how sociologists gain knowledge, let's look at three typical research techniques: participant observation, survey research, and the experiment.

Participant observation (often now called field research) is a study in which the researcher is or appears to be a participant in the activity or group that is being studied. *Street Corner Society* by William F. Whyte is a classic participant observation study. While a student at Harvard some years ago, Whyte decided he wanted to study a slum district of a large city. He walked around Boston until he came upon "Cornerville," an area that looked interesting to him. How should he study the area? He first tried a door-to-door questionnaire but was totally dissatisfied with this approach. After several other false starts, Whyte sought help from settlement house social workers in Cornerville, and they introduced him to "Doc." Doc was a native of Cornerville and knew everybody in the area. He took Whyte around as "my friend," and Whyte became involved in the community in ways that he never could have as an outsider. Shortly after, he rented a room in Cornerville, further establishing himself in the community. He found that as he got to know key members of groups, he could get what he wanted from other members of the group. He learned how to join in streetcorner conversations, and it wasn't long before Doc told him that he was as much a fixture on the street corner as the lamppost.

Everything did not go smoothly, however. On one occasion Whyte was talking about police payoffs to a gambling operator. When he became too inquisitive, the gambler became suspicious. On another occasion while talking with some Cornerville people, he decided to swear and use obscenities like they did. The conversation immediately stopped, and he was gently reminded that although they talked that way, they knew that he did not.

Whyte's relationship with Doc changed as his research continued. At first Doc was a friend and entrée into situations and groups. Later Doc became more of a collaborator as he helped Whyte interpret what he was seeing. In Whyte's case, many of the citizens in Cornerville knew he was something more than just another fellow on the street. It was reasonably well known that he was "working on a book." However, he was well enough integrated into the community that the knowledge that he was observer as well as a participant didn't seem to change the way people behaved around him. By using participant observation Whyte learned things about Cornerville that he probably never could have otherwise. Through participant observation he was able to analyze "the structure and functioning of the community through intensive examination of some of its parts—*in action*."[6]

We touched on **survey research**, a very common social science research technique, in discussing reactive studies. The survey involves the systematic collection of information from or about people through the use of self-administered questionnaires or interviews.[7] The researcher is interested in the general characteristics of a sample or in some experience or event in which they have been involved. Surveys generally fall into one of two categories: descriptive surveys and causal-explanatory surveys.

A *descriptive* survey is like a photograph in that it provides a numerical picture or description of certain characteristics of a group of people. A descriptive survey might investigate voting behavior or attitudes and opinions. Or a descriptive survey may tell us how often certain traits or conditions occur in a particular group. A recent descriptive survey of my college sociology class provides the following profile:

Size of class:	247
Year in school:	
Freshman	2%
Sophomore	4%
Junior	56%
Senior	36%
Graduate student	2%
Hometown:	
Sacramento area	58%
Elsewhere in the state or country	42%
Employment status:	
Not working	32%
Working part-time	43%
Working full-time	25%
Sex:	
Male	62%
Female	38%

(continued on p. 14)

[6]William Foote Whyte, *Street Corner Society* (Chicago: University of Chicago Press, 1943; 2d ed., 1955). Also see a good summary of Whyte's work in *The Origins of Scientific Sociology*, by John Madge (New York: Free Press, 1962), Chapter 7.

[7]I found the following research methods texts especially helpful: Julian Simon, *Basic Research Methods in the Social Sciences* (New York: Random House, 1969), Chapter 6; Denzin, *The Research Act*, Chapter 8 (see footnote 5); Herbert Hyman, *Survey Design and Analysis* (New York: Free Press, 1955); and Earl Babbie, *The Practice of Social Research* (Belmont, California: Wadsworth, 1975).

Age:

Range of 19 to 58
Average 23

Marital status:

Single	66%
Married	26%
Divorced/separated	8%

I asked the class in this survey to rank the following behaviors from 1 (most deviant) to 9 (least deviant):

forgery
armed robbery
prostitution
homicide
arson
homosexual act
rape
suicide
shoplifting

I took the students' ranks for each behavior, added them up, and divided the total by the number of students (247). This gave me a set of average ranks:

Behavior	Rank
Homicide	1.7
Rape	2.6
Armed robbery	3.7
Arson	4.2
Suicide	4.9
Homosexual act	6.3
Forgery	6.6
Prostitution	7.5
Shoplifting	7.8

The responses were analyzed one step further by controlling for sex. That is, the group was divided into males and females, and the attitudes of each group about the nine behaviors were examined.

Males		Females	
Behavior	Rank	Behavior	Rank
Homicide	1.7	Homicide	1.6
Rape	2.7	Rape	2.3
Armed robbery	3.7	Armed robbery	3.7
Arson	4.3	Arson	4.0
Suicide	4.7	Suicide	5.1
Homosexual act	5.8	Forgery	6.1
Forgery	6.9	Homosexual act	7.2
Prostitution	7.7	Prostitution	7.2
Shoplifting	7.8	Shoplifting	7.7

As you can see, the lists are similar, but there are a few differences. Armed robbery has identical scores in each group, for example, and several others are very close. The two groups differ most on the homosexual act. The males see it as more deviant than the females do. The males also see suicide as more deviant than the females do. On the other hand, the females see rape, forgery, and prostitution as more deviant than the males do.

If we wanted to analyze this information further, controls for age, marital status, and year in school could be introduced to see how each subgroup scored. A descriptive survey, then, provides us with a numerical description of a group or category of people.

The *causal-explanatory* survey studies the relationships between sets of relevant variables. (A variable is a condition that changes or has different values, such as I.Q., weight, temperature, number of arrests, and so on.) The idea is to see whether change in one variable is linked with change in another variable. The next step is to see whether change in one variable *explains* change in another variable. Consistent explanations may then lead to inferences about cause. In its attempt to manipulate and link appropriate factors, the causal-explanatory survey is a more ambitious undertaking than the descriptive survey.

To take a simple example, suppose we want to measure the idea that religiosity is related to delinquent behavior. That is, if a person is religious, that person is less likely to become a juvenile delinquent; a person who isn't religious is more likely to become a delinquent. This is a reasonably straightforward idea that we could try to test. A causal-explanatory survey to examine this question might look like this: As an operational definition of religiosity we will use church attendance. Then we select two groups of people. One is a group of one hundred, fifteen-year-old males who are heavy church attenders—they go to church two or three times a week. Assuming that church attendance is a good measure, they are obviously very religious. Group two is a group of one hundred, fifteen-year-old males who have never attended church. So we have two groups: one apparently very religious, the other not religious. The next step is to look into the backgrounds of these boys for evidence of delinquent behavior. We try to find out whether they have been hard to handle at school, have been arrested, or have been in correctional institutions. We would predict that if religiosity is related to delinquency, then group one will turn out to be disgustingly good kids, and members of group two will be in all sorts of trouble. But several outcomes are possible. Consider these categories:

1. Those males who are very religious are not delinquent
2. Those males who are not religious are delinquent
3. Those males who are very religious are delinquent
4. Those males who are not religious are not delinquent

If our idea is correct that if one is religious he is less likely to become a delinquent, then we would expect our subjects generally to fall into categories 1 and 2. But what if we are wrong? In that case our subjects might fall generally into categories 3 and 4. This would mean that there seems to be a relationship between religiosity and delinquency but it is the reverse of the one we predicted (delinquents are religious, nondelinquents are not). Or our subjects might be scattered rather equally across all four categories. This would mean that there is apparently *no* relationship between religiosity and delinquency as we tried to measure them.

There's more to a causal-explanatory survey, but this example illustrates some of the essentials of this type of study. The important point is that attempts are made to link or find relationships between variables in order to get to explanation and cause.

The **experiment** represents a third kind of research technique. In an experiment, the researcher manipulates one variable (the causal or **independent variable**) and watches for changes in the other variable (the effect or **dependent variable**). For example, find two groups of people in good health. Then have one group run forty miles a day while the other group does no physical exercise. Finally, watch the two groups for incidence of heart disease. The independent variable, exercise, is manipulated for two groups, and one watches for changes in the dependent variable, heart disease.

As you can see, the experiment searches for explanatory or causal relationships. In this it is like the causal-explanatory survey discussed earlier. The basic difference between the survey and the experiment is that the survey takes the world as it comes—surveys it without altering it. The experiment, on the other hand, systematically alters or manipulates aspects of the world in order to see what changes follow.[8] Suppose you are interested in the relationship between studying and academic performance—that is, you want to improve your grades. You could keep a record of how much you study for each test and the grades you get. This would be a type of survey. Or you could systematically vary your studying—ten hours for one test, twenty hours for another, forty hours for a third—and check the effect on your grades. This would be an experiment.

Several students and I performed an experiment that centered upon two ideas. First, the women's liberation movement was receiving wide attention in our area, and we were interested in the viewpoints college women held on some of the issues of the movement. Second, we were interested in response bias. For example, will your responses to a questionnaire or interview be the same if you are questioned by a white as compared to a black? By a young person as compared to an older person? By a man as compared to a woman? Probably not. Your responses on the questionnaire vary, not so much because of the questions asked (although that is important, too), but because of *who* is asking them. This, of course, greatly affects the accuracy of the study.

Most research projects center upon a **hypothesis**, which is a statement or proposition used to guide an investigation or study. The hypothesis for our study stated: "Response to statements concerning women's roles will be affected by the sex of the interviewer." A series of items dealing with these attitudes were collected, and ninety married college women were interviewed. They were asked whether they agreed or disagreed with statements such as "A woman's place is in the home," "Motherhood and a career should not be mixed," "Males have higher I.Q.'s and better abilities than females." The subjects were selected randomly and

---

[8]This comes from Simon's discussion in *Basic Research Methods in the Social Sciences*, Chapter 16, p. 229 (see footnote 7).

were separated into two groups by the flip of a coin. Half of the subjects were contacted by a male interviewer; the other half were asked the same questions by a female interviewer. When we analyzed their answers, we found that the response to the male interviewer was much different from the response to the female interviewer. I'll return to this later, but for now consider this question: Would you anticipate a pro-women's liberation response to the male interviewer ("the enemy") or to the female interviewer ("one of us"), and why?

Let's review some of the factors in this study. We were trying to test a cause-effect relationship. The sex of the interviewer was the independent variable, or cause; the women's response on the items was the dependent variable, or effect. By having a man interview one group and a woman interview the other group, we manipulated or altered the independent variable. By selecting the sample randomly we hoped to control for factors we weren't interested in but that might affect the results.

The term **random sample** has been used several times and perhaps should be explained further. The subjects of our study were women, but to interview all the women in the U.S. was impossible. So we really narrowed it down to a group of 900 women living in a campus housing project. It can be seen that this represents substantial compromises. In return for specifying a group we could manage, we lost other geographical areas as well as age, education, and marital status differences. Almost any attempts at reducing down from a large group will involve a compromise of sorts, although not necessarily as severe as ours. Nine hundred was still too large for us. We wanted a small sample of 90, but at the same time we wanted it to be representative of the total group. How to do this? If all people in the sample were alike we could pick anybody—the first 90 we found—and it wouldn't matter. But people aren't alike—they vary tremendously. To be a good one, our sample of 90 had to show the same variations and peculiarities as the original 900. A random sample in which each element has an equal chance of being selected should, we decided, give us what we want. This could be done in a practical way by placing 900 names in a barrel, scrambling them, and then picking out 90. The way we did it was to start with an address (apartment 7) and go to every tenth apartment after that (17, 27, 37, 47, etc.). This gave us a one-in-ten sample, or 90 out of 900. Remember that because a sample is smaller than the original universe some accuracy is lost. A sample is an *approximation* of the whole, but it is a necessary approximation because of the impossibility of dealing with the whole. Sampling is an essential part of the scientific method. Poor sampling technique has more than once led a scientist astray.

In describing our project to others, we included details of the characteristics of the subjects and interviewers and the questions that were asked, as well as the errors or weaknesses of the study. The major weakness, by the way, lies in the area of controls. For example, it was assumed that the interviewer's sex was the cause of the differing responses, but the cause could have been a difference in the personalities of the two interviewers or in the clothes they were wearing or something else that had not been controlled. We should have used more interviewers of both sexes and of varying types. It may be that *another* cause produced the apparent effect we noted, or perhaps *several* causes (of which the interviewer's sex was only one) were operating. The study should be repeated by others to verify the results, and when it is, controlling for the additional factors we missed would be appropriate[9]

In the last few pages we have described three research techniques: participant observation, survey research, and the experiment. You might find it interesting and challenging to try out one or more of these techniques. For example, take one of these groups you belong to (athletic team, dorm group, social club, political organization, or whatever), and study it. A short questionnaire could give you a descriptive survey of attitudes on the death penalty, political conservatism, types of deviant behavior, or presidential candidates. Or, more informally, as participant observer, watch the group in action. Who interacts with whom? Who are the leaders of the group and why? Is disruption caused by the same people, or is it spread throughout the group? Are some people left out by the rest of the group? See whether, by using controlled observation, you can discover something about the group that you were not previously aware of.

Problems in Social Science Investigation

We have been describing sociological research efforts—how sociologists come to know what they know. We have found that working within the general guidelines of science, they develop special techniques to study human behavior. All sciences do the same thing. And for the natural sciences these procedures have worked beautifully. The explosion of knowledge in the natural sciences in the last several decades attests to the value of the scientific mode of inquiry. But do these techniques work as well in the social sciences? So far, they don't seem to.

There are numerous explanations offered for the different levels of results in the natural and social sciences. One explanation has it that because the natural sciences historically got a head start on the social sciences, they are further ahead at this point. If this explanation is accurate, then as the social sciences age and gather more maturity and sophistication in their techniques and theories, they may reach a higher level of performance.

In February, 1979, we had a total eclipse of the sun. Astronomers handled it beautifully—they told us when it would happen, how long it would last, and what we should expect to see depending on where we were watching from. They compounded that achievement by telling us when the *next* eclipse of the same type would happen—February 16, 2017! Then they asked a social scientist to tell them about social conditions in the U.S. in 2017—family size, migration patterns, form of government, crime patterns, economic conditions, types of social movements, popular social problems, and so on. The social scientist told them he would check out his data and get back to them in 2018. . . .

---

[9]For more detail on this study, see Judson R. Landis, Daryl Sullivan, and Joseph Sheley, "Feminist Attitudes as Related to Sex of the Interviewer," *Pacific Sociological Review*, vol. 16, no. 3 (July 1973), pp. 305–314.

There is probably something to this, but there are other issues as well. A more basic explanation has to do with the nature of the subject matter—in the case of the social sciences, *people*. Variations in humans and their behavior are vast. Multiple causation is the rule, not the exception, and digging out all the related factors is always difficult and often impossible. Social scientists are convinced that their subject matter is more complex than that of natural scientists. Whether social scientists are right about this can be argued, but there are certainly complicating factors introduced when the subject matter of the study is people. For one thing, the study of people is an *interactive* process. When oxygen, force fields, a laser beam, or light rays are studied, they probably do what they always do. The fact of their being studied is unlikely to change their behavior. But when people are studied, they usually know it, and the process of being studied may change their behavior. (We commented on this earlier in discussing reactive and nonreactive studies.) For example, look at a study done some years ago at the Hawthorne Works of the Western Electric Company. Some researchers were interested in increasing production among women who wired electrical relays. They experimented with two groups. For one group, lighting was improved so they could see their work better. For the other group nothing was done. Output improved equally in *both* groups. Next, lighting was reduced to the point where the workers had difficulty seeing what they were doing. But there was no decrease in efficiency or speed of production! What was going on? It became apparent that there was much more to working efficiency than just physical working conditions. In fact, the workers were responding to *being studied* by the researchers, and this had more effect on their output than changing supposedly important physical factors. This finding, sometimes called the *Hawthorne effect,* was the impetus for a series of studies dealing with psychological and social aspects of the work situation.[10]

The problem begins with multiple causation of human behavior, and now we find that one of these causes is one *we* introduce by trying to study it. It is difficult enough as it is, and we make it worse (more complicated) by looking at it.

Another problem when people are the subject matter is that of introducing *controls*. People vary across so many factors that it becomes difficult to take all of them into account. Look again at the survey of delinquency and religiosity I suggested a few pages back. The two groups should be of the same social class, same age, same sex, and so on. In fact, they should be the same on *everything* except the two variables being studied— delinquency involvement and religiosity (church attendance). And that's not possible.

Social scientists are involved in the unique situation of *humans studying humans,* and this leads to problems. It is hard to be objective under the best of circumstances, and here scientists are studying people like themselves. If it were oxygen or laser beams, one would be less likely to identify with the subject. But in social science the subject is people, and scientists may identify with their feelings, their reactions, their beliefs. I suppose we are asking, Can people possibly be objective and unbiased when, in effect, they are studying *themselves*? This question has

[10]The Hawthorne–Western Electric studies are summarized by Madge in *The Origins of Scientific Sociology*, Chapter 6 (see footnote 6).

bothered social scientists for decades, and their responses to it vary. Some believe that one can put aside biases and beliefs and become a dispassionate observer. Others say no—humans can't study other humans and be objective. If this last group is right, there isn't much future for social science. Who's right? Well, certainly there are problems with objectivity when studying humans. Most social scientists probably see this as another variable present in their studies that needs to be taken into account but one that by itself doesn't compromise the scientific effort. Valuable knowledge about human behavior has been achieved and will continue to be achieved in spite of the various problems we have just outlined.

We have described how sociologists use the techniques of science to gain knowledge and some of the problems they encounter along the way. You may have the impression by now that sociologists tend to be super scientists bustling about in white coats guided by the principles of empiricism and a value-free science. Well, it's not necessarily so. There has always been a strong humanistic theme in sociology. Rather than just describe human activity, humanists attempt to interpret and focus on the meaning, value, and richness of life. At the center of the humanistic approach is the conviction that all people have dignity and worth. The sociologist as humanist is concerned about human welfare and conduct and wants to improve the lot of people in general. Humanism and science may be cooperative, but there are certain sharp contrasts between them. The scientist encourages value-free observation; the humanist believes that values are an essential part of the study of humans. The scientist studies what is; the humanist is concerned about what ought to be. These differerces have led some philosophers to the view that if there is too great an emphasis in a society on science and technology, humanistic values and the well-being of the society are seriously challenged. At this point suffice it to say that sociology contains both of these sometimes conflicting viewpoints—the scientific and humanistic. We will return to this issue in Chapter 12.

Sociological Theories

Besides research methods, the other major instrument used to gain knowledge is theory. A theory is a coherent set of propositions used to explain a class of phenomena. Scientists develop theories to explain that aspect of the world that they are studying. They then attempt to test the theories with information or data that they collect. Theories are crucially important, for scientific research is organized around them. If the theory is reasonably accurate, it will explain many of the phenomena with which it is concerned. If it does not, then it is not much good, and eventually a better theory, one that explains more, will replace it.

In the second century A.D., a Greek scholar named Ptolemy published a theory stating that the earth was the center of the universe and the other planets rotated in complicated ways around it. This was *the* theory and had strong support in the scientific and religious communities. But it did not explain the movements of the planets as well as it should have. Some 1,300 years later the Polish astronomer Copernicus began publishing papers that outlined a new theory—that the sun was the center of the universe and the earth and other planets rotated around the sun. It was a revolutionary idea. In the years after Copernicus died in 1543, Kepler, Galileo, and others made continued observations enabling them to refine the theory that Copernicus had suggested. There was substantial opposition to the new theory because it challenged some beliefs that were very important to the Catholic Church. In fact, Galileo was imprisoned for a time because of his support of the theory. It slowly became accepted, however, because it was a better explanation for phenomena than the Ptolemaic theory before it had been.

All disciplines have competing theories that attempt to explain the phenomena that are important to that discipline, and sociology is no exception. In the following paragraphs I will briefly outline some of the major theories in sociology. The theories we will examine are functional analysis, conflict theory, and symbolic interaction. Remember that this is a brief summary of fairly complex theories. Keep in mind also that there are variations in how each theory is defined and that there is some overlap between them.

Functional Analysis   The key terms in **functional analysis** are structure and function. A good way of understanding functional analysis is to start with a biological analogy. If one looks at the human body, one sees that numerous functions must be performed—breathing and eating, for example—in order for the organism to survive. To perform these functions, structures have developed—nose, lungs, digestive tract, and so on. Functional analysis holds that society can be analyzed in the same manner. Societies (and groups) need to perform certain functions to maintain their existence. They must have people, they must care for the sick, the young must be socialized, there must be distribution of goods and services. Structures develop to perform these functions—a family system to control reproduction, an educational system to train the young, economic and medical institutions to carry out other functions. This theory holds that structure and function are closely linked, and that they are the crucial factors in understanding and explaining society. Again, functional analysis explains a given pattern of activity by defining its contribution (function) to the group or society of which it is a part. Functional analysis tends to emphasize social equilibrium, stability, and the integration of the elements of society. One of the criticisms of this theory is that it has a conservative bias; in its emphasis on social order, functional analysis tends to ignore conflict and social change.

Several terms commonly used in functional analysis should be clarified. *Function* refers to an act that contributes to the existence of a unit (breathing and eating for the life of the organism). *Dysfunction* is the opposite—an act that leads to change or destruction of a unit (cancer in an organism). *Manifest* function is an intended and recognized function. *Latent* functions are those that are unintended and unrecognized.

Try a functional analysis of a sociology class. Why *is* there such a class? It functions to pass on knowledge, viewpoints, and information. A structure has developed consisting of an instructor, forty-eight students, and a set of rules in order to facilitate this passing of knowledge. It also functions to provide the teacher with a job. Some feel a need for the function of finding out how well the knowledge is getting across, and the structure of tests and a grading system develops. Attending class is functional if the student wants to get a good grade; cutting class often is dysfunctional. Giving a test is functional in enabling the teacher to evaluate how the material is getting across. I have also found that the first big test given in a class is dysfunctional in that it changes the mood of the class. The rapport and mutual understanding that develop between teacher and students over six weeks is suddenly compromised, and an adversary relationship develops. A manifest function of the typical classroom procedure—teacher makes assignments, students listen and read, obey, memorize, and give back on tests what the instructor has said— is that it facilitates the learning process, it works better if it is done that way. A latent function of this procedure is that perhaps it trains students to take orders and become good bureaucrats in the large organizations they will join in the near future.

Now that you have some idea how it works, try a functional analysis of some events or behaviors—for example, prostitution, professional football, a funeral ceremony, or punishment for a crime. The discussion of institutions in Chapter 7 is the clearest example in this book of functional analysis, although it crops up in several other places as well.[11]

Conflict Theory   In contrast to the order and stability of functional analysis, another group of theorists focus on conflict and discord. In examining social interaction, conflict theorists ask who benefits and who is deprived. Conflict often arises as people compete for scarce resources such as wealth, status, power, or territory. Conflict also arises over differences in values and interests—for example, between superiors and subordinates, management and labor, in-groups and out-groups. **Conflict theory** suggests that competition and conflict are common in social interaction and the study of these processes is the most appropriate way to

[11]From among the numerous sources available on functional analysis, the following have been especially helpful: Neil Smelser, ed., *Sociology* (New York: Wiley, 1967), pp 706–708; and Robert Merton, *Social Theory and Social Structure*, 2d ed. (New York: Free Press, 1957). See the section on functional analysis in the *International Encyclopedia of the Social Sciences* for a summary and an excellent bibliography.

understand society. Some conflicts are minor and of little consequence. Others are deeply felt and may result in the division of society into two hostile classes as suggested by Marx, or even war between nations.

Getting back to our sociology class, what would conflict theorists see? The testing and grading system necessary to facilitate the passage of information creates a system of domination (instructor) and subordination (students) and sets up conflicting interests. Consequently, the conflict theorist would not be at all surprised with the sudden change in mood as the first test is given. Competition for scarce resources (A's) leads to predictable types of behavior: cheating to get grades, memorization of masses of soon-to-be forgotten material, and rivalries with other students. The conflict theorist might also call attention to the tendency of the educational system to reinforce the current stratification system. Students from lower-class backgrounds who often have less adequate educational preparation may do less well in college classes, receive lower grades or perhaps flunk out, and because of this obtain lower-level jobs, and as a consequence, stay near the bottom of the social-class ladder.

Try using conflict theory on some events or behaviors—prostitution, professional football, or punishment for a crime. Ask who benefits and who is deprived. Conflict theory will come up several times in this book, probably most clearly in Chapters 5 and 6 in the discussion of stratification, the consequences of stratification, power, prejudice, and discrimination.[12]

Symbolic Interaction **Symbolic interaction** theory focuses on interaction between people, on the processes by which individuals come to develop viewpoints about themselves and relate to their associates. In comparison with functional analysis and conflict theory (which examine social structure in groups, institutions, and societies), symbolic interaction theory narrows the focus to person-to-person interaction. People interpret and define the symbols, gestures, and words of people around them, and they modify their own behavior accordingly. It is this activity that the symbolic interactionist is interested in. Symbolic interactionists see social life as *process*. They are interested in describing patterns of interaction, how parties to the interaction interpret what is going on, the use of signs, symbols, and other forms of communication, the meanings actions have for others, and the processes of socialization and development of the self.

Let's return once more to the sociology class, this time as symbolic interactionists. We would be interested in the type of interaction between instructor and students and would look at the signals (verbal and nonverbal bits of communication) that pass back and forth. Suppose a difficult point is being made. The instructor attempts to evaluate how well the class is getting the point and adjusts the lecture according to his or her interpretations of the students' responses. Back in the corner is a student totally disgusted with this instructor, and yet class participation is required. Notice the way the student balances competing values—hostility,

[12]For a background on conflict theory see the works of Karl Marx; Lewis Coser, *The Functions of Social Conflict* (Glencoe, Ill.: Free Press, 1956); Ralf Dahrendorf, *Class and Class Conflict in Industrial Society* (Stanford, Calif.: Stanford University Press, 1959); and see the section on conflict in the *International Encyclopedia of the Social Sciences* for an overview and bibliography.

deference, and desire for an A—in his gestures, tone of voice, body language, asides to other students, and so on.

The instructor has a particular self-concept—how is it expressed in his or her behavior? One instructor is informal and innovative; another is vastly self-confident, secure in the knowledge that he is the best instructor in the Western world. A student in the classroom who has always seen herself as an A student gets a C on a test. What responses does she make that help her maintain her original self-concept? If a change in mood appears after the first test, the symbolic interactionist would be interested in how it is expressed by students and how the instructor reacts to it. The symbolic interactionist, knowing that interaction is a two-way process, would be interested not only in changes in the students, but also in how the instructor changes as a consequence of his or her interaction with the class.

I tend to favor the symbolic interactionist approach more than functional analysis or conflict theory, so it should be no surprise to you that it will come up frequently in this book. The following examples come to mind: the discussion of nonreactive techniques in Chapter 1, all of Chapter 2 on socialization and self, parts of the discussion of groups in Chapter 4, self-fulfilling prophecy throughout, much of Chapter 11 on deviation (labeling theory is based on the symbolic interactionist approach), and many other places as well.[13]

These theories represent contrasting approaches used to explain or organize the material of sociology. Each theory emphasizes certain aspects and ignores others, and each has particular strengths and weaknesses. It is a good idea when reading sociology to be aware of the author's theoretical perspective, for it will suggest to you why certain factors are stressed and others are not.

Is It Common Sense?

Students of introductory sociology, and many others as well, frequently describe and consequently dismiss sociology as mere common sense. Or, worse, they say, "Sociologists describe what we all knew anyway in language that none of us can understand."

Unfortunately, there may be some truth to this statement, especially the indictment for obscure and complicated language. Sociologists might benefit if they learned to use more four-letter words and fewer twenty-four-letter ones. The belief, however, that sociology deals only with common sense is, I think, inaccurate. One reason people say that is because sociologists deal with contemporary human behavior, patterns of interaction between people. Since most of us are humans, we feel quite familiar with the topic. We think that atoms and rockets and the theory of relativity are one thing, but when it comes to understanding people, we're all experts.

In some aspects of human behavior our experiences and our intuition may serve us well. None of us, however, has experienced all situations. Because we live in a particular society, area, social class, and community, at a particular time in history, our experiences are necessarily limited. We in fact know much less about

---

[13]See the works of Charles Cooley or George H. Mead (see index) or a social psychology text such as *Social Psychology,* 4th ed., by Alfred Lindesmith, Anselm Strauss, and Norman Denzin (Hinsdale, Ill.: Dryden Press, 1975) for more on symbolic interaction.

human behavior than we think. For example, let's return to the study of women's attitudes, described earlier. The women were more pro-women's liberation to the male interviewer. To the female interviewer asking the same questions, they were much less pro-women's liberation. Did you guess right? Perhaps you did and had a logical explanation as well, but a peculiarity of common sense is that it can provide a rationale for almost *any* response. I takes a more sophisticated analysis to predict human behavior accurately and to answer the complex questions of why people do what they do. To further put what we know by means of common sense in perspective, try this adaptation of Gerald Maxwell's social awareness test. How well does your common sense serve you?[14] (The answers are at the bottom of this page.)

"Social Awareness" Test Are the following true or false?

1. The arrest rate for people between the ages of fifteen and nineteen is more than *double* the arrest rate of those aged twenty-five to twenty-nine.
2. Because of discrimination and depressed living conditions, more blacks commit suicide proportionately than whites.
3. With the exception of movie stars, people who divorce are slow to remarry.
4. Land is generally less expensive in the suburbs than in other parts of the city.
5. Women, being somewhat more emotional, are more likely to commit suicide than men.
6. There are more Hindus in the world than Protestants.
7. Cities are where the jobs are; consequently, there are generally more men than women in cities.
8. Children from divorced or unhappy homes are usually more careful in selecting a mate and make better marriages.
9. Panic is a common response for people confronted by disaster.
10. People with some college education are more likely to attend church than are people with only a high-school education.

This Book

This book focuses on the *concepts* of sociology. Concepts provide a way of generalizing about phenomena. Sociologists use concepts—role, motivation, anticipatory socialization, culture, in-group, cult, institution, mob—to help them organize and

[14] Gerald Maxwell describes a social awareness test that he has devised (*The American Sociologist,* November 1966, pp. 253–254). I have used his title as well as one or two of his questions.

Answers to "Social Awareness" test:

1. True. (See *Uniform Crime Reports—1977.*)
2. False. See pp. 170 and 339.
3. False. Divorced persons are generally more likely to marry than single persons of the same age.
4. True. See p. 248.
5. False. See p. 339.
6. True. See p. 214.
7. False. See p. 240.
8. False. Couples whose parents had unhappy marriages have a greater proneness to divorce.
9. False. See p. 311.
10. True. See p. 220.

understand the events they are studying. In fact, one could say that the major task of sociology (and probably other disciplines as well) is to build concepts—that is, to isolate certain unifying, abstract qualities that underlie and thus "explain" behavior. This book attempts to gather together some of the major concepts of sociology and define and illustrate them. Not all concepts are included, but the important ones are.

The discussion of concepts that follows is divided into three major sections. These discuss (1) the individual in society, (2) the organization of society, and (3) society in flux, under the headings Socialization and Culture, Social Organization, and Social Change and Social Deviation. The last chapter provides a sort of "sociology of sociology"— brief descriptions of some of the dominant ideas and crosscurrents of the discipline at this point in its development.

1 Socialization and Culture

In this section, we discuss how the infant develops into a social being. The socialization process is of major importance. Through this process values are transmitted from one generation to the next, and infants grow and learn to adapt to their environments. The *self,* the person's conception of what and who he or she is, slowly emerges from interaction with others. Through this interaction, individuals are introduced to norms, and roles, behaviors that are expected of them in specific situations and positions. This personal and social development takes place within the context of a specific culture. The culture provides a set of behaviors, traditions, customs, habits, and skills that also become a part of the individual. These processes—socialization, development of the self, internalization of norms, roles, and other aspects of the culture—are particularly evident in young children, although they continue to be important throughout life.

2 Socialization and Self

Few people spend much time thinking about the transformation they went through in the process of becoming mature human beings. Not only are we not concerned with the steps required to carry us from an early blob of protoplasm to a complicated, interacting individual, but it is even hard for us to believe that we were ever at the stage of egg and sperm. Beyond a certain idle curiosity as we watch a baby grow up, we take these changes in the developing human for granted. They are like the phases of the moon or the coming of summer—they seem to just happen.

However, if one decides to analyze the development of the individual in some detail, several approaches are available. A biological approach would emphasize physiological maturation. As a man's hair changes from brown to gray to gone, so does the person grow and mature in other ways. This approach might suggest that maturity is merely a matter of changes in cells, and that given enough time, these changes produce a mature social being.

But there is much more to human development than just the biological and physiological changes. Interaction with other humans is of critical importance. Isolation from (or inadequate) human interaction can affect our normal growth in a number of ways. Examples of extreme isolation are unusual, but occasionally such cases are described. Some years ago, Kingsley Davis described the cases of Anna and Isabelle who, because they were illegitimate children, were kept in nearly total isolation the first years of their lives.[1] Anna's mother was mentally retarded and left Anna alone in an attic room most of the time. Isabelle's mother was a deaf mute who stayed in a dark room with Isabelle, shut off from the rest of the family. When Anna was discovered, she was about six years old and could not walk, talk, or do anything that showed intelligence. She was in bad physical condition as well. After about two years in a county home she had learned to walk, understand simple commands, feed herself, and achieve some neatness, but she still did not speak. She spent the next three years of her life (she died at the age of ten and a half) in a private home for retarded children, and here she made some further progress. Her hearing and vision were normal, and she walked and ran fairly well. She could bounce and catch a ball, string beads, identify a few colors, and build with blocks. And she finally began to develop speech. She attempted conversations with others, although she spoke in phrases rather than in sentences. In summary, when Anna was found at the age of six, she had the mental capacity of a newborn infant. Four and a half years later she had progressed to a mental level of two and a half or three years.

Isabelle was six and a half years old when she was found. Like Anna, Isabelle was in bad shape both physically and mentally when she was discovered. For speech she made a strange croaking sound. She reacted to strangers, especially men, with much fear and hostility. In many ways she behaved like a deaf child, and her mental capacity was no more than that of a six-month-old baby. Specialists working with her at first believed her to be feebleminded and uneducable. An intensive training program was started. At first it seemed hopeless, but gradually Isabelle began to respond. Then suddenly she began to learn rapidly. Two months after starting to speak, she was putting sentences together. Sixteen months later she had a vocabulary of 1,500–2,000 words and was asking complicated questions. She covered in two years the stages of learning that ordinarily require six. Her I.Q. tripled in a year and a half. Davis concluded his description of Isabelle by noting that she was over fourteen years old and had passed the sixth grade. She was bright, cheerful, and energetic, and her teachers reported that she participated in school activities as normally as other children.

What do these cases tell us? It seems apparent that inadequate social interaction (near isolation in these cases) inhibits the development of the individual. Although they were six years old, neither Anna nor Isabelle had developed beyond the infant level, and both were believed to be feebleminded. Yet when effective interaction with others began, both girls progressed. In Isabelle's case the development was remarkable. This is probably because she had concentrated and expert training from the beginning and because she learned language quickly. Perhaps this

[1]This section is summarized from "Final Note on a Case of Extreme Isolation," by Kingsley Davis, *American Journal of Sociology* 52 (1947), pp. 432–437. Also see Bruno Bettelheim, "Feral Children and Autistic Children," *American Journal of Sociology* 64 (March 1959), pp. 455–467.

is the key. Or perhaps Anna was more isolated—Isabelle's mother stayed with her while Anna was often by herself. Or perhaps Isabelle's mental capacity was superior to Anna's to begin with. This we don't know. But in each case the effect of inadequate social interaction on human development is clearly demonstrated. Sociologists are convinced that the development of the individual is, at least in part, a *social* process.

Socialization: A Social Process

The process by which the organism becomes a social being is called socialization. **Socialization** refers to the learning of expectations, habits, skills, values, beliefs, and other requirements necessary for effective participation in social groups. Biological maturity is necessary, hereditary factors may set limits, and the process takes place in a physical environment, but the crucial aspect of socialization is that it is a social process. The individual develops through interaction in the social environment; the social environment determines the result. This is not to imply that if baby Reggie Jackson and baby Leonard Bernstein had been switched in the nursery shortly after birth, Bernstein would have played right field for the New York Yankees and Jackson would have directed the New York Philharmonic. We would have to look at other factors as well, and biology and heredity certainly play an important part. The exact extent of the role of biological factors is hard to determine. In fact, there is a heated and interesting debate going on now on this very issue—biology versus social environment. Edward Wilson, an entomologist from Harvard, proposed in a book published in 1975 that a new science called **sociobiology** be established. Sociobiology is defined as "the systematic study of the biological basis of all forms of social behavior, including sexual and parental behavior, in all kinds of organisms, including man." Sociobiologists are convinced that the behavior of lower organisms is biologically determined, and they believe that the same may be true of much of human behavior. In their writings they cite apparent genetic constraints on human social behavior in such areas as choice of sexual partners (the incest taboo and homosexuality), sex roles, aggression, kinship rules, and infant development.[2] The ideas of the sociobiologists are controversial (some say inflammatory); they have delighted some social scientists and threatened and angered others. Probably most social scientists recognize that biology places certain limits or conditions on human development. Beyond this, however, social scientists and especially sociologists believe that the crucial elements for understanding human behavior are the social environment and social interaction. By and large (according to sociologists) these are the primary determinants of who we are.

By **social interaction** we mean the process of being aware of others when we act, of modifying our behavior in accordance with others' responses. Social interac-

---

[2]Edward C. Wilson's books include *Sociobiology: The New Synthesis* (Cambridge, Mass.: Harvard University Press, 1975), and *On Human Nature* (Cambridge, Mass.: Harvard University Press, 1978). His newer book devotes much more attention to human behavior than his earlier book did. Also see *Society* 15 (September/October 1978). The whole issue is on sociobiology. The quote above comes from p. 10 of the *Society* issue. Also see numerous reviews in the popular press (for example, *Time* and *Newsweek* during September and October 1978) and in *Contemporary Sociology* 5 (November 1976).

tion occurs in a variety of ways, and its patterns are complex. When a student asks a teacher a question, he speaks differently than he does when he talks to the student next to him in class. The teacher evaluates the question as fairly sophisticated, and this affects his response to the student. If the interaction continues, each response is modified and determined by the response of the other immediately preceding it. The pattern of interaction may be affected by manner, body language, deference, relative status, degree of acquaintance, eye contact, and numerous other factors in addition to the spoken words. Social interaction occurs between two people—husband and wife, strangers on the street—and in groups and even large organizations. Try watching some examples of social interaction, and see whether you can identify the more subtle aspects of communication. How do the parties show agreement and disagreement, interest and boredom, and happiness and unhappiness through the use of body language, spatial distance, and facial expressions?

Socialization is continuous—it takes place throughout life, starting as soon as the infant leaves the womb and continuing until death. It occurs through interaction with other humans. We could call these other humans *agents of socialization.* Who they will be depends on one's place in the life span. For the baby, the socialization agents are the parents, who begin very early to communicate accepted and expected modes of behavior to the infant. Brothers and sisters also become socialization agents. An aspect of the socialization process can be observed in children as they pretend to be mothers, fathers, airplane pilots, or truck drivers. They are already anticipating and playing future roles. Later, peers become socialization agents, and, regardless of whether they are school friends or members of a delinquent gang or teammates on the football team, their influence becomes very important. Still later, one's colleagues on the job, one's spouse, and even one's own children become agents of socialization. Also, indirect influences such as vicarious participation or involvement in what we are reading or watching on TV continually play a part in the socialization process. In fact, in our interaction with others, we all become agents of socialization.

As you can see, socialization is extremely important. Through this lifelong process we gradually take specific points of view. Our views of religion, politics, and sports, style of family life, how to commit certain crimes, and how to raise children are all learned through the socialization process. I throw a volleyball to my seven-year-old son. He catches it in his hands and throws it back. Very easy, he doesn't even think about it. But suppose I throw the ball to a French or English boy—what happens? If the throw is above his shoulders, he will probably "head" it back to me. If it's lower he will control the ball with his legs and feet and kick it back to me. Each child has been socialized—has learned—to respond in a certain way. They respond differently because different things are emphasized where each child lives. But again, the socialization process "tracks" them into a certain response.

Another part of us that comes with socialization is illustrated in a study by Philip Goldberg.[3] Goldberg took articles in six fields—law, city planning, elemen-

---

[3]This study is described in "Are Women Prejudiced Against Women?" by Philip Goldberg, *Trans-Action* 5 (April 1968), pp. 28–30.

tary education, dietetics, linguistics, art history—and asked a group of college women to evaluate each article. The catch was that Goldberg manipulated the names of the authors of the articles. For half the women, the author of an article was a man ("John McKay"); for the other half of the women, the *same* article was by a woman ("Joan McKay"). In other words, the women were reading the same six articles, but in half the cases the authors were listed as men, and in the other half the authors were women. What happened? In nearly all cases, the women rated the article supposedly written by the man *higher* than the same article supposedly written by a woman! Several fields were selected by Goldberg because they were traditionally viewed as women's areas (elementary education, dietetics), but even here, articles supposedly written by men were ranked higher than those supposedly written by women. The explanation is inescapable: Women have been socialized to see themselves as inferior to men. A major goal of the women's liberation and equal rights movements is to counteract this "inferior woman" socialization, in women as well as in men.

Socialization may be better understood as occurring at two levels—primary and secondary. According to Berger and Luckmann, **primary socialization** refers to the first socialization an individual undergoes in childhood, through which he becomes a member of society. **Secondary socialization** refers to any subsequent process that inducts an already socialized individual into new sectors of his or her society.[4] Primary socialization usually takes place in the family. Here, the individuals have no choice about the important or significant socializing agents—they almost automatically and inevitably accept and internalize the family's view of the world. As primary socialization proceeds, the child's referents move from specific to general. A progressive abstraction occurs whereby at one stage the child understands that her parent specifically wants her to do certain things (for example, not play with food), and at a later stage she understands that people in general expect her to behave in certain ways (to use correct manners and not play with food). It is through primary socialization that the individual's first world is constructed. Consequently, according to Berger and Luckmann, it is the most important, for the basic structure of all secondary socialization must resemble that of primary socialization. Primary socialization ends when the "generalized other" has been established.[5]

Secondary socialization takes over where primary socialization leaves off and involves the individual's moving into and internalizing knowledge of new areas or sectors of life. Secondary socialization takes place when the individual decides to learn to read or to type, to take up sky-diving, to become a police officer, or to raise a family. Secondary socialization does not need an emotionally charged atmosphere to succeed, nor does it presuppose a high degree of identification, and its contents do not possess the quality of inevitability. In secondary socialization, the individual can be more objective than in primary socialization.

---

[4]This discussion follows that contained in *The Social Construction of Reality,* by Peter Berger and Thomas Luckmann (Garden City, N.Y.: Doubleday, 1966), especially pp. 129–147.

[5]See Mead's ideas about the "generalized other" on p. 38.

A person entering a new profession illustrates adult secondary socialization; an example is the steps in the socialization of the new police officer, outlined by Arthur Niederhoffer. The rookie patrolman proudly accepts the symbols of his new job—uniform, revolver, and badge. At police academy he learns about law, police procedures, human relations, rules and regulations, first aid, and how to fire weapons. He graduates, becomes a patrolman, faces a hostile and unappreciative public, and reality shock occurs. The more experienced officers tell him that in order to become a real policeman, he will have to forget everything he learned at the academy. The patrolman learns a new language, he learns to treat people differently in different areas of the city, and he learns to react to people's language, attitudes, and dress as well as to their criminal behavior. He learns when to enforce the law and when to look the other way. He learns how to make an arrest effectively, and he learns about graft. According to Niederhoffer, his attitudes change the longer he is on the force; if the officer has a college education but is slow to get promoted, he becomes more and more cynical. And generally as officers near retirement they become less cynical.[6]

Resocialization and Anticipatory Socialization

Socialization at the adult level (secondary socialization) is usually of a gradual nature; that is, the changes in the individual are more minor than those which occurred during primary socialization. Occasionally, however, major modifications or reconstructions of people are attempted. This could be called **resocialization.** It usually represents a concentrated effort by a group or organization. For example, look at prisons. Individuals commit crime, are caught, convicted, and sent to reformatories if they are young or to prisons if they are older. The idea is that the discomfort of their confinement will help them see the error of their ways, counseling and training programs there will help them change their behavior, and criminals will be resocialized into good citizens.

What actually happens? Resocialization certainly does take place, but it is far more diversified than one might imagine. Prisons are very effective crime schools for some prisoners. Regardless of the inmates' expertise upon entering, they can improve their crafts while inside. Through association with other inmates, they can learn new skills and techniques of crime. They can set up networks of important criminal friends and contacts for when they are released. Inmates learn a new language in prison. For example, "gleaning," "low riders," "bonaroos," "shots," "politicians," "merchants," "hoods," and "toughs" are prison slang for types of convicts.[7] The inmates learn new sexual practices, sometimes against their will, and they must learn how to get what they want in a society that is not at all like the

[6]See Arthur Niederhoffer, *Behind the Shield: The Police in Urban Society* (Garden City, N.Y.: Doubleday, 1967).

[7]There are numerous books and articles on prison life that describe the language or argot of inmates. For example, see Gresham Sykes, *Society of Captives* (New York: Atheneum, 1958). The example I have used here comes from *The Felon,* by John Irwin (Englewood Cliffs, N.J.: Prentice-Hall, 1970), pp. 66–85. Also Peter Letkemann, *Crime as Work* (Englewood Cliffs, N.J.: Prentice-Hall, 1973).

one they are used to. Some inmates even *like* prison—they have found a new home. These inmates find it easier to get along inside than outside, and they take steps to make sure they can return quickly once they are released. These people, too, have been resocialized. Draft resisters and others convicted of minor offenses may also be resocialized into a criminal role while in prison.

When marines or soldiers go through basic training, they are being resocialized. Recruits are taught to get up at times when they would ordinarily be going to bed, to cut their hair in peculiar ways, and to spend enormous amounts of time on the maintenance and appearance of their shoes, clothing, and equipment. They are told that a patch of dirt, rock, and sand outside the barracks is in fact a plot of grass that must be raked and cleaned every morning. They are taught to obey authority unquestioningly, that the individual is unimportant, and to act as a unit with their fellow recruits at all times.

There are other examples of major changes in people. The Patty Hearst the world learned about in the months after her kidnapping by the SLA was not the Patty Hearst known to her family and friends. Somehow she had been quickly and effectively resocialized. Brainwashing of war prisoners through isolation and sensory deprivation is another type of resocialization. One technique used by the Chinese in Korea to lower morale was to allow only collection notices, divorce subpoenas, "Dear John" letters, and other demoralizing mail to get to the prisoners. They held back positive letters and let the negative ones through.[8] Organizations such as Alcoholics Anonymous, dedicated to helping people recover from dependence on alcohol, are also involved in attempts at resocialization.

When a person adopts the values, behavior, or viewpoints of a group he or she would like to belong to, but does not yet, this is called **anticipatory socialization.** This is a common occurrence and explains the behavior of the lower-class person who develops middle-class values, or the behavior of the gung-ho military recruit who wants to become an officer, or the new behaviors and viewpoints of law or med students who anticipate becoming doctors or lawyers. Anticipatory socialization has the interesting function of easing the transition from one stage in life to another. When individuals practice for a new role ahead of time, their assumption of the new role is probably much less difficult. On the other hand, if the new stage in life is never reached, the trauma may be even greater than a sudden, unprepared-for change would have been.

Self and Personality

Psychology and sociology are most closely linked when they attempt to define the individual and explain developmental processes. A separate discipline, social psychology, has developed and deals with theories of socialization and individual development. Self and personality are the major concepts in this analysis. The words are similar in meaning, but **personality** is a somewhat more general term and

---

[8] *The Brain Benders,* by Charles Brownfield (New York: Exposition Press, 1972), has an interesting description and analysis of brainwashing. Brownfield deals with the actual occurrence in wartime and with scientific experiments. The example cited here comes from p. 55.

may be defined as the sum total of the physical, mental, emotional, social, and behavioral characteristics of an individual. **Self** refers to one's awareness of and ideas and attitudes about one's own personal and social identity. Psychologists are perhaps more inclined to use the term *personality;* sociologists generally prefer to use *self.* My interest in the following paragraphs is to explain how sociologists view the self, but first, here is a brief summary of some of the psychological perspectives.

Generally, psychologists have placed more emphasis on hereditary and biological factors in personality development, whereas sociologists focus on social interaction and the social environment. Psychologists place more emphasis on early childhood than do sociologists. Although there are numerous psychological theories, the most famous ideas are those of Sigmund Freud. Freud (1856–1939) was a Viennese physician and founder of psychoanalysis. According to Freud, the personality is made up of three major components: the id, the ego, and the superego.[9] The **id** is the most primitive aspect of the personality and represents the basic instinctual drives with which the person is born. Sexual and aggressive desires in the id constantly seek expression. The **ego** is the acting self; it is the mediator between the id and the outside world. Whereas the id operates by a pleasure principle—maximizing pleasure for the organism—the ego operates by a reality principle—balancing the instinctual needs of the organism against the conditions in the surrounding environment. The **superego** is an internalized set of rules and regulations that represent the values and ideas of society initially interpreted for individuals by their parents. The superego, commonly referred to as the conscience, is the aspect of personality that controls behavior. Don't think of id, ego, and superego as three little people running around in your head, but rather as three sets of processes whose sometimes conflicting purposes combine to function as personality. Freud believed that the individual passed through a series of psychosexual stages and that personality was fixed very early in life, around the age of six. Unlike Freud, sociologists believe that although the early years are extremely important, socialization and development of self are lifelong processes. Since Freud was a psychoanalyst and was working with people who were mentally ill, he emphasized the restricting nature of parents and society, and the conflict aspects of group life. Sociologists have focused more on the positive roles played by parents and groups in socialization and development of self.

With this brief view of Freud as introduction, let's turn to sociological theories of the self. Sociologists believe that self-development is rooted in social behavior, and not in biological, hereditary, or instinctual factors. The self is developed during the socialization process. Through interaction and association with others, you as an individual develop an image of *what you are.* This involves a perception of your role requirements and your position and behavioral expectations in the various social groupings with which you identify. As Charles H. Cooley put it, the word *self* means simply that which is designated in common speech by the pronouns of the first person singular, *I, me, mine,* and *myself.*[10] Aspects of one's self might

[9]For more detail, see Calvin Hall and Gardner Lindzey, *Theories of Personality* (New York: Wiley, 1957).

[10]Charles Horton Cooley's books are *Human Nature and the Social Order* (New York: Charles Scribner's, 1902) and *Social Organization* (New York: Charles Scribner's, 1909).

include: I am male, I am a college student, I am of medium height, I am athletic, I am usually happy, I am intelligent. The self might include as well: I can never do anything right, I am not worth much, nobody listens to me, I am inadequate, I am unloved, I am not as capable as my older brother.

Individuals develop these images or viewpoints about themselves from the way others respond to them. More specifically, they develop them from the way *they think* others are responding to them. Development of the self is a two-way interactive process that takes place throughout the period of socialization, the entire life span. Development of the self is an extremely subjective process involving interpretations of others' evaluations. Current evaluations are based on past evaluations, so that earlier mistakes become additive. A father may continually tell his daughter that she is extremely intelligent. This becomes part of her self, one of the ways she views herself, and she behaves and has certain expectations because of it. If she flunks bonehead English as a college freshman, contradictory information comes in. What happened? She makes excuses and rationalizes her failure in order to support the view of self that she had held. She will probably seek reinforcement from other sources (father, girl friend, I.Q. test scores) to support her self-view. If evidence is lacking or reinforcement becomes harder to find (other bad grades, low I.Q. test scores), this part of her self-conception will probably begin to change.

Aspects of self constantly undergo change. Often these changes occur slowly. Occasionally changes may be more rapid, sudden, and dramatic as we mentioned earlier in cases of resocialization of inmates of prisons and concentration camps and recruits in military basic training. All of these changes are a result of our evaluations of others' evaluations of us.

Charles H. Cooley described the development of the self in his concept, the **looking-glass self.** The looking-glass self contains three elements: the imagination of our appearance to the other person, the imagination of his judgment of that appearance, and some sort of self-feeling, such as pride or mortification. Suppose, for example, a person eating in a crowded restaurant accidentally knocks his plate off the table. It makes a huge crash, and the food spills all over him. According to Cooley, he first "steps outside himself" and observes himself from the viewpoint of others in the room (" . . . a well-dressed fellow with spaghetti all over him . . . "). Next, still examining himself as object, he imagines that others are evaluating his behavior (" . . . must be a rather clumsy and awkward person . . . "). Finally, the individual as subject develops feelings and reactions to these imaginary evaluations of himself as object. He gets embarrassed, his face reddens, and he tries unsuccessfully to pretend it didn't happen. The process is made more interesting when we note that probably the same things would have happened if the person had been the only one in the restaurant. We are carrying our judges around with us in our head, and they are constantly evaluating our behavior.

George Herbert Mead[11] described the development of the self this way: Individuals will conceive of themselves as they believe significant others conceive of them. They will then tend to act in accordance with expectations they impute to these significant others concerning the way "people like them" should act. As children develop the ability to examine and control their behavior in accordance

---

George Orwell tells the story of the English police officer on duty in a Burmese town who is told one day that an elephant has run amok, is ravaging the bazaar, and has killed a native—"caught him with its trunk, put its foot on his back and ground him into the earth." The officer gets a rifle and seeks out the elephant. When he finds the elephant, he realizes immediately that he ought not to shoot him—the elephant is eating peacefully and is not dangerous. "But at that moment I glanced round at the crowd that had followed me. It was an immense crowd, two thousand at the least and growing every minute. I looked at the sea of yellow faces all happy and excited over this bit of fun, all certain that the elephant was going to be shot. They did not like me, but with the magical rifle in my hands I was momentarily worth watching. And suddenly I realized that I should have to shoot the elephant after all. The people expected it of me and I had got to do it; I could feel their two thousand wills pressing me forward, irresistibly. Here was I, the white man with his gun, standing in front of the unarmed native crowd—seemingly the leading actor of the piece; but in reality I was only an absurd puppet pushed to and fro by the will of those yellow faces behind."

The officer did not want to shoot the elephant, but he did, many times, and the elephant finally died. Later there was much discussion about whether he had done the right thing. "The older men said I was right, the younger men said it was a damn shame to shoot an elephant for killing a coolie. And afterwards I was very glad that the coolie had been killed; it put me legally in the right and it gave me a sufficient pretext for shooting the elephant. I often wondered whether any of the others grasped that I had done it solely to avoid looking a fool."

Excerpts from "Shooting an Elephant" in *Shooting an Elephant and Other Essays* by George Orwell are reprinted by permission of Harcourt Brace Jovanovich, Inc.

---

[11]George Herbert Mead's writings include *Mind, Self, and Society* (Chicago: University of Chicago Press, 1934) and "The Genesis of the Self and Social Control," from *International Journal of Ethics* 35 (April 1925), pp. 251–273.

with others' views and attitudes about their behavior, they are learning to "take the role of the other." At this first stage of development (called *primary socialization* by Berger and Luckmann), children do not cooperate with others and relate only to specific individuals such as parents and perhaps an older brother or sister or a teacher—persons whom Mead described as **significant others.** Later, as individuals develop they are less likely to continue to react to individual others and learn instead to react more to a less personalized grouping of others. This grouping of others, which Mead called the **generalized other,** represents the sum of the viewpoints of the social group or community of people to which one belongs. The second stage of development (secondary socialization) begins, then, when children are mature enough to cooperate with others in joint activities and to be able to react to the idea of people in general rather than to specific others.

Although our internalized attitudes of others are crucial, they do not determine all behavior. Mead made a distinction between two aspects of the self, the "I" and the "me." The "I" represents the subjective, acting self, which may initiate spontaneous and original behavior. The "me" sees self as object and represents a conception of others' attitudes and viewpoints toward self. The "I" is freer, more innovative; the "me" is more conventional. "I" behaves, "me" judges and evaluates. "I" is in part governed by "me" but not completely. The abstract scrawling on the wall or in the dirt by the young child might represent "I" behavior; the same child's in-school drawing of the houses or trees that seem to please the teacher so much would be closer to "me" behavior. The driver involved in an auto accident who leaps out of the car and punches the other driver, swears at the passenger, and kicks a passing dog is probably showing us the "I" aspect of self, while another passenger who goes to the nearest phone to call the highway patrol illustrates the "me." Or imagine the football player about to catch a punt as a group of monstrous players from the other team race down the field to smash him. The player's "I" says, "I don't want to catch that thing. It's coming down hard and is going to hurt my hands; look at all those guys going to tackle me—I think I'll let the ball bounce off my helmet." The "me," however, says, "Oh no you don't—lot of people watching. You're supposed to *catch* that ball and *run* with it. The team and the coach are depending on you. *Do* it!"

The Importance of Language

It was also Mead who first emphasized that socialization and development of the self could not occur without *language.* Indeed, it is argued that it is largely language that distinguishes humans from other animals. The essential factor in language and symbolic communication is that a symbol arouses in one's self the same meaning it arouses in another. Primitive communication begins with a conversation of gestures, such as the mating dance of birds, the snarl of dogs, the roar of lions, or the cry of an infant. At this level, meanings of gestures are not shared. To be sure, the gestures may bring forth a response in some observer (another dog or lion, the infant's parent), but the important fact, according to Mead, is that the gesture does not arouse in the actor the same response it arouses in the observer. For example, a very young baby feels discomfort and cries. The parent interprets this as hunger and feeds the baby. If the parent is right, this is communication of a sort, but for the baby, the act of crying had no communicative intent; it was merely a biological response. This represents primitive communication because the meanings were not shared by both parties.

As children mature they learn to use symbols and words. The words are poorly formed at first, and probably only a parent could understand them, but they are the beginnings of language—something beyond primitive communication. As their use of language improves, children learn that what they say and do elicits responses from others. Language allows them to replace behavior with ideas—they can now say they are hungry rather than acting it out by crying or pointing at food. Language allows them to think, makes possible the internalization of attitudes of others, and allows individuals to control their responses to others. We can imagine an internal conversation in the child: "I would really like to have ice cream and cake, but my parents seem to like me better if I eat that other stuff they put out. . . ." Mead suggests that the use of symbolic communication continues to develop, and through language individuals are able to think, to develop shared social meanings, to take themselves as objects and evaluate their own behavior as they think others do. In sum, then, language makes possible the development of mind and self.

Definition of the Situation

An important principle of socialization and self-concept is that our understanding of reality is subjective and socially structured. We respond to what we *think* is so, rather than what really is so. When we peer into Cooley's looking glass the view may be quite distorted, but we believe what we see. Two ideas, *definition of the situation* and *self-fulfilling prophecy,* help illustrate this point.

Sociologist W. I. Thomas introduced **definition of the situation** by saying, "If men define situations as real, they are real in their consequences." The point he was making is that reality is socially structured and that people respond as much or more to the meaning a situation has for them as to the objective features of a situation. If a student defines passing a certain exam as the most important thing in the world, then for her it is, and she goes to great extremes to ensure that she does. People define certain races as inferior and certain cultural beliefs or practices (cannibalism, polygamy) as peculiar, regardless of the objective reality of the situation. Or recall the old club initiation stunt. The victim is blindfolded and fed cold cooked spaghetti. Halfway through the meal he is told he is eating worms. What happens? He gags and is sick to his stomach. Why? He responds to what he thinks is true. That response has been socially defined and includes what his feeders tell him, how important initiation is to him, and what his background has taught him regarding the relative merits of angleworms and spaghetti. Even worse and horrible to consider, suppose we feed our friend angleworms and tell him it's spaghetti. That, I'm afraid, would work too.

The **self-fulfilling prophecy** is an extension of the idea of definition of the situation. A self-fulfilling prophecy occurs when a *false* definition of a situation evokes a new behavior that makes the originally false conception come *true*. [12] A student is worried that she will flunk an exam. This makes her so nervous and anxious that she is unable to study effectively, and she flunks the exam. Or police believe Gorples to be very criminal types. Consequently, more police patrols and surveillance are concentrated in those sections of the city where the Gorples live. Increased police surveillance leads to greater visibility and reporting of crime, so the crime rate of Gorples increases. As Merton explains, "confident error generates its own spurious confirmation."[13] If we look carefully, we can see this phenomenon frequently in everyday situations.

Robert Rosenthal performed several interesting experiments that illustrate what we are discussing here.[14] In one experiment six students were given five rats each. They were told that their rats were very bright ones bred especially for running a maze. Six other students were given five rats each and were told that their rats were genetically inferior and probably would be poor at running through mazes. Then both groups of students attempted to train their rats to run the maze. What the students didn't know was that there were no "bright" rats and no "dull" rats—they were all the same with equal capacities for learning. What happened? Well, right from the beginning of the training the "bright" rats performed better. The "dull" rats made little progress and sometimes would not even budge from the starting position in the maze. And there were differences on more than just perfor-mance. The students found the "bright" rats to be brighter, more pleasant, and more likeable than the "dull" rats. The self-fulfilling prophecy explains what happened this way: The students with "bright" rats helped, coaxed, and encour-aged their animals to do what they expected them to, and the "dull" rats got little encouragement. Or perhaps the students so expected "brights" to do well and "dulls" to do poorly that that is what they saw—regardless of what was actually happening.

In another experiment, Rosenthal and Lenore Jacobson tested the intelligence of some elementary school children in San Francisco.[15] They told the children's teachers that based on tests, twenty percent of the children were identified as "academic spurters." They told the teachers the children's names and that they could be expected to do well in school. As with the rats in the earlier study, the children were all alike. The "spurters" were *not* of higher intelligence, but in fact Rosenthal and Jacobson had chosen them at random. The children were tested again later in the year, and the teachers evaluated the students. You can guess what

---

[12]This discussion of definition of the situation and self-fulfilling prophecy follows that of Robert Merton in *Social Theory and Social Structure,* 2d ed. (New York: Free Press, 1957), pp. 421–436.

[13]Merton, *Social Theory and Social Structure,* p. 128 (see footnote 12).

[14]The study is first reported in "The effect of Experimenter Bias on the Performance of the Albino Rat," by Robert Rosenthal and Kermit Fode, *Behavioral Science* 8 (July 1963), pp. 183–189. The discus-sion here is summarized from another report, "Teacher Expectations for the Disadvantaged," by Rosen-thal and Lenore Jacobson, *Scientific American* 218 (April 1968), pp. 19–23.

[15]This is summarized from "Teacher Expectations for the Disadvantaged," mentioned in footnote 14. Also see Rosenthal and Jacobson's book *Pygmalion in the Classroom: Teacher Expectation and Pupils' Intellectual Development* (New York: Holt, Rinehart and Winston, 1968).

happened. The students labeled "academic spurters" were described as happier than other students, more curious, more interesting, more appealing, and better adjusted. They also showed greater gains in intelligence than the other children. The teachers acted in terms of what they thought to be true (definition of the situation) and behaved so that what was expected to occur did occur (self-fulfilling prophecy).[16] Again, the point is that our reality is subjective and is socially structured.

In the paragraph above I used the term **labeling,** which is an important one in sociology. Labeling refers to the tendency of people to stamp or type or categorize others. Often these categories are negative, and the process of labeling is important for precisely the reasons we have just been discussing. If one is labeled bright, dull, academic spurter, stupid, ex-con, deviant, lesbian, mentally ill, or sex offender, it is bound to have an effect on that individual. The label may be accurate or it may be false. But as we have just discovered, accuracy is of little consequence because reality is subjective and people believe what they are told. Labeling leads to different treatment by others (who respond to the label rather than to the individual), to effects on the individual's self-concept, and perhaps to a self-fulfilling prophecy. We will return to labeling in more detail in a later chapter on deviant behavior.

SUMMARY

Our study of sociology starts with the assumption that humans are social animals. The obvious question is, how do they become that way? In this chapter we have discussed some of the processes that sociologists feel are important and essential if we are to understand how one changes from a blob of matter into a complex, interacting, social being.

The process through which this transformation occurs is called socialization. During socialization, the self is developed. The self is the individual's set of images about what he or she is. Its development is a social process; it arises out of our interpretations of others' reactions to us. Several theories were examined that describe in detail how the self is developed. Cooley's explanation involves the looking-glass self; Mead describes self-growth through significant others, the generalized other, and taking the role of the other. In Mead's view, language is a complex method of symbolic communication that is essential in socialization and in development of the self.

Although the individual is a combination of biological, hereditary, and social

[16]We mentioned in Chapter 1 the importance of verification in science, and the Rosenthal study provides an interesting sidelight in this regard. When the study appeared in 1968 it drew wide interest. Then, a series of critical reviews appeared taking Rosenthal to task for the research methods he used in his study. Next, numerous attempts were made to repeat Rosenthal's study on other samples. Some researchers have been able to repeat his findings and conclusions, many have not been able to do so, and the debate goes on about the original study. If you would like to get involved in the discussion, see Glen Mendels and James Flanders, "Teachers' Expectations and Pupil Performance," *American Educational Research Journal* 10 (Summer 1973), pp. 203–212, which describes a replication and cites most of the other attempts and critiques up to 1973.

factors, sociologists focus their studies on interaction in the social environment. The social environment is the stage or setting in which socialization and self-development take place. The emphasis throughout this chapter has been on interaction and on interpretation and internalization of others' reactions to us. The effect of the social environment on the individual is also a very subjective process. There are substantial variations in how individuals perceive, interpret, and react to their social environment. Suppose twenty people observe an accident at a busy intersection, and then each person writes a description of what happened. How many different descriptions might we get? Probably at least ten or fifteen, maybe even twenty (or more, if we have a few schizophrenics in the group). Or observe how different students react to a good or bad grade on an exam—again, there is a great variation. The effect of the social environment, then, is a very subjective and interpretive phenomenon; no two people react in exactly the same way. Differences multiply because future perceptions and interpretations are based on past perceptions and interpretations. In like manner, socialization and development of the self are building processes that take place throughout the life span.

Four readings follow that will help illustrate some of the concepts we have discussed in this chapter. In an excerpt from her book *The Story of My Life,* Helen Keller, who was deaf and blind from early childhood, recalls meeting her new teacher and beginning her education. This reading illustrates how important language and symbolic communication are in the processes of socialization and self-development. The second reading is an excerpt from Malcolm X's autobiography in which he describes how some events that occurred during his early teens seemed to have a great and lasting impact on him. In the third reading, a sad story about the death of a boy, Jean Mizer illustrates socialization, agents of socialization, and the self-fulfilling prophecy. An interview with Jerome Kagan provides some cross-cultural viewpoints on child development and continues the debate on the importance of the early years of life.

Reading 2.1

The Story of My Life

HELEN KELLER

Socialization is defined as the process by which the organism becomes a social being—the learning of habits, skills and other requirements for effective participation in social groups. Socialization is a continuing process and occurs through interaction with other humans—parents, teachers, friends.

Helen Keller was deaf and blind from early childhood. In this excerpt from one of her books, she describes the period when her new teacher first arrived and a new form of learning began to take place.

From *The Story of My Life* by Helen Keller. Reprinted by permission of Doubleday & Company, Inc.

The most important day I remember in all my life is the one on which my teacher, Anne Mansfield Sullivan, came to me. I am filled with wonder when I consider the immeasurable contrasts between the two lives which it connects. It was the third of March, 1887, three months before I was seven years old.

Have you ever been at sea in a dense fog, when it seemed as if a tangible white darkness shut you in, and the great ship, tense and anxious, groped her way toward the shore with plummet and sounding-line, and you waited with beating heart for something to happen? I was like that ship before my education began, only I was without compass or sounding-line, and had no way of knowing how near the harbour was. "Light! give me light!" was the wordless cry of my soul, and the light of love shone on me in that very hour.

I felt approaching footsteps. I stretched out my hand, as I supposed to my mother. Someone took it, and I was caught up and held close in the arms of her who had come to reveal all things to me, and, more than all things else, to love me.

The morning after my teacher came she led me into her room and gave me a doll. The little blind children at the Perkins Institution had sent it and Laura Bridgman had dressed it; but I did not know this until afterward. When I had played with it a little while, Miss Sullivan slowly spelled into my hand the word "d-o-l-l." I was at once interested in this finger play and tried to imitate it. When I finally succeeded in making the letters correctly I was flushed with childish pleasure and pride. Running downstairs to my mother I held up my hand and made the letters for doll. I did not know that I was spelling a word or even that words existed; I was simply making my fingers go in monkey-like imitation. In the days that followed I learned to spell in this uncomprehending way a great many words, among them pin, hat, cup and a few verbs like sit, stand and walk. But my teacher had been with me several weeks before I understood that everything has a name.

One day, while I was playing with my new doll, Miss Sullivan put my big rag doll into my lap also, spelled "d-o-l-l" and tried to make me understand that "d-o-l-l" applied to both. Earlier in the day we had had a tussle over the words "m-u-g" and "w-a-t-e-r." Miss Sullivan had tried to impress it upon me that "m-u-g" is mug and that "w-a-t-e-r" is water, but I persisted in confounding the two. In despair she had dropped the subject for the time, only to renew it at the first opportunity. I became impatient at her repeated attempts and, seizing the new doll, I dashed it upon the floor. I was keenly delighted when I felt the fragments of the broken doll at my feet. Neither sorrow nor regret followed my passionate outburst. I had not loved the doll. In the still, dark world in which I lived there was no strong sentiment of tenderness. I felt my teacher sweep the fragments to one side of the hearth, and I had a sense of satisfaction that the cause of my discomfort was removed. She brought me my hat, and I knew I was going out into the warm sunshine. This thought, if a wordless sensation may be called a thought, made me hop and skip with pleasure.

We walked down the path to the well-house, attracted by the fragrance of the honeysuckle with which it was covered. Some one was drawing water and my teacher placed my hand under the spout. As the cool stream gushed over one hand she spelled into the other the word water, first slowly, then rapidly. I stood still, my whole attention fixed upon the motions of her fingers. Suddenly I felt a misty consciousness as of something forgotten—a thrill of returning thought; and some-how the mystery of language was revealed to me. I knew then that "w-a-t-e-r" meant the wonderful cool something that was flowing over my hand. That living word awakened my soul, gave it light, hope, joy, set it free! There were barriers still, it is true, but barriers that could in time be swept away.

I left the well-house eager to learn. Everything had a name, and each name gave birth to a new thought. As we returned to the house every object which I touched seemed to quiver with life. That was because I saw everything with the strange, new sight that had come to me. On entering the door I remembered the doll I had broken. I felt my way to the hearth and picked up the pieces. I tried vainly to put them together. Then my eyes filled with tears; for I realized what I had done, and for the first time I felt repentance and sorrow.

I learned a great many new words that day. I do not remember what they all were; but I do know that mother, father, sister, teacher were among them—words that were to make the world blossom for me, "like Aaron's rod, with flowers." It would have been difficult to find a happier child than I was as I lay in my crib at the close of that eventful day and lived over the joys it had brought me, and for the first time longed for a new day to come.

I recall many incidents of the summer of 1887 that followed my soul's sudden awakening. I did nothing but explore with my hands and learn the name of every object that I touched; and the more I handled things and learned their names and uses, the more joyous and confident grew my sense of kinship with the rest of the world.

When the time of daisies and buttercups came Miss Sullivan took me by the hand across the fields, where men were preparing the earth for the seed, to the banks of the Tennessee River, and there, sitting on the warm grass, I had my first lessons in the beneficence of nature. I learned how the sun and the rain make to grow out of the ground every tree that is pleasant to the sight and good for food, how birds build their nests and live and thrive from land to land, how the squirrel, the deer, the lion and every other creature finds food and shelter. As my knowledge of things grew I felt more and more the delight of the world I was in. Long before I learned to do a sum in arithmetic or describe the shape of the earth, Miss Sullivan had taught me to find beauty in the fragrant woods, in every blade of grass, and in the curves and dimples of my baby sister's hand. She linked my earliest thoughts with nature, and made me feel that "birds and flowers and I were happy peers."

I had now the key to all language, and I was eager to learn to use it. Children who hear acquire language without any particular effort; the words that fall from others' lips they catch on the wing, as it were, delightedly, while the little deaf child must trap them by a slow and often painful process. But whatever the process, the result is wonderful. Gradually from naming an object we advance step by step until we have traversed the vast distance between our first stammered syllable and the sweep of thought in a line of Shakespeare.

At first, when my teacher told me about a new thing I asked very few ques-tions. My ideas were vague, and my vocabulary was inadequate; but as my knowl-edge of things grew, and I learned more and more words, my field of inquiry broadened, and I would return again and again to the same subject, eager for further information. Sometimes a new word revived an image that some earlier experience had engraved on my brain.

I remember the morning that I first asked the meaning of the word, "love." This was before I knew many words. I had found a few early violets in the garden and brought them to my teacher. She tried to kiss me: but at that time I did not like to have any one kiss me except my mother. Miss Sullivan put her arm gently round me and spelled into my hand, "I love Helen."

"What is love?" I asked.

She drew me closer to her and said, "It is here," pointing to my heart, whose beats I was conscious of for the first time. Her words puzzled me very much because I did not then understand anything unless I touched it.

I smelt the violets in her hand and asked, half in words, half in signs, a question which meant, "Is love the sweetness of flowers?"

"No," said my teacher.

Again I thought. The warm sun was shining on us.

"Is this not love?" I asked, pointing in the direction from which the heat came. "Is this not love?"

It seemed to me that there could be nothing more beautiful than the sun, whose warmth makes all things grow. But Miss Sullivan shook her head, and I was greatly puzzled and disappointed. I thought it strange that my teacher could not show me love.

A day or two afterward I was stringing beads of different sizes in symmetrical groups—two large beads, three small ones, and so on. I had made many mistakes, and Miss Sullivan had pointed them out again and again with gentle patience. Finally I noticed a very obvious error in the sequence and for an instant I concentrated my attention on the lesson and tried to think how I should have arranged the beads. Miss Sullivan touched my forehead and spelled with decided emphasis, "Think."

In a flash I knew that the word was the name of the process that was going on in my head. This was my first conscious perception of an abstract idea.

For a long time I was still—I was not thinking of the beads in my lap, but trying to find a meaning for "love" in the light of this new idea. The sun had been under a cloud all day, and there had been brief showers; but suddenly the sun broke forth in all its southern splendour.

Again I asked my teacher, "Is this not love?"

"Love is something like the clouds that were in the sky before the sun came out," she replied. Then in simpler words than these, which at that time I could not have understood, she explained: "You cannot touch the clouds, you know; but you feel the rain and know how glad the flowers and the thirsty earth are to have it after a hot day. You cannot touch love either; but you feel the sweetness that it pours into everything. Without love you would not be happy or want to play."

The beautiful truth burst upon my mind—I felt that there were invisible lines stretched between my spirit and the spirits of others.

Questions 2.1

1. Without language and communication, socialization cannot take place. Discuss.
2. What natural skills were developed by Helen Keller during the period discussed in this article? Could she have learned these skills without the help of others? Is the same true for a person who doesn't have the handicaps that Helen Keller had?

Reading 2.2

Mascot

MALCOLM X

Socialization involves many things. Part of it is learning that you are male or female, short or tall, black or white; a major part is learning how people react to you *because* you are male or female, short or tall, black or white. These reactions and interpretations become an important part of the self. Many people probably do not recall the stage in the socialization process when they became aware of their sex or race. In order to remember, one must be very perceptive, and the new learning must be so unique or unexpected that it creates a lasting impression. In this excerpt from his autobiography, Malcolm X recalls learning what it means to be black in America.

... They told me I was going to go to a reform school. I was still thirteen years old.

But first I was going to the detention home. It was in Mason, Michigan, about twelve miles from Lansing. The detention home was where all the "bad" boys and girls from Ingham County were held, on their way to reform school—waiting for their hearings.

The white state man was a Mr. Maynard Allen. He was nicer to me than most of the state Welfare people had been. He even had consoling words for the Gohannas and Mrs. Adcock and Big Boy; all of them were crying. But I wasn't. With the few clothes I owned stuffed into a box, we rode in his car to Mason. He talked as he drove along, saying that my school marks showed that if I would just straighten up, I could make something of myself. He said that reform school had the wrong reputation; he talked about what the word "reform" meant—to change and become better. He said the school was really a place where boys like me could have time to see their mistakes and start a new life and become somebody everyone would be proud of. And he told me that the lady in charge of the detention home, a Mrs. Swerlin, and her husband were very good people.

They were good people. Mrs. Swerlin was bigger than her husband, I remember, a big, buxom, robust, laughing woman, and Mr. Swerlin was thin, with black hair, and a black mustache and a red face, quiet and polite, even to me.

They liked me right away, too. Mrs. Swerlin showed me to my room, my own room—the first in my life. It was in one of those huge dormitory-like buildings where kids in detention were kept in those days—and still are in most places. I discovered next, with surprise, that I was allowed to eat with the Swerlins. It was the first time I'd eaten with white people—at least with grown white people—since the Seventh Day Adventist country meetings. It wasn't my own exclusive privilege, of course. Except for the very troublesome boys and girls at the detention home, who were kept locked up—those who had run away and been caught and brought back, or something like that—all of us ate with the Swerlins sitting at the head of the long tables.

They had a white cook-helper, I recall—Lucille Lathrop. (It amazes me how these names come back, from a time I haven't thought about for more than twenty years.) Lucille treated me well, too. Her husband's name was Duane Lathrop. He worked somewhere else, but he stayed there at the detention home on the weekends with Lucille.

I noticed again how white people smelled different from us, and how their food tasted different, not seasoned like Negro cooking. I began to sweep and mop and dust around in the Swerlins' house, as I had done with Big Boy at the Gohannas'.

They all liked my attitude, and it was out of their liking for me that I soon became accepted by them—as a mascot, I know now. They would talk about anything and everything with me standing right there hearing them, the same way people would talk freely in front of a pet canary. They would even talk about me, or about "niggers," as though I wasn't there, as if I wouldn't understand what the word meant. A hundred times a day, they used the word "nigger." I suppose that in their own minds, they meant no harm; in fact they probably meant well. It was the same with the cook, Lucille, and her husband, Duane. I remember one day when Mr. Swerlin, as nice as he was, came in from Lansing, where he had been through the Negro section, and said to Mrs. Swerlin right in front of me, "I just can't see how those niggers can be so happy and be so poor." He talked about how they lived in shacks, but had those big, shining cars out front.

And Mrs. Swerlin said, me standing right there, "Niggers are just that way. . . ." That scene always stayed with me.

It was the same with the other white people, most of them local politicians, when they would come visiting the Swerlins. One of their favorite parlor topics was "niggers." One of them was the judge who was in charge of me in Lansing. He was a close friend of the Swerlins. He would ask about me when he came, and they would call me in, and he would look me up and down, his expression approving, like he was examining a fine colt, or a pedigreed pup. I knew they must have told him how I acted and how I worked.

What I am trying to say is that it just never dawned upon them that I could understand, that I wasn't a pet, but a human being. They didn't give me credit for having the same sensitivity, intellect, and understanding that they would have been ready and willing to recognize in a white boy in my position. But it has historically been the case with white people, in their regard for black people, that even though we might be *with* them, we weren't considered *of* them. Even though they appeared to have opened the door, it was still closed. Thus they never did really see *me*.

This is the sort of kindly condescension which I try to clarify today, to these integration-hungry Negroes, about their "liberal" white friends, these so-called "good white people"—most of them anyway. I don't care how nice one is to you; the thing you must always remember is that almost never does he really see you as he sees himself, as he sees his own kind. He may stand with you through thin, but not thick; when the chips are down, you'll find that as fixed in him as his bone structure is his sometimes subconscious conviction that he's better than anybody black.

But I was no more than vaguely aware of anything like that in my detention-home years. I did my little chores around the house, and everything was fine. And each week-end, they didn't mind my catching a ride over to Lansing for the afternoon or evening. If I wasn't old enough, I sure was big enough by then, and nobody ever questioned my hanging out, even at night, in the streets of the Negro section.

I was growing up to be even bigger than Wilfred and Philbert, who had begun to meet girls at the school dances, and other places, and introduced me to a few. But the ones who seemed to like me, I didn't go for—and vice versa. I couldn't dance a lick, anyway, and I couldn't see squandering my few dimes on girls. So mostly I pleasured myself these Saturday nights by gawking around the Negro bars and restaurants. The jukeboxes were wailing Erskine Hawkins' "Tuxedo Junction," Slim and Slam's "Flatfoot Floogie," things like that. Sometimes, big bands from New York, out touring the one-night stands in the sticks, would play for big dances in Lansing. Everybody with legs would come out to see any performer who bore the magic name "New York." Which is how I first heard Lucky Thompson and Milt Jackson, both of whom I later got to know well in Harlem.

Many youngsters from the detention home, when their dates came up, went off to the reform school. But when mine came up—two or three times—it was always ignored. I saw new youngsters arrive and leave. I was glad and grateful. I knew it was Mrs. Swerlin's doing. I didn't want to leave.

She finally told me one day that I was going to be entered in Mason Junior High School. It was the only school in town. No ward of the detention home had ever gone to school there, at least while still a ward. So I entered their seventh grade. The only other Negroes there were some of the Lyons children, younger than I was, in the lower grades. The Lyons and I, as it happened, were the town's only Negroes. They were, as Negroes, very much respected. Mr. Lyons was a smart, hardworking man, and Mrs. Lyons was a very good woman. She and my mother, I had heard my mother say, were two of the four West Indians in that whole section of Michigan.

Some of the white kids at school, I found, were even friendlier than some of those in Lansing had been. Though some, including the teachers, called me "nigger," it was easy to see that they didn't mean any more harm by it than the Swerlins. As the "nigger" of my class, I was in fact extremely popular—I suppose partly because I was kind of a novelty. I was in demand, I had top priority. But

I also benefited from the special prestige of having the seal of approval from that Very Important Woman about the town of Mason, Mrs. Swerlin. Nobody in Mason would have dreamed of getting on the wrong side of her. It became hard for me to get through a school day without someone after me to join this or head up that—the debating society, the Junior High basketball team, or some other extracurricular activity. I never turned them down.

And I hadn't been in the school long when Mrs. Swerlin, knowing I could use spending money of my own, got me a job after school washing the dishes in a local restaurant. My boss there was the father of a white classmate whom I spent a lot of time with. His family lived over the restaurant. It was fine working there. Every Friday night when I got paid, I'd feel at least ten feet tall. I forget how much I made, but it seemed like a lot. It was the first time I'd ever had any money to speak of, all my own, in my whole life. As soon as I could afford it, I bought a green suit and some shoes, and at school I'd buy treats for the others in my class—at least as much as any of them did for me.

English and history were the subjects I liked most. My English teacher, I recall —a Mr. Ostrowski—was always giving advice about how to become something in life. The one thing I didn't like about history class was that the teacher, Mr. Williams, was a great one for "nigger" jokes. One day during my first week at school, I walked into the room and he started singing to the class, as a joke, " 'Way down yonder in the cotton field, some folks say that a nigger won't steal." Very funny. I liked history, but I never thereafter had much liking for Mr. Williams. Later, I remember, we came to the textbook section on Negro history. It was exactly one paragraph long. Mr. Williams laughed through it practically in a single breath, reading aloud how the Negroes had been slaves and then were freed, and how they were usually lazy and dumb and shiftless. He added, I remember, an anthropological footnote on his own, telling us between laughs how Negroes' feet were "so big that when they walk, they don't leave tracks, they leave a hole in the ground."

. . . Then, in the second semester of the seventh grade, I was elected class president. It surprised me even more than other people. But I can see now why the class might have done it. My grades were among the highest in the school. I was unique in my class, like a pink poodle. And I was proud; I'm not going to say I wasn't. In fact, by then, I didn't really have much feeling about being a Negro, because I was trying so hard, in every way I could, to be white. Which is why I am spending much of my life today telling the American black man that he's wasting his time straining to "integrate." I know from personal experience. I tried hard enough. . . .

That summer of 1940, in Lansing, I caught the Greyhound bus for Boston with my cardboard suitcase, and wearing my green suit. If someone had hung a sign, *"hick,"* around my neck, I couldn't have looked much more obvious. They didn't have the turnpikes then; the bus stopped at what seemed every corner and cowpatch. From my seat in—you guessed it—the back of the bus, I gawked out of the window at white man's America rolling past for what seemed a month, but must have been only a day and a half.

When we finally arrived, Ella met me at the terminal and took me home. The house was on Waumbeck Street in the Sugar Hill section of Roxbury, the Harlem of Boston. I met Ella's second husband, Frank, who was now a soldier; and her brother Earl, the singer who called himself Jimmy Carleton; and Mary, who was very different from her older sister. It's funny how I seemed to think of Mary as Ella's sister, instead of her being, just as Ella is, my own half-sister. It's probably because Ella and I always were much closer as basic types; we're dominant people, and Mary has always been mild and quiet, almost shy.

Ella was busily involved in dozens of things. She belonged to I don't know how many different clubs; she was a leading light of local so-called "black society." I saw and met a hundred black people there whose big-city talk and ways left my mouth hanging open.

I couldn't have feigned indifference if I had tried to. People talked casually about Chicago, Detroit, New York. I didn't know the world contained as many Negroes as I saw thronging downtown Roxbury at night, especially on Saturdays. Neon lights, nightclubs, poolhalls, bars, the cars they drove! Restaurants made the streets smell—rich, greasy, down-home black cooking! Jukeboxes blared Erskine Hawkins, Duke Ellington, Cootie Williams, dozens of others. If somebody had told me then that some day I'd know them all personally, I'd have found it hard to believe. The biggest bands, like these, played at the Roseland State Ballroom, on Boston's Massachusetts Avenue—one night for Negroes, the next night for whites.

I saw for the first time occasional black-white couples strolling around arm in arm. And on Sundays, when Ella, Mary, or somebody took me to church, I saw churches for black people such as I had never seen. They were many times finer than the white church I had attended back in Mason, Michigan. There, the white people just sat and worshiped with words; but the Boston Negroes, like all other Negroes I had ever seen at church, threw their souls and bodies wholly into worship.

Two or three times, I wrote letters to Wilfred intended for everybody back in Lansing. I said I'd try to describe it when I got back.

But I found I couldn't.

My restlessness with Mason—and for the first time in my life a restlessness with being around white people—began as soon as I got back home and entered eighth grade.

I continued to think constantly about all that I had seen in Boston, and about the way I had felt there. I know now that it was the sense of being a real part of a mass of my own kind for the first time.

The white people—classmates, the Swerlins, the people at the restaurant where I worked—noticed the change. They said, "You're acting so strange. You don't seem like yourself, Malcolm. What's the matter?"

I kept close to the top of the class, though. The top-most scholastic standing, I remember, kept shifting between me, a girl named Audrey Slaugh, and a boy named Jimmy Cotton.

It went on that way, as I became increasingly restless and disturbed through the first semester. And then one day, just about when those of us who had passed were about to move up to 8-A, from which we would enter high school the next year something happened which was to become the first major turning point of my life.

Somehow, I happened to be alone in the classroom with Mr. Ostrowski, my English teacher. He was a tall, rather reddish white man and he had a thick mustache. I had gotten some of my best marks under him, and he had always made me feel that he liked me. He was, as I have mentioned, a natural-born "advisor," about what you ought to read, to do, or think—about any and everything. We used to make unkind jokes about him: why was he teaching in Mason instead of somewhere else, getting for himself some of the "success in life" that he kept telling us how to get?

I know that he probably meant well in what he happened to advise me that day. I doubt that he meant any harm. It was just in his nature as an American white man. I was one of his top students, one of the school's top students—but all he could see for me was the kind of future "in your place" that almost all white people see for black people.

He told me, "Malcolm, you ought to be thinking about a career. Have you been giving it thought?"

The truth is, I hadn't. I never had figured out why I told him, "Well, yes, sir, I've been thinking I'd like to be a lawyer." Lansing certainly had no Negro lawyers —or doctors either—in those days, to hold up an image I might have aspired to. All I really knew for certain was that a lawyer didn't wash dishes, as I was doing.

Mr. Ostrowski looked surprised, I remember, and leaned back in his chair and clasped his hands behind his head. He kind of half-smiled and said, "Malcolm, one of life's first needs is for us to be realistic. Don't misunderstand me, now. We all here like you, you know that. But you've got to be realistic about being a nigger. A lawyer—that's no realistic goal for a nigger. You need to think about something you *can* be. You're good with your hands—making things. Everybody admires your carpentry shop work. Why don't you plan on carpentry? People like you as a person—you'd get all kinds of work."

The more I thought afterwards about what he said, the more uneasy it made me. It just kept treading around in my mind.

What made it really begin to disturb me was Mr. Ostrowski's advice to others in my class—all of them white. Most of them told him they were planning to become farmers. But those who wanted to strike out on their own, to try something new, he had encouraged. Some, mostly girls, wanted to be teachers. A few wanted other professions, such as one boy who wanted to become a county agent; another, a veterinarian; and one girl wanted to be a nurse. They all reported that Mr. Ostrowski had encouraged what they had wanted. Yet nearly none of them had earned marks equal to mine.

It was a surprising thing that I had never thought of it that way before, but I realized that whatever I wasn't, I *was* smarter than nearly all of those white kids. But apparently I was still not intelligent enough, in their eyes, to become whatever *I* wanted to be.

It was then that I began to change—inside.

I drew away from white people. I came to class, and I answered when called upon. It became a physical strain simply to sit in Mr. Ostrowski's class.

Where "nigger" had slipped off my back before, wherever I heard it now, I stopped and looked at whoever said it. And they looked surprised that I did.

I quit hearing so much "nigger" and "What's wrong?"—which was the way I wanted it. Nobody, including the teachers, could decide what had come over me. I knew I was being discussed.

In a few more weeks, it was that way, too, at the restaurant where I worked washing dishes, and at the Swerlins'. . . .

Questions 2.2

1. Malcolm X believes he was treated as a "mascot." What does he mean by this? Why was he treated this way? Discuss.
2. Outline the important aspects of socialization that occurred during the period described by Malcolm X. Who were the socialization agents in this section?
3. Review Chapter 2, and using examples from Malcolm X, illustrate development of the self using Cooley's and Mead's theories.

Reading 2.3

Cipher in the Snow

JEAN E. MIZER

Socialization and development of self are interactive processes that are critically important in the growth and future of every individual. Seldom, however, are these processes so graphically and dramatically displayed as they are in this reading. Jean Mizer was a school teacher in Idaho when she wrote this memoir of a personal experience.

It started with tragedy on a biting cold February morning. I was driving behind the Milford Corners bus as I did most snowy mornings on my way to school. It veered and stopped short at the hotel, which it had no business doing, and I was annoyed as I had to come to an unexpected stop. A boy lurched out of the bus, reeled, stumbled, and collapsed on the snowbank at the curb. The bus driver and I reached him at the same moment. His thin, hollow face was white even against the snow.

"He's dead," the driver whispered.

I didn't register for a minute. I glanced quickly at the scared young faces staring down at us from the school bus. "A doctor! Quick! I'll phone from the hotel. . . ."

"No use. I tell you he's dead." The driver looked down at the boy's still form. "He never even said he felt bad," he muttered, "just tapped me on the shoulder and said, real quiet, 'I'm sorry. I have to get off at the hotel.' That's all. Polite and apologizing like."

Reprinted from the November 1964 issue of *NEA Journal* by permission of the National Education Association and the author.

At school, the giggling, shuffling morning noise quieted as the news went down the halls. I passed a huddle of girls. "Who was it? Who dropped dead on the way to school?" I heard one of them half-whisper.

"Don't know his name; some kid from Milford Corners," was the reply.

It was like that in the faculty room and the principal's office. "I'd appreciate your going out to tell the parents," the principal told me. "They haven't a phone and, anyway, somebody from school should go there in person. I'll cover your classes."

"Why me?" I asked. "Wouldn't it be better if you did it?"

"I didn't know the boy," the principal admitted levelly. "And in last year's sophomore personalities column I note that you were listed as his favorite teacher."

I drove through the snow and cold down the bad canyon road to the Evans place and thought about the boy, Cliff Evans. His favorite teacher! I thought. He hasn't spoken two words to me in two years! I could see him in my mind's eye all right, sitting back there in the last seat in my afternoon literature class. He came in the room by himself and left by himself. "Cliff Evans," I muttered to myself, "a boy who never talked." I thought a minute. "A boy who never smiled. I never saw him smile once."

The big ranch kitchen was clean and warm. I blurted out my news somehow. Mrs. Evans reached blindly toward a chair. "He never said anything about bein' ailing."

His step-father snorted. "He ain't said nothin' about anything since I moved in here."

Mrs. Evans pushed a pan to the back of the stove and began to untie her apron. "Now hold on," her husband snapped. "I got to have breakfast before I go to town. Nothin' we can do now anyway. If Cliff hadn't been so dumb, he'd have told us he didn't feel good."

After school I sat in the office and stared bleakly at the records spread out before me. I was to close the file and write the obituary for the school paper. The almost bare sheets mocked the effort. Cliff Evans, white, never legally adopted by step-father, five young half-brothers and sisters. These meager strands of information and the list of D grades were all the records had to offer.

Cliff Evans had silently come in the school door in the mornings and gone out the school door in the evenings, and that was all. He had never belonged to a club. He had never played on a team. He had never held an office. As far as I could tell, he had never done one happy, noisy kid thing. He had never been anybody at all.

How do you go about making a boy into a zero? The grade school records showed me. The first and second grade teachers' annotations read "sweet, shy child"; "timid but eager." Then the third grade note had opened the attack. Some teacher had written in a good, firm hand, "Cliff won't talk. Uncooperative. Slow learner." The other academic sheep had followed with "dull"; "slow-witted"; "low I.Q." They became correct. The boy's I.Q. score in the ninth grade was listed at 83. But his I.Q. in the third grade had been 106. The score didn't go under 100 until the seventh grade. Even shy, timid, sweet children have resilience. It takes time to break them.

I stomped to the typewriter and wrote a savage report pointing out what education had done to Cliff Evans. I slapped a copy on the principal's desk and another in the sad, dog-eared file. I banged the typewriter and slammed the file and crashed the door shut, but I didn't feel much better. A little boy kept walking after me, a little boy with a peaked, pale face; a skinny body in faded jeans; and big eyes that had looked and searched for a long time and then had become veiled.

I could guess how many times he'd been chosen last to play sides in a game, how many whispered child conversations had excluded him, how many times he hadn't been asked. I could see and hear the faces and voices that said over and over, "You're dumb. You're dumb. You're nothing, Cliff Evans."

A child is a believing creature. Cliff undoubtedly believed them. Suddenly it seemed clear to me: When finally there was nothing left at all for Cliff Evans, he collapsed on a snowbank and went away. The doctor might list "heart failure" as the cause of death, but that wouldn't change my mind.

We couldn't find ten students in the school who had known Cliff well enough to attend the funeral as his friends. So the student body officers and a committee from the junior class went as a group to the church, being politely sad. I attended the services with them, and sat through it with a lump of cold lead in my chest and a big resolve growing through me.

I've never forgotten Cliff Evans nor that resolve. He has been my challenge year after year, class after class. I look up and down the rows carefully each September at the unfamiliar faces. I look for veiled eyes or bodies scrouged into a seat in an alien world. "Look, kids," I say silently, "I may not do anything else for you this year, but not one of you is going to come out of here a nobody. I'll work or fight to the bitter end doing battle with society and the school board, but I won't have one of you coming out of here thinking himself into a zero."

Most of the time—not always, but most of the time—I've succeeded.

Questions 2.3

1. How does the self-fulfilling prophecy apply in this situation?
2. Who were the agents of socialization in this story? Why did they define Cliff Evans as they did?

Reading 2.4
A Conversation with Jerome Kagan

SATURDAY REVIEW

The importance of the first year or two of life in determining intelligence and learning capacity is emphasized by numerous experts, including Freud, Piaget, and many learning theorists. Jerome Kagan believed it, too, until he discovered a village in Guatemala in which the children broke all the rules of development. What follows is an interview with Kagan by the editors of *Saturday Review* on his research. Jerome Kagan is a professor of human development at Harvard University.

SR   *What happened in Guatemala to make you reverse your thinking?*
Kagan   I found myself in a thirteenth-century, pre-Columbian village, located on the shores of Lake Atitlan. I saw 850 Indians, poor, exploited, alienated, bitter, sick. I saw infants in the first years of their lives completely isolated in their homes, because parents believe that sun and dust and air or the gazes of either pregnant women or men fresh with perspiration from the field will cause illness. It's the evil-eye belief. So the infants are kept in the hut. Now these are bamboo huts, and there are no windows, so the light level in this hut at high noon in a perfectly azure sky is what it should be at dusk. Very dark. Although parents love their children —mothers nurse on demand and hold their infants close to their bodies—they don't talk or interact with them. And there are no toys. So at one and one-half years of age, you have a very retarded child.
SR   *What are the children like?*
Kagan   Not only are they quiet, somber, motorically passive, and extremely fearful, but on tests of maturational and intellectual development, they are four or five months behind American children.
SR   *What kinds of tests do you use?*
Kagan   Here's an example of a maturational test. Take a child nine months of age, cover an object with a cloth, and then, through sleight of hand, remove the object. We know from Piaget's work that if he pulls off the cloth and the object's not there, he shows surprise, indicating that he knows the object should be there. That ability should occur somewhere in the last third of the first year. None of the Guatemalan babies showed this until 18 months of age. We also know that babies in the Western world become frightened of strangers at about eight months. It's called "stranger anxiety." You won't get that [in Guatemala] until the middle of the second year. In the Western world children begin to talk about 12 and 18 months. The Guatemalan kids don't talk until about two and a half to three years. If I had seen infants like the Guatemalans in America prior to my experience, I would have gotten very upset, called the police, had the children removed, and begun to make gloomy statements about the fact that it was all over for these children.
SR   *But they do recover.*
Kagan   That's the paradox. The 11-year-olds in this Guatemalan village are beautiful. They're gay, alert, active, affective, just like 11-year-olds in the United States. They're *more* impressive than Americans in a set of "culture-fair" tests— where the words and the materials are familiar. For example, we asked them, "What is brown, hard, and found near the shore of the lake?" And they'd say, "a wharf." They have no problem with this. In reasoning, memory, inference, deduction, and perception, these children at 11—who, we must assume, were "ghosts" as infants—had recovered. Therefore, one must conclude that the first two years of life do not inexorably doom you to retardation and that there's much more

potential for recovery than Western psychologists have surmised, including me. I didn't go to Guatemala to prove this; I found it a complete surprise.

SR   *Don't the experiments that Harry Harlow [a psychologist at the University of Wisconsin] conducted with monkeys contradict that conclusion?*

Kagan   They did until last year, when Harlow published a very important report. He took monkeys and put them in isolation for six months, and they emerged with the expected bizarre, abnormal, crazy behavior. But this time he placed them with normal infant female monkeys three months younger than themselves for 26 weeks (seven months). He reports that after seven months they could not be distinguished from normal monkeys. If we can do this in seven months with a creature less complex than we, then certainly it does not require an enormous stretch of immagination to believe that in nine years a human infant, treated less bizarrely, can recover.

SR   *Any human studies to support your findings?*

Kagan   Freda Rebelsky spent several years in eastern Holland, where there is a middle-class, stable, nuclear family arrangement. In this small part of this very small country, it's local custom to isolate a child for the first ten months. He's put in a room outside the house; he's tightly bound—no mobiles, no toys, and minimal interaction. Like our Guatemalan children. He emerges at one year absolutely retarded, but at five years of age he's fully recovered.

SR   *But what about René Spitz's [a professor of psychiatry at the University of Colorado] observations?*

Kagan   Spitz made his observations on South American children in an orphanage. He saw ghostlike (what he called "marasmic") children much like the ones I saw. They lacked both stimulation and affection, so he made the same mistake many analysts have made and concluded their retardation was due to lack of affection. It's not affection, because my infants in San Marcos are on their mothers' bodies three-quarters of the day, and they get lots of physical holding, lots of skin contact. So it's not the love, but the input, that's important.

SR   *If you kept the infant or the monkey deprived for a longer period of time, would there be permanent effects?*

Kagan   We don't know. I am not saying that there is no treatment you can give a child from which he cannot recover. That is obviously too strong. We do have extreme case-history reports: for instance, a mother locked her kid up in a closet for six years. He emerged mute but still managed to learn language later. But I'm trying to be a reasonably cautious person. What I can say with confidence—and had I not had this experience, I would have resisted it—is that an abnormal experience in the first two years of life in no way affects basic intellectual functions or the ability to be affectively normal—to experience gaiety and sadness, guilt and shame.

SR   *What implications do you see for American schools?*

Kagan   I think my work suggests we've got to stop the very early, and I think, premature rank-ordering of children in grades one, two, and three. We decide too soon. Poor children enter the school system (a) with less motivation, because they see less value in intellectual activity, and (b) one or two years behind in the emergence of what I call executive-cognitive functions (what Piaget would call concrete operational thinking). They are going to get there, but they are a year or two behind. We arbitrarily decide that age seven is when the race starts, so you have a larger proportion of poor than of privileged children who are not yet ready for school instruction. And then we classify them, prematurely. Let's use the example of puberty. Suppose we decided that fertility was important in our society and that fertility should occur at age 13. Then if you're not fertile at 13, we conclude that you are never going to be fertile, and we give you a different kind of life. It's illogical, because that 13-year-old who is not fertile now will be next year.

SR   *In other words, learning does not follow the same pattern in every child.*

Kagan   Yes. We used to think that all learning was continuous—like a "freight train." There is a series of closely connected cars: you start at car one and do certain things; then you jump to car two, and you carry your baggage with you. But now let me substitute an analogy that makes more sense: development as a series of lily pads. I choose that because lily pads are farther apart, because each child dumps a lot of baggage in traversing the lily pads (he doesn't have to carry everything with him), and because he can skip some of the lily pads. American psychologists have surmised that you could never walk unless you crawled. Now we know that is false. I could prevent a child from crawling—bind him up until he was two and then unbind him—and we know he would walk. He wouldn't have to crawl. Now maybe that analogy holds for a lot more in mental development than we have surmised.

SR   *How has the public reacted to your rather optimistic conclusions?*

Kagan   What I say is often misunderstood. When I say kids can catch up, people say that can't be right, because they know that a poor child always remains retarded relative to a middle-class child in the school system. But these people— most Americans—are confusing relative and absolute standards. Absolute retardation refers to a lack of certain fundamental motor, affective, and intellectual skills that are basic to our species. They include crawling, walking, standing, speaking, inference, and reasoning. Now if a child isn't walking by three, he is absolutely retarded. If a child cannot remember four numbers when he is ten years old, he is absolutely retarded.

SR   *Then what is "relative retardation"?*

Kagan   If kids don't have certain culturally arbitrary skills—like being able to read—they are retarded relative to some other reference group. When we say a Mexican-American child from a ghetto is retarded, we mean relative to that arbitrary reference which is the middle-class child. The analogy of physical development should make that distinction clearer. There are natural skills like walking or running which you get better at each year; if a child of ten cannot run as fast as a three-year-old, we worry about it. So it makes sense to say that this ten-year-old is physically retarded. But would we ever say that a ten-year-old who can't play hockey is retarded? Well, when it comes to intellectual skills, that's exactly what we do; we say if this child can't multiply, he is retarded. But multiplication is like hockey; no child's going to know how to multiply unless you teach him how to multiply. See the mistake we make? In the physical area we never confuse relative with absolute retardation. But in the mental area we do.

SR   *Given the vast implications of your study, where do you plan to go from here?*

Kagan   I want to see schools begin to serve the needs of society. Ancient Sparta needed warriors, Athens needed a sense of the hero, the ancient Hebrews needed knowledge of the Testament, nineteenth-century Americans needed managers and technicians—and the schools responded beautifully in each case by providing the kind of people the society needed. What do we need now? I believe that we need to restore faith, honesty, humanity. And I am suggesting in deep seriousness that we must, in the school, begin to reward these traits as the Spartans rewarded physical fitness. I want children rank-ordered on the basis of humanism as we rank-order on the basis of reading and mathematics. I'm dead serious. When I was a kid, deportment was always a grade. In a funny way, I want that, but instead of deportment, I want him graded on humanism: How kind is he? How nurturant is he?

SR   *But aren't we getting back then to the same problem of sorting?*

Kagan   Every society must sort its children according to the traits it values. We will never get away from that. A society needs a set of people whom it can trust in and give responsibility to for the management of its capital and resources, for the health of its people, the legal prerogatives of its people, the wars of its people. The function of the school system is in fact to prepare this class.

Questions 2.4

1. Isolation in the early years of life leads to retardation. Discuss.
2. Can socialization occur without interaction, or is some kind of social interaction actually occurring between the Guatemalan infants and their parents?
3. Different socialization patterns in different societies still result in normal, nonretarded children. Discuss.
4. If it is true that learning does not follow the same pattern in every child, what implications does this have for our school systems?

3 Norms, Roles, Culture

A sociology instructor is lecturing to a class of college freshmen and sophomores. At one point in her lecture, she asks a student to help her illustrate a point by standing up. The student is belligerent and upset at being interrupted in his reading of the school newspaper. The student replies that he would rather not help and that the teacher should ask someone else. The teacher asks the student once more to please help her with the experiment and to stand up. The student replies in a louder voice that he doesn't think much of this stupid class or the teacher, and he is not about to participate in some silly experiment. The now angry teacher responds, "Either stand up or get out of this classroom!" The student replies, "I'm not standing up—and if you want me out of here you'll have to throw me out!" The two then glare at each other for what seems like a year.

If we were watching the scene and could take our eyes off the principal characters, we would notice that the rest of the class is behaving strangely. Nearly all appear to be very uncomfortable, many are obviously embarrassed. They are twisting and squirming and are avoiding meeting the eyes of the instructor. At the beginning of the confrontation some may have laughed nervously; now all are quiet. They act as if they are trying to deny that what is happening is actually happening. . . . Why?

Society and Social Structure

We learned in Chapter 1 that sociology studies the origin, development, organization and functioning of human society. At its most general, the term society refers to human association and the existence of social relationships. This is too general for our use, however, because it suggests that any set of people interacting could be called a society. A more precise definition states that a **society** is a continuing number of people living in a specific area who are relatively organized, self-sufficient and independent, and share a common culture. Continuing means that there is some permanence to the society. The number of people can vary greatly —American society numbers more than 220 million people while there are other societies that number less than 1000 people. By *organized* we mean that there is some systematization and structure to the patterns of social interaction. A society occupies an area; it has boundaries that separate it from other societies. In part these boundaries are what we usually think of—an ocean, a river, a mountain, or a line drawn on a map. The essential point, however, is that these are *social* boundaries —the vast majority of the social interactions of a society take place within a particular area. Finally, each society, because of its particular cultural beliefs, habits, and traditions, has certain unique characteristics that distinguish it or make it different from other societies.

As you can see, several of the terms in our definition involve matters of degree. There is often much interaction between societies, and probably no society is totally independent of others. Although interpretation will always be necessary, I think this definition should give us a reasonably good idea of what is meant by society. There are other uses of the term that don't fit our definition. Special interest groups such as professional organizations (Society for the Study of Social Problems), political groups (John Birch Society), social clubs (Second Street Skateboard Society), and other groups are *not* societies in the sociological sense. And whatever it is that those people have whose pictures appear in the "society" pages of the newspapers, it isn't society. None of these groups alone constitutes a society; all of them are part of a society.

How do sociologists study human society? Let's suggest for a moment that any given society has a form, a composition, a structure. Imagine society to be like a building with many parts—wood, steel, bricks, and concrete—all somehow attached together into a coherent structure. Look at the end product and you see a five-story building, but there are actually thousands of elements that make up the whole. It is not a group of random parts, but a network, a structure. Now take society as a building. The many parts are people, and they are held together by the ways they relate to each other, their relationships to each other. The people of society, just like the steel and concrete of the building, are held together in very specific ways.

We can take the five-story building apart to examine its elements, and we can do the same with a society. As we look at the ways people relate to each other we find that these ways fit consistent patterns. The same important elements seem to appear again and again. **Social structure** refers to the network of ways people relate to each other in society. Sociologists study human society by concentrating on social structure. The important elements of social structure appear to be norm, status, role, group, and institution. Norm, status, and role will be discussed in this chapter, group and institution in later chapters.

Norms

All societies have rules that specify what people should do in specific situations. Sociologists call these shared standards for behavior **norms.** Norms describe the accepted or required behavior for a person in a particular situation. When a person gets into a car, that person unconsciously begins to behave according to a whole set of norms relating to driving procedure. In America the driver knows that he or she should drive on the right side of the road, pass on the left, signal before turning, and so on. The norms vary from place to place, but they always exist. These shared standards for behavior allow us to predict what other people will do. Without even thinking about it or knowing him or her, I know how the driver of the car approaching me will behave. The system of norms allows us to predict what other people will do in specific situations and to pattern our own behavior accordingly.

Where do norms come from? Like much of what we discuss in this book, norms emerge through the process of social interaction. As people interact, they come to understand that certain ways of behaving are proper and acceptable, and that other ways are improper and unacceptable. Norms develop out of this growing network of beliefs and values that people have about the way things should happen. Some values—for example, the sanctity of life, the importance of telling the truth—reflect widely held beliefs and are a part of custom and tradition. The norms that emerge relating to these values are also a part of custom and tradition. Other norms are of shorter duration and may reflect the values of a particular group. As values change, norms change. For example, norms dealing with fashion in clothes and in slang seem to change continually.

It is disturbing when the normative system breaks down and predictability of behavior vanishes. Norm breakdown occurs when there are conflicting sets of norms and when groups and societies change. We see norm breakdown most vividly during periods of rapid social change, such as wars or disasters. When norms cease to be effective at controlling people's behavior, we say that a state of normlessness is present. One tends to lose all sense of stability, security, and orderliness when norms break down. Imagine the consternation if we did not know what to expect of that oncoming driver—if we had *no* idea what he or she was going to do.

This may explain the strange behavior of the students in the classroom. There are norms that govern the student-teacher relationship. These norms are so obvious and ingrained that we do not even think about them. Characteristically, norms do not become apparent until they are violated. According to norms dealing with student-teacher relationships, the student will show respect for the teacher, will laugh at his or her jokes, and will generally obey the authority that the teacher represents. That is, students will respect any reasonable demands made by the teacher without resorting to mutiny. When, as in our example above, behavior is contrary to the norms, the situation becomes uncomfortable for others. Instructors who have tried this "stand up" experiment on classes (with the aid of a willing villain) report that the experience is almost as hard on the two of them (instructor and villain), who know it's a fake, as it is for the rest of the class, who don't know that it has been set up. Thus even planned and legitimate norm violation may be hard on individuals when done in the context of a group that is unaware of the new definitions.

Other experiments in norm violation have been devised.[1] For example, get somebody you don't know very well in a game of ticktacktoe. Invite the other person to make the first move. After he or she makes a mark, you erase it, move it to another square, and make your own mark. Act as if nothing unusual has happened. Or select a person (not a family member or very close friend) and during the course of an ordinary conversation, and without indicating that anything unusual is happening, bring your face closer to the other person's until your noses are almost touching. The first experiment deals with norms concerning game playing, and the second with norms concerning spatial invasion or the appropriate distance between people. In each case, the subject will react noticeably (and possibly unpredictably) because common norms that ordinarily one doesn't even think about are suddenly being violated.

Types of Norms

Norm strength varies greatly. One way of determining the relative strength of norms is by the sanctions that the norms carry. A **sanction** is the punishment one receives for violation of a norm or the reward one receives for correct norm performance. Sanctions take a variety of forms: a look on someone's face, an "A" on an exam, a sharp word from a spouse or boss, a kind word from a parent, a traffic ticket from a police officer, a life sentence in a penitentiary. Norms that are most important to a society, that tend to be obeyed without question, and that have harsh sanctions if they are violated are called **mores.** In our society, norms dealing with taking another's life, eating human flesh, and sexual activity with one's parents are examples of mores. Mores are often traditional norms that are a part of the customs of a society—"things have always been that way." When a society feels it neces-

---

[1]These and other examples are contained in *Studies in Ethnomethodology,* by Harold Garfinkel (Englewood Cliffs, N.J.: Prentice-Hall, 1967).

sary (perhaps because increasing violations mean that the informal sanctions aren't working), mores may be translated into written law. Whether written or unwritten, the emotional force of mores is strong—they still represent the "musts" of behavior.

There are also norms dealing with what we *should* do rather than what we *must* do. These norms are less obligatory than mores, and the sanctions for violation are milder in degree. People may look at us rather strangely if we violate these norms, but they probably will not lock us up or banish us. These norms are called **folkways**.[2] Practices such as shaking hands when meeting someone or norms regulating the type of clothes one wears would be considered folkways. A student coming to class in a bathing suit and golf shoes would probably be allowed to stay in spite of the obvious violation of the folkways. At the same time there would likely be ample private discussion of the student's character and intelligence.

A further distinction should be made between ideal norms and statistical norms. **Ideal norms** refer to what people agree *should* be done. **Statistical norms** refer to what they *actually* do. Ideal norms indicate that cheating on tests, premarital sexual intercourse, and falsifying one's income tax are wrong. However, statistical norms—what people are actually doing—would indicate that a substantial number of people are performing these activities. Often, amazingly enough, these are the same people who previously told us these things were wrong. It shouldn't surprise us that there may be quite a discrepancy between talk and action—or, "Do as I say, not as I do. . . ."

Norm Conflict

As we said earlier, norms develop out of a set of beliefs and values that people have about the way things should happen. Norms probably develop first at the group level when specific friendship groups, clubs, work groups, clans, organizations, or communities of people establish rules. Often these rules are informal and unwritten. Sometimes, if the people have sufficient power, their rules may become written in the form of laws.

Norms vary in how widely they are supported. For example, norms dealing with taking a human life, stealing property, or eating human flesh are probably looked at the same way by most people in United States society. On the other hand, since norms emerge from groups and since each group has its own interests and viewpoints, we shouldn't be at all surprised to see norm conflict—the norms of one group conflicting with the norms of another. People who have been taught the norm of not killing other people may find themselves as soldiers being trained to kill. The norms of the consumer often conflict with the norms of the manufacturer. Car owners want a vehicle that runs cheaply, looks beautiful, is safe, and won't fall apart in the first six months. The manufacturer is interested more in reducing costs per unit and cutting corners where possible. One would hope that the producers of the food you eat are as concerned about its purity and wholesomeness as you are when you eat it. Perhaps they're not, however; consider that laws and

[2]The terms "folkways" and "mores" were introduced by William Graham Sumner in *Folkways* (Boston: Ginn, 1907). (Later, some editions have appeared in paperback.)

agencies (Food and Drug Administration, for example) are necessary to *force* food producers to maintain standards. So, because different groups have conflicting viewpoints and motivations, norm conflict is bound to occur.

Examples of conflict over norms are not hard to find. There seems to be almost constant conflict over norms dealing with sexual conduct. Prostitution is not unknown in our society, although it is against the law nearly everywhere. Groups upset by the existence of prostitution get together to stamp it out. Other groups get together to defend prostitution. Police agencies often don't know whether to attempt to enforce laws prohibiting prostitution or to ignore its existence. For a time, narcotics laws defined possession and use of marijuana as a serious crime. In parts of society a different set of norms existed that didn't view marijuana as dangerous and encouraged its use. The energy crisis and the related effort to conserve fuel led in 1973 and 1974 to a law lowering the speed limit to fifty-five miles per hour. Highways and cars are designed for high speeds, and drivers are used to going faster than fifty-five, so there are problems with the law. In some areas, even with a continuing energy crisis so many drivers ignore the speed law that enforcement has become almost impossible.

Society's laws usually reflect its mores, but sometimes they don't. As we have said, it is natural for different segments of society to disagree on norms. Occasionally, however, a minority or special interest group gains enough power to manipulate laws. Also, sometimes change in norms is rapid, and change in laws does not keep pace. When either of these situations occurs, laws may not reflect the mores of society. Usually, when laws and mores are in conflict, mores will win in the long run. The prohibition laws in the 1920s and 1930s apparently did not reflect the mores of the country, and the laws were flagrantly violated until they were changed. Recently, as a result of the norm conflict over marijuana use, marijuana laws have been modified. A 1976 California law states that a person found to be carrying less than an ounce of marijuana will be issued a citation (similar to a traffic ticket) and will have to pay a small fine. People carrying more than an ounce may be arrested, but penalties have been reduced considerably. Another approach is for police to give enforcement of existing laws low priority. This won't resolve all norm conflict, but it represents an attempt to achieve a compromise between conflicting viewpoints. It will be interesting to see what happens on highway speed limits. Will the law be changed, will it remain, with drivers and enforcement agencies alike ignoring it, or will driving habits (norms) gradually change to conform to the slower speeds?

Status and Role

When students and an instructor walk into class the first day of the semester, they know without thinking what to expect of each other and how each will behave. They know these things even though they have not seen each other before. The students know that the instructor will stand in front of the class behind a lectern, probably call roll, assign reading, and dismiss them early the first day. The instructor knows that, unless the class is required, students will be shopping around. They will be trying to decide whether to take this class, and their decision will be based on course content, the viewpoint and personality of the instructor, the amount and type of work required, or how the instructor is known to grade.

We know these things about each other partly because of the system of norms discussed previously. The concepts of status and role are closely related to norms, and they play a major part in the situation described above. By **status** we mean a position in society or in a group. There are innumerable positions that one may occupy—teacher, student, police officer, president, football player, father, wife, convict. Furthermore, each of us may occupy several positions at once—teacher, handball player, father, husband, and so on. By **role** we mean the behavior of one who occupies a particular status. As Robert Bierstedt puts it, a role is what an individual *does* in the status he or she occupies; statuses are occupied, roles are played.[3]

A set of norms surrounds each status and role. These norms, called **role requirements,** describe the behavior expected of persons holding a particular position in society. Recalling our earlier example, the behavior of the student who refused to stand up was disturbing because it was unpredictable. He was occupying the status or position of student, but the role he played—his behavior—was contrary to the expected behavior of a person in that status. His behavior was outside the limits set by the norms or role requirements.

Within the boundaries set by the role requirements, there is often extensive variation in how a role is played. On a football team, status would refer to the positions, role to the behavior of the incumbent of the position. One status would be quarterback. Role requirements of quarterbacks are generally that they call the plays, direct the team, and try to move the ball down the field. But now look at the actual performance of several quarterbacks. One passes frequently, another

[3]Robert Bierstedt, *The Social Order,* 4th ed. (New York: McGraw-Hill, 1974), Chapter 9.

seldom passes but runs with the ball often, and a third does neither but usually blocks. Compare four or five of your instructors in their role behavior. Although all occupy the status of college professor, no doubt their behavior varies markedly. One paces the floor, another stays behind the podium while lecturing. One demands class discussion, the next dislikes having lectures interrupted. One has beautifully organized and prepared lectures, and another has a disorganized, stream-of-consciousness presentation put together on the way to class. Or compare the behavior of the last three Presidents of the United States. Again we see marked differences in role within a given status. These differences in behavior obviously occur because people holding the same status define the role differently. This should sound familiar because it's essentially the idea we had in mind in discussing definition of the situation in the last chapter. As a result of a particular pattern of socialization, each individual defines status and role in a particular way. Each individual brings to the situation a specific personality and set of skills, interests, and abilities. Therefore, although each status carries with it certain role requirements, there is still variation and flexibility in actual behavior.

Role—behavior that is suited to a particular status—varies not only because of the style of a particular quarterback, college professor, or President. Roles must be seen in an *interaction* setting. While behaving, people are always socially interacting with others, and consequently their behavior adjusts to and is modified by the responses of others. This continues the viewpoint introduced in the previous chapter in which we pointed out that socialization and self-development occur through the process of social interaction. Roles we play are shaped by others' reactions to us: After comments and complaints from an unhappy class, the unprepared, stream-of-consciousness professor mentioned above may modify his or her performance. It is a common occurrence to go into a situation prepared for one sort of role only to find that in the process of the interaction, another sort of behavior is necessary.

Achieved and Ascribed Status

How do we happen to occupy the statuses that we do? Some, probably most, statuses are earned or achieved in some way, and hence these are called **achieved statuses**. Astronaut, policeman, college professor, and truck driver represent achieved statuses. Some statuses are automatically conferred on us with no effort or choice on our part. These are **ascribed statuses.** One's sex, race, and nationality are ascribed (although occasionally some changes can be made). Sometimes it is difficult to tell whether a status is ascribed or achieved. Take the student who feels forced to go to college because of the wishes of his or her parents—is the status of student ascribed or achieved? Or how about statuses that a child inherits from his or her parents, such as political and religious affiliations—are they ascribed or achieved?

Statuses are stratified or ranked at a number of levels. Some statuses are of high rank and bring much prestige to the occupant. Doctor, board director of a large corporation, college president, author, artist, scientist, and movie star are statuses that have high value and prestige in our society. Evaluation of positions is usually determined by the requirements that one must have to fill that status—extensive education, wealth, beauty, skill, or some other extraordinary characteristic. Sometimes this ranking is based on a societal tradition that automatically ranks certain characteristics above others, such as being of a particular sex, race, or religion, or born in a particular aristocratic family. Sometimes having high ascribed status makes it easier to obtain desired achieved statuses. For example, a child born in a middle-class family (ascribed status) will have a better chance of becoming a doctor or scientist (achieved status) than will a lower-class child. Sometimes having high ascribed status is limiting, however. People who are members of royalty may find that their freedom is severely restricted. They must always live their ascribed status (Queen of England) and decline to pursue a perhaps more attractive achieved status (college professor?).

Role Strain and Role Conflict

Problems may occur when a person must play several roles simultaneously, or when one role requires a person to perform in several different ways. These situations are called role conflict and role strain, and they may lead to personal stress and discomfort. **Role strain** refers to the situation in which there are differing and conflicting expectations regarding one's status or position. A student may experience role strain when he compares the expectations of his parents (study, get A's, prepare for a vocation, practice frugality in all things) with the expectations of his fraternity brothers (be social, be active in fraternity affairs, be athletic). Police officers who are trained to arrest people who have committed crimes probably feel role strain when they are ordered by superiors who do not want to make a bad situation worse to stand by and watch looting take place during a riot. A typical situation on college campuses leads to role strain for young professors. Their students expect them to be good teachers, but the school tells them that keeping their jobs and getting promoted will depend on how many articles and books they publish. Doing one takes valuable time from the other—what do you do?

Role conflict occurs when a person occupies several statuses or positions that have contradictory role requirements. Here there is not the confusion or disagreement about the requirements of a single role that we saw in the first case. The requirements of the roles are clearly understood—the problem is that the requirements of two or more roles are contradictory. Imagine the dilemma of a police officer invited by friends to a party where marijuana is being smoked. Police officers are trained to respond to violations of the law with the authority of their position, both on and off duty. But the officer is a normal citizen who is expected by friends —and who wants—to behave like everyone else at the party and have fun. The requirements of the two roles are clearly contradictory. Doctors seldom treat members of their own families because of the role conflict that may occur. Similarly, the football coach whose son is trying out for the team experiences conflict between the contradictory requirements of two different roles—coach and father. And finally, if we have ever marvelled at the phenomenon of the champion tennis player beating everyone in the world except her future husband, we should have recognized and sympathized with her attempt to resolve her role conflict.

Other Cultures, Other Norms

Normative behavior varies from one place to another. Actions that are correct and expected in one part of the world are wrong and peculiar in another part of the world. Appropriate behavior in one country is inappropriate in another. Social scientists use the concept of *culture* to understand and explain these phenomena. Before defining culture, it might be well to illustrate some aspects of culturally related behavior. There are many examples, but the following come to mind.

Every four years, writers from England and Europe flock to the United States to observe a very peculiar ritual the like of which is unknown throughout the rest of the civilized world. These strange ceremonies are written up and read about by disbelieving audiences everywhere. The tribal celebrations being enacted are called locally the "American political conventions." Strange indeed.

Imagine that you are dropped onto a small South Sea island, and your only possession is a golf club—a number 2 iron. To avoid being eaten alive you have to explain the function and purpose of the golf club to the natives. Where do you start?

In the summer of 1978 two British men on a picnic with an Egyptian airline hostess in Saudi Arabia had car trouble and flagged down a police car for assistance. The two men were immediately arrested and later deported to England. The problem? Under Islamic law it is illegal for a man to be alone with a woman to whom he is not married.

Anthropologists specialize in the study of cultural patterns in different societies, especially in primitive or preliterate societies, and in their studies they have made many discoveries that seem strange to Americans. They describe a society in which very fat women are highly regarded. Women in this society spend weeks in fattening sheds where they eat starchy, fatty foods and have their bodies greased to make them more attractive. On festival day they are paraded before the king, who chooses the fattest and heaviest as his mate. Very peculiar people. But imagine for a moment that you have to explain to a member of that society the popularity in America of the various dieting and health spas where men and women spend great sums of money to lose weight.

Some Indian tribes living along the Amazon have an interesting reaction to childbirth. The woman breaks off from work in the fields and returns home for only two or three hours to give birth to the child. Meanwhile, her husband has been lying at home in a hammock, tossing about and groaning as if in great pain. Even after the birth when the woman has returned to the fields, the husband remains in bed with the baby to recuperate from his ordeal. It appears that pain is determined by something more than the nature of the wound.

Anthropologist Margaret Mead visited three primitive tribes in New Guinea and wrote about them in her book *Sex and Temperament.* First, Mead describes the mountain-dwelling Arapesh, among whom both the men and the women behave in a way that Americans would describe as maternal or feminine. Both parents devote their lives to raising the children. The men are gentle, and there is complete cooperation between both sexes at all times. Next, Mead describes a cannibalistic tribe living on a river, the Mundugumor. Here both the men and the women behave in a way that Americans would describe as masculine. Men and women work in the fields together and are aggressive individualists. Finally, Margaret Mead describes the lake-dwelling Tchambuli. In this society the men behave in a manner that Americans define as feminine or maternal, and the women are masculine by our standards. The women spend the days fishing and weaving, and they have all the power. The men spend their time dancing in ceremonies, dressing and making themselves up, and in artistic endeavors. The men gossip, quarrel, and get very jealous of each other over the affections of a woman. The women's attitude toward the men is one of kindly tolerance and appreciation—they watch the shows that the men put on.

We tend to believe that certain patterns of behavior and temperament are automatically, necessarily related to sex. We may believe that to be male is to naturally behave a certain way, and that female behavior is innate as well. The point of Mead's research is that the relationship between sex and the corresponding behavior and temperament is not necessarily biological but is determined by the society in which one lives—as are body shape and size preference, taste in food or art, belief in a supreme being, nature of recreational activity, and many other characteristics.

Culture

By **culture** we mean that complex set of learned and shared beliefs, customs, skills, habits, traditions, and knowledge common to the members of a society. Culture is viewed as the social heritage of a society. According to anthropologist Clyde Kluckhohn, culture represents the distinctive way of life of a group of people, their complete design for living.[4] So, society (as we learned at the beginning of this chapter) refers to an organized, independent, continuing number of people living in a specific area, and culture refers to the learned, shared patterns of beliefs and behaviors common to that people.

For social scientists, the concept of culture is very important. The culture is shared by the members of a society and is learned through the socialization process. In fact, the socialization process is the process whereby one learns and internalizes the norms and roles of the culture in which one lives. The culture determines for us what we will want to eat, whom we will like or hate, what we will fear (snakes and mice, but not evil spirits), how we will express our emotions, how we will dress (blue jeans and bikinis, but not turbans or saris), our manners, and how we will celebrate New Year's Eve. In the previous chapter, I mentioned that when I throw a volleyball to my son, he catches it with his hands and throws it back, but a ball thrown to a French or English child is likely to be headed or kicked back. We can now see that these are *cultural* differences. In American culture, ball sports emphasize the use of hands—catching and throwing in basketball, baseball, volleyball, and handball, for example. In France and England and many other cultures, the major sport is soccer, which emphasizes controlling the ball with one's feet and head.

---

[4]Clyde Kluckhohn, "The Study of Culture," in *The Policy Sciences,* edited by Daniel Lerner and Harold D. Lasswell (Stanford, Calif.: Stanford University Press, 1951), p. 86.

The distinction is frequently made between the material and nonmaterial aspects of a culture. **Material culture** refers to the concrete things that a society creates and uses—screwdriver, house, classroom, desk, car, plane, telephone. **Nonmaterial culture** refers to the more abstract creations of a society, such as customs, laws, ideas, values, and beliefs. The nonmaterial culture would include beliefs about religion and courtship, ideas about democracy and communism, definitions of good manners, and rules for driving a car.

Certain aspects of any given culture are unique to that culture. Some striking contrasts in cultures were shown earlier in this chapter. However, many aspects are shared with other cultures. General patterns recur frequently—a family system, the incest taboo, a system of religion. Variation in culture traits and patterns is more likely to occur in certain specific practices than in general patterns. Cultures constantly change as old traits and patterns die out and new ones are introduced through invention from within or diffusion from some other culture. Soccer is becoming popular in the United States. Many school children are playing it, a professional soccer league has been started, a soccer player won a superstar competition, and several famous international players are now playing for United States teams. Those ball-handling differences I mentioned may disappear in a few years. Some cultures change rapidly, others slowly, but change is inevitable.

Culture and Personality

Personality and temperament vary from one culture to another. As we noted, Margaret Mead described a variety of relationships between sex and temperament in three primitive societies. Ruth Benedict, in her book *Patterns of Culture,* describes two distinct character traits she observed in her comparison of primitive societies in North America. The Zuni are described as "Apollonian" in that they are extremely self-controlled. They emphasize formality, sobriety, and inoffensiveness, they are not individualistic, and they are traditional, frowning on anything new or different. The Kwakiutl, on the other hand, are described as "Dionysian" in that they emphasize self-gratification to excess. They are wildly ceremonious and strive for ecstasy, which is achieved through complete loss of self-control. Benedict reports that dancers were sometimes tethered by four ropes so that they might not do irreparable damage to themselves in their frenzy.

David Riesman in *The Lonely Crowd* describes the effect of culture on personality in a somewhat different manner. His subject is American character, and he describes how character and personality change as other aspects within the culture change. According to Riesman, three types of social character have been dominant in American society. In earlier years the dominant type of character was *tradition-directed.* In a tradition-directed culture, behavior is carefully controlled. Routine orients and occupies the lives of everyone. Ritual, religion, and custom are dominant. New solutions are not sought, and change is very slow. Later, the *inner-directed* type of character appeared. Inner-directed people are taught early in life to have an inward focus, with emphasis on the self and its needs and gratifications. Other persons are not of crucial importance. Individuals may be internally driven toward such ideals as power and wealth; they are encouraged to set their own goals and to be on their own. Their lives are concerned with self-mastery and accomplishment. Finally and more recently, the *other-directed* type of character appeared. The chief interest for other-directed people is to be liked by other people. According to Riesman, other-directed people have built-in radar systems that search out the reactions and feelings of others so that they may adapt themselves to them. These people are more concerned with conformity, are shallower, friendlier, more unsure of themselves, and more demanding of approval from others. The peer group is all-important, as is the front that one puts up. Riesman believes that these types of character result from other changes within the culture, such as population growth or change, along with changes in economic, industrial, and agricultural techniques, and urbanization. Again the major point for us is that the culture people live in plays a major part in determining who they are and how they behave, including patterns of personality and character.

Stanley Milgram designed an experiment to test cultural differences in conformity.[5] He had subjects listen to two tones and then tell him which tone was longer. Each experiment involved six subjects. Five of the subjects, however, were confederates of the experimenter. The five confederates answered first, and their decisions on the tones were heard by the real subject, who answered last. The confederates were instructed to give wrong answers on about half the trials. What does the subject (number 6) do when he hears the five others respond one way and he hears the tones another way? The subject is faced with the clear choice of being independent and giving the right answer regardless of what the others say, or conforming and going along with the group. Milgram tried his experiment on one hundred French students in Paris and one hundred Norwegian students in Oslo. He found that the Norwegians were more conforming, the French more independent. The differences weren't large, but they were consistent. Through a number of trials under varied conditions the Norwegians voted with the group more often than did the French. By way of explanation, Milgram describes Norwegian society as highly cohesive. The Norwegian tends to identify with the group and has a strong sense of social responsibility. The French, on the other hand, show much less consensus in their social and political life and more of a tradition of dissent and critical argument. Milgram's research demonstrates cultural differences in personality characteristics between what many would consider to be very similar nationality groups.

American males have one of the highest heart-disease rates in the world. By contrast, Japanese males have one of the lowest rates. There is obviously a cultural factor at work here, but which cultural factor is it? For years scientists thought the explanation to be diet. The Japanese diet of fish and rice is much lower in cholesterol than is the American diet of meat and dairy products. However, a nine-year study completed in 1975 of 4,000 Japanese-Americans living in this country found another cultural factor to be the culprit.[6] The key turned out to be *lifestyle.* The Japanese living in the U.S. who maintained their traditional lifestyle—downplaying individual competition and accepting their place in family and society—had low heart-attack rates *regardless* of what they ate, how much they smoked, their blood pressure, or their weight. Those Japanese who adopted the American life-

---

[5]For a more complete report of this study see Stanley Milgram, "Nationality and Conformity," *Scientific American* 205 (December 1961), pp. 46–51.

[6]This study was done at the School of Public Health at the University of California at Berkeley and reported in newspapers and news magazines beginning in August 1975.

style (or personality) and became impatient, aggressive, hard driving, competitive go-getters were five times as likely to have heart attacks as those who maintained Japanese ways. The Japanese culture is apparently better able to protect the individual against the effects of pressure and stress. Unhappily, then, one's culture dictates not only how one will live, but also how and why one will die.

Ethnocentrism and Cultural Relativism

Ethnocentrism describes a type of prejudice that says simply, my culture's ways are right and other cultures' ways, if they are not like mine, are wrong. Racism (a particular race is superior to others) and sexism (one sex is superior) are related to ethnocentrism but are more specific types of prejudice. Informal practices and formal policies (who gets hired, who gets paid most) may emerge to support racism, sexism, and ethnocentrism, as well as other types of prejudice. The ethnocentric person says that the familiar is good and the unfamiliar or foreign is bad. An ethnocentric person in the United States might maintain, among other things, that non-Christians are barbarians, that Eskimo tribes practicing sexual hospitality are totally lacking in moral fiber, that anybody who eats dogmeat, horsemeat, or people is not civilized, that democracy is the only way of government, and generally that we are doing other cultures a favor when we go in and Americanize them.

Being ethnocentric to some degree is difficult to avoid. Informally, in interacting with family and friends, and formally through a kind of indoctrination in the educational system, we are frequently taught that our ways are best and, at least by implication, others' ways are less good. The mass media encourage ethnocentrism by treating the foreign and unfamiliar in terms of easily recognized stereotypes. It is probably true that ethnocentrism is impossible to escape, as it is encouraged in one way or another by most of the institutions (family, church, schools, government) in any society. This is at least partly because there are positive functions to ethnocentrism. Ethnocentrism probably leads to greater group solidarity, loyalty, and patriotism, and a certain degree of ethnocentrism may be essential for the survival of a culture. The effects of ethnocentrism are complicated —as we reinforce our belief in the goodness of our own ways, we make unfair and often derogatory judgments about the beliefs of others.

Even social scientists (who should know better) sometimes run into difficulty when studying other cultures. Since most social scientists are white middle-class representatives of the dominant culture, they may have a tendency to describe phenomena that are different—Amish, Eskimos, delinquent gangs—from the viewpoint of their own value system rather than from the viewpoint of the people they are studying. As you come across descriptions of research in this book and elsewhere, see if the research seems to have been influenced by ethnocentrism. See if you can detect ethnocentrism in the choice of topic, the way the reasearch is done, or in the interpretation of results.

Related to ethnocentrism but opposite in meaning is the concept of **cultural relativism.** Cultural relativism suggests that each culture be judged from its own viewpoint without imposing outside standards of judgment. Behaviors, values, and beliefs are relative to the culture in which they appear. The cultural relativist believes that what is right in one society may be wrong in another and that what is considered civilized in one society may be seen as barbaric in another, but that basically judgments should not be made about the "goodness" or "badness" of traits in cultures other than one's own. The point is that although cultures share many values, beliefs, and behaviors, there are also differences between cultures. When one evaluates particular traits, one should do it from the viewpoint of the society in which they appear.

Subculture and Contraculture

Most societies, especially large, complex societies like the United States, have groups that, by their traits, beliefs, or interests, are somewhat separated and distinct from the rest of society. Members of such a group may share many of the characteristics of the dominant culture, but they have some of their own specific customs or ways as well. If these groups have definite boundaries and if their differences with the rest of society have some permanence, they are called **subcultures.** Sociologists generally use the term *subculture* to refer to groups that stand out in that some of their values and customs are different from or even at odds with those of the rest of society. The sociologist asks such questions as: How do the subculture's values differ from those of the dominant culture? Is there conflict? Does the dominant culture attempt to change the subculture? What does the subculture do to maintain its separate identity?

Some religious groups, the Amish for example, seem to qualify as subcultures. A major problem for the Amish, as for many subcultures, is to maintain their identity, even their existence, in the face of a dominant culture frequently hostile to their beliefs. The opposition of the Amish to electricity (which meant no lights at night on their horse-drawn carriages) and their opposition to any formal education beyond the eighth grade brought well-publicized confrontations with the authorities in several Midwestern states. Other examples of subcultures might include terrorist organizations, college students, Hare Krishnas, Chicanos, the Hutterites, professional baseball or football players, and sociologists.

The line of distinction between culture and subculture is not always clear. Some believe that over a period of time societies go through a melting-pot experience, in which different nationality, racial, and interest groups become so mixed and merged together that their subcultural differences cease to exist. The result of the melting-pot experience would be a society representing a mix of the remnants of former subcultures.

A society that has a number of subcultures with relatively equal size and power so that they tend to balance one another is often referred to as a *pluralist* society. Each group is limited in its power and influence by the power and influence of other groups, and the result is an interesting balance of power that reduces the likelihood of anybody having a monopoly of influence and increases the chances for freedom for everybody.

There is an element of conflict in some subcultural behavior, and this led Milton Yinger to propose the term **contraculture.**[7] The central element in a con-

---

[7] J. Milton Yinger, "Contraculture and Subculture," *American Sociological Review* 25 (October 1960), pp. 625–635. Also see an analysis by Ruth Shonle Cavan, "The Concepts of Tolerance and Contraculture as Applied to Delinquency," *Sociological Quarterly* 2 (1961), pp. 243–258, and an empirical test by Dean S. Dorn, "A Partial Test of the Delinquency Continuum Typology: Contracultures and Subcultures," *Social Forces* 47 (March 1969), pp. 305–314.

traculture is the idea of opposition to or conflict with the norms and values of the dominant culture. Contracultures are groups whose behavior is disintegrative and destructive to society. Urban lower-class youth who band together in gangs have been called a delinquent subculture, but in many cases contraculture would be the more appropriate term. Albert Cohen, Walter Miller, and other sociologists have studied these gangs and have described them as groups that are distinct from the rest of society. They have their own set of values and beliefs, and often these are in conflict with those of the rest of society. The frequent result is that individuals following the contraculture's norms find themselves locked up in the society's jails. Other examples of contracultures would include revolutionary groups (such as the Symbionese Liberation Army) whose opposition to society is expressed through the use of violence to bring about social change. In summary, subculture is the more general term, contraculture the more specific. All contracultures are subcultures, but only those subcultures that include the element of conflict and destructiveness toward society would be called contracultures.

SUMMARY

In the first chapter in this section on socialization and culture, we focused on how individuals develop into social beings. In this chapter, we have turned our attention from individuals and the processes of socialization and self-development to the stage or setting where these processes take place. This setting is called the social environment, and we have introduced concepts that can be used to examine the social environment in more detail. Individuals exist in specific societies and cultures. Further, individuals will occupy numerous positions, be governed by rules, and behave in a variety of ways that are sometimes appropriate, sometimes inappropriate, but seldom unusual. The basic fact in this chapter is that individuals' membership in a given society and culture, whose patterns and customs developed long before them and will probably long outlive them, affects and explains much of their behavior.

Norms are the rules of society. We operate effectively and behavior becomes predictable because of them. Norm breakdown occasionally occurs, and when it does, it may produce crises both for society and for individuals. Norms vary in strength—"shoulds" are called folkways, "musts" are called mores. There are group norms and societal norms, and sometimes these sets of norms are in conflict. When this happens, it produces problems for people who are influenced by the conflicting sets of norms. A status is a position in society, and role describes the behavior of one who occupies a status. Norms define the boundaries for role requirements, but within these boundaries there is variation in how the role is actually performed. Statuses, which may be either achieved or ascribed, are ranked in value or prestige. When a person occupies several statuses with contradictory role requirements, role conflict may occur. Role strain may result for one who tries to play a role that includes conflicting expectations.

Society is defined as a continuing number of people living in a specific area who are relatively organized, self-sufficient, and independent, and who share a common culture. Culture is made up of the learned, shared patterns of behavior and knowledge common to a society. There are material and nonmaterial aspects to a culture. Subcultures refer to groups that share many of the traits of the dominant culture but have some unique customs and traits as well. Our cultural and subcultural affiliations are of crucial importance in determining who we are and what we do. The concept of ethnocentrism helps us to understand the familiar tendency to assume that the world everywhere is the same as it is here, and that if by some chance it's not, it should be. On the other hand, cultural relativism is an attitude that judges each culture from its own viewpoint.

The first of the following four readings illustrates several characteristics of norms. Norms come in a variety of types—written laws, unwritten customs, myths, and legends. Norms are culture-bound—they are tied to a given culture, and there is often great variation from one culture to another. In "The Mysterious Drop in Japan's Birth Rate," Koya Azumi describes how a superstition or myth exerts normative power. The second article also deals with norms. Stanley Milgram describes what happens in an experimental situation when subjects are faced with conflicting norms: Should they follow orders and hurt someone, or should they respond to the cries of pain and disobey orders? In his classic article, "One Hundred Percent American," Ralph Linton deals with the problem of whether new elements of the American culture are introduced from within through invention or are adapted from other cultures through the process of diffusion. The final article in this section is an excerpt from a novel by an anthropologist in which she describes some of the cultural patterns of the Tiv of northern Nigeria and her reactions to them.

Reading 3.1
The Mysterious Drop in Japan's Birth Rate
KOYA AZUMI

Norms and roles exist in a cultural context. What is "normative"—the expected behavior—in one culture will not be in another. Norms come in a variety of forms, from written laws to informal agreements. Even superstitions and myths may represent values that act as norms when they suggest or require that people behave in specific ways at certain times or under certain conditions.

Sociologist Koya Azumi describes how in Japan in the mid-twentieth century, an ancient superstition exerts the normative power to change population rates.

In 1966, the birth rate in Japan suddenly plunged to a record low of 13.7 per thousand—down almost half a million births from the preceding year. This decline

Published by permission of Transaction, Inc., from *Transaction,* Vol. 5, No. 6. Copyright © 1968 by Transaction, Inc.

in births—26 percent in one year—was extraordinary. Such a birth-rate plunge would have exceeded the wildest hopes of the countries that are frantically trying to limit their populations. But in Japan, a prosperous and heavily industrialized country that is *not* trying to limit its population, the drop seemed to make no sense.

None of the usual explanations for a rapid birth decline seemed to work. A quick survey of the country showed that Japan in 1966 was no different from Japan in 1965 or 1967—and the number of births in 1967 increased by 50 percent over 1966. The year 1966 was marked by no war, no sudden shifts in prosperity, and no change in the legal codes that might have influenced reproductive behavior.

Furthermore, the decline could not be ascribed to any sudden lack of sexual activity. In fact, during the last half of 1965 the number of induced abortions rose sharply. This suggests that people were still engaging in their usual sexual activities but that, for some reason, they were determined not to have children.

This determination first became evident in the birth statistics for January 1966. In December 1965 the birth rate stood at a steady 17.3; by the end of January it had fallen to 14.6. In a single month, the Japanese made their birth rate fall by a spectacular 16 percent. True, with modern contraceptive methods (and, as a last resort, modern abortion methods), people have greater control over their reproductive lives. But under no normal circumstances do they choose to exercise this control to the extent that the Japanese did in the last nine months of 1965 and the first three months of 1966.

This was not the first time that the Japanese birth rate had fallen sharply. But this was the first time it had done so without apparent reason. The birth rate took a sharp plunge in the 1950s, for example, but that was in response to deliberate government policy. Such a policy was necessary because by 1947, two years after the end of World War II, the Japanese rate had risen to 34.4 per thousand—a figure comparable to the current high rates in countries like Taiwan, Cuba, and Ceylon. The Japanese government was alarmed. To stop this dangerous trend toward over-population, the government launched a massive birth-control campaign. It adopted family planning as national policy and began to spread birth-control information and materials throughout the country. Legal restrictions against abortion were eased—so much so that abortion became available to almost any woman who wanted it.

The desire to limit family size was apparently there, for contraception soon became accepted and widespread. Within 10 years, the birth rate had actually halved—a decline unprecedented in Japan or anywhere else. If it had continued at this pace, within a few decades there would have been no births at all. But by 1957, the rate stabilized at between 17 and 18 live births per thousand per year.

On the basis of that sustained low rate, demographers predicted that by the 1980s the Japanese population would hit a ceiling of about 110 million. Then a cycle of depopulation would begin.

The nationalistic Japanese, faced with the declining vigor of an increasing older population and the long-term threat of possible depopulation, might have been expected to respond to this prospect by starting to plan larger families. But instead, in 1966, they reduced their birth rate even beyond the sustained low figure that had prevailed for the past nine years.

A Bad Year for Girls

Why then, against all logical expectations to the contrary, did the Japanese apparently declare a moratorium on child-bearing in 1966? The answer lies in an ancient superstition.

The superstition is rooted in the ancient lunar-solar calendar of Chinese origin. This old calendar, although abandoned by the Japanese in 1872 in favor of the Gregorian calendar used in the West, is still very much a part of Japanese thinking. It is composed of two circular systems—one a decimal system of 10 "trunks" and the other a duodecimal system of 12 "twigs." The trunks carry the names of natural objects or elements, and the twigs carry the names of animals. Every 60 years, when the "fire" period of the first system coincides with the "horse" period of the second, a new cycle of history begins. The first year of each new cycle is called a year of Hinouema.

What explains Japan's sudden birth-rate decline in 1966 is the fact that 1966 was a year of Hinouema. For according to the superstition, any girl born in such a year will be of harsh temperament and invite misfortune—in other words, she will have great difficulty finding a husband. The Japanese just weren't taking that chance. Rather than conceiving children on the chance that they would be boys and thus immune to the misfortunes of Hinouema, many Japanese decided to wait till next year. During 1965 and early 1966, they practiced rigorous birth control. And failing that, they were quite prepared to resort to abortion to make certain that they brought no unlucky daughters into the world.

Recurrent Declines

Plainly, the Hinouema superstition has withstood industrialization, mass education, and the growth of science and technology, as well as the passage of time. But how can we be sure that it was responsible for the birth decline of 1966? The answer is that the persistence of the superstition and its link to the birth rate can be shown statistically. For example, government figures indicate that the 1966 decline was greatest in the traditional, rural areas.

Since the phenomenon is also a recurrent one, the case for superstition becomes even stronger. The last time a year of Hinouema came around was in 1906. Predictably, the birth rate declined—from 31.1 per thousand in 1905 down to 29.6 in 1906. The next year, it rose rapidly to about 34. Something else very peculiar happened in 1906: The sex ratio at birth became noticeably unbalanced. Normally, each year there are slightly more boys than girls born, but in 1906 the number of boys so far exceeded the number of girls that the usual ratio was definitely upset. In 1905, the sex ratio of boys to girls was 102.7 to 100. In 1906, the year of Hinouema, the ratio jumped to 108.7 to 100. Then in 1907, it returned to 102.7 to 100—a normal figure.

The explanation circulated at the time laid the sudden increase in boys to a mysterious force of nature that compensates for the loss of men during war. And Japan had concluded a war against Russia the year before. But there is some reason to doubt that such an increase in male births really occurs after a war. For example, the American demographer C. T. McMahan tested this expectation against actual birth statistics in the United States following both world wars and found no such increase.

McMahan's findings suggest that Japan's apparent proportionate increase in male births following the Russo-Japanese War may need a skeptical second look. How can we be sure that such an increase occurred? In other words, how reliable are Japan's birth statistics for 1906?

False Statistics

It turns out that in 1906, like today, the responsibility for registering the vital events of birth, marriage, and death rested with Japan's heads of household. This fact, plus the fact that 1906 was a year of Hinouema, may help explain the peculiar activity of the 1906 birth rate. Household heads may simply have responded to the Hinouema superstition by failing to register the births of girls born in 1906. Since there was no vigorously enforced time requirement for registration, these household heads could easily have registered these girl children as having been born in 1905 or in 1907. If this had happened, we would expect the over-registration of girls in those years to depress the sex ratio—and the 102.7-to-100 figure that prevailed during both these years *was,* although within the normal range, slightly below average. (The figures for 1904 and 1908 give male rates of 105.1 and 104.6 respectively.) By this very rational method of accommodating to an irrational belief, then, Japanese parents—in their effort to shield their newborn daughters from the stigma of Hinouema—likely falsified the birth statistics for 1906.

By 1966, the next unlucky year, the Japanese no longer needed to falsify the birth statistics. Modernization had brought family planning within the reach of almost everyone. But in the 60 years since 1906, Japan had also undergone other radical changes: Illiteracy had been wiped out, the agricultural population had dwindled from about two-thirds to less than one-fourth of the labor force, and a modern industrial economy had evolved. In addition, most of the women who were of child-bearing age in 1966 were modern women, born after 1930. All of this should have helped quash the Hinouema superstition. If, as sociologists believe, modernization means demystification, secularization, and rationalization, then the Japanese of 1966 should have been free of the idea that a woman's year of birth can determine her personality and even her life chances.

But the birth-rate plunge of 1966 showed that the superstition was still very much alive. Modernization, it appears, served only to provide the Japanese with more efficient ways to propitiate the same old deities. The Japanese of 1906 concealed female births, and the Japanese of 1966 *prevented* them. But the motivation —to avoid the year of Hinouema—was still the same.

Of course, it is not fair to conclude that *all* the Japanese who avoided having children in 1966 because it was the year of Hinouema were themselves superstitious. Perhaps they merely felt that *others* believed in the superstition and that this might be enough to hinder the chances of girls born in that year. But whether the potential parents of 1966 themselves believed in the superstition, or whether they merely thought that others believed in it, they acted *as if* they believed it by postponing many of the births that normally would have occurred that year.

Despite the plunging birth rate, there were still a great many girls born in 1966. Perhaps Hinouema's 1966 children will have sufficiently fortunate lives to dilute the superstition, or to dispel it completely. In any case, most of them will still be around to see what happens the next time a new cycle begins, in the year 2026. It will be interesting to watch the birth rate then, and to see whether Japan's Hinouema superstition can survive the turn of still another century.

Questions 3.1

1. What types of norms are described here—folkways, mores, or both? What are the sanctions for norm violation?
2. What conditions in society seem to be more conducive to maintaining traditional beliefs and norms? What conditions seem more conducive to dropping traditional beliefs and norms?
3. Make a list of situations in the United States that are similar to that in Japan described by Azumi. That is, list those superstitions, myths, and customs that exert normative power to the extent that they change behavior (birth rates, crime rates, drinking rates, buying rates, etc.) under certain conditions (time of the year, phase of the moon, etc.).

Reading 3.2
Some Conditions of Obedience and Disobedience to Authority

STANLEY MILGRAM

Stanley Milgram is a social psychologist and professor at City University of New York. In this excerpt from one of his research papers he describes what happens when people are faced with conflicting norms. Milgram's research question is this: If a person tells a second person to hurt a third person, under what conditions will the second person refuse to obey?

The situation in which one agent commands another to hurt a third turns up time and again as a significant theme in human relations. It is powerfully expressed in the story of Abraham, who is commanded by God to kill his son. It is no accident that Kierkegaard, seeking to orient his thought to the central themes of human experience, chose Abraham's conflict as the springboard to his philosophy.

War too moves forward on the triad of an authority which commands a person to destroy the enemy, and perhaps all organized hostility may be viewed as a theme and variation of the three elements of authority, executant, and victim. We describe an experimental program, recently concluded at Yale University, in which a particular expression of this conflict is studied by experimental means.

Adapted from *Human Relations,* February 1965, pp. 57–76. Reprinted by permission of the author. A more thoroughgoing analysis of the experiments described in this article may be found in Stanley Milgram's *Obedience to Authority,* published by Harper & Row, 1974. A 45-minute film depicting the experiments is available to educational groups. It is entitled *Obedience* and is distributed by the New York University Film Library, 41 Press Annex, Washington Square, New York, N.Y. 10003.

In its most general form the problem may be defined thus: if X tells Y to hurt Z, under what conditions will Y carry out the command of X and under what conditions will he refuse. In the more limited form possible in laboratory research, the question becomes: if an experimenter tells a subject to hurt another person, under what conditions will he refuse to obey. The laboratory problem is not so much a dilution of the general statement as one concrete expression of the many particular forms this question may assume.

One aim of the research was to study behavior in a strong situation of deep consequence to the participants, for the psychological forces operative in powerful and lifelike forms of the conflict may not be brought into play under diluted conditions.

This approach meant, first, that we had a special obligation to protect the welfare and dignity of the persons who took part in the study; subjects were, of necessity, placed in a difficult predicament, and steps had to be taken to ensure their wellbeing before they were discharged from the laboratory. Toward this end, a careful, post-experimental treatment was devised and has been carried through for subjects in all conditions.

The subjects used in all experimental conditons were male adults, residing in the greater New Haven and Bridgeport areas, aged 20 to 50 years, and engaged in a wide variety of occupations. Each experimental condition described in this report employed 40 fresh subjects and was carefully balanced for age and occupational types. The occupational composition for each experiment was: workers, skilled and unskilled: 40 percent; white collar, sales, business: 40 percent; professionals: 20 percent. The occupations were intersected with three age categories (subjects in 20s, 30s, and 40s, assigned to each condition in the proportions of 20, 40, and 40 percent respectively).

The focus of the study concerns the amount of electric shock a subject is willing to administer to another person when ordered by an experimenter to give the "victim" increasingly more severe punishment. The act of administering shock is set in the context of a learning experiment, ostensibly designed to study the effect of punishment on memory. Aside from the experimenter, one naive subject and one accomplice perform in each session. On arrival each subject is paid $4.50. After a general talk by the experimenter, telling how little scientists know about the effect of punishment on memory, subjects are informed that one member of the pair will serve as teacher and one as learner. A rigged drawing is held so that the naive subject is always the teacher, and the accomplice becomes the learner. The learner is taken to an adjacent room and strapped into an "electric chair."

The naive subject is told that it is his task to teach the learner a list of paired associates, to test him on the list, and to administer punishment whenever the learner errs in the test. Punishment takes the form of electric shock, delivered to the learner by means of a shock generator controlled by the naive subject. The teacher is instructed to increase the intensity of electric shock one step on the generator on each error. The learner, according to plan, provides many wrong answers, so that before long the naive subject must give him the strongest shock on the generator. Increases in shock level are met by increasingly insistent demands from the learner that the experiment be stopped because of the growing discomfort to him. However, in clear terms the experimenter orders the teacher to continue with the procedure in disregard of the learner's protests. *Thus, the naive subject must resolve a conflict between two mutually incompatible demands from the social field. He may continue to follow the orders of the experimenter and shock the learner with increasing severity, or he may refuse to follow the orders of the experimenter and heed the learner's pleas. The experimenter's authority operates not in a free field, but against evermounting counter-vailing pressures from the person being punished.*

A few technical points need to be considered before the findings of the study are described. For the purpose of delivering shock, a simulated shock generator is used, with 30 clearly marked voltage levels that range from 15 to 450 volts (and each activated by one of 30 individual level switches set in a horizontal line). The naive subject is given a sample shock of 45 volts to convince him of the authenticity of the instrument. The generator bears verbal designations that range from "Slight Shock" to "Danger: Severe Shock."

The responses of the victim are standardized on tape, and each protest is coordinated to a particular voltage level on the shock generator. Starting with 75 volts the learner begins to grunt and moan. At 150 volts he demands to be let out of the experiment. At 180 volts he cries out that he can no longer stand the pain. At 300 volts he refuses to provide any more answers to the memory test, insisting that he is no longer a participant in the experiment and must be freed. In response to this last tactic, the experimenter instructs the naive subject to treat the absence of an answer as equivalent to a wrong answer, and to follow the usual shock procedure. The experimenter reinforces his demand with the statement: "You have no other choice, you must go on!" (This imperative is used whenever the naive subject tries to break off the experiment.) If the subject refuses to give the next higher level of shock, the experiment is considered at an end. A quantitative value is assigned to the subject's performance based on the maximum intensity shock he administered before breaking off. Thus any subject's score may range from zero (for a subject unwilling to administer the first shock level) to 30 (for a subject who proceeds to the highest voltage level on the board). For any particular subject and for any particular experimental condition the degree to which participants have followed the experimenter's orders may be specified with a numerical value, corre-sponding to the metric on the shock generator.

This laboratory situation gives us a framework in which to study the subject's reactions to the principal conflict of the experiment. Again, this conflict is between the experimenter's demands that he continue to administer the electric shock, and the learner's demands, which become increasingly more insistent, that the experi-ment be stopped. The crux of the study is to vary systematically the factors believed to alter the degree of obedience to the experimental commands, to learn under what conditions submission to authority is most probable, and under what conditons defiance is brought to the fore.

This series consisted of four experimental conditions. In each condition the victim was brought "psychologically" closer to the subject giving him shocks.

In the first condition (Remote Feedback) the victim was placed in another room and could not be heard or seen by the subject, except that, at 300 volts, he pounded on the wall in protest. After 315 volts he no longer answered or was heard from.

The second condition (Voice Feedback) was identical to the first except that voice protests were introduced. As in the first condition the victim was placed in an adjacent room, but his complaints could be heard through a door left slightly ajar, and through the walls of the laboratory. It is difficult to convey on the printed page the full tenor of the victim's responses, for we have no adequate notation for vocal intensity, timing, and general qualities of delivery. Yet these features are crucial to producing the effect of an increasingly severe reaction to mounting voltage levels. In general terms, however, the victim indicates no discomfort until the 75-volt shock is administered, at which time there is a light grunt in response to the punishment. Similar reactions follow the 90- and 105-volt shocks, and at 120 volts the victim shouts to the experimenter that the shocks are becoming painful. Painful groans are heard on administration of the 135-volt shock, and at 150 volts the victim cries out, "Experimenter, get me out of here! I won't be in the experiment any more! I refuse to go on!" Cries of this type continue with generally rising intensity, so that at 180 volts the victim cries out, "I can't stand the pain," and by 270 volts his response to the shock is definitely an agonized scream. Throughout, he insists that he be let out of the experiment. At 300 volts the victim shouts in desperation that he will no longer provide answers to the memory test; and at 315 volts, after a violent scream, he reaffirms with vehemence that he is no longer a participant. From this point on, he provides no answers, but shrieks in agony whenever a shock is administered; this continues through 450 volts. Of course, many subjects will have broken off before this point.

The third experimental condition (Proximity) was similar to the second, except that the victim was now placed in the same room as the subject, and 1½ feet from him. Thus he was visible as well as audible, and voice cues were provided.

The fourth, and final, condition of this series (Touch-Proximity) was identical to the third, with this exception: the victim received a shock only when his hand rested on a shockplate. At the 150-volt level the victim again demanded to be let free and, in this condition, refused to place his hand on the shockplate. The experimenter ordered the naive subject to force the victim's hand onto the plate. Thus obedience in this condition required that the subject have physical contact with the victim in order to give him punishment beyond the 150-volt level.

Forty adult subjects were studied in each condition. The data revealed that obedience was significantly reduced as the victim was rendered more immediate to the subject.

Expressed in terms of the proportion of obedient to defiant subjects, the findings are that 34 percent of the subjects defied the experimenter in the Remote condition, 37.5 percent in Voice Feedback, 60 percent in Proximity, and 70 percent in Touch-Proximity.

If the spatial relationship of the subject and victim is relevant to the degree of obedience, would not the relationship of subject to experimenter also play a part? There are reasons to feel that, on arrival, the subject is oriented primarily to the experimenter rather than to the victim. He has come to the laboratory to fit into the structure that the experimenter—not the victim—would provide. He has come less to understand his behavior than to *reveal* that behavior to a competent scientist, and he is willing to display himself as the scientist's purposes require. Most subjects seem quite concerned about the appearance they are making before the experimenter, and one could argue that this preoccupation in a relatively new and strange setting makes the subject somewhat insensitive to the triadic nature of the social situation. In other words, the subject is so concerned about the show he is putting on for the experimenter that influences from other parts of the social field do not receive as much weight as they ordinarily would. This overdetermined orientation to the experimenter would account for the relative insensitivity of the subject to the victim, and would also lead us to believe that alterations in the relationship between subject and experimenter would have important consequences for obedience.

In a series of experiments we varied the physical closeness and degree of surveillance of the experimenter. In one condition the experimenter sat just a few feet away from the subject. In a second condition, after giving initial instructions, the experimenter left the laboratory and gave his orders by telephone; in still a third condition the experimenter was never seen, providing instructions by means of a tape recording activated when the subjects entered the laboratory.

Obedience dropped sharply as the experimenter was physically removed from the laboratory. The number of obedient subjects in the first condition (Experimenter Present) was almost three times as great as in the second, where the experimenter gave his orders by telephone. Twenty-six subjects were fully obedient in the first condition, and only 9 in the second. Subjects seemed able to take a far stronger stand against the experimenter when they did not have to encounter him face to face, and the experimenter's power over the subject was severely curtailed.

Moreover, when the experimenter was absent, subjects displayed an interesting form of behavior that had not occurred under his surveillance. Though continuing with the experiment, several subjects administered lower shocks than were required and never informed the experimenter of their deviation from the correct procedure. (Unknown to the subjects, shock levels were automatically recorded by an Esterline-Angus event recorder wired directly into the shock generator; the instrument provided us with an objective record of the subjects' performance.) Indeed, in telephone conversations some subjects specifically assured the experimenter that they were raising the shock level according to instruction, whereas in fact they were repeatedly using the lowest shock on the board. This form of behavior is particularly interesting: although these subjects acted in a way that clearly undermined the avowed purposes of the experiment, they found it easier to handle the conflict in this manner than to precipitate an open break with authority.

Experiments in this series show that the physical *presence* of an authority is an important force contributing to the subject's obedience or defiance. Taken together with the first experimental series on the proximity of the victim, it would appear that something akin to fields of force, diminishing in effectiveness with increasing psychological distance from their source, have a controlling effect on the subject's performance. As the victim is brought closer, the subject finds it harder to administer shocks to him. When the victim's position is held constant relative to the subject, and the authority is made more remote, the subject finds it easier to break off the experiment. This effect is substantial in both cases, but manipulation of the experimenter's position yielded the more powerful results. Obedience to destructive commands is highly dependent on the proximal relations between authority and subject.

One general finding that merits attention is the high level of obedience manifested in the experimental situation. Subjects often expressed deep disapproval of shocking a man in the face of his objections, and others denounced it as senseless and stupid. Yet many subjects complied even while they protested. The proportion of obedient subjects greatly exceeded the expectations of the experimenter and his colleagues. At the outset, we had conjectured that subjects would not, in general, go above the level of "Strong Shock." In practice, many subjects were willing to administer the most extreme shocks available when commanded by the experimenter. For some subjects the experiment provides an occasion for aggressive release. And for others it demonstrates the extent to which obedient dispositions are deeply ingrained, and are engaged irrespective of their consequences for others. Yet this is not the whole story. Somehow, the subject becomes implicated in a situation from which he cannot disengage himself.

The departure of the experimental results from intelligent expectation, to some extent, has been formalized. The procedure was to describe the experimental situation in concrete detail to a group of competent persons, and to ask them to predict the performance of 100 hypothetical subjects. For purposes of indicating the distribution of break-off points judges were provided with a diagram of the shock generator, and recorded their predictions before being informed of the actual results. Judges typically underestimated the amount of obedience demonstrated by subjects.

What is the limit of such obedience? At many points we attempted to establish a boundary. Cries from the victim were inserted; not good enough. The victim claimed heart trouble; subjects still shocked him on command. The victim pleaded that he be let free, and his answers no longer registered on the signal box; subjects continued to shock him. At the outset we had not conceived that such drastic procedures would be needed to generate disobedience, and each step was added only as the ineffectiveness of the earlier techniques became clear. The final effort to establish a limit was the Touch-Proximity condition. But the very first subject in this condition subdued the victim on command, and proceeded to the highest shock level. A quarter of the subjects in this condition performed similarly.

The results, as seen and felt in the laboratory, are to this author disturbing. They raise the possibility that human nature, or—more specifically—the kind of character produced in American democratic society, cannot be counted on to insulate its citizens from brutality and inhumane treatment at the direction of malevolent authority. A substantial proportion of people do what they are told to do, irrespective of the content of the act and without limitations of conscience, so long as they perceive that the command comes from a legitimate authority.

Questions 3.2

1. How is role strain illustrated in this article?
2. What conflicting norms did the subjects face? How did they resolve the conflicts?
3. Under what conditions were subjects most likely to comply with the experimenter's instructions? Why?
4. A number of the principles or characteristics of scientific inquiry are outlined in Chapter 1. Show how these principles are illustrated in Milgram's research.

Reading 3.3

One Hundred Percent American

RALPH LINTON

The content of a culture—skills, customs, material objects, and nonmaterial ideas—comes from several sources. Some aspects of culture appear spontaneously and are developed from within the culture through the process of invention. Much more, however, is borrowed from other cultures through the usually unconscious process of diffusion. Anthropologist Ralph Linton wrote this passage some years ago. It is often quoted and still remains a classic at demonstrating the importance of diffusion. Much of what we thought was "one hundred percent American" actually came long ago from societies we never heard of.

There can be no question about the average American's Americanism or his desire to preserve this precious heritage at all costs. Nevertheless, some insidious foreign ideas have already wormed their way into his civilization without his realizing what was going on. Thus dawn finds the unsuspecting patriot garbed in pajamas, a garment of East Indian origin; and lying in a bed built on a pattern which originated in either Persia or Asia Minor. He is muffled to the ears in un-American materials; cotton, first domesticated in India; linen, domesticated in the Near East; wool from an animal native to Asia Minor; or silk, whose uses were first discovered by the Chinese. All these substances have been transformed into cloth by a method invented in Southwestern Asia. If the weather is cold enough he may even be sleeping under an eiderdown quilt invented in Scandinavia.

On awakening he glances at the clock, a medieval European invention, uses one potent Latin word in abbreviated form, rises in haste, and goes to the bathroom. Here, if he stops to think about it, he must feel himself in the presence of a great American institution; he will have heard stories of both the quality and frequency of foreign plumbing and will know that in no other country does the average man perform his ablutions in the midst of such splendor. But the insidious foreign

From *The American Mercury*, April 1937, pp. 427–429. Reprinted by permission of the publisher.

influence pursues him even here. Glass was invented by the ancient Egyptians, the use of glazed tiles for floors and walls in the Near East, porcelain in China, and the art of enameling on metal by Mediterranean artisans of the Bronze Age. Even his bathtub and toilet are but slightly modified copies of Roman originals. The only purely American contribution to the ensemble is the steam radiator.

In this bathroom the American washes with soap invented by the ancient Gauls. Next he cleans his teeth, a subversive European practice which did not invade America until the latter part of the eighteenth century. He then shaves, a masochistic rite first developed by the heathen priests of ancient Egypt and Sumer. The process is made less of a penance by the fact that his razor is of steel, an iron-carbon alloy discovered in either India or Turkestan. Lastly, he dries himself on a Turkish towel.

Returning to the bedroom, the unconscious victim of un-American practices removes his clothes from a chair, invented in the Near East, and proceeds to dress. He puts on close-fitting tailored garments whose form derives from the skin clothing of the ancient nomads of the Asiatic steppes and fastens them with buttons whose prototypes appeared in Europe at the close of the Stone Age. This costume is appropriate enough for outdoor exercise in a cold climate, but is quite unsuited to American summers, steam-heated houses, and Pullmans. Nevertheless, foreign ideas and habits hold the unfortunate man in thrall even when common sense tells him that the authentically American costume of gee string and moccasins would be far more comfortable. He puts on his feet stiff coverings made from hide prepared by a process invented in ancient Egypt and cut to a pattern which can be traced to ancient Greece, and makes sure they are properly polished, also a Greek idea. Lastly, he ties about his neck a strip of bright-colored cloth which is a vestigial survival of the shoulder shawls worn by seventeenth-century Croats. He gives himself a final appraisal in the mirror, an old Mediterranean invention, and goes downstairs to breakfast.

Here a whole new series of foreign things confront him. His food and drink are placed before him in pottery vessels, the popular name of which—china—is sufficient evidence of their origin. His fork is a medieval Italian invention and his spoon a copy of a Roman original. He will usually begin the meal with coffee, an Abyssinian plant first discovered by the Arabs. The American is quite likely to need it to dispel the morning-after effects of overindulgence in fermented drinks, invented in the Near East; or distilled ones, invented by the alchemists of medieval Europe. Whereas the Arabs took their coffee straight, he will probably sweeten it with sugar, discovered in India, and dilute it with cream, both the domestication of cattle and the technique of milking having originated in Asia Minor.

If our patriot is old-fashioned enough to adhere to the so-called American breakfast, his coffee will be accompanied by an orange, domesticated in the Mediterranean region, a cantaloupe domesticated in Persia, or grapes, domesticated in Asia Minor. He will follow this with a bowl of cereal made from grain domesticated in the Near East and prepared by methods also invented there. From this he will go on to waffles, a Scandinavian invention, with plenty of butter, originally a Near-Eastern cosmetic. As a side dish he may have the egg of a bird domesticated in Southeastern Asia or strips of the flesh of an animal domesticated in the same region, which have been salted and smoked by a process invented in Northern Europe.

Breakfast over, he places upon his head a molded piece of felt, invented by the nomads of Eastern Asia, and, if it looks like rain, puts on outer shoes of rubber, discovered by the ancient Mexicans, and takes an umbrella, invented in India. He then sprints for his train—the train, not the sprinting, being an English invention. At the station he pauses for a moment to buy a newspaper, paying for it with coins invented in ancient Lydia. Once on board he settles back to inhale the fumes of a cigarette invented in Mexico, or a cigar invented in Brazil. Meanwhile, he reads the news of the day, imprinted in characters invented by the ancient Semites by a process invented in Germany upon a material invented in China. As he scans the latest editorial pointing out the dire results to our institutions of accepting foreign ideas, he will not fail to thank a Hebrew God in an Indo-European language that he is a one hundred percent (decimal system invented by the Greeks) American (from Americus Vespucci, Italian geographer).

Questions 3.3

1. While it is true that many material objects have come to us through diffusion, most of the nonmaterial aspects of American culture are original and the products of invention. Discuss.
2. This article was written in 1930; the same sort of statements could not be made today. Discuss. To prove the point, draw up a list of aspects of American culture developed through invention.
3. Analyze Linton's article, using the terms "ethnocentrism" and "cultural relativism."

Reading 3.4
Return to Laughter

ELENORE S. BOWEN

This excerpt from the book *Return to Laughter* describes the patterns of kinship and marriage—in this case, polygamy—of an African society. Patterns of culture that are quite different from our own are illustrated as well as the concepts ethnocentrism and cultural relativism. Elenore Bowen is the pen name of anthropologist Laura Bohannan who wrote the novel *Return to Laughter* after working among the Tiv of northern Nigeria.

"You feed Ihugh, therefore you *are* his mother." Udama corrected me firmly but quite patiently now that she saw I meant no insult. "Listen, Redwoman, if a woman dies, do her children become motherless? Is not the woman who feeds them and cares for them their mother? Therefore these are not merely matters of birth. They are matters of deed as well. You and I, we are both Ihugh's mother; therefore his children are *our* grandchildren. But there is more. Kako has put some of his youngest wives in my hut, for me to watch and care for; therefore they are my wives as well. Ihugh's wife I treat as I treat them; therefore she is my wife and she is your wife, and her children are our children."

Dazed, but convinced I was struggling along the right track, I ventured a deduction. "Then, if Rogo calls me 'my mother,' it is because I feed him. But if he calls me 'my mother-in-law,' it is because . . ."

"Because he respects you, but must nevertheless say to you things you will not like."

"I sat on a teak root." In my own ears this did not sound very coherent, but Udama followed with the same facility Rogo had used in the original connection. "And some young man told you you must not," she finished. "Therefore of course he called you 'mother-in-law,' or it would have been rude."

Udama meditated into her pipe. I wrestled with the implications of this dual aspect of kinship, by birth and by deed. She was the first to rouse herself. "You must learn more of these matters, Redwoman, or you will be like a child among us, a child who knows nothing of life, nor of death, nor of birth." She scrabbled among the ashes looking for a coal to relight her pipe. "You know Ava and her wives?"

I nodded. Everyone knew Ava and her wives. They were the model household of the community, one every husband cited when his wives disagreed. Ava was a tall, rather light-skinned woman who was one of the leading dancers and song-leaders at all successful wedding parties. She was also the senior of five wives who lived with their husband and children alone in a homestead not very far from Kako's. The women were fast friends. Indeed, it was Ava who had picked out all the others. She saved up forty or fifty shillings every few years, searched out an industrious girl of congenial character, then brought her home and presented her to her husband: "Here is your new wife."

Ava's husband always welcomed her additions to his household and he always set to work to pay the rest of the bridewealth, for he knew perfectly well that Ava always picked hardworking, healthy, handsome, steady women who wouldn't run away. Many men envied him. Thanks to Ava he had peace and quiet in his home and did not, like so many others, have to spend time and money chasing after truant wives. My feelings were more mixed. If, before I came out here, I had expected to feel sorry for anyone in a polygamous household, it was the women. But these women did very well. It was their husband I felt sorry for. We tend to think of the henpecked husband as a rather weak character. But what man can stand up against five united women? If Ava's husband raised his voice to any one of his wives, all of them refused to cook for him. If he bought one of them a cloth, he had to buy four other identical cloths. Discipline of the wives was in Ava's hands, and stayed there. When the poor man got drunk one day and struck one wife for nagging—well, until he had given many and expensive presents to all his wives, the five of them slept barricaded in one hut. Yes, I knew Ava.

"One of Ava's wives," Udama went on, "will soon bear a child. I will be the midwife, and I shall call you, for I would have you see for yourself what it means to have co-wives to help you and to know that if you die in labour there are those who will care for your children."

A few days later, Ava herself stuck her head into my reception hut and called me without ceremony. "Come, Redwoman, my wife is in labour. Udama told me to fetch you while she banked her fire." The three of us walked to Ava's homestead. Her husband was sitting in his reception hut, whittling aimlessly away at a stick and pretending not to be anxious. It was his twelfth child, he told me, but this wife's first. He greeted Udama with relief.

We went inside the hut. The mother-to-be was sitting on a very low reclining chair, looking quite composed while all her co-wives bustled about her. Udama, after a brief and expert examination, announced that there was plenty of time. She and Ava began to lecture me on the benefits of being one of many wives.

"When an only wife has a child, who will help her so she may rest? Who will feed her husband and her other children? Who will tend her farm and bring her firewood so she may be warm? Who will comfort her in labour and who will stop her cries?"

No adult should be so weakminded as to cry out with pain. The two times when people will yell out, circumcision and childbirth, someone stands behind to clap a hand over the mouth at the first scream. Hard, perhaps, but certainly easier on their relatives and neighbours. I could not, however, even for sake of argument protest that any of the other services they mentioned could be performed by any other relatives. I had been there long enough to know that no kinsman will take over the duties of another; it would be considered wrong, and these were the duties of no one but a co-wife.

"Never," said Ava severely, "let your husband rest with one wife. Men are lazy. If they have one woman to cook for them, they are content. If you leave it to your husband, you'll never get another wife to help you carry the firewood and the water or to look after you when you are ill. And if you do nag him into it, he'll pick up the first good-looking wench he sees. You can't trust a man to inquire into a woman's character and industry. Let a man pick his own mistresses; he knows what he wants there. But they're all bunglers when it comes to choosing wives."

"That," Udama interpolated, "is why a man's father selects his first wife."

"And the first wife," Ava continued, "should get the rest herself, like me."

I replied mildly that men in our country generally couldn't afford more than one wife at a time. "Earn the money yourself by going to market," Ava advised. "It only takes a small chicken to start with, if you're a good trader." I explained that we had a law against it as well. Udama stopped Ava's incredulity. "Indeed, I think it must be so. Rogo told Ihugh that very few Europeans have even one wife because the bridewealth is very high and anyhow they don't have enough women to go around."

There was a stifled cry from the chair and conversation stopped. Two of the wives held her back in her chair, a third pressing back her head and holding a hand over her mouth. Ava and Udama were busy for a long time, mixing herbs, massaging, giving encouragement. Finally, at sunset, Udama called out to the father, "A boy." He flapped happily in the background while the new mother was led outside to be washed, and the baby made uncomplimentary noises about the hot water in which Udama washed him. An elder appeared. Ava told me he had come to 'remove the blood' from all of us who had been inside the hut during the birth. I found myself lined up with the other women and having my legs brushed with a wet and squawking chicken while the elder mumbled his incantation. It was a unique sensation.

Ava gave Udama the salt, palm oil and camwood that are the midwife's due and we went home.

"A very easy birth," she commented as we parted. I had not thought it so, nor, by the looks of her, had the mother. Perhaps it was easier if one didn't know there were such things as anaesthetics. One must make shift to endure unavoidable pain. But it wasn't just a matter of suffering. I remembered what the government and mission doctors had told me about deliveries gone wrong and about the damage caused by native midwifery even when there were no complications.

I also remembered that my great-grandmother had her first child alone with her husband on the frontier; in her diary she had longed for another woman then. I tried to imagine her surrounded by four co-wives, and could not. More generally, though, I could see that where we multiply specialists and services, these people multiplied personal relationships and perhaps in this way were closer to my great-grandmother than I was. But not in detail, not my great-grandmother with co-wives. What she wanted of her husband wasn't readily shareable.

Here people looked for little in marriage. A man would turn to his sixteenth cousin twice removed before he turned to his wife. Here the important ties were between blood relatives. Again I remembered Ihugh's pessimistic lecture by the roadside: women bring trouble between friends and relatives and age mates. Perhaps it was woman's only remedy against such an attitude—to club together, as co-wives, when they were far from their own relatives. Certainly a woman in trouble turned to her guardian or her brother and not to her husband.

I was beginning to understand what they did. I could not understand what they felt. I could admire the way co-wives got on together and still know that I, born and reared as I had been, could never take such a relationship. I would have all the wrong emotions.

Questions 3.4

1. Compare the role expectations of the Tiv wife, as described in this article, and the American wife of the 1970s.
2. What examples of ethnocentrism can be found in this article? Why are people ethnocentric? What functions does ethnocentrism perform in societies?
3. Outline the positive aspects of the Tiv family patterns from both male and female viewpoints.

11 Social Organization

In preceding chapters we have looked at basic units of analysis used by sociologists to understand, describe, and explain human behavior. In this section our view becomes more general. If we combine these basic units and move to a higher level of abstraction, we come to the concept of social organization. If, in a like manner, we were analyzing football, we could first look at the basic elements—players, a ball, a marked-off field, and maybe some spectators. But our description is helped a great deal if we move to the next level and describe a football game, because it is now necessary to look beyond the elements and deal with the combination of the setting, the rules, shared expectations, and interaction patterns of participants—in other words, the social organization present that allows twenty-two players, six officials, and 20,000 observers to mutually participate in and get something out of the same event.

As there is an extensive degree of organization to a football game, so there is to society. The basic elements of a society are a number of people and an inhabitable geographical area. But no understanding of a society is obtained until we study the patterns of interaction and organization that are characteristic of the people. We see that cities exist (why do they?), that highways link cities, that educational facilities are developed, that some individuals are more highly valued than others, that governments run the cities. These things don't just happen by accident; they are evidences that there is organization to society. People cooperate, interact, and share expectations and mutual interests, and there is a structure or system to society much as there is to a building or a machine or a football game—parts link together to form a complex whole. The **social organization** of society is frequently referred to as a *social fabric,* an integrated set of norms, roles, cultural values, and beliefs through which people interact with each other, individually and through groups. The terms *social organization* and *social structure* (which we discussed in Chapter 3) are very similar concepts and are often used interchangeably. Although *social structure* can be used to refer more to a stable network of elements through which people relate to each other and *social organization* can be used to refer more to the continually changing ordering and coordination of human activities, it is probably not worthwhile to try to make a distinction between the terms.

Studying various aspects of the social organization and social structure of society is the central task of sociology. We undertake this analysis in a variety of ways. It is as if we were looking at a subject, society in this case, through a number of windows. Each window is of a different shape, size, thickness, and color of glass. So, though we are looking at the same subject, each approach gives a somewhat different viewpoint, emphasizing certain aspects and ignoring others. The following chapters will analyze the social organization of society through several windows. Groups will be the topic of Chapter 4, and several types of groups will be discussed in detail. Chapters 5 and 6 will deal with types of social differentiation. Chapter 5 will focus on social class, and Chapter 6 on race, ethnicity, sex, and age categories. In Chapter 7 we will discuss institutions as the sociologist sees them. And Chapter 8 will cover population and ecology.

4 Groups

The group is a major unit of analysis for sociologists. A group, simply defined, is a collection of people. Not all collections of people, however, are defined as groups. Are the people on a bus a group? How about red-haired people between the ages of thirty and forty-five? Or what about the students at a large university? At the same time, collectivities that *are* defined as groups may vary tremendously in some characteristics. Your family, my sociology department, a college's football team or a sorority, and the President's Cabinet could probably be defined as groups, but they are quite different in many dimensions—size, complexity, type of interaction, division of labor. Much of the study of social organization, therefore, could be described as centering around two questions: What constitutes a group, and how is the group developed? What are the different types of groups?

Why Study Groups?

Sociologists study groups for several reasons. The division of labor and sharing of interests and jobs that occurs in groups makes it possible to complete tasks that would be impossible for individuals alone. Far more important for the sociologist, however, is the role the group plays in the socialization and development of the individual. To a great degree, we feel that a person *is* the sum of the groups he or she belongs to. Transmission of culture and learning of values, attitudes, and ways of behaving and believing occur mainly in groups. As we have pointed out in Chapters 2 and 3, socialization and development of self and personality are interactive processes. Individuals interact with others and modify their own behavior according to their interpretations of the responses of others. These others are individuals—mother, father, teacher, a significant other person. These others are also groups. Most of the socialization process, both primary and secondary, takes place in *groups.* First the family, then the classroom group, the team or club, the social group, the professional organization, and numerous other voluntary and involuntary associations influence and shape the individual.

The group is more than just the sum of the people who belong to it. Perhaps a good example of this is to compare a family of five people with five people we pick at random on the street. Even if we set each "group" in front of the fire or TV or around the same dinner table and start them interacting, the differences between the two would be clear. We would shortly see that the real family group had developed a set of norms, roles, and relationships to each other that went far beyond the five people. Because of the presence of this network of relationships and understandings that exists in groups, the impact or power of the group in influencing the individual is extensive.

To get a better idea of the importance of groups, imagine the effects on two people of belonging to the following contrasting groups. One person is raised in a family in which competitiveness is valued—family members are constantly competing with each other and with outsiders. The other is raised in a family in which competition is discouraged. One is raised in a family that pursues artistic endeavors, and the other in a family that prefers athletics. One is a Jehovah's Witness, the other a member of a Unitarian church. One is a member of a rock group, the other is a member of a chamber music group. One is on the high school basketball team, the other is on the yearbook staff. One goes to the University of California at Berkeley, the other goes to West Point. One goes through basic training in the Marine Corps, the other joins the Peace Corps. One is raised in a modern western family, the other in a primitive tribal family.

You're probably thinking, "Sure the Berkeley grad is a lot different from the West Point grad, but they had some of those differences before, so one chose Berkeley and the other West Point." That's probably true, but those differences too can be explained by other earlier group memberships and experiences. Each set of group experiences prepares and inclines the person toward another set, then another set, and so on. Or, consider this example. Here is a forty-six-year-old doctor at the top of his field who climbs mountains, builds sailboats, races sports cars, writes books, and is a male chauvinist pig. How did this super achiever get this way? Was he born this way? Certainly not, says the sociologist. Study his socialization patterns through numerous group contexts, and you will find the answer. It may not be easy, but the basic explanations are in the complicated interaction between group and individual.

Groups are important, then, for the ways they affect and shape the individual. We can also study the way groups interact with other groups, how they affect and shape each other. Groups with mutual interests may find themselves supporting each other's activities. Likewise, groups are frequently in conflict with other groups. Since groups are often organized around common interests, and since other groups' interests are bound to be somewhat different, group conflict is almost commonplace. We can quickly think of conflict between employer and employee groups, between political groups, between consumer and business groups, and so on. The level of conflict may vary from easily tolerated disagreement at one extreme to serious, prolonged attempts to eradicate the other group at the other extreme.

Groups and Non-Groups

Sociologists say that a **group** exists when you have a number of people who (1) have shared or patterned interaction and (2) feel bound together by a "consciousness of kind" or a "we" feeling. "Consciousness of kind," a phrase coined by Franklin Giddings, refers to the individual's awareness of important similarities between himself and certain others and to the awareness that the individual and other group members have common loyalties, share at least some similar values, and see themselves as set apart from the rest of the world because of their membership in this particular group. There are tremendous varieties, sizes, and shapes of groups. A group may be as small as two people or almost infinitely large. Groups may be simple in structure or exceedingly complex; they may involve close, intimate relationships between members or more distant and infrequent personal contacts. In other words, the definition of group—patterned interaction and "we" feeling—may fit an enormous variety of situations: a family, a basketball team, a sociology class, IBM, or General Motors.

This definition of groups, imprecise as it may seem, allows us to distinguish groups from other types of collectivities of people, which we could call non-groups. One type of non-group, which we will call an **aggregate** (or aggregation), consists of a number of people clustered together in one place. Examples of aggregates might be all the people in New York City, or the pedestrians at a busy intersection waiting for the light to change to "walk," or all the people in North America, or the passengers on a jet from New York to San Francisco. A second useful non-group, called a **category**, consists of a number of people who have a particular characteristic in common. Examples of categories would be all females, or all red-haired people, or all pilots, or all teenagers, or all whites.

Although we have called them non-groups, aggregates and categories may be transformed into groups should they develop patterned interaction among members and consciousness of kind. For example, let's examine our aggregate of ten

Group members have common loyalties

people waiting at the intersection for the light to change to "walk." Then suppose it *doesn't* change—for five, ten, even fifteen minutes the light refuses to budge from "wait." The pedestrians, strangers until now, begin talking to each other about the impossible situation. Should they race across through traffic against the light? Where's the cop?—you can never find one when you really need one. Some interaction takes places, and a consciousness of kind develops—a group of good people being victimized by a lousy, mechanical light. Or, take the passengers on the jet from New York to San Francisco, another aggregate. Somewhere over Pennsylvania the pilot says to himself, "I'm sick and tired of flying to San Francisco all the time; I guess I'll go to the North Pole." The passengers, who did not know each other before, begin to interact, possibly in an agitated manner, and by the time they reach the Arctic Circle there would probably be highly developed interaction.

Categories may also become groups. All the red-haired people between the ages of thirty and forty-five would constitute a category, as would all carpenters of Irish ancestry. But suppose the middle-aged redheads decided to get together and put out a journal telling of their common problems and aspirations. Or suppose the Carpenters of Irish Ancestry decide it's time to start an organization (CIA?), have a convention, and elect officers. In each case we might have a category developing into a group. These sound farfetched, but the point is that sociologists study both groups and non-groups (categories and aggregates), and the lines between these collectivities are somewhat fluid and easily crossed.

The study of people and society is a large task. It is made more manageable if the whole is broken down into more basic parts. Much of our study is of various types of groups, and the rest of this chapter will be devoted to this. We can also divide a society into categories (males, upper-class blacks, teenage white females) and aggregates (a crowd, a city). This makes our analysis easier (smaller units) and more precise (the units now have some characteristics in common). In later chapters we will examine categories and aggregations.

Types of Groups

The New York Times has described one of the most unusual clubs in the world made up of a small number of usually serious scientists stationed at the South Pole. It is called the "300 Club." Those who want to join must wait until the temperature is at least 100 degrees Fahrenheit below zero, then strip completely nude and dash 100 yards across the ice to a marker designating the South Pole and 100 yards back to the scientific hut. Anyone surviving becomes a member of this very exclusive group.

The criteria that determine a group are broad. In some groups membership is automatic and the participant has no choice; in others the option is open and individuals may join or not as they wish. These two types are labeled involuntary and voluntary groups. **Involuntary groups** might include the family one is born into or the army platoon one is drafted into. **Voluntary groups** would include any of a vast number that the member may exercise some choice in joining—lodges, fraternities, bridge clubs, student governments, political organizations. **In-groups** and **out-groups** are labels applied on the one hand to groups that *I* belong to, that *I* identify with, that are *my* groups, as opposed to groups that I do not belong to or identify with and that may even be alien to me. Again the examples are numerous and could involve the dimensions of family, race, religion, occupation, age, sex, political viewpoint, and many others.

Reference groups are groups that serve as models for our behavior, groups whose perspectives we assume and mold our behavior after. A reference group may be made up of people one associates with or knows personally, or it may be an abstract collectivity of individuals who represent models for our behavior. Each individual will belong to many reference groups. As a teacher I would have certain reference groups, as a sociologist others, as a husband others, and as a handball player still others. One's **peer group** is made up of people of relatively the same age, interests, and social position with whom one has reasonably close association and contact. A peer group may consist of a class at school, a street gang, or an occupational group such as the members of a college sociology department or a group of lawyers in a law firm. Not all the members of a peer group are necessarily friends, but the peer group exercises a major role in the socialization process. During adolescence, it may be *the* major socializing agent.

Groups whose members come predominantly from one social-class level are called **horizontal groups.** Examples of horizontal groups would include almost any organization formed along occupational lines—an association of doctors, carpenters, or prostitutes. If a group includes members from a variety of social classes, it could be called a **vertical group.** Vertical groups are more difficult to find in American society, since many divisions are made along social-class lines. A church congregation might constitute a vertical group, and in some cases an army platoon made up of draftees would include members from a variety of social classes. Groups are also categorized according to their longevity. A group brought together to perform a single, short-term task could be called a **temporary group,** whereas a longer-lasting collectivity like a family could be called a **permanent group.** Groups are defined as open or closed according to the ease of gaining membership. A white fraternity is often a **closed group** as far as a black male is concerned, but the U.S. Army is probably a very **open group** for the same individual. Now, what type of group is the "300 Club"?

Primary and Secondary Groups

A family and a draftee's army platoon are involuntary groups, but they are quite different sorts of groups. A basketball team and the members of a large college class are voluntary groups, but again they are very different. Groups vary along a number of dimensions, and one of the most important of these is how primary or secondary each group is. For example, a family and a basketball team are more primary than an army platoon and a large college class. Primary groups play an important role in human development. Most of the socialization process—learning society's norms and roles, development of the self—takes place in small primary groups. The **primary group** was first described by C. H. Cooley as referring to groups in which contacts between members are intimate, personal, and face-to-face. A great part of the individual's total life experience is bound up in the group and is known to other group members. The primary type of relationship is one involving deep and personal interaction and communication. This interaction is an end in itself—primary groups often exist because of the value of the primary relationship rather than because of other specific goals or tasks. People conform in primary groups because of strong informal norms—for example, fear of being ostracized, scorned, or ridiculed—rather than because of any formal written rules.

A **secondary group,** on the other hand, is more impersonal. Interaction is more superficial and probably based on utilitarian goals. That is, the person is less important than a particular skill he or she may offer the group. Interaction and communication are based on the value of one's particular skill rather than on interest in one's general personal qualities. It is probably most helpful to see the concepts of primary and secondary as opposite ends of a continuum. The completely primary or completely secondary group may seldom be found. Rather, groups vary in their degree of primariness or secondariness. Moving from primary to secondary along the continuum we might see these groups: a married couple, an extended family including parents and grandparents, a basketball team, a sorority, a professional organization or labor union, the employees of a large corporation.

Small Groups

The study of small groups has long been a central interest of sociology and social psychology. Small groups have become popular in a number of areas recently. Small groups are used as vehicles for treatment—group therapy has proven to be a useful mechanism for change in prisons, mental hospitals, and organizations dealing with alcoholism and drug usage. Sensitivity training groups and encounter groups have become popular on college campuses and with large organizations as techniques for improving communication, interaction, and self-understanding. The small class is believed to work better than the large class in the educational process.

Small groups, as we are describing them here, combine a primary type of interaction with a task orientation. Achievement of the task—better education, self-understanding, improved communication and management skills—is facilitated by the primary group atmosphere. Social scientists have done extensive research on small groups. In the following paragraphs we will discuss ways of studying small groups and some of the characteristics of small group behavior.

Small groups are studied in a variety of ways. Each method focuses on a different perspective of small group interaction. Robert Bales has developed a technique called **interaction process analysis (IPA)**.[1] In this technique, the interaction of group members is observed and categorized by researchers as they watch the group through one-way windows or monitor their behavior with tape recorders. A basic assumption of IPA is that groups function to solve problems. Four main problems confronting small groups are:

1. Adaptation to outside factors that influence the group (control by or cooperation with others).
2. Instrumental control over performing group tasks (assigning jobs, making decisions).
3. Expression and management of group members' feelings (expressing dissatisfaction or pleasure, dealing with interpersonal problems, relieving tension).
4. Development and maintenance of group integration (cohesion, willingness to do things, satisfaction).

Group members interact in a variety of ways (verbally, with gestures, through facial expressions) to solve the problems confronting them. The researchers studying the group break this interaction down into small parts or *acts*. An act may be verbal or nonverbal behavior and must be communicated to at least one other person in the group. An act can come from a long interaction or a short one. For example, a discussion between two people may result in only one act, whereas in another situation one sentence may involve two or three acts. Typically, a sentence or an independent clause in a sentence is considered an act.

The IPA observer then places each act into one of twelve categories. This classification of bits of interaction into predetermined categories is really IPA's major distinguishing feature. Table 4.1 outlines the twelve act categories and four general areas into which the act categories fall. It also shows a profile of the responses of a typical group, which we will discuss more in a moment.

The coach of a professional basketball team is talking to the team at halftime. They look like a small group, so let's try IPA on them. Their problem seems to be that they are behind the Boston Celtics by thirty-nine points. Little does the coach know that, in IPA language, their plight can be defined in terms of four problems. The major problem as the coach sees it is *adaptation to outside factors:* the darn Celtics, the hostile crowd, the uneven floor. *This* is the problem he must deal with.

[1]Bales's major work is *Interaction Process Analysis* (Cambridge, Mass.: Addison-Wesley, 1950). Shepherd's summary of Bales's work has been especially helpful: see Clovis Shepherd, *Small Groups* (San Francisco: Chandler, 1964), pp. 27–36. Also see Michael Olmsted, *The Small Group* (New York: Random House, 1959), pp. 117–132, and *The Small Group,* 2d ed. by Michael Olmsted and Paul Hare (New York: Random House, 1978).

But it is also likely that the halftime discussion will involve *instrumental control over performing group tasks* (someone must stop the Celtics' center, who has already scored fifty points); *expression and management of feelings* (Fogarty, who is guarding the Celtics' center, kicks the water cooler across the locker room); and *development and maintenance of group integration* (the coach explains that the team must stand together and help Fogarty out in this difficult time). Now, observe the discussion and check off the acts as they occur. Most of the coach's remarks fall in the answers area. He *gives suggestions* and *opinions* (suggests that Blatt stop shooting at the wrong basket, tells Ragley that his broken arm seems to be hindering his dribbling, and reminds Henson that they are playing basketball, not football). The assistant coach *gives information*—shooting percentages and number of rebounds. Fogarty *asks for information* regarding how to keep the opposing center from scoring so much. Martinez provides *tension release* by telling what he did on his summer vacation. The coach *shows tension* and *antagonism* by telling Martinez to shut up or he will punch his lights out. But the team leaves the halftime talk on a positive note: They *show solidarity* by crowding together and clasping hands before stumbling back onto the court.

　　Although most groups are more sophisticated and their interaction more complicated than that of our hapless basketball team, the example does illustrate how group interaction might be recorded by the IPA observer. At this point, we should look again at Table 4.1. The right-hand column shows a profile of the responses of a typical group. For example, when the interaction that occurs in a typical group is broken down into acts, roughly fifty-six percent of these acts will be answers of one sort or another. Many groups are not typical, of course, so there may be substantial differences in the percentages of different groups. As might be expected, satisfied and dissatisfied groups differ. In satisfied groups, there are more suggestions and fewer requests for information than in dissatisfied groups. The biggest difference, however, is in positive and negative reactions. Dissatisfied groups have about three times as much disagreement and only one-third as much agreement as satisfied groups. The normal group has an average ratio of about two instrumental acts (questions and answers) to one social-emotional act (positive and

Table 4.1　Interaction Process Analysis (IPA) Categories

Act Categories	General Areas	Typical Group Response
1. Shows solidarity 2. Shows tension release 3. Shows agreement	Positive reactions	25%
4. Gives suggestion 5. Gives opinion 6. Gives information	Answers	56
7. Asks for information 8. Asks for opinion 9. Asks for suggestion	Questions	7
10. Shows disagreement 11. Shows tension 12. Shows antagonism	Negative reactions	12

negative reactions). However, there can be different interpretations of the same pattern of response: If the ratio is higher than two to one, it may mean that the group wants to get a particular job done quickly and efficiently. Or it could mean that the group members are anxious about their feelings toward each other and have decided that steady work is the best way to keep out of each others' hair. A ratio of less than two instrumental acts to one social-emotional act may mean that the group is avoiding its work or that the group is interested in reducing conflict and developing warmth and cohesion.

There appears to be an optimum pattern for most effective group performance. If the percentage of answers rises too high, the group may get the feeling of a dictated decision. If the percentage of answers drops too low, the group may be seen as a waste of time. Typically, groups have two positive reactions to each negative reaction. Too many negative reactions and the group turns into a name-calling session; too many positive reactions and it becomes a mutual admiration society.

According to Bales's observations, the life history of a group moves through several stages. In the beginning stage the group focuses on problems of orientation (facts and information). In the middle stage the group is concerned with problems of evaluation (opinions). In the final stage the group deals with problems of control and decision (suggestions).

This should give some idea of Bales's IPA. As you can see, this method involves counting and classifying each bit of interaction in an experimental problem-solving group. It differs from other approaches in that a large amount of detailed factual material is collected. Critics of this type of research on small groups are dubious about the created-in-the-laboratory nature of these experiments; they suggest that in real life small groups may behave differently from the way they behave in labs. Perhaps you should pick a group and try it out to see whether the categories and percentages that Bales suggests really fit.

J. L. Moreno developed a technique called **sociometry** that provides a quite different way of studying small groups. Here the focus is more on the *who* of interaction rather than on the *what*. Sociometry looks not at the nature or type of interaction, as Bales's IPA does, but at the direction of interaction—who interacts with whom. Members of the group being studied are asked questions like, "Who is your best friend in the group?" or "Who would you most like to work with on an important project?" The patterns and directions of interaction are then graphed as in Figure 4.1. This figure represents a sociogram of the members of a volunteer fire department. Each member of the group was asked three questions: "Who would you most prefer to have help you fight a fire?" "Who would you most prefer to have help you plan a social function?" and "Who is your best friend in the department?" The lines and arrows in the sociogram represent the resulting choices. For example, fireman 13 chose fireman 11, firemen 1 and 7 named each other, and so on. Not all the selections are shown in this sociogram in order to keep it from getting too complicated. Those near the center of the sociogram were chosen more often—fireman 11 was named twenty-eight times, fireman 9 fourteen times, fireman 4 not at all. Several typical sociometric patterns appear in this figure. Fireman 4 was not chosen and is called an *isolate*. Firemen 5, 10, and 13 were named

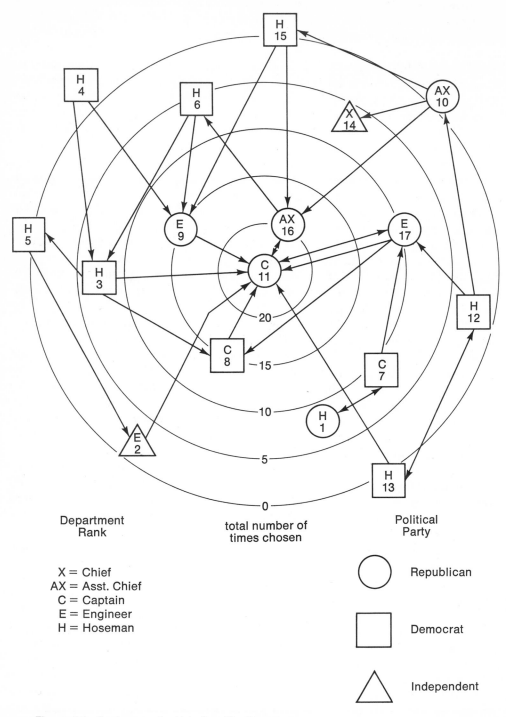

Department
Rank

total number of
times chosen

Political
Party

X = Chief
AX = Asst. Chief
C = Captain
E = Engineer
H = Hoseman

◯ Republican

▢ Democrat

△ Independent

Figure 4.1 Sociogram of a Volunteer Fire Department.

only once each and are near-isolates or *neglectees.* Fireman 11 was chosen by nearly everybody and is termed a *star.* Rank in the department and political preference are shown in the sociogram to see whether these explain patterns of selection. One of the assistant chiefs was more popular than the chief, and the three captains are all near the center of the sociogram. Hosemen, the lowest rank, are consistently around the edge. More detail on fireman 11 indicates that aside from being a Republican and a captain, he is one of two men in the department with a college degree, he is the third oldest member, he is one of five Catholics, he has the highest social-class standing in the department, and he participates actively in departmental activities.

As a technique for the study of groups, sociometry presents both advantages and disadvantages. On the positive side, it helps uncover informal interaction and friendship patterns, and helps to identify variables associated with leadership and social isolation. On the negative side, sociometry is somewhat static and, unless repeated often, does not take into account the fluid and rapidly changing nature of group structure. It is an effective technique for mapping interaction but does not provide an in-depth analysis of that interaction.

Another way of studying small groups is by means of **participant observation.** Here, the researcher joins the group being studied and becomes involved in its activities—one learns about the group by becoming part of it. (See the discussion of Whyte's participant observation study of Cornerville in Chapter 1, page 12.) We can see that participant observation is often less controlled and provides less of the sort of detail that either IPA or sociometry gives. A talented observer, however, can use participant observation to achieve an analysis of more depth, can uncover meanings of actions, and can present a dynamic picture of a group's behavior. I have a feeling that if I were studying a group—the Hell's Angels, the SLA, the Pittsburgh Steelers, and the President's cabinet come to mind—I'd learn more through participant observation than I would through IPA or sociometry. Essentially, though, the method to use depends on the type of group being studied and on what it is you want to find out. In participant observation, the observer always has to be cautious in order that his or her presence in the group doesn't unduly change the group's behavior and that he or she doesn't become so much a part of the group that objectivity is lost. Both of these are crucial problems that the participant observer has to face.

Small Group Research

The following paragraphs summarize some small group research that I have found particularly interesting. Social psychologists have long been fascinated by conformity, and a number of studies have examined the effects of group pressure on individual judgment and behavior. (Milgram's study of conformity in France and Norway discussed on page 71 is an example of this.) A stationary light in a dark room appears to move; this is called the *autokinetic effect.* Muzafer Sherif asked subjects to judge how far the light moved. When small groups were tested, they quickly arrived at agreement on the light's movement—a group norm. When the members were tested individually, they stuck to the earlier established group norm. When other subjects were tested individually *first* (no group norm available), their judgments of the light's movement were more variable and erratic. In other studies, Solomon Asch asked small groups of people to compare the length of lines. Some members of the group were stooges, or confederates of the researcher. The stooges were instructed to make obviously wrong selections—two lines that were of different lengths were said to be the same. In studies involving eight stooges and one subject, the subject was faced with the choice of going along with the majority or making an independent judgment. Many avoided stress and simply went along with the majority.[2]

There is variation in how small groups handle deviants. Laboratory experiments indicate that if one person continues to disagree with or block a position on which the rest of the group agrees, there is a tendency to reject the deviant. In another study of Quaker work groups and army basic training squads, however, another pattern emerged. Robert Dentler and Kai Erikson found that in some groups, deviant behavior helps maintain group equilibrium, and attempts to alienate a member whose behavior was deviant were resisted. Mentally ill (schizophrenic) members of basic-training squads were taken care of by the other recruits. Others performed the deviant's duties, they became very protective of him, and when he was finally hospitalized, other squad members became disturbed and angry at his removal.

Leadership and other roles in small groups follow certain predictable patterns. Two types of leaders generally appear: the task leader and the social-emotional leader. The *task leader* possesses skills or characteristics that the group values highly, but he or she is not highly approachable. The *social-emotional leader* is highly approachable; he or she is the one to whom other group members can complain, show affection, or in other ways express feelings. The social-emotional leader may have some influence on the task leader. Other group roles are described by the terms *nice guys, ignored,* and *rejected. Nice guys* are approachable—not as much as the social-emotional leader but enough that their membership and contributions are valued. Those *ignored* are members who are usually inactive; they are an unknown quantity to the rest of the group. Those *rejected* are members perceived as unapproachable because they have no skills or characteristics valued by the group or because of hostile or confusing behavior on their part.[3]

A study of deviants in small groups was concerned with finding out whether the deviant's rank in the group would affect the punishment he received. Twenty-five members of a college fraternity's pledge class were divided into four groups. Each group was told by an officer of the fraternity that another member of the fraternity had violated some rules and would have to be punished. The identity of the offender (independent variable) was changed for each group, and each group was asked to determine the appropriate punishment (dependent variable). Here are the descriptions of the four offenders:

---

[2]Muzafer Sherif, *The Psychology of Social Norms* (New York: Harper, 1936). Solomon Asch. "Effects of Group Pressure on the Modification and Distortion of Judgment," in *Groups, Leadership and Men,* edited by M. H. Guetzkow (Pittsburgh: Carnegie, 1951), and S. Asch, "Studies of Independence and Conformity: A Minority of One Against a Unanimous Majority," *Psychological Monographs* 70, no. 9 (1956), Whole No. 416.

[3]The studies discussed in this and the previous paragraph are summarized by Shepherd in *Small Groups,* pp. 69 and 74–79 (see footnote 1).

Offender for Group 1. Highest social position, fraternity officer, very well liked, task and social-emotional leader.

Offender for Group 2. High social position, best liked member of the sophomore class, social-emotional leader.

Offender for Group 3. Not identified by name—just as "a member of the sophomore class."

Offender for Group 4. Low social position, not very well liked.

The groups were told that the deviant had duplicated and sold fraternity files. They were given twenty minutes to discuss the case and were told to individually and anonymously write down the appropriate punishment. Group 1 all felt the deviant should give a formal apology. Group 2 felt the deviant should be given a one-month to one-semester suspension. Group 3 felt a one-semester suspension to be appropriate with one member voting for a one-year suspension. Most of the members of group 4 felt the deviant should not be allowed to eat or sleep in the house, and one member voted for expulsion from the fraternity. We see that deviants are punished not so much according to what they have done, but according to their position or status in the group. The high-ranking individuals were lightly punished; the low-ranking person's punishment bordered on ostracism—he was physically removed from group activity. As the author of the study puts it, "The higher the position of a person within a group, the more lenient will be his punishment for deviance; the reason for this being that the higher the social position of a person, the more value he has to the group and the more they would have to lose by rejecting him."[4]

Some of the effects and constraints that small groups have on behavior can be seen in the actions of people on juries. The jury usually quickly selects a person of high status (wealth and/or education) as foreman. People of high status are more

---

How do juries reach decisions? Sometimes in strange and peculiar ways. The jury of ten women and two men at the trial of the Chicago Seven (seven young men charged with inciting a riot during the 1968 Democratic convention) argued and horse-traded for four days before they could reach a verdict. At first a majority of eight favored convicting all of the defendants while three jurors insisted on complete acquittal. Agreement was finally reached late at night with each group holed up in a separate hotel room. One juror reported that "Feelings were so high, with the two groups against each other, we just didn't feel at ease in there in the jury room together." After much argument, ". . . we agreed we should not be a hung jury. We decided to compromise, and it was just a question of how to compromise." Another juror who favored convicting all and admitted that there was not one of the defendants she really liked said, "Half a chicken is better than none at all. We were all anxious to go home." The jury found five of the seven defendants guilty.

Reported in *Time*, March 2, 1970, pp. 8–11.

---

[4]Lowell W. Gerson, "Punishment and Position: The Sanctioning of Deviants in Small Groups," *Case Western Reserve Journal of Sociology,* vol. 1 (1967), pp. 54–62.

active on the jury—they talk more, have more influence, and are seen as more competent. Low-status people tend to defer to the higher-status members. Men are more active on juries, but women are better jurors—they take more care in considering testimony. Jurors are very reluctant to come back without a verdict. The self-confidence of witnesses often has more effect on the jury than the logic or soundness of what they say. Juries often try the lawyer rather than the person he or she is representing. Finally, the mere fact of a person's being brought to trial makes him or her suspect in the eyes of the jury, in spite of the presumption of innocence in our court system.[5]

Formal Organizations

The new director of the Department of Motor Vehicles (DMV) ran head-on into a problem recently. He had DMV workers paint "no parking" in Chinese in no-parking areas around the DMV buildings. There were already signs in English and Spanish as part of a program to help people unfamiliar with English. The director was proud and the local newspaper published a picture of the new signs. But the next day they were gone, painted over. It seems that a grounds supervisor had also seen the picture in the newspaper, had checked around and couldn't find the necessary work order for having the signs painted, and had them painted over. The next day the director had the signs painted in Chinese again, but only after he had obtained the necessary work order. "It was his first real experience with bureaucracy, and he lost it to the paper pushers," reported a spokesperson.

Large-scale formal organizations are an essential part of modern society. These organizations, often called **bureaucracies,** arise as societies' activities become increasingly planned rather than spontaneous. People discovered long ago that if several people got together and planned an activity—building a car, educating a student—they often got the job done more rapidly and efficiently than if each pursued the task in his or her own way, spontaneously and haphazardly. Arthur Stinchcombe defines a formal organization as any social arrangement in which the activities of some people are systematically planned by other people in order to achieve some special purpose. Those who plan the activities automatically have authority over the others. Formal organizations seem to arise in societies with a money economy that are pursuing complex tasks requiring the coordinated efforts of a number of people. As the size of the organization increases, administrative tasks multiply, and this encourages further bureaucratization. There is an enduring quality about these organizations—people leave, but like the building they worked in, their jobs and the organization remain, seemingly forever.[6]

Some years ago, sociologist Max Weber identified the characteristics of an abstract or pure form of bureaucracy. (1) There is a precise division of labor, so that

---

[5]For more detail on these and other studies of jury behavior, see Hans Toch, ed., *Legal and Criminal Psychology* (New York: Holt, Rinehart and Winston, 1961).

[6]See Arthur Stinchcombe, "Formal Organizations" in *Sociology: An Introduction,* 2d ed., edited by Neil Smelser (New York: Wiley, 1973). Also see Peter Blau and Marshall Meyer, *Bureaucracy in Modern Society,* 2d ed. (New York: Random House, 1971), and H. H. Gerth and C. W. Mills, *From Max Weber: Essays in Sociology* (New York: Oxford University Press, 1958).

each individual in the organization is a specialist—an expert in performing a specific task. (2) There is a hierarchy of authority, a chain of command in which each individual is clearly in control of some and clearly responsible to others. (3) There is an exhaustive and consistent system of rules designed to assure uniformity in the performance of every task. (4) Social relationships between individuals in the organization, especially between superiors and their subordinates, are formal and impersonal. (5) The bureaucracy is technically highly efficient, much like a machine. (6) Employees are highly trained for their task; they are, in turn, protected from arbitrary dismissal—their job constitutes a career with possibilities for advancement according to seniority and/or achievement.

Weber was talking about how bureaucracies in an abstract sense might operate. Formal organizations in fact do not necessarily resemble Weber's description on all or even most points. In any organization, much that is unplanned occurs. The chain of command is often circumvented. Shortcuts reduce bureaucratic red tape in a variety of ways. Relationships between individuals are often personal and informal. Organizations occasionally are grossly inefficient. In fact, to counteract the somewhat negative view that many people have of the huge bureaucracy, organizations often consciously attempt to look and act less formal, less bureaucratic. Nevertheless, Weber's description provides us with a useful abstraction of the general characteristics of large organizations.

The bureaucracy I'm most familiar with is a university. If Max Weber wandered through our institution, he would probably note the following. *Division of labor, specialization:* There are groundskeepers, secretaries, computer operators, librarians, janitors, and professors. The professors teach specific courses in specific areas, and these courses seldom overlap. In the sociology department I teach criminology, and another person teaches courses on Middle Eastern societies. We are both sociologists, yet he knows little about my area and I even less about his. We are all highly specialized. *Hierarchy of authority:* There is an authority ladder in each section. There is a massive organizational chart for the college (which in fact looks like a map of the Los Angeles freeway system and I'm certain is understood by no one). Hierarchy runs from students (at the bottom) to professors to department heads to associate deans to deans to associate vice presidents to vice presidents to the president. Each must answer to the one above. *System of rules:* Classes must be added or dropped by a certain day. Grades must be turned in by professors in a certain way by a certain time. Lists of rules describe how students may complain about injustices and how faculty may deal with unruly students. A faculty member wishing to leave campus to go to a professional meeting in another city must fill out a pile of forms weeks in advance of the trip. People are promoted by a mathematical model so complex that it defies comprehension. *Relationships are formal and impersonal:* All are handled alike, people in the same circumstances must be handled the same—the rules say so. We are all cogs in a large machine, and the machine works better if it does not have to concern itself with exceptions. People I know well become members of committees (budget, promotion, grievance), and suddenly they become very formal and impersonal. *The bureaucracy is highly efficient:* I have a feeling that if Max looked at our operation, he would pass on this one. Well, perhaps we *are* efficient. We have an assembly-line process with which we mass-educate thousands of students. We take flocks of uneducated high school seniors and after only four years of subjecting them to some forty sophisticated courses of instruction, we produce educated people. *Highly trained employees, protected from dismissal:* Most of the faculty have Ph.D.'s or the equivalent in their area of specialization. After being with the organization for a set number of years, tenure (protection from dismissal) is granted.

But there is another side—the nonbureaucratic side of bureaucracies, the informal organization in the formal organization. Our institution has that as well. Specialization breaks down somewhat as instructors, because of changing enrollment patterns, move into new teaching areas. It is common knowledge that contrary to the hierarchy of authority, the university is really run by the secretaries. They are here everyday, they work longer hours, they have more knowledge about how the place really works, and they end up making or influencing many of the decisions. Informal small primary groups arise within the organization that counteract formality and impersonality. Often these cut across the authority structure as well. Several faculty lunch groups constantly meet to pass on information and to plan strategy. A phone call to the right person (usually a secretary) quickly cuts through the system of rules and bypasses miles of red tape. The typical organization is so large that it cannot keep track of bits and pieces. Many professors do not turn in travel plans; they know that they could leave for months and never be missed. And efficiency? The car manufacturer proudly counts the number of units manufactured—3,000 cars today. What they don't tell us is that 2,500 broke down within a mile of the assembly line. Our institution graduates 2,000 people a year, but there is growing concern over the inability of many of the graduates to read and understand the diploma they receive. . . .

I have perhaps exaggerated to make the point—bureaucracies and large organizations have typical formal characteristics that develop because of their size and functions. They also have typical informal characteristics that develop because of the needs of the people that work in the organizations.

Types of Organizations

People who study organizations often come to the conclusion that organizations can be categorized. Two typologies are shown in Table 4.2. Weber categorized organizations according to their authority and internal structure, whereas Katz and Kahn typed organizations according to the type of function they performed.

Charisma, which is a basic factor in Weber's charismatic retinue, refers to a certain superior quality an individual may have that sets him or her apart from others. This individual is viewed as superhuman and capable of exceptional acts—the sort of person you might follow to the ends of the earth if you were asked to.

Remember when you encounter typologies that the categories are seldom as clearly cut and exclusive in real life as they appear to be in a table. A given organization may cut across or be included in several categories because it may, in its various parts, show several structures or perform a variety of functions. For example, I think again of the university where I work. It is an adaptive organization, but it is a production and maintenance organization as well. Although it is

Table 4.2 Types of Organizations

Weber—Based on Type of Authority and Structure	Characteristics	Examples
Charismatic retinue	Made up of the followers and disciples of a charismatic leader	Followers of civil rights leader Martin Luther King, Jr.; Reverend Moon's Unification Church; Jim Jones's People's Temple; followers of a great scientist or artist
Feudal administration	Separate from but responsible to a parent organization; has local autonomy to act in terms of own interests; is obligated to superiors, but there is no constant flow of orders or supervision	New-car dealerships; chain or franchised stores, agencies, or theaters
Modern bureaucracy	Close to Weber's characteristics of bureaucracy: specialization, hierarchy of authority, system of rules, formality	Governmental agencies, large public utilities, military organizations
Modern professional organization	Bureaucratic but with more individual freedom, more decentralization of responsibility once the individual's competency is certified	Universities, large hospitals

Katz and Kahn—Based on Type of Function		
Production or economic organization	Creates wealth, manufactures goods, makes things or produces services that are consumed by society	General Motors, IBM, an advertising agency, Pacific Telephone
Maintenance organization	Socializes people for their roles in other organizations and in society	Churches, schools, health and welfare organizations, rehabilitation and reform organizations
Adaptive organization	Creates knowledge, develops theories, applies information to existing problems	Universities, research organizations, organizations dealing with the arts
Managerial or political organization	Judges, coordinates, and controls people; generates and allocates power	Federal and state government, pressure groups, labor unions, special interest groups

Arthur Stinchcombe, "Formal Organizations" (see footnote 6); Daniel Katz and Robert Kahn, *The Social Psychology of Organizations* (New York: Wiley, 1966), Chapter 5; and Richard H. Hall, *Organizations: Structure and Process* (Englewood Cliffs, N.J.: Prentice-Hall, 1972), Chapter 2.

probably basically a modern professional organization, parts show the modern bureaucracy at its extreme, some of the administration is definitely feudal, and perhaps one could even find a charismatic leader complete with followers or disciples (most likely the football coach during a winning season).

Formal Organizations—Consequences and Concerns

Parkinson's Law: The Formula of 1,000
Any enterprise with more than 1,000 employees becomes a self-perpetuating empire, creating so much internal work that it no longer needs any contact with the outside world.

A proliferation in society of large organizations and the bureaucratic values of efficiency and rationality will have consequences, some obvious, some less so. Large organizations allow the performance of tasks that could not otherwise be accomplished. There is undoubtedly greater efficiency in producing products. At the same time, alienation may result when workers see themselves as small cogs in a huge, impersonal machine. Stinchcombe states that in societies dominated by formal organizations, people tend to become specialists in particular activities. Educational institutions respond by encouraging students to concentrate on learning a specific technique or skill rather than attaining a broader, more general education. In societies dominated by formal organizations, a larger percentage of a person's social relationships is planned instead of spontaneous. Interaction is more superficial, and emotions play less of a part in social relationships of this type. People are judged more by what they *do* (actions) than by what they *are* (their more permanent qualities). To put it another way, interaction of all types, on the job or off, is more secondary, less primary. Some analysts of modern society have commented with concern on the decline in the number of primary groups with which one can affiliate. They argue that groups and contacts are becoming increasingly secondary in modern industrialized countries like the United States.

There have been many attempts to categorize societies, and often these attempts involve the variables of modernization and industrialization. Anthropologist Robert Redfield contrasted folk and urban societies. He used the term *folk societies* to describe isolated villages in less-industrialized countries, which were small, homogeneous, relatively self-contained, and largely based on subsistence activities. *Urban societies* referred to modern Western industrialized nations. Redfield saw folk and urban as opposite ends of a continuum along which societies at various degrees of development could be placed. Sociologist Emile Durkheim used the terms *mechanical solidarity* and *organic solidarity* to describe types of social cohesion that occur in small, homogeneous, preindustrial societies and in modern industrialized societies. Mechanical solidarity is likely to exist in a small homogeneous society and describes uniformity among people and lack of differentiation or specialization. Organic solidarity is likely to exist in complex societies, which are characterized by more specialization and division of labor, and consequently, increasing individualism. Ferdinand Toennies also described two contrasting types of societies with the terms *Gemeinschaft* and *Gesellschaft*. The **Gemeinschaft** is a more primary and closely knit society in which relationships are personal and informal and there is a commitment or identification with the community. The **Gesellschaft** is a more secondary society based on contractual arrangements, bargaining, a well-developed division of labor, and rational thought rather than emotion. Relationships between people are impersonal and utilitarian.

Many who feel as Cooley did that primary group relationships are of great importance in the socialization process and the development of the self and personality, are concerned that the increasing secondariness or *Gesellschaft*-like nature of modern societies will have serious effects on the developmental processes. Some would no doubt point to high rates of divorce, rising crime and delinquency, increased mental illness, and other individual and group pathologies as consequences of restricted primary-group contacts. Others would argue that these conditions are merely the consequences of any modern, complex society. Moreover, the huge, complicated, multi-layered bureaucracies that perform tasks for us today are highly efficient even though somewhat impersonal. To idealize the *Gemeinschaft* society, they would argue, is unrealistic and shows a lack of understanding of the positive aspects of the large organizations of today. They would conclude that there is not really more pathology (crime, marital breakup, mental illness); our efficient bureaucracies just do a better job of ferreting it out and letting us know about it.

About twenty years ago William H. Whyte, Jr., wrote *The Organization Man,* in which he painted a rather gloomy picture of how large organizations were affecting people's lives. Americans have long been guided by what has been called the Protestant Ethic—the idea that pursuit of individual salvation through hard work, thrift, and competitive struggle is the heart of the American achievement. According to Whyte, a new ethic has emerged as a consequence of the proliferation of large organizations. Now the young person going out into the world believes that to make a living he must do what somebody else tells him to do. The idea of individual achievement and the encouragement of personal creativity is disappearing. Instead, the guiding values of the organization man include a belief in the group as source of creativity, in belongingness and togetherness, and in the value of fitting in. These phrases are part of the organizational ethic: "Be a compromiser." "Maintain group solidarity at all costs." "Don't rock the boat." "The unorthodox can be dangerous." The organization man is conforming and "well-rounded"; he looks at his company this way:

> Be loyal to the company and the company will be loyal to you. After all, if you do a good job for the organization, it is only good sense for the organization to be good to you, because that will be best for everybody. There are a bunch of real people around here. Tell them what you think and they will respect you for it. They don't want a man to fret and stew about his work. It won't happen to me. A man who gets ulcers probably shouldn't be in business anyway.[7]

The goals of the organization and the goals of the individual are the same. People don't buck the system; they cooperate with it.

Where did the organization man come from? He was produced by a society that is now geared to the large organization. The educational system, which is increas-

---

[7]William H. Whyte, Jr., *The Organization Man* (Garden City, N.Y.: Doubleday, 1956), p. 143.

ingly influenced by business, is the first step. The university curriculum has become more practical, vocational, and job oriented, with a declining emphasis on liberal arts and the humanities. And the organization man ten years later? He lives an outgoing friendly life of inconspicuous consumption in suburbia where he joins clubs, has kids, plays golf, and where all the houses, cars, appliances, lawns, and even people tend to look alike.

And if the individual messes up, can't hack it, gets disgusted, and drops out, whose fault is it? The organization's? Certainly not. It's the *individual's* fault—he or she doesn't fit in. Our worship of organizations bothers Whyte, and he objects to the emerging values and behaviors that result.

Is it really as bad as he says? It's hard to accurately calculate the effects of formal organizations, since they are so much a part of our lives, but remember, he wrote *The Organization Man* more than twenty years ago, and we are certainly a far more bureaucratized society now.

Can Formal Organizations Change?

In sometimes interesting ways, formal organizations modify their forms and structures and change their philosophies. For example, bureaucracies have long had a basic belief in specialization—the simpler the task, the better and more efficiently it can be performed. (See Weber's first characteristic of bureaucracy.) Break the job down into its basic parts. Make it simple, precise, and repetitive, and the worker can't possibly mess it up. Well, this sort of approach to tasks—three turns on the same nut with the same wrench 3,000 times a day—may *be* more efficient, but people don't like it. They get bored, job satisfaction goes down, and absenteeism goes up. The new fad in management is to reverse the cherished specialization ethic and *enrich* jobs, make them more interesting, more varied, not so repetitive. This view has been widely picked up by industry and by business graduate schools. The new pitch is that jobs should be meaningful, self-fulfillment is a worthwhile goal, and work groups are important for improving job satisfaction. Workers will take more pride in the product if they can follow it all the way through, performing a variety of tasks toward its completion.

They may be right, and it certainly sounds like a more enlightened approach to the work situation. But a skeptic might inquire as to management's reasons for this new approach. Companies like to feel they are progressive. And, of course, it's good for the image—current ads portray the happy Swedish automobile workers who get to follow a car to complete construction. You just *know* that's a better car. Industry can be humanistic after all. But the clincher for the organization is the economic payoff. Improved worker morale means less absenteeism, employee turnover, and sabotage, and improved quality of product. The best of all possible worlds exists if organizations can improve their image and cut costs at the same time. Imagine the company's dilemma, however, if the new program increases worker morale, happiness, and self-fulfillment—but efficiency and output are unchanged or reduced.

Bureaucratic formal organizations are dominant today; every year more and more people work for them. But what of the future? Will the classic bureaucratic structure described by Max Weber continue to be the prevailing mode of social organization? A number of experts, including Alvin Toffler and Warren Bennis, think not. Toffler predicts that in the future we will witness not the triumph, but the breakdown of bureaucracy.[8] He calls the organization of the future the "ad-hocracy" (from the Latin, *ad hoc:* meant for a particular purpose or goal). A number of factors are leading to the demise of old-style bureaucracy. Mergers, organizational upheavals, and internal reorganizations are occurring at rapidly increasing rates, and this is disrupting once-stable bureaucratic rules and structures. Individuals' places in the organization are less stable—they are shifted from one task to another. There is a rapid increase in project or task-force management. Teams are put together to perform specific short-term tasks, and when finished the teams are disassembled and the people are reassigned, "exactly like mobile playgrounds." It is this particular characteristic that Toffler means by his term "ad-hocracy." Weber's hierarchy of authority is collapsing also, and the chain of command is altered. The rapidity of events and the need for quick actions mean that decisions are being made at all levels without waiting for higher-ups to approve.

Like Toffler, Warren Bennis believes that bureaucracies worked well in stable societies for routine tasks. But with the rapid change of today, those characteristics —routine, stability—are disappearing. The future will see adaptive, short-term, rapidly changing, temporary systems—task forces that solve specific problems. Gone will be permanence and enduring relationships between an individual and the organization. Gone will be the powerful hierarchies of authority that kept the individual in line. Loyalties will be to one's profession rather than to the organization. All of this, according to Toffler, is caused basically by the rapidity of change. To keep pace, organizations will adapt and change their structure and hence,

---

[8]The ideas of Toffler and Bennis in this and the following paragraphs are summarized from *Future Shock,* by Alvin Toffler (New York: Random House, 1970), Chapter 7.

ad-hocracy. But what's the price? Much is unforeseen, but Toffler and Bennis suggest that there will be strains on the adaptability of people. We should anticipate substantial social strains and psychological tensions, and many will experience "future shock" as the future arrives too soon.

Several factors might be remembered as we consider Bennis's and Toffler's speculations about the formal organization of the future. Weber's general characteristics of bureaucracy should not blind us to the fact that individual differences in organizations (as in people) are vast. Some are more affected by change and more responsive to it than others. For example, educational institutions are probably more likely to react to demands for change than are military organizations. Bureaucracies may be responsive to change in one area but resist it in another. The auto industry changes styles yearly, but its responses to suggestions of environmentalists come more slowly. Some organizations generate member loyalty more easily than others. Compare turnover rates in several organizations with which you are familiar. Short-term task groups probably do work well in some situations, but to generalize is risky. And finally, organizations traditionally have been very slow to change. Problems inherent in industrial bureaucracies have been discussed for well over one hundred years, yet little has changed. Today we are more bureaucratized than ever—large formal organizations are the handmaidens of mass society. Under these conditions it is hard to imagine that the changes predicted by Toffler and Bennis will take place, but time will tell.

SUMMARY

The social organization or *social fabric* of a society is woven of cultural norms, values, beliefs, and patterns of behavior through which people interact with each other. The analysis and description of this social organization is a major area of study for sociologists. The analysis of the social organization of a society can be approached from a number of viewpoints. The viewpoint we have taken in this chapter introduces the concepts of group, category, and aggregation. A group exists when a number of people have shared or patterned interaction and feel bound together by a consciousness of kind. A collectivity of people lacking these traits is called a *category* (if they have a particular characteristic in common) or an *aggregate* (if they are located in a specific area).

Sociologists categorize groups in a variety of ways. Of special importance are primary groups, small groups, secondary groups, and formal organizations. Ways of studying small groups were described as well as some of the effects small groups have on their members. Characteristics of past, present, and future bureaucracies were compared. By categorizing and analyzing specific types of groups we are better able to understand and explain the variety, importance, and effect of the group affiliations that individuals have. With the number of different types of groups we have discussed here, it is probably clear that a given group will cut across types and carry several labels. I work for a large formal organization in which I am a member of a sociology department that could be described as a reference group, a peer group, an in-group, a voluntary group, a horizontal group, a permanent group, a closed group (depending on the job market and how many professors are seeking the California climate), and sometimes more a primary group, sometimes more a secondary group.

Three readings follow. The first is an excerpt from the book *Tally's Corner* by Elliot Liebow. This is a study of black streetcorner men, and the selection here describes a particular pattern of primary relationships and small group life. The second reading, by Elinor Langer, describes a large, formal organization. Her article on the New York Telephone Company illustrates many of the characteristics of bureaucracy that we have discussed. The third reading shows how the characteristics of large organizations can be seen even in such a seemingly nonbureaucratic setting as that of religious salvation and conversion.

Reading 4.1
Friends and Networks

ELLIOT LIEBOW

Primary relationships take a variety of forms—a couple dating, a family, maybe an athletic team, or a work group in a large organization. In this excerpt from *Tally's Corner*, Elliot Liebow describes the primary relationships existing among lower-class black streetcorner men in Washington, D.C.

More than most social worlds, perhaps, the streetcorner world takes its shape and color from the structure and character of the face-to-face relationships of the people who live in it. Unlike other areas in our society, where a large portion of the individual's energies, concerns and time are invested in self-improvement, career and job development, family and community activities, religious and cultural pursuits, or even in broad, impersonal social and political issues, these resources in the streetcorner world are almost entirely given over to the construction and maintenance of personal relationships.

On the streetcorner, each man has his own network of these personal relationships and each man's network defines for him the members of his personal community. His personal community, then, is not a bounded area but rather a web-like arrangement of man-man and man-woman relationships in which he is selectively attached in a particular way to a definite number of discrete persons. In like fashion, each of these persons has his own personal network.

At the edges of this network are those persons with whom his relationship is affectively neutral, such as area residents whom he has "seen around" but does not know except to nod or say "hi" to as they pass on the street. These relationships are limited to simple recognition. Also at the edges are those men and women, including former friends and acquaintances, whom he dislikes or fears or who dislike or fear him. These relationships are frequently characterized by avoidance but the incumbents remain highly visible and relevant to one another.

In toward the center are those persons he knows and likes best, those with whom he is "up tight": his "walking buddies," "good" or "best" friends, girl friends, and sometimes real or putative kinsmen. These are the people with whom he is in more or less daily, face-to-face contact, and whom he turns to for emergency aid, comfort or support in time of need or crisis. He gives them and receives from them goods and services in the name of friendship, ostensibly keeping no reckoning. Routinely, he seeks them out and is sought out by them. They serve his need to be with others of his kind, and to be recognized as a discrete, distinctive personality, and he, in turn, serves them the same way. They are both his audience and his fellow actors.

It is with these men and women that he spends his waking, nonworking hours, drinking, dancing, engaging in sex, playing the fool or the wise man, passing the time at the Carry-out or on the streetcorner, talking about nothing and everything, about epistemology or Cassius Clay,[9] about the nature of numbers or how he would "have it made" if he could have a steady job that paid him $60 a week with no layoffs.

So important a part of daily life are these relationships that it seems like no life at all without them. Old Mr. Jenkins climbed out of his sickbed to take up a seat on the Coca-Cola case at the Carry-out for a couple of hours."I can't stay home and play dead," he explained, "I got to get out and see my friends."

In general, close friendships tend to develop out of associations with those who are already in one's network of personal relationships: relatives, men and women who live in the area and spend much of their time on the street or in public places, and co-workers. The result is that the streetcorner man, perhaps more than others in our society, tends to use the same individuals over and over again: he may make a friend, neighbor and co-worker of his kinsman, or a friend, co-worker and kinsman of his neighbor. A look at some of the personal relationships can illustrate the many-stranded aspects of friendship and the bi-directional character of friendship on the one hand, and kinship, neighbor, co-worker and other relationships on the other.

When Tonk and Pearl got married and took an apartment near the Carry-out, Pearl's brother, Boley, moved in with them. Later, Pearl's nephew, J. R., came up from their hometown in North Carolina and he, too, moved in with them. J. R. joined Tonk and Boley on the streetcorner and when Earl told Tonk of some job openings where he worked, Tonk took J. R. with him. These three, then, were kinsmen, shared the same residence, hung out together on the streetcorner, and two of them—for a time at least—were co-workers.

Preston was Clarence's uncle. They lived within a block of each other and within two blocks of the Carry-out. Clarence worked on a construction job and later got Preston a job at the same place. Tally, Wee Tom and Budder also worked

[9]Cassius Clay is now known as Muhammad Ali.

at the same construction site. The five men regularly walked back from the job to the streetcorner together, usually sharing a bottle along the way. On Friday afternoons, they continued drinking together for an hour or so after returning to the streetcorner. Tally referred to the other four men as his "drinking buddies."

Tally had met Wee Tom on the job. Through Tally, Wee Tom joined them on the walk home, began to hang around the Carry-out and finally moved into the neighborhood as well. Budder had been the last to join the group at the construction site. He had known Preston and Clarence all along, but not well. He first knew Tally as a neighbor. They came to be friends through Tally's visits to the girl who lived with Budder, his common-law wife, and his wife's children. When Tally took Budder onto the job with him, Budder became a co-worker and drinking buddy, too. Thus, in Tally's network, Wee Tom began as co-worker, moved up to drinking buddy, neighbor and finally close friend; Budder from neighbor and friend to co-worker. Importantly, and irrespective of the direction in which the relationships developed, the confluence of the co-worker and especially the neighbor relationship with friendship deepened the friend relationship.

One of the most striking aspects of these overlapping relationships is the use of kinship as a model for the friend relationship. Most of the men and women on the streetcorners are unrelated to one another and only a few have kinsmen in the immediate area. Nevertheless, kinship ties are frequently manufactured to explain, account for, or even to validate friend relationships. In this manner, one could move from friendship to kinship in either direction. One could start with kinship, say, as did Preston and Clarence or Boley and Tonk and build on this, or conversely, one could start with friendship and build a kin relationship.

The most common form of the pseudo-kin relationship between two men is known as "going for brothers." This means, simply, that two men agree to present themselves as brothers to the outside world and to deal with one another on the same basis. Going for brothers appears as a special case of friendship in which the usual claims, obligations, expectations, and loyalties of the friend relationship are publicly declared to be at their maximum.

Sea Cat and Arthur went for brothers. Sea Cat's room was Arthur's home so far as he had one anywhere. It was there that he kept his few clothes and other belongings, and it was on Sea Cat's dresser that he placed the pictures of his girl friends (sent "with love" or "love and kisses"). Sea Cat and Arthur wore one another's clothes and, whenever possible or practical, were in one another's company. Even when not together, each usually had a good idea of where the other was or had been or when he would return. Generally, they seem to prefer going with women who were themselves friends; for a period of a month or so, they went out with two sisters.

Sea Cat worked regularly; Arthur only sporadically or for long periods not at all. His own credit of little value, Arthur sometimes tried to borrow money from the men on the corner, saying that the lender could look to his "brother" for payment. And when Sea Cat found a "good thing" in Gloria, who set him up with a car and his own apartment, Arthur shared in his friend's good fortune. On the streetcorner or in Sea Cat's room, they laughed and horsed around together, obviously enjoying one another's company. They cursed each other and called each other names in mock anger or battle, taking liberties that were reserved for and tolerated in close friends alone.

The social reality of the pseudo-kinship tie between those who are "going for brothers" is clearly evident in the case of Richard and Leroy. Richard and Leroy had been going for brothers for three months or so when Leroy got in a fight with a group of teenagers and young adults. Leroy suffered serious internal injuries and was hospitalized for more than a month. One week after the fight, Richard and one of the teenagers who had beaten up Leroy, and with whom both he and Leroy had been on friendly terms, got into a fight over a private matter having nothing to do with Leroy, and Richard killed the teenager. Richard was immediately arrested and the police, acting on information from the dead boy's friends, relatives, and others in the community, charged him with first degree murder for the premeditated revenge killing of one who had beaten up "his brother." But when it was established that Leroy and Richard were not related in any way the charge was dropped to murder in the second degree. The dead boy's friends and relatives were outraged and bewildered. To them, it was clearly a premeditated and deliberate killing. Hadn't Richard and Leroy been going for brothers? And hadn't Leroy been badly beaten by this same boy just eight days earlier?

Questions 4.1

1. What is meant by "going for brothers"?
2. Why would the relationships described in this reading be referred to as primary rather than secondary?
3. Give examples of peer group, reference group, and primary group from this reading.
4. What methods did Liebow apparently use to study the relationships on Tally's corner? What other methods could have been used, and what are the advantages and disadvantages of each?

Reading 4.2

Inside the New York Telephone Company

ELINOR LANGER

Formal organizations are everywhere in modern industrialized societies. It has been estimated that more than ninety percent of the work force in the U.S. is employed in formal organizations. In Max Weber's typology, the New York Telephone Company is a good example of a *modern bureaucracy.* Journalist Elinor Langer worked for the phone company, and here she describes how a large bureaucratic organization works.

From October to December 1969 I worked for the New York Telephone Company as a Customer's Service Representative in the Commercial Department. My office was one of several in the Broadway-City Hall area of lower Manhattan, a flattened, blue-windowed commercial building in which the telephone company occupies three floors. The room was big and brightly lit—like the city room of a large newspaper—with perhaps one hundred desks arranged in groups of five or six around the desk of a Supervisor. The job consists of taking orders for new equipment and services and pacifying customers who complain, on the eleven exchanges (although not the more complex business accounts) in the area between the Lower East Side and 23rd Street on the North and bounded by Sixth Avenue on the West.

My Supervisor is the supervisor of five women. She reports to a Manager who manages four supervisors (about twenty women) and he reports to the District Supervisor along with two other managers. The offices of the managers are on the outer edge of the main room separated from the floor by glass partitions. The District Supervisor is down the hall in an executive suite. A job identical in rank to that of the district supervisor is held by four other men in Southern Manhattan alone. They report to the Chief of the Southern Division, himself a soldier in an army of division chiefs whose territories are the five boroughs, Long Island, Westchester, and the vast hinterlands vaguely referred to as "Upstate." The executives at————Street were only dozens among the thousands in New York Tel alone.

Authority in their hierarchy is parceled out in bits. A Representative, for example, may issue credit to customers up to, say, $10.00; her supervisor, $25.00; her manager, $100.00; his supervisor, $300.00; and so forth.

... Securing the position was not without hurdles. I was "overqualified," having confessed to college; I performed better on personnel tests than I intended to do; and I was inspected for symptoms of militance by a shrewd but friendly interviewer who noticed the several years' gap in my record of employment. "What have you been doing lately?" she asked me. "Protesting?" I said: "Oh, no, I've been married," as if that condition itself explained one's neglect of social problems. She seemed to agree that it did.

The Representative's course is "programmed." It is apparent that the phone company has spent millions of dollars for high-class management consultation on the best way to train new employees. The two principal criteria are easily deduced. First, the course should be made so routine that any employee can teach it. The teacher's material—the remarks she makes, the examples she uses—are all printed in a loose-leaf notebook that she follows. Anyone can start where anyone else leaves off. I felt that I could teach the course myself, simply by following the program. The second criterion is to assure the reproducibility of results, to guarantee that every part turned out by the system will be interchangeable with every other part. The system is to bureaucracy what Taylor was to the factory: it consists of breaking down every operation into discrete parts, then making verbal the discretions that are made.

Soon acting out the right way to deal with customers became more important than self-instruction. The days were organized into Lesson Plans, a typical early one being: How to Respond to a Customer if You Haven't Already Been Trained to Answer His question, or a slightly more bureaucratic rendering of that notion.

Sally explained the idea, which is that you are supposed to refer the call to a more experienced Representative or to the Supervisor. But somehow they manage to complicate this situation to the point where it becomes confusing even for an intelligent person to handle it. You mustn't say: "Gosh, that's tough, I don't know anything about that, let me give the phone to someone who does," though that in effect is what you do. Instead when the phone rings, you say: "Hello. This is Miss Langer. May I help you?" (The Rule is, get immediate "control of the contact" and hold it lest anything unexpected happen, like, for instance, a human transaction between you and the customer.)

He says: "This is Mr. Smith and I'd like to have an additional wall telephone installed in my kitchen."

You say: "I'll be very glad to help you, Mr. Smith (Rule the Second: Always express interest in the Case and indicate willingness to help), but I'll need more information. What is your telephone number?"

He tells you, then you confess: "Well, Mr. Smith, I'm afraid I haven't been trained in new installations yet because I'm a new representative, but let me give you someone else who can help you." (Rule the Third: You must get his consent to this arrangement. That is, you must say: *May* I get someone else who can help you? *May* I put you on hold for a moment?)

The details are absurd but they are all prescribed. What you would do naturally becomes unnatural when it is codified, and the rigidity of the rules makes the Representatives in training feel they are stupid when they make mistakes. Another lesson, for example, was: What to Do if a Customer Calls and Asks for a Specific Person, such as Miss Smith, another Representative, or the Manager. Whatever the facts, you are to say "Oh, Miss Smith is busy but I have access to your records, may I help you?" A customer is never allowed to identify his interests with any particular employee. During one lesson, however, Sally said to Angela: "Hello, I'd like immediately to speak to Mrs. Brown," and Angela said, naturally, "Hold the line a minute, please. I'll put her on." A cardinal sin, for which she was immediately rebuked. Angela felt terrible.

Company rhetoric asserts that this rigidity does not exist, that Representatives are supposed to use "initiative" and "judgment," to develop their own language. What that means is that instead of using the precise words "Of course I'll be glad to help you but I'll need more information," you are allowed to "create" some individual variant. But you must always (1) express willingness to help and (2) indicate the need for further investigation. In addition, while you are doing this, you must always write down the information taken from the customer, coded, on a yellow form called a CF-1, in such a way as to make it possible for a Representative in Florida to read and translate it. "That's the point," Sally told us. "You are doing it the same way a rep in Illinois or Alaska does it. We're one big monopoly."

The logic of training is to transform the trainees from humans into machines. The basic method is to handle any customer request by extracting "bits" of information: by translating the human problem he might have into bureaucratic language so that it can be processed by the right department. For instance, if a customer calls and says: "My wife is dying and she's coming home from the hospital today and I'd like to have a phone installed in her bedroom right away," you *say*, "Oh, I'm very sorry to hear that sir, I'm sure I can help you, would you be interested in our Princess model? It has a dial that lights up at night," meanwhile *writing* on your ever-present CF-1: "Csr wnts Prn inst bdrm immed," issuing the order, and placing it in the right-hand side of your work-file where it gets picked up every fifteen minutes by a little clerk.

The knowledge that one is under constant observation (of which more later) I think helps to ensure that contacts are handled in this uniform and wooden manner. If you varied it, and said something spontaneous, you might well be overheard; moreover, it is probably not possible to be especially human when you are concentrating so hard on extracting the bits, and when you have to deal with so many bits in one day.

Sometimes the bits can be extraordinarily complicated. A customer (that is, CSR) calls and says rapidly, "This is Mrs. Smith and I'm moving from 23rd Street to 68th Street, and I'd like to keep my green Princess phone and add two white Trimlines and get another phone in a metallic finish and my husband wants a new desk phone in his study." You are supposed to have taken that all down as she says it. Naturally you have no time to listen to how she says it, to strike up a conversation, or be friendly. You are desperate to get straight the details.

The dehumanization and the surprising degree of complication are closely related: the number of variables is large, each variable has a code which must be learned and manipulated, and each situation has one—and only one—correct answer. The kind of problem we were taught to handle, in its own language, looks like this:

A CSR has: IMRCV EX CV GRN BCHM IV

He wants: IMRCV WHT EX CV WHT BCHM IV

This case, very simplified, means only that the customer has regular residential phone service with a black phone, a green one, and an ivory bell chime, and that he wants new service with two white phones and a bell chime. Nonetheless, all these items are charged at differing monthly rates which the Representative must learn where to find and how to calculate; each has a separate installation charge which varies in a number of ways; and, most important, they represent only a few of the dozens of items or services a customer could possibly want (each of which, naturally, has its own rates and variables, its own codes).

He could want a long cord or a short one, a green one or a white one, a new party listed on his line, a special headset for a problem with deafness, a touch-tone phone, and on and on and on. For each of the things he could possibly want there would be one and only one correct charge to quote to him, one and only one right way to handle the situation.

Observers at the phone company. They are everywhere. I became aware of a new layer of Observation every day. The system works like this. For every five or six women there is, as I have said, a Supervisor who can at any moment listen in from the phone set on her desk to any of her Representatives' contacts with a customer. For an hour every day, the Supervisor goes to a private room off the main floor where she can listen (herself unobserved) to the conversations of any of her "girls" she chooses. The women know, naturally, *when* she is doing this but not *whose* contact she is observing.

Further off the main floor is a still more secret Observing Room staffed by women whose title and function is, specifically, Observer. These women "jack in" at random to any contact between any Representative and a customer: their job is basically to make sure that the Representatives are giving out correct information. Furthermore, these observers are themselves observed from a central telephone company location elsewhere in the city to make sure that they are not reporting as incorrect information which is actually correct. In addition the Observers make "access calls" by which they check to see that the telephone lines are open for the customers to make their connections. This entire structure of observation is, of course, apart from the formal representative-supervisor-manager-district-supervisor-division-head chain of managerial command. They are, in effect, parallel hierarchical structures.

One result of the constant observation (the technology being unbounded) is that one can never be certain where the observation stops. It is company policy to stress its finite character, but no one ever knows for sure. Officials of the Communications Workers of America have testified, for instance, that the company overindulged in the wired-Martini stage of technology, bugging the pen sets of many of its top personnel. At——— Street there were TV cameras in the lobby and on the elevators. This system coexists with the most righteous official attitude toward wiretapping. Only supervisors and managers can deal with wiretap complaints; Federal regulations about the sanctity of communications are posted; and the overt position toward taps, in the lower managerial echelons, is that they are simply illegal and, if they exist, must be the result of private entrepreneurship (businesses bugging one another) rather than Government policy.

"If someone complains about a tap," Sally said, "I just ask them: Why would anyone be tapping your phone?" Consciousness of the Government's "internal security" net is simply blacked out. Nonetheless, the constant awareness of the company's ability to observe creates unease: Are the lounge phones wired into the Observing structure? Does the company tap the phones of new or suspicious personnel? Is union activity monitored? No one can say with confidence.

The system of Observers is linked with the telephone company's ultimate weapon, the Service Index by which Errors are charted and separate units of the company rated against each other. Throughout training—in class and in our days on the floor—hints of the monumental importance of the Index in the psychic life of the employees continually emerged. "Do you know how many Errors you're allowed?" Sally would ask us. "No Errors"—proud that the standard was so high. Or: "I can't afford an Error"—from my supervisor, Laura, on the floor, explaining why she was keeping me roped in on my first days on the job. But the system was not revealed in all its parts until the very end of training when as a *pièce de résistance* the manager, Y, came in to give a little talk billed as a discussion of "Service" but in fact an attempt to persuade the class of the logic of observation.

Y was a brooding, reserved man in his mid-twenties, a kind of Ivy League leftover who looked as if he'd accidentally got caught in the wrong decade. His talk was very much like Sally's. "We need some way to measure Service. If a customer doesn't like Thom McCann shoes he can go out and buy Buster Brown. Thom

McCann will know something is wrong. But the phone company is a monopoly, people can't escape it, they have no other choice. How can we tell if our product, Service, is good?" He said that observation was begun in 1924 and that, although the Company had tried other methods of measuring service, none had proved equally satisfactory. Specifically, he said, other methods failed to provide an accurate measure of the work performance of one unit as opposed to another.

. . . The company gave every woman a Christmas present: a little wooden doll, about four inches tall, with the sick-humor look that was popular a few years ago and still appears on greeting cards. On the outside the doll says "Joy is . . ." and when you press down the springs a little stick pops up that says "Extensions in Color" (referring to the telephone extension we were trying to sell). Under that label is another sticker, the original one, which says "Knowing I wuv you." The doll is typical of the presents the company distributes periodically: a plastic shopping bag inscribed with the motto "Colorful Extensions Lighten the Load"; a keychain with a plastic Princess telephone saying "It's Little, It's Lovely, It Lights"; plastic rain bonnets with the telephone company emblem, and so forth.

It is obvious that the gifts are all programmed, down to the last cherry-filled chocolate, in some manual of Personnel Administration that is the source of all wisdom and policy; it is clear from their frequency that a whole agency of the company is devoted to devising these gimmicks and passing them out.

Another characteristic of the telephone company is a kind of programmed "niceness" which starts from the top down but which the women internalize and mimic. For management the strategy is clear (the Hawthorne experiments, after all, were carried out at Western Electric): it is, simply, make the employees feel important. For trainees this was accomplished by a generous induction ceremony complete with flowers, films, a fancy buffet, and addresses by top division representatives, all of which stressed the theme: the company cares about you.

The paternalism, the "niceness," filters down and is real. Employees are on a first-name basis, even the women with the managers. The women are very close to one another, sharing endless gossip, going on excursions together, and continually engaging in ceremonial celebration of one another's births, engagements, promotions. The generosity even extends to difficult situations on the job. I have, for example, seen women voluntarily sharing their precious closed time when one of them was overcommitted and the other slightly more free.

The women have a strangely dissociated attitude toward company operations that aren't working well. What company *policy* is—that is, the way they learn things are supposed to be—gets pressed into their heads so much that they get a little confused by their simultaneous understanding that it isn't really working that way at all. I pointed that out a lot to see what would happen. For instance our lesson books say: "Customers always get Manhattan directories delivered with their regular installations." I said, in class: "Gee, that's funny, Sally, I had a telephone installed recently and I didn't get any phone books at all." Sally would make sure not to lose control and merely repeat: "Phone books are delivered with the regular installations."

Questions 4.2

1. Illustrate Weber's characteristics of bureaucracy with examples from the description of the phone company.
2. What are the disadvantages and advantages—to employees, to the general public—of the bureaucratic characteristics of the phone company?
3. Illustrate different types of groups (voluntary-involuntary, in-out, reference, etc.) with examples from the description of the phone company.
4. "Organizations consciously make attempts to look and act less formal, less bureaucratic. . . ." Does the New York Telephone Company do this? If so, how?
5. Draw a comparison between the phone company and a formal organization that you are familiar with, such as the college or university you are attending. How are they similar and how different? Would your formal organization work better or worse if it was more like the phone company?

Reading 4.3

Counting Souls

DAVID ALTHEIDE and JOHN JOHNSON

We learned in this chapter that formal organizations arise as society's activities become increasingly planned rather than spontaneous. In modern society, social processes are organized, and behavior and image are managed. It is believed that the more something is organized, planned, and bureaucratized, the less chance there is for failure or for results contrary to the organization's goals to occur. How widespread *is* this tendency to bureaucratize?

The Billy Graham Crusade is a widely publicized and recognized fundamentalist and evangelical movement. Graham claims to have encouraged more than one million people to "step forward for Christ." Is it the charisma of Billy Graham that leads to these amazing results? Certainly Graham's personal magnetism is important, but, according to a recent study by two sociologists, the *organizational* structure of the Crusade is a central factor in its success. It is perhaps startling to realize that in its own way an evangelical movement can be as organized as the New York Telephone Company—even the salvation and conversion process can be bureaucratized.

In May 1974, the Billy Graham Evangelical Association (BGEA) crusade visited Phoenix, Arizona. Two professors from Arizona State, David Altheide and John Johnson, studied the crusade and focused on the activities of the religious counselors. These counselors are local volun-

These excerpts are reprinted from "Counting Souls: A Study of Counseling at Evangelical Crusades" by David L. Altheide and John M. Johnson in PACIFIC SOCIOLOGICAL REVIEW, Vol. 20, No. 3 (July 1977), pp. 331, 332, 333, 335, 340 by permission of the Publisher, Sage Publications, Inc.

teers who are trained by the BGEA and whose function is to assist converts as they make their decisions for Christ.

All counselors involved in one of the BGEA crusades are drawn from the local area
where the crusade is held. All undergo an extensive instructional and training
program, typically conducted in two or three hour sessions over a period of four
to six weeks. This "Christian Life and Witness Course" is presented under the
auspices of preparing Christians to cope with any problem or situation. When
translated into the organizational context of the impending crusade, however, the
instruction is more concrete, immediate, and practical. Counselors receive instructions on how to recognize the coded name tags, coded hand signals to be used
during the altar call, how to fill out daily statistical break-downs, what brand of
mint to chew immediately prior to encountering a new convert to make one's
breath less offensive, and many other bits of knowledge necessary to insure a
smooth performance. Most important, however, counselors receive instructions
about their interactions with, and classifications of, prospective converts, and the
crucial follow-up contacts as well.

Counselors begin their work after the singing, testimonials, collection, and
Billy Graham's sermon, which culminates in the altar call. At the moment of
Graham's invitation to "come forward to Christ," counselors and choir members
begin moving forward to an area usually in front of the speaker's platform or
rostrum. To a naive member of the audience or a television viewer, this movement
creates an illusion of a spontaneous and mass response to the invitation. Having
been assigned seating in strategic areas of the auditorium or arena and given
instructions on the staggered time-sequencing for coming forward, the counselors
move forward in such a fashion so as to create the illusion of individuals "flowing"
into the center of the arena from all quarters, in a steady outpouring of individual
decision. Unless an outsider or observer of these events has been instructed to look
for the name tags and ribbons worn by those moving forward, it is all too easy to
infer from these appearances the "charismatic" impact of Graham and his invitation. These strategies promote the respectability of making a public commitment
and represent methods calculated to manipulate the consent of the passive, the
uncertain, the wary, and the indecisive.

Following the ceremonial benediction, the public portion of the crusade is
terminated, and those standing in the area in front of the rostrum are asked to
remain for an additional message. At this point, a sizable majority of those in front
of the rostrum represent the counselors, choir, and staff of the crusade. During this
additional message, new converts are informed that they will be immediately
contacted by a person standing close to them, to give Billy's "massive evangelism"
a more personal and individual touch. Though the new converts are unaware of
this, by this point virtually all those in the area have been "paired-off" with one
another on the basis of sex and approximate age. This is accomplished by a combination of self-selection, standardized assignment procedures, and the silent hand
signals of "Advisors" who are at this point managing the performance. Indeed,
many of the new converts have been specifically "followed" by a given counselor

since leaving their seats. (Counselors are instructed, for example, to bow their heads and close their eyes at the beginning of the final prayer of the sermon, but to reopen their eyes immediately to keep track of individuals who may begin moving forward during the prayer.) Following this final message, the process of translating mass to personal evangelism begins with the counselor's work; at first, a hand on a shoulder, a smile, and a welcome.

Religious counseling to evangelical converts involves the production of a step-by-step protocol. Confidential crusade training manuals containing the standard operating procedures variously depict eight to ten broad steps, but each of these is further broken down into as many as seventeen additional subcategories. These steps are standardized so as to effect a warm and friendly welcome, a direct introduction to Christ through mutual prayer and scripture reading. They afford enough opportunity for expression so that the convert maintains a sense of participation in the interaction, while winning the convert's confidence. They direct counselors to make an assessment of the convert's commitment and to elicit and record the information needed for the follow-up. The encounter is ended by introducing the convert to one of the roaming Advisors (typically a local minister), hopefully in time to minister to another. The progressive enactment of the BGEA protocol, similar to those used by door-to-door encyclopedia salesmen, is partially contingent on passing through a series of "check-off points" where the convert's verbal responses partially influence what occurs next. If all goes smoothly, and the counselor has efficaciously followed the rules about being warm, congenial, friendly, and yet not too talkative, the encounter will consume eight to fourteen minutes. This time sequence is partially based on the BGEA understandings about how long the people have been there to this point (i.e., perhaps two to three hours), their transportation problems, and so on. But counselors will, if judged necessary, spend up to 60 to 90 minutes or more with the new convert, explaining and encouraging the decision for Christ. For the most part, however, religious counseling in the evangelical context is not designed to "convince" or "persuade" individuals, but to obtain information needed for the follow-up. The more personal follow-up, always made within 48 hours by phone, visit, or letter, is seen as a more appropriate context for persuasion.

In addition to learning about the practical aspects of putting on a crusade, counselors also receive extensive doctrinal instruction and preparation. . . .

. . . The general purpose of the counselor training courses is to insure that all have a standardized knowledge of the scriptures which, given the organizational conception of the conversion process, is defined as utilitarian in evangelical terms. This training involves attending the classes, memorizing key scriptural passages, learning which Biblical passages correspond to a listing of common problems or questions converts express, and so forth. The instruction includes scriptural references to expressions of doubt, the devil's first attack on a young Christian, and even possible "reasons" for such (e.g., the possible "blindness" of Jewish converts). But these instructions about the literal truth of the scriptures are also seen to contain possible sources of "trouble" for a counselor. They are, therefore, combined with some accommodative "ground rules" to enhance the success of the immediate organizational purpose. When counseling Jewish converts, for example, the point is made not to frighten them with the prospect of hell punishment at this time, and to side-step all discussions of this as well as the Trinity and Virgin Birth. The immediate objective is to encourage the decision, and record the needed information for the follow-up. In fact, given the limited time available, counselors are advised to generally avoid doctrinal argument and proselytizing altogether. By using methods such as these, then, the absolutist morality of the fundamentalist beliefs becomes intertwined with the accommodative morality of everyday life and practical affairs. . . .

. . . As noted previously, the pamphlet used by the counselor to instruct the convert is ordered by progressive steps. Before the counselor turns the page for the next step, he queries the convert about his understanding at that point. If the convert understands, he turns the page for the next one; if not, further clarification will be forthcoming before going on. At the concluding portion of the final step, the convert learns by way of a citation from Romans (10:9) that if one has acknowledged with his lips the fact that Jesus is Lord (which was required to progress beyond step three), then one's salvation has been assured. If, for whatever reason, the convert were to respond in an obviously negative way at some point in this process, that is, as opposed to an expression of uncertainty, then the convert's responses to the earlier steps are used to point out the "inconsistency" of the latter response.

The evangelical conversion process is both personal and organizational, and thereby combines a mixture of personal feelings and rationally organized procedures. Converts may cry, but the counselor who beckons him toward eternal life does so calmly and with a rational plan of action.

Questions 4.3

1. In what ways has the BGEA Crusade bureaucratized its operation? How do these compare with the characteristics of bureaucracy outlined by Weber?
2. *Why* would the Crusade become bureaucratic? What does it gain by doing this?
3. What problems might arise when an organization like the BGEA Crusade becomes bureaucratic?

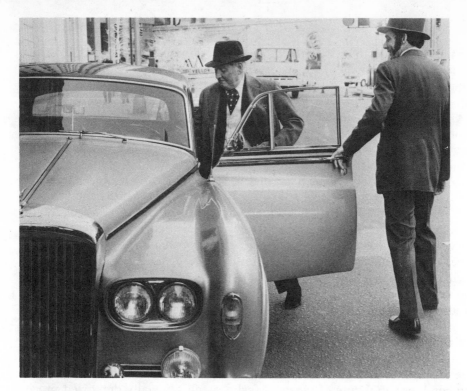

5 Social Differentiation: Social Class

Sociologists study groups and non-groups in order to understand the social organization of society. The previous chapter dealt with groups —specifically, small primary groups and large formal organizations. In this chapter our attention turns to non-groups. Many sociologists spend much of their time specializing in the study of *categories* of people—people who have a particular characteristic in common but who do not constitute a group. Those who specialize in the study of older people, an age category, are called gerontologists. Others study race, ethnic, religious, social-class, and sex categories.

The process of defining, describing, and distinguishing between different categories of people is called *social differentiation.* People differ across a range of variables, and some of these categories we find ourselves in automatically—age, sex, race. Other categories have a greater degree of flexibility and to a certain extent one's position can be changed—social class, religion. (Recall the discussion of ascribed and achieved status in Chapter 3.)

As we pointed out in the previous chapter, members of a category may become a group if they become involved in shared or patterned interaction and feel bound together by a consciousness of kind. People belonging to categories—race, religion, age, sex—obviously share common values and interests, and the formation of smaller groups along these lines naturally follows. This chapter and the next, however, focus on categories in the larger sense, and we will examine what sociologists know about the general characteristics of social-class, race, ethnic, age, and sex categories.

Social Stratification

Semper Anglia—A dignified English solicitor-widower with a considerable income had long dreamed of playing Sandringham, one of Great Britain's most exclusive golf courses, and one day he made up his mind to chance it when he was traveling in the area.

Entering the clubhouse, he asked at the desk if he might play the course. The club secretary inquired, "Member?" "No, sir." "Guest of a member?" "No, sir." "Sorry."

As he turned to leave, the lawyer spotted a slightly familiar figure seated in the lounge, reading the London *Times.* It was Lord Parham. He approached and, bowing low, said, "I beg your pardon, your Lordship, but my name is Higginbotham of the London solicitors Higginbotham, Willingby and Barclay. I should like to crave your Lordship's indulgence. Might I play this beautiful course as your guest?"

His Lordship gave Higginbotham a long look, put down his paper and asked, "Church?" "Church of England, sir, as was my late wife." "Education?" "Eton, sir, and Oxford." "Sport?" "Rugby, sir, a spot of tennis and number 4 on the crew that beat Cambridge." "Service?" "Brigadier, sir, Coldstream Guards, Victoria Cross and Knight of the Garter." "Campaigns?" "Dunkirk, El Alamein and Normandy, sir." "Languages?" "Private tutor in French, fluent German and a bit of Greek."

His Lordship considered briefly, then nodded to the club secretary and said, "Nine holes."

The study of **social stratification** arises out of the recognition that people are ranked or evaluated at a number of levels. As the geologist finds layers in the earth when examining a cross section, so the sociologist finds layers in the social world.

People are *unequal*—they are constantly evaluated and ranked by others on a number of criteria. The idea exists that we are all created equal, but what is really meant is that we all have an equal chance to become unequal. Even that is not true, though, because some people have an obvious head start and others are blocked from the time they are born. For example, imagine two boys, Billy and Tommy. *Billy* is the one-year-old son of black parents in rural Mississippi, his parents are tenant farmers, the family income is less than $3,000 a year, he has six brothers and sisters, and neither of his parents went beyond the eighth grade in school.

Tommy is the one-year-old son of white parents in Scarsdale, New York. His father is a surgeon, his mother is an author, the family income is over $50,000 a year, he has one brother, and both his parents are college graduates. Now map out each boy's future. What are the chances of each living to the age of six? Of graduating from high school? Of going to college? Of going to an Ivy League school? Of receiving regular medical and dental care? Of living to the age of sixty-five? Of getting married while still in his teens? Of having many children? Of having an arrest record? Of going to prison? Of having his name in *Who's Who in America?* Two healthy, happy, bouncing babies, but their life chances are vastly different.

Parallel Stratification Systems

Most societies have more than one system of stratification. These several or parallel stratification systems are based on different factors. The system we usually use when discussing social class is based on occupation, education, wealth, power, and prestige. We could refer to this as socioeconomic status. Another stratification system might be based on race—individuals are ranked high or low purely on the basis of racial characteristics. We see this kind of stratification in the United States and to a greater extent in South Africa. Age, sex, and religion may be the bases for other stratification systems. In some societies, older people automatically have higher status than younger people. In Northern Ireland in the late 1960s and 1970s, the battles between the Protestants and Catholics frequently made news. Northern Ireland is religiously stratified: Protestants have higher status than Catholics.

When there are a number of parallel stratification systems, an individual will be ranked in several different systems at the same time. One may be ranked in terms of race, then in terms of socioeconomic factors, then in terms of age, and so on. And though the stratification systems are parallel, they are not necessarily equal. The status of an American black who is upper-class in terms of wealth and occupation may be roughly equivalent to the status of a white who is middle-class in wealth and occupation. The discrepancy is explained by the existence of two stratification systems—one that ranks a person according to socioeconomic status, a second according to race.

Our society, then, is stratified in numerous ways. In the remainder of this chapter and in the next chapter we will examine several ways by which people are categorized and stratified. The subject of this chapter will be socioeconomic stratification. The following chapter will deal with race, ethnic, sex, and age categories.

Socioeconomic Status and Social Class

Status symbols vary by country and by sex. A poll published in Paris in August 1975 found that the most admired symbols of status for French women were (1) a chauffeur-driven car, (2) a set of jewels, and (3) an ocean cruise. The status symbols ranked highest by French men were (1) the Legion of Honor medal, (2) a private swimming pool, and (3) a live-in maid.

The ultimate in the U.S. in 1978? Perhaps a Patek Phillippe pocket watch ($48,000), a Piaget watch (up to $64,000), or Gucci loafers ($79); a castle in Germany, Ireland, or Spain; certainly a car—a Porsche or Mercedes-Benz, a Ferrari 365 GT4 ($54,000), or for more comfort, a Rolls Royce Camargue ($96,000).

Status based on socioeconomic factors represents one of the major systems of stratification. Following the ideas of Max Weber, socioeconomic status is usually determined by wealth power, and prestige.[1]

Wealth

Generally, when comparing and evaluating people, we rank those higher who have the greater *wealth* and store of material possessions—type and size of house, area of residence, make and number of cars, quality of clothes, and so on. In a society that places value on wealth and material possessions, it becomes important to allow others to find out how well-off one really is, and so we have status symbols. These are visible symbols of having made it. If a person drives a Rolls Royce, Lincoln Continental, or exotic foreign car with a low-numbered license plate, lives in Beverly Hills or on Park Avenue, is mentioned in the society pages, winters in Palm Springs and summers in Switzerland, then we have a pretty good idea of where he belongs on the social-class ladder. The game gets complicated, however, when status symbols change or become generally available. Then it becomes more difficult to tell who ranks where. Only the Internal Revenue Service knows for sure.

Table 5.1 Family Income and Education, 1977

	Family Income				
	$3,000–3,999	$6,000–6,999	$10,000–14,999	$25,000–49,999	$50,000 and Over
Median school years completed by head of family	9.1	10.6	12.3	13.2	16.5

U.S. Bureau of the Census, *Statistical Abstract of the United States, 1978* (99th ed.), Washington, D.C., p. 454.

Table 5.2 School Years Completed and Lifetime (Age 18 to Death) Income, 1972

School Years Completed	Lifetime Income
Less than eight years	$280,000
Eight years	344,000
Four years high school	479,000
Four years college	758,000

U.S. Bureau of the Census, *Statistical Abstract of the United States, 1975* (96th ed.), Washington, D.C., p. 123.

[1]H. H. Gerth and C. W. Mills, *From Max Weber: Essays in Sociology* (New York: Oxford University Press, 1958), Chapter 7.

Table 5.3   Race, Education, and Family Income, 1977

| | Family Income | | |
Race and Education	Under $3,000	$5,000– 6,999	$25,000 and Over
White families	3%	6%	25%
Less than eight years education	6	15	7
Four years college	1	2	50
Black families	8	13	10
Less than eight years education	11	17	5
Four years college	0	4	36

U.S. Bureau of the Census, *Statistical Abstract of the United States, 1978* (99th ed.), Washington, D.C., p. 457.

Wealth is strongly correlated with education, income, and occupation, and when socioeconomic status is measured, these other factors are usually included. Income refers to current earning capacity, whereas wealth refers more to an accumulation of money and property over time. some of the relationships between income and education are shown in Tables 5.1, 5.2, and 5.3. Table 5.1 shows the median number of school years completed by the head of the family for different levels of family income. Table 5.2 illustrates how total lifetime income varies with education. Table 5.3 again shows the relationship between education and income. In addition, the data in Table 5.3 remind us of parallel stratification systems by introducing the variable of race. It can be seen that increased education leads to increased family income, but the effect is greater for whites than for blacks.

Power

People are also ranked according to the amount of *power* we think they have. Individuals who run things, who make the important decisions in our cities or at a national level, whether they are formally elected or informally appointed, are accorded high status by those who know of the power they exercise. Elected government officials, advisers to presidents, and consultants in high, mysterious-sounding positions are automatically given high status because we know that they are at or near the centers of power.

Power is a fascinating variable that stimulates numerous questions: Who has it? How did they get it? How is it used? How is power distributed in society? Some analysts of American society believe that power is concentrated in the hands of a few people who are not directly responsible to others. For example, C. Wright Mills saw classes or layers of power in society. At the top, power lies in the hands of "the warlords, the corporation chieftains, and the political directorate," who tend to work together to form a power elite in America.[2] According to Mills, decisions are made in this country by a few people, and they govern a fragmented mass of people who are impotent in any power sense. Between the elite and the mass is a group whose power is a semi-organized stalemate. The middle is visible but

[2]See C. Wright Mills, *The Power Elite* (New York: Oxford University Press, 1959).

neither represents the mass nor has any real effect on the elite. The elite is highly organized and made up of military leaders (admirals and generals), politicians, and business leaders. Mills suggests that a system in which so much power is held by a few who are not responsible to anyone but themselves is both immoral and irresponsible.

Some suggest that it is basically wealth (accompanied by the related variables of education and occupation) that establishes a person's position in society, and that this wealth *leads* to power. Wealth is not shared equally in our society and it never has been. In 1972, the wealthiest one percent of the population had twenty-one percent of the personal wealth. As the data in Table 5.4 indicate, the top fifth of the population control far more than their share of national income, and the poorest fifth have only five percent of the national income. To put it another way, one-fifth of the population in the United States has nearly half of the income, and this relationship has not changed at all in more than twenty years.

In his book *Who Rules America?*, William Domhoff agrees with Mills that power lies with an elite. For Domhoff, however, the elite is the upper class. This upper class in the United States is a governing class "which owns a disproportionate amount of a country's wealth, receives a disproportionate amount of a country's yearly income, and contributes a disproportionate number of its members to the controlling institutions and key decision-making groups of the country." Excessive wealth and income are the key—having these (which other classes do not) allows the upper class to *control* other individuals and institutions. This upper-class elite has well-established ways of training and preparing new members for future service. Bright young people are processed into the upper class by means of "education at private schools, elite universities, and elite law schools; through success as a corporation executive; through membership in exclusive gentlemen's clubs; and through participation in exclusive charities."[3]

It is Domhoff's thesis that the leaders of the executive branch of the federal government are either members of the upper class or former employees of institutions controlled by members of the upper class. He cites an impressive array of evidence that describes who has the wealth and how it is used to control power. Domhoff traces the occupants of various government positions and finds, for

Table 5.4 Proportion of Income Received by Each Fifth of the Population

	1950	1977
Top fifth	43%	42%
Second fifth	23	24
Third fifth	17	18
Fourth fifth	12	12
Bottom fifth	5	5

U.S. Bureau of the Census, *Statistical Abstract of the United States, 1978* (99th ed.), Washington, D.C., p. 455.

[3]Both quotes in this paragraph come from *Who Rules America?* by G. William Domhoff (Englewood Cliffs, N.J.: Prentice-Hall, 1967), p. 5.

example, that members of the upper-class power elite dominate the President's Cabinet, especially in Departments of State, Treasury, Defense, Commerce, and even Labor. Of the thirteen men who were Secretary of Defense or Secretary of War between 1932 and 1964, eight have been listed in the *Social Register,* and six of the eight people who were Secretary of State in the same period were members of the upper-class power elite.[4] Through the CIA and other agencies, the power elite have manipulated intellectuals by giving money to individuals, schools, and foundations to exert influence, to start organizations, to hold conferences and publish magazines and books. As a consequence, the elite manages ideas, co-opts potential critics, and spreads its influence internationally.

The central issue for the power elite theorists is this: Is it right and proper for so much power to be held by so few, especially in a society that believes itself to be democratic and equalitarian? A second issue concerns the nature of the decisions made by the elite: Are these decisions good for the country or good only for the elite? Domhoff's view on this point is clear as he states that no matter how much the elite may plead otherwise, "they are primarily self-interested partisans, their horizons severely limited by the ideologies and institutions that sustain and justify their privilege, celebrity, and power."[5]

Pluralist theories of power stand in stark contrast to the power-elite theories of Mills and Domhoff. According to pluralist theories, power is spread among many groups and is amorphous and unorganized. There is continuous competition and conflict for power between elites with the result that they tend to neutralize each other. Moreover, the power groups are very specialized so that no single elite has absolute authority. Some have political power, some have economic power, some military or religious power. Political parties, numerous voluntary associations (such as the PTA, League of Women Voters, ACLU, and labor unions), Congress and state governments, and finally even the voters exercise power. The pluralist view, then, is that power is complicated and many-faceted. Numerous groups, none of which gains ascendancy over the rest, share and compete for it.[6] Who is right? The debate between the pluralists and the power-elite theorists is interesting and lively. Domhoff's evidence is convincing. Arnold Rose's book, *The Power Structure,* expresses the pluralist view and is comprehensive, widely used, and has received much favorable comment. It would be pleasant for us if there were a balance of power in our democratic society—and perhaps that's the way it is. However, recent revelations regarding Vietnam, Watergate, and the activities of the CIA provide additional evidence for those who think otherwise.

Prestige

Prestige means distinction or reputation and refers to how we subjectively evaluate others. It is usually connected to a position that one holds in society. Some positions have high prestige (doctor, Supreme Court justice), others carry lower

[4]G. William Domhoff, *Who Rules America?*, pp. 97–99 (see footnote 3).

[5]This is from Domhoff's later book, *The Higher Circles* (New York: Random House, 1970), p. 275.

[6]For the pluralist view see David Riesman, Nathan Glazer, and Reuel Denny, *The Lonely Crowd* (Garden City, N.Y.: Doubleday, 1953); Suzanne Keller, *Beyond the Ruling Class: Strategic Elites in Modern Society* (New York: Random House, 1963); and Arnold Rose, *The Power Structure* (New York: Oxford University Press, 1967).

prestige (shoe shiner, garbage collector). Prestige—distinction in the eyes of others —is less concrete than wealth and power. It is no less important, however. In fact, if they had the opportunity to choose, many would probably rather have prestige than wealth.

In 1947, North and Hatt had a national cross section of people evaluate a series of occupations as "excellent," "good," "average," "somewhat below average," or "poor." This resulted in an occupational prestige scale that has been widely used by sociologists.[7] The study has been repeated and updated numerous times since 1947, and the occupational prestige scores have remained amazingly consistent. Table 5.5 compares several occupations and their prestige scores from the first North-Hatt study with some scores from a study in California done in 1967. The highest prestige rating an occupation can obtain by the North-Hatt method is 100, the lowest is 20. The California study included some deviant occupations that didn't appear in the earlier study.

There appears to be permanence and stability in how people view occupations —most of them show similar scores twenty years later. On the other hand, a few do change as their importance and notoriety fluctuate (lawyer, nuclear physicist, minister). In the California study the college students generally tended to rank uneducated occupations (except for bartender) lower than the non-college adults did. The college students also were less condemning of the deviant occupations than were the non-college adults.

Table 5.5 Prestige Scores for Selected Occupations

| | Original North-Hatt 1947 | California Study 1967 | |
| | | College Students | Non-college Adults |
Occupation			
U.S. Supreme Court Justice	96	96	93
Doctor	93	96	96
State governor	93	91	93
College professor	89	89	90
Lawyer	86	94	90
Minister	86	79	80
Nuclear physicist	86	95	95
Public school teacher	78	78	80
Railroad engineer	77	68	75
Electrician	73	74	73
Policeman	67	68	69
Carpenter	65	66	70
Garage mechanic	62	57	64
Barber	59	59	63
Store clerk	58	55	57
Truck driver	54	54	59
Bartender	44	52	45
Gambler	—	39	30
Prostitute	—	29	23
Racketeer	—	28	23

[7]Cecil North and Paul Hatt, "Jobs and Occupations: A Popular Evaluation," *Opinion News* 9(September 1947), pp. 3–13.

As Davis and Moore have mentioned, the prestige and status accorded one's position are determined by its scarcity or importance to society and by the amount of training or talent needed to obtain the position.[8] Logically, we would expect that one holding a position high in prestige would receive greater financial rewards than would one in a position of less prestige. This is usually true, but not always. A carpenter or plumber often makes more money than a teacher, but the teacher, whose skill requires more training, has higher occupational prestige (this may make the teacher *feel* better, but won't pay the bills).

People in the situation just described—material wealth but low prestige, or vice versa—are victims of **status inconsistency.** They are status-inconsistent because the factors that determine their ranks in society are not consistent with each other. If we recall that there are many stratification systems—race, religion, age, sex, as well as socioeconomic factors—it is clear that there are many possibilities for status inconsistency. Examples of status-inconsistent people in the U.S. would include a college-educated carpenter, a wealthy business executive with an eighth-grade education, a Catholic President, or a person of recent wealth but no prestige. The problem for the status-inconsistent person is that he behaves toward others in terms of his high rank (wealthy business executive) but others tend to behave toward him in terms of his low rank (eighth-grade education). Some sociologists report that status inconsistency may lead to other things: stress, political liberalism, involvement in social movements, withdrawal, or psychosomatic illness.[9]

[8]Kingsley Davis and Wilbert Moore, "Some Principles of Stratification," *American Sociological Review* 10 (April 1945), pp. 242–249.

[9]See Gerhard Lenski, "Status Crystallization: A Non-Vertical Dimension," *American Sociological Review* 19 (August 1954), pp. 405–413; Gerhard Lenski, "Status Inconsistency and the Vote: A Four Nation Test," *American Journal of Sociology* 32 (April 1967), pp. 298–302; and "Status Consistency and Right-Wing Extremism," *American Sociological Review* 32 (February 1967), pp. 86–92.

How Many Social Classes?

A variety of factors, then, produce a layered society. The question of just exactly *how many* layers or social classes exist has long been of interest to sociologists. Karl Marx was an economic determinist in that he felt that a person's position in the economic structure of society determined his life style, his values, his beliefs, and his behavior. In his writings in the mid-nineteenth century, Marx described societies as composed of two classes, the *bourgeoisie,* or capitalists, and the *proletariat,* or workers. The bourgeoisie controls the capital, the means of production. The proletariat owns only their own labor. Marx saw a continuing struggle between these two classes leading to the overthrow of the bourgeoisie by the proletariat, a classless society, and socialism as a new system of government.

Studies of social class in the United States have produced varying results. Lloyd Warner studied a New England community and discovered six social classes. August Hollingshead, using a technique similar to Warner's in a Midwestern town, found five social classes. Joseph Kahl also developed a system of five social classes. According to Kahl, the upper two classes (upper and upper-middle) account for about ten percent of the population and include the "big people," the important people. The other three classes (lower-middle, working, and lower) account for about ninety percent of the population and include the "little" or "common people." Others have performed similar studies of a number of communities, and the results are often the same—five or six social classes. Table 5.6 outlines a typical American community in terms of six social classes, and describes some of the characteristics of each social class.

Other students of stratification believe that it distorts the picture to speak in terms of specific social classes, whether it be two, three, five, six, nine, or whatever. It is more accurate, they feel, to speak of a stratification continuum, consisting of many rankings with small gradations between them (much like a thermometer) and with no readily discernible social-class categories. Logically, this approach makes sense and may be the most accurate description of the way things really are. However, since people seem to believe in social classes, and since teachers and researchers often find it easier to make distinctions among several broad categories than among numerous slightly differing gradations, we usually view stratification in terms of specific classes. Most often this involves the Warner or Kahl categories or a similar modification.[10]

Determining Social Class

Sociologists have developed several ways of determining social-class rank. These methods include the subjective, reputational, and objective techniques. In the *subjective* method, the person is asked what social class he thinks he belongs

---

[10]In this section we have directly or indirectly referred to several classic works in stratification. Lloyd Warner's study of Newburyport, Massachusetts, was first described in Lloyd Warner and Paul S. Lunt, *The Social Life of a Modern Community* (New Haven, Conn.: Yale University Press, 1941). Robert S. Lynd and Helen M. Lynd described stratification in a Midwestern city in *Middletown* (New York: Harcourt, 1959) and *Middletown in Transition* (New York: Harcourt, 1963). So did August Hollingshead in *Elmtown's Youth,* first published in 1949 and now available as *Elmtown's Youth and Elmtown Revisited* (New York: Wiley, 1975). Stratification along a continuum is discussed by John Cuber and William Kenkel in *Social Stratification in the United States* (New York: Appleton-Century-Crofts, 1954).

Table 5.6   Social Class Portrait of a Typical American Community

Class	Proportion of Community	Characteristics
Upper-upper	1–2%	These people have wealth, power, and social repute gained through long residence in the community, a prominent family name, and an Ivy League education. One can only be born or occasionally marry into this level. Lineage is important. There is reverence for the past and graceful living.
Lower-upper	1–2	These people have wealth and power, but the tradition of upper-classness is lacking. Money is too new, and there is no prominent old family name. Several generations of breeding, right schools, careful marriages, and hope may get them into upper-upper.
Upper-middle	10–12	These are professionals and successful merchants who may belong to the country club and will have college degrees, but from the state university instead of Ivy League schools. They have less wealth and prestige than classes above, but they are still important people. They are career-oriented joiners.
		▲ Important People—"Big" People ▲ ▼ Common People—"Little" People ▼
Lower-middle	33	These small businessmen, salesmen, clerks, and foremen have average income and education (high school plus) and white-collar jobs. They are active in fraternal, veterans, and religious organizations, are religious, family-centered, and moralistic, and live the Protestant Ethic: frugality, respectability, thrift, and hard work.
Upper-lower	33	These are blue-collar workers who earn less, probably didn't graduate from high school, and are more likely to be employees than employers. They belong to trade unions and aim at getting by. Their jobs are routine and uninteresting, a way to earn a living only.
Lower-lower	15–20	These are unskilled workers who dropped out of school early and are frequently unemployed. They married young and quickly had more children than the family could afford to support. They have unhappy marriages and cramped and dilapidated housing, and they see the world as a dog-eat-dog jungle. They are pessimistic, resigned, and apathetic.

Summarized from Harold M. Hodges, Jr., *Social Stratification* (Cambridge, Mass.: Schenkman Publishing Co., 1964), pp. 60–70; and from Joseph Kahl, *The American Class Structure* (New York: Holt, Rinehart and Winston, 1957), Chapter 7.

to. This seems a rather crude method, but many argue as Marx did that the world is divided along class lines and that a person's social-class identification is very much a part of his or her self-image—it is much of what he or she *is*. This view holds that social class is important to people, that these people therefore have a high degree of class consciousness, and that they should be able to place themselves accurately in the social-class spectrum.

The *reputational* method involves finding out what others think. People from the community are selected to act as prestige judges, and these judges in turn evaluate others in the community. Social class becomes what selected people say it is. This method is similar to the subjective technique, and again it hinges on community members' class consciousness. The *objective* method differs from other methods in that individuals are evaluated in terms of certain specific factors that sociologists assume are related to social class. For example, Warner examined four factors when he used the objective technique: the individual's occupation, his or her source of income, the type of house, and the area of the city in which he or she lives. By knowing these facts about a person, Warner felt that he could objectively place him or her in a specific social class. Other objective factors that have been used include years of education, amount of income, type of possessions, even type and quality of home furnishings.

Using any of these methods, especially the objective, may give the impression that social class is a very clear-cut phenomenon and that each person can be adequately plugged in. This, of course, is an oversimplification. The categories are not precise and are not always related one to another. For example, in what social class do we put the status-inconsistent person whose occupational prestige is low, income is high, who lives in an apartment in a slum, and is a college graduate— and when we ask her, she says she doesn't believe in social class?[11]

Social Class and Behavior

When the *Titanic* sank in 1912, three percent of the women in First Class died, but forty-five percent of the women in Third Class perished. It was supposed to be women and children into the life boats first, but the death rate was higher for children in Third Class than for men in First Class.[12] We saw at the beginning of this chapter that the life chances of Tommy and Billy were affected drastically by their social class. It is clear that social class is related to numerous patterns of behavior. For example, we would expect patterns of consumption to vary by social class. Table 5.7 shows how ownership of cars and appliances varies by level of income.

Other less obvious differences between social classes have been studied. Lower-class people seem oriented more toward taking pleasures in the present than toward planning for future goals. Middle-class people are more prone to defer gratification. There seems to be a link between low status and prejudice. That is,

[11]Methods of determining social class and critiques of these methods are covered in more detail in Harold M. Hodges, *Social Stratification* (Cambridge, Mass.: Schenkman, 1964), Chapter 5.

[12]Walter Lord, *A Night to Remember* (New York: Holt, Rinehart and Winston, 1955).

Table 5.7   Income and Consumption Patterns, 1974

Percentage of House- holds Owning:	Income		
	Under $3,000	$10,000– 14,999	$25,000 and Over
Two or more cars	6%	37%	67%
Central air conditioning	8	18	39
Freezer	20	37	48
Color TV	32	67	84
Washing machine	51	77	89

U.S. Bureau of the Census, *Statistical Abstract of the United States, 1977* (98th ed.), Washington, D.C., p. 462.

lower-class people are more likely than middle-class people to be intolerant of minorities and foreigners.[13]

Studies of social class and mental illness have found that psychoses, particularly schizophrenia and manic-depressive disorders, are more prevalent among lower-class than middle-class people. Middle-class people, on the other hand, are more likely to be neurotic (or so diagnosed by psychiatrists) than are lower-class people. There are class differences in treatment as well. Middle-class people are likely to have psychotherapy, highly qualified practitioners, and more thorough treatment of mental illness. Lower-class people are more often treated by interns and less qualified practitioners and are more likely to be subjected to questionable procedures (shock treatments, lobotomies, and drugs).[14]

Voting behavior is affected by many factors, and social class is certainly one of them. Lower-class people are more likely to vote Democratic, and middle- and upper-class people are more likely to vote Republican. In addition, middle-class people are more likely to vote than are lower-class people. Turning to deviant behavior, we find that homicide is more prevalent among lower-class people than among middle-class people in the United States and throughout the world. Assault is also a lower-class phenomenon.[15]

Several sociologists have studied social-class variations in patterns of leisure and recreation. Hodges found in his survey of "Peninsula People" that upper-class people watched television an average of sixteen minutes per week night, whereas lower-lower-class people watched an average of 180 minutes a night. Thirty-three percent of the uppers said that they never watched television, while only six percent of the lower-lowers said they never watched. Reading books and magazines increases as one goes up the social-class ladder. The higher one's social class, the more one is likely to be involved in sports as a participant; the lower one's class, the more likely that person is to be involved as a spectator. Al Clarke compared

[13]The research on prejudice is summarized by Hodges in *Social Stratification*, pp. 210–220 (see footnote 11).

[14]A. B. Hollingshead and F. C. Redlich, *Social Class and Mental Illness: A Community Study* (New York: Wiley, 1958). For a general summary, see Hodges, *Social Stratification*, pp. 223–227 (see footnote 11).

[15]Marshall Clinard and Robert Meier discuss the data on homicide in *Sociology of Deviant Behavior*, 5th ed. (New York: Holt, Rinehart and Winston, 1979), p. 199.

Table 5.8   Income and Participation in Outdoor Recreation, 1972

Percentage of People Participating in:	Income	
	Under $8,000	$15,000 and Over
Sailing	15%	51%
Golf	13	47
Hunting	43	18
Fishing	38	18
Waterskiing	21	35
Picnicking	36	21
Tennis	22	37
Bicycling	27	28

Department of Interior, Bureau of Outdoor Recreation, *Outdoor Recreation.* Reprinted from *Social Indicators, 1976* (Washington, D.C.: U.S. Government Printing Office, 1977), p. 513.

upper- and lower-class people and found that the uppers favored playing bridge, watching movies, and going to museums, while the lowers liked playing poker, watching baseball, and going to the zoo.[16] Participation in outdoor recreation activites also varies by income, as shown in Table 5.8.

In terms of the way they raise their children, middle-class parents are probably more permissive, lower-class parents more rigid. Melvin Kohn reports that middle-class mothers value self-control, dependability, and consideration, while lower-class mothers value obedience and the ability in a boy to defend himself. The middle-class child is raised in an atmosphere in which achievement and getting ahead are encouraged. The lower-class child is raised in an atmosphere that emphasizes the immediate and the concrete, that focuses on getting by, and that counsels the child to shy away from the new or unfamiliar. We should note here that there is much change in social-class-linked childrearing practices. What is fashionable or correct at one time may change drastically a few years later.[17]

Many of the current theories attempting to explain delinquent and criminal behavior are based on social class. Walter Miller, for example, argues that lower-class juveniles who become delinquents do so because of the lower-class value system. Lower-class values and beliefs important to lower-class youth include trouble, toughness, smartness, excitement, fate, and autonomy (resistance to being bossed or controlled). Miller believes that the more marked presence of these values in the lower class than in other social classes makes it inevitable that many lower-class children will run afoul of the law. In a way he is saying that we have two different cultures—middle-class and lower-class—but the *laws* in United States society emerge solely from the middle-class culture, and therefore one should expect that most *illegal* behavior will come from the lower-class culture.

[16]Hodges, *Social Stratification,* p. 161 (see footnote 11), and Alfred C. Clarke, "The Use of Leisure and Its Relation to Levels of Occupational Prestige," *American Sociological Review* 21 (June 1956), pp. 301–306.

[17]See Hodges' discussion in *Social Stratification,* Chapter 8, especially pp. 178–186 (see footnote 11). Melvin Kohn's research is discussed by Hodges, pp. 181–182. Also see Melvin Kohn's book, *Class and Conformity* (Homewood, Ill.: Dorsey Press, 1969).

The rather pessimistic inference from this theory is that the only way to make it is to become middle-class.

Several other theories examine the social-class-linked motivations for delinquency in a slightly different way. Albert Cohen and Richard Cloward and Lloyd Ohlin agree that ours is a middle-class-based society, but they do not believe that it is a lower-class value system or culture that leads one to delinquency. Rather, they feel that the basic problem arises out of the lower-class individual's attempt to move into the middle class. It is Cohen's view that most who try to make it will not. Anticipating failure, their reaction is to invert the middle-class system—to do just the opposite of what middle-class people say is correct. The result is malicious, nonutilitarian, frequently criminal behavior. Cloward and Ohlin agree with Cohen up to the point of the reaction of inverting the values of the middle class to spite them. Cloward and Ohlin believe that the lower-class individuals still want to make it and that when they see they cannot succeed legally, they decide to try it illegally. They become involved, therefore, in utilitarian property crime, which allows them to collect the good things, the symbols of status associated with middle-class culture. Regardless of whether the theorists agree on particulars, the important factor in all of these theories is that they are based on social class. The social class to which people belong apparently provides them with a characteristic view of the world that does much to determine their behavior.

The theories discussed above deal only with lower-class crime and may leave one with the impression that all crime is committed by lower-class people. This is a common error that is made if one looks only at arrest figures, which *are* higher among the lower class. Middle-class people commit different types of crime— fraud, embezzlement, white-collar offenses—that are less easily detected and punished. Also, middle-class people have the financial resources to deal with the law, to avoid arrest to begin with, and to obtain better legal defense should arrest occur. Typically, the middle-class juvenile delinquent is informally apprehended and returned to his or her parents, whereas the lower-class delinquent is formally arrested and sent to a juvenile hall. The actual extent of hidden middle-class crime is hard to assess. It may be that if all offenses could be known, the differences between social classes would be only in types of offenses, not in number of offenses.[18]

As you might expect, the likelihood of being a *victim* of crime also varies by social class. The pattern is a curious one, however, as can be seen in Table 5.9. As income increases, the chances of being a victim of theft (larceny-theft, burglary, auto theft) increase, but the chances of being a victim of violent crime (homicide, assault, rape) decrease.

[18]The original works referred to in this section include William C. Kvaraceus and Walter B. Miller, *Delinquent Behavior: Culture and the Individual* (Washington, D.C.: National Education Association, 1959); Walter Miller, "Lower-Class Culture as a Generating Milieu of Gang Delinquency," *Journal of Social Issues* 14 (1958), pp. 5–19; Albert K. Cohen, *Delinquent Boys: The Culture of the Gang* (New York: Free Press, 1955); and Richard Cloward and Lloyd Ohlin, *Delinquency and Opportunity* (New York: Free Press, 1960). These and other class-related theories of delinquency are summarized in Hodges, *Social Stratification,* Chapter 10 (see footnote 11), and in many textbooks on criminology—for example, Walter C. Reckless, *The Crime Problem,* 5th ed. (New York: Appleton-Century-Crofts, 1973), Chapter 2.

A recent study supports the idea of little relationship between class and criminality. See "The Myth of Social Class and Criminality: An Empirical Assessment of the Empirical Evidence" by Charles Tittle, Wayne Villemez, and Douglas Smith, *American Sociological Review* 43 (October 1978), pp. 643–656.

Table 5.9   Crime Victims and Income, 1974

Annual Family Income	Rate per 1,000 People 12 and Over	
	Violent Crime	Crimes of Theft
Under $3,000	54	81
$10,000–14,999	28	94
$25,000 and over	25	128

Social Indicators, 1976 (Washington, D.C.: U.S. Government Printing Office, 1977), p. 248.

Social Mobility

Horizontal social mobility refers to movement from one occupation to another within the same social class. If an architect becomes a minister, or if the mail carrier becomes a carpenter, we would say that horizontal social mobility has occurred—occupational change but no change in social class. The term is also used by sociologists to describe geographical mobility, moving one's home from one place to another. Vertical social mobility is more relevant to our discussion here, however. **Vertical social mobility** refers to movement up or down the social-class ladder, movement from one rank to another.

Societies with unlimited possibilities for vertical social mobility are described as *open.* Those with no possibilities for mobility are called *closed.* In reality, all societies rank somewhere between the extremes of completely open and completely closed. India's system of stratification, for example, is closer to the closed end of the continuum. Lines between levels or castes are often firmly drawn; moving from the caste into which one is born may be difficult if not impossible. Some have suggested that we have a type of caste system in the United States relative to blacks and whites. That is, there is a firm line between black and white stratification systems, and although a black may rise within the black class system, he is either blocked from the white system or is automatically assigned low rank in the white system. In societies with stratification systems that rank more toward the open end of the continuum, mobility from one level to another may be both possible and frequent.

Examining mobility in a given country is a complicated procedure. Americans, for example, have traditionally looked at their own system as completely open. Mobility and achievement were available to anyone who worked hard and led a clean life. We *know* that the rags-to-riches, Horatio Alger story is *true* and *we* can make it too. America is not like other countries where class lines are difficult to cross. In fact and contrary to these beliefs, mobility is very much the same in all modern industrialized countries. The dramatic leap from rags to riches is a rare occurrence indeed. Mobility, when it occurs, is usually in a series of small steps and possibly over several generations. There is more mobility within classes (horizontal mobility) than between classes (vertical mobility). There seems to be more upward vertical mobility than downward, but though many are mobile, few move very far.

A recent study of mobility of men and women in the United States reported an interesting finding: women are more mobile, both upward and downward, through marriage than men are through occupations. Men are much more likely to inherit their fathers' statuses than are women. Because our society lacks mechanisms for women to directly inherit occupations, they are freer to marry into statuses both above and below their origins.[19]

If I have convinced you that it is difficult but you still want to become upwardly mobile without relying completely on luck, there are a few general rules to follow. Defer gratification, marry late, and have a small family if you must have a family. If you live in a small town, leave. Vertical mobility is easier in middle-sized and large cities. If you are an immigrant to the United States, be Japanese, Jewish, or Scottish. These groups are more mobile than other immigrant groups, who more often than not come in at the bottom of the social-class ladder and stay there. In modern societies in which skills and knowledge are increasingly important, education is essential for upward mobility. In the United States a college degree helps. For some it is not only the degree, but the right school—Harvard, Yale, Radcliffe, Princeton—that is essential to mobility. Finally, if all else fails in your quest for upward mobility, marry someone who has followed the above rules.

But before you decide for sure to move up, beware of the consequences. Sociologists have been studying the social-psychological effects of upward mobility. One result of uprooting oneself from the past and moving to a new level is that it becomes difficult to form satisfying relationships. One is alone, a **marginal person** between two worlds and a member of neither. Another view agrees that socially mobile people are isolates, but argues that they were isolates to begin with. They were unhappy and isolated, and this led to attempts at mobility, so they are really no worse off. A third view of the situation (and the one that is most accurate according to current research on social mobility) is that socially mobile people have few problems because they are so anxious to get to the next level that they adopt the patterns of behavior of that level long before they ever get there (anticipatory socialization). Consequently, they are accepted and much at home when they finally arrive.[20]

In a society that is oriented upward, downward mobility is hard to take. Studies cite relationships between downward mobility and both suicide and mental illness (especially schizophrenia). The same factors that are related to upward mobility are related in their converse to downward mobility. Marrying early, having a large family, or failing to get an education may do it. Personal factors may help: business failure, sickness, or rejection of the ethic that says that climbing the social ladder is important.

Poverty and Welfare

Earlier in this chapter we learned that wealth is an important variable in determining social class and that wealth is not equally shared in American society. The top twenty percent of the population controls forty-two percent of the national in-

[19]Ivan Chase, "A Comparison of Men's and Women's Intergenerational Mobility in the United States," *American Sociological Review* 40 (August 1975), pp. 483–505.

[20]See the discussion of social mobility and its effects in *Social Stratification in America* by Leonard Beeghley (Santa Monica, Calif.: Goodyear, 1978), pp. 311–318. Also see Hodges, *Social Stratification*, Chapters 12 and 13, especially p. 266.

come, but the poorest twenty percent have only five percent of the national income (see Table 5.4, page 133). This calls our attention to one of this country's major social issues: poverty. Poverty is a major social issue because of the links between it and crime, delinquency, self-esteem, mental illness, educational opportunities, physical health, life expectancy, infant mortality, and numerous other factors.

The United States government has developed a definition of poverty that is based on the amount of money needed to buy a nutritionally adequate diet (assuming that no more than one-third of the family income is used for food). The poverty line varies according to family size, location, and the value of the dollar. In 1977, for example, the poverty line for a single person was an annual income of $3,075; for a non-farm family of four it was $6,191. In 1977, twenty-five million people (roughly twelve percent of the population) were below the poverty line. Large as that number is, it is not nearly the whole picture of poverty in this country. The poverty line refers to a so-called survival income, and there are many people who are above the poverty line but who don't have a normal or acceptable standard of living. They may live in dwellings without electricity or running water, or in conditions in which, although they may be able to survive, they know that most of the rest of the people in the country live far better than they do. It is difficult to arrive at an accurate estimate of how many poor and near-poor there are, but the bottom twenty percent of the population is the figure often used. Roughly forty-three million people would fall into this category, and as we can see from Table 5.4, they were no better off in 1977 than they were in 1950. In each year they had only five percent of the total income although they represented twenty percent of the population.

Who are the poor? Obviously poverty doesn't strike all equally. The characteristics of the poor show them to be the young and the elderly, members of ethnic and racial minorities, women who are heads of households, the illiterate and unemployable, and the disabled and handicapped. Poverty is higher in certain parts of the country, primarily in rural areas and in the South.

How does a society that sees itself as a land of opportunity deal with the existence of poverty? In curious and interesting ways. One approach is to hide it. The poor are located in areas we don't see and consciously avoid. The sick and aged are almost by definition invisible. The subject is not popular and won't be found on prime-time television except for an occasional documentary. The poor have no economic or political clout. The poor are a large but essentially anonymous and hidden group; we try to deny their existence.

Another way of dealing with an unwelcome problem is to blame the victim. William Ryan begins his book *Blaming the Victim* with the story of actor Zero Mostel impersonating a pompous senator investigating the origins of World War II. The climax of the senator's investigation comes when he booms out with triumph and suspicion, "What was Pearl Harbor *doing* in the Pacific?" Exactly. The poor are poor because they are lazy, unintelligent and lack motivation, tend to drink and have loose morals, can't manage money, and don't want to work anyway. Blaming the victim releases the non-victims from responsibility for the victim's plight. Recent studies have found that many Americans (often, a majority of those asked) believe that (1) most people on welfare who can work don't try to find jobs,

(2) many people on welfare are not honest about their need, (3) many mothers on welfare have babies to increase their welfare payments. In fact, studies of those on welfare show that all of these beliefs are *incorrect.*[21]

Why do we have these beliefs about the poor? Probably because Americans fervently believe in the work ethic. All able-bodied people should work, their income should come from work, and the more hard-working they are the better people they are. Work is good—even if it is low-paying, exhausting, and degrading temporary work. There is also a welfare ethic, which emphasizes that no one should take money unless absolutely necessary. This leads to suspicions regarding welfare recipients, more extensive monitoring to find suspected welfare cheaters, and confirmation of the view that people who take charity were bad people to begin with.

Finally, we should recognize that poverty is *functional.* The existence of the poor and their exploitation benefits other Americans in many ways. The poor do society's dirty work—the dirty, dangerous, undignified, and menial jobs. They work for low wages, and as domestics, for example, they make life easier for the middle and upper classes. The existence of poverty creates all sorts of jobs and occupations to service the poor—social workers, police officers, ministers, pawn shop operators, and the peacetime army (which recruits heavily from the poor). The poor help the economy by purchasing goods that the more affluent don't want —day-old food, second-hand clothes, and deteriorating merchandise. In many ways, then, the existence of poverty is advantageous to the non-poor segment of American society.[22]

Welfare

The welfare system was devised ostensibly to assist the victims of poverty, to help them fare well in society. The idea of welfare has been around for a long time. Originally, churches were the primary agencies for charity and relief giving, but as the urban labor class grew, attempts to control the poor emerged. In 1351 under King Edward III of England, a law established maximum wages, required the unemployed to work for whoever demanded, restricted the travel of workers, and forbade charity to the able bodied. In large part, these have become the basic features of welfare in America today.[23]

Public program social welfare expenditures in 1976 were more than $331 billion. These programs included aid for families with dependent children (AFDC), Medicaid, aid for the aged, the blind, and the disabled, food stamps, veterans' aid, workmen's compensation, black lung benefits, and so on. The list of programs is long, and the amount of money spent is substantial and increasing sharply.

[21]The major sources I am using in this section on poverty are Leonard Beeghley, *Social Stratification in America* (Santa Monica, Calif.: Goodyear, 1978), Chapter 8; Jonathan Turner and Charles Starnes, *Inequality: Privilege & Poverty in America* (Pacific Palisades, Calif.: Goodyear, 1976); Jerome Skolnick and Elliott Currie, *Crisis in American Institutions,* 3d ed. (Boston: Little, Brown, 1976); and William Ryan, *Blaming the Victim,* rev. ed. (New York: Random House, 1976). Facts on money and numbers come from *Statistical Abstract, 1978.*
The study of welfare beliefs and facts is discussed in Beeghley, pp. 135–138.

[22]Herbert Gans, "The Positive Functions of Poverty," *American Journal of Sociology* 78 (September 1972), pp. 275–289; and Beeghley, *Social Stratification in America,* p. 140.

[23]Turner and Starnes, *Inequality: Privilege & Poverty in America,* p. 122.

Critics of the welfare system, however, believe that in spite of the huge amounts of money spent, the system actually operates to *perpetuate* poverty. Those statutes that Edward III established over 600 years ago helped him *control* the poor. Piven and Cloward argue that our current system has the same intent—to regulate and exploit the poor. During periods when high unemployment leads to public unrest, welfare programs are expanded to absorb and pacify the masses. At times of political and economic stability and low unemployment, welfare rolls are narrowed, forcing people into low-paying jobs in the labor market.[24]

Turner and Starnes suggest that we really have two systems operating, a *wealthfare* system and a *welfare* system. The wealthfare system enables the middle and especially the upper class to maintain their privileged position by allowing them to avoid taxation and by giving them and the businesses they own and operate direct cash payments and subsidies. The wealthfare system is an example of the exercise of power, and it works through the intricacies of the federal tax system. A quick example: In 1968 a family with an income of less than $2,000 a year paid twenty-seven percent of its income in taxes; a family with an income of over $50,000 a year paid less than seven percent of its income in taxes. In which case was the tax bite more painful? Who does the system work for?

The welfare system exists, according to Turner and Starnes, because it appears to be a humanitarian effort to keep people from starving, it is politically necessary because the numbers of poor give them some power and they may revolt, and it is a nice balance to and keeps attention diverted from the far more expensive wealthfare system. The welfare system perpetuates poverty by keeping payments low, by forcing people to work in any available job, and by diffusing any collective power the poor may have.[25]

What is the answer? Recognition that poverty is a problem that we want to solve and redistribution of wealth and resources, perhaps through a guaranteed annual income—maybe in these ways inequality could be reduced. But we cannot be hopeful about the prospect. If our analysis is accurate, the middle and upper classes benefit from the system as it exists. Poverty is unpleasant, but the alternative to it—massive changes in existing education, government, and economic institutions—and the threat changes suggest is more unpleasant for the affluent to consider, and power resides with privilege. Again we must consider power—who has it, how it is used, for whose benefit.

SUMMARY

Sociologists study the social organization of society by studying groups and non-groups. The subject of the previous chapter was groups. The characteristics of groups were discussed as well as the variations in behavior in small and large groups. This chapter focuses on social differentiation. What we have done here is examine characteristics that make people *different*. People fall into a number of

---

[24]Frances Piven and Richard Cloward, "The Relief of Welfare," in Skolnick and Currie, *Crisis in American Institutions,* 3d ed. Also see Beeghley, *Social Stratification in America,* pp. 139–140.
[25]Turner and Starnes, *Inequality: Privilege & Poverty in America,* pp. 62–63, and 93.

categories—age, sex, race, social class, religion—by which they differ. These are not groups as we discussed them earlier; they are non-groups, *categories,* very large collectivities of people.

A central point here is not only that people are separated into categories, but that these categories are *ranked.* People act as though some are better and some are worse than others. This introduces the idea of social stratification—in all societies people are ranked across a number of variables. In this chapter we have focused on the ranking relative to socioeconomic status.

The important variables in socioeconomic status are wealth, power, and prestige. Wealth, income, and education are separate variables but closely related. Several interesting debates run through the discussion of social class. Who has the power in the United States? The power elite theorists (Mills, Domhoff) have one answer; the pluralists (Reisman, Rose) have another answer. What does American class structure look like? Here again it depends on whom you ask. Some see a continuum with no specific classes; others see three, four, five, six, or even more reasonably well-defined classes.

We found that social class is related to numerous aspects of behavior—voting, mental illness, recreation patterns, homicide, prejudice, child-rearing patterns, suicide, consumption patterns, and delinquency. Vertical social mobility refers to movement up or down the social-class ladder. Analysis of social mobility in the United States indicates that Horatio Alger doesn't live here anymore—few people move very far up or down the ladder.

Some forty million people are poor or near-poor in this country. Their poverty and the ways society deals with it are a major social issue for Americans. Analysis of the welfare system suggests that although it was established to help the poor, it may actually operate to perpetuate poverty.

In the next chapter this analysis of social differentiation will continue as we direct our attention to other categories: race, ethnicity, sex, and age.

The following readings focus on several ideas raised in this chapter. Norman Podhoretz describes his own first awareness of social class and his encounter with a teacher who encouraged him to be socially mobile. The second article, from David Halberstam's *The Best and the Brightest,* examines some of the characteristics of power and influence.

Reading 5.1
Making It: The Brutal Bargain
NORMAN PODHORETZ

There is much variation in how conscious people are of social class. In societies where class lines are strictly drawn, there is probably greater class consciousness. In such societies the individual is likely to have a well-developed sense of his own class position, of others who are like him, and of those who rank higher or lower. In societies where class is more fluid and lines are easily crossed, there is probably less class consciousness. And in any society, some individuals are more conscious of class than are others.

Norman Podhoretz is an author and editor of *Commentary* magazine. In this selection from his book, *Making It,* Podhoretz describes his growing awareness of social class. Podhoretz was of lower- or working-class background, but he encountered an English teacher who decided he was a "gem in the rough and took it upon herself to polish [him] to as high a sheen as she could manage. . . ." This process illustrates a growing class consciousness and the processes and problems of upward social mobility as well.

I

One of the longest journeys in the world is the journey from Brooklyn to Manhattan—or at least from certain neighborhoods in Brooklyn to certain parts of Manhattan. I have made that journey, but it is not from the experience of having made it that I know how very great the distance is, for I started on the road many years before I realized what I was doing, and by the time I did realize it I was for all practical purposes already there. At so imperceptible a pace did I travel, and with so little awareness, that I never felt footsore or out of breath or weary at the thought of how far I still had to go. Yet whenever anyone who has remained back there where I started—remained not physically but socially and culturally, for the neighborhood is now a Negro ghetto and the Jews who have "remained" in it mostly reside in the less affluent areas of Long Island—whenever anyone like that happens into the world in which I now live with such perfect ease, I can see that in his eyes I have become a fully acculturated citizen of a country as foreign to him as China and infinitely more frightening.

That country is sometimes called the upper middle class; and indeed I am a member of that class, less by virtue of my income than by virtue of the way my speech is accented, the way I dress, the way I furnish my home, the way I entertain and am entertained, the way I educate my children—the way, quite simply, I look and live. It appalls me to think what an immense transformation I had to work on myself in order to become what I have become: if I had known what I was doing I would surely not have been able to do it, I would surely not have wanted to. No wonder the choice had to be blind; there was a kind of treason in it—treason toward my family, treason toward my friends. In choosing the road I chose, I was pronouncing a judgment upon them, and the fact that they themselves concurred in the judgment makes the whole thing sadder but no less cruel.

When I say that the choice was blind, I mean that I was never aware—obviously not as a small child, certainly not as an adolescent, and not even as a young man already writing for publication and working on the staff of an important intellectual magazine in New York—how inextricably my "noblest" ambitions were tied to the vulgar desire to rise above the class into which I was born; nor did I understand to what an astonishing extent these ambitions were shaped and defined by the standards and values and tastes of the class into which I did not know I wanted to move. It is not that I was or am a social climber as that term is commonly used. High society interests me, if at all, only as a curiosity; I do not wish to be a member of it; and in any case, it is not, as I have learned from a small experience of contact with the very rich and fashionable, my "scene." Yet precisely because social climbing is not one of my vices (unless what might be called celebrity climbing, which very definitely *is* one of my vices, can be considered the contemporary variant of social climbing), I think there may be more than a merely personal significance in the fact that class has played so large a part both in my life and in my career.

But whether or not the significance is there, I feel certain that my long-time blindness to the part class was playing in my life was not altogether idiosyncratic. "Privilege," Robert L. Heilbroner has shrewdly observed in *The Limits of American Capitalism,* "is not an attribute we are accustomed to stress when we consider the construction of *our* social order." For a variety of reasons, says Heilbroner, "privilege under capitalism is much less 'visible,' especially to the favored groups, than privilege under other systems" like feudalism. This "invisibility" extends in America to class as well.

No one, of course, is so naïve as to believe that America is a classless society or that the force of egalitarianism—powerful as it has been in some respects—has ever been powerful enough to wipe out class distinctions altogether. There was a moment during the 1950s, to be sure, when social thought hovered on the brink of saying that the country had to all intents and purposes become a wholly middle-class society. But the emergence of the civil-rights movement in the 1960s and the concomitant discovery of the poor—to whom, in helping to discover them, Michael Harrington interestingly enough applied, in *The Other America,* the very word ("invisible") that Heilbroner later used with reference to the rich—has put at least a temporary end to that kind of talk. And yet if class has become visible again, it is only in its grossest outlines—mainly, that is, in terms of income levels—and to the degree that manners and style of life are perceived as relevant at all, it is generally in the crudest of terms. There is something in us, it would seem, which resists the idea of class. Even our novelists, working in a genre for which class has traditionally been a supreme reality, are largely indifferent to it—which is to say, blind to its importance as a factor in the life of the individual.

In my own case, the blindness to class always expressed itself in an outright and very often belligerent refusal to believe that it had anything to do with me at all. I no longer remember when or in what form I first discovered that there was such a thing as class, but whenever it was and whatever form the discovery took, it could only have coincided with the recognition that criteria existed by which I and everyone I knew were stamped as inferior: we were in the *lower* class. This was not a proposition I was willing to accept, and my way of not accepting it was to dismiss the whole idea of class as a prissy triviality.

Given the fact that I had literary ambitions even as a small boy, it was inevitable that the issue of class would sooner or later arise for me with a sharpness it would never acquire for most of my friends. But given the fact also that I was on the whole very happy to be growing up where I was, that I was fiercely patriotic about Brownsville (the spawning ground of so many famous athletes and gangsters), and that I felt genuinely patronizing toward other neighborhoods (especially the "better" ones like Crown Heights and East Flatbush which seemed by comparison colorless and unexciting)—given the fact, in other words, that I was not, for all that I wrote poetry and read books, an "alienated" boy dreaming of escape, my confrontation with the issue of class would probably have come later rather than sooner if not for an English teacher in high school who decided that I was a gem in the rough and took it upon herself to polish me to as high a sheen as she could manage and I would permit.

I resisted—far less effectively, I can see now, than I then thought, though even then I knew that she was wearing me down far more than I would ever give her the satisfaction of admitting. Famous throughout the school for her altogether outspoken snobbery, which stopped short by only a hair (and sometimes did not stop short at all) of an old-fashioned kind of patrician anti-Semitism, Mrs. K. was also famous for being an extremely good teacher; indeed, I am sure that she saw no distinction between the hopeless task of teaching the proper use of English to the young Jewish barbarians whom fate had so unkindly deposited into her charge and the equally hopeless task of teaching them the proper "manners." (There were as many young Negro barbarians in her charge as Jewish ones, but I doubt that she could ever bring herself to pay very much attention to them. As she never hestitated to make clear, it was punishment enough for a woman of her background —her family was old-Brooklyn and, she would have us understand, extremely distinguished—to have fallen among the sons of East European immigrant Jews.)

For three years, from the age of thirteen to the age of sixteen, I was her special pet, though that word is scarcely adequate to suggest the intensity of the relationship which developed between us. It was a relationship right out of *The Corn Is Green,* which may, for all I know, have served as her model; at any rate, her objective was much the same as the Welsh teacher's in that play: she was determined that I should win a scholarship to Harvard. But whereas (an irony much to the point here) the problem the teacher had in *The Corn Is Green* with her coalminer pupil in the traditional class society of Edwardian England was strictly academic, Mrs. K.'s problem with me in the putatively egalitarian society of New Deal America was strictly social. My grades were very high and would obviously remain so, but what would they avail me if I continued to go about looking and sounding like a "filthy little slum child" (the epithet she would invariably hurl at me whenever we had an argument about "manners")?

Childless herself, she worked on me like a dementedly ambitious mother with a somewhat recalcitrant son; married to a solemn and elderly man (she was then in her early forties or thereabouts), she treated me like a cruelly ungrateful adolescent lover on whom she had humiliatingly bestowed her favors. She flirted with me and flattered me, she scolded me and insulted me. Slum child, filthy little slum child, so beautiful a mind and so vulgar a personality, so exquisite in sensibility and so coarse in manner. What would she do with me, what would become of me if I persisted out of stubbornness and perversity in the disgusting ways they had taught me at home and on the streets?

To her the most offensive of these ways was the style in which I dressed: a T-shirt, tightly pegged pants and a red satin jacket with the legend "Cherokees,

S.A.C." (social-athletic club) stitched in large white letters across the back. This was bad enough, but when on certain days I would appear in school wearing, as a particular ceremonial occasion required, a suit and tie, the sight of those immense padded shoulders and my white-on-white shirt would drive her to even greater heights of contempt and even lower depths of loving despair than usual. *Slum child, filthy little slum child.* I was beyond saving; I deserved no better than to wind up with all the other horrible little Jewboys in the gutter (by which she meant Brooklyn College). If only I would listen to her, the whole world could be mine: I could win a scholarship to Harvard, I could get to know the best people, I could grow up into a life of elegance and refinement and taste. Why was I so stupid as not to understand?

II

In those days it was very unusual, and possibly even against the rules, for teachers in public high schools to associate with their students after hours. Nevertheless, Mrs. K. sometimes invited me to her home, a beautiful old brownstone located in what was perhaps the only section in the whole of Brooklyn fashionable enough to be intimidating. I would read her my poems and she would tell me about her family, about the schools she had gone to, about Vassar, about writers she had met, while her husband, of whom I was frightened to death and who to my utter astonishment turned out to be Jewish (but not, as Mrs. K. quite unnecessarily hastened to inform me, *my* kind of Jewish), sat stiffly and silently in an armchair across the room squinting at his newspaper through the first pince-nez I had ever seen outside the movies. He spoke to me but once, and that was after I had read Mrs. K. my tearful editorial for the school newspaper on the death of Roosevelt —an effusion which provoked him into a full five-minute harangue whose blasphemous contents would certainly have shocked me into insensibility if I had not been even more shocked to discover that he actually had a voice.

But Mrs. K. not only had me to her house; she also—what was even more unusual—took me out a few times, to the Frick Gallery and the Metropolitan Museum, and once to the theater, where we saw a dramatization of *The Late George Apley,* a play I imagine she deliberately chose with the not wholly mistaken idea that it would impress upon me the glories of aristocratic Boston.

One of our excursions into Manhattan I remember with particular vividness because she used it to bring the struggle between us to rather a dramatic head. The familiar argument began this time on the subway. Why, knowing that we would be spending the afternoon together "in public," had I come to school that morning improperly dressed? (I was, as usual, wearing my red satin club jacket over a white T-shirt.) She realized, of course, that I owned only one suit (this said not in compassion but in derision) and that my poor parents had, God only knew where, picked up the idea that it was too precious to be worn except at one of those bar mitzvahs I was always going to. Though why, if my parents were so worried about clothes, they had permitted me to buy a suit which made me look like a young hoodlum, she found it very difficult to imagine. Still, much as she would have been embarrassed to be seen in public with a boy whose parents allowed him to wear a zoot suit, she would have been somewhat less embarrassed than she was now by the ridiculous costume I had on. Had I no consideration for her? Had I no consideration for myself? Did I want everyone who laid eyes on me to think that I was nothing but an ill-bred little slum child?

My standard ploy in these arguments was to take the position that such things were of no concern to me: I was a poet and I had more important matters to think about than clothes. Besides, I would feel silly coming to school on an ordinary day dressed in a suit. Did Mrs. K. want me to look like one those "creeps" from Crown Heights who were all going to become doctors? This was usually an effective counter, since Mrs. K. despised her middle-class Jewish students even more than she did the "slum children," but probably because she was growing desperate at the thought of how I would strike a Harvard interviewer (it was my senior year), she did not respond according to form on that particular occasion.

"At least," she snapped, "they reflect well on their parents."

I was accustomed to her bantering gibes at my parents, and sensing, probably, that they arose out of jealousy, I was rarely troubled by them. But this one bothered me; it went beyond banter and I did not know how to deal with it. I remember flushing, but I cannot remember what if anything I said in protest. It was the beginning of a very bad afternoon for both of us.

We had been heading for the Museum of Modern Art, but as we got off the subway, Mrs. K. announced that she had changed her mind about the museum. She was going to show me something else instead, just down the street on Fifth Avenue. This mysterious "something else" to which we proceeded in silence turned out to be the college department of an expensive clothing store, De Pinna. I do not exaggerate when I say than an actual physical dread seized me as I followed her into the store. I had never been inside such a store; it was not a store, it was enemy territory, every inch of it mined with humiliations. "I am," Mrs. K. declared in the coldest human voice I hope I shall ever hear, "going to buy you a suit that you will be able to wear at your Harvard interview." I had guessed, of course, that this was what she had in mind, and even at fifteen I understood what a fantastic act of aggression she was planning to commit against my parents and asking me to participate in. Oh no, I said in a panic (suddenly realizing that I *wanted* her to buy me that suit), I can't, my mother wouldn't like it. "You can tell her it's a birthday present. Or else I will tell her. If I tell her, I'm sure she won't object." The idea of Mrs. K. meeting my mother was more than I could bear: my mother, who spoke with a Yiddish accent and whom, until that sickening moment, I had never known I was so ready to betray.

To my immense relief and my equally immense disappointment, we left the store, finally, without buying a suit, but it was not to be the end of clothing or "manners" for me that day—not yet. There was still the ordeal of a restaurant to go through. Where I came from, people rarely ate in restaurants, not so much because most of them were too poor to afford such a luxury—although most of them most certainly were—as because eating in restaurants was not regarded as a luxury at all; it was, rather, a necessity to which bachelors were pitiably condemned. A home-cooked meal was assumed to be better than anything one could possibly get in a restaurant, and considering the class of restaurants in question (they were really diners or luncheonettes), the assumption was probably correct.

In the case of my own family, myself included until my late teens, the business of going to restaurants was complicated by the fact that we observed the Jewish dietary laws, and except in certain neighborhoods, few places could be found which served kosher food; in midtown Manhattan in the 1940s, I believe there were only two and both were relatively expensive. All this is by way of explaining why I had had so little experience of restaurants up to the age of fifteen and why I grew apprehensive once more when Mrs. K. decided after we left De Pinna that we should have something to eat.

The restaurant she chose was not at all an elegant one—I have, like a criminal, revisited it since—but it seemed very elegant indeed to me: enemy territory again, and this time a mine exploded in my face the minute I set foot through the door. The hostess was very sorry, but she could not seat the young gentleman without a coat and tie. If the lady wished, however, something could be arranged. The lady (visibly pleased by this unexpected—or was it expected?—object lesson) did wish, and the so recently defiant but by now utterly docile young gentleman was forthwith divested of his so recently beloved but by now thoroughly loathsome red satin jacket and provided with a much oversized white waiter's coat and a tie—which, there being no collar to a T-shirt, had to be worn around his bare neck. Thus attired, and with his face supplying the touch of red which had moments earlier been supplied by his jacket, he was led into the dining room, there to be taught the importance of proper table manners through the same pedagogic instrumentality that had worked so well in impressing him with the importance of proper dress.

Like any other pedagogic technique, however, humiliation has its limits, and Mrs. K. was to make no further progress with it that day. For I had had enough, and I was not about to risk stepping on another mine. Knowing she would subject me to still more ridicule if I made a point of my revulsion at the prospect of eating non-kosher food, I resolved to let her order for me and then to feign lack of appetite or possibly even illness when the meal was served. She did order—duck for both of us, undoubtedly because it would be a hard dish for me to manage without using my fingers.

The two portions came in deep oval-shaped dishes, swimming in a brown sauce and each with a sprig of parsley sitting on top. I had not the faintest idea of what to do—should the food be eaten directly from the oval dish or not?—nor which of the many implements on the table to do it with. But remembering that Mrs. K. herself had once advised me to watch my hostess in such a situation and then to do exactly as she did, I sat perfectly still and waited for her to make the first move. Unfortunately, Mrs. K. also remembered having taught me that trick, and determined as she was that I should be given a lesson that would force me to mend my ways, she waited too. And so we both waited, chatting amiably, pretending not to notice the food while it sat there getting colder and colder by the minute. Thanks partly to the fact that I would probably have gagged on the duck if I had tried to eat it—dietary taboos are very powerful if one has been conditioned to them—I was prepared to wait forever. And, indeed, it was Mrs. K. who broke first.

"Why aren't you eating?" she suddenly said after something like fifteen minutes had passed. "Aren't you hungry?" Not very, I answered. "Well," she said, "I think we'd better eat. The food is getting cold." Whereupon, as I watched with great fascination, she deftly captured the sprig of parsley between the prongs of her serving fork, set it aside, took up her serving spoon and delicately used those two esoteric implements to transfer a piece of duck from the oval dish to her plate. I imitated the whole operation as best as I could, but not well enough to avoid splattering some partly congealed sauce onto my borrowed coat in the process. Still, things could have been worse, and having more or less successfully negotiated my way around that particular mine, I now had to cope with the problem of how to get out of eating the duck. But I need not have worried. Mrs. K. took one bite, pronounced it inedible (it must have been frozen by then), and called in quiet fury for the check.

Several months later, wearing an altered but respectably conservative suit which had been handed down to me in good condition by a bachelor uncle, I presented myself on two different occasions before interviewers from Harvard and from the Pulitzer Scholarship Committee. Some months after that, Mrs. K. had her triumph: I won the Harvard scholarship on which her heart had been so passionately set. It was not, however, large enough to cover all expenses, and since my parents could not afford to make up the difference, I was unable to accept it. My parents felt wretched but not, I think, quite as wretched as Mrs. K. For a while it looked as though I would wind up in the "gutter" of Brooklyn College after all, but then the news arrived that I had also won a Pulitzer Scholarship which paid full tuition if used at Columbia, and a small stipend besides. Everyone was consoled, even Mrs. K. Columbia was at least in the Ivy League.

The last time I saw her was shortly before my graduation from Columbia and just after a story had appeared in the *Times* announcing that I had been awarded a fellowship which was to send me to Cambridge University. Mrs. K. had passionately wanted to see me in Cambridge, Massachusetts, but Cambridge, England, was even better. We met somewhere near Columbia for a drink, and her happiness over my fellowship, it seemed to me, was if anything exceeded by her delight at discovering that I now knew enough to know that the right thing to order in a cocktail lounge was a very dry martini with lemon peel, please.

III

Looking back now at the story of my relationship with Mrs. K. strictly in the context of the issue of class, what strikes me most sharply is the astonishing rudeness of this woman to whom "manners" were of such overriding concern. (This, as I have since had some occasion to notice, is a fairly common characteristic among members of the class to which she belonged.) Though she would not have admitted it, good manners to Mrs. K. meant only one thing: conformity to a highly stylized set of surface habits and fashions which she took, quite as a matter of course, to be superior to all other styles of social behavior. But in what did their superiority consist? Were her "good" manners derived from or conducive to a greater moral sensitivity than the "bad" manners I had learned at home and on the streets of Brownsville? I rather doubt it. The "crude" behavior of my own parents, for example, was then and is still marked by a tactfulness and a delicacy that Mrs. K. simply could not have approached. It is not that she was incapable of tact and delicacy; in certain moods she was (and manners apart, she was an extraordinarily loving and generous woman). But such qualities were neither built into nor expressed by the system of manners under which she lived. She was fond of quoting Cardinal Newman's definition of a gentleman as a person who could be at ease in any company, yet if anything was clear about the manners she was trying to teach me, it was that they operated—not inadvertently but by deliberate design—to set one at ease *only* with others similarly trained and to cut one off altogether from those who were not.

While I would have been unable to formulate it in those terms at the time, I think I must have understood perfectly well what Mrs. K. was attempting to communicate with all her talk about manners; if I had not understood it so well, I would not have resisted so fiercely. She was saying that because I was a talented boy, a better class of people stood ready to admit me into their ranks. But only on one condition: I had to signify by my general deportment that I ackowledged them as *superior* to the class of people among whom I happened to have been born. That was the bargain—take it or leave it. In resisting Mrs. K. where "manners" were concerned—just as I was later to resist many others—I was expressing my refusal to have any part of so brutal a bargain.

But the joke was on me, for what I did not understand—not in the least then and not for a long time afterward—was that in matters having to do with "art" and "culture" (the "life of the mind," as I learned to call it at Columbia), I was being offered the very same brutal bargain and accepting it with the wildest enthusiasm.

I have said that I did not, for all my bookishness, feel alienated as a boy, and this is certainly true. Far from dreaming of escape from Brownsville, I dreaded the thought of living anywhere else, and whenever my older sister, who hated the neighborhood, began begging my parents to move, it was invariably my howls of protest that kept them from giving in. For by the age of thirteen I had made it into the neighborhood big time, otherwise known as the Cherokees, S.A.C. It had by no means been easy for me, as a mediocre athlete and a notoriously good student, to win acceptance from a gang which prided itself mainly on its masculinity and its contempt for authority, but once this had been accomplished, down the drain went any reason I might earlier have had for thinking that life could be better in any other place. Not for nothing, then, did I wear that red satin jacket to school every day. It was my proudest possession, a badge of manly status, proving that I was not to be classified with the Crown Heights "creeps," even though my grades, like theirs, were high.

And yet, despite the Cherokees, it cannot be that I felt quite so securely at home in Brownsville as I remember thinking. The reason is that something extremely significant in this connection had happened to me by the time I first met Mrs. K.: without any conscious effort on my part, my speech had largely lost the characteristic neighborhood accent and was well on its way to becoming as neutrally American as I gather it now is.

Now whatever else may be involved in a nondeliberate change of accent, one thing is clear: it bespeaks a very high degree of detachment from the ethos of one's immediate surroundings. It is not a good ear alone, and perhaps not even a good ear at all, which enables a child to hear the difference between the way he and everyone else around him sound when they talk, and the way teachers and radio announcers—as it must have been in my case—sound. Most people, and especially most children, are entirely insensitive to such differences, which is why anyone who pays attention to these matters can, on the basis of a man's accent alone, often draw a reasonably accurate picture of his regional, social, and ethnic background. People who feel that they belong in their familiar surroundings—whether it be a place, a class, or a group—will invariably speak in the accent of those surroundings; in all likelihood, indeed, they will never have imagined any other possibility for themselves. Conversely, it is safe to assume that a person whose accent has undergone a radical change from childhood is a person who once had fantasies of escaping to some other world, whether or not they were ever realized.

But accent in America has more than a psychological or spiritual significance. "Her kerbstone English," said Henry Higgins of Eliza Doolittle, "will keep her in the gutter to the end of her days." Most Americans probably respond with a sense of amused democratic superiority to the idea of a society in which so trivial a thing as accent can keep a man down, and it is a good measure of our blindness to the pervasive operations of class that there has been so little consciousness of the fact that America itself is such a society. While the broadly regional accents—New England, Midwestern, Southern—enjoy more or less equal status and will not affect the economic or social chances of those who speak in them, the opposite is still surely true of any accent identifiably influenced by Yiddish, Italian, Polish, Spanish —that is, the languages of the major post-Civil War immigrant groups (among which may be included American-Irish). A man with such an accent will no longer be confined, as once he would almost automatically have been, to the working class, but unless his life, both occupational and social, is lived strictly within the milieu in whose tone of voice he speaks, his accent will at the least operate as an obstacle to be overcome (if, for example, he is a schoolteacher aspiring to be a principal), and at the most as an effective barrier to advancement (if, say, he is an engineer), let alone to entry into the governing elite of the country. (For better or worse, incidentally, these accents are not a temporary phenomenon destined to disappear with the passage of the generations, no more than ethnic consciousness itself is. I have heard third-generation American Jews of East European stock speaking with thicker accents than their parents.)

Clearly, then, while fancying myself altogether at home in the world into which I was born, I was not only more detached from it than I realized; I was also taking action—and of very fundamental kind—which would eventually make it possible for me to move into some other world. Yet I still did not recognize what I was doing—not in any such terms. My ambition was to be a great and famous poet, not to live in a different community, a different class, a different "world." If I had a concrete image of what greatness would mean socially, it was probably based on the famous professional boxer from our block who had moved to a more prosperous neighborhood but still spent his leisure time hanging around the corner candy store and the local poolroom with his old friends (among whom he could, of course, experience his fame far more sharply than he could have done among his newly acquired peers).

But to each career its own sociology. Boxers, unlike poets, do not undergo a cultural change in the process of becoming boxers, and if I was not brave enough or clever enough as a boy to see the distinction, others who knew me then were. "Ten years from now, you won't even want to talk to me, you won't even recognize me if you pass me on the street," was the kind of comment I frequently heard in my teens from women in the neighborhood, friends of my mother who were fond of me and nearly as proud as she was of the high grades I was getting in school and the prizes I was always winning. "That's crazy, you must be kidding," I would answer. They were not crazy and they were not kidding. They were simply better sociologists than I.

As, indeed, my mother herself was, for often in later years—after I had become a writer and an editor and was living only a subway ride away but in a style that was foreign to her and among people by whom she was intimidated—she would gaze wistfully at this strange creature, her son, and murmur, "I should have made him for a dentist," registering thereby her perception that whereas Jewish sons who grow up to be successes in certain occupations usually remain fixed in an accessible cultural ethos, sons who grow up into literary success are transformed almost beyond recognition and distanced almost beyond a mother's reach. My mother wanted nothing so much as for me to be a success, to be respected and admired. But she did not imagine, I think, that she would only purchase the realization of her ambition at the price of my progressive estrangement from her and her ways. Perhaps it was my guilt at the first glimmerings of this knowledge which accounted for my repression of it and for the obstinacy of the struggle I waged over "manners" with Mrs. K.

For what seemed most of all to puzzle Mrs. K., who saw no distinction between taste in poetry and taste in clothes, was that I could see no connection between the two. Mrs. K. knew that a boy from Brownsville with a taste for Keats was not long for Brownsville, and moreover would in all probability end up in the social class to which she herself belonged. How could I have explained to her that I would only be able to leave Brownsville if I could maintain the illusion that my destination was a place in some mystical country of the spirit and not a place in the upper reaches of the American class structure?

Saint Paul, who was a Jew, conceived of salvation as a world in which there would be neither Jew nor Greek, and though he may well have been the first, he was very far from the last Jew to dream such a dream of transcendence—transcendence of the actual alternative categories with which reality so stingily presents us. Not to be Jewish, but not to be Christian either; not to be a worker, but not to be a boss either; not—if I may be forgiven for injecting this banality out of my own soul into so formidable a series of fantasies—to be a slum child but not to be a snob either. How could I have explained to Mrs. K. that wearing a suit from De Pinna would for me have been something like the social equivalent of a conversion to Christianity? And how could she have explained to me that there was no socially neutral ground to be found in the United States of America, and that a distaste for the surroundings in which I was bred, and ultimately (God forgive me) even for many of the people I loved—and so a new taste for other kinds of people— how could she have explained that all this was inexorably entailed in the logic of a taste for the poetry of Keats and the painting of Cézanne and the music of Mozart?

Questions 5.1

1. What is the function of the manners that Mrs. K. sought to teach?
2. What was the "brutal bargain"? Mr. Podhoretz rejected the "brutal bargain" but later accepted it—how and why?
3. Identify the symbols of class that concerned Mrs. K.
4. What were the strains or problems that upward social mobility presented for Mr. Podhoretz?
5. From information presented in this article, develop a convincing argument that (a) America has an open class system, and (b) America has a closed class system.

Reading 5.2

The Best and the Brightest

DAVID HALBERSTAM

Where do the leaders of the country come from? Some are elected by the people, of course, but some are appointed to high office. What of these people—what are they like? What do they have in common? Who selects them and why? David Halberstam sheds some light on these questions in this excerpt from *The Best and the Brightest*, his book about the men and decisions in the years leading up to and into the Vietnam war. Halberstam is a Pulitzer Prize–winning journalist whose work has appeared in the *New York Times*, *Harpers*, the *Atlantic Monthly*, and numerous other publications.

A cold day in December. Long afterward, after the assassination and all the pain, the older man would remember with great clarity the young man's grace, his good manners, his capacity to put a visitor at ease. He was concerned about the weather, that the old man not be exposed to the cold or to the probing questions of freezing newspapermen, that he not have to wait for a cab. Instead he had guided his guest to his own car and driver. The older man would remember the young man's good manners almost as clearly as the substance of their talk, though it was an important meeting.

In just a few weeks the young man would become President of the United States, and to the newspapermen standing outside his Georgetown house, there was an air of excitement about every small act, every gesture, every word, every visitor to his temporary headquarters. They complained less than usual, the bitter cold notwithstanding; they felt themselves a part of history: The old was going out and the new was coming in, and the new seemed exciting, promising.

On the threshold of great power and great office, the young man seemed to have everything. He was handsome, rich, charming, candid. The candor was part of the charm: he could beguile a visitor by admitting that everything the visitor proposed was right, rational, proper—but he couldn't do it, not this week, this month, this term. Now he was trying to put together a government, and the candor showed again. He was self-deprecating with the older man. He had spent the last five years, he said ruefully, running for office, and he did not know any real public officials, people to run a government, serious men. The only ones he knew, he admitted, were politicians, and if this seemed a denigration of his own kind, it was not altogether displeasing to the older man. Politicians *did* need men to serve, to run the government. The implication was obvious. Politicians could run Pennsylvania and Ohio, and if they could not run Chicago they could at least deliver it. But politicians run the world? What did they know about the Germans, the French, the Chinese? He needed experts for that, and now he was summoning them.

The old man was Robert A. Lovett, the symbolic expert, representative of the best of the breed, a great surviving link to a then unquestioned past, to the wartime and postwar successes of the Stimson-Marshall-Acheson years. He was the very embodiment of the Establishment, a man who had a sense of country rather than party. He was above petty divisions, so he could say of his friends, as so many of that group could, that he did not even know to which political party they belonged. He was a man of impeccable credentials, indeed he passed on other people's credentials, deciding who was safe and sound, who was ready for advancement and who was not. He was so much a part of that atmosphere that he was immortalized even in the fiction of his class. Louis Auchincloss, who was the unofficial laureate of that particular world, would have one of his great fictional lawyers say: "I've got that Washington bug. Ever since I had that job with Bob Lovett. . . ."

. . . Robert Lovett understood power, where it resided, how to exercise it. He had exercised it all his life, yet he was curiously little known to the general public. The anonymity was not entirely by chance, for he was the embodiment of the public servant—financier who is so secure in his job, the value of it, his right to do it, that he does not need to seek publicity, to see his face on the cover of a magazine or on televison, to feel reassured. Discretion is better, anonymity is safer: His peers know him, know his role, know that he can get things done. Publicity sometimes frightens your superiors, annoys congressional adversaries (when Lovett was at Defense, the senior members of the Armed Services committees never had to read in newspapers and magazines how brilliant Lovett was, how well he handled the Congress; rather they read how much he admired the Congress). He was the private man in the public society *par excellence.* He did not need to impress people with false images. He knew the rules of the game: to whom you talked, what you said, to whom you did not talk, which journalists were your kind, would, without being told, know what to print for the greater good, which questions to ask, and which questions not to ask. He lived in a world where young men made their way up the ladder by virtue not just of their own brilliance and ability but also of who their parents were, which phone calls from which old friends had preceded their appearance in an office. In a world like this he knew that those whose names were always in print, who were always on the radio and television, were there precisely because they did *not* have power, that those who did hold or had access to power tried to keep out of sight. He was a twentieth-century man who did not hold press conferences, who never ran for anything. The classic insider's man.

He was born in Huntsville, Texas, in 1895, the son of Robert Scott Lovett, a general counsel for Harriman's Union Pacific Railway, a railroad lawyer, a power man in those rough and heady days, who then became a judge, very much a part of the power structure, the Texas arm of it, and eventually a member of the Union Pacific board of directors and president of the railway. His son Bob would do all the right Eastern things, go to the right schools, join the right clubs (Hill School, Yale, Skull and Bones). He helped form the Yale unit of pilots which flew in World War I, and he commanded the first U.S. Naval Air Squadron. He married well, Adele Brown, the beautiful daughter of James Brown, a senior partner in the great banking firm of Brown Brothers.

Since those post-college years were a bad time for the railways, he went to work for Brown Brothers, starting at $1,080 a year, a fumbling-fingered young clerk who eventually rose to become a partner and finally helped to arrange the merger of Brown Brothers with the Harriman banking house to form the powerful firm of Brown Bros., Harriman & Co. So he came naturally to power, to running things, to knowing people, and his own marriage had connected him to the great families. His view of the world was a banker's view, the right men making the right decisions, stability to be preserved. The status quo was good, one did not question it.

He served overseas in London, gaining experience in foreign affairs, though like most influential Americans who would play a key role in foreign affairs entering government through the auspices of the Council on Foreign Relations, the group which served as the Establishment's unofficial club, it was with the eyes of a man with a vested interest in the static world, where business could take place as usual, where the existing order could and should be preserved. He saw the rise of Hitler and the coming military importance of air power; when he returned to America he played a major role in speeding up America's almost nonexistant air defenses. He served with great distinction during World War II, a member of that small inner group which worked for Secretary of War Henry Stimson and Chief of Staff George C. Marshall ("There are three people I cannot say no to," Lovett would say when asked back into government in the late forties, "Colonel Stimson, General Marshall and my wife"). That small group of policy makers came from the great banking houses and law firms of New York and Boston. They knew one another, were linked to one another, and they guided America's national security in those years, men like James Forrestal, Douglas Dillon and Allen Dulles. In 1947, after Acheson had resigned as Undersecretary of State, Marshall (who was then head of State) chose Robert Lovett as his successor, and in 1950 he became Secretary of Defense.

So that cold December day Kennedy was lunching with a man who not only symbolized a group, the Establishment, and was a power broker who carried the proxies for the great law firms and financial institutions, but was also tied to a great and seemingly awesome era. If Kennedy, as he always did in that period, complained that he knew no experts, that was no problem; the Establishment had long lists and it would be delighted to co-operate with this young President, help him along. It was of course above politics.

Kennedy believed in the Establishment mystique; there had, after all, been little debunking of it in early 1960. Rarely had there been such a political consensus on foreign affairs: containment was good, Communism was dangerous, there was of course the problem of getting foreign aid bills through Congress, bills which would help us keep the Third World from the Communists. Besides, he was young, and since his victory over Nixon was slimmer than he had expected, he needed the backing of this club, the elitists of the national security people. And he felt at ease with them: after Chester Bowles and Adlai Stevenson and all the other Democratic eggheads pushing their favorite causes, Lovett, who seemingly pushed no causes and had no ideology, was a relief.

The meeting continued pleasantly, Caroline darting in and out, carrying a football, emphasizing to Lovett the youth and the enormity of the task before this man. Lovett had a feeling that he was taking too much of the President-elect's time, but he found that just the opposite was true. Kennedy tried hard to bring Lovett into the government, to take a job, any job (earlier Kennedy had sent Clark Clifford as a messenger with the offer to serve as Secretary of the Treasury, which Lovett turned down). Lovett, who had not voted for Kennedy, could have State, Defense, or Treasury ("I think because I had been in both State and Defense he thought he was getting two men for the price of one," Lovett would later say). Lovett declined regretfully again, explaining that he had been ill, bothered by severe ulcers, and each time after his last three government tours he had gone to the hospital. Now they had taken out part of his stomach, and he did not feel he was well enough to take on any of these jobs. Again Kennedy complained about his lack of knowledge of the right people, but Lovett told him not to worry, he and his friends would supply him with lists. Take Treasury, for instance—there Kennedy would want a man of national reputation, a skilled professional, well known and respected by the banking houses. There were Henry Alexander at Morgan, and Jack McCloy at Chase, and Gene Black at the World Bank. Doug Dillon too. Lovett said he didn't know their politics. Well, he reconsidered, he knew McCloy was an independent Republican, and Dillon had served in a Republican Administration, but, he added, he did not know the politics of Black and Alexander at all (their real politics of course being business). At State, Kennedy wanted someone who would reassure European governments: they discussed names and Lovett pushed, as would Dean Acheson, the name of someone little known to voters, a young fellow who had been a particular favorite of General Marshall's—Dean Rusk over at Rockefeller. He handled himself there very well, said Lovett. The atmosphere was not unlike a college faculty, but Rusk had stayed above it, handled the various cliques very well.

Then the meeting was over, and the young man guided the older man through the throng of waiting reporters, saying that he had asked Mr. Lovett to come down and have lunch with him to see if he could get him for State, Defense or Treasury. (That night Lovett's old friend Arthur Krock, the *New York Times* columnist, called him to ask, "My God, is there any truth in it—it's going all over town," and Lovett answered, "Oh, I think he was just trying to make me feel good.") Since it was cold and there were no taxis, Kennedy gave Lovett his own car and driver, having failed to give him State, Defense or Treasury.

Questions 5.2

1. Suppose you aspire to be appointed to high government position. On the basis of this reading, what would be the most appropriate things for you to do?
2. Be a pluralist for a moment and explain the situation described in this article in ways that are consistent with pluralist power theory.
3. Be a power-elite theorist and explain the situation described in this article from that viewpoint.

6 Social Differentiation: Race, Ethnicity, Sex, Age

The previous chapter introduced the idea of social differentiation. Social differentiation refers to the fact that people in society fall into categories because of their age, sex, race, social class, and numerous other characteristics. Study of these categories is very helpful because it gives us a more precise picture of society, of the characteristics that bind people together, and of how these affect their behavior.

We found that social differentiation leads to social stratification. People tend to *rank* other people according to the categories into which they fall. In Chapter 5 we discussed stratification produced by socioeconomic factors. Socioeconomic status can be described as an achieved status because there is some flexibility in the ranking—one can perhaps move up or down the social class ladder. In this chapter we look at categories that are more tightly drawn. These are automatically conferred on the individual, and there is little that can be done about it. These are best described as ascribed statuses.

Minority Status

The term **minority status** is an important one and is very useful in trying to understand how people interact with each other. Minority status means much more than to say that a person is of a certain age, race, gender, or ethnic group. Black, female, over sixty-five, or Mexican-American names a category of people, but minority status describes one's position in society, how one is likely to be treated by others.

We will find in this chapter that groups with minority status are dealt with differently than other groups. Often they are treated as lower in social ranking and subject to domination by other segments of the population. Desired objectives are denied to them: education, occupations, elected positions, voting rights. Minority status may mean not being allowed to go certain places or do certain things.

It is important to understand that minority status is a social condition, not necessarily a statistical one. A minority could represent a majority of a society's population, but they have minority status because of the way they are viewed and treated by other segments of society. For example, women in the United States are a numerical majority but have minority status because they are not treated on a level of equality with men. For years the black population in South Africa has had minority status even though they greatly outnumber the white population, which has dominated them. In most instances minority groups do represent a smaller proportion of the population—blacks and Hispanic-Americans in the United States, for example—but it is important to recall the *social* nature of minority status.

Where do definitions of minority status come from? Who decides? A number of factors are probably at work. Some decisions about minority status arrive through custom and tradition. Those people who get someplace first tend to be proprietary about their good fortune and may look down on those who come later. Some groups blend in more easily or appear to. If their skin color and language are the same and their cultural backgrounds are similar to those of the society they are entering, their differences will be less apparent, and they will be more likely to escape minority status. And we learned in the last chapter of the importance of wealth and power. Assume that there is limited access to the good things in life —it follows that those with wealth and power will want to protect their positions by denying access to them by others. By labeling and treating categories of people differently—as of lower quality—they are effectively removed as threats to established positions of privilege. The creation and maintenance of minority status might work much the same as the treatment of the poor that we discussed in Chapter 5.

Race and Ethnicity

We learned in the previous chapter that people differ and are ranked by such socioeconomic factors as wealth, education, occupation, power, and prestige. People also differ and are ranked by their race and ethnicity. A person's race and ethnic affiliation confer on him or her a status or position in society—and sometimes this is a minority status.

Race is a vague and ambiguous term. It is generally defined as people bound together by hereditary physical features. The difficulty with the category of race is that practically no pure races exist. Substantial biological mixing has blurred boundaries to the point that it is difficult to outline uniform hereditary physical features. Scientists attempting to define race have come up with systems for anywhere from three racial categories to more than thirty. Three definitions of race—biological, legal, social—seem to intermingle.[1] A biological definition is based on observable physical features such as skin color, hair texture, and eye color, or on differences in gene frequencies. The legal definition is carried by the laws of states or nations. The law in one of our states has defined a black as a person who had "one-eighth or more Negro blood," and in other states a black is a person with "any ascertainable trace of Negro blood." The social definition refers to what members of society feel to be the important distinctions about race. Brewton Berry has suggested that in the United States the social definition of a black is anyone who identifies himself as black or who has any *known* trace of black ancestry. It can be seen from this that the term *race* is not a particularly precise term, but it is nevertheless widely used.

A sociology class is shown slides of people who identify themselves as blacks but who, because of an absence of typical racial characteristics, don't *look* like blacks. The class (which is predominantly white) is asked to identify the race or nationality of the light-skinned, straight-haired people on the slides, and the guesses range across the globe. Finally the class is told, "they are all American Negroes." The reaction is astonishment, of course, because "they don't look like blacks." This illustrates several things, among them the difficulty of defining race, the blurring of racial boundaries, and the importance of the social definition—once the class is told that the people on the slides identify as blacks (probably because of some black ancestry), to the class they *are* blacks. No question about it, regardless of how they look.

When race is discussed, the question of racial differences inevitably comes up. That is, do races biologically differ in I.Q., in achievement, in susceptibility to diseases, in perception? The haziness in definitions of race supplies part of the answer: If the boundaries of race are unclear, how can any statements about racial differences be made? Nevertheless, they are, as witness the current controversy over inherent racial I.Q. differences. A conclusion to this discussion that is favored by most social scientists is that there are no significant differences *caused* by race. There are numerous differences among people caused by cultural, social, and geo-

---

[1]This distinction is suggested by Brewton Berry in *Race and Ethnic Relations,* 3d ed. (Boston: Houghton Mifflin, 1965), Chapter 2.

graphic factors, however, and these are often incorrectly identified as racial differences. For example, certain gene frequencies and blood characteristics have developed in particular areas of the world. Population groups migrating from those areas—regardless of race—carry these characteristics to other parts of the world. Apparently, a specific blood characteristic that has survival value in areas of high malaria incidence has developed in populations in parts of Africa and the Middle East. This same blood characteristic also leads to sickle-cell anemia, a disease that has victimized blacks in the United States. Is sickle-cell anemia linked to race? No, because non-blacks who have migrated to other parts of the world from those same areas of Africa and the Middle East may also have it. Likewise, differences in attitude, achievement, and perception are explained by cultural differences—one culture emphasizes achievement, another tranquility, one is aggressive, another encourages passivity, and so on. In short, social scientists argue from a cultural determinist viewpoint and reject the idea of racially caused differences. Many people remain unconvinced, however, and the argument will undoubtedly continue.

Ethnicity or *ethnic group* are more useful terms than *race,* at least from the sociological viewpoint. **Ethnicity** refers to people bound together by cultural ties. These cultural ties may have several origins. When nationality groups immigrate to a new area, their ties to their previous culture may remain strong. Religious beliefs may also provide the basis for ethnicity, and examples in the United States might include Jews, the Amish, and the Hutterites. The term *ethnicity* is useful because it appropriately brings the focus on cultural similarities, which to the social scientist are more important and have more explanatory power than racial similarities.

Prejudice and Discrimination

Prejudice has been defined as an unfavorable attitude toward a person or thing, prior to, or not based on, actual experience. A prejudiced person ignores the individual and his particular qualities or characteristics, and groups the person with others who happen to have the same skin color (brown or yellow), or speak with the same accent (New England), or have the same type of name (Cohen, Greenberg), or come from the same part of the country (South).

Prejudice tends to be generalized. People who are prejudiced against one group will probably be prejudiced against others. Some years ago E. L. Hartley asked college students what they thought of Canadians, Turks, Swiss, French, Jews, atheists, Irish, Negroes, Wallonians, Pireneans, Danireans, and other groups. He found that people who were prejudiced against blacks were also likely to be prejudiced against Jews, Wallonians, and Danireans. Now there are about fourteen million Jews in the world, but no Wallonians or Danireans. Hartley used these fictitious groups to see how people would react to groups they knew nothing about. He found that people tend to generalize their prejudices.[2]

Discrimination is actual behavior unfavorable to a specific individual or group. When people desire equality of treatment and are denied it, they are being discrim-

[2]E. L. Hartley, *Problems in Prejudice* (New York: Kings Crown Press, 1946).

inated against. Discrimination occurs when a person is denied a desired position or right because of irrelevant factors—for example, when skin color is used to determine eligibility to vote, or when religious affiliation is used to determine where one may reside.

Prejudice and discrimination are usually associated but not always. The situation gets complicated when people think one way but behave another way. Robert Merton attempted to describe what happens by suggesting four categories of people.[3]

Unprejudiced non-discriminator or all-weather liberal: confirmed and consistent liberal; not prejudiced; doesn't discriminate; believes in American creed of justice, freedom, equality of opportunity, and dignity of the individual.

Unprejudiced discriminator or fair-weather liberal: thinks in terms of expediency; not prejudiced but keeps quiet when bigots are about; will discriminate for fear that to do otherwise would "hurt business"; will make concessions to the intolerant.

Prejudiced non-discriminator or fair-weather illiberal: timid bigot; doesn't believe in the American creed but conforms to it when slightest pressure is applied; hates minorities but hires them to obey the law.

Prejudiced discriminator or all-weather illiberal: a bigot, pure and unashamed; doesn't believe in the American creed and doesn't hesitate to tell that to others; believes it is right and proper to discriminate, so does.

The origins of prejudice are explained in varying ways. Some psychologists believe that there is a certain type of personality—called an *authoritarian personality*—that is especially prone to prejudice.[4] The authoritarian personality is also ethnocentric, rigidly conformist, and worships authority and strength. According to psychologists, the authoritarian personality can most often be traced to faulty emotional development born of harsh discipline and lack of affection and love from one's parents during childhood. Most sociologists believe that prejudice, like other attitudes and behaviors, is learned in interaction with others, mainly in the family, and that personality is not as important as the social or cultural situation in which one interacts. We learn race prejudice in the same way we learn how to eat with a fork, study for a test, or drive a car. Also, certain life situations affect how this learning takes place. For example, people who are downwardly mobile—moving from middle to lower class—show more intense feelings of prejudice toward blacks and Jews; and in times of rapid social change, prejudice and discrimination may become more intense and more generalized.

Sociologists also associate stereotyping with prejudice. In **stereotyping,** we apply a common label and set of characteristics to all people in a certain category, even though none or only some of the people in that category fit the image we are applying. The stereotyped male college professor is absent-minded, smokes a pipe, is an extreme liberal, wears horn-rimmed glasses and a tweed jacket with elbow patches, and generally is not much in touch with the real world. This image is applied to everyone in the college professor category even though most do not fit

[3]Robert K. Merton, "Discrimination and the American Creed," in *Discrimination and National Welfare,* edited by R. M. MacIver (New York: Harper & Brothers, 1949), pp. 99–126. Also see Berry's summary in *Race and Ethnic Relations,* 3d ed., pp. 300–302 (see footnote 1).

[4]T. W. Adorno et al., *The Authoritarian Personality* (New York: Harper & Row, 1950).

the part. Professors will probably survive their stereotype without serious damage because the characteristics of the stereotype are not particularly bad in our society. Also, a person *chooses* as an adult to become a college teacher and, therefore, to enter a stereotyped category.

A black, on the other hand, who is stereotyped from birth as ignorant, lazy, dirty, happy-go-lucky, morally primitive, emotionally unstable, and fit only for menial work, can be psychologically damaged by the effects of the lifelong stereotype. When others react to us on the basis of such stereotypes, it strongly affects our self-concepts—the way we see ourselves. This again is the self-fulfilling prophecy, which we discussed several times earlier. Remember what happened to the "bright" rats and "dull" rats? Or what happened when teachers thought some of their students were "academic spurters"? (See pages 40–41.)

Several theories have been offered to explain prejudice and discrimination. One such theory explains conflict between unlike groups in terms of scapegoating. If attention can be focused on some out-group, this may strengthen the boundaries and unity of the in-group. It is suggested that the Nazis' attack on the Jews before and during World War II had this motivation. Marxist theory holds that economic competition is the best explanation for prejudice and discrimination. When access to desired goods or valued positions in society is limited, discrimination against certain categories of people helps ensure that others can more easily dominate and obtain their goals. By reducing the status of others to second-class citizens, by eliminating certain people from highly valued jobs, education, and access to wealth, we can guarantee that our own path is free of obstacles. Some have said that the conflict that arises when unlike groups meet may be best and most simply explained as resulting from a struggle for status between competing groups.

The common areas of discrimination in the United States include employment, education, housing, and, to a lesser extent, voting. In the following paragraphs we will take a brief look at some patterns of prejudice and discrimination as they affect blacks, Indians, Hispanic-Americans, and Jews.

Blacks

There were twenty-five million blacks in the United States in 1977 or roughly 11.5 percent of the population. Blacks have been a part of American history from its beginning; the economy of the earliest days of our settlement was based on slavery. We are still trying to overcome the effects that the culture of slavery had on blacks and whites in America. Certain dates stand out:

1619 Twenty blacks purchased from a Dutch ship
1644 First slaves imported directly from Africa
1861–1865 Civil War with emancipation as a major issue
1865 Legal abolition of slavery by the Thirteenth Amendment to the Constitution
1896 *Plessy* v. *Ferguson* decision by the Supreme Court supports "separate but equal" doctrine
1918–on Black migration from the rural South to jobs in the urban North
1954 *Brown* v. *Board of Education* decision by the Supreme Court states that "separate facilities are inherently unequal"
1956 Montgomery bus boycott led by Martin Luther King, Jr.

1960–1965 Passive resistance, sit-ins, demonstrations
1965–1970 Urban riots, beginning of black militancy, and "Black Power"
1970s Prison riots, widespread disagreement over busing to achieve school desegregation

The Kerner (riot commission) Report in 1968 stated that "our nation is moving toward two societies, one black, one white—separate and unequal." Some examples of how separate and unequal status affects other conditions of life are shown in Table 6.1.

Jobs, Income, Unemployment   Median income for white families in 1977 was $16,-740; for black and other families, it was $10,142 (see Table 6.2). The unemployment rate for blacks was about double that of whites (twelve percent compared to six percent annual average for 1977). The jobless rate for black teenagers was thirty-seven percent for 1977, but the comparable figure for white teenagers was about fifteen percent. Blacks represented a larger proportion of the poverty group in 1977 than in 1959 despite the fact that average income had gone up. In other words, the economic position of blacks had improved, but it had improved much faster for whites. Another sign of economic difficulties is the fact that the percentage of black soldiers in the Army's enlisted ranks doubled between 1970 and 1978 to a record

Table 6.1   Comparison by Race on Selected Characteristics

	White	Black
Birthrate per 1,000 people, 1976	14	21*
Life expectancy, 1976		
Males	70	64*
Females	77	73*
Infant deaths per 1,000 live births, 1976	13	24*
Caloric intake per day, 1972	2,072	1,810
Percent illiterate, 1969	.7	3.6
Homicide victims per 100,000 people, 1976		
Males	11	83*
Females	3	18*
Suicide victims per 100,000 people, 1976		
Males	26	16*
Females	9	5*
Percent unemployed, 1977	6	12*
Percent below poverty line, 1977	9	29*
Mental hospital admissions per 100,000 people, 1970		
Males	299	648*
Females	184	453*
Percent of households living in crowded conditions, 1974	5	13*
Percent of families earning under $3,000, 1977	3	10
Percent of families earning $25,000 and over, 1977	24	11
Percent completing 4 years of college, 1977	16	7

*For this category, designation is "black and other"; blacks make up about ninety percent of this group.

U.S. Bureau of the Census, *Statistical Abstract of the United States, 1978* (99th ed.), Washington, D.C.; from Census Bureau documents; and from *Social Indicators, 1976.*

high of twenty-eight percent. Blacks continued to move into white-collar jobs in the 1970s but at a slower pace than in the 1960s. Black men in white-collar jobs rose slightly from twenty-two percent in 1970 to twenty-three percent in 1977; for black women the percentage rose from thirty-six percent in 1970 to forty-four percent in 1977.[5]

Table 6.2   Median Income (in 1977 dollars) and Race

	White Families	Black and Other Families
1950	$ 8,672	$ 4,704
1960	11,940	6,610
1970	15,975	10,169
1977	16,740	10,142

U.S. Bureau of the Census, *Statistical Abstract of the United States, 1978* (99th ed.), Washington, D.C., p. 452.

A recent study analyzed occupation, unemployment, and income in the United States and concluded that some whites, particularly in the South, continue to benefit from the subordinate position of blacks. Because of the subordinate position of blacks, these whites (in white-collar and higher-income jobs) gain higher occupational status, lower unemployment, higher family income, and reduced labor costs. The author of the study concluded that in recent American history, the improvement in racial equality has been grossly exaggerated. Some whites (who appear to be of high status and income) will continue to oppose advancement of blacks due to their own self-interests.[6]

Education   Blacks receive less education than whites in the United States as Tables 6.3 and 6.4 indicate. The gap is closing but slowly. The Supreme Court outlawed segregated schools in the *Brown v. Board of Education* decision in 1954, but integration of schools did not proceed very rapidly; more than two-thirds of Southern black children were still attending all-black schools in 1968. However, a dramatic change did take place between 1968 and 1974. In 1974 only eight percent

Table 6.3   Median School Years Completed and Race

	White	Black
1960	10.9	8.0
1970	12.2	9.9
1977	12.5	11.4

U.S. Bureau of the Census, *Statistical Abstract of the United States, 1978* (99th ed.), Washington, D.C., p. 143.

[5]Much of the data in this and following paragraphs comes from the comprehensive report, "The Social and Economic Status of the Black Population in the United States: An Historical View, 1790–1978," *Current Population Reports* Series P-23, no. 80, published by the U.S. Bureau of the Census (Washington, D.C.: U.S. Government Printing Office, 1979), and from *Statistical Abstract of the United States, 1978.*

[6]George Dowdall, "White Gains from Black Subordination in 1960 and 1970," *Social Problems* 22 (December 1974), pp. 162-183.

of Southern black children were still in schools in which all students were minorities (blacks, Asians, Spanish-Americans), whereas in the North and West fourteen percent of black students were in such schools. More black students were in mainly white schools in 1974 in the South than in the North and West. These statistics reveal that, despite a tendency to accuse Southerners in discussing racism in America, all areas of the nation share the guilt. Housing (especially *de facto*) segregation has certainly been increasing much more repidly in the ghettos of Northern cities than it has been in the South.

In the mid-1970s the issue of busing was more heated than ever. Several controversial reports by James S. Coleman provoked much discussion. A 1966 Coleman report concluded that deprived students did better educationally when their classmates came from backgrounds emphasizing educational achievement. The idea was to improve the educational chances of blacks by busing them from their poor school districts to higher quality white school districts. Many court decisions, many complicated school board plans, and many demonstrations later, people on both sides of the issue continue to wonder if busing will work.[7] However, this education available to blacks has not significantly improved their performance, and many whites are moving to private schools in the cities or public schools in the suburbs. Far from desegregating schools, busing seems to be resegregating them. Coleman completed another report in 1975 in which he too concluded that this desegregation may be increasing segregation. He cited new research showing that desegregation has little, if any, effect on students' performance in many of the participating schools. It now seems that the importance of family background in determining educational achievement was seriously underestimated in the early studies. Moving an educationally deprived student to an educationally rich school is fine, but apparently the important factor is the student's family background, which does not change.

The picture is brighter at colleges and universities. College enrollment increased more rapidly for blacks than for whites between 1970 and 1974. Black enrollment increased by fifty-six percent; white enrollment increased by fifteen percent. A gap remains, however. The proportion of young blacks enrolled (eighteen percent) was still below that of young whites (twenty-five percent).

Housing   Finding adequate housing is difficult for blacks. First there were restrictive laws, and now tacit agreements keep blacks out of the better districts in most cities and suburbs of the North, West, and South. Because middle-class whites are leaving the cities for the suburbs, *de facto* segregation is turning the inner cities into black ghettos. Blacks isolated in these areas find their housing, their public facilities, and their schools automatically segregated and made inadequate by the lowered tax base, the backwardness (and often helplessness) of city government, and the exploitation or apathy of absentee landlords and local business people.

[7]See the editorial by Norman Cousins in *Saturday Review,* 24 January 1976. The report of James S. Coleman et al. is "Equality of Educational Opportunity" (Washington, D.C.: U.S. Government Printing Office, 1966).

Voting, Elected Officials   Blacks have been denied the vote for years in the South. However, implementation of the Civil Rights Act, calling for federal voting regis- trars in the South, seemed to change this form of discrimination. Voter registration figures in eleven Southern states in 1960 indicated that sixty-one percent of the eligible whites were registered, whereas only twenty-nine percent of the eligible blacks were registered. By 1976, however, sixty-eight percent of the whites and sixty-three percent of the blacks were registered. In 1970, there were fewer than 1500 black office holders. In July 1978, 4,503 blacks were holding office in forty- four states and the District of Columbia. However, blacks still account for fewer than one percent of all elected officials. The increase in elected officials has been most predominant in the South. Numerous black legislators, 135 black mayors, and two black lieutenant governors had been elected by 1975.

American Indians

In the middle and late nineteenth century, Americans believed in Manifest Destiny, the doctrine that it was the destiny of the United States to expand its territory and enhance its political, economic, and social influence over the whole of North America. And so, the original occupants of the land, the American Indi- ans, were killed, captured, displaced, and placed on reservations as settlers moved west. It was too bad, as one Army general who supervised the removal of the Indians put it—they were a brave and proud people but they finally realized that it was their destiny to "give way to the insatiable progress of our race. . . . "[8]

In his book, *Custer Died for Your Sins,* Vine Deloria, Jr., discusses an interesting paradox in American society. Americans are told not to trust Communist countries, for they do not keep treaty commitments. We fought in Vietnam for years and thousands of people lost their lives ostensibly because the United States had to keep its commitments in Southeast Asia. The paradox is this: At the very time that we were spending $100 billion keeping commitments in Vietnam, the United States government was also breaking the oldest Indian treaty, the Pickering treaty of 1794 with the Seneca tribe of the Iroquois Nation. In fact, as far as breaking treaties is concerned, it is doubtful if anybody can beat our record. Deloria reports that "America has yet to keep one Indian treaty or agreement despite the fact that the U.S. government signed over 400 such treaties with Indian tribes."[9]

Desirable land has been systematically taken from Indians, and they are then relocated on reservations in less desirable areas. Indians held 138 million acres in 1887; this had been reduced to 55 million acres by 1970, and to 52 million by 1976. If formerly undesirable land becomes desirable (because of the discovery of oil or coal deposits, a river to be used for power or irrigation, a location for a power plant, or a ripe area to be developed for settlement or recreation), further relocation and manipulation of Indian rights and lands follows.

The 1970 Census reported there are approximately 800,000 American Indians. Median family income was $5,800 a year, Indian unemployment was higher than

---

[8]General Carleton's views on Manifest Destiny and the Indians are quoted by Dee Brown in *Bury My Heart at Wounded Knee* (New York: Holt, Rinehart & Winston, Bantam Books, 1971), p. 31

[9]Vine Deloria, Jr., *Custer Died for Your Sins* (New York: Macmillan, 1969), pp.28–29.

for other groups, and the income of thirty-three percent of Indian families was below the poverty level. Median years of schooling received by Indians was 9.8, and thirty-three percent were high school graduates. Living conditions on reservations have long been substandard. Life expectancy of Indians lags about seven years behind that of whites. Death statistics provide further evidence of the effects of minority status. Indians are less likely to die of heart disease and cancer than other Americans but about three times as likely to die of accidents. Indians have a high birth rate (about two and a half times that of whites), but Indian deaths in infancy and early childhood are about double that of other Americans. Indian deaths from cirrhosis of the liver are more than double the national average, by homicide more than triple, and by tuberculosis four times the national average. Indian alcoholism and suicide rates are also very high, and suicide is especially high for Indians in their late teens and twenties.[10] Dr. Bertram Brown, a director of the National Institute of Mental Health, has stated that Indians suffer greatly the effects of isolation and alienation from society brought on by the general neglect of many generations. American racism and bigotry have an adverse effect on mental health. The Indian has been the victim of this abuse longer than any other American.

Hispanic-Americans

Americans of Spanish origin have become this country's fastest growing minority. Census figures put the number of Hispanics in the United States in 1978 at twelve million. If illegal aliens are included, the figure increases to nineteen million. Population projections suggest that the Hispanic population may outnumber blacks within the next decade. The major unifying factors for Hispanic-Americans are their religion (Roman Catholicism) and their language, but many diversities exist as well. Seven million Hispanics are of Mexican origin and have settled in the West and Southwest (probably nearly two million in Los Angeles alone). Some 700,000 Hispanics have come from Cuba, more than half of whom have settled in the Miami area. More than one million Hispanics from Puerto Rico are living in the New York City area. Americans of Spanish origin are divided by several factors including nationality differences and the consequent rivalries that these lead to, and differences in conditions of immigration—how recent, how well to do, how upwardly mobile, and so on.

Hispanic-Americans, however, uniformly face the conditions that seem to accompany minority status. Their income is lower and their unemployment rate higher than that of whites. Twenty-two percent of families of Spanish origin were below the poverty level in 1977 (compared to about ten percent for other American families). Many Chicanos in the West are migrant workers performing farm labor in the fields of California and Oregon. Farm labor is seasonal, uncertain, underpaid, and subject to bad working conditions. Hispanic-Americans are much underrepresented in political and governmental positions. In 1978 there were no Hispanics in the Senate and five in the House of Representatives compared to sixteen blacks and

---

[10]The information on birth and death rates and causes comes from "Natality and Mortality of American Indians Compared with U.S. Whites and Nonwhites," by Charles Hill and Mozart Spector, *Public Health Reports*, vol. 86 (March 1971), pp. 229–246.

Table 6.4   Level of Education for People 25 Years Old and Older, 1977

Percent of the Population with:	Whites	Blacks	Hispanic-Americans		
			Mexican-Americans	Puerto Ricans	Cubans
Less than five years of school	3%	10%	23%	19%	11%
Four years of high school or more	67	46	34	31	49

U.S. Bureau of the Census, *Statistical Abstract of the United States, 1978* (99th ed.), Washington, D.C., p. 144.

twenty-two Jews in the House. Hispanics hold three percent of the jobs in federal government, whereas blacks have sixteen percent. Hispanics are low in voter registration—less than forty percent of those eligible are registered. Perhaps the most serious problem for Hispanic-Americans is in the area of education. They have a high dropout rate as can be seen in Table 6.4. The central issue is language and the necessity for bilingual education. Look, for example, at the Southwest, where the Mexican-American is the largest culturally distinct minority group. According to a May 1972 report by the U.S. Commission on Civil Rights, schools in the Southwest exclude the Chicanos' Spanish language, exclude their Mexican heritage, and discourage their participation in school affairs. Nearly fifty percent of the Mexican-American first graders do not speak English as well as the average Anglo first grader. They have to learn a new language in addition to the other material being taught. By the twelfth grade, sixty-three percent of all Chicano students read at least six months below grade level. Before the end of the twelfth grade, forty-seven percent of the Chicanos will have left school. Only seven percent of the secondary schools in the Southwest had a course in Mexican-American history. More than four million persons in the Southwest identify Spanish as their mother tongue, but the schools (seventy-five percent of the elementary, ninety percent of the secondary) communicate with parents (send notices, conduct meetings) only in English.

The debate over bilingual education centers around the following dilemma: Should all be demanded to speak English, which means that many are sure to fall behind and drop out, or should bilingual programs be established, with the result that many students will have little skill in English in a specialized technological society in which knowledge of English is essential?[11]

Jews

There are approximately fourteen million people of the Jewish faith in the world. There are six million Jews in the United States or roughly three percent of our population. Religion is the foundation, but being Jewish also involves an ethnic and cultural identity. Unfortunately, persecution has been a consistent factor in Jewish cultural history. They were forced off their land and driven into other areas as early as the sixth century B.C. Especially sharp conflict between Christians and Jews emerged after the third century A.D. Starting around the tenth century Jews

[11]See the article on Hispanic-Americans in *Time,* October 16, 1978, pp. 48-61. Some of the numbers came from *Statistical Abstract of the United States, 1978.*

were segregated into ghettos, at first voluntarily, then on a compulsory basis. In 1555, the Pope decreed that Jews must be segregated strictly in their own quarter of the city surrounded by a high wall with gates closed at night. Jews were forced out of certain occupations and denied citizenship. They were used as scapegoats to distract people's attentions from other issues and to promote national unity. This was played to its most horrible extreme during World War II with the extermination of six million Jews in Germany.

The consequences of minority status for Jews in the United States do not seem to be as severe as they are for other groups that we have looked at. This is probably because Jews are less visible than most minority groups and because they have been more upwardly mobile through their emphasis on education and participation in the professions. Jews have faced certain types of prejudice and discrimination in the United States. For a time, certain jobs were not open to Jews. Colleges and universities, especially in the Eastern United States, had quotas covering the percentage of Jews they would accept. As recently as 1958, thirty-three percent of the real estate agents in a large Midwestern city reported they did not want to rent to Jews, and a study of 3,000 resorts across the country in the same year found that twenty-two percent discriminated against Jews. In the late 1960s and 1970s, such overt discrimination against Jews probably declined, although anti-Jewish prejudice remains. Of some current concern are the quotas and preferential treatment being received by some groups in education and employment which, it is argued, favors one minority to the exclusion of others.

Jews represent a powerful interest group that the government must consider in its policies toward Israel and the Middle East, and occasionally, events evoke memories of the atrocities in Germany and galvanize Jewish political action groups —most recently, the 1978 march in Skokie, Illinois, by members of the American Nazi Party.

Patterns of Interaction

When populations that differ by race or ethnicity meet, a number of different types of reactions may occur. Some of these reactions are quite peaceful, others are not.[12] **Annihilation** refers to the elimination of one group by another. This may be done intentionally, such as the Nazis' treatment of the Jews or United States policies toward Indians in the nineteenth century. The practice of deliberately exterminating a whole race or ethnic group is called *genocide.* Annihilation may occur unintentionally when one group brings disease that decimates the other group. Again, American Indians are examples as they fell victim in great numbers to illnesses brought over by European settlers. **Expulsion** refers to the removal of a group from the territory in which it resides. Japanese on the West Coast during World War II were removed from their homes and placed in detention camps, and yes, American Indian tribes were forced from their homes onto reservations. **Segregation** refers

---

[12]These paragraphs on patterns of interaction are drawn from Berry, *Race and Ethnic Relations,* 3d ed., Chapters 7–12 (see footnote 1).

to the setting apart of one group. It is not as extreme as expulsion, but the separation is nevertheless obvious. The segregation may be physical—a separate area of the city—or it may be social as when people living together are constrained in how and with whom they may interact. Segregation (from the minority's viewpoint) may be involuntary—blacks in America—or voluntary. Avoidance (voluntary self-segregation) occurs when a culture such as the Amish in America wants to maintain its identity and uniqueness against the onslaught of the dominant culture and therefore voluntarily separates itself.

Assimilation and amalgamation represent less violent patterns of interaction between unlike groups. **Assimilation** refers to the mixing and merging of unlike cultures so that two groups come to have a common culture. When two cultures meet, one outcome would be that each culture adopts some of the other's traits so that the result is a true melting pot—the emergence of a new culture different from either of the old cultures. More often, however, assimilation means that the incoming or minority culture adapts to the dominant culture. **Amalgamation** refers to biological (rather than cultural) mixing. Amalgamation seems invariably to accompany the meeting of racial and ethnic groups, despite the best efforts of some societies (the United States, for example) to legislate against it. The **marginal person** is defined as a person who is between two antagonistic cultures, a product of both but a member of neither. Studies indicate that in some cases the consequences of marginality may be severe—personality disturbance, feelings of inferiority. Marginality is often defined as a product of amalgamation, but it may also result from cultural mixing (the Southern rural migrant to the urban North, for example).

Cultural pluralism describes a pattern of interaction in which unlike cultures maintain their own identity and yet interact with each other relatively peacefully. Switzerland is usually cited as the best example of pluralism in that peoples of several nationalities and religions and even three or four different languages are able to get along peacefully. According to Brewton Berry, few countries have been able to successfully accomplish a system of pluralism. Some minorities at some times in the United States have voiced a preference for cultural pluralism, but the dominant culture seems to look either toward integration or toward discrimination and segregation.

Minority Group Reactions

The patterns of interaction described above are usually dictated by the dominant group. What then of minority group reactions to domination? Gordon Allport has outlined some types of reactions in his book, *The Nature of Prejudice.* [13] The simplest response is to *deny membership* in the minority group—members of one race pass as members of another, people change their names to get rid of their ethnic identification. Similarly, **acculturation** refers to attempts by members of minority groups to assimilate, to blend in and take on as many characteristics of the dominant culture as possible. Hiding resentment in *withdrawal* and passivity—"a mask of

[13]See Gordon Allport, *The Nature of Prejudice* (Garden City, N.Y.: Doubleday, 1958) Chapter 9.

contentment"—is another reaction *Secession* refers to the formal withdrawal of a group of people from a political, religious, or national union. The South seceded prior to the Civil War, and the citizens of Quebec have been considering secession from the rest of Canada. *Self-hatred* may develop, and the minority group may then identify with the dominant group. Studies of Nazi concentration camps showed that after years of suffering, inmates began identifying with the guards. The prisoners wore bits of the guards' clothing, they became anti-Semitic, and in general they adopted the mentality of the oppressor. Likewise, if blacks value light skin more than dark, they may be accepting whites' evaluation of skin pigmentation. Self-hate may lead to aggression against one's own group, as when a segment of the minority that thinks of itself as being a higher class takes out its frustrations on a lower-ranked segment. Minorities sometimes show greater *prejudice* against other minorities, and in other cases the opposite reaction—greater *sympathy.*

A *strengthening of in-group ties* is another reaction of minorities to domination. **Nativism** is a type of rejection of the dominant culture in which people attempt to improve their own existence by eliminating all foreign persons, objects, and customs. This has been seen recently in the United States with slogans such as "Black Power" and "Don't buy where you can't work," and by the focus on the development of ethnic identity through emphasizing the minority's cultural and historical roots. Minorities may react to domination by using *aggression.* The aggression may be individual and reflected in crime patterns, or it can be collective and culminate in urban disturbances or riots. In milder form, the aggression may appear in the literature and humor of the minority group as it makes fun of or shows its bitterness toward the majority group. In fact, humor is a common way of expressing feelings about other groups. In the following not very representative examples, who is putting down whom?

> A black woman from Harlem wins the Irish sweepstakes and decides to buy a fur coat. She tries on a coat at Saks Fifth Avenue and it comes down to her ankles. As she looks at herself in the mirror, she turns to the saleslady and says, "Do you think this makes me look too Jewish?"
>
> A priest and a rabbi are each driving down a New York street. The rabbi stops at a light and the priest runs into him. An Irish cop comes up to the priest and asks, "Ah Father, how fast might the rabbi have been going when he backed into you?"
>
> Dick Gregory: "I sat in at this place for three years and when they finally waited on me I found out they didn't have what I wanted."
>
> What do you have when you cross a WASP and a chimpanzee? A three foot tall, blond company president.

Female and Male

Is a person upper-middle class or lower-middle class? Is an American Indian a white? Difficult questions, but female and male—no problem at all with the sex category. There are arguments over how many social classes exist, to say nothing of the problem of determining the social class of a particular individual. The answer depends on the variables and method of analysis that are used. The boundaries of race and ethnicity are blurred—in many cases the best answer seems to be that people are what they define themselves to be. Sex categories are more easily defined, at least biologically. This is one distinction that people have felt confident about for ages. And if occasional doubts do pop up, a scientific test can be applied. One of the more intriguing parts of the Olympics is the sex test that is used to make sure that males are not masquerading as females.

The paradox in this situation is that although people confidently feel and always have felt that they have a clear grasp of the biological fact, until recently few have considered the *social* consequences of sex differences. Karl Marx wrote about the consequences of social-class differences over one hundred years ago, and he wasn't the first. The consequences of racial differences have been a central issue in the United States for decades. But the consequences of the minority status produced by sex differences have only recently—perhaps in the last ten years— become a topic drawing widespread and serious attention.

Socialization and Sex Roles

Thirty pairs of parents were questioned within twenty-four hours after the birth of their first child and were asked to "describe your baby as you would to a close relative." Hospital information on the babies showed that the fifteen boy babies and the fifteen girl babies *did not differ* on such objective data as birth length, weight, irritability, etc. But the parents said that girl babies were softer, littler, more beautiful, prettier, finer featured, cuter, and more inattentive than the boy babies. The fathers tended to label or stereotype the babies in this fashion more than the mothers. The authors of the study suggest that sex-typing, and sex-role socialization have already begun at birth.[14]

How could this be? One day after birth and already babies are showing definite sex differences in terms of physical appearance and temperament. The answer, of course, is that *it isn't so.* People assume that males and females are born with different abilities and temperaments. People assume it to be so, and then behave as if it *were* so. We tend to act toward children one way if they are male, another way if they are female. We expect them to be a certain way, and they turn out that way. The self-fulfilling prophecy rides again.

To place the assumption about so-called inherited sexual characteristics in correct perspective, recall Margaret Mead's description of sex and temperament among the Arapesh, Mundugumor, and Tchambuli (page 68). There was great variety in the behavior of the sexes in those societies. Compared with sex roles in America, roles were modified and reversed. The explanation is not that these societies are strange and peculiar, but more simply that the sex roles learned in those societies are different from those learned here.

Like other roles, sex roles are learned through the socialization process. It is possible that in our society the teaching of sex roles starts even earlier than the teaching of other roles. As we saw above, parents immediately start acting differently toward their children based on their sex. Look at their toys: Boys get tractors,

---

[14]Jeffrey Rubin, Frank Provenzano, and Zella Luria, "The Eye of the Beholder: Parents' Views on Sex of New Borns," *American Journal of Orthopsychiatry* 44 (July 1974), pp. 512–519.

trucks, tools, guns, athletic equipment; girls get dolls, cooking sets, play perfume and cosmetic kits, pretty clothes. Friends and grandparents, scandalized to hear that the mother concerned about sex typing bought her son a doll, were only partly mollified to find that at least it was a boy doll. Few families escape the typing. Our family stopped at a gas station in southern France in which the pumps were operated by a female attendant. Our four-year-old son Jeff studied the situation for a long time and finally said: "What's that lady doing working in the gas station? I don't like it—it doesn't look too good." Jeff's mother: "They can work there too. They can work anywhere." Jeff: "No, they are supposed to go to the store and stuff. . . ." And that from a child of parents who should know better.

The schools continue the pattern. Textbooks from Dick and Jane on up portray boys in active, aggressive, so-called masculine roles and girls in passive, tender, so-called feminine roles. A study of teachers in nursery schools found that they spent more time with the boys in the class than with the girls. Boys were encouraged to work harder on academic subjects. They were given more rewards and more directions in how to do things. Boys were given instructions, then encouraged to complete the task themselves. If the girls did not quickly get the idea, the teacher would often intervene and do the task for them. There was one exception: The teachers did pay more attention to the girls on feminine-sex-typed activities such as cooking. Even here girls got praise and assistance, whereas boys received detailed instructions. The boys were given more attention, and the environment was much more of a learning experience for them than it was for the girls.[15]

Another group of researchers working in the Boston area found that sex-role differences were well developed in the majority of children by the age of five. The children knew which personality traits were "masculine" and which were "feminine." They knew which jobs were for men and which were for women. The

[15]Lisa Serbin and Daniel O'Leary, "How Nursery Schools Teach Girls to Shut Up," *Psychology Today* 9 (December 1975), p. 57.

experimenters developed a curriculum that attempted to make the children more flexible in their assumptions about the sexes. The outcome of the program was mixed. To the researchers' surprise, many of the fifth- and ninth-grade boys with whom they worked became *more* stereotyped in their views of women and more rigid and outspoken about what they thought to be women's place. The effects on the girls in the program were more positive, showing attitude change away from typical stereotypes and increased self-esteem.[16] The researchers are hopeful about the school program they tested, but it's not enough by itself. The socialization agents include family, peers, teachers, literature, entertainment, mass media, and the whole social tradition that socializes people to believe in the inherent psychological, temperamental, and attitudinal differences between the sexes. It should not surprise us at all that boys grow up to be doctors and mechanics and girls grow up to keep house, have babies, and take care of their families. They have been socialized into these roles from the very beginning.

Consequences of Sex-Role Typing

The results of sex-role typing are many and varied, and not all the benefits are for males. The male is restricted in how he may show emotion—he is strong and silent, he does not show weakness, and he keeps his feelings under careful rein, at least outwardly. The female has far greater freedom to express emotion. The male is subject to much more stress and pressure to achieve and be successful. This is probably part of the reason why males have a shorter life expectancy, more heart disease, higher rates of suicide and hospitalization for mental illness and related pathologies. (See Table 6.1, page 170.) Women have been much less involved in crime and deviant behavior than have men, and this too is related to sex-role differences. Some men would like to change roles, to be househusbands, staying home and cooking, working in the garden, and taking care of the kids. What are their chances in a society that sets up sex roles like ours does?

The major consequence of sex-role typing, however, is that women are not able to participate fully in American society, a society in which they make up fifty-one percent of the members. People are becoming more sensitive to the unfairness of this situation, and women's frustration is increasing.

There is ample evidence of the effects of sex typing. Table 6.5 shows the years of education completed by males and females in the U.S. in 1977. An interesting contrast appears. More women then men graduate from high school, but more men

Table 6.5   Years of School Completed by Sex, 1977

	Males	Females
High school graduate	32%	40%
One to three years college	14	13
Four years or more college	19	12

U.S. Bureau of the Census, *Statistical Abstract of the United States, 1978* (99th ed.), Washington, D.C., p. 144.

[16]This research is summarized by Carol Tavris in "It's Tough to Nip Sexism in the Bud," *Psychology Today* 9 (December 1975), p. 58. Ms. Tavris states that the full report of this research by Marcia Guttentag is available in *Undoing Sex Stereotypes* by Marcia Guttentag and Helen Bray (New York: McGraw-Hill, 1976).

go on to and graduate from college. A high school education is seen as adequate for many women, but the ambitious male goes on to improve his career chances.

The percentage of workers with income and how much they earn is shown in Table 6.6. The proportion of men working has not changed much in twenty-seven years, while the proportion of women working has gone up substantially. But now check their income—how fast is that gap closing?

Table 6.6 Median Income of Employed People Over Fourteen, by Sex

	Males		Females	
	Percent with Income	Median Income	Percent with Income	Median Income
1950	90%	$2,570	43%	$ 953
1960	91	4,080	56	1,261
1970	92	6,670	67	2,237
1977	93	10,123	75	3,941

U.S. Bureau of the Census, *Statistical Abstract of the United States, 1978* (99th ed.), Washington, D.C., p. 463.

Next, compare income level for the same occupation, as in Table 6.7. It is apparent that for the same category of job, women are paid far less than men.

Table 6.7 Median Income by Occupation of Year-round Full-time Workers Over Fourteen in 1976, by Sex

	Males	Females
Professional and technical	$16,939	$11,072
Teachers	15,285	11,113
Sales workers	14,586	6,272
Clerical	12,843	8,128
Craft workers	13,638	7,765
Laborers	10,104	7,613

"Money Income in 1976 of Families and Persons in the United States," *Current Population Reports*, Series P–60, no. 114.

Women represent about forty percent of the work force but generally have lower skilled and lower paying jobs. Women are always well represented at the sales and clerical level but seldom higher up. Even when a woman does the same work as a man, she gets paid less for it, as we saw above. There have never been any female Supreme Court justices, and there have been only three female Cabinet members. Women represent more than fifty percent of the nation's registered voters but hold five percent of the elective positions. In 1977 there were eighteen women in the House of Representatives (out of more than four hundred), and in 1979 there was one woman in the Senate (out of one hundred). Women make up about seven percent of the nation's lawyers and about nine percent of the nation's doctors. Women constitute eight-five percent of the elementary school teachers but only twenty-one percent of the principals; in high schools the number of female principals drops to three percent. Female representation in higher education follows the same pattern. In 1976 women were well over fifty percent of the high school graduates, but they accounted for only forty-four percent of the bachelor's degrees, forty-six percent of the master's degrees, and twenty-three percent of the doctorates.

Is Change Coming?

Instead of citing "Man of the Year" as usual, in 1975 *Time* gave its annual award to "Women of the Year" in recognition of gains that certain women specifically and the women's movement in general had made in the past two or three years. Gains cited for women by late 1975 included the following: According to a Harris poll, Americans favored "most of the efforts to strengthen and change women's status in society" by a margin of sixty-three percent to twenty-five percent. Five years previously when the same question had been asked, it was forty-two percent to forty-one percent. The first woman state governor had been elected (Grasso, Connecticut) and there was a woman on the President's Cabinet (Hills, Department of Housing and Urban Development). Women's enrollment in business schools (the path to top management positions) was up sharply between 1971 and 1975—five to nineteen percent at Stanford, six to thirty-three percent at Columbia. Numbers of women going to medical school and law school are increasing as well. In 1975, twenty-five percent of entering medical students were women compared to eleven percent in 1971. In law school the percentage rose from eight and one-half percent to twenty percent.

Change has also occurred in other areas. The United Methodist Church had ordained nearly 600 women by 1975, up from 300 in 1970; the United Presbyterian Church has ordained over 200 women, compared with about 100 in 1972. Ninety-two percent of the jobs in the military are now open to women, and of 2.1 million people in the military in 1977, some 119,000 (six percent) were women.[17] Many police departments across the country now have women in jobs equal to those of male police officers. Women's participation in organized sports is increasingly legitimized. Women are finally eligible to win large prizes on the professional tennis circuit, and girls are participating in soccer and baseball Little Leagues. Even in crime, where males have a substantial lead, women seem to be struggling toward parity. Arrests of males were up thirteen percent between 1968 and 1977; arrests of females for the same period were up fifty-eight percent.[18]

Is equality, then, just around the corner? Obviously not. Look back at the facts —forty-nine governors are male, ninety-three percent of the nation's lawyers and eighty percent of the law school students are males, and so on. A few women get there; most do not. In 1978, *Fortune* Magazine conducted a survey of the 1,300 top companies and found only one chief executive (Katherine Graham of the Washington Post Co.) and only ten female high executives out of a total of 6,400 officers and directors. Further, the number isn't growing—in the previous survey in 1973,

[17]Much of the data in this and the previous two paragraphs comes from *Time*, 5 January 1976, pp. 6–16. *Statistical Abstract of the United States*, 1978 has also been helpful.

[18]Information on arrests comes out from the *Uniform Crime Reports*, 1978, which is put out annually by the FBI.

there were eleven women on the list.[19] Often, the achievements of the successful are widely publicized, perhaps unintentionally giving the impression of great gains. Even those women who are successful inevitably have horror stories to tell of the subtle pressure and overt discrimination used against them. A woman is still usually paid less than a man for the same work, regardless of level.

Although the Equal Rights Amendment (ERA) was close to ratification in 1979 with only three more states needed, it was stalled, and it appeared that it might not gain the necessary votes. Help came in 1978 when Congress granted an extension of the ratification period to July 1982. There seem to be several reasons why the ERA has had trouble in being ratified. According to Gloria Steinem, those in favor of the amendment felt it couldn't fail to pass and did not work hard enough to get out the vote. There is also some uncertainty about the consequences of enactment of the amendment. Some feminists and some lawyers are dubious about its quality and feel that it might not work toward the best interests of the women's movement. Finally, there are factional disputes and differences of opinion among women. Some who value the traditional wife-and-mother role fear the amendment and have organized against it. Besides being an honest reflection of how many women feel about the situation, this allows many legislators to get themselves off the hook by directing attention away from their own prejudices to "the wishes of my constituents."

The greatest success of the women's movement has been in raising people's awareness of the existence of sex-role stereotypes and sex discrimination. Change is occurring, and the progress in reducing education and job discrimination is consistent if not dramatic. Changing traditional patterns of socialization for the young and resocializing adults is difficult at best. Even sociologists (who should know better) are culprits. As recently as ten years ago the subject was foreign to us—it was seldom a textbook topic or a research interest. We weren't paying any attention either.

But change is coming. Lucy Komisar of NOW said several years ago, "If the 1960s belonged to the blacks, the next ten years are ours." Some who look at the gains of the past several years congratulate themselves that the glass of equality is now half full. Many others observe more somberly that the glass is still half empty.

The Elderly

Airline pilots are protesting policies that stipulate mandatory retirement at age sixty. Hope Bagger at the age of seventy was called for jury duty but then told to go home because she was too old. Mrs. Bagger, now eighty-six, is an active member of the Gray Panthers, an organization seeking to remedy the way society treats old people. In some parts of the world old age is seen as a virtue, life in its very highest

---

[19]*Fortune* 98 (July 17, 1978), p. 59, includes detailed sketches of the ten who made it.

form. The elderly are revered and are well cared for by society as a whole. In this country the elderly find that they are forced to retire, have trouble getting other jobs, and are exploited if they do get work. As one member of the Gray Panthers put it, the young seem to feel that old people descended from outer space. They forget that the elderly have a past and a future.

A baby born in 1900 had a life expectancy of forty-eight years; a child born today has a life expectancy of more than seventy years. There were 23.5 million people sixty-five and older in the United States in 1977, and the number will continue to increase. Many of the elderly are poor and out of work, over fifty percent are widowed, the suicide rate of older males is high, and age often compounds the effects of other minority statuses.

Aging affects people both physically and socially. In a general sense, physical aging begins in people around the age of thirty and continues throughout the life span. Certain body functions, muscle tone and strength, and the senses all reach their peaks around thirty and decline thereafter. Although many people tend to view it as such, aging is not a disease. People are more likely to die as they get older because the body becomes more vulnerable to outside influences, less adaptable, and more affected by stress and crisis.[20]

Social aging is more treacherous, yet potentially easier to deal with than physical aging. Social aging refers to the attitudes we have about older people. We are indoctrinated with the idea that the old are different and inferior from the rest of us. We stereotype the aged, and they are victims of prejudice and discrimination. In fact, American society treats the elderly with the same sort of stereotyping, the same institutionalized discrimination as that based on sex and race. The old are thought to be unintelligent, asexual, unemployable, mentally ill, and hard to get along with. The fact that many if not most older people are *not* this way is beside the point. We continue to retire them before they want to, refuse to hire them, and pay them less when they do get a job. And the self-fulfilling prophecy suggests to us that if people are viewed and treated a certain way long enough, they tend to become that way.

What do the elderly want? Our stereotypes about aging again help us. A life of leisure—sit out the last twenty years on the porch swing or in front of the tube. Grow old gracefully. A time of disengagement. Relax now—the important things are done. On the contrary, to remain in optimal health old people need what people need: work to do, money to live on, a place to live in, and other people to care whether they live or die. Society should recognize that the elderly are an important resource.[21]

As with other victims of minority status before them, the elderly are becoming politically active. It probably starts with consciousness raising and moves to more militant stands on issues through collective action. Groups like the Gray Panthers,

[20]Anita Harbert and Leon Ginsberg, *Human Services for Older Adults: Concepts & Skills* (Belmont, Calif.: Wadsworth, 1979), Chapters 1 and 2.

[21]Alexander Comfort, "Age Prejudice in America," *Social Policy*, November/December 1976, pp. 3–8.

the National Retired Teachers Association, the National Council of Senior Citizens, and the American Association of Retired Persons have formed a gray lobby of enormous strength in Washington. They have not lost a major campaign. The gray lobby defeated the AMA on Medicare, the big businesses on forced retirement, and the taxpayer groups on social security.[22]

It is important, then, that the elderly not be viewed as recent arrivals from outer space. They *do* have a past and a future. And remember that unlike other minority statuses, this is one that is going to happen to *all* of us—if we're fortunate.

SUMMARY

This is the second of two chapters on social differentiation. Here we examined the characteristics of race, ethnic, and sex categories. Social differentiation refers to the dividing of people into categories according to some social or biological characteristic such as race, sex, social class, or religion. We found earlier that social differentiation often leads to social stratification. That is, these categories are ranked; some are seen as better than others.

One common theme that runs through the discussion of these categories is that of minority status. The fact that categories are ranked and the consequences of this ranking to those who are on the *low* end of it were the central topics of this chapter. Prejudice, discrimination, and stereotyping are commonly used to reaffirm the status ranking that one believes in. They help people keep others "in their place." We examined the types of reactions that occur when populations of different races or ethnic backgrounds meet as well as the reactions of minority groups to discrimination.

We examined a number of statistical examples of differential treatment— differences in education, jobs, income, life chances, crime and deviant behavior, sickness, and others. Less easily statistically displayed but more important as a human concern is the effect that continued differential treatment has on *how one sees onself.* Some concepts studied earlier—socialization, role, self-concept, self-fulfilling prophecy—help us understand the critical significance of minority status for the individual's development.

The first of the readings that follow, an excerpt from John Howard Griffin's *Black Like Me,* describes the interaction of people who are racially different. In the second reading, Sandra Bem summarizes her research on the differences between sex-typed and androgynous males and females. The final reading is an excerpt from *Bury My Heart At Wounded Knee,* a book by Dee Brown, which describes the consequences for the American Indians of the western expansion of the United States between 1860 and 1890.

[22]David H. Fischer, "Books Considered," *The New Republic,* December 2, 1978, pp. 31–36.

Reading 6.1
Black Like Me

JOHN HOWARD GRIFFIN

Race relations—relationships between people of differing racial categories—is a major area of sociological study. Often the focus is on the
prejudice and discrimination that occur when people who differ by race or
ethnicity come in contact with each other. Prejudice ignores the individual
and his or her particular qualities or characteristics and groups the person
with others who happen to have the same skin color, have the same
religious beliefs, come from the same part of the country or world, or have
some other characteristic in common. Discrimination refers to actual behavior unfavorable to a specific individual or group.

The following is from John Howard Griffin's book *Black Like Me.*
Griffin is a white man who temporarily darkened his skin with chemicals
and then traveled through the Deep South as a black.

November 14

In the bus station lobby, I looked for signs indicating a colored waiting room,
but saw none. I walked up to the ticket counter. When the lady ticket-seller saw
me, her otherwise attractive face turned sour, violently so. This look was so unexpected and so unprovoked I was taken aback.

"What do you want?" she snapped.

Taking care to pitch my voice to politeness, I asked about the next bus to
Hattiesburg.

She answered rudely and glared at me with such loathing I knew I was receiving what the Negroes call "the hate stare." It was my first experience with it. It is
far more than the look of disapproval one occasionally gets. This was so exagger-
atedly hateful I would have been amused if I had not been so surprised.

I framed the words in my mind: "Pardon me, but have I done something to
offend you?" But I realized I had done nothing—my color offended her.

"I'd like a one-way ticket to Hattiesburg, please," I said and placed a ten-dollar
bill on the counter.

"I can't change that big a bill," she said abruptly and turned away, as though
the matter were closed. I remained at the window, feeling strangely abandoned but
not knowing what else to do. In a while she flew back at me, her face flushed, and
fairly shouted: "I *told* you—I can't change that big a bill."

"Surely," I said stiffly, "in the entire Greyhound system there must be some
means of changing a ten-dollar bill. Perhaps the manager—"

She jerked the bill furiously from my hand and stepped away from the window. In a moment she reappeared to hurl my change and the ticket on the counter

with such force most of it fell on the floor at my feet. I was truly dumbfounded by this deep fury that possessed her whenever she looked at me. Her performance was so venomous, I felt sorry for her. It must have shown in my expression, for her face congested to high pink. She undoubtedly considered it a supreme insolence for a Negro to dare to feel sorry for her.

I stooped to pick up my change and ticket from the floor. I wondered how she would feel if she learned that the Negro before whom she had behaved in such an unladylike manner was habitually a white man.

With almost an hour before bus departure, I turned away and looked for a place to sit. The large, handsome room was almost empty. No other Negro was there, and I dared not take a seat unless I saw some other Negro also seated.

Once again a "hate stare" drew my attention like a magnet. It came from a middle-aged, heavy-set, well dressed white man. He sat a few yards away, fixing his eyes on me. Nothing can describe the withering horror of this. You feel lost, sick at heart before such unmasked hatred, not so much because it threatens you as because it shows humans in such an inhuman light. You see a kind of insanity, something so obscene the very obscenity of it (rather than its threat) terrifies you. It was so new I could not take my eyes from the man's face. I felt like saying: "What in God's name are you doing to yourself?"

A Negro porter sidled over to me. I glimpsed his white coat and turned to him. His glance met mine and communicated the sorrow, the understanding.

"Where am I supposed to go?" I asked him.

He touched my arm in that mute and reassuring way of men who share a moment of crisis. "Go outside and around the corner of the building. You'll find the room."

The white man continued to stare, his mouth twisted with loathing as he turned his head to watch me move away.

In the colored waiting room, which was not labeled as such, but rather as *Colored Café,* presumably because of interstate travel regulations, I took the last empty seat. The room was crowded with glum faces, faces dead to all enthusiasm, faces of people waiting.

December 1

I developed a technique of zigzagging back and forth. In my bag I kept a damp sponge, dyes, cleansing cream and Kleenex. It was hazardous, but it was the only way to traverse an area both as Negro and white. As I traveled, I would find an isolated spot, perhaps an alley at night or the brush beside a highway, and quickly apply the dye to face, hands and legs, then rub off and reapply until it was firmly anchored in my pores. I would go through the area as a Negro and then, usually at night, remove the dyes with cleansing cream and tissues and pass through the same area as a white man.

I was the same man, whether white or black. Yet when I was white, I received the brotherly-love smiles and the privileges from whites and the hate stares or obsequiousness from the Negroes. And when I was a Negro, the whites judged me fit for the junk heap, while the Negroes treated me with great warmth.

As the Negro Griffin, I walked up the steep hill to the bus station in Montgomery to get the schedule for buses to Tuskegee. I received the information from a polite clerk and turned away from the counter.

"Boy!" I heard a woman's voice, harsh and loud.

I glanced toward the door to see a large, matriarchical woman, elderly and impatient. Her pinched face grimaced and she waved me to her.

"Boy, come here. Hurry!"

Astonished, I obeyed.

"Get those bags out of the cab," she ordered testily, seeming outraged with my lack of speed.

Without thinking, I allowed my face to spread to a grin as though overjoyed to serve her. I carried her bags to the bus and received three haughty dimes. I thanked her profusely. Her eyebrows knitted with irritation and she finally waved me away.

I took the early afternoon bus for Tuskegee, walked through a Southern town of great beauty and tranquility. The famed Tuskegee Institute was, I learned, out of the city limits. In fact the major portion of the Negro residential area is out of the city limits—put there when the city fathers decided it was the simplest way to invalidate the Negro vote in local elections.

The spirit of George Washington Carver hangs strongly over the campus—a quiet, almost hauntingly quiet area of trees and grass. It radiates an atmosphere of respect for the work of one's hands and mind, of human dignity. In interviews here, my previous findings were confirmed: with the exception of those trained in professions where they can set up independent practice, they can find jobs commensurate with their education only outside the South. I found an atmosphere of great courtesy, with students more dignified and more soberly dressed than one finds on most white campuses. Education for them is a serious business. They are so close to the days when their ancestors were kept totally illiterate, when their ancestors learned to read and write at the risk of severe punishment, that learning is an almost sacred privilege now. They see it also as the only possible way out of the morass in which the Negro finds himself.

Later that afternoon, after wandering around the town, I turned back toward the Institute to talk with the dean. A white man stood in front of a Negro recreation parlor near the college entrance gates and waved to me. I hesitated at first, fearing he would be just another bully. But his eyes pleaded with me to trust him.

I crossed slowly over to him.

"Did you want me?" I asked.

"Yes—could you tell me where is Tuskegee Institute?"

"Right there," I said, pointing to the gates a block away.

"Aw, I know it," he grinned. I smelled whisky in the fresh evening air. "I was just looking for an excuse to talk to you," he admitted. "Do you teach here?"

"No, I'm just traveling through," I said.

"I'm a Ph.D.," he said uncomfortably. "I'm from New York—down here as an observer."

"For some government agency?"

"No, strictly on my own," he said. I studied him closely, since other Negroes were beginning to watch us. He appeared to be in his early fifties and was well enough dressed.

"How about you and me having a drink?" he said.

"No, thanks," I said and turned away.

"Wait a minute, dammit. You people are my brothers. It's people like me that are your only hope. How do you expect me to observe if you won't talk to me?"

"Very well," I said. "I'll be glad to talk with you."

"Hell, I've observed all I can stomach," he said. "Let's us go get just roaring blinko drunk and forget all this damned prejudice stuff."

"A white man and a Negro," I laughed. "We'd both hear from the merciful Klan."

"Damned right—a white man and a Negro. Hell, I don't consider myself any better than you—not even as good, maybe. I'm just trying to show some brotherhood."

Though I knew he had been drinking, I wondered that an educated man and an observer could be so obtuse—could create such an embarrassing situation for a Negro.

"I appreciate it," I said stiffly. "But it would never work."

"They needn't know," he whispered, leaning close to me, an almost frantic look in his eyes as though he were begging not to be rejected. "I'm going to get soused anyway. Hell, I've had all this I can stand. It's just between you and me. We could go into the woods somewhere. Come on—for brotherhood's sake."

I felt great pity for him. He was obviously lonely and fearful of rejection by the very people he sought to help. But I wondered if he could know how offensive this over-weaning "brotherhood" demonstration was. Others stood by and watched with frowns of disapproval.

At that moment a Negro drove up in an old car and stopped. Ignoring the white man, he spoke to me. "Would you like to buy some nice fat turkeys?"

"I don't have any family here," I said.

"Wait a minute there," the white man said. "Hell, I'll buy all your turkeys . . . just to help out. I'll show you fellows that not all white men are bastards. How many've you got in there?" We looked into the car and saw several live turkeys in the back seat.

"How much for all of them?" the white man asked, pulling a ten-dollar bill from his wallet.

The vendor looked at me, puzzled, as though he did not wish to unload such a baggage on the generous white man.

"What can you do with them when you get them out of the car?" I asked.

"What're you trying to do," the white man asked belligerently, "kill this man's sale?"

The vendor quickly put in: "No . . . no, mister, he's not trying to do that. I'm glad to sell you all the turkeys you want. But where you want me to unload them? You live around here?"

"No, I'm just an observer. Hell, take the ten dollars. I'll give the damned turkeys away."

When the vendor hesitated, the white man asked: "What's the matter—did you steal them or something?"

"Oh, no sir . . ."

"You afraid I'm a cop or something?"

The unpardonable had been said. The white man, despite his protestations of brotherhood, had made the first dirty suggestion that came to his mind. He was probably unaware of it but it escaped none of us. By the very tone of his question he revealed his contempt for us. His voice had taken on a hard edge, putting us in our place, as they say. He had become just like the whites he decried.

"I didn't steal them," the turkey man said coldly. "You can come out to my farm. I've got more there."

The white man, sensing the change, the resentment, glared at me. "Hell, no wonder nobody has any use for you. You don't give a man a chance to be nice to you. And damn it, I'm going to put that in my report." He turned away grumbling. "There's something 'funny' about all of you." Then he raised his head toward the evening sky and announced furiously: "But before I do anything else, I'm going to get drunk, stinking drunk."

He stamped off down the road toward open country. Negroes around me shook their heads slowly, with regret. We had witnessed a pitiful one-man attempt to make up for some of the abuses the man had seen practiced against the Negro. It had failed miserably. If I had dared, I would have gone after him and tried to bridge the terrible gap that had come between him and us.

Instead, I walked to the street lamp and wrote in my notebook.

"We must return to them their lawful rights, assure equality of justice—and then everybody leave everybody else to hell alone. Paternalistic—we show our prejudice in our paternalism—we downgrade their dignity."

It was too late to visit the dean of Tuskegee, so I went to the bus station and boarded a bus for Atlanta, via Auburn, Alabama.

The trip was without incident until we changed buses at Auburn. As always, we Negroes sat at the rear. Four of us occupied the back bench. A large, middle-aged Negro woman sat in front of us to the left, a young Negro man occupied the seat in front of us to the right.

At one of the stops, two white women boarded and could find no place to sit. No gallant Southern white man (or youth) rose to offer them a place in the "white section."

The bus driver called back and asked the young Negro man and the middle-aged Negro woman to sit together so the white women could have one of the seats. Both ignored the request. We felt the tensions mount as whites craned to stare at us.

A redheaded white man in a sports shirt stood up, faced the rear and called to the Negro. "Didn't you hear the driver? Move out, man."

"They're welcome to sit here," the Negro said quietly, indicating the empty seat beside him and the one beside the woman across the aisle.

The driver looked dumbfounded and then dismayed. He walked halfway to the rear and, struggling to keep his voice under control, said: "They don't want to sit with you people, don't you know that? They don't want to—is that plain enough?"

We felt an incident boiling, but none of us wanted the young Negro, who had paid for his ticket, to be forced to vacate his seat. If the women did not want to sit with us, then let one of the white men offer his seat and he could come and sit with us. The young Negro said no more. He gazed out the window.

The redhead bristled. "Do you want me to slap these two jigaboos out of their seats?" he asked the driver in a loud voice.

We winced and turned into mummies, staring vacantly, insulating ourselves against further insults.

"No—for God's sake—please—no rough stuff," the driver pleaded.

One of the white women looked toward us apologetically, as though she were sorry to be the cause of such a scene. "It's all right," she said. "Please . . ." asking the driver and the young man to end their attempts to get her a seat.

The redhead flexed his chest muscles and slowly took his seat, glaring back at us. A young teen-ager, sitting halfway to the front, sniggered: "Man, he was going to slap that nigger, all right." The white bully was his hero, but other whites maintained a disapproving silence.

At the Atlanta station we waited for the whites to get off. One of them, a large middle-aged man, hesitated, turned and stepped back toward us. We hardened ourselves for another insult. He bent over to speak to the young Negro. "I just wanted to tell you that before he slapped you, he'd have had to slap me down first," he said.

None of us smiled. We wondered why he had not spoken up while whites were still on the bus. We nodded our appreciation and the young Negro said gently: "It happens to us all the time."

"Well, I just wanted you to know—I was on your side, boy." He winked, never realizing how he had revealed himself to us by calling our companion by the hated name of "boy." We nodded wearily in response to his parting nod.

I was the last to leave the bus. An elderly white man, bald and square of build, dressed in worn blue work clothes, peered intently at me. Then he crimped his face as though I were odious and snorted, "Phew!" His small blue eyes shone with repugnance, a look of such unreasoning contempt for my skin that it filled me with despair.

It was a little thing, but piled on all the other little things it broke something in me. Suddenly I had had enough. Suddenly I could stomach no more of this degradation—not of myself but of all men who were black like me. Abruptly I turned and walked away. The large bus station was crowded with humanity. In the men's room, I entered one of the cubicles and locked the door. For a time I was safe, isolated; for a time I owned the space around me, though it was scarcely more than that of a coffin. In medieval times, men sought sanctuary in churches. Nowadays, for a nickel, I could find sanctuary in a colored rest room. Then, sanctuary had the smell of incense-permeated walls. Now it had the odor of disinfectant.

The irony of it hit me. I was back in the land of my forefathers, Georgia. The town of Griffin was named for one of them. Too I, a Negro, carried the name hated by all Negroes, for former Governor Griffin (no kin that I would care to discover) devoted himself heroically to the task of keeping Negroes "in their place." Thanks in part to his efforts, this John Griffin celebrated a triumphant return to the land from which his people had sprung by seeking sanctuary in a toilet cubicle at the bus station.

I took out my cleansing cream and rubbed it on my hands and face to remove the stain. I then removed my shirt and undershirt, rubbed my skin almost raw with the undershirt, and looked into my hand mirror. I could pass for white again. I repacked my duffel, put my shirt and coat back on and wondered how I could best leave the colored rest room without attracting attention. I guessed it was near midnight, but the traffic in and out remained heavy.

Oddly, there was little of the easy conversation one generally hears in public rest rooms, none of the laughter and "woofing." I waited, listening to footsteps come and go, to the water-sounds of hand-washing and flushing.

Much later, when I heard no more footsteps, I stepped from my cubicle and walked toward the door that led into the main waiting room. I hurried into the crowd unnoticed.

The shift back to white status was always confusing. I had to guard against the easy, semiobscene language that Negroes use among themselves, for coming from a white man it is insulting. It was midnight. I asked a doorman where to find a room for the night. He indicated a neon sign that stood out against the night sky —YMCA, only a block or so away. I realized that though I was well dressed for a Negro, my appearance looked shabby for a white man. He judged me by that and indicated a place where lodging was inexpensive.

Questions 6.1

1. "A caste system accurately describes America's relations between the races...." Discuss.
2. Describe the forms of racism (differential treatment because of race) that took place in the incident with the white "observer" and in the incident on the bus.
3. Analyze and explain Griffin's experiences in terms of (a) prejudice and discrimination, and (b) status differences.

Reading 6.2
Androgyny vs. the Tight Little Lives of Fluffy Women and Chesty Men
SANDRA LIPSITZ BEM

The traditional sex-role structure of our society demands that men be masculine and women be feminine. But not everyone is a victim of this rigid sex typing. Some people are "androgynous," meaning that they describe themselves as having about an equal balance of masculine and feminine traits. How do androgynous and sex-typed people differ? Which type is more adaptable? Which is better adjusted? Which is more restricted in behavior? Sandra Bem's interesting research described in this paper attempts to answer these questions and suggests that the consequences of being androgynous may be very positive for *both* males and females. Dr. Bem is a psychology professor at Stanford University.

In American society, men are supposed to be masculine, women are supposed to be feminine, and neither sex is supposed to be much like the other. If men are independent, tough and assertive, women should be dependent, sweet and retiring. A womanly woman may be tender and nurturant, but no manly man may be so.

For years we have taken these polar opposites as evidence of psychological health. Even our psychological tests of masculinity and femininity reflect this bias: a person scores as *either* masculine *or* feminine, but the tests do not allow a person to say that he or she is both.

I have come to believe that we need a new standard of psychological health for the sexes, one that removes the burden of stereotype and allows people to feel free to express the best traits of men and women. As many feminists have argued, freeing people from rigid sex roles and allowing them to be *androgynous* (from "andro," male, and "gyne," female), should make them more flexible in meeting new situations, and less restricted in what they can do and how they can express themselves.

In fact, there is already considerable evidence that traditional sex typing is unhealthy. For example, high femininity in females consistently correlates with high anxiety, low self-esteem, and low self-acceptance. And although high masculinity in males has been related to better psychological adjustment during adolescence, it is often accompanied during adulthood by high anxiety, high neuroticism, and low self-acceptance. Further, greater intellectual development has quite consistently correlated with cross-sex typing (masculinity in girls, femininity in boys). Boys who are strongly masculine and girls who are strongly feminine tend to have lower overall intelligence, lower spatial ability, and show lower creativity.

In addition, it seems to me that traditional sex typing necessarily restricts behavior. Because people learn, during their formative years, to suppress any behavior that might be considered undesirable or inappropriate for their sex, men are afraid to do "women's work," and women are afraid to enter "man's world." Men are reluctant to be gentle, and women to be assertive. In contrast, androgynous people are not limited by labels. They are able to do whatever they want, both in their behavior and their feelings.

A Measure of Androgyny

I decided to study this question, to see whether sex-typed people really were more restricted and androgynous people more adaptable. Because I needed a way to measure how masculine, feminine, or androgynous a person was, I developed the Bem Sex Role Inventory (BSRI), which consists of a list of 60 personality characteristics: 20 traditionally masculine (ambitious, self-reliant, independent, assertive); 20 traditionally feminine (affectionate, gentle, understanding, sensitive to the needs of others); and 20 neutral (truthful, friendly, likable). I gave a list of 400 such traits to a group of undergraduates, who rated the desirability of each characteristic either "for a man" or "for a woman." I drew the final list for the BSRI from those characteristics that both males and females rated as being significantly more desirable for one sex than for the other.

The masculine, feminine and neutral characteristics appear in random order on the test, and a person indicates on a scale of one ("never or almost never true") to seven ("always or almost always true") how accurate each word is as a self-description. The difference between the total points assigned to masculine and feminine adjectives indicates the degree of a person's sex typing. If masculinity and feminity scores are approximately equal, the individual has an androgynous sex role.

My colleagues and I have given the BSRI to more than 1,500 undergraduates at Stanford University. Semester after semester, we find that about 50 percent of the students adhere to "appropriate" sex roles, about 15 percent are cross-sex typed, and about 35 percent are androgynous.

With the BSRI in hand, we were in a position to find out whether sex-typed people really were restricted and androgynous people really more adaptable. Our strategy was to measure a number of behaviors that were stereotypically either masculine or feminine. We selected these particular actions to represent the very best of what masculinity and femininity have come to stand for, and we felt that any healthy adult should be capable of them. We predicted that sex-typed people would do well only when the behavior was traditionally considered appropriate for his or her sex, whereas those who were androgynous would do well regardless of the sex-role stereotype attached to the particular action.

The masculine behaviors that we selected were independence and assertiveness. The study of independence brought students to the lab for what they thought was an experiment on humor. In fact, they were there to test conformity versus independence of judgment. Karen Rook and Robyn Stickney placed each person in a booth equipped with microphones and earphones, and showed him or her a series of cartoons that had been rated earlier for humorous quality. As a new cartoon appeared on the screen, the students heard the experimenter call on each person in turn for his or her rating. Although they believed that they were hearing each other's voices, they were in fact listening to a preprogrammed tape. To provoke the students into conformity, the tape included 36 trials during which the taped voices answered the experimenter falsely, agreeing that a particular cartoon was funny when it wasn't, or vice versa.

The Limitations of Femininity

We predicted that feminine women would be less independent than anyone else, and we were right. They were far more likely to conform to the incorrect taped judgments than masculine men or androgynous students of either sex. Only 33 percent of the feminine women were very independent (more independent than the average of all students), compared to 70 percent of the masculine and androgynous students.

Jeffrey Wildfogel carried out a similar study to measure assertiveness. He called students on the telephone with an unreasonable request: when would they be willing to spend over two hours, without pay, to fill out a questionnaire about their reactions to various insurance policies for students? At no time did he actually ask *whether* the people he called would be willing to participate. He simply assumed that they would, and asked them to indicate when they would be available.

In this situation, agreeing would cost a person time, effort and inconvenience, but refusing required the student to assert his or her preferences over those of the caller. The preliminary results confirmed our expectation that feminine women would find it harder to be assertive than anyone else. When Wildfogel asked the students later how difficult it was to turn the caller down, 67 percent of the feminine women said that they found it very difficult, compared to only 28 percent of the masculine men and androgynous students.

The feminine behaviors that we selected all measured the extent to which a person was willing to be responsible for or helpful toward another living creature. We expected that this time the masculine men would be at a disadvantage.

In the first study, Jenny Jacobs measured how responsive people were toward a six-week-old kitten. When students came to the lab, Jacobs explained that she wanted to see how different activities would affect their moods. Actually, we wanted only to determine their reaction to the kitten. For one of the activities, therefore, we put a kitten into the room and asked the student to respond to it in any way he or she wished. We simply recorded how often the student touched or petted the kitten. Later on in the experiment, we gave each person the opportunity to do anything in the lab room that he or she wanted: play with the kitten, read magazines, work puzzles, play with a three-dimensional tilting maze, or whatever. This time we measured how much the students played with the kitten when they didn't have to.

As expected, the masculine men were less playful than anyone else. Only nine percent of them showed a high level of playfulness with the kitten, compared to 52 percent of all the other students. But there was an unexpected result: the androgynous women played with the kitten more often than feminine women, who are presumably so fond of small, cuddly things, 64 percent to 36 percent.

Macho Males and Cuddly Babies

We conducted two further tests—this time with human beings instead of kittens. Carol Watson and Bart Astor measured how responsive people would be toward a six-month-old baby. The student thought the study was about babies' reactions to strangers, but actually we observed the students' reactions to the baby. We left each person alone with the infant for 10 minutes while the experimenter and one of the baby's parents watched from a one-way mirror. We recorded what each person did, such as how often he or she talked to the baby, smiled at it, or picked it up. Once again, the masculine men were the least likely to play much with the baby. Only 21 percent of them were highly responsive, compared to half of all the other students. And this time the feminine women did respond warmly, but no more than the androgynous women.

The last experiment, conducted by Wendy Martyna and Dorothy Ginsberg, explored people's reactions to a person with emotional problems. The students came to the lab in pairs for what they thought was a study of acquaintance, and they drew lots so that one would be a "talker" and the other a "listener." In fact, the talker was our confederate who delivered a memorized script of personal problems. The listener was allowed to ask questions or to make comments, but never to shift the focus of the conversation away from the talker. We recorded the listener's reactions, such as how often he or she nodded and made sympathetic comments, and later we asked each listener how concerned he or she felt about the talker's problems.

Again, the masculine men were the least responsive; only 14 percent of them were above average in reacting sympathetically or in showing concern, compared to 60 percent of the other students. And the feminine women reacted most strongly to the talker, showing more concern than even the androgynous women.

The pattern of results for these five experiments suggests that rigid sex roles can seriously restrict behavior. This is especially the case for men. The masculine men did masculine things very well, but they did not do feminine things. They were independent and assertive when they needed to be, but they weren't responsive to the kitten, or the baby, or to a person in need. In other words, they lacked the ability to express warmth, playfulness and concern, important human—if traditionally feminine—traits.

Similarly, the feminine women were restricted in their ability to express masculine characteristics. They did feminine things—played with the baby, responded with concern and support for the troubled talker—but they weren't independent in judgment or assertive of their own preferences. And for some reason, they didn't respond to the kitten; perhaps feminine women also are afraid of animals.

In contrast, the androgynous men and women did just about everything. They could be independent and assertive when they needed to be, and warm and responsive in appropriate situations. It didn't matter, in other words, whether a behavior was stereotypically masculine or feminine; they did equally well on both.

The Rigid Bars of Sex Roles

In order to find out whether sex-typed people actually avoid opposite-sex behavior, Ellen Lenney and I designed a study in which people could choose an action to perform for pay. We said that we were going to photograph them for a later study, and that we didn't care at all how well they did each activity. In fact, we gave them only one minute for each performance, long enough for a convincing photo, but not long enough for them to complete the task.

Then we gave the students 30 pairs of activities, and asked them to select one from each pair to act out for pay. Some of these pairs pitted masculine activities against feminine ones (oiling a hinge versus preparing a baby bottle); some pitted feminine against neutral (winding yarn into a ball versus sorting newspapers by geographical area); and some pitted masculine against neutral (nailing boards together versus peeling an orange).

We predicted that masculine men and feminine women would consistently avoid the activity that was inappropriate for their sex, *even though it always paid more.* We were right. Such individuals were actually ready to lose money to avoid acting in trivial ways that are characteristic of the opposite sex. That was particularly true when the person running the experiment was a member of the opposite sex. In that case, fully 71 percent of the sex-typed students chose highly stereotyped activities compared to only 42 percent of the androgynous students.

We went one step further, because we wondered how sex-typed people would feel about themselves if they *had* to carry out an opposite-sex activity. We asked all the students to perform three masculine, three feminine, and three neutral activities while we photographed them, and then they indicated on a series of scales how each activity made them feel about themselves. Masculine men and feminine women felt much worse than androgynous people about doing a cross-sex task. Traditional men felt less masculine if they had to, say, prepare a baby bottle, and traditional women felt less feminine if they had to nail boards together. When the experimenter was a member of the opposite sex, sex-typed students were especially upset about acting out of role. They felt less attractive and likeable, more nervous and peculiar, less masculine or feminine, and didn't particularly enjoy the experience.

Androgyny Is Destiny

This research persuades me that traditional concepts of masculinity and femininity do restrict a person's behavior in important ways. In a modern complex society like ours, an adult has to be assertive, independent and self-reliant, but traditional femininity makes many women unable to behave in these ways. On the other hand, an adult must also be able to relate to other people, to be sensitive to their needs and concerned about their welfare, as well as to be able to depend on them for emotional support. But traditional masculinity keeps men from responding in such supposedly feminine ways.

Androgyny, in contrast, allows an individual to be both independent and tender, assertive and yielding, masculine and feminine. Thus androgyny greatly expands the range of behavior open to everyone, permitting people to cope more effectively with diverse situations. As such, I hope that androgyny will some day come to define a new and more human standard of psychological health.

Questions 6.2

1. List the behavioral consequences of being masculine men and feminine women. How does self-concept relate to this discussion?
2. How would you produce an androgynous person? Use concepts such as self and socialization in your discussion.
3. Who benefits more from being androgynous, men or women? Why? Argue each side.

Reading 6.3

Wounded Knee

DEE BROWN

In his book, *Bury My Heart at Wounded Knee,* Dee Brown writes about the critical period between 1860 and 1890, the thirty years during which the culture and civilization of the American Indian was destroyed. Brown tells the story in an unusual way—he uses the viewpoint and the words of the victims, the Indians. The story is a haunting and depressing one and includes descriptions of the long walk of the Navahos, the war to save the buffalo, the war for the Black Hills, the flight of the Nez Perces, and Geronimo, the last of the Apache chiefs. The following excerpt from Brown's book describes the end of it, the "battle" at Wounded Knee Creek in South Dakota in late December of 1890. The Indians' lands were gone then, their chiefs were dead or imprisoned, their own numbers decimated by thirty years of battles, by disease, by living on crowded reservations in unfamiliar places, and by heartbreak. In early December 1890 the great chief Sitting Bull was assassinated. Then . . .

As soon as Big Foot learned that Sitting Bull had been killed, he started his people toward Pine Ridge, hoping that Red Cloud could protect them from the soldiers. En route, he fell ill of pneumonia, and when hemorrhaging began, he had to travel in a wagon. On December 28, as they neared Porcupine Creek, the Minneconjous sighted four troops of cavalry approaching. Big Foot immediately ordered a white flag run up over his wagon. About two o'clock in the afternoon he raised up from his blankets to greet Major Samuel Whitside, Seventh U.S. Cavalry. Big Foot's blankets were stained with blood from his lungs, and as he talked in a hoarse whisper with Whitside, red drops fell from his nose and froze in the bitter cold.

Whitside told Big Foot that he had orders to take him to a cavalry camp on Wounded Knee Creek. The Minneconjou chief replied that he was going in that direction; he was taking his people to Pine Ridge for safety.

Turning to his half-breed scout, John Shangreau, Major Whitside ordered him to begin disarming Big Foot's band.

"Look here, Major," Shangreau replied, "if you do that there is liable to be a fight here; and if there is, you will kill all those women and children and the men will get away from you."

Whitside insisted that his orders were to capture Big Foot's Indians and disarm and dismount them.

"We better take them to camp and then take their horses from them and their guns," Shangreau declared.

"All right," Whitside agreed. "You tell Big Foot to move down to camp at Wounded Knee."

The major glanced at the ailing chief, then gave an order for his Army ambulance to be brought forward. The ambulance would be warmer and would give Big Foot an easier ride than the jolting springless wagon. After the chief was transferred to the ambulance, Whitside formed a column for the march to Wounded Knee Creek. Two troops of cavalry took the lead, the ambulance and wagons following, the Indians herded into a compact group behind them, with the other two cavalry troops and a battery of two Hotchkiss guns bringing up the rear.

Twilight was falling when the column crawled over the last rise in the land and began descending the slope toward Chankpe Opi Wakpala, the creek called Wounded Knee. The wintry dusk and the tiny crystals of ice dancing in the dying light added a supernatural quality to the somber landscape. Somewhere along this frozen stream the heart of Crazy Horse lay in a secret place, and the Ghost Dancers believed that his disembodied spirit was waiting impatiently for the new earth that would surely come with the first green grass of spring.

At the cavalry tent camp on Wounded Knee Creek, the Indians were halted and children counted. There were 120 men and 230 women and children. Because of the gathering darkness, Major Whitside decided to wait until morning before disarming his prisoners. He assigned them a camping area immediately to the south of the military camp, issued them rations, and as there was a shortage of tepee covers, he furnished them several tents. Whitside ordered a stove placed in Big Foot's tent and sent a regimental surgeon to administer to the sick chief. To make certain that none of his prisoners escaped, the major stationed two troops of cavalry as sentinels around the Sioux tepees, and then posted his two Hotchkiss guns on top of a rise overlooking the camp. The barrels of these rifled guns, which could hurl explosive charges for more than two miles, were positioned to rake the length of the Indian lodges.

Later in the darkness of that December night the remainder of the Seventh Regiment marched in from the east and quietly bivouacked north of Major Whitside's troops. Colonel James W. Forsyth, commanding Custer's former regiment, now took charge of operations. He informed Whitside that he had received orders to take Big Foot's band to the Union Pacific Railroad for shipment to a military prison in Omaha.

After placing two more Hotchkiss guns on the slope beside the others, Forsyth and his officers settled down for the evening with a keg of whiskey to celebrate the capture of Big Foot.

The chief lay in his tent, too ill to sleep, barely able to breathe. Even with their protective Ghost Shirts and their belief in the prophecies of the new Messiah, his people were fearful of the pony soldiers camped all around them. Fourteen years before, on the Little Bighorn, some of these warriors had helped defeat some of these soldier chiefs—Moylan, Varnum, Wallace, Godfrey, Edgerly—and the Indians wondered if revenge could still be in their hearts.

"The following morning there was a bugle call," said Wasumaza, one of Big Foot's warriors who years afterward was to change his name to Dewey Beard. "Then I saw the soldiers mounting their horses and surrounding us. It was announced that all men should come to the center for a talk and that after the talk they were to move on to Pine Ridge agency. Big Foot was brought out of his tepee and sat in front of his tent and the older men were gathered around him and sitting right near him in the center."

After issuing hardtack for breakfast rations, Colonel Forsyth informed the Indians that they were now to be disarmed. "They called for guns and arms," White Lance said, "so all of us gave the guns and they were stacked up in the center." The soldier chiefs were not satisfied with the number of weapons surrendered, and so they sent details of troopers to search the tepees. "They would go right into the tents and come out with bundles and tear them open," Dog Chief said. "They brought our axes, knives, and tent stakes and piled them near the guns."

Still not satisfied, the soldier chiefs ordered the warriors to remove their blankets and submit to searches for weapons. The Indians' faces showed their anger, but only the medicine man, Yellow Bird, made any overt protest. He danced a few Ghost Dance steps, and chanted one of the holy songs, assuring the warriors that the soldiers' bullets could not penetrate their sacred garments. "The bullets will not go toward you," he chanted in Sioux. "The prairie is large and the bullets will not go toward you."

The troopers found only two rifles, one of them a new Winchester belonging to a young Minneconjou named Black Coyote. Black Coyote raised the Winchester above his head, shouting that he paid much money for the rifle and that it belonged to him. Some years afterward Dewey Beard recalled that Black Coyote was deaf. "If they had left him alone he was going to put his gun down where he should. They grabbed him and spinned him in the east direction. He was still unconcerned even then. He hadn't his gun pointed at anyone. His intention was to put that gun down. They came on and grabbed the gun that he was going to put down. Right after they spun him around there was the report of a gun, was quite loud. I couldn't say that anyone was shot, but following that was a crash."

"It sounded much like the sound of tearing canvas, that was the crash," Rough Feather said. Afraid-of-the-Enemy described it as a "lightning crash."

Turning Hawk said that Black Coyote "was a crazy man, a young man of very bad influence and in fact a nobody." He said that Black Coyote fired his gun and that "immediately the soldiers returned fire and indiscriminate killing followed."

In the first seconds of violence, the firing of carbines was deafening, filling the air with powder smoke. Among the dying who lay sprawled on the frozen ground was Big Foot. Then there was a brief lull in the rattle of arms, with small groups of Indians and soldiers grappling at close quarters, using knives, clubs, and pistols. As few of the Indians had arms, they soon had to flee, and then the big Hotchkiss guns on the hill opened upon them, firing almost a shell a second, raking the Indian camp, shredding the tepees with flying shrapnel, killing men, women, and children.

"We tried to run," Louise Weasel Bear said, "but they shot us like we were buffalo. I know there are some good white people, but the soldiers must be mean to shoot children and women. Indian soldiers would not do that to white children."

"I was running away from the place and followed those who were running away," said Hakiktawin, another of the young women. "My grandfather and grandmother and brother were killed as we crossed the ravine, and then I was shot on the right hip clear through and on my right wrist where I did not go any further as I was not able to walk, and after the soldier picked me up where a little girl came to me and crawled into the blanket."

When the madness ended, Big Foot and more than half of his people were dead or seriously wounded; 153 were known dead, but many of the wounded crawled away to die afterward. One estimate placed the final total of dead at very nearly three hundred of the original 350 men, women, and children. The soldiers lost twenty-five dead and thirty-nine wounded, most of them struck by their own bullets or shrapnel.

After the wounded cavalrymen were started for the agency at Pine Ridge, a detail of soldiers went over the Wounded Knee battlefield, gathering up Indians who were still alive and loading them into wagons. As it was apparent by the end of the day that a blizzard was approaching, the dead Indians were left lying where they had fallen. (After the blizzard, when a burial party returned to Wounded Knee, they found the bodies, including Big Foot's, frozen into grotesque shapes.)

The wagonloads of wounded Sioux (four men and forty-seven women and children) reached Pine Ridge after dark. Because all available barracks were filled with soldiers, they were left lying in the open wagons in the bitter cold while an inept Army officer searched for shelter. Finally the Episcopal mission was opened, the benches taken out, and hay scattered over the rough flooring.

It was the fourth day after Christmas in the Year of Our Lord 1890. When the first torn and bleeding bodies were carried into the candlelit church, those who were conscious could see Christmas greenery hanging from the open rafters. Across the chancel front above the pulpit was strung a crudely lettered banner: PEACE ON EARTH, GOOD WILL TO MEN.

Questions 6.3

1. Describe the treatment of the Indians in terms of the patterns of interaction described in the text. What is the pattern today?
2. Discuss the concept of Manifest Destiny: What might have caused it to appear? Were there other victims in addition to the Indians? What are the consequences of this doctrine for its adherents as well as its victims? Is this doctrine still with us?
3. Research the Indian situation in your area—what tribe lived there and what happened to them?

7 Institutions

So far we have peered through several windows in order to discover the social organization of society. One view of social organization is through study of the nature and structure of groups. Analysis of the characteristics of categories and social differentiation provides another view. In this chapter, the study of social institutions will provide us with a third perspective.

One way of understanding social institutions as a concept is to describe the emergence of an institution. All societies have certain constant and important central needs or problems that must be dealt with. A society, if it wants to survive, must deal with such issues as reproduction of the species, socialization of the young, distribution of goods and services, care for the sick, and so on. Norms and roles emerge to organize and regulate behavior the society deems appropriate. And so, a system of social

Troeltsch

relationships, a pattern of organization develops. **Social institutions**, then, refer to this organized system of social relationships, common to all societies, which emerges to deal with certain basic problems.[1]

Take an example. The basic societal problem of reproduction of the species leads to the development of particular patterns of behavior. A society supports some of these behaviors (perhaps heterosexual contact) and discourages others (perhaps indiscriminate mating outside of marriage). This reflects the development of norms: consistent views about the way things should and should not be done. The development of these norms and roles whereby the experimental becomes expected, the spontaneous becomes formalized, is the process of *institutionalization*. As this proceeds and the system of social relationships becomes more and more organized, an institutional area emerges—in this case the institution of the *family*.

The study of social organization makes a good deal more sense if we integrate several of the concepts we have studied. For example, merge the concepts of social institutions and groups as in Table 7.1. Certain basic problems lead to the development of corresponding institutional areas. Next, groups perform the functions that are important to the institutional area. Two important factors—the individual's interests and the institutional norms—come together in groups. These groups are of various sizes and complexities—from large, formal organizations to small, personal, primary groups.

Let's follow an example across Table 7.1. People in most societies are concerned with life after death and seek an explanation for the unknown or uncertain in life. Great power or faith may be invested in an idol or a god or a person or an idea. At first experimentally and spontaneously, then more consistently, and finally in a formalized fashion, norms and roles emerge defining behaviors and beliefs felt to be appropriate in that society. This could be called the institutional area of religion. In America the institution of religion is organized around norms favoring Christianity. Groups perform the functions essential to the institutional area. Large organizations such as the Catholic, Presbyterian, and Baptist churches of America, and small groups such as a Wednesday evening Bible study or a Sunday school group make up the *locus* in which individual interests and institutional norms intersect. It is in these groups that the institutional norms are played out. This same pattern is repeated in other institutional areas, as can be seen in the table.

In some institutional areas—particularly the family—smaller groups are all-important and assume the major, almost exclusive, role. In other institutional areas, especially economic and governmental, larger groups play a major role. The important fact, however, is that we can combine group and institution to understand social organization.

As you look at Table 7.1, it becomes apparent that institutional areas are not necessarily separate and isolated from each other. In fact, there is a good deal of overlap between them. Socialization of the young takes place in the family, and in educational and religious institutions as well. Groups from many institutional areas (science, health care, religion, education, leisure, government) fill economic

---

[1] This benefits from the discussion of social institutions by S. N. Eisenstadt in the *International Encyclopedia of the Social Sciences* (New York: Crowell, Collier, and Macmillan, 1968), 14: 409–429.

Table 7.1   Institutions in the United States

Basic Problem or Issue Faced by Society	Institutional Area	Institutional Organization or Large Organizations	Institutional Units or Small Groups
Reproduction of the species	Family	Planned Parenthood; an organization of marriage counselors	My family
Socialization and training of the young	Education	University of California; Boston school system	A kindergarten class; a graduate seminar
Explanation for the unknown or uncertain	Religion	Catholic church; the Council of Churches	Wednesday evening Bible study group; a Sunday school group
Distribution of goods and services	Economics	General Motors; IBM	Several assembly line workers installing brakes on Fords; the steno pool handling the Phillips account
Development of rules and regulations to govern people's behavior	Government	U.S. Senate; State Assembly	Township subcommittee on dogcatching
Use of free time; time away from work	Leisure	Professional Golfers Assoc.; NCAA; Sacramento Recreation Association	A professional basketball team; a bowling team
Care and treatment of the sick	Health care	Massachusetts General Hospital; Kaiser Health Plan	Doctors and nurses on a cardiac ward; technicians in a medical lab
Collection and organization of empirical knowledge	Science	National Science Foundation; Salk Institute	Several astronomers studying the universe; a group of biologists experimenting with virus strains

functions—scientists, doctors, priests, teachers, professional basketball players, and lawyers are earning a living. So these institutional areas are overlapping circles, each intersecting with others in sometimes complicated ways.

Since the institutional areas are interrelated, we should expect that change in one institutional area will be related to change in another. Child labor laws, reform movements, and the organization of labor led to shorter work days and work weeks and much greater free time, which in turn led to the development of the institutional area of leisure. Increased employment of women (economic) has had effects on the family. The increase of women's rights in general is having a tremendous impact as women are admitted and treated as equals in all institutional areas. An economic decline in the 1970s had consequences for higher education—college students became more concerned about getting jobs and moved to business administration and other job-related majors and away from the liberal arts and social sciences. Politicians running for office must contend with the effect of economic factors on voting behavior. When Russia launched its first Sputnik in 1957, many people in the United States became concerned that we had "fallen behind." One response was a renewed emphasis on science in schools: change in one area (education) in order to bring change in another (science). So it is clear that, although we have introduced the institutional areas as separate entities, they are closely related and intersect at many points. As we said earlier, the social organization of society is best seen as a social fabric—a network of norms, roles, and values through which people interact individually and in groups, and this point is evident again as we examine social institutions.

Although the same institutional areas are found in many societies, they may not *look* the same in every society. The mountain-dwelling Arapesh of New Guinea and the campus-dwelling college students of America both operate within the institutional area of the family, for example, which involves elaborate procedures for courtship, marriage, and raising of children, and yet the specific practices of the two societies are vastly different. Not only will the content be different, but the same institutional area in different societies may, at least to an extent, focus on different cultural concerns and serve different functions.

Institutions change, as do all aspects of human behavior. Change in institutions probably occurs more slowly than the behavior and values of smaller elements like groups and individuals. Institutional change also varies from one society to another. To make a comparison of extremes, modern industrialized countries, for the most part, change more rapidly than primitive preliterate societies. Even within one society, one institutional area may change slowly, another rapidly. We will discuss this topic of social change in more detail in Chapter 9.

In summary, social organization can be examined at several levels. We can understand people's behavior by focusing on the dynamics and characteristics of group behavior and on the particular types of groups people belong to. We can also understand behavior by focusing on the attitudes, values, norms, procedures, and symbols that are part of certain institutional areas. Finally, the analysis is improved further by combining concepts and observing that groups operate in the context of the norms, roles, and values of an institutional area. To get a better idea of how the concept of institution is applied to specific areas of human behavior, the remainder of this chapter will examine two institutional areas in more detail: family and religion.

Family

Sociologists have always looked with great interest on the institution of the family. This is mainly because we tend to see the family as the most basic of all institutions, and perhaps also because there are such tremendous variations in family practices from one culture to another. These variations never cease to fascinate people, and ethnocentrism plays a part in this fascination. Many people are convinced that their own way is the right and best way, and they are amazed to find other people behaving differently. This ethnocentrism is unfortunate. Perhaps these issues can be placed in better perspective if we examine cross-culturally some of the similarities and differences in family structure.

Structural Variabilities: How Do Family Structures Differ?

Anthropologists, after studying primitive societies all over the world, report that the structure of the family is almost infinitely variable. Imagine almost anything, and there is probably at least one society someplace that practices it (and the people there would be aghast if they knew the strange things *we* were doing).

It all starts (usually) by mating. This may involve extensive dating leading up to the fateful act. Or a woman may inherit a husband—often a dead sister's widower. Or you may buy a spouse or two. Or you may fall in love. Or you may capture someone. On the east coast of Greenland, the man goes to the woman's tent, grabs her by the hair, and drags her off to his tent. Violent scenes result because single women there always act very shy and resistant to marriage. Otherwise they might lose their reputation for modesty and be considered loose women.

Or parents may have the obligation of arranging marriages for their children. Chinese Empire law from around 1700 stated that a family elder who failed to find a husband for any young woman belonging to his household was condemning her to an unfulfilled life, and was liable to receive publicly eighty blows with the bamboo.[2] In India if a young woman's parents had been unable to find a husband for her as late as three years after she had reached puberty, then she could arrange a marriage for herself, but in doing this she would bring great disgrace on her family. Normally the marriage partner was chosen by the parents together. In China, however, it was typical for the final decision on a prospective husband to be made by the young woman's father, and for the mother to select her son's future wife. Correct order had to be observed in marrying off children—eldest children must be found mates first. This led to problems if the eldest child was unattractive or if younger children were especially attractive and precocious. This in turn forced desperate parents to trickery, switching one daughter for another at the last minute. Recall from the Bible that Jacob thought that he had married Rachel but found out the next morning that the bride that he had spent the night with was her elder sister Leah.

At any rate, whom you may date, buy, inherit, be forced upon, or capture is determined by whether your society practices **endogamy** (marriage within a certain group) or **exogamy** (marriage outside that certain group). In the United States we practice both. We forbid marriage within the immediate family, and it is necessary to marry an outsider: exogamy. At the same time interracial marriages are often discouraged, and some religious groups encourage their members to marry people of the same faith: endogamy. The number of spouses you may have at one time varies depending on the culture in which you live. Two major types of marriage are called monogamy and pologamy. **Monogamy** means one husband for one wife at a time. It is estimated that most people in the world practice monogamy.

[2]The discussion in this paragraph is taken in part from David and Vera Mace, *Marriage: East and West* (Garden City, N.Y.: Doubleday, 1960), pp. 141–142.

The United States is technically monogamous, but with our high rate of divorce and family instability it might be more accurate to say that we practice a type of serial, consecutive, or musical-chairs monogamy. **Polygamy** means plural marriage and includes three types: pologyny, polyandry, and group marriage. **Polygyny** refers to the practice of one man having several wives at a time. G.P. Murdock studied 250 societies and found that polygyny was the preferred form of marriage in seventy-seven percent of them, although, as mentioned above, most people in the world practice monogamy.[3] Even in polygynous societies, most people practice monogamy. Although both sexes favor polygyny in such societies, the wealthy are more able to afford it and are more likely to practice it. **Polyandry** refers to the very rare practice of one woman having several husbands, and group marriage describes the practice of mutual marriage between several men and several women. Polyandry, when it occurs, is usually found in poor societies with a shortage of women. Occasionally such societies kill female babies to keep the population down. When the woman becomes pregnant, deciding which husband is the father is a problem. This is usually solved by some sort of ceremony—possibly by shooting arrows at a distant target and designating the owner of the nearest arrow to be the father.

Family practices vary in many other ways in societies across the world. Where do newlyweds live after marriage? They may be expected to live with the husband's family, or with the wife's family, or to alternate between the husband's and wife's families. In some societies (such as the United States) the couple is expected to live apart from both families. How is ancestry traced? In some societies it's traced through males, in others through females, and in still others through both sides equally. As to who has the formal power and legal authority in the family and makes the decisions, in **patriarchal** societies it is the male and in **matriarchal** societies, the female. It is interesting to note that many of the different practices we have mentioned arise at least partially in reaction to the incest taboo. All societies deny sexual access between certain family members, and these restrictions are called incest taboos. The particular lines of the taboo vary from one society to another. To help regulate the situation, various rules—residence, descent, etc.— were developed. It should be clear by now that almost any imaginable practice exists in some society somewhere. Anything and everything seem to work.

A number of other terms have emerged that help describe aspects of family structure. The family one is born into is called the **family of orientation.** The family of which one is a parent is called the **family of procreation. The nuclear family,** a much-used term today, refers to the married couple and their children. The **conjugal family** is one related by marital ties; the **consanguine family** is one related by blood ties. Finally, **extended** and **compound families** differ from the nuclear family in that the extended family includes more than two generations in close association or under the same roof, and the compound family refers to marriages involving multiple spouses—several wives and/or husbands at the same time.

In summary, we could describe the peculiar American family as a nuclear, monogamous, patriarchal, conjugal, exogamous structure practicing marriage by romance.

[3]George P. Murdock, *Social Structure* (New York: Macmillan, 1949), p. 28.

Functional Uniformities: How Are Families Alike?

The institution of the family exists in all societies in some form. Therefore it must serve a purpose, fill basic needs, and perform essential tasks. Those who have studied family institutions have discovered a number of such functions, some obvious and important and some less obvious. An obvious function of the family is to provide for continuation of the species. Societies, to exist, need people; the institution of the family functions to control reproduction. A second function of the family is control of sex expression. The family institution attempts to deal with powerful sexual needs and desires by defining the who, when, where, why, and how of sexual activity.

A third function of the family is to care for and socialize children. The baby cannot survive without the substantial care that the family provides. Socialization of the young by the family transmits the culture and prepares the child for participation in the adult world. Much of the child's later life is patterned on family models. It is possible that personal pathology and individual unhappiness will follow from inadequate family models or a bad family atmosphere. It may frequently be the case that the child is the defenseless target of the parents' own frustrations, anxieties, neuroses, and maladjustments.

The family may also function to provide close affectional and emotional ties for the individual. In some societies, many groups and associations may perform this function, but in mass, industrialized, secondary societies such as the United States, the family may be one of the few remaining places where primary relationships are possible. The family also functions to provide placement or status ascription. The family we are born into provides us with a *place* in society. If a person is a Protestant, middle-class, Midwestern, American Democrat, it is more than likely to be because he or she inherited certain statuses—religion, social class, region, nationality, political preference—from his or her family of orientation.

These are some of the functions of the family, and there are probably others. These functions are not necessarily completely separate from each other—reproduction of the species and control of sex expression would seem to be related. And further, other institutions may serve some of the same functions the family institution serves. The institution of education certainly deals with socialization of the young and transmission of culture, as does the institution of religion.

Family in America

The American family today is smaller than it used to be in several ways. On the average there are fewer children. The birth rate continued to drop in the early and mid 1970s. It reached a low of 14.8 per 1,000 people in 1976 and then rose slightly in 1977 to 15.3 and was still at that level in mid-1979. Birth control techniques and changing values have led to fewer large families. The American family is also small in that it is a nuclear rather than an extended family. The extended family of a century ago had aunts, uncles, parents, grandparents, and children all assembled under the same roof. Compare that with the nuclear family of today and think of the differences in roles, division of labor, diffusion of responsibilities, child care, expression of affection and emotion, and individual freedom. The change from the extended to the nuclear family brought tremendous changes in the roles of individual family members. The family of today is segregated: Each segment of that large extended family of one hundred years ago now lives by itself as a separate family unit.

Today's family is probably more egalitarian and less patriarchal. People share authority more than they used to, and women are making many of the important decisions. The woman has developed equality in other ways relating to family structure. She is more likely to be working outside the home while married. The possibility of career has given her alternatives to early marriage or even marriage at all. If she does marry, she has a greater choice in the type of role she may play as wife.

The family of today is more urban, more geographically mobile, and less rigid or orthodox in religious beliefs. The family used to be the all-powerful institution, but gradually other institutions—religious, educational, governmental—have become involved in some of the functions that the family formerly handled exclusively. So far this has resulted not in the disappearance of the family but in increased emphasis on or importance of the remaining functions that the family fills and a jealous guarding of them: "Sex education in the schools?? Certainly not! Keep it in the home where it belongs!" As mentioned before, it may be that one of the major functions of the family in mass society is to provide for the affectional and emotional needs of people. The family is nearly the last refuge of the true primary type of relationship, and if it is accurate to call this a basic social need, then this function of the family becomes exceedingly important as other functions decrease in importance.

Pursuing this point a bit further, let's examine a recent study that explored some of the correlates of individual happiness. Angus Campbell conducted an interview survey of 2,000 adults that related people's happiness, satisfaction, and stress to their family situation.[4] Campbell and his colleagues studied nine categories of people in various stages of the life cycle. These categories included young people about to be married, married people with children, married people without children, divorced people, widows, and those who never married. The researchers found that single women were happier than single men. As Campbell puts it, the old stereotype of the carefree bachelor and anxious spinster is backwards; you are more likely to find carefree spinsters and anxious bachelors. The researchers also found that married people were happier and more satisfied with their lives than single (unmarried, divorced, or widowed) people. The newly married without children showed the highest levels of satisfaction. Parenthood produces stress, however—happiness and satisfaction ratings drop when children arrive. The ratings then remain only average until the children are eighteen, and at that point the parents' happiness and satisfaction ratings again begin to rise. Many couples decide to stay childless, and these couples, especially the husbands, report high satisfaction with life and little stress. Campbell and his colleagues found that people whose marriages fail are miserable being single, and most of them remarry soon. Divorce seems to hit women harder as they are forced to work and care for children with little emotional and economic support. They feel the greatest stress and pressure

---

[4]See Angus Campbell, "The American Way of Mating: Marriage Si, Children Only Maybe," *Psychology Today*, vol. 8, no. 12 (May 1975), pp. 37-43. Also see Angus Campbell, Philip Converse and Willard Rodgers, *The Perceived Quality of Life* (New York: Russell Sage, 1975).

of any group. The conclusion? If the findings of this study can be generalized, then it seems that marriage is an important factor in definitions of happiness and satisfaction in life for both sexes. Children put a crimp in things: Happiness levels tend to drop when they arrive, and the desire to have children is apparently decreasing. This research seems to support the idea that a major function of the family today is to provide affectional ties and emotional support to the married couple.

Several dramatic changes have occurred in recent years that may have far-reaching consequences for the future of the family. A 1977 Census Bureau paper reports an increase in the proportion of never-married adults. This trend started in the 1960s and has continued into the 1970s. This is especially notable in age groups where most people have traditionally married. In 1977, forty-five percent of the women and sixty-four percent of the men aged twenty to twenty-four were still single, and the percentage single in the twenty-five to twenty-nine bracket had also increased between 1970 and 1977. People who do marry are marrying later. The median age at first marriage continued to rise in 1977 for both men and women, as can be seen in Table 7.2. The changes are slight from year to year, but this is as high as the median age of marriage has been since the 1940s. The marriage rate reached a low of 10.0 per 1,000 people in 1976. Then it began increasing gradually until in mid-1979 it was 10.4. And finally, the Census Bureau reports that the proportion of never-married young people who maintain their own household has increased. Some are living with others, many are living alone. In 1977, twenty-one percent of American households were one-person households.[5]

Table 7.2 Median Age at First Marriage, by Sex

	Male	Female
1890	26.1	22.0
1930	24.3	21.3
1940	24.3	21.5
1950	22.8	20.3
1956	22.5	20.1
1960	22.8	20.3
1970	23.2	20.8
1975	23.5	21.1
1977	24.0	21.6

U.S. Bureau of the Census, "Marital Status and Living Arrangements: March 1977," *Current Population Reports*, Series P–20, no. 323.

So much for marriage patterns. What about divorce? Marriage and divorce rates in the U.S. are shown in Table 7.3. The divorce rate continues to increase. Between the mid-1950s and the mid-1960s the rate had changed little. After 1965 the divorce rate began to go up, and in the 1970s it increased sharply. There were

[5] Numerous Census Bureau documents were used for this section on marriage and divorce. Especially see "Marital Status and Living Arrangements: March 1977," *Current Population Reports*, Series P-20, no. 323 (Washington, D.C.: U.S. Government Printing Office, 1978); monthly and yearly *Vital Statistics* reports; and *Statistical Abstract of the United States, 1978.*

Table 7.3   Divorce and Marriage in the United States (Rates per
1,000 People)

	Marriage	Divorce
1920	12.0	1.6
1930	9.2	1.6
1940	12.1	2.0
1950	11.1	2.6
1960	8.5	2.2
1970	10.6	3.5
1972	11.0	4.1
1974	10.5	4.6
1976	10.0	5.0
1979 (12 mo.	10.4	5.2
to end of Apr.)		

U.S. Bureau of the Census, *Statistical Abstract of the United States, 1978*
(99th ed.), Washington, D.C., p. 59; and *Vital Statistics.*

1.1 million divorces in 1978 (and 2.2 million marriages). Divorce is rising in many countries, but the United States continues to have one of the highest rates in the world. Why? Among the many explanations offered, the following seem most convincing. Divorce is becoming more and more accepted. It is not the stigma it once was, and people are much more inclined to use it today. Laws have changed. By late 1975, twenty-four states had no-fault divorce laws making divorces much easier to obtain. Another explanation has to do with the emphasis on individuality and happiness. Parties to a marriage that isn't working are less likely to want to stick with it today than they used to be. The view is that if you're not happy, then get out and try again, or try something else. The woman (as well as the man) knows that she has a good chance to make a meaningful life for herself in some other way than by staying in a bad marriage. And with fewer children, perhaps fewer marriages are kept together "for the sake of the children." Unmarried people living together also separate of course, and in the late 1970s courts were faced with several difficult cases that were essentially requests to have the legal benefits of divorce (community property and alimony payments) extended to people who had never married.

The American family in the late 1970s, then, is many things. Young people seem to be postponing marriage, perhaps because of unstable economic conditions, perhaps because a new variety in living arrangements enables people to enjoy primary group benefits without the necessity of a traditional marriage. A recent study of the Common Market countries of western Europe found that the people who rated themselves happiest were those who were living together without being married. People who do marry, marry later. Some population analysts take this as a hopeful sign. Maybe Americans are being more careful about selecting mates. Taking more time and marrying at a later age may lead to more stable marriages in the long run, and perhaps today's high divorce rates will begin to decline. At any rate, if the marriage is not happy, it is likely to be dissolved quickly. There are more single-parent families due to both divorce and to single people being allowed to adopt children. The nuclear family (two parents plus children) is a major part of American family life, but it continues to shrink in size as the birth rate drops. The retired couple in their sixties and seventies represents another facet of the American family, one whose numbers are growing substantially as our population grows older and as the birth rate decreases. Other agencies or groups may develop to help fill family functions. And maybe the current popularity of sensitivity-training and encounter groups in general is a search for the primary relationship that has been typically fulfilled by the family.

Perhaps, then, we see two contrasting threads in the American family. One is an experimental, postponing-or-never-marrying, alternative-life-style thread; the other is the traditional nuclear family, progressing from young to middle-aged parents with their children to elderly retired couples. Time has changed the nuclear family—it is a smaller unit with more equal relationships between partners. Although the two threads are contrasting, they also intersect: Many people may find themselves first being experimental and later following a more traditional path as their own needs and definitions undergo change.

And what of the family of the future? In a recent report, Jean Lipman-Blumen painted the following picture of the American family of the next two decades.[6] There will be fewer of the typical nuclear families that consist of two parents and one or more children. Instead, there will be more single-parent families. This will occur, she feels, because marriage and remarriage rates will continue to decline while divorce rates will continue to climb. More single-parent families will combine with others in the future for shelter, food, child care, and companionship. Lipman-Blumen feels that the smaller families of the future will be less segregated than those of today—they will get together for mutual support and cooperation. Shortened work weeks will have men at home more, which will mean that they will be playing a more real (and less ceremonial) role in the family. Women will be working more, meaning that household tasks will be more shared in the family of the future.

Another look at the future is provided by Charles Zastrow.[7] He sees the family being significantly affected by technological changes, and consequently, he imagines the possibility of human embryo transplants, test-tube babies, manipulation of the genetic code to control aging and disease, and even cloning, in which an identical new organism (a biological carbon copy) is produced from the nucleus of a single cell. It is hard to believe that these things could happen, and yet scientists report that in only a few more years (perhaps by 1984?) they could be a reality. Zastrow believes that technological changes will encourage the family of the future to experiment with new forms. There will be more childless couples. Parents will put off child-rearing until after retirement, when they have more time—test-tube babies and adoption will allow parents to be of any age. Professional parents will

---

[6]This is taken from Jean Lipman-Blumen, "Changing Sex Roles: Their Implications for Family Structure" (paper presented at the Pacific Sociological Association Meeting, San Diego, California, March 1976.) Jean Lipman-Blumen is affiliated with the Women's Research Program at the National Institute of Education.

[7]Charles H. Zastrow, "Dramatic Changes Foreseen in the American Family of Tomorrow," *International Journal of Sociology of the Family*, vol. 3 (March 1973), pp. 93–101.

be trained and licensed and have the responsibility of raising the children of those who do not want to or are unable to. Marriage patterns will also become more experimental, thinks Zastrow, and will include such variations as serial marriages (successive temporary alliances), contract marriages, trial marriages, open marriages, group or communal marriages, and homosexual marriages and adoptions. In addition, the single life may become more romanticized and idealized in the future with the result that more people will never marry.

Could an institution that has changed so slowly for two hundred years now change so rapidly? Could these things happen? In fact, some of them already have —marriage patterns in the 1970s have become quite experimental, and more people are remaining single or marrying later. During 1978, the world witnessed the first human embryo transplant, and there was much debate over the wisdom of manipulating the genetic code. In his book *Future Shock,* Alvin Toffler warned us that more innovations and changes are taking place now than at any time in human history. Will this also be true of the family, or is it more resistant to change? It will be interesting to see.

Religion

Like the family, religion has appeared in all societies, although its form varies greatly from society to society. To get an idea of the variation, look at Tables 7.4 and 7.5. Table 7.4 shows a breakdown of the religious population of the world. Table 7.5 shows recent membership figures in the United States. Not all of America's churches are included in Table 7.5—only those with memberships of at least 500,000 are listed. View the figures in these tables with a certain amount of care. Religious bodies count membership in different ways. For example, some churches count all baptized persons including infants, while others count only those people who have attained full membership (usually meaning that they are over thirteen years of age). Accuracy of religious membership data varies by religious body and by country. In light of this, these figures should be taken as no more than general estimates.

Table 7.4   Religious Population of the World, 1976

Christian		955,000,000
Roman Catholic	541,000,000	
Eastern Orthodox	87,000,000	
Protestant	328,000,000	
Jewish		14,000,000
Muslim		538,000,000
Shinto		60,000,000
Taoist		30,000,000
Confucian		186,000,000
Buddhist		250,000,000
Hindu		524,000,000

The 1976 Encyclopaedia Britannica Book of the Year and *The 1977 World Almanac.*

Table 7.5 Membership in Selected Religious
Bodies in the United States, 1976

Adventist Churches	510,000
Assemblies of God	1,200,000
Baptist	26,970,000
Churches of Christ	2,400,000
Churches of God	700,000
Disciples of Christ	1,300,000
Eastern Orthodox	4,190,000
Episcopal	2,900,000
Jehovah's Witnesses	540,000
Jewish	6,100,000
Latter-Day Saints	2,800,000
Lutheran	8,200,000
Methodist	12,900,000
Pentecostal Assemblies	500,000
Presbyterian	3,800,000
Roman Catholic	48,900,000
United Church of Christ	1,840,000

The Yearbook of American Churches (1974, 1976) and *The 1977
World Almanac.*

All countries have at least one religion, although not all people are religious. Ethnocentrism relates to our discussion of religion as it does to our discussion of the family. The lack of acceptance of others' ways of doing things, the hostility to difference, is probably even more pronounced with regard to religion. Whereas people with peculiar practices (different from ours) in marriage, family, clothing, or eating are seen as different, primitive, or ignorant, people of different religious beliefs are frequently seen as evil, pagan, or guided by the devil. Great rivalries and conflicts have occurred between religious groups, for religious faith and conviction can be a powerful force. Knowing that "it's God's will" or that "God is on our side" gives a justification and motivation for behavior that is difficult to duplicate by any other means.

Religion: Elements, Conflict, Functions

Sociologists who study religion are not concerned with the possible truth or falsity of religious beliefs. They are interested in what people believe and especially in what believing does for people. Although there is great variation among religions, a discussion of some common definitions and descriptions may help our understanding of the institution of religion. Religion may be described as a unified system of beliefs, feelings, and behaviors related to things defined as sacred. Societies define things as sacred—objects (a tree, the moon, a cross, a book), animals, ideas (science, communism, democracy), people (Buddha, Christ, saints). When things become sacred, they are endowed with a special quality or power and are treated with awe, reverence, and respect. Beliefs about the sacred things develop, and often what people choose to believe is of a supernatural quality. A set of appropriate feelings—reverence, happiness, sadness, fear, terror, ecstasy—are established. Finally, behaviors (or rituals) are developed consistent with the beliefs and feelings—confessional, rosary, communion, dietary laws, or the content of a particular worship service.[8]

Religion may be examined from several viewpoints, and two of the theories we discussed in Chapter 1 are useful here. The *conflict* perspective focuses on the role religion plays in social conflict. Contrasting religious beliefs have often been a source of conflict—take, for example, the battles between Protestants and Catholics in Northern Ireland over the past decade or so. Religious differences may also become the basis for political differences as currently in the Middle East. Karl Marx was critical of religion because of people's tendency to use it in times of uncertainty or stress. Marx described religion as the opiate of the masses because he felt that it took their minds off their real problems in favor of the other-worldly answers of Christianity. The working class's real problem in Marx's view was its manipulation and exploitation by the wealthy industrialists—the bourgeoisie—in capitalist economic systems. Religion was a needless distraction that could only slow the workers' revolt and subsequent freedom from oppression.

Religion plays an important role in social conflict according to conflict theorists because the dominant religion in society usually represents the dominant social class. The dominant religion supports the status quo, offers justifications for existing class lines, and operates to make working-class and lower-class people satisfied with their condition. The conflict between social classes may lead to the emergence of specific religious groups that represent specific class interests. A recent example is the People's Temple of the Rev. Jim Jones, which reportedly drew much of its membership from the ranks of the disaffected and alienated in society. According to the conflict perspective, a consequence of the development of class-based reli-

[8]Much of our discussion in this section is drawn from Charles Glock and Rodney Stark, *Religion and Society in Tension* (Chicago: Rand McNally, 1965). This definition of religion is close to that of Glock and Stark. In their book, Glock and Stark trace the background of their definition, which includes the works of Durkheim, Yinger, Parsons, Nottingham. and Williams.

gions is that often what appear to be religious differences between opposing religious groups (for example, Protestants and Catholics in Northern Ireland) actually turn out to be class differences. One religious group represents money and propertied people, and the other represents the working class. Conflict, then, is a central element in the discussion of religion according to this viewpoint.

Functional analysis is a second way of examining religion. This approach focuses on the functions that religion offers for society. First, religion provides a way for people to deal with the unknown; it supplies some measure of certainty in an uncertain world. There are a number of things we cannot explain. There are many other things that can be explained and understood but are still difficult to accept —the certainty of death, the loss of loved ones. Religion enables people to adjust to these situations by providing a sacred, supernatural being or object to explain the unknowable; religion provides a belief system to deal with situations difficult to accept—for the certainty of death, a life after death. Anthropologists have noted that sacred rituals and beliefs are usually found in situations that are hardest to control, where there is most uncertainty. Our own appeals for divine guidance and support usually come at intervals when uncertainty is present: when the jet accelerates for takeoff, or just before a particularly difficult test.

Religion also functions to provide people with a perspective, a viewpoint, a way of looking at the world. It provides value orientations as to how the world ought to be; it gives meaning to life. Max Weber held that people are motivated by ideologies or beliefs that stem in great part from religious origins, and that these are more basic than the economic values believed by Marx to be so important. In his classic work *The Protestant Ethic and the Spirit of Capitalism,* Weber's analysis of history led him to the conclusion that the beliefs surrounding Protestantism were central to the rise of capitalism. For example, Protestant values encourage the view that work is a calling: to work hard is virtuous, acquisition is supported, sobriety is encouraged. Far from being a needless distraction, religion is the source, according to Weber, of many of a society's most basic values, perspectives, and orientations to the world.

Religion may serve an integrative function in that it promotes solidarity. People with similar beliefs and viewpoints are drawn together, are more unified than those without this common experience. The presence of religion does not guarantee solidarity within a society, however, as other factors are also important. Many societies—the United States, for example—have several religions, and these may be in conflict with each other. In this case there may be a degree of solidarity among those of the same faith but an absence of solidarity in the society— religion may prove to be disintegrative for society even though it is integrative for the individual.

Religion may function as an agency of social control. We noted earlier that religion provides people with a value orientation, a perspective on life, a view of the world. From shared viewpoints, common agreements arise as to what people should and should not do. Since these norms emerge from a religious base, the church becomes involved in ensuring that they are observed. They may be informally encouraged or enforced, or they may be enacted into law. For example, many religions provide for the education of the young in schools run by the church. Some churches do not recognize marriages that take place outside the church. The clergy perform marriages and engage in marriage counseling. A little more indirectly, through pressure groups and lobbies, religions are involved in ensuring the passage or rejection of laws that they feel are crucial; laws dealing with liquor, pornography, abortion, and birth control are recent examples in the United States. In countries where there is less separation of church and state, religious organizations and their representatives are more directly involved with government in determining right and wrong.

In a variety of ways, then, organized religious groups assert moral authority and attempt to provide guidance—they act as agents of social control. Problems may arise when values and viewpoints on issues change, as they have, for example, on legalized abortion and birth control in the United States. Formal church doctrines change much more slowly than the values and attitudes of the people change. The result is that the social control function of the church is compromised when its members no longer hold its values. It is likely that if this occurs on many issues, the authority of the church will be seriously undermined. In fact, a report published in March 1976, relates how this happened recently. In 1968, Pope Paul VI ruled against the use of artificial birth control by Catholics. Earlier in the 1960s the Second Vatican Council had made church reforms that were well accepted by Catholics in the United States. However, the Pope's 1968 ruling was, according to Andrew Greeley, who studied the consequences and authored the report, "as far as the American church goes, one of the worst catastrophes in religious history." The birth control ruling did serious damage to the authority of the church and to the credibility of the Pope. Apparently as a consequence of the ruling, between 1963 and 1974 weekly attendance at Mass dropped from seventy-one to fifty percent, monthly confession dropped from thirty-eight to seventeen percent, families who favored a son becoming a priest dropped from sixty-three to fifty percent, parochial school enrollment dropped from 5.6 million to 3.5 million, and so on. The Pope's ruling was issued to restore faith in the church, but, in pushing a view no longer held by most members, it in fact badly weakened it.[9]

These four functions—to explain the unknown or uncertain, to provide a perspective or viewpoint, to afford solidarity, and to exercise social control—represent some of the more obvious functions of religion. These are not mutually exclusive, and there are others as well. It is interesting to note here while we are discussing functions that *magic* in primitive societies and *science* in more advanced societies serve many of the same functions as religion. In fact, it is sometimes difficult to distinguish between what is magic, science, or religion.

Religious Organizations

So far we have examined the elements of religion (beliefs, feelings, and behavior related to sacred objects) and some of the functions religion may serve. Religion may also be studied from the viewpoint of the organizational structure of religious groups. What we know about bureaucracies and large organizations may be applied

---

[9]This project was researched by the National Opinion Research Center in Chicago, directed by Andrew Greeley. See Andrew Greeley, William McCready, and Kathleen McCourt, *Catholic Schools in a Declining Church* (Mission, Kan.: Sheed & Ward, 1976).

to churches. Terminology has been developed to describe different types of church organization. One distinction that is commonly made is between church and sect. The **church** is large and highly organized, represents and supports the *status quo,* is respectable, and membership is automatic—one is born into the church. The **sect,** on the other hand, is smaller and less organized, and membership is voluntary. Members of sects usually show greater depth and fervor in their religious commitment than members of churches. The sect is more closely associated with the lower classes, the church with the middle and upper classes. The sect usually arises because of protest when church members become disaffected. They may feel that the church is too compromising or religiously too conservative, or in some other way is not responding to the wishes or convictions of its membership. The disaffected, deciding they would rather switch than fight, establish a sect based on purity of belief and the individual religious needs of its membership.[10]

Yinger sees church and sect as two types on a continuum of religious organizations. He adds several other types, including denomination and cult, as is shown in Table 7.6. The **denomination** appeals to a somewhat smaller category of people than the church—a racial ethnic, or social-class grouping. Yinger defines **cult** as a small, short-lived, often local group, frequently built around a dominant leader. Cults and sects arise, it is argued, because people feel deprivation in some form— poverty, ill health, value conflict, anomie. It is this deprivation that leads to the

Table 7.6   Religious Organizations

Church	Large—universal appeal—very respectable—members are born into it—supports the status quo and existing non-religious (secular) institutions—formal structure	Example: Roman Catholic Church of the Middle Ages
Denomination	Less universal appeal but organized around class, racial, or regional boundaries—conventional and respectable—less emotionalism and fervor than is shown in the sect—mainly middle class—stable, organized, and at peace with secular institutions	Examples: Presbyterian Church, Lutheran Church
Sect	Smaller—arises out of protest—membership is voluntary—uncompromising on religious doctrine—more emotional—less formal organization—more withdrawn from society and at war with secular institutions—it alone "has truth"—mainly lower class	Examples: pentecostal and evangelical movements, Jehovah's Witnesses
Cult	Smallest—less organized, somewhat formless and often short term—frequently centered around a charismatic leader—concerned mainly with problems of the individual (loneliness, alienation)—more exotic ritual—may focus on the religious (salvation) or on the more secular (self-improvement, self-awareness)	Examples: snake worshipers, People's Temple, urban store-front churches

[10]These paragraphs on types of religious organizations make use of material from Glock and Stark, *Religion and Society in Tension,* Chapter 13 (see footnote 8), and from J. Milton Yinger's book, *Religion, Society and the Individual* (New York: Macmillan, 1957), Chapter 6, especially pp. 142–155.

formation of new religious movements. Once formed, the movement may later die out, or it may become larger, more established and conservative, and move to another category of organization—from cult to sect to denomination, for example.

COMING OUT OF THE CULTS

Many young adults, some say as many as two or three million, have become involved in cults in the 1970s. Psychologists Margaret Thaler Singer studied several hundred people who had recently left groups such as the Children of God, the Unification Church of Reverend Moon, the Divine Light Mission, and the Church of Scientology. The people were generally middle and upper-middle class, around twenty-three years old, with some college education. Many joined cults during periods of depression and confusion, when life seemed meaningless. Cults supplied ready-made friendships and decisions about life. Exclusion of family and other outside contacts, rigid moral judgments of the unconverted outside world, and restriction of sexual behavior all worked to increase followers' commitment to the goals of the group and in some cases to its powerful leader. Indoctrination by the cult gradually eliminated any conflicting ties or information.

Coming out of the cult was not easy. Cult life usually provided a twenty-four hour schedule of work and ritual; members had tasks and purpose, their life was planned. After leaving, members felt at loose ends; they became depressed over the years they had lost. Some felt guilt over being involved in deception, especially over recruitment and fund-raising. They were lonely—leaving a cult meant leaving friends and the intimacy of sharing a signficant experience. Ex-cultists found it hard to make decisions for themselves, they became indecisive. Many also tended to slip back into altered trancelike states of consciousness—"spaceing out" or floating. Cult-encouraged thought patterns continued: don't question, don't doubt, accept uncritically and passively. Some were fearful of the cult. They worried about retaliation for leaving and even over chance street meetings with cult friends. Ex-cultists also experienced difficulty in their relationships with family and friends. They felt that "people were staring." Difficult questions were asked or implied: How could you do it? Why didn't you leave? Further, returnees often want to talk to people about the positive effects of the cult experience, the good things that happened. Yet, they feel that outsiders refuse to hear anything but the bad.

Adapted from "Coming Out of the Cults," by Margaret Thaler Singer, *PSYCHOLOGY TODAY*, January 1979, pp. 72–82. Copyright © 1979 Ziff-Davis Publishing Co.

Religion in America

To a sociologist looking at religion in the United States, certain aspects stand out. In America as in other countries there is *differential involvement* in religious activities. If we take church attendance as a measure of religious involvement, we find that women are more active than men, Catholics more than Protestants, college-educated more than those with high school education or less, people over thirty more than those under thirty, and people in the East most and people in the West least. Middle- and upper-class people attend and participate in church activities more than those of the lower class. Lower-class people tend to show greater intensity and emotion in religious feeling. Religious groups seem to be stratified according to social class. Episcopalians, Congregationalists, and Jews tend to be of higher social class than Presbyterians and Methodists, who in turn tend to rank higher than Baptists and Catholics. This ranking in great part reflects ethnic or national origin and recency of migration to the United States. However, a recent study challenges earlier findings, which tended to place Catholic immigrants low on the stratification totem pole. The National Opinion Research Center reported in October 1975 that Jewish and Catholic ethnics were doing better than Protestants whose ancestors came to the United States much earlier. The study examined income level by religious group as is shown in Table 7.7. In education as well, Jews (14 years) and Catholics (12.5 years) were above the national average of 11.1 years of schooling for all whites. The religion and social-class picture is complicated by the apparent tendency of Americans to change their religious affiliation as they move up the social-class ladder.[11]

Table 7.7   Income and Religious Affiliation

	Yearly Household Income in 1974 Dollars
Jews	$13,340
Irish Catholics	12,426
Italian Catholics	11,748
German Catholics	11,632
Polish Catholics	11,298
Episcopalians	11,032
Methodists	10,103
Baptists	8,693

Great *religious diversity* characterizes this country. The United States has no official state-supported religion. America, unlike some countries, has attempted to maintain a separation between church and state. Broadly speaking, three religious bodies—Protestant, Catholic, and Jewish—dominate. However, there are numerous Protestant denominations, of which the largest are Baptist, Methodist, Lutheran, and Presbyterian, as well as a multitude of sects and cults. Some authorities have noted this diversity in American religious groups and have argued that, on the contrary, the differences are in name only. They believe that there is a growing consensus on religious beliefs and that we are approaching a common religion in America that is eroding the traditional differences between Protestantism, Catholicism, and Judaism. Glock and Stark tested this idea by asking a number of members of Protestant and Catholic churches about their beliefs. They conclude that great diversity *does* exist, not only between Protestants and Catholics but between various Protestant denominations as well. In fact, Glock and Stark believe that the differences between various Protestant denominations are so great that it is inappropriate to speak of "Protestants"—there is no such thing as a unified Protestant religion. Some of the results of Glock and Stark's research are shown in Table 7.8.

[11]George Gallup conducts a yearly poll on church attendance. Family income and occupational status as related to denomination are provided by Galen Gockel, "Income and Religious Affiliation: A Regression Analysis," *American Journal of Sociology*, vol. 24, no. 6 (May 1969), pp. 632–647. The NORC study (again directed by Greeley) was reported in newspapers and news magazines in late October 1975.

It is apparent from these data that members of different Protestant denominations have marked differences in belief. These differences are reflected in numerous areas and seem to indicate that a common American religion, at least in terms of beliefs, does not now exist.[12] On the other hand, Protestantism, Catholicism, and Judaism in the United States are probably peculiarly American. Often they differ markedly from their antecedents in other countries. The melting pot has modified traditional religions so that they all probably reflect the cultural values of the United States. In this sense, at least, there is a "common American religion," and we will return to this when we discuss the secularization of American religion.

In the late 1970s the White House was occupied by a President who was a born-again Christian, and numerous people on the national scene from Watergate conspirators to athletic heroes publicly became religious. The United States appears to be going through a religious revival of sorts with renewed interest in fundamentalist, pentecostal, and evangelical types of experiences. Some traditional churches have discovered, often to their embarrassment, that many of their members found themselves attracted toward more emotional and exotic religious conduct—faith healing, speaking in tongues, mass revival meetings, and so on. Young people seem to be especially attracted to and active in evangelical movements. At the same time, an increasing interest has developed in Eastern religions and mysticism. Religion and religious organizations seem to be continually in the public eye. Members of Hare Krishna chanted in the streets . . . the government investigated Scientology . . . Reverend Moon's Unification Church held mass rallies, there were charges of brainwashing converts, and parents attempted to kidnap their children back . . . the People's Temple at Jonestown in Guyana was the site of a mass suicide. Religious behavior in general seemed to fragment and take many different forms. As we will see in a moment, overall church attendance did not increase in the late 1970s—it

Table 7.8   Percentage of Members of Various Religious Groups Who Held the Following Beliefs to Be "Completely True"

	Congregationalists	Methodists	Presbyterians	Missouri Lutherans	Southern Baptists	Catholics
Belief in the existence of God	41%	60%	75%	81%	99%	81%
Belief that Jesus was born of a virgin	21	34	57	92	99	81
Belief in life after death	36	49	69	84	97	75
Belief in the existence of the Devil	6	13	31	77	92	66
Belief in original sin	2	7	21	86	43	68

Adapted from Charles Glock and Rodney Stark, *Religion and Society in Tension* (Chicago: Rand McNally, 1965), Chapter 5.

[12]For a more complete analysis of this topic, see Glock and Stark, *Religion and Society in Tension,* Chapters 4, and 5 (see footnote 8).

was the *form* of religious expression that was undergoing change. Great diversity continues to characterize religion in America.

Religion in America is *losing functions.* Other institutions are taking over the traditional functions that religion has served. Education and socialization of the young is handled for the most part by educational institutions rather than by the church. More dramatic is the rise in the importance of science. Today we tend to put our faith in science rather than religion when dealing with the unknown or uncertainty. Scientific knowledge increasingly forces a redefining of religious beliefs. How do you describe heaven when rockets and spaceships are racing through the universe to the moon and beyond? What is the soul when hearts and possibly even brains can be transplanted from one body to another? Today it seems that we look to science for the answers rather than to religion—the scientist is more of a folk hero than is the minister. We might predict that either religion will change to adapt to a scientific world or that religion will have ever decreasing influence. Some religious organizations, in a spirit of "if you can't lick 'em, join 'em," are attempting to develop new functions to replace those they have lost. Usually this means becoming more "this-worldly" and less "other-worldly." The new church looks like a social work agency, and religious leaders frequently lead the way in speaking out on social issues. Ministers and priests put their bodies on the line in the 1960s in civil rights demonstrations in the South. Individual representatives of the church have, among other things, spoken out on the draft and the war in Southeast Asia and have been active in the farm labor movement in California and the Southwest. Churches have provided food and shelter for youth "doing their own thing." It is frequently noted that the minister in the pulpit sounds more as though his college degree were in psychology or sociology than in theology.

These trends may not be widespread or even widely accepted in the very churches in which they are taking place. Some argue that these changes are certain guarantees of the decline of religion. After all, formerly churches were offering something different, a special way of looking at the world unattainable elsewhere. Now the church is no different from other secular organizations and loses any unique appeal it might have had. Others believe, however, that in a changing world, religion too must change or run the risk of becoming irrelevant to modern people.

Finally, the *secularization of American religion* bears discussion. By secular we mean nonspiritual, nonsacred, this-worldly. Americans seem to be religious and nonreligious at the same time. Millions of Bibles are sold yearly, and polls indicate that over ninety percent of Americans say they believe in God, and yet fifty-three percent of the people asked could not name one of the four authors of the first four books of the New Testament. Americans believe in prayer, in heaven and hell, and in life after death, and yet church attendance has dropped from forty-nine percent in a given week in 1958 to forty percent in 1971, and remains at about that level (forty-one percent in 1978). In 1957, ninety-seven percent of Americans identified with a religious denomination. Yet at about the same time a panel of outstanding Americans, when asked to rate the most significant events in history, gave first place to Columbus's discovery of America. Christ's birth or crucifixion came in fourteenth, tied with the discovery of the X ray and the Wright brothers' first

THE TNEVNOC CULT

The 1970s have witnessed a profusion of new religious movements, and as these groups have grown in size and wealth, there has been a parallel spread of alarm at the tactics by which they recruit and hold members. Allegations of deception, seduction, hypnosis, brainwashing, and other forms of mind control are made.

David Bromley and Anson Shupe argue that characteristics of this "cult menace" are not new but have been a persistent feature in our history. They describe the Tnevnoc cult, a once-powerful and widespread religious movement of the nineteenth century. Young women at school were openly recruited and induced to commit themselves totally to the cult. Once they had joined the Tnevnocs, they had to surrender all aspects of their former lives: All possessions were taken away; all luxuries and even basic amenities were eliminated; members had their hair cut off; they could not own or look into mirrors; they were permitted no outside visitors during the first year; they could write no more than four letters a year; they could not associate with the opposite sex; and they had to accept cult leaders in parental roles. Cult life was relentless and consuming: Members were wakened at 4:30 A.M. and spent a long day at manual labor mixed with meditation, mind-numbing chanting, and compulsory religious ceremonies. Like the Hare Krishna they carried prayer beads, which they used in their repetitive, monotonic chanting. In a bizarre ceremony involving ritualistic cannibalism, Tnevnocs consumed food that symbolically represented parts of the dead founder's body. All loyalty had to be channeled to the cult and its leaders. In one macabre nuptial ceremony, members were required to become the living brides of the dead cult leader.

The group that Bromley and Shupe are talking about is not all that obscure. It is a Roman Catholic convent (*Tnevnoc* spelled backwards). The description doesn't mention the other side of the picture—the sense of majesty, purpose, and personal fulfillment that nuns feel, or the order, stability, and integration of the convent as a social organization. The methods may seem strange but socialization and resocialization take place in elite military units, communes, convents, religious groups, and social movements seeking radical social change. These groups seek the total commitment of their members, which means detachment from former lifestyles and attachment to new ones. Society's response to what it sees groups doing depends on the group's *degree of legitimacy.* The less the degree of a group's legitimacy, the more objections a society raises to its behavior. Much as the Unification Church, Hare Krishna, and Children of God are currently labeled "cults," the Catholic Church once was perjoratively lumped with groups such as the Mormons and Masons despite enormous doctrinal and organizational diversity. Bromley and Shupe suggest that groups that seek to initiate sweeping social change become the focus of hysterical reactions well out of proportion to the real threat they present and that most religious movements through American history have gradually accommodated to the larger society.

Adapted from "The Tnevnoc Cult" by David G. Bromley and Anson D. Shupe, Jr., with the permission of *Sociological Analysis* and the authors.

flight.[13] Religion used to be of vital significance; it guided the pioneers' way of life. People read the Bible regularly at family gatherings. It was the law, and its teachings were carefully followed. As society changes in other ways, so does religious observation. Today people join churches and say they are religious, but perhaps the meaning and reasons have changed. Although many remain religious in the traditional sense, many others are religious for social and secular reasons—it looks right, it makes one respectable. Religion is used to get other desired things. Belonging to the right church will help the aspiring businessman make the right contacts, meet the right people, have the right friends. Athletic teams pray before games; even the U.S. Marine Corps holds special religious services before shooting the rifle on qualification day. We seem to feel that if we have religion—belong or go to church—other good things will happen to us. The result is an increasing secularization of American religion. As Will Herberg puts it, contemporary American religion is *man-centered*. People, not God, are the beginning and end of the spiritual system of much of present-day American religiosity. The result is a religiousness without religion, a way of sociability or belonging rather than a way of orienting one's life to God.[14]

Making categorical statements about religion in America is risky business, however. Some seventy-five percent of the American people believe that "religion is losing it influence." And on the other hand, as we noted, there seems to be a resurgence of interest, especially among young people, in evangelical and Eastern religions. Next to the secular strain of religion is another strain emphasizing its spiritual and emotional aspects. This seems to be the keynote of religion in America: great variation in belief and practice.

SUMMARY

The major topics of the previous chapters in this section on social organization were groups, categories, and social differentiation. These concepts permit the study of a number of different types of collectivities of people. In this chapter we moved to another, somewhat more abstract level, and focused on social institutions. Sociologists define an institution as a system of social relationships, an organized way of doing things that meets certain basic needs of society. All societies have basic needs—reproduction of the species and socialization of the young, for example. Consequently, many of the same institutions—family, religion, education, government, economics—appear in all societies, although the content of a given institution may vary from one society to another. As societies develop and change, other institutions, such as science and leisure, may emerge.

Sociological research and study is more apt to be concerned with specific institutions than it is with the concept itself. The major part of this chapter has

[13]Figures on attendance come from the Gallup Poll, 1978. Other facts in this section come from Will Herberg's interesting book, *Protestant-Catholic-Jew* (Garden City, N.Y.: Doubleday, Anchor Books, 1960), Chapter 1. Also Glock and Stark, *Religion and Society in Tension*, Chapter 4 (see footnote 8).

[14]Herberg, *Protestant-Catholic-Jew*, Chapter 11, especially p. 268 (see footnote 13).

presented an analysis of the family and religion in order to illustrate the application of the concept of institution to specific areas of human behavior. In the section on the family, cross-cultural variations were examined. The constants or uniformities were discussed, and it was observed that the family everywhere seems to fulfill similar functions. Finally, we examined the family in America in terms of current trends and prospects for the future.

In our analysis of religion, we outlined those common elements and functions that religions seem to have. Religious organizations were analyzed using Yinger's typology of church and sect. A description of religion in America included discussion of differential involvement, religious diversity, loss or change in functions, and the apparent secularization of American religion.

Five readings follow. The three short excerpts from books by Ruth Benedict, Margaret Mead, and David and Vera Mace illustrate that within a given institution, the cultural variability is vast. Benedict describes courtship among the Dobu, Mead describes courtship among the Mundugumor, and the Maces relate an interview with some young women in India who cast American courtship patterns in an unusual light. In the fourth reading, Jane Howard wonders if friends can be family and if good families have common characteristics. The final article, by Nathan Gerrard, deals with serpent-handling religions. Gerrard again makes the point that there is great diversity in practices within a given institution. More importantly, we again see the combination of several methods of analysis—social class and institution—with one concept helping to explain the characteristics of the other.

Reading 7.1
Courtship among the Dobu
RUTH BENEDICT

Although the same institutions are common to many societies, the specific content of an institutional area may vary greatly from one society to another. The institutional area of the family is no exception.

Marriage is set in motion by a hostile act of the mother-in-law. She blocks with her own person the door of her house within which the youth is sleeping with her daughter, and he is trapped for the public ceremony of betrothal. Before this, since the time of puberty, the boy has slept each night in the houses of unmarried girls. By custom his own house is closed to him. He avoids entanglements for several years by spreading his favours widely and leaving the house well before daylight. When he is trapped at last, it is usually because he has tired of his roaming and has settled upon a more constant companion. He ceases to be so careful about early rising. Nevertheless he is never thought of as being ready to undertake the indigni-

From *Patterns of Culture* by Ruth Benedict, copyright renewed 1962 by Ruth Valentine, pp. 133–135. Reprinted by permission of the publisher, Houghton Mifflin Company.

ties of marriage, and the event is forced upon him by the old witch in the doorway, his future mother-in-law. When the villagers, the maternal kin of the girl, see the old woman immobile in her doorway, they gather, and under the stare of the public the two descend and sit on a mat upon the ground. The villagers stare at them for half an hour and gradually disperse, nothing more; the couple are formally betrothed.

From this time forward the young man has to reckon with the village of his wife. Its first demand is upon his labour. Immediately his mother-in-law gives him a digging-stick with the command, "Now work." He must make a garden under the surveillance of his parents-in-law. When they cook and eat, he must continue work, since he cannot eat in their presence. He is bound to a double task, for when he has finished work on his father-in-law's yams he has still to cultivate his own garden on his own family land. His father-in-law gets ample satisfaction of his will to power and hugely enjoys his power over his son-in-law. For a year or more the situation continues. The boy is not the only one who is caught in this affair, for his relatives also are loaded with obligations. So heavy are the burdens upon his brothers in providing the necessary garden stuff and the valuables for the marriage gift that nowadays young men at their brother's betrothal escape from the imposition by signing up with the white recruiter for indentured labour.

Reading 7.2
Courtship among the Mundugumor

MARGARET MEAD

Girls of this age are also divided by their experience; some are married and living in the houses of their mothers-in-law, some have been successfully kept at home by jealous fathers. While the betrothed girls may be fretting over the indignity of having husbands too young to copulate with them, or too old to be desirable, the unbetrothed girls are fretting because their fathers follow them about everywhere and never permit them any privacy. Temporary alliances are sometimes formed in pursuance of love-affairs, but for the most part each pair of Mundugumor lovers acts in complete secrecy. The implications of a love-affair are so dangerous that it is inadvisable to trust anyone. In the face of all Mundugumor conflicts about arranged marriages there exists a violent preference for individual selection of one's mate. Children who have been accustomed to fight even for their first drops of milk do not docilely accept prescribed marriages arranged for other people's convenience. Almost every girl, betrothed or not, goes about with her skin polished and her grass skirt gay and stylish, with her eye out for a lover, and boys and men are watchful for the slightest sign of favour. The love-affairs of the young unmarried people are sudden and highly charged, characterized by passion rather than by tenderness or romance. A few hastily whispered words, a tryst muttered as they pass on a trail, are often the only interchange between them after they have chosen each other and before that choice is expressed in intercourse. The element of time and discovery is always present, goading them towards the swiftest possible cut-and-run relationship. The words in which a slightly older man advises a boy give the tone of these encounters: "When you meet a girl in the bush and copulate with her, be careful to come back to the village quickly and with explanations to account for your disappearance. If your bow-string is snapped, say that it caught on a passing bush. If your arrows are broken, explain that you tripped and caught them against a branch. If your loin-cloth is torn, or your face scratched, or your hair disarrayed, be ready with an explanation. Say that you fell, that you caught your foot, that you were running after game. Otherwise people will laugh in your face when you return." A girl is similarly advised: "If your ear-rings are torn out of your ears, and the cord of your necklace broken, if your grass skirt is torn and bedraggled, and your face and arms scratched and bleeding, say that you were frightened, that you heard a noise in the bush and ran and fell. Otherwise people will taunt you with having met a lover." Foreplay in these quick encounters takes the form of a violent scratching and biting match, calculated to produce the maximum amount of excitement in the minumum amount of time. To break the arrows or the basket of the beloved is one standard way of demonstrating consuming passion; so also is tearing off ornaments, and smashing them if possible.

Before she marries, a girl may have a number of affairs, each characterized by the same quick violence, but it is dangerous. If the matter is discovered the whole community will know that she is no longer a virgin, and the Mundugumor value virginity in their daughters and brides. Only a virgin may be offered in exchange for a virgin, and a girl whose virginity is known to be lost can be exchanged only for one whose exchange value has been similarly damaged. However, if a man marries a girl and then discovers she is not a virgin, he says nothing about it, for his own reputation is now involved and people would mock him. Sometimes the bush meetings are varied by an accepted lover's slipping into the girl's sleeping basket at night. Fathers may, if they wish, sleep with their adolescent daughters until they marry, and mothers have a similar right to sleep with their sons. Particularly jealous fathers and particularly possessive mothers exercise this privilege. Often, however, two girls are allowed to sleep together in a basket; if one of the pair is away, the other temporarily has the basket to herself. If she receives a lover in her sleeping basket, she risks not only discovery but actual injury, for an angry father who discovers the intruder may fasten up the opening of the sleeping-bag and roll the couple down the house-ladder, which is almost perpendicular and some six or seven feet in height. The bag may receive a good kicking and even a prodding with a spear or an arrow before it is opened. As a result, this method of courtship, although very occasionally resorted to by desperate lovers in the wet seasons when the bush is flooded, is not very popular. Young men relate with bated breath the most conspicuous mishaps that have befallen their elders, mishaps so uproariously humiliating and damaging to pride and person that they have become sagas of mirth. While the lover from another hamlet will therefore seldom risk a tryst within the house, new relationships between people temporarily housed together are often set up in this way, where the risk is much smaller.

Reading 7.3

Marriage East and West

DAVID AND VERA MACE

"Tell us," said Kusima, "about the young people in the West. We want to know how *they* get married."

Night was falling at the close of a sultry Indian day. A cool, refreshing breeze playfully caressed the glittering black tresses of the girls' hair and set their gay saris fluttering. All teen-agers, they had been invited along by our host because we had expressed a desire to know what Indian young people thought about love and marriage. The girls, ten of them, were squatting on the veranda floor in a wide circle. Being awkward Westerners who couldn't sit comfortably on folded legs, we had been provided with low stools.

We gave as good an account as we could of how our young people are free to meet each other and have dates; how a boy and girl will fall in love; and how, after a period of going steady, they become engaged and then get married. We knew that young people in the East live a very restricted life, and have their marriages arranged for them by their parents, so we felt a little relieved that they had chosen to question us about our delightful romantic traditions. We didn't want to make them *too* envious, but we naturally were glad to demonstrate our superiority in this matter of finding a mate.

When we had finished, there was a meditative silence. Concluding that they had been impressed, we decided to start a discussion.

"Wouldn't you like to be free to choose your own marriage partners, like the young people do in the West?"

"Oh no!" several voices replied in chorus.

Taken aback, we searched their faces.

"Why not?"

"For one thing," said one of them, "doesn't it put the girl in a very humiliating position?"

"Humiliating? In what way?"

"Well, doesn't it mean that she has to try to look pretty, and call attention to herself, and attract a boy, to be sure she'll get married?"

"Well, perhaps so."

"And if she doesn't want to do that, or if she feels it's undignified, wouldn't that mean she mightn't get a husband?"

"Yes, that's possible."

"So a girl who is shy and doesn't push herself forward might not be able to get married. Does that happen?"

"Sometimes it does."

"Well, surely that's humiliating. It makes getting married a sort of competition in which the girls are fighting each other for the boys. And it encourages a girl to pretend she's better than she really is. She can't relax and be herself. She has to make a good impression to get a boy, and then she has to go on making a good impression to get him to marry her."

Before we could think of an answer to this unexpected line of argument, another girl broke in.

"In our system, you see," she explained, "we girls don't have to worry at all. We *know* we'll get married. When we are old enough, our parents will find a suitable boy, and everything will be arranged. We don't have to go into competition with each other."

"Besides," said a third girl, "how would we be able to judge the character of a boy we met and got friendly with? We are young and inexperienced. Our parents are older and wiser, and they aren't as easily deceived as we would be. I'd far rather have my parents choose for me. It's so important that the man I marry should be the right one. I could so easily make a mistake if I had to find him for myself."

Another girl had her hand stretched out eagerly.

"But *does* the girl really have any choice in the West?" she said. "From what I've read, it seems that the boy does all the choosing. All the girl can do is to say yes or no. She can't go up to a boy and say 'I like you. Will you marry me?' can she?"

We admitted that this was not the done thing.

"So," she went on eagerly, "when you talk about men and women being equal in the West, it isn't true. When our parents are looking for a husband for us, they don't have to wait until some boy takes it into his head to ask for us. They just find out what families are looking for wives for their sons, and see whether one of the boys would be suitable. Then, if his family agree that it would be a good match, they arrange it together."

Questions 7.1, 7.2, 7.3

1. The variabilities or differences are obvious, but describe the uniformities or similarities among Dobu, Mundugumor, and U.S. institutions of the family.
2. To the extent that you can, describe the Dobu and Mundugumor using rules of marriage, residence, descent, authority, and so on.
3. Evaluate the Indian women's critique of American practices. Where are they right, and where do they misinterpret or misunderstand? What are the advantages and disadvantages of the Indian system of marriage?

Reading 7.4
Families

JANE HOWARD

Do family members need to be related by blood? Not necessarily, according to Jane Howard. Relatives sometimes fail to be friends, but with luck, friends can be transformed into relatives, members of one's clan. Further,

good families, whether they be related by blood or friendship, seem to
have certain characteristics in common.

Jane Howard, author of several best-sellers, studied some 200 family
groups. Out of this came her book *Families,* from which the following
excerpt is taken.

Call it a clan, call it a network, call it a tribe, call it a family. Whatever you call
it, whoever you are, you need one. You need one because you are human. You
didn't come from nowhere. Before you, around you, and presumably after you, too,
there are others. Some of these others must matter a lot—to you, and if you are
very lucky, to one another. Their welfare must be nearly as important to you as
your own. Even if you live alone, even if your solitude is elected and ebullient, you
still cannot do without a clan or a tribe.

The trouble with the clans and tribes many of us were born into is not that
they consist of meddlesome ogres but that they are too far away. In emergencies
we rush across continents and if need be oceans to their sides, as they do to ours.
Maybe we even make a habit of seeing them, once or twice a year, for the sheer
pleasure of it. But blood ties seldom dictate our addresses. Our blood kin are often
too remote to ease us from our Tuesdays to our Wednesdays. For this we must rely
on our families of friends. If our relatives are not, do not wish to be, or for whatever
reasons cannot be our friends, then by some complex alchemy we must try to
transform our friends into our relatives. If blood and roots don't do the job, then
we must look to water and branches, and sort ourselves into new constellations,
new families. . . .

If some of our friends are not in effect part of our family, then they ought to
be, and soon. Friendships are sacred and miraculous, but they can be even more
so if they lead to the equivalent of clans. If the important people in my life discern
in my friend a fraction of the worth that I do, and if those who matter to him can
understand his affinity for me, then we are on our way: the dim but promising
outline of a new sort of family emerges.

I have been hearing quite a bit of talk about "support systems." The term is
not among my favorites, but I can understand its currency. Whatever "support
systems" may be, the need for them is clearly urgent, and not just in this country.
Are there not thriving "megafamilies" of as many as three hundred people in
Scandinavia? Have not the Japanese for years had an honored, enduring—if perhaps by our standards rather rigid—custom of adopting non-relatives to fill gaps
in their families? Should we not applaud and maybe imitate such ingenuity? And
consider our own Unitarians. From Santa Barbara to Boston they have been ear-
nestly dividing their congregations into arbitrary "extended families" whose members are bound to act like each other's relatives.

As a member in reasonable standing of six or seven tribes in addition to the
one I was born to, I have been trying to figure which characteristics are important
for families to have.

1) Good families have a chief, or a heroine, or a founder—someone around whom
   others cluster, whose achievements and example spur others on to like feats.
2) Good families have a switchboard operator—someone who keeps track of what all
   the others are up to. This person feels driven to keep scrapbooks and photography
   albums up to date so that the clan can see proof of its own continuity.

3) Good families are much to all their members, but everything to none. They have many outside interests—parents are nearly as devoted to what they do outside as they are to each other and their children. Curiosity and passion are contagious. Everbody, where they live, is busy.

4) Good families are hospitable. They are generous with honorary memberships for friends, whom they urge to come early and often and to stay late. There is the sense that surrounding relatives and friends may at any time become part of the inner circle.

5) Good families deal squarely with direness. Pity the family that supposes it can avoid for long the woes to which all flesh is heir. Lunacy, bankruptcy, suicide, and other unthinkable fates sooner or later afflict the noblest of clans with an undertow of gloom.

6) Good families prize their rituals. Nothing welds a family more than these. Rituals are vital especially for clans without histories, because they evoke a past, imply a future, and hint at continuity. A clan becomes more of a clan each time it gathers to observe a fixed ritual, grieves at a funeral, and devises a new rite of its own.

7) Good familes are affectionate.

8) Good families have a sense of place—if not a home, then a set of totems and icons that make short-term quarters feel like home. Rooms with stoves or fireplaces and round tables which inspire good conversation will help.

9) Good families, not just the blood kind, find some way to connect with posterity. It is a sadly impoverished tribe that does not allow access to, and make much of, some children. Those without children might build homes, plant trees, write books or symphonies or laws, but even so there should be children nearby.

10) Good families honor their elders. The wider the age range, the stronger the tribe.

Questions 7.4

1. How do Howard's characteristics of "good families" fit with the standard functions of the family? Are certain of the functions emphasized more than others? Is Howard suggesting certain new functions?
2. According to Howard, whoever you are, you need a family. Why?
3. How should "family" in Howard's sense (a group formed by both blood and friendship ties) be defined? Develop an adequate definition.

Reading 7.5
The Serpent-Handling Religions of West Virginia

NATHAN L. GERRARD

There is great diversity in religious practices, as this article by sociologist Nathan Gerrard makes clear. Gerrard feels that a group's religious practices are at least partly explained by the social class of the members. He also outlines the functions that the serpent-handling religions seem to provide for their members.

. . . And these signs shall follow them that believe; In my name shall they cast out devils; they shall speak with new tongues; They shall take up serpents; and if they drink any deadly thing, it shall not hurt them; they shall lay hands on the sick and they shall recover. Mark 16:17–18.

In Southern Appalachia, two dozen or three dozen fundamentalist congregations take this passage literally and "take up serpents." They use copperheads, water moccasins, and rattlesnakes in their religious services.

The serpent-handling ritual was inaugurated between 1900 and 1910, probably by George Went Hensley. Hensley began evangelizing in rural Grasshopper Valley, Tenn., then traveled widely throughout the South, particularly in Kentucky, spreading his religion. He died in Florida at 70—of snakebite. To date, the press has reported about 20 such deaths among the serpent-handlers. One other death was recorded last year, in Kentucky.

For seven years, my wife and I have been studying a number of West Virginia serpent-handlers, primarily in order to discover what effect that unusual form of religious practice has on their lives. Although serpent-handling is outlawed by the state legislatures of Kentucky, Virginia, and Tennessee and by municipal ordinances in North Carolina, it is still legal in West Virginia. One center is the Scrabble Creek Church of All Nations in Fayette County, about 37 miles from Charleston. Another center is the Church of Jesus in Jolo, McDowell county, one of the most poverty-stricken areas of the state. Serpent-handling is also practiced sporadically elsewhere in West Virginia, where it is usually led by visitors from Scrabble Creek or Jolo.

The Jolo church attracts people from both Virginia and Kentucky, in addition to those from West Virginia. Members of the Scrabble Creek church speak with awe of the Jolo services, where people pick up large handfuls of poisonous snakes, fling them to the ground, pick them up again, and thrust them under their shirts or blouses, dancing ecstatically. We attended one church service in Scrabble Creek where visitors from Jolo covered their heads with clusters of snakes and wore them as crowns.

Serpent-handling was introduced to Scrabble Creek in 1941 by a coal miner from Harlan, Ky. The practice really began to take hold in 1946, when the present leader of the Scrabble Creek church, then a member of the Church of God, first took up serpents. The four or five original serpent-handlers in Fayette County met at one another's homes until given the use of an abandoned one-room school house in Big Creek. In 1959, when their number had swelled several times over, they moved to a larger church in Scrabble Creek.

Snakebites, Saints, and Scoffers

During the course of our seven-year study, about a dozen members of the church received snakebites. (My wife and I were present on two of these occasions.) Although there were no deaths, each incident was widely and unfavorably publicized in the area. For their part, the serpent-handlers say the Lord causes a snake to strike in order to refute scoffers' claims that the snakes' fangs have been pulled. They see each recovery from snakebite as a miracle wrought by the Lord —and each death as a sign that the Lord "really had to show the scoffers how dangerous it is to obey His commandments." Since adherents believe that death brings one to the throne of God, some express an eagerness to die when He decides they are ready. Those who have been bitten and who have recovered seem to receive special deference from other members of the church.

The ritual of serpent-handling takes only 15 or 20 minutes in religious sessions that are seldom shorter than four hours. The rest of the service includes singing Christian hymns, ecstatic dancing, testifying, extemporaneous and impassioned sermons, faith-healing, "speaking in tongues," and foot-washing. These latter rituals are a part of the firmly rooted Holiness movement, which encompasses thousands of churches in the Southern Appalachian region. The Holiness churches started in the 19th century as part of a perfectionist movement.

The social and psychological functions served by the Scrabble Creek church are probably very much the same as those served by the more conventional Holiness churches. Thus, the extreme danger of the Scrabble Creek rituals probably helps to validate the members' claims to holiness. After all, the claim that one is a living saint is pretentious even in a sacred society—and it is particularly difficult to maintain in a secular society. That the serpent-handler regularly risks his life for his religion is seen as evidence of his saintliness. As the serpent-handler stresses over and over, "I'm afraid of snakes like anybody else, but when God anoints me, I handle them with joy." The fact that he is usually not bitten, or if bitten usually recovers, is cited as further evidence of his claim to holiness.

After we had observed the Scrabble Creek serpent-handlers for some time, we decided to give them psychological tests. We enlisted the aid of Auke Tellegen, department of psychology, University of Minnesota, and three of his clinical associates: James Butcher, William Schofield, and Anne Wirt. They interpreted the Minnesota Multiphasic Personality Inventory that we administered to 50 serpent-handlers (46 were completed)—and also to 90 members of a conventional-denomination church 20 miles from Scrabble Creek. What we wanted to find out was how these two groups differed.

What we found were important personality differences not only between the serpent-handlers and the conventional church members, but also between the older and the younger generations within the conventional group. We believe that these differences are due, ultimately, to differences in social class: The serpent-handlers come from the nonmobile working class (average annual income: $3000), whereas members of the conventional church are upwardly mobile working-class people (average annual income: $5000) with their eyes on the future.

But first, let us consider the similarities between the two groups. Most of the people who live in the south central part of West Virginia, serpent-handlers or not, have similar backgrounds. The area is rural, nonfarm, with only about one-tenth of the population living in settlements of more than 2500. Until recently, the dominant industry was coal-mining, but in the last 15 years mining operations have been drastically curtailed. The result have been widespread unemployment. Scrabble Creek is in that part of Appalachia that has been officially declared a "depressed area"—which means that current unemployment rates there often equal those of the Depression.

There are few foreign-born in this part of West Virginia. Most of the residents are of Scottish-Irish or Pennsylvania Dutch descent, and their ancestors came to the New World so long ago that there are no memories of an Old World past.

Generally, public schools in the area are below national standards. Few people over 50 have had more than six or seven years of elementary education.

Religion has always been important here. One or two generations ago, the immediate ancestors of both serpent-handlers and conventional-church members lived in the same mining communities and followed roughly the same religious practices. Today there is much "backsliding," and the majority seldom attend church regularly. But there is still a great deal of talk about religion, and there are few professed atheists.

Hypochondria and the Holy Spirit

Though the people of both churches are native-born Protestants with fundamentalist religious beliefs, little education, and precarious employment, the two groups seem to handle their common problems in very different ways. One of the first differences we noticed was in the ways the older members of both churches responded to illness and old age. Because the members of both churches had been impoverished and medically neglected during childhood and young adulthood, and because they had earned their livelihoods in hazardous and health destroying ways, they were old before their time. They suffered from a wide variety of physical ailments. Yet while the older members of the conventional church seemed to dwell morbidly on their physical disabilities, the aged serpent-handlers seemed able to cheerfully ignore their ailments.

The serpent-handlers, in fact, went to the opposite extreme. Far from being pessimistic hypochondriacs like the conventional-church members, the serpent-handlers were so intent on placing their fate in God's benevolent hands that they usually failed to take even the normal precautions in caring for their health. Three old serpent-handlers we knew in Scrabble Creek were suffering from serious cardiac conditions. But when the Holy Spirit moved them, they danced ecstatically and violently. And they did this without any apparent harm.

No matter how ill the old serpent-handlers are, unless they are actually prostrate in their beds they manage to attend and enjoy church services lasting four to six hours, two or three times a week. Some have to travel long distances over the mountains to get to church. When the long sessions are over, they appear refreshed rather than weary.

One evening an elderly woman was carried into the serpent-handling church in a wheelchair. She had had a severe stroke and was almost completely paralyzed. Wheeled to the front of the church, she watched everything throughout the long services. During one particularly frenzied singing and dancing session, the fingers of her right hand tapped lightly against the arm of the chair. This was the only movement she was able to make, but obviously she was enjoying the service. When friends leaned over and offered to take her home, she made it clear she was not ready to go. She stayed until the end, and gave the impression of smiling when she was finally wheeled out. Others in the church apparently felt pleased rather than depressed by her presence.

Both old members of the conventional denomination and old serpent-handlers undoubtedly are frequently visited by the thought of death. Both rely on religion for solace, but the serpent-handlers evidently are more successful. The old serpent-handlers are not frightened by the prospect of death. This is true not only of those members who handle poisonous snakes in religious services, but also of the minority who do *not* handle serpents.

One 80-year-old member of the Scrabble Creek church—who did not handle serpents—testified in our presence: "I am not afraid to meet my Maker in Heaven. I am ready. If somebody was to wave a gun in my face, I would not turn away. I am in God's hands."

Another old church member, a serpent-handler, was dying from silicosis. When we visited him in the hospital he appeared serene, although he must have known that he would not live out the week.

The assertion of some modern theologians that whatever meaning and relevance God once may have had has been lost for modern man does not apply to the old serpent-handlers. To them, God is real. In fact, they often see Him during vivid hallucinations. He watches over the faithful. Misfortune and even death do not shake their faith, for misfortune is interpreted, in accordance with God's inscrutable will, as a hidden good.

Surprisingly, the contrast between the optimistic old serpent-handlers and the pessimistic elders of the conventional church all but disappeared when we shifted to the younger members of the two groups. Both groups of young people, on the psychological tests, came out as remarkably well adjusted. They showed none of the neurotic and depressive tendencies of the older conventional-church members. And this cheerful attitude prevailed despite the fact that many of them, at least among the young serpent-handlers, had much to be depressed about.

The young members of the conventional church are much better off, socially and economically, than the young serpent-handlers. The parents of the young conventional-church members can usually provide the luxuries that most young Americans regard as necessities. Many conventional-church youths are active in extracurricular activities in high school or are attending college. The young serpent-handlers, in contrast, are shunned and stigmatized as "snakes." Most young members of the conventional denomination who are in high school intend to go on to college, and they will undoubtedly attain a higher socioeconomic status than their parents have attained. But most of the young serpent-handlers are not attending school. Many are unemployed. None attend or plan to attend college, and they often appear quite depressed about their economic prospects.

The young serpent-handlers spend a great deal of time wandering aimlessly up and down the roads of the hollows, and undoubtedly are bored when not attending church. Their conversation is sometimes marked by humor, with undertones of cynicism and bitterness. We are convinced that what prevents many of them from becoming delinquent or demoralized is their wholehearted participation in religious practices that provide an acceptable outlet for their excess energy, and strengthen their self-esteem by giving them the opportunity to achieve "holiness."

Now, how does all this relate to the class differences between the serpent-handlers and the conventional-church group? The answer is that what allows the serpent-handlers to cope so well with their problems—what allows the older members to rise above the worries of illness and approaching death, and the younger members to remain relatively well adjusted despite their grim economic prospect—is a certain approach to life that is typical of them as members of the stationary working class. The key to this approach is hedonism.

Hopelessness and Hedonism

The psychological tests showed that the young serpent-handlers, like their elders, were more impulsive and spontaneous than the members of the conventional church. This may account for the strong appeal of the Holiness churches to those members of the stationary working class who prefer religious hedonism to reckless hedonism, with its high incidence of drunkenness and illegitimacy. Religious hedonism is compatible with a puritan morality—and it compensates for its constraints.

The feeling that one cannot plan for the future, expressed in religious terms as "being in God's hands," fosters the widespread conviction among members of the stationary working class that opportunities for pleasure must be exploited immediately. After all, they may never occur again. This attitude is markedly different from that of the upwardly mobile working class, whose members are willing to postpone immediate pleasures for the sake of long-term goals.

Hedonism in the stationary working class is fostered in childhood by parental practices that, while demanding obedience in the home, permit the child license outside the home. Later, during adulthood, this orientation toward enjoying the present and ignoring the future is reinforced by irregular employment and other insecurities of stationary working-class life. In terms of middle-class values, hedonism is self-defeating. But from a psychiatric point of view, for those who actually have little control of their position in the social and economic structure of modern society, it may very well aid acceptance of the situation. This is particularly true when it takes a religious form of expression. Certainly, hedonism and the associated trait of spontaneity seen in the old serpent-handlers form a very appropriate attitude toward life among old people who can no longer plan for the future.

In addition to being more hedonistic than members of the conventional church, the serpent-handlers are also more exhibitionistic. This exhibitionism and the related need for self-revelation are, of course, directly related to the religious practices of the serpent-handling church. But frankness, both about others and themselves, is typical of stationary working-class people in general. To a large extent, this explains the appeal of the Holiness churches. Ordinarily, their members have little to lose from frankness, since their status pretensions are less than those of the upwardly mobile working class, who are continually trying to present favorable images of themselves.

Because the young members of the conventional denomination are upwardly mobile, they tend to regard their elders as "old fashioned," "stick-in-the-muds," and "ignorant." Naturally, this lack of respect from their children and grandchildren further depresses the sagging morale of the older conventional-church members. They respond resentfully to the tendency of the young "to think they know more than their elders." The result is a vicious circle of increasing alienation and depression among the older members of the conventional denomination.

Respect for Age

There appears to be much less psychological incompatibility between the old and the young serpent-handlers. This is partly because the old serpent-handlers manage to retain a youthful spontaneity in their approach to life. Then, too, the young serpent-handlers do not take a superior attitude toward their elders. They admire their elders for their greater knowledge of the Bible, which both old and young accept as literally true. And they also admire their elders for their handling of serpents. The younger church members, who handle snakes much less often than the older members do, are much more likely to confess an ordinary, everyday fear of snakes—a fear that persists until overcome by strong religious emotion.

Furthermore, the young serpent-handlers do not expect to achieve higher socioeconomic status than their elders. In fact, several young men said they would be satisfied if they could accomplish as much. From the point of view of the stationary working class, many of the older serpent-handlers are quite well-off. They sometimes draw two pensions, one from Social Security and one from the United Mine Workers.

Religious serpent-handling, then—and all the other emotionalism of the Holiness churches that goes with it—serves a definite function in the lives of its adherents. It is a safety valve for many of the frustrations of life in present-day Appalachia. For the old, the serpent-handling religion helps soften the inevitability of poor health, illness, and death. For the young, with their poor educations and poor hopes of finding sound jobs, its promise of holiness is one of the few meaningful goals in a future dominated by the apparent inevitability of lifelong poverty and idleness.

Questions 7.5

1. What are the functions that the serpent-handling religions provide? Relate your discussion to the four functions covered in the text.
2. How are these functions related to the social class of the members?
3. Analyze the serpent-handlers in terms of religious organization—church, denomination, sect, etc.

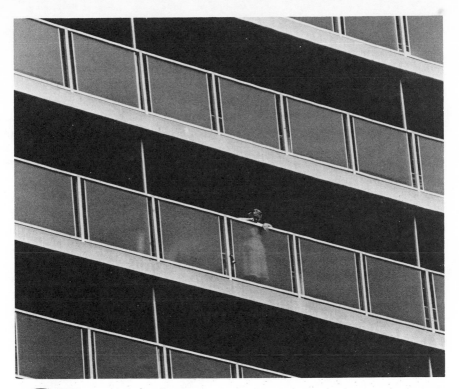

8 Population and Ecology

Previous chapters in this section on social organization have examined concepts dealing with groups, categories, aggregations, and institutions. In this chapter, we will show how social organization may be analyzed through the study of population and human ecology. Population refers to the number of people in a given unit, as in a state, society, world, or universe. **Human ecology** refers to the adaptation of people to their physical environment, their location in space. **Demography** is the study of human population, its distribution, composition, and change.

As an introduction to some of the important techniques and variables, suppose we try a demographic analysis of a college sociology class. What does the professor see as he looks out at the mass of eager young faces? The total population of the class selected is 130, of which eighty are females and fifty are males. There are four Afro-Americans, eleven

Asian-Americans, and 115 Caucasian-Americans. The age distribution of this "society" is overwhelmingly in the nineteen to twenty-three categories, with trace amounts in ages up to forty-five. Both birth and death rates for this "society" are exceedingly low. Apparently this represents a very healthy but nonfertile tribe. The life expectancy for the majority will be one semester, although for some it may be at least double that. Migration variables are peculiar for this tribe. Temporary immigration ("in-migration") occurs on those occasions when the class is planning to discuss sex or deviant behavior. Permanent emigration ("out-migration") occurs just before tests are scheduled or papers are due.

Ecologically, this class is also interesting. After several meetings, they arrange themselves in space consistently and predictably. There are occasional shifts as dating alliances change, but generally they sit in the same seats throughout the semester. Part of the patterning may be explained by classical ecological processes. Cooperation: X takes great notes, so she is constantly surrounded by A, B and C (at least I think that's the reason). Competition: When asked why they sit in front, several have said they pay more attention to what is being said and they feel the instructor is more likely to remember them; consequently, they will get better grades. Films of migrating apes have shown ecological processes at work: older males proceed in front, younger males at the rear, and females protected in the middle. Do these principles apply in your classroom?

Population

Population, then, involves the study of the numbers of people classified according to a series of variables. Demographers look at the total number of people in a society. They look at the sex ratio—the number of males per hundred females (a ratio of about sixty-three in the sociology class discussed above). Data are collected on the number of people in racial, ethnic, and religious categories. Age distributions are calculated. Birth rates and death rates are computed, as are indications of life expectancy. Migration affects the population of a society, so rates of migration—how many as well as who—are collected for those entering as well as leaving a country. Migration patterns within the country are examined also. Population growth for an area is determined by net migration (in-migration minus out-migration) plus natural increase (births minus deaths). Using these variables, a demographer might describe the United States as follows.

According to the Census Bureau, the population of the United States in February 1979 was approximately 220 million. The world population was over 4 billion. The **sex ratio** (number of males per 100 females) in 1975 in the United States was 94.9 (about ninety-five males for every hundred females). Regionally, New England and the Atlantic states have a low sex ratio (fewer males than females), and Mountain and Western states have a high sex ratio (more males than females). In 1970, New York and Massachusetts were lowest with sex ratios of less than 92; Alaska and Hawaii were highest with ratios of 119 and 108. American cities have more women than men—in central cities the sex ratio in 1970 was 90.7, while in rural areas it was 101.

Population pyramids in Figures 8.1 through 8.6 illustrate the distinctive age and sex profiles produced by different types of communities and countries. The first pyramid gives an age/sex profile for Norfolk, Virginia. Norfolk is a city with a large military base and, consequently, a concentration of young people, especially young males. The second pyramid describes Ann Arbor, Michigan, a college town. The third gives an age/sex profile of St. Petersburg, Florida, a city that attracts older, retired people.

Countries also produce distinctive population pyramids depending on their birth and death rates. Look at the population pyramids for the United States, Mexico, and Sweden. Mexico has a high birth rate and a young population, while Sweden has a low birth rate and a balanced population in terms of age. How does the United States compare with these countries? As you look at these six population profiles, imagine the types of problems and the social consequences that would go with each profile. What types of social services would be necessary given each profile?

Blacks made up about 11.5 percent of the American population in 1977, whereas Mexican-Americans accounted for about 6 percent and Asian-Americans less than 1 percent. In 1957 census data (which was the last time information on religion was collected), 66 percent reported that they were Protestant, 26 percent Catholic, and 3 percent Jewish. The median age of the population in the United States in 1970 was 28 years (a drop from 30 in 1950). The median age for males was 26.8, for females 29.3. There was variation between states as well, with Alaska having the youngest population (median age = 22.9) and Florida the oldest (32.3). By 1975, the median age of the U.S. population was moving up again, to 28.8, and in 1977 it was up to 29.4. There are proportionately more older people (age 65 and older) and more people in their twenties and thirties than there were 30 years ago. In 1977 there were 23.5 million elderly (age 65 and older) in the United States. Between 1970 and 1977, their numbers had increased by 3.5 million, but the population under the age of 5 *decreased* by almost 2 million. The fastest growing age group between 1970 and 1977 was the population between 25 and 34 years of age. The rapid growth of this group reflects the difference in the number of births during a period of relatively low fertility (the late 1930s) and a period of much higher fertility (the late 1940s).

As the proportion of young to elderly people indicates, the United States has a declining birth rate, or at least it did until 1977. Birth rates and death rates from 1930 to mid-1979 are shown in Table 8.1. The birth rate reached a high of 26 (per 1,000 people) in the late 1940s, remained around 24 through 1960, and then dropped until 1977. The general fertility rate—births per 1,000 women age 15 to 44—dropped to 65.8 in 1976. This was its lowest level in United States history (or at least since such records have been kept). The rate was higher in 1977 and 1978, but whether this signified a new trend or a short-term aberration in the rate was difficult to tell. Family size continues to decline—number of children per family was slightly over 1.8 in 1977, well below the replacement level of 2.1 children per family. *Replacement level* is defined as the average number of births per woman over her lifetime necessary for the population eventually to reach zero growth (which would take about seventy years). Population experts don't know whether this birth

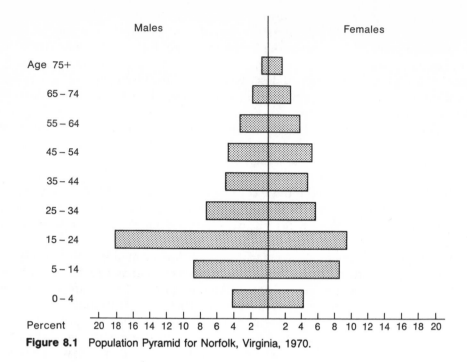

Figure 8.1 Population Pyramid for Norfolk, Virginia, 1970.

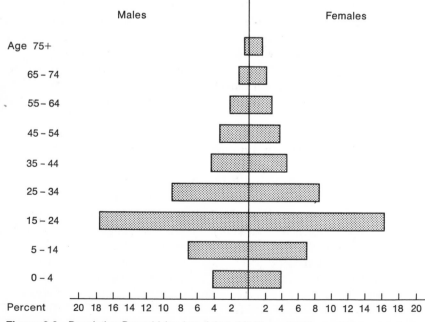

Figure 8.2 Population Pyramid for Ann Arbor, Michigan, 1970.

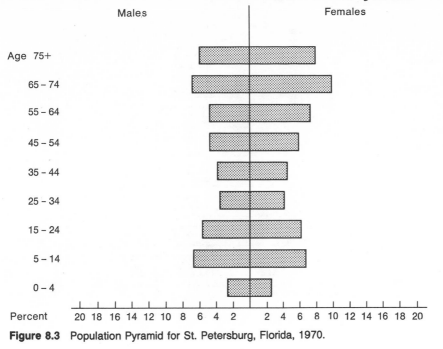

Figure 8.3 Population Pyramid for St. Petersburg, Florida, 1970.

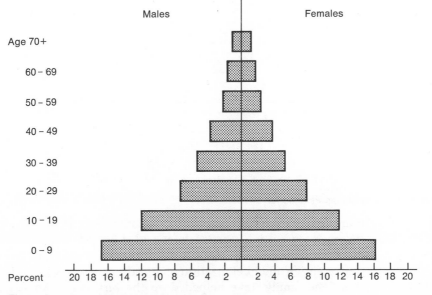

Figure 8.4 Population Pyramid for Mexico, 1970.

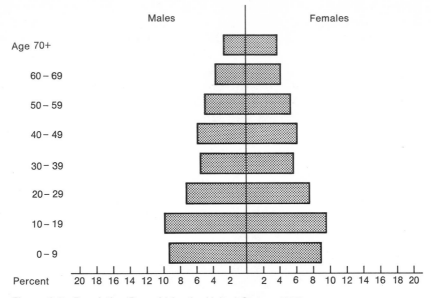

Figure 8.5 Population Pyramid for the United States, 1970.

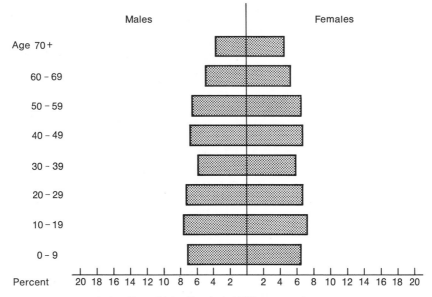

Figure 8.6 Population Pyramid for Sweden, 1970.

decline will continue, but they have come up with some reasons for why it is happening now. Women are getting married later and divorced more. Increased freedom of women to work means they are putting off marriage and child-rearing. Increased use of contraception and liberalization of abortion laws as well as changing viewpoints about the family have helped drop the birth rate. And finally, unemployment rates and a sluggish economy are also cited as contributing factors.

Forecasting the future of the American birth rate is at best a very precarious undertaking, as two researchers from California note. Nevertheless, June Sklar and Beth Berkov go out on a limb and predict that the dropping birth rate may be over and that the United States is likely to see a rise in reproduction. They state that the dropping fertility rate in this country was in great part caused by the postponement of marriage and childbearing by young women. Many of these women are getting to an age (late twenties through mid-thirties) at which they must have children soon if they are ever going to have them. This combined with the fact that large numbers of women born in the baby-boom years of the 1950s are now or will soon be in their mid-twenties suggests to Sklar and Berkov that the birth rates may rise sharply in the next few years. Increases in the birth rate in the United States in the late 1970s seems to support their contention.[1]

Let's compare the United States to other countries. Countries in Europe have about the same birth rates as the United States, whereas the birth rates of some countries (Mexico, Guatemala, Indonesia, India, Pakistan) more than double ours. The death rate in this country in 1978 was 8.7 per 1,000 people. Over a long period of time this rate has been dropping slowly, but it has remained nearly constant since the early 1950s (See Table 8.1.) European countries have about the same rate, but the rates in Nigeria, India, and Indonesia are about double ours. (Some of these comparisons are shown in Table 8.3 later in this chapter on page 255.) Life expectancy in America has slowly risen to its present point of around 74 years for whites (77 for females, 70 for males), and 68 years for non-whites (73 for females, 64 for males).

Table 8.1 Birth and Death Rates in the United States for Selected Years (per 1,000 People)

	Birth Rate	Death Rate
1930	21.3	11.5
1940	19.4	10.8
1950	23.9	9.6
1960	23.8	9.5
1970	18.2	9.4
1972	15.6	9.4
1974	14.9	9.1
1976	14.7	8.9
1977	15.3	8.8
1979 (12 mo. to end of Apr.)	15.3	8.6

U.S. Bureau of the Census, *Statistical Abstract of the United States, 1978* (99th ed.), Washington, D.C., p. 59; also "Population Profile of the United States: 1977" *Current Population Reports*, Series P–20, no. 324; and *Vital Statistics.*

[1]See June Sklar and Beth Berkov, "The American Birth Rate: Evidences of a Coming Rise," *Science,* 29 August 1975, pp. 693–700.

The figures in this section on population come from the Census Bureau and have been published in their *Current Population Reports,* or come from news releases on population projections and estimates. I have also used *Vital Statistics* and *Statistical Abstract of the United States, 1978.* The international data come from the Statistical Office of the United Nations as published in the *Statistical Yearbook* and the *Demographic Yearbook.*

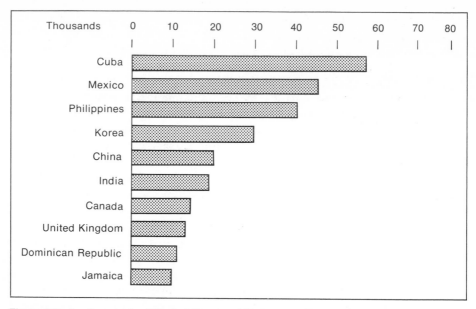

Figure 8.7 Immigrants, by Selected Country of Birth, 1977. *From U.S. Bureau of Census, Statistical Abstract of the the United States, 1978 (99th ed.), Washington, D.C.,* p. 85.

In 1977, approximately 462,000 people immigrated to the United States. Figure 8.7 shows the countries that contributed most of the immigrants to the United States in 1977. The yearly number of immigrants to this country has remained fairly constant since the 1960s.

Internally, Americans move around a great deal. Thirty-four percent of Americans did not live in the same house in 1978 as in 1975. Who is most likely to move? People in their twenties are very mobile—60 percent of 20- to 29-year-olds changed their homes between 1975 and 1978. People with at least some college education are more likely to move and to move farther than people with less education.

Migration in general is from farm to city and from city to suburb. However, demographers noticed an interesting new trend in the mid-1970s. For the first time in recent history, small communities grew faster than cities. This was coupled with increasing migration to *rural* areas. Rural counties that had lost population in the 1960s were gaining population in the 1970s. The Census Bureau reported in 1978 that nonmetropolitan areas continued to grow more rapidly than metropolitan areas. Even among those people moving to metropolitan areas, twice as many moved to suburbs as moved to the central cities between 1975 and 1977.

Population has always been concentrated around centers of industrialization and transportation, areas near important natural resources. This remains true, but it is interesting to note that migration arrows in the United States are pointing to rural and to sunbelt areas. People are moving out of the Northeast and North Central states and moving to the West and especially to the South. In the late 1970s the South's net in-migration exceeded that of the West. In another change in the middle and late 1970s, more blacks moved *to* the South instead of away from it.

Florida, California, and Texas gained the most people between 1970 and 1977, each having an average gain of over 200,000 people a year. No other state gained as much as 100,000 a year. Florida's growth has come mainly from in-migration. California and Texas have had many in-migrants, but over half their growth has been due to natural increase (births minus deaths). The *percentage* population change for selected states is shown in Table 8.2. It is apparent that population is becoming increasingly distributed in terms of recreation and leisure patterns. Sun and climate are the natural resources that are gaining new importance. By 1977, over half the population lived in the South and West. Forty percent of the population growth in this country between 1970 and 1977 occurred in just three states —California, Florida, and Texas.

Besides giving us a statistical description of collectivities, population data are useful in social planning. Population profiles in terms of age and sex enable planners to determine the number of schools needed, the number and proportion of apartments and homes to build, the type of recreation facilities required, the necessary facilities for the aged and for child care, and a number of other similar needs. When we hear that a group of city planners is developing a community with no schools (because there are no children), no tennis courts (because tennis is too strenuous), and many recreation centers and shuffleboard courts, it is apparent that the planners have designed a community for elderly retired people.

Human Ecology

Biologists have for some time studied the interrelationships and interdependence of plants and animals—the balance of nature. Living organisms are dependent on other organisms and pattern themselves in space accordingly. Why don't porcupines live in the desert? It may be because they would get sand in their quills, but it is certainly because their food supply—the bark of certain trees—does not grow

Table 8.2   Population Change in the United States 1970–1977

States Losing Population or Gaining Less Than the National Average of 6.4%	Percent Change	States Gaining Population	Percent Change
District of Columbia	−8.8%	Alaska	34.6%
New York	−1.7	Nevada	29.6
Rhode Island	−1.6	Arizona	29.3
Pennsylvania	−0.1	Florida	24.5
Ohio	0.4	Wyoming	22.2
Illinois	1.2	Idaho	20.3
Massachusetts	1.6	Utah	19.7
Iowa	1.9	Colorado	18.5
New Jersey	2.2	New Mexico	17.0
Connecticut	2.5	Hawaii	16.2

"Estimates of the Population of States: July 1, 1970 to 1977," *Current Population Reports*, Series P-25, no. 727.

in the desert. Likewise, all organisms live in certain places and patterns but not in others. Social scientists noticed that people too locate themselves in space in specific patterns, and this gave rise to the study of human ecology.

Flying over the United States, we see that people are not equally distributed but are grouped in clusters. There are fewer clusters in the West and more in the East. Most of the clusters are on rivers, lakes, or oceans. Highways run through the clusters, and various natural resources are nearby. There are fewer clusters where the climate is severe or the terrain rugged. People pattern themselves in space in predictable ways. They group together in cities, for in cities mutual cooperation and a complex division of labor allow people to accomplish much more than they could as isolated individuals. These cities are located to take maximum advantage of natural factors—waterways for transportation, resources for technological needs.

If we look more closely at the cities, we see that they also have consistent patterns. One city patterning first suggested by Ernest Burgess has five concentric circles or zones (see Figure 8.8). The small inner circle is called the *central business district* and contains the major stores, banks, offices, and government buildings, the downtown area of the city. The next circle is called the *zone in transition* and contains rundown buildings, slums, a high proportion of minority groups, some industry, and higher rates of unemployment. The third ring is called the working-man's zone and contains small apartment buildings and older single-dwelling units. The middle-class residential district is the fourth zone and contains better private residences and high-class apartments. Finally, the suburban or commuter's zone contains larger estates, golf courses, and makes up the upper-class residential district. Generally speaking, as one moves from Zone 1 (central business district) outward toward the suburbs, population density decreases, home ownership increases, the proportion of foreign-born decreases, social class rises, crime rate decreases, land cost decreases, and family size decreases. The pattern of the city may be affected by how fast the city develops, by the influence of cars, and by natural obstacles—hills, oceans, rivers. So a given city may not fit this design exactly, but many cities are close to this general pattern.

Other consistent city patterns have been suggested and are also described in Figure 8.8. Homer Hoyt feels that cities are more accurately described as sectors with a specific type of land use than as concentric zones. He believes that expensive high-rent areas follow patterns of city growth outward from the center like wedges of pie or spokes of a wheel. High-rent areas develop along the path of major streets, highways, or other major transportation lines. This type of growth outward could be along rivers or rapid transit systems, for example, and would often cut across the concentric circles suggested by Burgess.

Multiple nuclei describe a city in which a number of specialized centers or downtowns develop, each of which exerts dominance over its particular area. These centers may exist from the beginning of a city's development (as in London) or may develop later as the city grows and expands. Industry and residential areas grow up around each nucleus. Los Angeles, which has been called "a bunch of suburbs in search of a city," is an example of multiple-nuclei development.

More recent theories of city patterning include social area analysis and factorial

Concentric zone theory

Sector theory

District

1. Central business district
2. Wholesale light manufacturing
3. Low-class residential
4. Medium-class residential
5. High-class residential
6. Heavy manufacturing
7. Outlying business district
8. Residential suburb
9. Industrial suburb
10. Commuters' zone

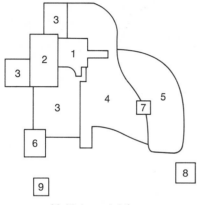

Multiple nuclei theory

Figure 8.8   Three Generalizations of the Internal Structure of Cities. *From C. D. Harris and Edward L. Ullman, Annals 242 (November 1945), 7–17.*

ecology. These techniques focus on a city's census tracts and obtain information across many variables (median rent, median education, percentage of the population married, employment, racial and ethnic mix, etc.) for each census tract. Tracts are then compared (usually by computer analysis) in an attempt to isolate the factors that distinguish between tracts and that explain city patterning. These techniques, because they use multiple dimensions, have more precision than the earlier theories and seem to have more explanatory power.[2]

[2]Original sources referred to in this section include: Ernest Burgess, "The Growth of the City," in Robert Park and Ernest Burgess, *The City* (Chicago: University of Chicago Press, 1925), p. 51; Homer Hoyt, *The Structure and Growth of Residential Neighborhoods in American Cities,* U.S. Federal Housing Administration (Washington, D.C.: U.S. Government Printing Office, 1939), Chapter 6; and C. D. Harris and Edward L. Ullman, "The Nature of Cities," *The Annals* 242 (November 1945), pp. 7–17.

Also see the discussion and summary of these theories in Noel Gist and Sylvia Fava, *Urban Society,* 6th ed. (New York: Thomas Y. Crowell, 1974), Chapter 6; or Ralph Thomlinson, *Urban Structure* (New York: Random House, 1969), Chapter 8.

How are these patterns explained? People arrange themselves in space according to social and cultural values that they believe to be important. It is apparent from previous paragraphs that economic competition has much to do with spatial arrangement in cities. Land is in greatest demand and, therefore, is most expensive in the center of the city. Banks, large stores, businesses, office buildings, and government buildings can afford the cost of locating here because of their importance, business volume, and/or financial base. Structures whose economic effect is less dramatic—homes, appartment buildings, schools, country clubs—are usually located away from the center of the city where land is cheaper. Other social values are also reflected. Many cities have set aside large green areas in those parts of the city where land is most expensive. Parks near the centers of London and Paris, the Boston Commons, and Central Park in New York are but a few of numerous examples illustrating that economic competition is not the sole determining factor in spatial arrangement. Racial and religious minority groups generally reside in separate areas of the city. This separation or segregation sometimes occurs by choice of the minority group, but more often it represents the wishes and values of the majority group. Social-class groupings also separate themselves into different parts of the city, and inevitably areas develop reputations that attract certain types of people and discourage others. As Otis and Beverly Duncan have pointed out, "spatial distances between occupation groups are closely related to their social distance."[3] In a variety of ways, then, we see that spatial arrangement reflects social and cultural values.

It is both important and interesting to note that spatial arrangement *affects* social interaction. People interact with those who live next door or across the street, unless it's a wide and busy street. People living toward the middle of the block have more social contacts than those living on corners. Friendships develop more on the side of the house where the driveway is located, especially if there are adjacent driveways—driveways are natural areas for gathering and talking. A family that doesn't mix or fit or is unfriendly often acts as a boundary; neighbors have difficulty interacting past this boundary as they would across a busy street. Such habits become so ingrained that when a new family moves into the house, it may inherit the previous family's reputation as a social boundary.[4]

William Michelson in his book *Man and His Urban Environment* outlines a number of factors that correlate with spatial arrangements in addition to those we have already mentioned. He finds, for example, that physical and social pathologies —crime and social and physical illness—are related to certain spatial factors. The health of women and their children living in self-contained houses was compared with the health of those living in three- and four-story apartments. The sickness rate of the apartment dwellers was fifty-seven percent greater than the sickness rate of those living in houses as measured by first-consultation rates for any ailment. The differences were attributed to the cramped space and greater isolation

[3]The article by Otis Dudley Duncan and Beverly Duncan, "Residential Distribution and Occupational Stratification," is quoted here from Thomlinson's book, *Urban Structure,* pp. 12–13 (see footnote 2).

[4]For a detailed description of these interaction patterns, see William H. Whyte, Jr., *The Organization Man* (New York: Simon and Schuster, 1956), Chapter 25.

of women in apartments removed from the ground. This conclusion is underlined by the fact that the women in apartments who did not have young children and were therefore able to come and go from their homes more freely had excellent health. High noise levels are related to the incidence of diseases that involve tension. Studies of overcrowding (many persons per room) and high density (many persons per acre) have found generally that *density* is more related to pathology than is overcrowding. For example, in one study (after controlling for other social characteristics) the researchers found in several instances that domestic internal overcrowding (that is, at home) was not related to students' achievement in school, but the number of families on the block (density) was. Michelson reminds us that although spatial arrangement may be important, its effects are modified by cultural values. Compare, for example, the way Japanese make use of internal and external space with how Americans make use of the same space.

Different types of people have different spatial preferences. Michelson reports that people who value convenience highly are likely to prefer more mixed land uses and small lot sizes; people who value individualism highly prefer larger lot sizes. People with cosmopolitan lifestyles desire more physical separation from neighbors and place less emphasis on being near facilities and services than do people whose interests are local. Research indicates that children up to about the age of seven, living in high-rise apartments cling much more closely to their parents than do children in single-family homes, who become independent at an earlier age. But past that age the patterns reverse—when they become more mobile, children living in high-rise apartment buildings spend much more time away from home than do children living in single-family houses. Finally, one study reports that although apartment dwellers do suffer more from noise disturbance than people living in homes, their main complaint is the restriction they feel on making noise themselves; this affects their leisure patterns and leads them to such sedentary practices as watching television.[5]

Ecologists use the terms *centralization, decentralization, segregation, invasion,* and *succession* to describe specific types of spatial arrangements. **Centralization** describes the tendency of people to gather around some central or pivotal point in a city. Centralization allows citizens to better fulfill social and economic needs and functions and is represented in most American cities by the central business district. **Decentralization,** on the other hand, refers to the tendency to move away from the central focus. Decentralization probably occurs at least partly because of dissatisfaction with certain of the consequences of centralization—traffic, crowds, noise, concrete, and so on—and is seen in the U.S. in the rush to the suburbs. **Segregation** refers to the clustering together of similar people. These similarities may be along the lines of occupation, race, religion, nationality, ethnicity, or education. **Invasion** refers to the penetration of one group or function into an area dominated by another group or function. **Succession** refers to the complete displacement or removal of the established group and represents the end product of

[5]See William Michelson, *Man and His Urban Environment* (Reading, Mass.: Addison-Wesley, 1970). The comments in these two paragraphs are drawn especially from pp. 98–99, 158, 161, and 193–195.

invasion. The invasion-succession process often produces tension, hostility, and sometimes overt conflict.[6]

A brief look at the ongoing drama of the local faculty dining room illustrates some of these ecological concepts. The room was originally segregated: faculty ate there, students ate elsewhere. Segregation also existed within the room: faculty generally sat on the south side of the room, and non-teaching staff—secretaries and administrators—sat on the north side of the room. As the college population grew, students were crowded out of other eating areas and began moving into the faculty room. Invasion had begun. Students found that the room made a convenient study area, and they brought stacks of books and papers, which further crowded out the faculty. Finally, the faculty gave up and moved elsewhere as the students took over the room. Alas, succession had occurred. . . .

Ecological arrangement in the United States has undergone change. This used to be a predominantly rural country; now most Americans live in cities or very near them. The number of people living on farms (7.8 million in 1977) has been declining over the past forty years as can be seen in Figure 8.9. As nations undergo technological and industrial development, probably it is inevitable that they become more and more urbanized. The transformation from rural to urban and the increased problems of the urbanized society have led to comparisons between the two ways of life. Urban life is seen as secondary, tense, complicated, and anonymous, and rural life is seen as primary, simple, peaceful, and benign. This tendency to idealize rural life may partially explain the current rush to the suburbs. Nostalgia for the rural existence may be based on fact or on wishful thinking, but some rural-urban behavioral differences do exist. There seems to be greater religious and political tolerance in cities and greater religious observance (church attendance) in rural areas. There is more change in cities, more stability in rural areas. There is a higher level of education and a lower birth rate in cities. There is more suicide, divorce, and a lower proportion of married people in the cities. Rates of mental illness, illegitimacy, and crime may be slightly higher in cities, but because cities keep statistics better than rural areas, we cannot be sure.[7] Technological change and the spreading influence of the mass media have in a sense given all—rural and urban dwellers alike—contact with a similar culture and set of values. The result is that many former differences between rural and urban people are rapidly disappearing.

A related ecological phenomenon is the exodus from the city to the suburbs, especially by whites. The area near the center of the city (zone in transition or workingman's zone) often offers the least expensive housing in the city. As a result, lower-class and minority group members migrate into these areas, and as they move in others who can afford it leave for the suburbs. The Bureau of the Census reported in 1970 that for the first time, suburbanites outnumbered city dwellers. This exodus continued throughout the 1970s. Between 1970 and 1977, the population of central cities declined by more than two and a half million people. Nine

[6]This is summarized from Thomlinson, *Urban Structure*, pp. 152–153 (see footnote 2).

[7]Rural-urban differences are discussed and summarized in Bernard Berelson and Gary Steiner's book, *Human Behavior* (New York: Harcourt Brace Jovanovich, 1964), pp. 606–607.

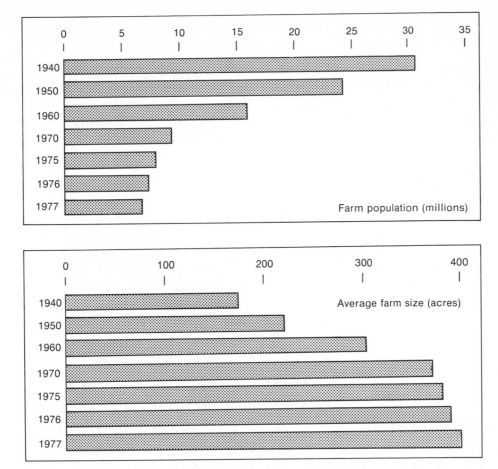

Figure 8.9 Changes in Farming: 1940 to 1977.   *From U.S. Bureau of the Census,* Statistical Abstract of the United States, 1978 *(99th ed.), Washington, D.C., p. 682.*

of the nation's ten largest cities in 1970 had lost population by 1973. As blacks and other minorities moved in, whites left. Between 1970 and 1977, whites living in central cities declined by four million while blacks living in central cities increased by almost one million. Several of our largest cities already have black majorities. The obvious result is that America is becoming more and more racially segregated. More and more schools are becoming all-white or all-black, and the gaps in understanding and tolerance between races seem to be widening rather than narrowing. The public school enrollments of Washington, D.C., Newark, Atlanta, San Antonio, New Orleans, Oakland, and Richmond, Virginia were all over seventy-five percent nonwhite and Hispanic in 1977. This increasing segregation is an urgent problem that American cities in particular and society in general must solve. We should note that all is not well even in white middle-class suburbia: Crime rates are going up in suburbs as fast as or faster than in city centers.

Another ecological trend occurring in the United States in the latter half of the twentieth century is the development of strip cities or megalopolises. One city and its suburbs merge and grow into an adjacent city and its suburbs. The eventual result is an unbroken series of cities for tens, and even hundreds of miles. Travelers at night over the East Coast report a constant chain of lights from north of Boston to south of Richmond, a 600-mile city. If urban or near-urban populations continue to grow, strip cities can be anticipated along the West Coast from San Francisco to San Diego, in the Midwest around the Great Lakes, in the Pacific Northwest, along both Florida coasts, and in many other places throughout the country.

Problem Aspects

As well as providing important information about the characteristics of societies, the study of population and human ecology calls attention to several important problems. One is what many feel will become our most serious social problem: the population explosion. For ages the human population remained fairly stable. Such things as disease, wars, and high rates of infant mortality kept births and deaths pretty much in balance. Then some 200 years ago a demographic transition occurred as death rates began to fall and population growth suddenly accelerated. A general overview of the growth of the human population over the past 10,000 years is shown in Figure 8.10.

Population increase in the last 200 years is more closely examined in Figure 8.11. The tremendous acceleration in growth since 1900 and especially since 1950 can clearly be seen.

Demographic transition refers to the movement of a population through three stages: (1) high birth rates and high death rates, (2) high birth rates and low death rates, and (3) low birth rates and low death rates. Western industrialized nations

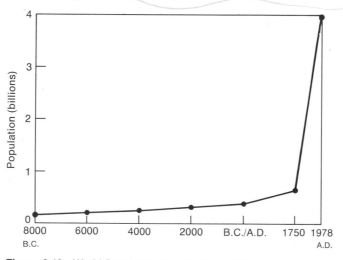

Figure 8.10   World Population Growth Since 8000 B.C.

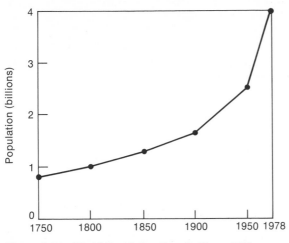

Figure 8.11   World Population Growth Since 1750.

are in the third stage, but nations in the underdeveloped regions of the world are generally in the second stage, which means rapid population growth. Table 8.3 shows birth rates, death rates, life expectancy, and population density for several underdeveloped or Third World nations and several industrialized or developed nations. Of the underdeveloped countries, Angola, Ethiopia, Nigeria, and Zaire remain on the fringes of the first stage. Their death rates are higher and life expectancy is lower than in other countries. The remaining underdeveloped nations are clearly in stage 2, just as the industrialized countries shown are clearly in stage 3—low birth and death rates. It is interesting to note that population density is not as closely related to industrialization as one might think. Some of the industrialized countries have high densities and some do not, and likewise with the nonindustrialized countries. If the nonindustrialized nations stay in stage 2, however, their population densities will probably increase substantially.

With increasing control of disease and death, population is exploding in many countries of the world. We mentioned earlier, for example, that the birth rate in Mexico is more than double that of the United States; Mexico's death rate, however, has dropped to the point where it is roughly the same as ours. The result of this lowered death rate but constant high birth rate is tremendous population growth. World population is growing at a rate of well over one million people per week. At current growth rates it is reported that in 600 years or so we will have about one square foot of land per person. (*Then* maybe further reproduction will be impossible.) Thomas Malthus said in 1789 that population would increase faster than would our ability to produce food and that we would run out of food. He may have been right, for in certain countries today, population pressure is linked to serious problems: poverty, disease, starvation, and war.

Many population experts are quite worried about this situation, and organizations all the way from the United Nations to your local Planned Parenthood Association are attempting to inform and enlighten people on the problem and on

Table 8.3   Birth Rates and Death Rates (per 1,000 People), Life Expectancy, and Population Density in Selected Countries

Underdeveloped Nations	Birth Rate	Death Rate	Life Expectancy at Birth		Density: Population per Square Kilometer
			Men	Women	
Angola	47	25	37	40	5
Egypt	36	12	52	54	37
Ethiopia	49	26	37	40	23
Guatemala	42	13	48	50	51
India	35	16	42	41	182
Iran	45	16	51	51	20
Mexico	42	9	63	67	30
Nicaragua	48	14	51	55	17
Nigeria	49	23	37	37	68
Zaire	45	21	42	45	11
Developed Nations					
Austria	12	13	67	75	90
Canada	15	7	69	76	2
England and Wales	13	12	69	75	326
France	15	10	69	76	97
Spain	18	8	70	75	70
Sweden	13	11	72	78	18
United States	15	9	68	76	23

Demographic Yearbook, 1975.

how to deal with overpopulation. Malthus thought later marriage might solve the problem. Today, birth control—the pill, abortion, sterilization—is seen as the answer. As we noted earlier in this chapter, birth rates in the United States have currently been reduced to the lowest levels in history. Whether this will continue is unknown. The rates will have to stay below the replacement level for some seventy years before population will indeed level off. Many American demographers continue to be cautious, believing that there is a population bomb latent, but not armed, in present society. A Zero Population Growth spokesman states, "The birth rate is notably fluid and capricious, strongly affected by such psychological factors as the economy or changing attitudes about the role of women." Some countries with high birth rates have encountered difficulty in introducing new population-control measures, especially when they run counter to local customs. Distrust of doctors, ignorance about biological facts or the consequences of overpopulation, desire for many sons to help farm the land, and numerous other cultural values have frustrated the efforts of people interested in population control. If the problem is ignored, or if we give up on it, it may be taken out of our hands; involuntary death control through starvation, war, or selective annihilation may be the last answer. Governmental intervention and national planning already occurring in some countries will have to become worldwide if this problem is to be effectively dealt with.

On the encouraging side, there is some evidence that perhaps the population bomb won't go off after all. Birth rates in some developing nations are beginning to decline. Ben Wattenberg has summarized research that reports some significant birth-rate drops between 1960 and 1970: South Korea from forty-one (per 1,000 people) to thirty-one, Taiwan from forty to twenty-eight, Costa Rica from forty-eight to thirty-three. Many of the declines were modest, but of the eighty-five nations with complete birth-registration data, seventy-eight reported declining rates. In mid-1978 Mexico reported a dramatic slowing in population growth, indicating that apparently the government's huge family planning program is working. A 1978 report from the United Nations states that although human numbers are growing, there are clear signs of a decline in fertility. R. M. Salas writes that in the 1970s "the world has experienced the beginning of a third wave in a series of fertility transitions. The first took place in Western Europe and North America in the 19th century; the second in Eastern Europe and Japan after World War II when population growth rates took a sharp downturn." Since the 1960s birth rates have fallen by approximately fifteen percent in three to four dozen developing nations. Why has this happened? Family planning movements may have had an effect as well as later marriage, increased literacy, and improved status of women. Whether this downward trend in fertility rates will continue long enough to have a decisive impact on world population growth remains to be seen. Even in the late 1970s, a few countries still restrict access to modern birth control methods according to the U.N., and in some countries, possession of contraceptives is still against the law.[8]

Some people optimistically suggest that population redistribution may be a helpful way of easing pressures in certain areas, and they cite as evidence high population densities in some countries (over 300 people per square kilometer in Belgium, Holland, and England and Wales, nearly 300 in Japan) and low population densities in other countries (two people per square kilometer in Canada and Australia, eleven per square kilometer in Russia, twenty-three in the United States). It is obvious, they suggest, that some countries are underpopulated and population redistribution would help. Paul Ehrlich disputes this and argues that overpopulation in a *world* problem, not a problem of individual countries, and redistribution of population will aggravate rather than solve the problem. More densely populated countries (such as Holland) are seldom self-sufficient and depend on the relatively underpopulated countries for resources and food. Measurements around the globe indicate that atmospheric dustiness is increasing by perhaps thirty percent per decade, and this poses a serious threat to the climatological balance. Fuels are being burned at rates that will exhaust estimated world reserves in well under a century. Pesticide residues are found everywhere, even in the fat of Antarctic penguins and in the Greenland ice cap. These facts indicate that the *world* has a population problem. Population distribution does present problems, especially in overcrowded urban areas, but the first priority in Ehrlich's opinion is not population redistribution but stopping population growth.[9]

[8]See Ben Wattenberg's article, "The Decline of the American Baby," *World,* 29 August 1972, pp. 20–23. Rafael M. Salas is executive director of the United Nations Fund for Population Activities, and the quote is from a newspaper excerpt (December 17, 1978) from the Fund's Annual Report by Atlas World Press Review.

[9]Paul Ehrlich has written a number of articles and several books on population and ecological problems. The ideas that I have summarized here come from Paul Ehrlich and John Holdren, "Why Do People Move?" which appeared in *Saturday Review,* 5 September 1970, p. 51.

Ecologists and urban sociologists call attention to other serious problems that are as difficult to solve as the population explosion. Specifically, they are worried about the ways we are using and destroying the environment. The automobile has taken over the American city. Most of the land area in our cities must be devoted to car-related functions—streets, highways, parking lots. With the advent of drive-in movies, drive-in restaurants, drive-in banks, drive-in stores, and now even drive-in church services, drive-in marriage ceremonies, and drive-in funeral parlors, it will soon be possible for people to go from birth to death almost without ever leaving their cars. Industries and the car are polluting our environment. Two rivers in Ohio were recently declared fire hazards. Chemicals developed to control insects have turned out to be more effective than was anticipated and are now destroying other forms of wildlife. Cities are becoming uglier, and urban sprawl is gutting the landscape. Cities are having increasing difficulty disposing of the huge amounts of garbage and refuse that people are producing (on the average, Americans produce more than four pounds of pure garbage per person per day). City centers are being abandoned, and we are creating slums at fantastic rates. More and more people feel that the city is an unfit place to live—only those live there who are forced to.[10]

Perhaps we came too quickly into an urban world. It is a fact that living in cities, especially large cities, is a relatively new experience. In 1800 only about three percent of the world's population lived in cities of 5,000 or more. By 1900, the proportion living in cities had grown to fourteen percent, and by 1950, to thirty percent.[11] The United States has changed from a sparsely settled rural country to an extremely urbanized nation. Possibly our problems are to be expected due to our lack of experience with the phenomenon of urbanization.

In his book *The Human Zoo*, zoologist Desmond Morris suggests that the human being is basically a tribal or small-group animal. People are used to interacting on a localized, interpersonal basis. Relatively recently in our history we have, because of population growth and economic advantage, been forced into a super-tribal or urban existence. Morris describes this new existence as "a human zoo." We have adapted well to some aspects of the super-tribe—the urban environment has stimulated "man's insatiable curiosity, . . . inventiveness, . . . intellectual athleticism." We have adapted less well to other aspects, however, and we see suicide, war, crime, mental illness, and destruction of the environment. The simple tribesman became a citizen, but according to Morris we have not had time to evolve into a new, genetically civilized species. We have adapted somewhat to our new environment through learning and conditioning, but biologically we are still simple tribal animals. Morris concludes, "If [man] is given the chance he may yet contrive to turn his human zoo into a magnificent human game-park. If he is not, it may proliferate into a gigantic lunatic asylum, like one of the hideously cramped menageries of the last century."[12]

---

[10]A detailed account of the problems facing cities is provided by Mitchell Gordon in his book *Sick Cities* (Baltimore: Penguin Books, 1965).

[11]This is summarized from Thomlinson, *Urban Structure*, pp. 46–48 (see footnote 2).

[12]Desmond Morris, *The Human Zoo* (New York: McGraw-Hill, 1969), especially Chapter 1. The quote is from page 248.

SUMMARY

In the previous chapters in this section on social organization we dealt with groups, categories, aggregations, and institutions. These are abstract concepts, but they are valuable for their capacity to describe and analyze the social organization of society. In this chapter, we continue to study social organization but in a somewhat different manner. The focus changes to population and human ecology, and we move from the abstract to the concrete.

Population and human ecology involve the study of numbers of people and their location in space. Population variables that are examined include birth and death rates, life expectancy figures, numbers of people in sex, age, race, ethnic, and religious categories, and migration rates. Ecological variables that are examined include study of city patterns (slums, suburbs, strip cities), ecological processes, reasons for spatial patterning, and consequences of spatial patterning. The study of population and human ecology supplies descriptive data about a society. These data, usually of a statistical nature, develop a picture of a society that often provides an interesting contrast to the picture supplied by the more abstract studies of groups and institutions. Finally, the study of population and ecology has today called attention to several serious problems facing us—overpopulation, urbanization, the destruction of the environment—and has encouraged development of the social planning needed to solve these problems.

Numerous books and articles have called attention to the almost insurmountable problems that the city faces. In the first of the two readings that follow, James and Carolyn Robertson describe the problems of a small California community and how the residents try to solve them. At the moment, overcrowded countries like India seem to have much more of a population problem than the United States. Wayne Davis in his article "Overpopulated America" suggests that, in fact, just the reverse is true. Given our numbers, our affluence, and our standard of living, we are in much more serious difficulty than India.

Reading 8.1
The Town of Last Resort—Mendocino
JAMES and CAROLYN ROBERTSON

The United States has changed from being a rural environment to being an environment dominated by cities. But cities have problems—pollution, crowding, traffic, inadequate services. In the 1970s many have come to the conclusions that cities don't work and that they are not particularly nice places to live. So people have headed back to small towns. Rural counties that were losing population in the 1960s were gaining population in the 1970s. In 1978, nonmetropolitan areas continued to grow more rapidly than metropolitan areas. And if the urbanites can't get away for good, maybe they can for the weekend at least—to the second home or just for a drive.

The rural small-town experience is valued today, so much so that it is getting harder and harder to find. Migration *out* of the city is placing tremendous pressures on the smaller communities as they try to maintain their identity and character. Most small communities do not have the resources to deal with invasion, but there are some successes. In *The Small Towns Book*, James and Carolyn Robertson write about the attempts of seven communities from across the country to cope with the pressures from outside. The following reading is adapted from their more detailed study of Mendocino, California.

Mendocino is a scenic day's drive from the San Francisco bay area on the rugged north coast of California. There are few places in California more attractive. It is perched on a bluff above the rocks and surf—at the very edge of the Pacific. It is a town of old houses, water towers, barns and chicken coops, plunked down in a spectacular countryside. In the little back alleys and in the empty lots are tangles of berries, flowering weeds, and nasturtiums gone wild. In spots, the old buildings lean on each other for support.

Mendocino was once a difficult-to-get-to lumber town settled by New Englanders, Finns, and Portuguese. A lumber mill, a few merchants and farmers made up the town. When the mill closed, the town went to sleep. In the late 1950s a San Francisco artist started the Mendocino Art Center and other artists soon followed. The tourists began coming—first a trickle, then a stream. Real estate offices, "prestige" homes, gift shops, a delicatessen, restaurants appeared. The town, for over a hundred years a home for children, ponies, and dogs, was invaded by outsiders.

> *This year we got tour busses for the very first time. It used to be we just got people who came here for the same reasons people came here to live. They loved the ocean, and they liked to walk in the open meadows, or in the woods around town. Or they combed the beaches. Maybe they brought paints and took a class at the Art Center—or just read a book. They were more like the rest of us. Now we're getting a different kind of tourist. I call them polyesters and double-knits. They come in motor homes. Or on Greyhound tour busses, and they don't seem to be satisfied with the town as it is. They are rewarding people who offer them a kind of entertainment or shopping that we've never had here and have no real use for. They need to be titillated. They don't take walks along the beach. They walk in my front yard. And they don't just come in the summertime anymore. They're coming all year long.*

Mendocino, like many other small communities, was discovered. Tourists, welcomed in smaller numbers, now appear to be changing the character of the town. Land developers have arrived. Property has become much more valuable and taxes are rising. Probably the most unfortunate consequence is the uncertainty and dissension among the residents themselves as they debate the town's future. Should Mendocino cash in on its sudden popularity or should it remain the private weatherbeaten small town of its past? These issues have split communities across the country as they struggle to deal with pressures from outside. Each community confronts its problems in unique ways. Mendocino's major events were the sewer, big money in town, the tax strike, and the chamber of anti-commerce.

The Sewer

In 1972 the Environmental Protection Agency informed the town that they must stop dumping untreated sewage in the ocean—they would have to build a sewer plant. The size of the sewer plant would determine how much the town could grow. In the debate over the town's sewer the first lines of contention between the advocates of development and the advocates of no more growth were drawn. Some residents didn't like what was happening to Mendocino but at the same time didn't want to restrict a person's freedom to do what they wanted to with their own property. Other residents who long awaited the town's revival felt the more development the better. Others saw their ideal of small town life being turned into a commercial bonanza, and they banded together to preserve Mendocino's "hometown" character.

The advocates of a bigger sewer won the first battle. The sewer would service areas not yet developed—Mendocino, it seems, would grow some more. But then things got complicated. The sewer was financed by a federal grant which required that certain conditions had to be met. For one thing, the sewer was not intended to be a stimulant to uncontrolled development of the town—there had to be a protective land-use plan for the town. In a subsequent battle over new development, the anti-development group found that certain federal requirements had not been met and they were able to obtain a state enforced moratorium on further development. Mendocino would not grow, at least not just yet.

Big Money in Town

In 1974 rumors began to circulate that someone was going to buy the old Mendocino Hotel on Main Street. A town landmark, the Hotel has a view of the ocean, old fashioned furniture, pretty good food, and bathrooms down the hall. The Hotel was bought by a wealthy Southern Californian who had fallen in love with Mendocino. He also bought other property in town and quickly became a major force in the community though still living in Southern California.

It's hard to tell how people feel about this. He gave a valuable piece of property to Mendocino and he remodeled the Hotel to high style California Victorian. But he doesn't live in Mendocino, his wealth comes from outside, and he is changing their town.

Other outside money began coming. Mendocino is seen as a good investment and they buy, paying high prices which drive property values up. It is the impact of this invasion of outside wealth which has had the most dramatic and potentially the most destructive effect on the little community.

The Tax Strike

In California taxes are levied by the County and are based on the value of real property. Most public revenue comes from those who own real estate. Property values are determined by improvements that may have been made to the property and by what similar properties in the area are selling for. In 1975 Mendocino

County re-assessed coastal properties and the property owners were notified by mail of the new value of their property.

The results were staggering. Property values had escalated by so much that taxes would increase by 4 to 10 times! Though citizens could appeal the new values, the procedure is time consuming and little understood. People were upset and many couldn't afford to pay their tax bills. They organized, held public meetings, and worked to get the word around. As the December 10th date for tax payment approached, a course of action developed. They decided on a tax strike—instead of sending tax money to the County, they sent teabags! Over a half million dollars in taxes were withheld. Nationwide attention was given to Mendocino's teabag tax protest.

The Chamber of Anti-Commerce

In September 1976 a market called Corners of the Mouth was told to vacate its premises. The owner of the building wanted to remodel and install an enlarged gift and antique shop. The market had been a popular place among the locals, a social center. Many doubted the need for another gift shop and saw the eviction of the Corners of the Mouth as one more blow to the hometown and another victory for tourism. Some of the residents of Mendocino had been pushed to the limit and they fought back. They developed SCAT—Sensible Citizens Against Tourism. They parked their cars in places normally used by tourists, put posters on the cars explaining why, and passed out information to visitors. The following letter was handed out.

An Open Letter to Visitors

First be assured that it is not you, personally, we are questioning. Person-to-person, had we a quiet context, we would probably become friends; certainly not enemies.

Our problem is that the flood of tourists recently has passed beyond what a small town can handle and still function as a community. Noise of automobiles drowns out sounds of the ocean, even late at night. We now smell exhaust instead of salt air. Streets are littered. Townspeople cannot find places to park. Many young, creative people have had their rents increased and must now move. Taxes are rising and many oldtimers now must sell. The quiet, creative ambience of the town is dissolving, replaced by a growing number of antique stores and other tourist-oriented businesses.

We realize growth is inevitable; most of us moved here realizing Mendocino had an active tourist industry already. We accept that visitors have a legal right to come here and that property owners have a legal right to develop their land as they see fit.

But we also profoundly cherish the fact that Mendocino is a living community; this is our home; families live here. This is still a creative center where artists, poets, actors and students come to live and work and experiment.

We do not mind a reasonable number of visitors, especially visitors who will pause long enough to get to know the town, the people—will trouble themselves to feel the real Mendocino beneath the commercial veneer. We mind the inundation of the town by hordes flashing through for a few minutes or hours. We mind the rapid and sudden investment in Mendocino-as-commercial-enterprise, especially by those who live elsewhere.

So we urge you to come here infrequently, sensitive to the fact that you are entering a fragile community of real people. If you do come back, we urge you to consider staying for more than a night or two—long enough to realize that basic functions of communities are deep and personal . . . and that window dressing is not the real product. Look for the authentic work of local people. Question what you buy, whether it is locally made, or just shipped here for the tourist industry.

Please do not encourage others to come here. Present facilities—and basic services— are overloaded. We do not want more facilities to further destroy the fragile fabric of community that still exists here. Consider—and we say this respectfully—your own backyard. If you spent the time and energy there that you are spending here, wouldn't you, your family, your neighborhood, and the planet, be better off? Then, perhaps we could someday visit you and have something to gain from it.

Community in America is getting to be a lost art. Commercial, phoney tourist traps are increasingly prevalent. Help us protect, maintain, and develop the former.

—The Mendocino SCAT Committee (Sensible Citizens Against Tourism)

The Town of Last Resort

A town is only partly real estate. It is also a network of enormously complex interactions between people. This network is a live thing, the thing that makes towns live. This network is a product of the collective history of the community, and of deeply personal beliefs and convictions held by each of its residents. To ignore this network when one is at work in the machinery of public affairs is to invite chaos.

Some of the people in and around Mendocino do not agree with SCAT. They believe it is morally wrong to move to a small community and then tell others to keep away. One writes, "Don't get mean with a tourist who has come here to find some beauty. How many of us have done the same, leaving behind the sad city? All we can do is grow, deal with knowledge, using life to determine what is valuable."

Other people in Mendocino who believe they are fighting for their homes do not agree. At their backs is the Pacific Ocean. At their doors are the promoters of tourism and land speculators. To them Mendocino is a town of last resort. There isn't anywhere else to go.

A small town is a fragile affair—it is easy to unbalance. But the issues are difficult: How many gift shops are enough? Should one sell property for less than it is worth? Should anyone stand in the way of progress? The battle in Mendocino will continue, for it reflects in a smaller arena many of the basic conflicts present in American Society.

Questions 8.1

1. What are the basic conflicts in Mendocino?
2. What sort of parallels can you draw between what is happening in Mendocino and the problems big cities face?
3. Imagine that you are a city planner. What kinds of statutes would you establish to keep what happened in Mendocino from happening in your community? Or would you want to?
4. Illustrate as many of the ecological processes as you can using Mendocino as example.

Reading 8.2
Overpopulated America

WAYNE H. DAVIS

Population pressure may be assessed by means of many different variables: number of people, population density, ability of the land to produce food, trends in birth rates and death rates. Wayne Davis introduces the variables of affluence and standard of living and suggests that they may be at least as important as number of people. He compares America's population problem to India's by using the concept of "Indian equivalents." Professor Davis teaches in the school of biological sciences at the University of Kentucky.

I define as most seriously overpopulated that nation whose people by virtue of their numbers and activities are most rapidly decreasing the ability of the land to support human life. With our large population, our affluence and our technological monstrosities the United States wins first place by a substantial margin.

Let's compare the U.S. to India, for example. We have 203 million people, whereas she has 540 million on much less land. But look at the impact of people on the land.

The average Indian eats his daily few cups of rice (or perhaps wheat, whose production on American farms contributed to our one percent per year drain in quality of our active farmland), draws his bucket of water from the communal well and sleeps in a mud hut. In his daily rounds to gather cow dung to burn to cook his rice and warm his feet, his footsteps, along with those of millions of his countrymen, help bring about a slow deterioration of the ability of the land to support people. His contribution to the destruction of the land is minimal.

An American, on the other hand, can be expected to destroy a piece of land on which he builds a home, garage and driveway. He will contribute his share to the 142 million tons of smoke and fumes, seven million junked cars, 20 million tons of paper, 48 billion cans, and 26 billion bottles the overburdened environment must absorb each year. To run his air conditioner we will strip-mine a Kentucky Hillside, push the dirt and slate down into the stream, and burn coal in a power generator, whose smokestack contributes to a plume of smoke massive enough to cause cloud seeding and premature precipitation from Gulf winds which should be irrigating the wheat farms of Minnesota.

In his lifetime he will personally pollute three million gallons of water, and industry and agriculture will use ten times this much water in his behalf. To provide these needs the U.S. Army Corps of Engineers will build dams and flood farmland. He will also use 21,000 gallons of leaded gasoline containing boron, drink 28,000 pounds of milk and eat 10,000 pounds of meat. The latter is produced and squandered in a life pattern unknown to Asians. A steer on a Western range eats plants containing minerals necessary for plant life. Some of these are incorporated into the body of the steer which is later shipped for slaughter. After being eaten by man these nutrients are flushed down the toilet into the ocean or buried in the cemetery, the surface of which is cluttered with boulders called tombstones and has been removed from productivity. The result is a continual drain on the productivity of range land. Add to this the erosion of overgrazed lands, and the effects of the falling water table as we mine Pleistocene deposits of groundwater to irrigate to produce food for more people, and we can see why our land is dying far more rapidly than did the great civilization of the Middle East, which experienced the same cycle. The average Indian citizen, whose fecal material goes back to the land, has but a minute fraction of the destructive effect on the land that the affluent American does.

Thus I want to introduce a new term, which I suggest be used in future discussions of human population and ecology. We should speak of our numbers in "Indian equivalents." An Indian equivalent I define as the average number of Indian citizens required to have the same detrimental effect on the land's ability to support human life as would the average American. This value is difficult to determine, but let's take an extremely conservative working figure of 25. To see how conservative this is, imagine the addition of 1000 citizens to your town and 25,000 to an Indian village. Not only would the Americans destroy much more land for homes, highways and a shopping center, but they would contribute far more to environmental deterioration in hundreds of other ways as well. For example, their demand for steel for new autos might increase the daily pollution equivalent of 130,000 junk autos which *Life* tells us that U.S. Steel Corp. dumps into Lake Michigan. Their demand for textiles would help the cotton industry destroy the life in the Black Warrior River in Alabama with endrin. And they would contribute to the massive industrial pollution of our oceans (we provide one-third to one-half the world's share) which has caused the precipitous downward trend in our commercial fisheries landings during the past seven years.

The per capita gross national product of the United States is 38 times that of India. Most of our goods and services contribute to the decline in the ability of the environment to support life. Thus it is clear that a figure of 25 for an Indian equivalent is conservative. It has been suggested to me that a more realistic figure would be 500.

In Indian equivalents, therefore, the population of the United States is at least four billion. And the rate of growth is even more alarming. We are growing at one percent per year, a rate which would double our numbers in 70 years. India is growing at 2.5 percent. Using the Indian equivalent of 25, our population growth becomes 10 times as serious as that of India. According to the Rienows in their recent book *Moment in the Sun,* just one year's crop of American babies can be expected to use up 25 billion pounds of beef, 200 million pounds of steel and 9.1 billion gallons of gasoline during their collective lifetime. And the demands on water and land for our growing population are expected to be far greater than the supply available in the year 2000. We are destroying our land at a rate of over a million acres a year. We now have only 2.6 agricultural acres per person. By 1975 this will be cut to 2.3, the critical point for the maintenance of what we consider a decent diet, and by the year 2000 we might expect to have 1.2.

You might object that I am playing with statistics in using the Indian equivalent on the rate of growth. I am making the assumption that today's child will live 35 years (the average Indian life span) at today's level of affluence. If he lives an American 70 years, our rate of population growth would be 20 times as serious as India's.

But the assumption of continued affluence at today's level is unfounded. If our numbers continue to rise, our standard of living will fall so sharply that by the year 2000 any surviving Americans might consider today's average Asian to be well off. Our children's destructive effects on their environment will decline as they sink ever lower into poverty.

The United States is in serious economic trouble now. Nothing could be more misleading than today's affluence, which rests precariously on a crumbling foundation. Our productivity, which had been increasing steadily at about 3.2 percent a year since World War II, has been falling during 1969. Our export over import balance has been shrinking steadily from $7.1 billion in 1964 to $0.15 billion in the first half of 1969. Our balance of payments deficit for the second quarter was $3.7 billion, the largest in history. We are now importing iron ore, steel, oil, beef, textiles, cameras, radios and hundreds of other things.

Our economy is based upon the Keynesian concept of a continued growth in population and productivity. It worked in an underpopulated nation with excess resources. It could continue to work only if the earth and its resources were expanding at an annual rate of 4 to 5 percent. Yet neither the number of cars, the economy, the human population, nor anything else can expand indefinitely at an exponential rate in a finite world. We must face this fact *now*. The crisis is here. When Walter Heller says that our economy will expand by 4 percent annually through the latter 1970s he is dreaming. He is in a theoretical world totally unaware of the realities of human ecology. If the economists do not wake up and devise a new system for us now somebody else will have to do it for them.

A civilization is comparable to a living organism. Its longevity is a function of its metabolism. The higher the metabolism (affluence), the shorter the life. Keynesian economics has allowed us an affluent but shortened life span. We have now run our course.

The tragedy facing the United States is even greater and more imminent than that descending upon the hungry nations. The Paddock brothers in their book, *Famine 1975!,* say that India "cannot be saved" no matter how much food we ship her. But India will be here after the United States is gone. Many millions will die in the most colossal famines India has ever known, but the land will survive and she will come back as she always has before. The United States on the other hand, will be a desolate tangle of concrete and ticky-tacky, of strip-mined moonscape and silt-choked reservoirs. The land and water will be so contaminated with pesticides, herbicides, mercury fungicides, lead, boron, nickel, arsenic and hundreds of other toxic substances, which have been approaching critical levels of concentration in our environment as a result of our numbers and affluence, that they may be unable to sustain human life.

Thus as the curtain gets ready to fall on man's civilization let it come as no surprise that it shall first fall on the United States. And let no one make the mistake of thinking we can save ourselves by "cleaning up the environment." Banning DDT is the equivalent of the physician's treating syphilis by putting a bandaid over the first chancre to appear. In either case you can be sure that more serious and widespread trouble will soon appear unless the disease itself is treated. We cannot survive by planning to treat the symptoms such as air pollution, water pollution, soil erosion, etc.

What can we do to slow the rate of destruction of the United States as a land capable of supporting human life? There are two approaches. First, we must reverse the population growth. We have far more people now than we can continue to support at anything near today's level of affluence. American women average slightly over three children each. According to the *Population Bulletin* if we reduced this number to 2.5 there would still be 330 million people in the nation at the end of the century. And even if we reduced this to 1.5 we would have 57 million more people in the year 2000 than we have now. With our present longevity patterns it would take more than 30 years for the population to peak even when reproducing at this rate, which would eventually give us a net decrease in numbers.

Do not make the mistake of thinking that technology will solve our population problem by producing a better contraceptive. Our problem now is that people want too many children. Surveys show the average number of children wanted by the American family is 3.3. There is a little difference between the poor and the wealthy, black and white, Catholic and Protestant. Production of children at this rate during the next 30 years would be so catastrophic in effect on our resources and the viability of the nation as to be beyond my ability to contemplate. To prevent this trend we must not only make contraceptives and abortion readily available to everyone, but we must establish a system to put severe economic pressure on those who produce children and reward those who do not. This can be done within our system of taxes and welfare.

The other thing we must do is to pare down our Indian equivalents. Individuals in American society vary tremendously in Indian equivalents. If we plot Indian equivalents versus their reciprocal, the percentage of land surviving a generation, we obtain a linear regression. We can then place individuals and occupation types on this graph. At one end would be the starving blacks of Mississippi; they would approach unity in Indian equivalents, and would have the least destructive effect on the land. At the other end of the graph would be the politicians slicing pork for the barrel, the highway contractors, strip-mine operators, real estate developers, and public enemy number one—the U.S. Army Corps of Engineers.

We must halt land destruction. We must abandon the view of land and minerals as private property to be exploited in any way economically feasible for private financial gain. Land and minerals are resources upon which the very survival of the nation depends, and their use must be planned in the best interests of the people.

Rising expectations for the poor is a cruel joke foisted upon them by the Establishment. As our new economy of use-it-once-and-throw-it-away produces more and more products for the affluent, the share of our resources available for the poor declines. Blessed be the starving blacks of Mississippi with their outdoor privies, for they are ecologically sound, and they shall inherit a nation. Although I hope that we will help these unfortunate people attain a decent standard of living by diverting war efforts to fertility control and job training, our most urgent task to assure this nation's survival during the next decade is to stop the affluent destroyers.

Questions 8.2

1. What point is Davis attempting to make by introducing the concept "Indian equivalents"?
2. Davis suggests that there are two approaches to America's problem of overpopulation. What are the difficulties likely to be encountered in following these two approaches?

III Social Change and Social Deviation

In Part II we dealt with the individual as a member of society and the social organization of society. We saw that social organization could be studied using the following concepts: group, category and aggregation, institution, population, and human ecology. In Part III we will focus on change and deviation in society. The concepts discussed in this section will suggest that all is not as predictable and organized as previous sections may have implied. Uncertainty and instability exist in all societies and are the result of a variety of factors. *Social change* occurs and affects the way individuals and groups relate to each other. If social change is rapid and extreme, the organization of society may break down and *social disorganization* may result. In some situations, behavior occurs that is spontaneous and unstructured but not necessarily disorganized. This type of behavior is called *collective behavior.* We learned in Part I that norms and roles describe what people are expected to do in certain situations and positions. But inevitably, many individuals do *not* behave in the ways they are expected to. Societies, in turn, devise ways to encourage or even force conformity. This leads us to the final topics of *deviant behavior* and *social control.*

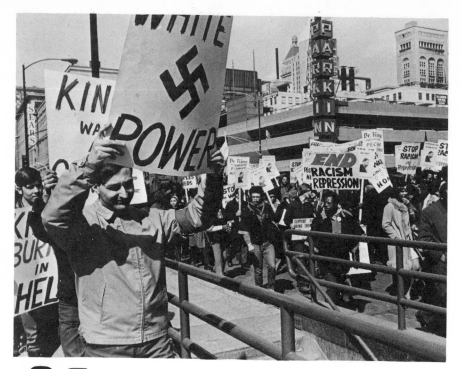

9 Social Change and Social Disorganization

In June, 1978, a British language expert reported that English is changing so much that in the future Americans and British people won't be able to understand each other without the help of a translator. American English is changing rapidly, and British English is retaining its more ancient character. Robert Burchfield, chief editor of the Oxford English dictionaries, states that since 1776 American English and British English have been on divergent courses and that their speakers should end up unintelligible to one another in another 200 years.

We have looked at the social organization of society for some five chapters now. At this point society may have the appearance of a well-oiled machine clickety-clicking along—groups interacting, highly polished institutions efficiently dealing with society's central issues and conducting business as usual, populations reproducing, and people continuing to pattern themselves in space in very predictable ways. Focusing on the social organization of society is an extremely important perspective, but it unfortunately implies that conditions are constant, that all behave as they are expected to, that there are never unpredictable occurrences or failures either in people or in social conditions.

The fact of the matter is that all is *not* constant—life is not the same today as it was yesterday. The following changes come to my mind. A supersonic jet (Concorde) is making regular flights to this country. It wasn't too long ago that it took more than twelve hours to cross the Atlantic by propeller plane; now it is just over three hours. Interest in the ozone layer, noise, and air pollution are recent concerns. A January 1976 marijuana law in California was an attempt to *decriminalize* a narcotics issue—imagine that happening three or four years earlier. A worldwide oil crisis means that the price of gasoline continues to rise rapidly and that international power alignments are being restructured. Who could have imagined OPEC and its current importance a decade ago? The women's movement has led to new rights and new roles and resocialization for many men and women. Watergate has brought a new view of presidential power and prerogative. The Supreme Court decisions on abortion and capital punishment have had far-reaching effects, and there is still much controversy about these issues.

The point is, of course, that all societies are dynamic and constantly changing. Some societies change more rapidly than others, and within a society some parts change more rapidly than other parts. Some changes may lead to improvement, to a better life for some or most of the members of society. Change may also lead to problems because, although some individuals and institutions will adjust rapidly, others will have difficulty adapting to change. We can anticipate that social change will occasionally lead to periods of social disorganization as old ways erode and collapse and new ways of behaving are developed.

Social change refers to significant alterations in social relationships and cultural ideas.[1] Social and cultural factors are combined in this definition because they

[1]See the chapter on social change by Alvin Boskoff in Howard Becker and Alvin Boskoff, *Modern Sociological Theory* (New York: Dryden Press, 1957).

are tightly interrelated. Changes in ideas and values quickly lead to changes in social relationships, and vice versa. Development of the ideas of science has led to new roles (astronauts, rocket experts) and changed social relationships. People's concerns about pollution led to new ideas and material inventions (smaller cars with fewer harmful emissions).

Social change takes place continually and, in modern society, at ever increasing rates. Change is such a constant factor in our existence that frequently we lose sight of its extent. One way to put change in perspective is to imagine that your own life started ten years earlier than it did or to compare your life experiences with those of your parents. Technological changes probably first come to mind—high-speed travel, voyages to outer space, atomic power, transplanting organs, a computerized society. But there are other sorts of changes as well. Look at the areas in which there would be contrasts for two people with only ten years difference in their ages: the changing role of women; the size of the family one is born into; different educational philosophies and techniques; control of certain diseases and life expectancy; likelihood of getting married and if so, at what age; to demonstrate for a cause or not, and if so, what cause (Vietnam, legalized abortion, civil rights?); whether to go to college, and if so, what major (social science or business administration?); amount of leisure time available and what to do with it; tastes in music (rock concerts or disco?); and so on. And if we can find these differences across ten years, imagine the contrast over twenty or thirty years.

Change factors are related to each other in complex patterns; often the path of influence is difficult to clearly detect. Development of the contraceptive pill (new idea, invention) led to changes (more freedom) in sexual behavior. Or did concerns with increased freedom for women and with family size lead to development of contraceptive devices? Keeping in mind the complex nature of social change, perhaps we can outline some of the major factors related to change.

Factors Related to Social Change

Various attempts have been made to relate social change to other factors in the physical and social environment.[2] Some of these hypothesized relationships seem farfetched; others seem more reasonable. For example, social change has been related to the biological characteristics of a nation. Adherents of master race theories believe that societies fortunate enough to be graced by the presence of a superior race will have greater progress (and more rapid social change) than will less fortunate nations. Sociologist Robert Bierstedt points out that such theories—present at all times in all societies—are only a primitive form of ethnocentrism. A more realistic approach might hold that people who differ by race or ethnicity have different social and cultural patterns, and certain mixtures of these in a given society could lead to greater or lesser conflict and, correspondingly, greater or lesser social change. Geographical factors may be related to change. Some countries are more favored by climate and natural resources, and this may affect their rates of

[2]This discussion is drawn in part from Robert Bierstedt, *The Social Order*, 4th ed. (New York: McGraw-Hill, 1974), Chapter 20.

Social change can be observed in many different ways. Compare the lists of the twenty most often watched TV programs in 1958–1959 and in 1978–1979.

1958–1959   **1978–1979**

  1 Gunsmoke   1 Laverne & Shirley
  2 Wagon Train   2 Three's Company
  3 Have Gun, Will Travel   3 Ropers
  4 Rifleman   4 Happy Days
  5 Danny Thomas   5 Mork & Mindy

  6 Maverick   6 Angie
  7 Wells Fargo   7 13 Queens Blvd
  8 Real McCoys   8 MASH
  9 I've Got a Secret   9 60 Minutes
 10 Wyatt Earp   10 Taxi

 11 Price Is Right   11 Charlie's Angels
 12 Red Skelton   12 All in the Family
 13 Zane Grey   13 Eight is Enough
 14 Father Knows Best   14 Little House on the Prairie
 15 Texan   15 Alice

 16 Wanted Dead or Alive   16 Barney Miller
 17 Peter Gun   17 ABC Sunday Movie
 18 Cheyenne   18 Love Boat
 19 Perry Mason   19 One Day at a Time
 20 Ernie Ford   20 S. Channing and Friends

What attitude changes are reflected here? Is it a transition from identifying with the frontier and the wild west to becoming a nation of city dwellers? Or is it a change in our patterns of escapism from the hard-riding, fast-shooting, macho man on horseback to urban, family-centered situation comedies? Or is it that we were more desperately in need of a laugh in the 1970s?

Lists courtesy of A. C. Nielsen, Inc.

technological advancement and social change. As we discussed in the previous chapter, demographic factors may lead to change. When a country faces population growth to the point of overcrowding, social relationships change, both within that society and with surrounding societies, which may be less crowded.

Social change may be related to the appearance of certain great men. Recall how societies, and even the world, were affected and changed by Hitler, Napoleon, Einstein, Lincoln, Karl Marx, and Julius Caesar. The course of events in the United States in the mid-twentieth century has been altered by men such as Franklin D. Roosevelt and Martin Luther King, Jr. It is sometimes argued that great men alone initiate significant social changes, but others maintain that such men are merely products of their society, and that if they had not appeared, someone else of the same caliber would have. The truth probably lies somewhere between these views.

The cultural and societal conditions might be seen as a stage where people perform, a few in unique ways having lasting effects, many others in more commonplace and predictable ways. And, certainly, the historical aspect cannot be overlooked as a factor in change. Many great men were made by historical conditions—accidents of history. Had they appeared at another time, they would probably have passed unnoticed.

Ideological and technological factors are related to social change. The appearance of and commitment to ideas of socialism, democracy, Christianity, science, or progress have led to major social changes. The industrial revolution of the eighteenth and nineteenth centuries was a major force for change in the United States and elsewhere; its dramatic consequences are still with us today. Technological innovations and inventions that have produced tremendous social change include the wheel, the car, the birth control pill, the atom bomb, the gun, the telephone, the airplane, and the computer. It is easy to point to the dramatic inventions that affect societies, probably because their emergence seems sudden, rather than slow and evolutionary as are many changes. Sometimes the effects of inventions are less obvious. Sociologist William Ogburn recorded numerous examples of the widespread effects of technological innovations.[3] The self-starter on cars aided in the emancipation of women: It allowed women to use cars on an equal basis with men. The invention of the elevator made possible the construction of tall apartment buildings. Living in these buildings, in turn, changed the family: Rearing of large families was more difficult, and consequently the urban birth rate declined. The invention of the cotton gin was a major factor leading to the Civil War. How? Ogburn suggests that invention of the cotton gin led to more slaves to cultivate more cotton, and the greater production led to increased trade with England. This in turn led the South, which supported free trade, into conflict with the economic interests of the North, which wanted protective tariffs and restricted foreign imports, and this conflict led to war. Invention of the six-shooter, barbed wire, and the windmill made possible the settling of the Great Plains. To imply that inventions have such far-reaching effects no doubt seems as much of an oversimplification as did the great men theory. The lesson probably is that we cannot single out any one element or invention in a culture and attribute change to it alone.

Social change is introduced in a culture through two processes: invention and diffusion. **Invention** refers to the creation of a new object or idea. Usually, although the end product of the invention (car, airplane, telescope) is new, the parts that make it up are not. The elements have been around and are now arranged or put together in a new way. **Diffusion** refers to the spread of objects or ideas from one society to another (Egypt to England) or from one group to another within the same society (upper class to lower class or black to white). Although innovation or invention attracts the most attention, most change is introduced through the process of diffusion. Remember Ralph Linton's "One Hundred Percent American" on pages 85–87?

To sum up the many factors related to social change, we could generalize and

---

[3]Ogburn's works include *Social Change* (New York: Viking Press, 1922, 1950); *The Social Effects of Aviation* (Boston: Houghton Mifflin, 1946); *Machines and Tomorrow's World,* rev. ed., Public Affairs Pamphlets, no. 25, 1946; and Ogburn and Nimkoff, *Sociology* 2d ed. (Boston: Houghton Mifflin, 1950).

say that social change represents the coming together of a number of events: The conditions in a particular culture at a given time in history and the change agent or catalyst (a particular person or the invention or diffusion of a new technique, object, or idea).

Rates of Change

Different segments of a given society frequently change at different rates. Ogburn called this condition **cultural lag.** A new element may be introduced requiring change in other areas of society, and when these other areas are slow to change, problems result. Faster cars were built in advance of highways that could handle them. Jumbo jets arrived before airports were constructed that could accommodate the increased passenger load. People's attitudes usually change far more rapidly than laws change, especially in the area of morality laws, and a cultural lag exists.

A society's receptivity to change is an important factor in the rate of social change. If a society has a strictly defined system of stratification or rigid institutional structure, change will be slower. If a society is isolated from others, change will be slower. Change will be more rapid in a society that emphasizes the values

---

Saudi Arabia sits atop the greatest reservoir of oil yet discovered on earth. In 1976, while working less than half her oil fields, the Saudi oil industry earned about $37.8 billion, or just over $100 million a day. This would allow the Saudis to buy (if they wanted):

all taxable real estate in Manhattan in 5 months, 27 days
General Motors in 4 months, 19 days
Bank of America in 2 weeks, 5 days
CBS in 7 days, 5 hours
all professional football teams in the U.S. in 4 days, 1 hour
Tiffany's in 5 hours, 49 minutes

In spite of this tremendous wealth, Saudi Arabia retains the characteristics of an underdeveloped country. The country lacks the schools, hospitals, roads, banks, factories, and farms that are the true bases of national wealth. One percent of the land grows food. About one person in eight can read Arabic. The life expectancy is about forty years and infant mortality is high—some Bedouin tribes still call all their sons Muhammad at birth and then, at the age of five, rename the minority who survive. The wheel was, in effect, introduced in Arabia only about fifty years ago, attached to the automobile.

Construction of roads, ports, buildings, schools, telephones, and so on, is now widespread. Improvement of social conditions will follow more slowly. *Imagine* the forces of social change focusing on this country as development of the rest of Saudi society tries to match the increasing flood of oil wealth.

From "The Arabian Ethos," by Peter A. Iseman, *Harpers* 256 (February 1978), pp. 37–56. Reprinted by permission of the Julian Bach Literary Agency, Inc. Copyright © 1978 by Peter A. Iseman. Reprinted from the February 1978 issue of Harper's Magazine.

of individualism and self-determination than in a society that emphasizes conformity and reverence for the past and custom. William Graham Sumner believed there is a basic resistance to change in all societies in that people are basically conservative and seek stability or "strain for consistency." Resistance to change is balanced to a certain extent by people's curiosity. They continue to seek new knowledge and better ways of doing things, so change must occur.

Planned Social Change and Social Movements

It may be that social change is an evolutionary process beyond our control—we are at the mercy of forces that we can do nothing about. Many people believe, however, that we can do something more than just describe and accept our social environment. Rather, the environment can actually be manipulated for our benefit. One view of the process of change, as expressed by William Graham Sumner, is that social change must be slow, and change in people's attitudes must precede change in legislation. Sumner believed that laws should not move ahead of the customs of the people, or, in his words, "stateways cannot change folkways." An opposite view is that new laws can lead the way—they can change people's attitudes and behavior in necessary and beneficial ways. From 1954 on, court decisions and legislative acts have attempted to change the pattern of interaction between the races in the United States. Civil rights groups in the 1960s, feeling that change had been too slow, tried sit-ins, nonviolent demonstrations, and passive resistance to speed up the process. Both sides—those who feel change is beyond control and those who feel that change can be planned and controlled—have fuel for their arguments. The latter group can state that the conditions of minorities in America have improved. The former group, however, can call attention to unanticipated changes that have also occurred: increasing violence between the races in the 1960s, and probably a hardening of racial attitudes on the part of many people. At any rate, social scientists today feel that change within limits can be a planned phenomenon. As a result, we see the development of commissions and agencies focusing on a number of areas where it is felt that planned social change is needed.

Social change may occur through a form of collective behavior called a social movement. A **social movement** is defined as a group of people acting with some continuity to promote or to resist a change in their society or group. Social movements are lasting rather than temporary, they have a distinctive perspective or viewpoint, they are oriented toward a specific goal or goals, and members have a sense of solidarity or *esprit de corps*.[4] Social movements seem to be especially popular in modern mass society. In mass society there is mass confusion; that is, there are a variety of viewpoints on every issue. The United States, like other mass societies, has a multiplicity of groups from numerous backgrounds, and each group has its own values, its own way of looking at things. Individual discontent, anxiety, and frustration about the condition of the world and about one's own chances are all conducive to social movements.[5] Mass communication exposes us to all the

[4]Ralph Turner and Lewis Killian, *Collective Behavior,* 2d ed. (Englewood Cliffs, N.J.: Prentice-Hall, 1972), p. 246.

[5]See C. Wendell King's book, *Social Movements in the United States* (New York: Random House, 1956), Chapter 1, for a discussion of social movements in mass society.

confusing aspects of the mass society and puts us immediately in touch with others who may also be frustrated and anxious and looking for a way to change things. The combination of these elements—complex societies with a variety of peoples and viewpoints, numbers of people who feel discontented or shortchanged, and a system of mass communication to tie them together—provides fertile soil for social movements.

Examples of social movements in the United States might include the following: the civil rights movement (which includes organizations like NAACP, CORE, Black Muslims, and Black Panthers), the student New Left (SDS), women's rights movements (NOW), peace movements, anti-communist movements (John Birch Society, Minutemen), religious movements (Billy Graham, Campus Crusade), and numerous others. Some of these movements are **revolutionary**, in that they demand a complete change in the social order. Others are **reform**, in that they seek modification in certain aspects of society.[6] Social movements of either type, however, provide an important impetus for social change.

Social movements frequently make use of public demonstrations to bring attention to the issue that they want to change. The anti-war movement of the 1960s and the gay rights movement of the 1970s are examples. Farmers descended on Washington, D.C., in several massive "tractorcades," most recently in early 1979, to bring attention to their economic problems. Sometimes, certain pressures lead groups that otherwise would not do so to use public protest as a means for change. The farmers may be one example of this, and "Anatomy of a Public Protest Action" describes another.

Often one social movement will develop to counter the effects of another. A current example centers upon legalization of abortion. As recently as 1966, abortion was illegal throughout the United States, although a few states would allow it if the mother's life were in danger. A social movement developed among people who, for a variety of reasons—rights of women, population control, objection to laws that discriminated against the poor—felt that abortion should be legalized. Pamphlets to citizens, letters to senators, articles in newspapers and magazines made people aware of the issue. In 1967, Colorado passed a liberalized abortion law, and soon California, New York, Hawaii, and other states followed. By early 1972, sixteen states and the District of Columbia had changed their laws. Then, in January, 1973, the U.S. Supreme Court overruled all state laws that prohibited or restricted women from obtaining abortions during the first three months of pregnancy. Seldom is social change, especially legal social change, so rapid, and seldom are the effects of a social movement so dramatic. There was an immediate outcry from those who objected to the Supreme Court's action. Groups of people began getting together ("Right to Life" is the name of one), and a social movement desiring restrictive abortion legislation started to develop. These groups gained power and reportedly were instrumental in the election and defeat of certain candidates for office in the late 1970s. Whether this movement will have the success of the earlier pro-abortion movement appears doubtful, but if the amount

[6]Turner and Killian give a brief discussion of reform and revolutionary movements in *Collective Behavior,* pp. 257–258 (see footnote 4).

ANATOMY OF A PUBLIC PROTEST ACTION

Independent truck drivers are generally viewed as middle class and politically conservative. They are not the type to get involved in challenging, confronting, mass protest actions. But on December 3, 1973, a group of owner-operator truckers blocked the entrance to the Delaware Memorial Bridge for seven hours. Two days later they blockaded the Ohio Turnpike and highways in several other states. The national guard and highway patrol broke up the blockades with force. Truck windshields were broken and trucks towed off highways. Some truckers were beaten and arrested.

Charles Bisanz studied the truckers and found them to be independent and self reliant. They have a belief in success through individual accomplishment, and they view trucking as a way of life. Social networks are developed by getting together at truck stops and by communicating through citizens' band radios. In December 1973, truckers were facing a severe economic squeeze—diesel fuel had suddenly become expensive, but the increases couldn't be passed back to the consumer because hauling rates were fixed by the ICC. Truckers felt they had no clout, that Congress didn't care about them. They also felt they had no exit; trucking was all they knew, and there were no other jobs available to them except perhaps unskilled work in factories. These feelings led to the blockade in early December. Widespread publicity of the blockades led to increased interaction among truckers and further confirmation of their problems. A nationwide shutdown took place from December 13 to 15, and again from January 31 to February 9, 1974. After eight days of the second shutdown, a rate increase was granted, and the independent truckers were given recognition by the government. Bisanz concludes by suggesting that when an individual (or group) is faced with frustration and threat to a way of life, the more cut off he perceives himself to be from established channels of institutional response and the fewer exits he perceives, the more likely it is he will engage in public protest actions as a strategy for change.

Adapted from "The Anatomy of a Mass Public Protest Action: A Shutdown by Independent Truck Drivers," by Charles Bisanz, *Human Organization* 36 (Spring 1977), pp. 62–66. Reprinted with permission of *Human Organization.*

---

of reaction and intensity of feeling are any indication, the movement is not likely to be short-lived.

Collective behavior experts feel that social movements have a life history. One description of the life span of movements sees them going through four stages.[7] The *preliminary* stage involves individual excitement, discontent, and unorganized and unformulated restlessness. Mechanisms of suggestion, imitation, and propaganda are important, and an "agitator" type of leader appears. The *popular* stage involves crowd or collective excitement or unrest. The unrest is now open and widespread, and *esprit de corps* and an ideology or viewpoint become important mechanisms. The leader at this stage is a "prophet" (who puts forth a general ideology) or a "reformer" (who focuses on specific evils and develops a clearly defined program). Eric Hoffer believes that the early stages of social movements are

---

[7]This description of the life history of a social movement is from Rex Hopper, "The Revolutionary Process: A Frame of Reference for the Study of Revolutionary Movements," *Social Forces* 28 (March 1950), pp. 270–279.

CHARISMATIC MOVEMENT
CONTINUING — EVEN IN
LEADER'S ABSENCE.

dominated by "true believers." These are people of fanatical faith for whom mass movements have an almost irresistible appeal. The true believer is ready to sacrifice his or her life for a cause, any cause.[8] The third or *formal* stage of the social movement involves the formulation of issues and formation of publics. The movement becomes "respectable" in order to gain wider appeal. Issues are discussed and debated. The leaders are "statesmen." The *institutional* stage involves the legalization of the movement; the movement becomes part of the society. The leaders are of the "administrator-executive" type.

Remember that this is a generalized description. Some movements follow this pattern, some do not. The time involved in any one stage is variable. The unsuccessful social movement disappears before it can progress through all stages. The successful social movement that attains its objectives must adapt and broaden its goals, or it too will die out.

Finally, the *charismatic* leader figures prominently in both sociological and popular literature. As we discussed in Chapter 4 (page 108), *charisma* refers to a certain quality an individual has that sets that person apart from other people. Charismatic leaders are treated as though they are superhuman and capable of exceptional acts. The charismatic movement follows the charismatic leader, who is a symbol for the movement and is above criticism.[9] Some movements are so closely identified with the leader that they have no goal beyond that of following the leader. Other movements, although they follow such a leader, have well-defined goals that allow the movement to continue even if the charismatic leader is lost. Examples of charismatic leaders might include Gandhi, Joan of Arc, Martin Luther King, Jr., Hitler, and Charles de Gaulle.

[8]See Eric Hoffer, *The True Believer* (New York: New American Library, 1951).
[9]See Turner and Killian, *Collective Behavior*, pp. 388–392 (see footnote 4), for a more detailed discussion of the charismatic movement.

> The first and most crucial task for the leaders of the Black Muslims is to keep the Movement a *movement* rather than permit it to become an institution. This does not mean that the Muslims must forsake structure and direction; on the contrary, they have one of the most effective organizational structures to be seen outside the military. But to lure the masses, they must seem to be going somewhere, not settling down. They must reflect and mobilize the masses' own dissatisfaction and urgency, building these into the corporate identity. A successful mass movement is always arriving, but never quite arrives.
>
> From *The Black Muslims in America*, rev. ed., by C. Eric Lincoln (Boston: Beacon Press, 1973).

Patterns of Social Change

Is there any pattern to social change? Is its course predictable? Some scholars think so. Some who have studied change in a number of societies conclude that all change is good and in the direction of progress; others argue very nearly the opposite. Some believe that societies, like people, go through a life cycle—youth, maturity, and decline. Sociologist Pitirim Sorokin devised a theory of change that states that societies fluctuate back and forth like a pendulum through three orientations: ideational, sensate, and idealistic. The **ideational culture** emphasizes feelings and emotions; it is more subjective, expressive, and religious, and sounds like Toennies' *Gemeinschaft*. The **sensate culture** emphasizes the senses; it is objective, scientific, materialistic, profane, and instrumental. Sorokin's sensate culture is more like Toennies' *Gesellschaft*. The **idealistic culture** is an intermediate stage emphasizing logic and rationality. Another interpretation of social change, by Karl Marx, was based on economic factors. He held that class conflict was the vehicle for social change. In his analysis of history, Marx saw societies progressing through a series of states ending inevitably in a form of communism and a classless society.

These speculations are interesting to examine, but they are only speculations. Perhaps the history of human beings is too short for scholars to accurately record permanent historical trends. And possibly we will find when we get to the proper place in history that social change follows no predictable pattern but occurs randomly and inevitably, in spite of our best efforts to modify its speed or direction.

Social Disorganization

Social disorganization refers to the breakdown of norms and roles with the result that customary ways of behaving no longer operate. Suppose the star halfback in the weekend football game is given the ball to run through the opposing team's line, but instead he turns and runs fifty yards the wrong way over his own goal line. The spectators are aghast. Several plays later, a player is running with the ball (in the right direction) only to be tackled by the referee. Again, consternation, because "that's not the way the game is played." The norms are so well known that when they are flagrantly violated and seem to be breaking down, effects on participants are marked. So unusual are these events that sometimes the "norm violators" become famous. A football player had broken loose on a touchdown run in a college game some years ago. No one had a chance to get him, when suddenly an opposing player who was out of the game and sitting on the bench raced onto the field and tackled the ball carrier. The incident made the sports pages throughout the country next day, and the two players (ball carrier and tackler from the bench) appeared on a nationwide television program a few days later to describe the great event. The event was remarkable because the game just isn't played that way.

But let's get back to the spectators at our peculiar game in which on every play something strange happens: a player runs the wrong way, the wrong person is tackled, eight players come into the game as substitutes but only three leave, and the quarterback runs up into the stands to lead cheers. How long would the spectators tolerate this behavior? It is my guess that very soon they would start leaving the stands. "This is ridiculous—the rules seem to change on every play— you don't know what to expect. . . ." In like manner, extensive breakdown in a society's norms and roles may produce a condition of social disorganization. Extreme social disorganization may lead to personal disorganization in which the individual becomes upset, disaffected, demoralized, and apathetic—he may want to "leave the game."

Social disorganization is often used to describe living conditions in ghetto and slum areas, which are damaged by the effects of poverty, anonymity, overcrowding, and absence of roots or ties to the community. The person living in these conditions may, like the person watching the peculiar football game, be disgusted at the way the game is being played and decide to leave or fight back. Socially disorganized inner cities have higher rates of crime, mental illness, infant mortality, disease, and family instability. This is not meant to imply that social disorganization causes these to occur, but rather that social disorganization describes a general set of conditions under which these social problems flourish.

Anomie has also been used to describe a generalized condition of normlessness. French sociologist Emile Durkheim used the concept of anomie to describe a condition in societies in which norms and rules governing people's aspirations and moral conduct had eroded.[10] There is loss of solidarity in that old group ties tend to break down, and there is a loss of consensus in that felt agreement on values and norms tends to disappear. It is difficult for individuals to know what is expected of them or for them to feel a sense of close identity with the group. Anomie describes a demoralized society in which norms are rapidly changing, uncertain, or conflicting. Durkheim felt that a particular type of suicide occurs in such societies: anomic suicide, in which the individual feels lost and disaffected due to an absence of clear-cut rules and standards for behavior. Durkheim believed that abrupt economic changes—sudden inflation or depression, poverty, or wealth—might lead to anomie. This concept has received much attention recently, especially from sociologists in the areas of criminology and delinquency. Although we will return to it later, the term *anomie* is being introduced here to describe a particular type

---

[10]Emile Durkheim, *Suicide,* translated by John A. Spaulding and George Simpson (New York: Free Press, 1951).

of social and personal disorganization that results when norms regulating people's aspirations and expectations begin to collapse.

Social disorganization may result from rapid social change. As social change takes place, new norms replace older ones, role behavior is modified, conflict in values occurs, and institutions assume different forms and functions. Individuals, groups, institutions, and societies must adapt to change, and for some of these it may be difficult, especially if change is rapid or if change is defined as unacceptable and is therefore resisted. In such situations we might anticipate social disorganization.

Some sociologists feel that the concept of social disorganization is not very useful. They maintain that the organization of society is constantly in flux, is always changing, and that the result is not disorganization but *reorganization.* They believe that we are really talking about another stage in the social change process rather than about social disorganization. Further, argue the critics of the concept, there is a tendency to apply the label of social disorganization to those things we dislike, to things that may contradict our own particular values or what we are used to. For example, suppose that in the United States we have high divorce and illegitimacy rates, birth control pills are freely available, and teenagers commit more crime than any other age group. Does this mean that the institution of the family in America is a victim of social disorganization, or that it is changing to a different form of organization? Is the current situation regarding relations between blacks and whites in America symptomatic of a disorganized society or of a society undergoing change and reorganization? Youth are challenging institutions of higher education throughout the country, and in other parts of the world as well. Does this mean we have social disorganization in the institution of education, or change and reorganization?

My view is that the concept of social disorganization may be helpful in identifying a particular stage that may occur in groups or institutions as they undergo change and reorganization. To produce social disorganization, rapid social change would probably be necessary. In my view, social disorganization involves confusion, disaffection, demoralization, disorientation for individuals—in short, personal disorganization as well. At the same time, it is important to avoid using the concept of social disorganization only to describe those conditions with which we disagree.

SUMMARY

In the previous section of this book, we focused on social organization, the *social fabric* of society. There is a tendency in studying social organization to emphasize the constant, recurring, normal, stable nature of society. In fact, however, all is not as organized, predictable, and fixed as previous sections may have implied. Change and deviation are present in all societies, and this section addresses itself to those topics.

This chapter dealt with the concepts of social change and social disorganization. Social change occurs at varying rates in all societies—on this at least there is general agreement. On some other issues there is more debate: Which, if any, factors are related to change? Can overall patterns of social change be identified? Is change automatic and inexorable or subject to man's intervention and control? Assuming that planned social change is possible, we have examined one vehicle through which such change occurs—the social movement. Finally, social disorganization is the condition that sometimes results when norms have broken down and behavior becomes unpredictable. Although there is some disagreement over the usefulness of the concept of social disorganization, it probably is helpful in describing what may happen in periods of rapid and traumatic social change.

In the first of the readings that follow, Robert Dryfoos describes social change among Eskimos and Indians in Canada. There are numerous factors that tend to encourage change. The article by Dryfoos illustrates the point that some cultures are more effective than others at resisting change. Most often, probably, change occurs slowly without creating much disturbance in the society in which it takes place. Occasionally, however, change may be sudden and far-reaching, with dramatic effects. Lauriston Sharp describes the consequences of the introduction of steel axes into a society of Australian aboriginals. For a look at social change in modern society we turn to an interview with futurist Alvin Toffler as he predicts the sort of changes we may see in the next few years.

Reading 9.1
Two Tactics for Ethnic Survival— Eskimo and Indian

ROBERT J. DRYFOOS, JR.

Social change takes place at varying rates, even within a given geographical area. Some cultures or subcultures are more successful than others at maintaining their identity in the face of a dominant culture that tends to absorb them. Both of these situations are described in anthropologist Robert Dryfoos's article on Eskimos and Indians in Canada.

On the isolated eastern shore of Hudson Bay, about 700 miles northwest of Montreal, lies the community of Great Whale River, Quebec. It cannot be reached by road. When the ice breaks up, in mid-May, the Hudson Bay Company boat makes its way bringing stock for the store. There is an aircraft landing strip, enabling weekly service from Montreal and twice weekly service from Moosonee, Ontario. But outside visitors are usually restricted to the federal or provincial authorities, police, doctors and dentists who serve the community.

At Great Whale River, subarctic temperatures of minus 50 degrees Fahrenheit are not uncommon during the short (six-hour) days of winter. Summer brings

18-hour days, balmy temperatures (up to 85), and swarms of flies and mosquitoes. The surrounding terrain is flat and sandy rising to low, rocky hills to the east and northeast. As the village lies only 100 miles south of the timber line, the trees are small and sparse. Berries grow in season, which is short. Life is hard. The community consists of about 450 Eskimos, 225 Indians and 100 Euro-Canadians. The latter include teachers, medical personnel, Hudson Bay Company employees, representatives of both the federal Canadian government and the Quebec government, and missionaries of the Anglican and Catholic churches. The Indians are trappers and hunters, trapping beaver and mink in the winter, hunting bear and smaller game year around. Although they now use rifles and shot guns, the Indians still hunt in the bush country to the east as they did in earlier times. The Eskimos are more frequently employed by the government and the Hudson Bay Company. They still hunt seal, and they too have adopted the rifle and shot gun to wound the animals initially before they are harpooned and landed. They have also continued to hunt whale and they trap in the summer, though none of this could be considered their major endeavor. The authorities recognize the difficulties of life in Great Whale River, and most of the people are eligible for and receive welfare payments and child allotments.

While both the Eskimo and the Indians have become settled residents of the village and have largely adopted the material culture of the white man, each group has maintained its own individuality and continues to speak its own language. And although very few rituals, practices or beliefs persist among members of the two native groups, considerable knowledge of the old ways still survives.

Remembrance of things past is the focus of this study; particularly the curious contrast between the remembrances of the Eskimos and the Indians of Great Whale River. The Eskimo has very largely left the past behind with his entry into the modern world; he looks back, if at all, to see a life of hardship and insecurity which he has little wish to perpetuate. Not so the Indian. His past is tenacious, and the days before the coming of the white man are meaningful, valued and well remembered. It is as if the bush still calls to him, and the old life holds something of the fascination of a "lost horizons" for the town-dwelling Indian.

The fact that sharp differences in recall do exist between the two native groups emerged in the course of a seven-month field study I conducted during the summers of 1964 and 1965. Why these differing perceptions should exist simultaneously is an intriguing question, especially as the history of contact with modern culture has been almost identical for each group in regard to both duration and intensity. Explanations involve the complex interplay between past and present, and among the three ethnic groups living side by side.

During my two summers in Great Whale River I interviewed approximately half the members of each native group, in most cases more than once. To try to insure that "no response" to questions about the past resulted from lack of traditional knowledge and not from unwillingness to answer, I attempted to establish a cordial relationship with each person I interviewed, and came to know some quite well. I also established good rapport with my interpreters, some of whom I used throughout the two summers, and relied heavily on their judgement in determining the truthfulness of the replies.

Among the Eskimos, only 12 percent were able to give information about former customs and beliefs, compared to 75 percent of the Indians. Not a single Eskimo under 35 could demonstrate any recall of the traditional ways; the average age for Eskimo informants was over 65. The average age for Indian informants was 42, and several Indian teen-agers as well as one child of 11 were able to give information about their past.

The amount and depth of knowledge retained shows a similar pattern. Members of both groups were asked for information about religion, rites of passage, rites of intensification, marriage and residence patterns, myths and legends, kinship, political organization and economic activities. The Indians were able to recall a total of about 85 such items, and almost invariably discussed them in considerable detail. The Eskimos recalled only 25 items, and could usually give only a skeletal version of the material they remembered.

In the traditional legends of both the Eskimos and the Indians there appears a great sea spirit which takes the form of a mermaid. Present-day experience with this mermaid is the closest to a survival of a traditional belief that I was able to discover. About 20 Indians reported that they, or someone they knew, had had some contact with the mermaid, whom they call Mentoxo—either seeing, hearing, or being affected in some way by this sea creature, in whose present existence they expressed belief. Only two Eskimos reported knowing of anyone who had encountered the Eskimo version of the mermaid, whom they call Tariup Inunga. (In most ethnographic literature this Eskimo spirit is known as Sedna, but none of the Eskimos at Great Whale River had ever heard this name, or were even able to pronounce it.) Several of the Indians who said they confronted Mentoxo dated these events within very recent years, whereas the two Eskimo reports of Tariup Inunga occurred perhaps 40 or 50 years ago.

The vitality of the past among the Indians is easily explained on one level: most Indian fathers say it is desirable for their children to learn of traditional Indian customs, and take pains to tell them about the "way things were done, and what we believed before the white man came." Practically every Eskimo, on the other hand, has dispensed with such teaching, explaining that the "old days have little value for today's children." This is true not just in the area of custom and belief, but for practical skills as well. Most Indian parents say it is valuable for the young men to be able to engage in "real" Indian activities, and teach their sons the proper techniques for hunting in the bush. Only a few Eskimo parents want their children to learn how to hunt sea mammals; most adults dismiss the idea, saying it is "too difficult for people today," or "hunting does not pay enough."

The harsh physical environment and the problems of sheer survival in traditional times may provide one clue to both what and how much of the past is recalled today. Although life was difficult for both peoples, the Eskimos faced an environment that was more continuously threatening than did the Indians. Certainly this is how it is viewed in retrospect: many more Eskimos than Indians comment that the old days were "bad," or that "there was great hunger and starvation many years ago." The Eskimos, then, may well have been more apt to recognize the advantages of Euro-Canadian culture and to welcome a way of life offering security and comfort. The Indians, with their less oppressive past, may have adopted the material culture of the white man less wholeheartedly, and this may have carried over to ideological areas as well. For example, although both groups are Christians today, the Eskimos appear to have internalized the Christian faith to a greater extent than the Indians.

Traditionally, both Indian and Eskimo culture was loosely structured, but some of the available ethnographies indicate that Indian culture was the more highly structured of the two and I would hold that this is one reason for its greater persistence. Today, Indians continue to view themselves as comprising a "tribe" or society; knowledge of the past functions as an integrating mechanism and helps to provide a sense of identity as members of an enduring, albeit fragmenting, society. The Eskimos have never considered themselves members of a cohesive group, so identification with the past would have little meaning from this point of view.

The favored position enjoyed by the Eskimos today in the eyes of the dominant white community, and the comparatively inferior status of the Indians, may well be significant in explaining their different regard for the past. I interviewed about three-fourths of the Euro-Canadian population during my study, and learned that they greatly favor the Eskimos. In general, Eskimos are regarded as more industrious and honest, practical and pragmatic, while Indians are often characterized as "dreamers." Both the Eskimos and the Indians are well aware of these attitudes; the Indians also believe they have less chance of being hired for wage labor than the Eskimos, and that they do not have equal access to government funds. Quite naturally, the Indians feel some resentment and hostility toward the white community as a result.

It is my belief that perpetuation of traditional knowledge serves the Indians as a relatively safe outlet for aggression against the whites. The passing on of stories, myths and beliefs of bygone days may also be seen as a nativistic movement, similar to the present-day mask-carving among the Onendaga, as suggested by Jean Hendry. The perpetuation of traditional knowledge may well serve to strengthen the Indians' image of themselves in the face of hostile white attitudes, especially vis-à-vis the Eskimos. Given their preferred status in relation to the Indians, the Eskimos would have no such reason to perpetuate the past, and might only alienate the dominant whites by doing so.

Shifting ecocultural patterns of the two groups may also suggest reasons for their differential recall of the past. Traditionally the Eskimos were oriented toward the sea, spending much of their time hunting seal and walrus on Hudson Bay. Today however, when an Eskimo leaves the village in the morning to hunt seal, he usually returns the same evening to a rather bustling village life. Hunting has become more and more a sideline activity, and at the urging of the white man during the last 20 to 25 years, the Eskimos have turned increasingly to various craft pursuits, especially soapstone-carving. (Soapstone-carving, formerly done only as a pleasant pastime during the long winter nights to ornament children's toys, was not a traditional economic activity of the Eskimos.) In other words, the Eskimo ecological orientation has shifted from the coast to the entirely novel one of the village; in this process, the traditional ties with the whole fabric of the past have been attenuated.

The ecocultural patterns of the Indian have not changed nearly so drastically, and he is still to some degree bush-oriented. The hunters and trappers of today must leave the village for extended periods to reach adequate game supplies—they cannot limit these activities to "off-business hours" as the Eskimos can. Indians are constantly reminded of their past by their present hunting and trapping patterns. Craft production is much less developed, though current efforts are being made to increase it. For the present, however, the Indians continue to think and talk largely in terms of their traditional bush orientation. The bush, and the old way of life that went with it, still linger as a powerfully nostalgic image to the Indians, even to those who never venture from the village now.

In summary, recollection of the past is meaningful to the Indians; it functions as a mechanism to make them "more Indian," to provide a sense of current identity. But the Eskimos have little interest in being "more Eskimo," and their past is being forgotten at an ever increasing rate.

Questions 9.1

1. Dryfoos suggests that the two groups—Indian and Eskimo—have changed at different rates. What types of evidence does he have for this conclusion?
2. What explanations are there for these different rates of change? Which of the factors related to change discussed in the text seem to fit best?
3. Which group—Eskimo or Indian—is held in higher regard by the dominant white community? Why? In your opinion, is this a typical or unusual occurrence when unlike races or ethnic groups come in contact?

Reading 9.2
Steel Axes for Stone Age Australians

LAURISTON SHARP

Social change occurs in all societies. Often change takes place without much disruption in the lives of people. Sometimes, however, change is extremely disturbing. This may be because the change is rapid and extensive, or because, regardless of the speed with which it takes place, people are unable to adapt to it. Social change that disrupts the order of a society may lead to social disorganization, possibly even the disintegration of the society. Anthropologist Lauriston Sharp describes what happened when missionaries gave steel axes to the Yir Yoront.

Excerpted from "Steel Axes for Stone Age Australians" by Lauriston Sharp, in *Human Problems in Technological Change,* edited by Edward H. Spicer, © 1952 by the Russell Sage Foundation, Publishers, New York.

Like other Australian aboriginals, The Yir Yoront group at the mouth of the Coleman River on the west coast of tropical Cape York Peninsula originally had no knowledge of metals. Technologically their culture was of the old stone age or paleolithic type; they supported themselves by hunting and fishing, obtaining vegetable foods and needed materials from the bush by simple gathering techniques. Their only domesticated animal was the dog, and they had no domesticated plants of any kind. Unlike some other aboriginal groups, however, the Yir Yoront did have polished stone axes hafted in short handles, and these implements were most important in their economy.

The production of a stone axe required a number of simple skills. With the idea of the axe in its various details well in mind, the adult men—and only the adult men—could set about producing it, a task not considered appropriate for women or children. First of all, a man had to know the location and properties of several natural resources found in his immediate environment: pliable wood, which could be doubled or bent over the axe head and bound tightly to form a handle; bark, which could be rolled into cord for the binding; and gum, with which the stone head could be firmly fixed in the haft. These materials had to be correctly gathered, stored, prepared, cut to size, and applied or manipulated. They were plentifully supplied by nature, and could be taken by a man from anyone's property without special permission. Postponing consideration of the stone head of the axe, we see that a simple knowledge of nature and of the technological skills involved, together with the possession of fire (for heating the gum) and a few simple cutting tools, which might be nothing more than the sharp shells of plentiful bivalves, all of which were available to everyone, were sufficient to enable any normal man to make a stone axe.

The use of the stone axe as a piece of capital equipment for the production of other goods indicates its very great importance in the subsistence economy of the aboriginal. Anyone—man, woman, or child—could use the axe; indeed, it was used more by women, for theirs was the onerous daily task of obtaining sufficient wood to keep the campfire of each family burning all day for cooking or other purposes and all night against mosquitoes and cold (in July, winter temperature might drop below forty degrees). In a normal lifetime any woman would use the axe to cut or knock down literally tons of firewood. Men and women, and sometimes children, needed the axe to make other tools, or weapons, or a variety of material equipment required by the aboriginal in his daily life. The stone axe was essential in making the wet-season domed huts, which keep out some rain and some insects; or platforms, which provide dry storage; or shelters, which give shade when days are bright and hot. In hunting and fishing and in gathering vegetable or animal food the axe was also a necessary tool; and in this tropical culture without preservatives or other means of storage; the native spends more time obtaining food than in any other occupation except sleeping.

In only two instances was the use of the stone axe strictly limited to adult men: Wild honey, the most prized food known to the Yir Yoront, was gathered only by men who usually used the axe to get it; and only men could make the secret paraphernalia for ceremonies, an activity often requiring use of the axe. From this brief listing of some of the activities in which the axe was used, it is easy to understand why there was at least one stone axe in every camp, in every hunting or fighting party, in every group out on a "walk-about" in the bush.

While the stone axe helped relate men and women and often children to nature in technological behavior, in the transformation of natural into cultural equipment, it also was prominent in that aspect of behavior which may be called conduct, primarily directed toward persons. Yir Yoront men were dependent upon interpersonal relations for their stone axe heads, since the flat, geologically recent alluvial country over which they range provides no stone from which axe heads can be made. The stone they used comes from known quarries four hundred miles to the south. It reached the Yir Yoront through long lines of male trading partners, some of these chains terminating with the Yir Yoront men, while others extended on farther north to other groups, having utilized Yir Yoront men as links. Almost every older adult man had one or more regular trading partners, some to the north and some to the south. His partner or partners in the south he provided with surplus spears, and particularly fighting spears tipped with the barbed spines of sting ray, which snap into vicious fragments when they penetrate human flesh. For a dozen spears, some of which he may have obtained from a partner to the north, he would receive from a southern partner one stone axe head.

Not only was it adult men alone who obtained axe heads and produced finished axes, but it was adult males who retained the axes, keeping them with other parts of their equipment in camp, or carrying them at the back slipped through a human hair belt when traveling. Thus, every woman or child who wanted to use an axe —and this might be frequently during the day—must get one from some man, use it promptly, and return it to the man in good condition. While a man might speak of "my axe," a woman or child could not; for them it was always "your axe," addressing a male, or "his axe."

This necessary and constant borrowing of axes from older men by women and children was done according to regular patterns of kinship behavior. A woman on good terms with her husband would expect to use his axe unless he were using it; a husband on good terms with his wives would let any one of them use his axe without question. If a woman was unmarried or her husband was absent, she would go first to her older brother or to her father for an axe. Only in extraordinary circumstances would she seek a stone axe from a mother's brother or certain other male kin with whom she had to be most circumspect. A girl, a boy, or a young man would look to a father or an older brother to provide an axe for her or his use, but would never approach a mother's brother, who would be at the same time a potential father-in-law, with such a request. Older men, too, would follow similar rules if they had to borrow an axe.

It will be noted that these social relationships in which the stone axe had a place are all pair relationships and that the use of the axe helped define and maintain the character of the relationships and the roles of the two individual participants. Every active relationship among the Yir Yoront involved a definite and accepted status of superordination or subordination. A person could have no dealings with any other on exactly equal terms. Women and children were dependent on, or subordinate to, older males in every action in which the axe entered.

The stone axe was an important symbol of masculinity among the Yir Yoront (just as pants or pipes are among ourselves). By a complicated set of ideas which we would label "ownership" the axe was defined as "belonging" to males. Everyone in the society (except untrained infants) accepted these ideas. Similarly spears, spear throwers, and fire-making sticks were associated with males, were owned only by them, and were symbols of masculinity. But the masculine values represented by the stone axe were constantly being impressed on all members of society by the fact that non-males had to use the axe and had to go to males for it, whereas they never borrowed other masculine artifacts. Thus, the axe stood for an important theme and ran all through Yir Yoront culture: the superiority and rightful dominance of the male, and the greater value of his concerns and of all things associated with him. We should call this androcentrism rather than patriarchy; the man ("andros") takes precedence over feminine values, an idea backed by very strong sentiments among the Yir Yoront. Since the axe had to be borrowed also by the younger from the older, it also represented the prestige of age, another important theme running all through Yir Yoront behavior.

The introduction of the steel axe indiscriminately and in large numbers into the Yir Yoront technology was only one of many changes occurring at the same time. It is therefore impossible to factor out all the results of this single innovation alone. Nevertheless, a number of specific effects of the change from stone axes to steel axes may be noted; and the steel axe may be used as an epitome of the European goods and implements received by the aboriginals in increasing quantity and of their general influence on the native culture. The use of the steel axe to illustrate such influences would seem to be justified, for it was one of the first European artifacts to be adopted for regular use by the Yir Yoront; and the axe, whether of stone or steel, was clearly one of the most important items of cultural equipment they possessed.

The shift from stone to steel axes provided no major technological difficulties. While the aboriginals themselves could not manufacture steel axe heads, a steady supply from outside continued; and broken wooden axe handles could easily be replaced from bush timbers with aboriginal tools. Among the Yir Yoront the new axe never acquired all the use it had on mission or cattle stations (carpentry work, pounding tent pegs, use as a hammer, and so on); and, indeed, it was used for little more than the stone axe had been, so that it had no practical effect in improving the native standard of living. It did some jobs better, and could be used longer without breakage; and these factors were sufficient to make it of value to the native. But the assumption of the white man (based in part on a realization that a shift from steel to stone axe in his case would be a definite regression) that his axe was much more efficient, that its use would save time, and that it therefore represented technical "progress" toward goals which he had set for the native was hardly borne out in aboriginal practice. Any leisure time the Yir Yoront might gain by using steel axes or other western tools was invested, not in "improving the conditions of life," and certainly not in developing aesthetic activities, but in sleep, an art they had thoroughly mastered.

Having acquired an axe head through regular trading partners of whom he knew what to expect, a man wanting a stone axe was then dependent solely upon a known and an adequate nature and upon his own skills or easily acquired techniques. A man wanting a steel axe, however, was in no such self-reliant position. While he might acquire one through trade, he now had the new alternative of dispensing with technological behavior in relation with a predictable trading partner and of turning instead to conduct alone in relation with a highly erratic missionary. If he attended one of the mission festivals when steel axes were handed out as gifts, he might receive one simply by chance or if he had happened somehow to impress upon the mission that he was one of the "better" bush aboriginals (their definition of "better" being quite different from that of his bush fellows). Or he might—but again almost by pure chance—be given some brief job in connection with the mission which would enable him to earn a steel axe. In either case, for older men a preference for the steel axe helped create a situation of dependence in place of a situation of self-reliance and a behavior shift from situations in technology or conduct which were well structured or defined to situations in conduct alone which were ill defined. It was particularly the older ones among the men, whose earlier experience or knowledge of the white man's harshness in any event made them suspicious, who would avoid having any relations with the mission at all, and who thus excluded themselves from acquiring steel axes directly from that source.

The steel axe was the root of psychological stress among the Yir Yoront even more significantly in other aspects of social relations. This was the result of new factors which the missionary considered all to the good: the simple numerical increase in axes per capita as a result of mission distribution; and distribution from the mission directly to younger men, women, and even children. By winning the favor of the mission staff, a woman might be given a steel axe. This was clearly intended to be hers. The situation was quite different from that involved in borrowing an axe from a male relative, with the result that a woman called such an axe "my" steel axe, a possessive form she never used for a stone axe. Furthermore, young men or even boys might also obtain steel axes directly from the mission. A result was that older men no longer had a complete monopoly of all the axes in the bush community. Indeed, an old man might have only a stone axe, while his wives and sons had steel axes which they considered their own and which he might even desire to borrow. All this led to a revolutionary confusion of sex, age, and kinship roles, with a major gain in independence and loss of subordination on the part of those able now to acquire steel axes when they had been unable to possess stone axes before.

The trading partner relationship was also affected by the new situation. A Yir Yoront might have a trading partner in a tribe to the south whom he defined as a younger brother, and on whom as an older brother he would therefore have an edge. But if the partner were in contact with the mission or had other easier access to steel axes, his subordination to his bush colleague was obviously decreased. Indeed, under the new dispensation he might prefer to give his axe to a bush "sweetheart" in return for favors or otherwise dispose of it outside regular trade channels, since many steel axes were so distributed between natives in new ways. Among other things, this took some of the excitement away from the fiesta-like tribal gatherings centering around initiations during the dry season. These had traditionally been the climactic annual occasions for exchanges between trading partners, when a man might seek to acquire a whole year's supply of stone axe heads. Now he might find himself prostituting his wife to almost total strangers in return for steel axes or other white men's goods. With trading partnerships weakened, there was less reason to attend the fiestas, and less fun for those who did. A decline in one of the important social activities which had symbolized these great gatherings created a lessening of interest in the other social aspects of these events.

The most disturbing effects of the steel axe, operating in conjunction with other elements also being introduced from the white man's several subcultures, developed in the realm of traditional ideas, sentiments, and values. These were undermined at a rapidly mounting rate, without new conceptions being defined to replace them. The result was a mental and moral void which foreshadowed the collapse and destruction of all Yir Yoront culture, if not, indeed, the extinction of the biological group itself.

From what has been said it should be clear how changes in overt behavior, in technology and conduct, weakened the values inherent in a reliance on nature, in androcentrism or the prestige of masculinity, in age prestige, and in the various kinship relations. A scene was set in which a wife or young son, his initiation perhaps not even yet completed, need no longer bow to the husband or father, who was left confused and insecure as he asked to borrow a steel axe from them. For the woman and boy the steel axe helped establish a new degree of freedom which was accepted readily as an escape from the unconscious stress of the old patterns, but which left them also confused and insecure. Ownership became less well defined, so that stealing and trespass were introduced into technology and conduct. Some of the excitement surrounding the great ceremonies evaporated, so that the only fiestas the people had became less festive, less interesting. Indeed, life itself became less interesting, although this did not lead the Yir Yoront to invent suicide, a concept foreign to them.

The bush Yir Yoront, still trying to maintain their aboriginal definition of the situation, accepted European artifacts and behavior patterns, but fit them into their totemic system, assigning them as totems to various clans on a par with original totems. There is an attempt to have the myth-making process keep up with these cultural changes so that the idea system can continue to support the rest of the culture. But analysis of overt behavior, of dreams, and of some of the new myths indicates that this arrangement is not entirely satisfactory; that the native clings to his totemic system with intellectual loyalty, lacking any substitute ideology; but that associated sentiments and values are weakened. His attitudes toward his own and toward European culture are found to be highly ambivalent.

The steel axe, like most European goods, has no distinctive origin myth, nor are mythical ancestors associated with it. Can anyone, sitting of an afternoon in the shade of a ti tree, create a myth to resolve this confusion? No one has, and the horrid suspicion arises that perhaps the origin myths are wrong, which took into account so little of this vast new universe of the white man. The steel axe, shifting hopelessly between one clan and the other, is not only replacing the stone axe physically, but is hacking at the supports of the entire cultural system.

During a wet season stay at the mission, the anthropologist discovered that his supply of tooth paste was being depleted at an alarming rate. Investigation showed that it was being taken by old men for use in a new tooth paste cult. Old materials of magic having failed, new materials were being tried out in a malevolent magic directed toward the mission staff and some of the younger aboriginal men. Old males, largely ignored by the missionaries, were seeking to regain some of their lost power and prestige. This mild aggression proved hardly effective, but perhaps only because confidence in any kind of magic on the mission was by this time at a low ebb.

For the Yir Yoront still in the bush a time could be predicted when personal deprivation and frustration in a confused culture would produce an overload of anxiety. The mythical past of the totemic ancestors would disappear as a guarantee of a present of which the future was supposed to be a stable continuation. Without the past, the present would be meaningless and the future unstructured and uncertain. Insecurities would be inevitable. Reaction to this stress might be some form of symbolic aggression, or withdrawal and apathy, or some more realistic approach.

Questions 9.2

1. What changes in the Yir Yoront culture followed the introduction of the steel axe?
2. Use the terms "social disorganization," "anomie," and "reorganization" to analyze and describe the condition of the Yir Yoront.
3. Why did the Yir Yoront have such difficulty adapting to the introduction of the steel axe?
4. What elements introduced into American culture have led to dramatic social change? As you list several, discuss why they didn't have the disastrous effect that introduction of the steel axe had for the Yir Yoront.

Reading 9.3
An Interview with Alvin Toffler

OMNI

Alvin Toffler added a concept to our language: future shock. Future shock is the dizzying disorientation brought on by the premature arrival of the future. Future shock is caused by the greatly accelerated rate of change in society. Social change occurs more and more rapidly in the modern world, and individuals, groups, even societies may be overwhelmed by it.

Toffler used the words *future shock* in an article he wrote in 1965. Later, in 1970, *Future Shock* became the title of his famous and widely read book. He continues to study the future and its impact on societies. In this interview with *Omni* magazine, Toffler discusses contrasting technologies and the hopes they offer for dealing with the future. He also relates his concerns that social change in the future be planned democratically rather than be captured by an elite.

OMNI　One of the most striking developments since *Future Shock* appeared is a much wider and deeper questioning of science and technology—not just concern about, say, the consequences of automation, but concern about all the values and goals of "progress." What do you make of this concern?

Toffler　When I was a child I saw the movie *Pasteur*. I can remember seeing many movies about Edison, Ehrlich, Alexander Graham Bell, and other great scientists, doctors, or technologists. They were always heroes. And they were *my* heroes.

By the late 1950s and early '60s, we began to get more Frankenstein images—images of scientists and engineers not as saviors, but as angels of doom. *Dr. Strangelove* appeared on the scene. Sinister figures. Today I know perfectly sweet, highly intelligent people who are so turned off by science and technology, so angry at what they regard as the arrogance and dogmatism of the men in white coats, that they would gladly lynch a few before breakfast.

This drastic change in public attitude reflects something far deeper happening today—a fundamental idea-quake, an upheaval in our whole view of reality. This is a change so deep it has no precedent in the past several hundred years. As a result, both science and technology—which until now have triggered so many revolutions—are themselves about to be revolutionized.

The industrial age began, one might say, with Newton and Descartes, the founding fathers of modern science. Newton told us that the entire universe was nothing more than a machine—a clock. Descartes told us we could eventually understand that clock if we took it apart, component by component, and studied the behavior of the pieces. What we have lived in during the past 300 years—until Einstein and the physicists began to challenge the mechanistic view—was not a scientific age, but a *scientistic* age.

We raised the scientist to the status of priest. We took from science not its emphasis on tentativity, on experiment, on skepticism, on imagination and daring hypothesis, but its mechanistic, tinker-toy notions of reality. We sought not tentative findings, which the next round of exploration could disconfirm, but "scientific laws." We reduced causality to a simple-minded search for a single cause. We viewed a fact not as a temporary metaphorical explanation that might prove useful, but as a fixed, static, single-sided phenomenon. We looked at things one way, instead of through multiple lenses.

Today all of this is under fire—not merely by antiscientific irrationalists and mystics, but by scientists themselves. They are breaking out of the old scientistic modes of thought and searching beyond established boundaries for new metaphors, new combinations of insight from both West and East. They are beginning to see science itself not as some relentless process, driven by its own mysterious inner imperatives, but as a social and cultural process we have created and that we, hopefully, can still shape.

I think that out of the raging war between "establishment science" and its critics—both inside and outside the science community—will come a new, far more flexible, modest, useful science of the future. This revolution in science will be part of a revolution in society as a whole. We are moving into a new civilization.

OMNI   A new civilization?

Toffler   Exactly.

OMNI   What do you mean?

Toffler   I mean that for 300 years we've been living in an industrial civilization. This period of human history is now over. We're moving swiftly out of—and beyond—industrialism toward a new phase that will be technological but no longer industrial.

OMNI   Aren't technological and industrial the same? We've always used these words almost interchangeably.

Toffler   No. The industrial age was based on a certain style of technology, on technologies representing a certain stage of development. Newtonian and Cartesian ideas were developed, elaborated, and applied to more and more fields during the period of early industrial development. And the two lines of development wrapped themselves together like a double helix. One one side, Scientism; on the other, Brute Force technology.

OMNI   Why "Brute Force"?

Toffler   Because industrial civilization, during its 300-year-long dominance of the planet, produced machines that were energy-hungry, machines that were ravenous and wasteful of raw materials, machines that were huge, machines that polluted heavily. Machines that were capital intensive.

This primitive, battering-ram kind of technology characterized the industrial age and made mass production possible. It gave rise to industries such as the textile, steel, auto, rubber, and rail and paid off in vastly improving the standard of life for hundreds of millions of human beings. It also raped and robbed others, but that is another part of the story. The fact is, industrialism increased the life span and solved the problem of hunger for a sizable chunk of the human race.

But at the same time, the Newtonian-Cartesian habit of looking at things through only a single lens meant we seldom stopped to think about side effects. A good friend of mine, Dr. Donald F. Klein, who is one of the world's top drug experts, is often asked whether this or that drug has a side effect. He shrugs and says, "No side effects, no central effect." You can't have one without the other.

But that's not how we've looked at technology historically. We've looked at its central effect—its ability to deliver a buck or a military bang—and said, "Aren't we smart?" We forgot to look at the side effects. Or we didn't want to look at them.

OMNI   How do you feel about the people who say it's time to stop technology?

Toffler   I can understand their anger, frustration, and fear. But I think the idea of "stopping technology" is both futile and immoral. I think there's a better way to achieve what most of these people want, anyway.

What we're seeing are increasing attacks on technology, not from Luddites, but from thoughtful people. They present a very powerful case, pointing out the atrocities and dangers that technology has trailed in its wake until now.

Of course, some critics are merely technophobes. They'd like the whole world to go back to some pretechnological age. They forget how life was for most human beings in those times. How short, brutal, and stultifying it was. How viciously anti-democratic society was. In my view, it's an attitude that goes with a full belly.

People in India or Burma, Guatemala or Colombia, can't afford to be as cavalier about stopping technology as some of the middle-class rebels of the sixties were.

There's something arrogant, anyway, about the idea of doing away with technology, as though it were ours to dispose of. We tend to think of it as a product of Western society, and we forget that it's also a product of Arab mathematics, of Chinese inventions, and so on. Science and technology are the common inheritance of the human race, and it's not for a few well-fed middle-class Westerners to say, "Let's pull the plug and begin again."

But the technophobes are really only a small, romantic group. Most people, by and large, do want science and technology in their future. But they want a new, more human science and technology. They want advances that are carefully thought through, carefully selected to minimize adverse side effects. And they want some say in the choice.

It has always seemed to me that both extremes in this debate are dangerous to our health and ought to be labeled as such. At one end, the blind "progress-manics" who want to push forward with the same kind of brute force technologies that have already imperiled the planet. At the other pole, the equally blind and arrogant past-glorifiers who want to go back to a past as prehuman as it was pretechnological.

What we need, even more desperately today than when I called for it in *Future Shock,* is a movement for *responsible* technology. That means a technology that recognizes our own limitations and the real or probable limitations of the biosphere.

OMNI   Isn't it really too late? Haven't we gone so far toward destroying the environment that nothing short of a screeching halt can now save us?

Toffler   No. I don't believe in apocalypse. I still believe that, over the long haul, we will pull through.

But, having said that, I also think the 1980s and '90s will see some terrible technological disasters if we continue on our present track. If we keep proliferating nuclear plants, siting them on geological faults or near volcanoes or dumping radioactive wastes into the seas and into the earth, somewhere along the line, despite all the fancy computer models and all the assurances we get from the experts, some unexpected series of human errors will occur. All those beautiful fail-safe systems will fail to prevent a tragedy because they themselves will prove irrelevant. You can't ever cover all possibilities.

If it isn't a nuclear catastrophe, who's to say it won't be something worse? We are beginning to play with genetic engineering, weather modification, and other high-powered technologies we know little about. Considering our abysmal environmental record with far more traditional, less powerful technologies, there is plenty of cause for concern.

But none of this means we should turn the clock back, that we should stamp out technology—which can't be done anyway—or that we should doom three-quarters of the human race to perpetual hunger or poverty in the interest of preserving the environment. What it does mean is that we can no longer play the technological game the way we have.

It's a new game, and Rule Number One is "proceed with extreme caution."
OMNI   You say we must proceed with caution, yet you've also often said that we
are on the edge of fantasic breakthroughs in science and technology for which we
are unprepared. Can you give us some examples. How do you foresee scientific and
technological development in the next twenty years?
Toffler   I think we'll see three separate, but converging, lines of development. I
call them "high-stream," "low-stream," and "out-of-the-stream" technologies.
The first of these—"high-stream"—depends on advanced theoretical knowledge or
on complex techno-engineering.

Under this heading, for example, I would include space exploration. Gerry
O'Neill at Princeton is still pressing for manned (and womanned) space colonies
and has mustered considerable political and intellectual support. Work is proceed-
ing on space manufacture—which will someday give rise to new processes and
materials that can't be duplicated on earth. Work on the space shuttle moves ahead.
Budgets will rise and fall, but we are irrevocably committed to space, in my
opinion, and that commitment is likely to deepen.

Similarly, while matters are confused because of the failure of the Law of the
Sea conferences to arrive at an international agreement, there is no doubt whatever
in my mind that we are about to take a historic step into the sea within the next
decade or two. We'll go from simply harvesting ocean life—i.e., fishing—to growing what we need—i.e., aquaculture. We'll also start taking manganese nodules off
the ocean floor. And we'll build semi-submersible floating platforms on which we
will put not only airports and oil refineries, but large numbers of people. We're
going to make our own islands and populate them. That was Bucky Fuller's dream
a generation ago.
OMNI   What new problems will this kind of high-stream development bring
with it?
Toffler   Just look at the political and international issues you raise when you
suddenly create a new island! To whom does it belong? Can it declare independence? Or join the UN? Environmentally, how do you carefully, cautiously develop these ocean resources without turning the seas into poisonous soup? How
do you avoid killing off the algae we depend on? How do you prevent overfishing?
Who has a right to the krill that populate the seas between Argentina and the
Antarctic?

Should American and other, multinational, corporations have the right to
plunge madly into the oceans, in a competitive race for profit, and be given wide-
open squatters' rights, or is the ocean—like technology—"the common heritage of
humanity," as the poor nations insist?

Many of these same questions will apply to operations in outer space as well
once manufacturing begins to take place there. And once the Pentagon and the
Soviets begin knocking down each other's satellites in earnest. Once again—
though we devote less money and brainpower to them—the social and political
questions linked to technology turn out to be far more important than the purely
technical or even scientific issues.
OMNI   What about genetic engineering? We've heard a lot lately about cloning-
and test tube babies. Is that "high-stream" science and technology, too?

Toffler Yes, I would include them under that heading. They certainly depend on advanced theoretical knowledge of biology. Years ago, at the time I described cloning and birth technology in *Future Shock,* most people thought it was wild speculation, science fiction. Today it's front page news. And it will be even bigger news in the near future.

When you get into genetic manipulation, you touch the life force itself. And like so many other breakthroughs, it has both its hideous risks and its positive side.

OMNI What's good about genetic engineering?

Toffler Genetic manipulation can yield cheap insulin. It can probably help us solve the cancer riddle. But, more important, over the very long run it could help us crack the world food problem.

You could radically reduce reliance on artificial fertilizers—which means saving energy and helping the poor nations substantially. You could produce new, fast-growing species. You could create species adapted to lands that are now marginal, infertile, arid, or saline. And if you really let your long-range imagination roam, you can foresee a possible convergence of genetic manipulation, weather modification, and computerized agriculture—all coming together with a wholly new energy system. Such developments would simply remake agriculture as we've known it for 10,000 years.

OMNI What's the downside?

Toffler Horrendous. Almost beyond our imagination. When you cut up genes and splice them together in new ways, you risk the accidental escape from the laboratory of new life forms and the swift spread of new diseases for which the human race has no defenses.

As is the case with nuclear energy, we have safety guidelines. But no system, in my view, can ever be totally fail-safe. All our safety calculations are based on certain assumptions. The assumptions are reasonable, even conservative. But none of the calculations tell what happens if one of the assumptions turns out to be wrong. Or what to do if a terrorist manages to get a hold of the crucial test tube.

A lot of good people are working to tighten controls in this field. NATO recently issued a report summarizing the steps taken by dozens of countries from the U.S.S.R. to Britain and the U.S. But what do we do about irresponsible corporations or nations who just want to crash ahead? And completely honest, socially responsible geneticists are found on both sides of an emotional debate as to how —or even whether—to proceed.

Farther down the road, you also get into very deep political, philosophical, and ecological issues. Who is to write the evolutionary code of tomorrow? Which species shall live and which shall die out? Environmentalists today worry about vanishing species and the effect of eliminating the leopard or the snail darter from the planet. These are real worries, because every species has a role to play in the overall ecology. But we have not yet begun to think about the possible emergence of new, predesigned species to take their place.

OMNI What about that old-fashioned species, *Homo sapiens?*

Toffler Well, what about us? Who is to redesign the human body? Who is to decide what your child and your grandchildren are going to look like? How shall we prevent such techniques from falling into the hands of the Hitlers of the future?

As usual, we are racing wildly ahead in the lab with innovations but crawling when it comes to social and political innovation. I think every dollar used for scientific and technical research and development ought to be matched by a dollar devoted to research and development on how to deal with the social and environmental consequences of that research.

We complain that political and social systems lag behind scientific and technological invention, but we put precious little money or brainpower to work on the problem of *social invention*. We're trying to cope with things like genetic engineering with obsolete regulatory concepts.

Not surprisingly, the guidelines and controls on genetic engineering are still only feeble at best. The geneticists (with some honorable exceptions) and the big drug companies (with fewer honorable exceptions) don't want anyone telling *them* what to do. They will want to play the game by the old laissez-faire rules.

OMNI   What other "high-stream" developments are ahead?

Toffler   Things are breaking loose on many other fronts—like brain research, for example. Dr. Jose Delgado, the man who once stopped a charging bull by sending radio waves to electrodes implanted in its brain, is now in Madrid, after having left Yale. I saw him recently at a UNESCO roundtable in Paris, and he predicts that within one year we'll see non-sensory communication from brain to brain—the direct input of electrical signals from one brain into another, bypassing the sense organs. This has staggering implications for our understanding of perception and communication. Delgado is speaking out, trying to tell us that revolutionary changes are about to explode. He says that before long we will have the ability to deliberately alter evolution of the human brain.

OMNI   Whew! If that is all "high-stream" development, what's "low-stream"? Give us some examples.

Toffler   Well, "low-stream" is technology that is designed to be more human, more responsive to local and community needs, less environmentally degrading. The people working on this say technology doesn't have to be big and wasteful. They point out that, where capital is scarce and labor plentiful, technologies should be deliberately labor-intensive. They say that the energy system must be decentralized and built on renewable sources.

This whole concept, as developed by E. F. Schumacher, is a constructive one, since it challenges the assumption that the technology that works in Birmingham will necessarily be good for Bombay or Brooklyn. It attacks the basic premises of brute force technology, and many of the underlying principles of industrialism.

I can give you one simple example of low-stream technology. A futurist friend of ours, M. S. Iyengar, some years ago headed up the Indian government's research laboratory in Assam. He looked for new processes that could be used by village people without much capital, without supporting staffs of Ph.Ds., without much energy input. He noticed that India was importing caffeine for pharmaceutical use, but that, at the same time, it was burning millions of tons of waste from its tea plantations. Now tea has a substance in it that is extremely similar to caffeine. So he invented a simple, cheap, village-scale machine for extracting this substance from tea waste. Then he invented a technology for using the waste from *that* process to make low-cost building materials.

I think we'll see much more of this approach in the years ahead, and that it will develop at the same time as our high-stream technologies, which will, themselves, begin to embody some of the same principles. Eventually, we'll see high-stream and low-stream begin to come together in appropriate systems.

OMNI You spoke of three main lines of development. What's the third?

Toffler In addition to "high-stream" and "low-stream" I would add what might be called "outside-the-stream" science and technologies—developments from fields that our scientific and engineering establishments today, for the most part, regard as kooky, weird, or unrespectable—beyond the pale.

OMNI Like what?

Toffler Like, for example, the new interest in the work of Nikola Tesla. Tesla was a genius who was supposed to share the Nobel prize with Edison but refused to appear on the same platform with that "tinkerer." Tesla believed that the earth itself could be used as an electrical conductor and that one could resonate electrical waves from point to point without wires or other connectors. For many years, Tesla has been a forgotten figure.

Today there are persistent reports that the Soviets, the American military, and others are doing strange things with low-frequency electromagnetic waves, based on Tesla's unconventional theories.

Two years ago, for example—on October 14, 1976, to be precise—radio communications around the world were disrupted by some mysterious influence. It turned out, as I understand it, that these were caused by secret Soviet experiments. The U.S., Canada, Britain, and the Scandinavian countries formally protested to the Russians. Intelligence sources reportedly now believe they were caused by waves originating at a Tesla magnifying transmitter in Riga, Latvia.

OMNI What about fields like parapsychology and the occult?

Toffler Well, this comes back to what I said at the beginning about the revolution in science itself. We are witnessing a slam-bang attack on rigid, restrictive conceptions of science. This is coupled with a demand that the frontiers of science be expanded to encompass many subjects that have until now been regarded as taboo.

Now, much of this—much of the interest, for example, in the occult, in irrationalism, mysticism, or parapsychology—is either naiveté or quackery. Millions of people, having lost faith in industrial civilization and its ruling ideas, are desperately searching for a new world view or a new religion. And many of them are extremely gullible, easy prey for the para-scientific hucksters and hoaxsters, for phony gurus and psychics.

Some people—dissatisfied with the criteria science uses to determine truth—use no criteria at all. They believe everything. . . .

OMNI What will this new civilization be like, and what role will technology play?

Toffler The shape of the new civilization will be determined by population and resource trends, by military factors, by value changes, by changes in family structure, by political shifts—not by technology alone. I'm not a technological determinist.

Nevertheless, the technological choices we make in the next five or ten years will have an extraordinary impact. If we choose to develop one energy system as against another, or one communications network as against another, we will drastically shape the world of our children. That's why we need a technological strategy.

OMNI   What do you mean, a technological strategy? Don't we have one?

Toffler   No. The U.S. has nothing remotely resembling a technological policy. My wife and I have just returned from Tokyo, where we met with, among others, people from MITI—their ministry of industry and trade. What interested us about the Japanese was *not* their very advanced research, but that this research was part of a larger plan.

They expect their manufacturing sector to decline and their service sector to grow as it has in many other nations. So they are busy inventing practical applications of advanced technology for the service sector of the economy.

OMNI   You have been quoted as advocating greater "citizen participation" in the making of major technological decisions. But isn't it naive to think that ordinary people, without scientific training, can make intelligent recommendations?

Toffler   I don't think untrained people can replace experts—on questions that need expert answers. But you don't need to be an expert to know what you want and you don't need to be an expert to make the kind of *value judgments* that technological policies are necessarily based upon.

I would put it the other way. I think it is naive, not to say anti-democratic, to go on letting major technological decisions—that will affect our lives and the lives of our children—be made by small elites from the business, government, and science communities.

Granted, we don't know much about how to get intelligent citizen participation in such matters. We lack the necessary social and intellectual technologies, so to speak. But I think we can invent them. In this respect, the Swedes may have something to teach us.

OMNI   What have they done?

Toffler   The Swedes were hard-hit by the energy squeeze of '73, and they decided they'd better have an energy policy and a lot more conservation. But they also recognized that if the policy came from the usual elites, and the people were not involved in formulating it, then no one would pay the slightest attention to it. So they tried to find a way to democratize it.

The immediate objection was, "What do ordinary people know about energy? They can't tell a solar cell from a fast-breeder reactor, so how can they make intelligent decisions?"

The Swedish government said, "OK, so the people don't know. Let's teach them." And it set up a program that, in effect, said that any Swede willing to spend ten one-hour sessions in a class learning about energy would have the right to make formal recommendations to the government.

Every political party from the right wing to the communists, every trade union, every adult education center, promptly offered its own ten-session courses on energy. The government people assumed that 10–15,000 Swedes might enroll. In fact, 70–80,000 signed up. That's like 2 million Americans sitting down, taking a crash course, and trying to learn something about a national problem.

I don't think this is a panacea. I'm not romantic about "the people." I don't think we can handle complex technological and scientific questions, or begin to control our own technological and scientific drive, without experts and scientists. But I also don't think we can afford to leave science and technology to "the best and the brightest."

If we do, we'll find the future has already been staked out in advance by small elites who got there first and colonized it for their own purposes. And that's dangerous.

OMNI Undemocratic maybe. But why dangerous?

Toffler Because the trajectory to the new civilization takes us through unknown territory.

At the end of the line, after a generation or two, we may very well have a much better, more decent, more democratic, and more humane world than we do now. But I don't believe getting there will be smooth and easy.

If history is any clue, the succession of civilizations is accompanied by bloodshed, disasters, and other tragedies. Our moral responsibility is not to stop the future, but to shape it, to channel our destiny in humane directions, and to try to ease the trauma of transition. One way to do that is to invite millions of people, especially the dispossessed and disfranchised, who are seldom consulted, to share in basic decisions.

This means giving them a stake in tomorrow. It means designing new institutions for controlling our technological lunge into the future. It means replacing our obsolete political structures. It means new decision-systems that are both future-oriented and, at the same time, broadly participative.

Only by opening the decision process, by democratizing our basic scientific and technological decisions, at least to a degree, can we hope to pass safely through the decades that stretch before us.

Questions 9.3

1. Describe and contrast the three technological levels described by Toffler.
2. "The prime mover in modern social change is technology." Discuss. What is Toffler's view on this question?
3. How should a society handle or deal with social change in Toffler's view?
4. Change in one area almost inevitably leads to change in other areas. Illustrate, using examples from the Toffler interview.

10 Collective Behavior

Collective behavior is group behavior that is spontaneous, unstructured, and unstable. It may be either sporadic and short term or more continuous and long-lasting.[1] Collective behavior is often hard to predict because it is not rooted in the usual cultural or social norms. Spontaneous and unstructured behavior is hard to observe or record objectively and is, therefore, difficult to study. Ethically and practically, the researcher cannot yell "Fire!" in a crowded theater, start a downtown riot, or produce a natural disaster and then observe how people behave. Although there have been some artificial or laboratory-created studies of rumor and panic, most studies of collective behavior by social scientists are after-the-fact analyses and discussions with people who happened to be involved. However, these

[1]Treatment of concepts in this chapter in general follows the description given by Ralph Turner and Lewis Killian in their book, *Collective Behavior,* 2d ed. (Englewood Cliffs, N.J.: Prentice-Hall, 1972).

studies have revealed that collective behavior, although spontaneous, is not as disorganized as it appears and, in fact, follows reasonably consistent patterns. Some of these patterns are examined in this chapter as we look at analyses of crowds (audiences, mobs), rumor, fads and fashions, mass hysteria, disaster behavior, publics, and public opinion.

Crowds

An outline of the major collective behavior concepts would start with the crowd. A **crowd** is a temporary collection of people in close physical contact reacting together to a common stimulus. For example, the passengers on the flight from New York to San Francisco whose pilot suddenly decides he would like to go to the North Pole might be transformed from an aggregation into a crowd (or even a mob). Crowds have certain characteristics in common. **Milling** usually occurs as a crowd is being formed. In one sense milling refers to the excited, restless, physical movement of the individuals involved. In a more important sense milling refers to a process of communication that leads to a definition of the situation and possible collective action. Not long ago, a Berkeley classroom suddenly started shaking with the first tremors of an earthquake. Almost at once the people began turning, shifting, looking at each other, at the ceiling, and at the instructor. They were seeking some explanation for the highly unusual experience and, whether spoken aloud or not, the questions on their faces were clear: "What is it?" "Did you feel it?" "What should we do?" Buzzing became louder talking, and someone shouted, "Earthquake!!!" The students began to get up and move toward the doors. Many continued to watch the ceiling. . . . Milling may involve the long buildup of a lynch mob, or the sudden reaction in a dark and crowded theater when someone shouts, "Fire!!!" Milling helps ensure the development of a common mood for crowd members.

When they are part of a crowd, people tend to be *suggestible.* They are less critical and will readily do things that they would not ordinarily do alone. This is in part because, as members of a crowd, they are *anonymous.* There is a prevailing feeling that it is the crowd that is responsible, not the individual. Once one becomes a member of an acting crowd, it is extremely difficult to step back, get perspective, and objectively evaluate what one is doing. Crowd members have a narrowed focus, a kind of tunnel vision. The physical presence of a crowd is a powerful force—people almost have to separate themselves from the crowd physically before they can critically examine their own behavior. There is also a *sense of urgency* about crowds. Crowds are oriented toward a specific focus or task: "We've got to do *this,* and we've got to do it *now!"* Some form of leadership usually appears in the crowd, but, as the mood of the crowd changes, the leadership may shift quickly from one individual or group to another.

There are many different types of crowds. Some are passive—those watching a building burn or those at the scene of an accident. Some are active—a race riot or a lynch mob. Some crowds have a number of loosely defined goals. Other crowds are focused on a specific goal. Turner and Killian distinguish between crowds that direct their action toward some external object—harassing a speaker until he leaves the platform or lynching a criminal—and expressive crowds, that direct their focus on the crowd itself—cheering at a football game or speaking in tongues at a church service.

Controlling the behavior of a crowd is difficult because of the mass of people involved and the spontaneous nature of their behavior. Some methods of dealing with a potentially riotous crowd have been suggested, however: Remove or isolate the individuals involved in the precipitating incident. Reduce the feelings of anonymity and invincibility of the individuals—force them to focus on themselves and the consequences of their action. Interrupt patterns of communication during the milling process by breaking the crowd into small units. Remove the crowd leaders if it can be done without use of force. Finally, attempt to distract the attention of the crowd by creating a diversion or a new point of interest, especially if this can be accomplished by someone who is considered to be in sympathy with the crowd.[2]

Audiences, Mobs, Riots

Audiences and mobs are specific types of crowds. An *audience* at a concert, football game, lecture, religious service, or burning building may usually be likened to a passive crowd. Emotional contagion is possible in such situations, and individuals are responsive in a group in ways that they would not be as individuals. Audiences at performances of rock and roll stars and in Pentecostal church services may

[2]For dimensions, types, and control of crowds, see Turner and Killian, *Collective Behavior,* Chapters 5–9 (see footnote 1).

become very expressive in a variety of possibly unpredictable ways. Comedians expect audiences to laugh at their jokes. But most comedians have "bits" that they do when audiences are unpredictable and don't laugh (Johnny Carson gets audience sympathy by jokingly mentioning his "war injuries"). Much of audience behavior is predictable, or at least predictably unpredictable. The football fan knows he is going to cheer at the game, the comedian's rejection bits are well prepared, and rock concerts are adequately staffed with police to protect the musicians, and with nurses to minister to the fans who pass out. At the same time, audiences demonstrate collective behavior characteristics in that their behavior is frequently spontaneous, and members are suggestible and anonymous.

A **mob** is a focused, acting crowd. It is emotionally aroused, intent on taking aggressive action. A lynch mob would be an example of such a crowd. A waterfight between several fraternities in Berkeley on a warm spring day in 1956 spontaneously turned into a panty raid. Thousands of eager young men marched with determination through the campus community methodically stealing panties from numerous sorority houses. Afterwards, many of the participants expressed amazement that they had been involved in such behavior. Mob behavior has occurred more recently when unusual events—a severe winter storm in New Jersey in February 1979, and power outages in New York City—have been followed by looting and vandalism.

A **riot** describes the situation in which mob behavior has become increasingly widespread and destructive. Riots may involve a number of mobs acting independently. Throughout our history, the United States has had riots over the issue of race: New York, 1863; Chicago, 1919; Detroit, 1943. In the 1960s, urban riots occurred with increasing frequency. The issues were social class and poverty as well as race. The Watts riot in Los Angeles in the summer of 1965 lasted six days. Nearly 4,000 people were arrested, and property damage was estimated at over $40 million. Thirty-four people were killed and over 1,000 people injured. Most of the killed and injured were blacks. In the Detroit riot in the summer of 1967 more than forty people died, and property damage was estimated at $50 million. The relatively minor incident that set off the week-long confrontation was the police closing of a "blind-pig," an after-hours tavern. A crowd collected as the police carted off the tavern's patrons, a stone was thrown, a shoe store was set on fire, and the riot was on. Campus disturbances occured in the late 1960s at San Francisco State, Berkeley, Harvard, Columbia, Cornell, and at a number of other schools. It is likely, however, that to call these occasions riots, as the press often did, is an exaggeration of what actually happened. Riots have taken place at prisons and sporting events. A highly unusual situation occurred in 1969 when a disagreement at a soccer match led to a riot, which in turn led to a short war between Honduras and El Salvador.

Social scientists have studied riots extensively since the activities of the 1960s. Ralph Conant has examined a number of urban conflicts, and he suggests four phases that describe the possible life history of a riot. Conant believes that not all civil disturbances go through all four stages—in fact, most do not even reach phase 3 but die out earlier. Typically, the temper or mood of the participants is ambivalent and unstable throughout the riot.

Phase 1—The precipitating incident: Some gesture, act, or event is taken by the community as concrete evidence of injustice. The incident—use of force by police, eviction of a tenant—is inflammatory because it is seen as typical of the antagonist. It is seen as ample excuse for striking back and tends to draw together a large number of people. In a community where there is much unrest, the precipitating incident may be a minor event to others, but it is very important to the members of the community.

Phase 2—Confrontation: More and more people gather. Individuals suggest targets for violence and attempt to focus crowd reaction, a process called *keynoting.* Other individuals attempt to calm the crowd and encourage moderation. Police officials may appear and attempt to disrupt the keynoting by dispersing the crowd. This may have the opposite effect and raise a hostile keynoter to an even more prominent position. Conant states that the outcome of phase 2 is of crucial importance. The temper of the crowd may calm, or it could escalate explosively. The response of civil authorities, of local leaders, and of news media (whether they over-report and sensationalize or show restraint) are all critical.

Phase 3—Roman holiday: Success of hostile keynoting and an explosion of activity mark the beginning of phase 3. The crowd, dominated now by younger people, begins moving. Conant describes their mood as an angry, gleeful intoxication. Buildings and cars are attacked. Targets are not necessarily random but more likely selected and patterned, representing objects that rioters resent or fear. Police are taunted and attacked. Later in phase 3, excitement subsides and systematic looting begins. According to Conant, behavior in the carnival-like atmosphere of the Roman holiday is explained at least in part by the amazing contradictions and ambivalences present in the urban ghetto: stores owned by hated white people and beloved contents of the stores; despised police and their admired weapons. This ambivalence extends to the riot participants, who show great changes in behavior. They can be violent one day and calm others the next day. These ambivalences toward violence and in mood make it unlikely that most riots will get to phase 4.

Phase 4—Siege: Polarization of the two sides signals the end of effective communication. Curfew is declared. Warlike acts occur. Snipers attack, buildings are firebombed, and a general state of siege exists.[3]

Panic and Mass Hysteria

Panic represents a particular type of reaction in a crowd situation. Sociologically, panic is defined as nonadaptive or nonrational flight resulting from extreme fear and loss of self-control. Usually there is a severe threat, a limited number of ways out, a feeling of being trapped. Flight in itself does not necessarily mean panic. Some flight is rational and sensible, as when people leave in an orderly manner an area that is threatened by hurricane or flood. Panic refers specifically to flight that is nonadaptive—people stampeding through a burning building and attempting to fight their way out a door that is already hopelessly blocked. Panic differs some-

---

[3]Ralph Conant, "Rioting, Insurrection, and Civil Disobedience," *The American Scholar* 37 (Summer 1968).

what from other forms of collective behavior in that, although it is frequently a result of the crowd situation (spontaneous and contagious), it is essentially an individualistic and competitive reaction. In panic, each person is desperately trying to obtain an objective on his or her own, and since many others are doing the same thing, there is a good chance that some will not make it.[4]

The Iroquois Theater fire in Chicago provides an extreme example of panic and its possible consequences. During a performance on a December afternoon in 1903, draperies on the stage caught fire. Somebody yelled "Fire," and most of the audience panicked. Actors and musicians attempted to calm the crowd, but to no avail. There were many exit doors, but some were poorly marked and some hard to open. People were crushed against doors and on stairways; others jumped to their death from fire escapes. The fire was not very serious, and the fire department arrived quickly—the panic lasted only eight minutes. The death toll, however, was 602.

Mass hysteria is in some ways similar to panic and describes the situation in which a particular behavior, fear, or belief sweeps through a large number of people —a crowd, a city, or a nation. Examples of mass hysteria might include fainting at a rock concert, the fear that flying saucers are after us or that the Martians are invading, or the belief that certain women are practicing witchcraft.

A SNAKE WITH BAD BREATH

A venomous snake has been haunting the people of the Pokharan desert area of Rajasthan in India. The snake, known as *peevana* or *piana*, is about twenty inches long. It steals into huts at dawn and delicately crawls onto the chest of someone asleep. It then opens its mouth wide and holds it in front of the sleeping person's nose, and the victim inhales the snake's poisonous breath. The snake appears to be sadistic as well—it lets its victims know of their fate by whipping them in the face with its tail as it slips away. Newspapers in Rajasthan recently reported that five persons fell victim to *peevana* in one village in a single day.

The *peevana* myth has endured for centuries. According to the local maharaja's gazette, the ruler once offered 1,000 rupees to anyone who could produce the reptile, dead or alive. No one has yet been able to.

Rumors

Rumor is a type of collective behavior that may or may not be crowd oriented. Much rumor is merely a form of person-to-person communication. Rumor is defined as unconfirmed, although not necessarily false, communication. It is often related to some issue of public concern. Rumors change constantly as they spread. They tend to grow shorter, more concise, and more easily told. Certain attractive details of the rumor become magnified. New details are manufactured to complete the story or to make it internally consistent. A rumor that Beatle Paul McCartney

[4]This discussion of panic is drawn from Duane Schultz, *Panic Behavior* (New York: Random House, 1964), and from Turner and Killian, *Collective Behavior,* Chapters 5 and 6 (see footnote 1).

LOOK—I DON'T CARE **WHAT** YOU STAND FOR.........
....I WANT SOMEONE WITH A
BIT OF **GLAMOR!**

had been killed in an automobile accident swept the country in the fall of 1969. Fans of the rock music group frantically sought further proof of Paul's demise by playing Beatle records backwards and by finding clues on album covers and in photographs of the group. Even several personal appearances by the supposedly dead Beatle did little to quash the rumor. In fact, some are still suspicious today of that fellow passing himself off as Paul McCartney. . . .

People pass or tell rumors for a variety of reasons. The rumor may fit with what we want to believe, with what we know to be true: "Teachers are absentminded" or "Sex education is Communist inspired." We may pass rumors on to increase our status in the eyes of others. If we were the first to get the news, we want others to know it. Or it's such a tremendous story that others are bound to think more of us when we tell it to them. Did you hear about the flying saucers over Minneapolis? About John F. Kennedy's sex life? About those giant birds perching on trees in the Southwest? About Bigfoot wandering through downtown Yakima? You *didn't?* Well, let me tell you. . . .

Rumor may have a variety of functions. It may be gossip and serve to enliven the Thursday afternoon bridge club, or it may provide a core of communication during a crowd's milling period and thus be the stimulus for crowd action.

There is a common assumption that rumors become less accurate as they are passed on. Taylor Buckner makes the point that in some situations rumors become *more* accurate. The important variables to consider are rumor set and interaction setting. Buckner suggests three rumor sets: critical, uncritical, and transmission. *Critical set* occurs when people have knowledge about the rumor's subject matter, have personal experience with it, or are habitually suspicious of rumors anyway. These people tend to eliminate inaccurate and irrelevant parts of rumors they hear and pass on only the most important parts. An *uncritical set* may exist when people have no knowledge about a situation, when passing the rumor fills a need, or during crisis situations when there is little information. People with an uncritical set may modify the rumor so it sounds better, change it to fit their own needs, devise totally new rumors to fit the situation, or in some other way contribute to the inaccuracy of the rumor. *Transmission set* means that the content of the rumor is irrelevant to the person. The person's only interest is to pass the rumor on. People who merely transmit a rumor forget or reword parts but usually do not purposely distort or correct the rumor.

Group characteristics—the interaction setting—also affect a rumor's accuracy. Buckner suggests that a rumor is heard more often and evaluated more carefully in a close, more primary group (college dorm, sorority, army unit, social club, clique) than in a more diffuse or secondary group. It also follows that the more interested and involved a group is with a rumor, the more the rumor is told and evaluated. The rumor that then-Beatle Paul McCartney was dead was undoubtedly more actively discussed among rock music and Beatles fans than it was in the board room at General Motors or among people pushing rumors about flying saucers. Buckner concludes that the multiple interaction likely to occur in a close, highly involved group combined with a critical set leads to increased accuracy in the rumor. However, if the critical set is missing, greater inaccuracy results.[5]

Fads, Crazes, and Fashions

> Rumor has it that Hollywood, the status symbol center of the universe, has a new thing. In the summer of 1978, no-chic became chic. The Rolls Royce and the Mercedes stayed in the garage, and the elite went to town in beat-up 1957 Chevies and Fords. No more Gucci and Vuitton satchels in the expensive restaurants—now it's nondescript knapsacks and duffel bags. And everyone is out jogging. Will it last?

Fads, crazes, and fashions are forms of collective behavior that are usually more widespread and long-lasting than crowd behavior. **Fads** (and *crazes*) refer to the relatively short-term obsessions that members of society or members of specific groups have toward certain mannerisms, objects, clothes, or ways of speaking. Among the current fads that come to mind are hot tubs, disco dancing, Mopeds, and science fiction movies. Past examples include the super ball, swallowing goldfish, the hula hoop, and stuffing phone booths. Fads and crazes may interest many and burn brightly for a while, but usually they die out quickly. **Fashions** are similar but are more widespread and last longer than fads and crazes. Examples of fashions might include the miniskirt, two-piece bathing suits, long hair on men, wide neckties, Mustang style in cars, ranch style in homes, and rock and folk rock in popular music.

Turner and Killian report an interesting peculiarity of fads and fashions: fashions follow the social-class structure, but fads do not necessarily follow the social-class structure. That is, fashions usually start at upper-class levels and seep

---

[5]H. Taylor Buckner, "A Theory of Rumor Transmission," in *Readings in Collective Behavior,* 2d ed., edited by Robert Evans (Chicago: Rand McNally, 1975), pp. 86–102. Also see Warren A. Peterson and Noel P. Gist's article, "Rumor and Public Opinion," *American Journal of Sociology* 57 (September 1951), pp. 159–167, for a summary and analysis of some theories on rumor.

downward. Fads, on the other hand, may appear anywhere in the class structure and may be adopted more quickly by members of lower social classes than by members of the upper classes. Since following fads and fashions brings prestige to people, fashion supports the *status quo* (the current prestige system), whereas fads may upset the *status quo* by granting prestige to people who otherwise have low status.[6]

Disasters

Studies of disasters provide us with data about collective behavior. A **disaster** situation is defined as one in which there is a basic disruption of the social context within which individuals and groups function, a radical departure from the pattern of normal expectations. Such a situation almost by definition results in collective behavior.[7]

Disaster research has focused on three times periods: immediately before the disaster, during the disaster, and after the disaster. Predisaster studies have noted that making people aware of impending disaster is extremely difficult unless the group concerned has already experienced a disaster—a flood, a bombing, or an earthquake. Otherwise, people do not take the warning seriously. They look around, note that others don't seem bothered, and define the situation as normal or at least not serious. During Hurricane Camille in Mississippi in August 1969, twenty-some people were killed in an apartment house where they had decided to ride out the storm and have a "hurricane party." People tend to interpret disaster cues as normal or familiar events.

Studies of behavior *during* the disaster indicate that, contrary to popular belief, panic and loss of control are rare. Flight is a frequent response, but it usually represents an adaptive rational reaction to the situation rather than panic. Studies of behavior *after* the disaster indicate that people tend to underestimate the scope and destructiveness of the disaster. Again, people define events in terms of the familiar and normal. Often those who had clearly defined tasks in case of disaster —civil defense workers, nurses—experience severe role conflict. The conflict is between helping people in general as they are trained to do or finding and helping family and loved ones. Frequently the latter choice is made. Various types of convergence behavior occur after a disaster. People flock *to* the disaster area. Within twenty-four hours after the atom bomb was dropped on Hiroshima, thousands of refugees streamed *into* the city. Airliners in trouble at major airports attract crowds of people to the scene. One such incident at New York's Kennedy Airport brought so much automobile traffic that emergency vehicles had difficulty reaching the scene. Communication lines become clogged with calls coming *into* disaster areas. Material convergence occurs as all sorts and varieties of material are shipped into the disaster area in an effort to help the victims. Within forty-eight

[6]Turner and Killian, *Collective Behavior*, pp. 152–153 (see footnote 1).

[7]This section on disaster is taken from Charles Fritz's chapter on disaster, which appears in Robert Merton and Robert Nisbet's book, *Contemporary Social Problems* (New York: Harcourt Brace Jovanovich, 1961), Chapter 14.

hours after a tornado in Arkansas, truckloads full of material began arriving. Among the mass of material that people sent were button shoes, derby hats, a tuxedo, and a carton of falsies. It took 500 workers two weeks to sort the material. After Hurricane Camille in 1969, a great variety of material poured into Mississippi. Authorities had to make television appeals to stop the shipments. The same thing happened after the February 1976 earthquake in Guatemala. Indians in an area heavily hit by the quake who usually eat corn and beans were sent canned goods they could not open and would not eat. They were also sent jars of peanut butter, boxes of cornflakes, and cans of anchovy paste. Other useless items piling up in warehouses after the quake included canned cherries, high-heeled shoes, see-through shirts, and wigs. A Red Cross official reported that the same thing happened after the 1970 Nicaragua earthquake and the 1973 Honduras hurricane and concluded that the public simply responds, partly out of a desire to be helpful in a bad situation, partly because they just want to empty their closets. Finally, the studies report that in many cases disaster as an immediate threat produces solidarity among those experiencing it. People tend to grow closer together as a result of their attempts to fight and survive the situation.

Publics and Public Opinion

Publics and public opinion represent another aspect of collective behavior. A **public** is a number of people who have an interest in, and difference of opinion about, a common issue. The public engages in communication and discussion (more often indirect than face-to-face) and, contrary to the crowd, the public is dispersed or scattered rather than in close physical contact. **Public opinion** refers to opinions held by a public on a given issue. **Propaganda** refers to attempts to influence and change the public's viewpoint on an issue.[8]

In a complicated mass society, a great number of issues appear, and each issue has its concerned interest group or public. Membership in these publics is transitory and constantly changing. Some members of a public are vitally interested, others only marginally. Members of a public may communicate by special magazines, newspapers, television, and letter writing. Professional football and baseball have a public, the National Rifle Association is a public, the American Medical Association is a public; the issues of socialized medicine, legalization of prostitution, and elimination of the death penalty all have publics. Some publics are widespread; if the issue is the type of job the President is doing, the whole nation may become the public. Other publics may be much smaller.

Public opinion is registered in a variety of ways. It is registered when an individual running for office is defeated. It is recorded in the letters-to-the-editor column of a newspaper or magazine that prints a story with which the public agrees or disagrees. More recently, public opinion polls have become a popular way of determining what the public is thinking. Polls are avidly followed by politicians

[8]For a comprehensive treatment of these concepts, see Turner and Killian, *Collective Behavior,* Chapters 10–12 (see footnote 1).

as well as by the man on the street. Polls have even been criticized because it is feared that some people look at the polls before deciding how to vote or what to think on a given issue.

There are many pitfalls in public opinion polling, and occasionally even the best pollsters go wrong. Probably the most famous miss was the *Literary Digest* poll of 1936, which predicted that Landon (Republican) would defeat Roosevelt (Democrat) for President. The *Literary Digest* obtained a biased sample by mailing ballots to people whose names, for the most part, were selected from telephone directories or from lists of automobile owners. Only forty percent of all homes had phones in 1936 and only fifty-five percent of all families had cars, so the magazine was sampling people who were economically well-off. Another error was introduced by *mailing* ballots—people of higher income and education are more likely to return mailed questionnaires than are people with low income and education. Ballots were mailed early (September) so that last-minute changes were missed. The upshot was that *Literary Digest* asked a group of reasonably well-to-do people (who generally tend to vote Republican) who they were going to vote for. Their prediction was so grossly wrong that it is given as the reason why the magazine went out of business.[9] A number of polls picked Dewey to beat Truman in 1948, and there was a tremendous uproar in England in June 1970, when the Tories decisively won an election that all the polls predicted would be won by Labour.

Since it is usually impossible in a public opinion poll to talk to all members of the public, a sample is taken. Frequently the success of the poll hinges on the accuracy of the sampling technique. The time at which the poll is taken is also important. Opinions change rapidly, and if the latest political poll is three or four weeks before the election, pollsters can expect to have missed many last-minute changes. A more basic fault in polling is that some people are very interested and know much about the issue, and others are only slightly interested and know little or nothing about the issue. Yet in most polls the responses of these two types are given the same weight. Other difficulties in sampling public opinion occur when people give pollsters answers they think the pollsters want, and when a person is a member of several conflicting publics at once, as most of us are. What if a member of the Catholic Church and mother of eleven kids is asked her opinion of government-supported artificial birth control? She may find herself a member of conflicting publics. Finally, as far as action is concerned, it is often much more important to know how a few powerful people or opinion leaders feel about an issue than it is to know what many relatively powerless people think.

In conclusion, let's examine how the public, public opinion, and propaganda might relate to a given issue, capital punishment. Members of the public interested in this issue would include policemen, prison officials, sociologists, psychologists, social workers, and future criminals. To obtain a measure of public opinion, Gallup might randomly select 1,000 people and ask them what they think about keeping the death penalty. The sample includes interested members of the public and disinterested bystanders, and all opinions are counted equally. (What if, for exam-

[9]This is summarized from Julian Simon's very complete discussion in his book *Basic Research Methods in Social Science* (New York: Random House, 1969), Chapter 8.

ple, we find that most of those who know most about capital punishment are opposed to it, and most of those who know least about it are in favor of it? What do we do?) Suppose we find (as Gallup did in 1978) that sixty-two percent of those polled want to keep the death penalty. The public in its various forms has spoken. Since the margin is not decisive, however, the other side decides to hire a public relations firm to persuade the public a little. Propaganda begins to appear. A public-interest story in a popular magazine tells how the family of an executed man is getting along. A newspaper story appears describing a famous case in which a condemned man was cleared of the crime he was supposed to have committed— but just too late. . . . An ex-warden of San Quentin is interviewed on a nationwide television news broadcast, and he relates in detail his opposition to the death penalty. A reporter, witness to an execution in the electric chair, describes it in vivid detail in a Sunday Supplement. The effectiveness of the propaganda will depend on its ability to reach the audience, on the sophistication of the audience, and on the receptiveness of the audience to the new viewpoint. Let's assume that the propaganda has been cleverly conceived, and a new sampling indicates that public opinion has changed—now only forty percent want to keep the death penalty. Still, nothing happens until power is applied. A lobbyist in Washington, D.C., working for the Anti-Death Penalty League, puts pressure on legislators. Thirty thousand anti-capital-punishment letters (all remarkably similar) flood in. Finally a new law is passed, more because of the League, lobby, and letters than because of public opinion. We can see from this imaginary and oversimplified example that boundaries of what constitutes a public are obscure, polls may be misleading, public opinion may change rapidly, propaganda is frequently very useful at building or changing public opinion, and finally, public opinion must be backed by political power if meaningful action is to result.

In June 1972 the U.S. Supreme Court ruled that the death penalty was unconstitutional. Polls indicated that the public still favored capital punishment and, due to public outcry and the reverse of some of the procedures outlined above, many states reinstituted the death penalty. Finally in July 1976 the U.S. Supreme Court seemingly reversed its earlier decision and upheld many of these laws.

SUMMARY

In the previous chapter in this section on change and deviation in society we dealt with social change and social disorganization. In this chapter we examined another form of activity that is outside the organized and ordinary—collective behavior. Collective behavior refers to spontaneous and somewhat unstructured actions by groups of people. A number of concepts and terms central to the study of collective behavior were discussed. We examined types of collectivities: crowds, audiences, and mobs. We described types of behaviors: rumor, panic, mass hysteria, fads, crazes, and fashions. Special situations involving collective behavior were noted: riots and disasters. Our discussion of collective behavior concluded with an analysis of publics, public opinion, and propaganda.

A riot is a situation in which mob behavior has become widespread and destructive. The first reading that follows is an excerpt from the U.S. Riot Commission's Report. It illustrates crowd, mob, and riot behavior in three American cities. A mob is a focused, acting crowd. A mob is hard to deal with once set in motion, but the next reading relates how one of the characters in Harper Lee's novel *To Kill a Mockingbird* distracted a lynch mob. A disaster situation is defined as one in which there is a radical departure from the pattern of normal expectations. In the last reading in this section, D. L. Webber describes what happened when Darwin, Australia, was hit by a cyclone.

Reading 10.1
U.S. Riot Commission Report

The following excerpts from the U.S. Riot Commission's report (the "Kerner Report") describe disturbances that took place in several cities in the summer of 1967. The riot in Tampa was mild in comparison with those in Newark and Detroit. In Newark, twenty-three died—a white detective, a white fireman, and twenty-one blacks. Damage was estimated at $10 million. In Detroit, forty-three persons were killed—thirty-three blacks and ten whites. Seventeen of the dead were looters. Damage was estimated at between $30 and $50 million. Together, these examples provide a composite of the life history of a riot. They also provide graphic illustrations of crowds and mobs.

Tampa
On Sunday, June 11, 1967, Tampa, Florida, sweltered in the 94-degree heat. A humid wind ruffled the bay, where thousands of persons watched the hydroplane races. Since early morning the Police Department's Selective Enforcement Unit, designed as a riot control squad, had been employed to keep order at the races.

At 5:30 P.M., a block from the waterfront, a photo supply warehouse was broken into. Forty-five minutes later two police officers spotted three Negro youths as they walked near the State Building. When the youths caught sight of the officers, they ducked into an alley. The officers gave chase. As they ran, the suspects left a trail of photographic equipment scattered from yellow paper bags they were carrying.

The officers transmitted a general broadcast over the police radio. As other officers arrived on the scene, a chase began through and around the streets, houses, and alleys of the neighborhood. When Negro residents of the area adjacent to the Central Park Village Housing Project became aware of the chase, they began to participate. Some attempted to help the officers in locating the suspects.

R. C. Oates, one of 17 Negroes on the 55-man Tampa police force, spotted

19-year-old Martin Chambers, bare to the waist, wriggling away beneath one of the houses. Oates called for Chambers to surrender. Ignoring him, Chambers emerged running from beneath the house. A white officer, J. L. Calvert, took up the pursuit.

Pursuing Calvert, in turn, were three young Negroes, all spectators. Behind one of the houses a high cyclone fence created a two-foot-wide alley twenty-five feet in length.

As Chambers darted along the fence, Officer Calvert rounded the corner of the house. Calvert yelled to him to halt. Chambers ignored him. Calvert pointed his .38 revolver and fired. The slug entered the back of Chambers and passed completely through his body. Raising his hands over his head, he clutched at the cyclone fence.

When the three youths running behind Officer Calvert came upon the scene, they assumed Chambers had been shot standing in the position in which they saw him. Rumor quickly spread through the neighborhood that a white police officer had shot a Negro youth who had had his hands over his head and was trying to surrender.

The ambulance that had been summoned became lost on the way. The gathering crowd viewing the bloody, critically injured youth grew increasingly belligerent.

Finally, Officer Oates loaded Chambers into his car and drove him to the hospital. The youth died shortly thereafter.

As officers were leaving the scene, a thunderstorm broke. Beneath the pelting rain, the spectators scattered. When an officer went back to check the area he found no one on the streets.

A few minutes after 7:00 P.M., the Selective Enforcement Unit, tired and sun-parched, reported in from the races. A half hour later a report was received that 500 persons were gathering. A police car was sent into the area to check the report. The officers could find no one. The men of the Selective Enforcement Unit were told to go home.

The men in the scout car had not, however, penetrated into the Central Park Village Housing complex where, as the rain ended, hundreds of persons poured from the apartments. At least half were teenagers and young adults. As they began to mill about and discuss the shooting, old grievances, both real and imagined, were resurrected: discriminatory practices of local stores, advantages taken by white men of Negro girls, the kicking in the face of a Negro boy by a white man as the Negro lay handcuffed on the ground, blackballing of two Negro high schools by the athletic conference.

When Officer Oates returned to the area he attempted to convince the crowd to disperse by announcing that a complete investigation would be made into the shooting. He seemed to be making headway when a young woman came running down the street screaming that the police had killed her brother. Her hysteria galvanized the crowd. Rock throwing began. Police cars driving into the area were stoned. The police, relying on a previous experience when, after withdrawal of their units, the crowd had dispersed, decided to send no more patrol cars into the vicinity.

This time the maneuver did not work. From nearby bars and tawdry night spots patrons joined the throng. A window was smashed. Haphazard looting began. As fluid bands of rioters moved down the Central Avenue business district, stores whose proprietors were particularly disliked were singled out. A grocery store, a liquor store, a restaurant were hit. The first fire was set.

Because of the dismissal of the Selective Enforcement Unit and the lack of accurate intelligence information, the police department was slow to react. Although Sheriff Malcolm Beard of Hillsborough County was in contact with the Department throughout the evening, it was not until after 11:00 P.M. that a request for deputies was made to him.

At 11:30 P.M. a recall order, issued earlier by the police department, began to bring officers back into the area. By this time, the streets in the vicinity of the housing project were lighted by the flames of burning buildings.

Falling power lines whipped sparks about the skirmish line of officers as they moved down the street. The popping noise of what sounded to the others like gunshots came from the direction of the housing project.

The officers did not return the fire. Police announced from a sound car that anyone caught armed would be shot. The firing ceased. Then, and throughout the succeeding two days, law enforcement officers refrained from the use of firearms. No officer or civilian suffered a gunshot wound during the riot.

Newark

Early on the evening of July 12, a cab driver named John Smith began, according to police reports, tailgating a Newark police car. Smith was an unlikely candidate to set a riot in motion. Forty years old, a Georgian by birth, he had attended college for a year before entering the Army in 1950. In 1953 he had been honorably discharged with the rank of corporal. A chess-playing trumpet player, he had worked as a musician and a factory hand before, in 1963, becoming a cab driver.

As a cab driver, he appeared to be a hazard. Within a relatively short period of time he had eight or nine accidents. His license was revoked. When, with a woman passenger in his cab, he was stopped by the police, he was in violation of that revocation.

From the high-rise towers of the Reverend William P. Hayes Housing Project, the residents can look down on the orange-red brick facade of the Fourth Precinct Police Station and observe every movement. Shortly after 9:30 P.M., people saw Smith, who either refused or was unable to walk, being dragged out of a police car into the front door of the station.

Within a few minutes at least two civil rights leaders received calls from a hysterical woman declaring a cab driver was being beaten by police. When one of the persons at the station notified the cab company of Smith's arrest, cab drivers all over the city began learning of it over their cab radios.

A crowd formed on the grounds of the housing project across the narrow street from the station. As more and more people arrived, the description of the beating purportedly administered to Smith became more and more exaggerated. The descriptions were supported by other complaints of police malpractice that, over the years, had been submitted for investigation—but had never been heard of again.

Several Negro community leaders, telephoned by a civil rights worker and informed of the deteriorating situation, rushed to the scene. By 10:15 P.M. the atmosphere had become so potentially explosive that Kenneth Melchior, the senior police inspector on the night watch, was called. He arrived at approximately 10:30 P.M.

Met by a delegation of civil rights leaders and militants who requested the right to see and interview Smith, Inspector Melchior acceded to their request.

When the delegation was taken to Smith, Melchior agreed with their observations that, as a result of injuries Smith had suffered, he needed to be examined by a doctor. Arrangements were made to have a police car transport him to the hospital.

Both within and outside of the police station the atmosphere was electric with hostility. Carloads of police officers arriving for the 10:45 P.M. change of shifts were subject to a gauntlet of catcalls, taunts and curses.

Joined by Oliver Lofton, administrative director of the Newark Legal Services Project, the Negro community leaders inside the station requested an interview with Inspector Melchior. As they were talking to the inspector about initiating an investigation to determine how Smith had been injured, the crowd outside became more and more unruly. Two of the Negro spokesmen went outside to attempt to pacify the people. There was little reaction to the spokesmen's appeal that the people go home. The second of the two had just finished speaking from atop a car when several Molotov cocktails smashed against the wall of the police station.

With the call of "Fire!" most of those inside the station, police officers and civilians alike, rushed out of the front door. The Molotov cocktails had splattered to the ground; the fire was quickly extinguished.

Inspector Melchior had a squad of men form a line across the front of the station. The police officers and the Negroes on the other side of the street exchanged volleys of profanity.

Three of the Negro leaders, Timothy Still of the United Community Corporation, Robert Curvin of CORE, and Lofton requested they be given another opportunity to disperse the crowd. Inspector Melchoir agreed to let them try, and provided a bullhorn. It was apparent that the several hundred persons who had gathered in the street and on the grounds of the housing project were not going to disperse. Therefore, it was decided to attempt to channel the energies of the people into a nonviolent protest. While Lofton promised the crowd that a full investigation would be made of the Smith incident, the other Negro leaders urged those on the scene to form a line of march toward the city hall.

Some persons joined the line of march. Others milled about in the narrow street. From the dark grounds of the housing project came a barrage of rocks. Some of them fell among the crowd. Others hit persons in the line of march. Many smashed the windows of the police station. The rock throwing, it was believed, was the work of youngsters; approximately 2,500 children lived in the housing project.

Almost at the same time, an old car was set afire in a parking lot. The line of march began to disintegrate. The police, their heads protected by World War I-type helmets, sallied forth to disperse the crowd. A fire engine, arriving on the scene, was pelted with rocks. As police drove people away from the station, they scattered in all directions.

A few minutes later a nearby liquor store was broken into. Some persons, seeing a caravan of cabs appear at city hall to protest Smith's arrest, interpreted this as evidence that the disturbance had been organized, and generated rumors to that effect.

However, only a few stores were looted. Within a short period of time the disorder ran its course.

(The next day) Reports and rumors, including one that Smith had died, circulated through the Negro community. Tension continued to rise. Nowhere was the tension greater than at the Spirit House, the gathering place for Black Nationalists, Black Power advocates, and militants of every hue. Black Muslims, Orthodox Muslims, and members of the United Afro-American Association, a new and growing organization that follows, in general, the teachings of the late Malcolm X, came regularly to mingle and exchange views. Anti-white playwright LeRoi Jones held workshops. The two police-Negro clashes, coming one on top of the other, coupled with the unresolved political issues, had created a state of crisis.

On Thursday, inflammatory leaflets were circulated in the neighborhoods of the Fourth Precinct. A "Police Brutality Protest Rally" was announced for early evening in front of the Fourth Precinct Station. Several television stations and newspapers sent news teams to interview people. Cameras were set up. A crowd gathered.

A Picket line was formed to march in front of the police station. Between 7:00 and 7:30 P.M. James Threatt, Executive Director of the Newark Human Rights Commission, arrived to announce to the people the decision of the mayor to form a citizens group to investigate the Smith incident, and to elevate a Negro to the rank of captain.

The response from the loosely milling mass of people was derisive. One youngster shouted "Black Power!" Rocks were thrown at Threatt, a Negro. The barrage of missiles that followed placed the police station under siege.

After the barrage had continued for some minutes, police came out to disperse the crowd. According to witnesses, there was little restraint of language or action by either side. A number of police officers and Negroes were injured.

As on the night before, once the people had been dispersed, reports of looting began to come in. Soon the glow of the first fire was seen.

Without enough men to establish control, the police set up a perimeter around a two-mile stretch of Springfield Avenue, one of the principal business districts, where bands of youths roamed up and down smashing windows. Grocery and liquor stores, clothing and furniture stores, drug stores and cleaners, appliance stores and pawnshops were the principal targets. Periodically police officers would appear and fire their weapons over the heads of looters and rioters. Laden with stolen goods people began returning to the housing projects.

Near midnight, activity appeared to taper off. The mayor told reporters the city had turned the corner.

As news of the disturbance had spread, however, people had flocked into the streets. As they saw stores being broken into with impunity, many bowed to temptation and joined the looting.

Without the necessary personnel to make mass arrests, police were shooting into the air to clear stores. A Negro boy was wounded by a .22 caliber bullet said to have been fired by a white man riding in a car. Guns were reported stolen from a Sears Roebuck store. Looting, fires, and gunshots were reported from a widening area. Between 2:00 and 2:30 A.M. on Friday, July 14, the mayor decided to request Governor Richard J. Hughes to dispatch the state police, and National Guard troops. The first elements of the state police arrived with a sizable contingent before dawn.

During the morning the governor and the mayor, together with police and National Guard officers, made a reconnaissance of the area. The police escort guarding the officials arrested looters as they went. By early afternoon the National Guard had set up 137 roadblocks, and state police and riot teams were beginning to achieve control. Command of anti-riot operations was taken over by the governor, who decreed a "hard line" in putting down the riot.

Detroit

On Saturday evening, July 22, the Detroit Police Department raided five "blind pigs." The blind pigs had had their origin in prohibition days, and survived as private social clubs. Often, they were after-hours drinking and gambling spots.

The fifth blind pig on the raid list, the United Community and Civic League at the corner of 12th Street and Clairmount, had been raided twice before. Once 10 persons had been picked up; another time 28. A Detroit Vice Squad officer had tried but failed to get in shortly after 10 o'clock Saturday night. He succeeded, on his second attempt, at 3:45 Sunday morning.

The Tactical Mobile Unit, the Police Department's Crowd Control Squad, had been dismissed at 3:00 A.M. Since Sunday morning traditionally is the least troublesome time for police in Detroit—and all over the country—only 193 officers were patrolling the streets. Of these, 44 were in the 10th Precinct where the blind pig was located.

Police expected to find two dozen patrons in the blind pig. That night, however, it was the scene of a party for several servicemen, two of whom were back from Vietnam. Instead of two dozen patrons, police found 82. Some voiced resentment at the police intrusion.

An hour went by before all 82 could be transported from the scene. The weather was humid and warm—the temperature that day was to rise to 86—and despite the late hour, many people were still on the street. In short order, a crowd of about 200 gathered.

A few minutes after 5:00 A.M., just after the last of those arrested had been hauled away, an empty bottle smashed into the rear window of a police car. A litter basket was thrown through the window of a store. Rumors circulated of excess force used by the police during the raid. A youth, whom police nicknamed "Mr. Greensleeves" because of the color of his shirt, was shouting: "We're going to have a riot!" and exhorting the crowd to vandalism.

By 7:50 A.M., when a 17-man police commando unit attempted to make the first sweep, an estimated 3,000 persons were on 12th Street. They offered no resistance. As the sweep moved down the street, they gave way to one side, and then flowed back behind it.

According to witnesses, police at some roadblocks made little effort to stop people from going in and out of the area. Bantering took place between police officers and the populace, some still in pajamas. To some observers, there seemed at this point to be an atmosphere of apathy. On the one hand, the police failed to interfere with the looting. On the other, a number of older, more stable residents, who had seen the street deteriorate from a prosperous commercial thoroughfare to one ridden by vice, remained aloof.

In an effort to avoid attracting people to the scene, some broadcasters cooperated by not reporting the riot, and an effort was made to downplay the extent of the disorder. The facade of "business as usual" necessitated the detailing of numerous police officers to protect the 50,000 spectators that were expected at that afternoon's New York Yankees–Detroit Tigers baseball game.

Numerous eyewitnesses interviewed by Commission investigators tell of the carefree mood with which people ran in and out of stores, looting and laughing, and joking with the police officers. Stores with "Soul Brothers" signs appeared no more immune than others. Looters paid no attention to residents who shouted at them and called their actions senseless. An epidemic of excitement had swept over the persons on the street.

. . . A rumor was threading through the crowd that a man had been bayoneted by the police. Influenced by such stories, the crowd became belligerent. At approximately 1:00 P.M. stonings accelerated. Numerous officers reported injuries from rocks, bottles, and other objects thrown at them. Smoke billowed upward from four fires, the first since the one at the shoe store early in the morning. When firemen answered the alarms, they became the targets for rocks and bottles.

At 2:00 P.M. Mayor Cavanagh met with community and political leaders at police headquarters. Until then there had been hope that, as people blew off steam, the riot would dissipate. Now the opinion was nearly unanimous that additional forces would be needed.

A request was made for state police aid. By 3:00 P.M. 360 officers were assembling at the armory. At that moment looting was spreading from the 12th Street area to other main thoroughfares.

Some evidence that criminal elements were organizing spontaneously to take advantage of the riot began to manifest itself. A number of cars were noted to be returning again and again, their occupants methodically looting stores. Months later, goods stolen during the riot were still being peddled.

A spirit of carefree nihilism was taking hold. To riot and to destroy appeared more and more to become ends in themselves. Late Sunday afternoon it appeared to one observer that the young people were "dancing amidst the flames."

Questions 10.1

1. Apply text definitions of crowd, mob, and riot to the cities described. Point out where "crowd" is the best description, where "mob" is the best description, and where "riot" is the best description.
2. List the common factors—the situations or occurrences that were present in each of the three city disturbances described.
3. "Urban riots may be seen as a type of social movement. . . ." Discuss (see Chapter Nine).

Reading 10.2

Maycomb Jail

HARPER LEE

A mob is a focused, acting crowd. It is emotionally aroused and intent on taking action. A mob is a powerful force, and it is difficult to change its direction. When the direction is changed (as it is in this fictional account), the change can be understood in collective behavior terms. Here, Scout and Jem Finch help their father, Atticus, protect a black man from a lynch mob in Harper Lee's novel *To Kill a Mockingbird.*

The Maycomb Jail was the most venerable and hideous of the county's buildings. Atticus said it was like something Cousin Joshua St. Clair might have designed. It was certainly someone's dream. Starkly out of place in a town of square-faced stores and steep-roofed houses, the Maycomb jail was a miniature Gothic joke one cell wide and two cells high, complete with tiny battlements and flying buttresses. Its fantasy was heightened by its red brick facade and the thick steel bars at its ecclesiastical windows. It stood on no lonely hill, but was wedged between Tyndal's Hardware Store and The Maycomb Tribune office. The jail was Maycomb's only conversation piece: its detractors said it looked like a Victorian privy; its supporters said it gave the town a good solid respectable look, and no stranger would ever suspect that it was full of niggers.

As we walked up the sidewalk, we saw a solitary light burning in the distance. "That's funny," said Jem, "jail doesn't have an outside light."

"Looks like it's over the door," said Dill.

A long extension cord ran between the bars of a second-floor window and down the side of the building. In the light from its bare bulb, Atticus was sitting propped against the front door. He was sitting in one of his office chairs, and he was reading, oblivious of the nightbugs dancing over his head.

I made to run, but Jem caught me. "Don't go to him," he said, "he might not like it. He's all right, let's go home. I just wanted to see where he was."

We were taking a short cut across the square when four dusty cars came in from the Meridian highway, moving slowly in a line. They went around the square, passed the bank building, and stopped in front of the jail.

Nobody got out. We saw Atticus look up from his newspaper. He closed it, folded it deliberately, dropped it in his lap, and pushed his hat to the back of his head. He seemed to be expecting them.

"Come on," whispered Jem. We streaked across the square, across the street, until we were in the shelter of the Jitney Jungle door. Jem peeked up the sidewalk. "We can get closer," he said. We ran to Tyndal's Hardware door—near enough, at the same time discreet.

In ones and twos, men got out of the cars. Shadows became substance as lights revealed solid shapes moving toward the jail door. Atticus remained where he was. The men hid him from view.

"He in there, Mr. Finch?" a man said.

"He is," we heard Atticus answer, "and he's asleep. Don't wake him up."

In obedience to my father, there followed what I later realized was a sickeningly comic aspect of an unfunny situation: the men talked in near-whispers.

"You know what we want," another man said. "Get aside from the door, Mr. Finch."

"You can turn around and go home again, Walter," Atticus said pleasantly. "Heck Tate's around somewhere."

"The hell he is," said another man. "Heck's bunch's so deep in the woods they won't get out till mornin'."

"Indeed? Why so?"

"Called 'em off on a snipe hunt," was the succinct answer. "Didn't you think a' that, Mr. Finch?"

"Thought about it, but didn't believe it. Well then," my father's voice was still the same, "that changes things, doesn't it?"

"It do," another deep voice said. Its owner was a shadow.

"Do you really think so?"

This was the second time I heard Atticus ask that question in two days, and it meant somebody's man would get jumped. This was too good to miss. I broke away from Jem and ran as fast as I could to Atticus.

Jem shrieked and tried to catch me, but I had a lead on him and Dill. I pushed my way through dark smelly bodies and burst into the circle of light.

"H-ey, Atticus!"

I thought he would have a fine surprise, but his face killed my joy. A flash of plain fear was going out of his eyes, but returned when Dill and Jem wriggled into the light.

There was a smell of stale whiskey and pigpen about, and when I glanced around I discovered that these men were strangers. They were not the people I saw last night. Hot embarrassment shot through me: I had leaped triumphantly into a ring of people I had never seen before.

Atticus got up from his chair, but he was moving slowly, like an old man. He put the newspaper down very carefully, adjusting its creases with lingering fingers. They were trembling a little.

"Go home, Jem," he said. "Take Scout and Dill home."

We were accustomed to prompt, if not always cheerful acquiescence to Atticus's instructions, but from the way he stood Jem was not thinking of budging.

"Go home, I said."

Jem shook his head. As Atticus's fists went to his hips, so did Jem's and as they faced each other I could see little resemblance between them: Jem's soft brown hair and eyes, his oval face and snug-fitting ears were our mother's, contrasting oddly with Atticus's graying black hair and square-cut features, but they were somehow alike. Mutual defiance made them alike.

"Son, I said go home."

Jem shook his head.

"I'll send him home," a burly man said, and grabbed Jem roughly by the collar. He yanked Jem nearly off his feet.

"Don't you touch him!" I kicked the man swiftly. Barefooted, I was surprised to see him fall back in real pain. I intended to kick his shin, but aimed too high.

"That'll do, Scout," Atticus put his hand on my shoulder. "Don't kick folks. No—" he said, as I was pleading justification.

"Ain't nobody gonna do Jem that way," I said.

"All right, Mr. Finch, get 'em outa here," someone growled. "You got fifteen seconds to get 'em outa here."

In the midst of this strange assembly, Atticus stood trying to make Jem mind him. "I ain't going," was his steady answer to Atticus's threats, requests, and finally, "Please Jem, take them home."

I was getting a bit tired of that, but felt Jem had his own reasons for doing as he did, in view of his prospects once Atticus did get him home. I looked around the crowd. It was a summer's night, but the men were dressed most of them, in overalls and denim shirts buttoned up to the collars. I thought they must be cold-natured, as their sleeves were unrolled and buttoned at the cuffs. Some wore hats pulled firmly down over their ears. They were sullen-looking, sleepy-eyed men who seemed unused to late hours. I sought once more for a familiar face, and at the center of the semi-circle I found one.

"Hey, Mr. Cunningham."

The man did not hear me, it seemed.

"Hey, Mr. Cunningham. How's your entailment gettin' along?"

Mr. Walter Cunningham's legal affairs were well known to me; Atticus had once described them at length. The big man blinked and hooked his thumbs in his overall straps. He seemed uncomfortable; he cleared his throat and looked away. My friendly overture had fallen flat.

Mr. Cunningham wore no hat, and the top half of his forehead was white in contrast to his sunscorched face, which led me to believe that he wore one most days. He shifted his feet, clad in heavy work shoes.

"Don't you remember me, Mr. Cunningham? I'm Jean Louise Finch. You brought us some hickory nuts one time, remember?" I began to sense the futility one feels when unacknowledged by a chance acquaintance.

"I go to school with Walter," I began again. "He's your boy, ain't he? Ain't he, sir?"

Mr. Cunningham was moved to a faint nod. He did know me, after all.

"He's in my grade," I said, "and he does right well. He's a good boy," I added, "a real nice boy. We brought him home for dinner one time. Maybe he told you about me, I beat him up one time but he was real nice about it. Tell him hey for me, won't you?"

Atticus had said it was the polite thing to talk to people about what they were interested in, not about what you were interested in. Mr. Cunningham displayed no interest in his son, so I tackled his entailment once more in a last-ditch effort to make him feel at home.

"Entailments are bad," I was advising him, when I slowly awoke to the fact that I was addressing the entire aggregation. The men were all looking at me, some had their mouths half-open. Atticus had stopped poking at Jem: they were standing together beside Dill. Their attention amounted to fascination. Atticus's mouth, even, was half-open, an attitude he had once described as uncouth. Our eyes met and he shut it.

"Well, Atticus, I was just sayin' to Mr. Cunningham that entailments are bad an' all that, but you said not to worry, it takes a long time sometimes . . . that you all'd ride it out together. . . ." I was slowly drying up, wondering what idiocy I had committed. Entailments seemed all right enough for living-room talk.

I began to feel sweat gathering at the edges of my hair; I could stand anything but a bunch of people looking at me. They were quite still.

"What's the matter?" I asked.

Atticus said nothing. I looked around and up at Mr. Cunningham, whose face was equally impassive. Then he did a peculiar thing. He squatted down and took me by both shoulders.

"I'll tell him you said hey, little lady," he said.

Then he straightened up and waved a big paw. "Let's clear out," he called. "Let's get going, boys."

As they had come, in ones and twos the men shuffled back to their ramshackle cars. Doors slammed, engines coughed, and they were gone.

I turned to Atticus, but Atticus had gone to the jail and was leaning against it with his face to the wall. I went to him and pulled his sleeve. "Can we go home now?" He nodded, produced his handerchief, gave his face a going-over and blew his nose violently.

"Mr. Finch?"

A soft husky voice came from the darkness above: "They gone?"

Atticus stepped back and looked up. "They've gone," he said. "Get some sleep, Tom. They won't bother you any more."

From a different direction, another voice cut crisply through the night: "You're damn tootin' they won't. Had you covered all the time, Atticus."

Mr. Underwood and a double-barreled shotgun were leaning out his window above the The Maycomb Tribune office.

It was long past my bedtime and I was growing quite tired; it seemed that Atticus and Mr. Underwood would talk for the rest of the night, Mr. Underwood out the window and Atticus up at him. Finally Atticus returned, switched off the light above the jail door, and picked up his chair.

"Can I carry it for you, Mr. Finch?" asked Dill. He had not said a word the whole time.

"Why, thank you, son."

Walking toward the office, Dill and I fell into step behind Atticus and Jem. Dill was encumbered by the chair, and his pace was slower. Atticus and Jem were well ahead of us, and I assumed that Atticus was giving him hell for not going home, but I was wrong. As they passed under a streetlight, Atticus reached out and massaged Jem's hair, his one gesture of affection.

Questions 10.2

1. Outline how mob and crowd characteristics are illustrated in this selection.
2. Describe in collective behavior terminology why and/or how the lynch mob was broken up.

Reading 10.3

Darwin Cyclone: An Exploration of Disaster Behavior

D. L. WEBBER

A disaster situation is defined as one in which there is a basic disruption of the social context within which individuals and groups function, a radical departure from the pattern of normal expectations. Studies of disasters provide us with data about a particular type of collective behavior. In this paper, D. L. Webber describes what was called Australia's greatest national disaster, the Darwin cyclone of 1974.

D. L. Webber is a psychologist with the Department of Health, Darwin. He and his family were in Darwin during the cyclone and remained to help with the emergency.

On Christmas eve 1974 Darwin was being battered by the fringe winds of Cyclone Tracy. By daylight on Christmas day the cyclone had passed through Darwin wrecking the city. Cyclonic winds exceeding 217 km per hour at their peak had brought about the greatest disaster in Australian history. Forty-nine people were dead and 16 others were missing, presumed dead, on the harbour. More than 140 people were admitted to hospital, mostly on Christmas day, and over 500 people were treated at Outpatients for injuries sustained during the cyclone. Countless others were treated at suburban emergency health centres for lacerations and injuries. As the city struggled to its feet on Christmas day it was without power, water, sewerage, or any communication contacts to the suburbs. Approximately $500 million damage had been done to buildings and facilities. Massive destruction and damage to housing left much of the population homeless. Roads were blocked, debris was everywhere, and it continued to rain.

Some weeks before 24 December 1974 there had been a cyclone alert that had ended as an anticlimax. There had in fact been no major cyclone strike in Darwin since 1937. There was no doubt about the current situation however. The Bureau of Meteorology was on full alert, regular warnings were broadcast, emergency

From "Darwin Cyclone: An Exploration of Disaster Behavior," by D. L. Webber, AUSTRALIAN JOURNAL OF SOCIAL ISSUES, February 1976. Reprinted by permission of the Australian Council of Social Service.

advice given, and later people were cautioned to take cover as destructive winds would begin in a few hours. Many heeded this advice. Some even booked into hotels or moved to larger buildings.

It was Christmas eve, an earlier cyclone had passed away, and many people had no experience of cyclones. Despite the advice of authorities and the example of those who took precautions, a substantial portion of the population either went to parties or got undressed as usual and simply went to bed. For very many people there was a complete misperception of the situation.

Cyclone Strike

By 11 PM Christmas eve, roofs were being lost from buildings and trees were being uprooted. By 2 AM Christmas day the power was off and radio stations had failed. People were now experiencing the nerve shattering sound of sheet iron grinding and scratching as it was hurled about by the wind. The thudding and exploding sound of beams falling, walls collapsing and heavy airborne objects smashing through houses was everywhere. Many houses simply disintegrated about the occupants. Faced with an immediate threat to life people sought shelter wherever they could find it. Some hid in baths, others lay on floors or under beds. As their houses were swept away some were able to shelter in cars parked between house piers. Most could only lie where they were, hang on and hope.

The sense of isolation during the cyclone was extreme. It was a common feeling that one was at the centre of the destruction and that other areas could not be so badly off. Only later did people realize that the destruction was almost city wide. As might be expected fear was a fairly universal and justifiable experience. Dissociation also occurred. Some people, whose houses were reasonably intact, wandered about inside in a dissociated state looking out of windows.

Post Cyclone

With the approach of dawn the winds abated and people realized they could come out of hiding. Most were simply relieved that the ordeal was over and that they were alive. Immediately neighbours and friends were checked and given aid. Shelter had to be found for children and others. As the only major buildings in most suburbs were the schools, an exodus of people began to these buildings. Some were able to grab a few personal items, others had sense enough to bring a little food. Many just arrived in night attire or in what clothing they could quickly gather. A major social and community crisis existed.

In the meantime key personnel, maintenance crews, tradesmen and the like reported for duty as soon as they could. The hospital and police station had continued to work throughout. Water and emergency power had to be restored to such places. At dawn plant and machinery at the works depot were operating and emergency procedures that had been adopted were being implemented. Front end loaders and graders began clearing major roads; the evacuation of the sick continued.

News of the disaster had by this stage reached the outside world. The government had been notified and the National Disaster Organization moved into action. Following a review of the situation a full scale evacuation of the city was ordered.

Over the next few days more than 25,000 people were moved to southern centres by air while nearly 10,000 others left Darwin by road. The greatest natural disaster in Australia had been followed by the greatest mass movement of civilian personnel in its history. During this process, food, water, clothing, medicines and other basic needs had to be met for thousands now forced to accommodate themselves in schools and elsewhere. Behind the scenes local professionals, technicians, tradesmen and others strove to tackle these problems.

Social and Individual Breakdown

The trauma experienced by family units in their efforts to survive, the mass destruction of homes, the termination of jobs for many in the private sector and the breakdown of public facilities were too much for many people. After they reached safety shock set in. Hundreds milled about looking stunned and unable to act. With others panic had already taken over. They dropped all and simply drove off down the North-South Highway. By 7 AM Wednesday there was a stream of traffic heading out of the city. In their haste to leave many people left wardrobes full of clothes, personal possessions, valuables and pets. Often not even readily accessible tins of food were packed. The stream of evacuees moving down the highway was to increase over the next day. Fortunately for them relief parties were ready and waiting at towns and hamlets on the route. Free fuel, food and assistance was provided at these points.

For the thousands seeking refuge at the schools, stress, anxiety, and lack of communications began to tell. There had been no radio contact since 1:40 AM Wednesday. The ABC could not resume local broadcasting for 36 hours. No official communication existed to the suburbs and the people. Collective anxiety was expressed about where the cyclone might be or whether it would come back. Stories of destruction in other parts of town and the numbers killed were quickly passed on and exaggerated; the situation was ripe for the spread of rumours. Many common experiences were misinterpreted and became the basis of these rumours. One such rumour concerned a supposed outbreak of gastroenteritis in the population. This had its origin in the large number of people suffering gastric upset immediately after the cyclone as a result of stress.

As in all sudden emergencies an immediate and far reaching change in personal goals and the status of people occurred. New priorities were established. Skills were revalued in terms of immediate needs, and role and status changes were called for on the part of many. Suddenly plumbers, plant operators, cooks, nurses and the like became more essential than petty bureaucrats. A town that had thrived as a basically bureaucratic structure with well ordered clerical hierarchies could not make the transition to a new order. Hundreds were disorientated, panic stricken and without any apparent social place in the city. The stage was set for mass panic and exit.

Other signs of social breakdown began to show. Looting began in the early hours of Wednesday 25th and was to continue as a problem throughout. Scapegoats were looked for. Even the Bureau of Meteorology was being blamed for the situation. As the stress continued prejudices became heightened, fighting and violence broke out, and petty crime increased.

For those with a clearly defined role or the ability to adopt a new role the task of meeting immediate needs was immense. Such people worked with only a few hours' sleep for several days. As the emergency continued and the central disaster organization worked non-stop to deal with the situation, the effects of a break-down in cooperative behaviour and its replacement by competitive behaviour on the part of large numbers of citizens became all too apparent.

Following the decision to evacuate by air as many people as possible from the city to southern centres, much of the competitive behaviour now became focused on this aspect as the great bulk of the population tried to escape. Women fought to get on planes, others grabbed nearby children so that they might get priority. Those women who were staying behind or helping directly in the emergency had other women approach them with a view to using their children for evacuation priority. As social dislocation continued and anxiety and panic mounted evacu-ation centres were sometimes mobbed and gates to planes rushed. On occasion order had to be restored by police resorting to a show of arms. The height of the disruption came with family units breaking up, men feigning injuries to get evacu-ated and some even dressing up as women.

Of the many who were evacuated and the few who remained, those who stayed seemed to suffer less emotional trauma and adjusted quicker to their circum-stances. Those who were evacuated had the additional stress associated with the evacuation to cope with. At the airport children and adults often milled for hours awaiting aircraft seats. Confusion, crowding and stress heightened anxiety. Sleep-ing on wet floors or standing in rain for hours, anxious mothers or separation from families did little for most children. Under continued stress, mothers often could not attend effectively to the needs of their children.

Discussion and Conclusion

The basic behaviour patterns that emerged in response to Cyclone Tracy were shock, apathy, psychosomatic reactions, anxiety and panic. Sleeplessness, loss of appetite and heightened sensitivity to wind and sound also occurred. Exhaustion, depression and grief reactions were common later. Detachment and the sense of attack on personal image through home and property loss were noticeable. Loss of public communication and rumours affected the course of events for many days. The wholesale substitution of competitive behaviour for cooperative behaviour threatened the entire social fabric. The aftermath of the cyclone continues and will do so for a long time.

Recognition of these emotional factors and the implementation of programmes to cope with them have been a feature of situations elsewhere. *Unfortunately no such programmes were implemented at Darwin.* On the whole the crisis was approached as essentially a physical crisis by authorities and public alike, with only belated recognition that there were social overtones. A small group of personnel provided mental health resources at the local hospital. This was much too small a group to handle Australia's largest natural disaster. Although general welfare aid in the form of food, clothing and bedding, together with personnel to organize and implement relief programmes were rushed to the city, there was no infusion of mental health personnel and no opportunity for the one or two that were on hand to either influence or advise administration. Australia's greatest peace time emotional crisis had passed by without even preliminary recognition that it was indeed an emotional and social as well as physical crisis.

To the writer it appears axiomatic that where basic social units such as family structures are collapsing in response to a disaster, efforts should be directed towards re-establishing such units, and developing a sense of social cohesion. Care should be exercised not to accelerate such breakdown by unnecessarily separating families, or isolating children. Evacuation of the injured, unfit and other appropriate elements of the population was essential as a first step in dealing with the disaster. The continued freighting out of disturbed and upset people many days after the event, instead of providing local support and treatment first, is questionable.

Questions 10.3

1. In what ways does the behavior in Darwin fit with the general characteristics of disaster discussed in the text? In what ways does it differ?
2. List the collective behavior concepts involved in the study of disaster. Give examples of each from the Darwin cyclone.

11 Deviation and Social Control

Experts tell us that no two people have the same fingerprints. People differ from each other in their appearance and behavior as well. Variation in behavior occurs even though we have norms and roles that specify what *should* happen and what people *should* do in almost any given situation. Social differentiation is not only tolerated but expected in social interaction. We expect people to be different from ourselves in behavior and appearance, and we would be very surprised if they were not. At a particular point, however, when differences from a group norm become great enough, social differentiation becomes social deviation.

Defining Deviation

There are a number of ways of defining deviation. Sometimes deviation and normality are defined statistically. Those around the average are considered normal, and those at the extremes are seen as deviant. If average height for American males is 5'10", then males from 5'7" to 6'2" are probably viewed as normal, and a fellow 6'8" or 5'2" is considered deviant. Since most people have an I.Q. of between 95 and 115, that I.Q. level is "normal," and a genius with an I.Q. of 145 or a moron with an I.Q. of 55 are both deviants. Because most Americans are heterosexual and fewer are homosexual, heterosexuality is normal and homosexuality is deviant, if viewed statistically. Sociologists, however, generally do *not* look at deviation as a statistical phenomenon.

A more common way of defining deviation is to liken it to a disease. This approach is especially common to people in general, but is also used by many social scientists. Deviation is something that a person has that we wish he or she could get over, like a cold or the measles. People wonder, "What is *wrong* with Susan? Why does she continue to screw up? She must be crazy. . . ." For years social scientists have viewed the deviant person as one who behaves differently because something is wrong with that person. The problem may be biological, psychological, or familial, or the problem may be with living conditions. With careful study, what is wrong can be discovered and perhaps corrected. The medical analogy fits well with this view of deviation—find the nature of the illness and prescribe a cure.

Labeling Theory

A 6'8" basketball player for the University of Arkansas, sporting collar-length hair and a long drooping mustache, fouled out of three straight games. Before his next one, against Baylor, he decided to trim his hair and shave his mustache. In the Baylor game he was called for only two fouls. Two nights later, against Texas Tech, the neat, trim player played forty minutes and was still around at the end of a 93–91 double-overtime victory that knocked Tech out of the Southwest Conference lead.

The haircut? The shave?

"I think they helped," the player stated. "I hate to say it, but I guess the hairstyle did affect the refs."

In the last several decades a theory of deviation competing with the "disease" theory has come to prominence. *Labeling theory,* as it's called, sees deviant behavior as a product of group definitions. Becoming a deviant involves a labeling process —one is a deviant because a particular group labels him or her as such.[1] As with the basketball player, the focus changes from an examination of why the individual does peculiar things to an examination of why these things are called deviant. In 1919 lawmakers succeeded in passing the Eighteenth Amendment to the U.S. Constitution, which made sale or manufacture of intoxicating beverages a crime. In 1933, the Twenty-first Amendment repealed the Eighteenth and decreed that drinkers were no longer criminal. Which was the majority view? Probably the

---

[1]This discussion of the labeling aspect of deviation is drawn from Howard S. Becker, *Outsiders* (New York: Free Press, 1963), Chapter 1. Also see his Chapter 8 for a discussion of rule creators and rule enforcers.

The case of the hairy basketball player was described in *Sports Illustrated,* 16 Febuary 1976.

latter, but the important point is that both amendments were results of the actions of rule makers who defined the same act as deviant and criminal at one time, and permissible at another time. In other words, it is labeling groups that determine who and what is deviant; *deviation is socially defined.*

Why are some acts labeled as deviant and others not? Sometimes the rule makers are motivated by moral or religious beliefs. They are strongly convinced that acts like drinking alcohol, smoking marijuana, or legalizing abortion are morally wrong and then make tremendous efforts to see their beliefs written into law. You can probably think of examples in American history, some quite recent, in which people have successfully crusaded for a cause that ultimately became law.

Perhaps rule makers are motivated by profit. If new clean air standards are going to mean retooling a company's whole assembly line and $5 million in research and development, then you can be fairly sure that the company may spend about $3 million fighting and delaying that law. Or turn it around. Imagine that I just invented an ingenious little catalytic converter that makes exhaust air *cleaner* than normal air, and I am lobbying for a law to get my invention placed on all cars. Would you believe me if I told you that I am motivated solely by concern for the environment?

Sometimes the rule makers are interested in supporting the *status quo* and protecting vested interests. Often, young politicians recently elected to Congress arrive in Washington with the idea of changing the entrenched seniority rules in the House and Senate. But the club remains. Some of the opposition to the Equal Rights Amendment probably reflects concern for vested interests and the *status quo.*

So, all sorts of motivations and justifications are used by rule makers to make rules. The result is a set of personal judgments about what is "right" and "wrong," which become justification for attempts to control people's behavior. Now rule enforcers take over. They seek out and punish those who violate the rules. Howard Becker refers to rule creators and rule enforcers, people whose profession centers around defining and regulating deviant behavior, as moral entrepreneurs. Labeling theory looks at it this way: Some people *make* rules, others *enforce* them, and out of this process certain individuals are *labeled* deviant. It is a *social* process.

To whom does the deviant label get applied? Well, not to everyone equally of course. It depends in part on the *seriousness* of the act. On very serious behaviors (homicide, armed robbery) about which there is general agreement, the deviant label is quickly and formally applied. If the act is less serious (belching in public, dressing very strangely), the deviant label, if applied at all, will be applied more slowly and perhaps informally. It also depends on the *vulnerability* of the person being labeled. Lower-class people and minorities are more likely to be labeled than others. It depends as well on *visibility.* If the act is obvious and occurs in full view of others, it is more likely to get a reaction.

These and other factors interact in complicated ways. Thus, in the view of the labeling theorists, calling people deviant may be an arbitrary and capricious act— telling us more about the person doing the labeling than about the person being labeled. Take the hairy basketball player once more. As you recall, he cut his hair and no more fouls were called. Tell me, which of the following was he: (1) a mild-mannered, peaceful, and orderly player victimized by referees who have a bias against grubby-long-haired-hippie types; or (2) a brutal "hatchet man" whose behavior became less visible to the rule enforcers (referees) when he cut his hair? We'll never know.

A recent example of the labeling process in action has been provided by Stanford psychologist David Rosenhan. Rosenhan and seven colleagues view themselves as quite sane, but for the purposes of an experiment each went to the admissions office of a mental hospital and told the same story: They were hearing unclear voices that seemed to be saying words like *empty, hollow,* and *thud.* That was enough for the admitting psychiatrists at twelve of the hospitals; Rosenhan and his friends were diagnosed as schizophrenic and admitted. The label was applied, and it stuck. The diagnoses were not questioned by other staff members, and the pseudo-patients were incarcerated for between seven and fifty-two days before being released. Although they behaved calmly and normally in the hospital, they were continually given pills (a total of nearly 2,100) to "help" them. None were released as cured—"in remission" was the final diagnosis. When a label is successfully applied, the individual's behavior is defined in ways that are consistent with the label. While in the hospitals, the pseudo-patients took careful notes about what was happening—hospital staff either ignored this or saw it as evidence of insane compulsiveness. The pseudo-patient's normal behavior was either over-looked entirely or profoundly misinterpreted. Often they would approach hospital staff with reasonable questions. In response, nurses and attendants would move hurriedly away, eyes averted. Psychiatrists also ignored the questioners. This sort of depersonalization is a predominant characteristic in labeling situations. Rosen-han is discouraged about the inability to correctly diagnose mental illness; but more to the point of our study of labeling is his comment that once a label is applied to people it sticks, a mark of inadequacy forever.[2]

---

[2]For the complete report, see "On Being Sane in Insane Places," by D. L. Rosenhan, in *Science,* 19 January 1973, pp. 250–258. *Saturday Review* also has a good summary of the research in the 24 February 1973 issue, pp. 55–56.

NORMAL
FINGER-PRINT

DEVIANT
FINGER-PRINT

Since deviation is socially defined, it should not surprise us to find that some-times the normal zone of behavior is rather wide and other times it is quite narrow. Moreover, what is defined as deviant by one group may be defined as normal by another. The definition of deviation depends on the variable being defined and the group doing the defining. What is deviant in hair length would vary depending on which of the following groups was doing the defining: the U.S. Marine Corps, college students, hippies, barbers, or an association of baldheaded men. For most males, height of over 6'6" is deviant, but for basketball players, height of below 6'1" is deviant and 6'3" to 7' is normal.

Sociologists, while recognizing that biological and psychological factors may play a part, emphasize that deviant behavior is learned behavior, developed through socialization. **Deviant behavior** is developed and learned through interac-tion with others. The behavior of a member of an urban delinquent gang could be described as conforming rather than deviant behavior. He is conforming to gang norms when he defends his turf, builds a zip gun, and saves face by fighting rather than backing down to a threat. His "deviant" behavior is learned and is as conform-ing in its own way as is the behavior of the middle-class college student who conforms to the styles, behavior, and attitudes of those around her.

Categories of Deviation

It is often hard for people to reach agreement on what is deviant and what is normative. There are great differences of opinion in evaluating such things as hair length, sexual behavior, fashion, types of dissent, patriotism, and so on. At the same time, there are some behaviors and characteristics about which there is more general agreement. In the following paragraphs we will briefly examine some of these categories of deviation.

Individuals who lack intelligence to the extent that they are unable to perform normal tasks expected of people their age are victims of *mental deficiency*. Current practice defines five levels of mental deficiency or retardation: *borderline* (I.Q. range of 83–68), *mild* (67–52), *moderate* (51–36), *severe* (35–20), and *profound* (below 20). The extent of mental retardation in the United States is estimated at approximately 3 percent of the population. More than half of the retarded receive special educational services, and a great majority of those in the 50-to-80 I.Q. levels make a satisfactory adjustment in the community at the adult level. Those with I.Q. levels between 25 and 50 are viewed as trainable in that they can learn certain skills necessary for living in the home, neighborhood, or sheltered workshop. They will, however, need some care and supervision throughout life. About 5 percent of all retarded fall in the profoundly retarded category and require complete care and supervision throughout life. Mental deficiency, especially severe retardation, may be related to genetic factors, birth trauma, or diseases of the mother prior to birth. Many instances of retardation, particularly at the higher I.Q. levels (50–80), seem to be related to factors in the social environment.[3]

Mental illnesses are commonly classified in two categories: neuroses and psychoses. Neuroses are the mildest and most common; psychoses are more severe and less common. The neurotic is anxious, nervous, compulsive, but generally able to function adequately in society. The psychotic loses touch with reality. The psychotic may have hallucinations, incoherent speech and thought, or delusions of persecution; or he may withdraw into a dream world. Psychoses fall into two categories: organic and functional. Organic disorders are those caused by brain injury, hereditary factors, or physiological deterioration (as a result of aging or the effects of alcoholism or syphilis). Functional disorders are those without organic cause; they are based on environmental factors. Functional disorders represent a reaction to such things as stress or rejection, or they may possibly be a chosen alternative to an unlivable and intolerable world. Examples of functional disorders include schizophrenia and manic-depressive psychoses. Social scientists generally are more interested in the functional psychoses because of their relationship to social factors. It is important to note that these categories (organic and functional) are not clear-cut or mutually exclusive. Some research has indicated, for example, that hereditary factors affect schizophrenia and that psychoses resulting from aging may be as much related to social isolation (functional) as to physiological deterioration (organic).[4]

It is difficult to estimate the exact number of neurotics in the United States. Some say we are all a little neurotic; other estimates of the number of neurotics in the population run from a high of forty percent to a low of five percent. It has been estimated that there are over two million psychotics in the United States. Half of all hospital beds in the country are used in the care of mental patients, and at current rates one person in ten will be hospitalized for mental illness sometime during his or her life. It is easy to see why mental illness has been called America's *major* health problem.

[3]This is summarized from *Psychology 73/74 Encyclopedia* (Guilford, Conn.: Dushkin Publishing Group, 1973), pp. 166–169.

[4]A more detailed discussion of mental illness, as well as of alcoholism, narcotics, and suicide, appears in Marshall Clinard's and Robert Meier's *Sociology of Deviant Behavior,* 5th ed. (New York: Holt, Rinehart and Winston, 1979).

Drinking alcoholic beverages is relatively common in the United States, but excessive drinking, or *alcoholism,* is viewed as deviant behavior. A 1964 study reported that sixty-eight percent of Americans over eighteen drink, and a 1976 Gallup poll put it at seventy-one percent. Some general characteristics of drinkers are shown in Table 11.1. It should be noted that although more men than women drink, the percentage of women drinkers is increasing rapidly in the United States. Drinking and alcoholism are not identical. Some groups have relatively high alcohol consumption rates but little alcoholism. The major factors here are the group associations and cultural factors associated with drinking.

There are several types of drinkers. *Social drinkers* drink when the occasion suggests or demands it and are relatively indifferent to alcohol—they can take it or leave it. Some social drinkers drink regularly, others infrequently. *Heavy drinkers* drink more frequently and consume greater quantities when they drink. They occasionally become intoxicated. *Acute alcoholics* have much trouble controlling their use of alcohol. They may go on weekend binges or drunks. They have sober periods, but they rely more and more on alcohol. *Chronic alcoholics* drink constantly. They "live to drink, drink to live." It is difficult if not impossible for them to hold jobs, and their health will inevitably be affected. It is estimated that there are 5.5 million problem drinkers in the United States, and most of these would be termed chronic alcoholics. Of an estimated ten million arrests in 1977, approximately 3.3 million were for offenses directly related to alcohol (drunkenness, drunk driving, and disorderly conduct). Sociologists believe that alcoholism is a learned behavior, since drinking patterns tend to be associated with occupational groups, social classes, religious categories, and nationalities.

Use of *narcotics* is a central issue in American society. Drug use is viewed as deviant in a Protestant ethic society dominated by the values of hard work, self-control, and self-discipline. But use of drugs is widespread. Many youth are using marijuana, amphetamines, and LSD and other hallucinogens. Their elders are using tranquilizers, pep pills, and sleeping pills. In the 1960s, drugs, like rock music, became a part of the culture of many youth groups. As young people became more

Table 11.1 Who Drinks Alcohol?

	Highest Proportion of Drinkers	Lowest Proportion of Drinkers
Income	High income	Low income
Education	College	7th grade or less
Residence	Large city	Small city
Religion	Jews, Catholics, Lutherans	Other large Protestant denominations
Age	21–39	60 and over
Sex	Male	Female
State	Alaska, D.C., Hawaii, California, Washington	Iowa, Minnesota, Nebraska, South Dakota, North Dakota

Marshall Clinard and Robert Meier, *Sociology of Deviant Behavior*, 5th ed. (New York: Holt, Rinehart and Winston, 1979), Chapter 10; and the National Institute on Alcohol Abuse and Alcoholism.

interested in drugs, adults became more concerned about drugs, at least about those the young people were using. The result is a classic example of conflicting views about what is deviant behavior and what is not. Concern about drug usage resulted in passage of new drug control laws and stricter enforcement of older laws. One consequence is that there were more than 640,000 arrests for drug abuse in 1977. This represented an increase of 183 percent in ten years (since 1968)—the largest increase of any crime category. Between 1973 and 1977, however, drug abuse arrests *dropped* by seven percent. This could mean that usage is declining. It is far more likely, though, that this means that attitudes toward use of milder drugs, especially marijuana, are moderating, that laws are changing, and that enforcement of existing drug laws is easing.[5]

Suicide is viewed as deviant behavior in the United States, as it is in most societies dominated by Christian and/or Jewish religions. Reactions vary, however. Some countries have called suicide a crime and have buried suicides in special cemeteries. In some Oriental societies suicide is looked upon with less disfavor. Ceremonial self-destruction, known as *hara-kiri,* has long been a custom in Japan. Several states in the United States have classified attempted suicide as a crime, but it is unlikely that this has any deterrent effect, except possibly to insure the success of the attempt. It is estimated that 27,000 Americans committed suicide in 1976, a rate of 12.5 per 100,000 people. Probably at least five times as many attempt suicide as actually commit it.[6]

Suicide rates in selected countries are shown in Table 11.2. Patterns of deviant behavior often vary substantially from one country to another, and this is certainly true of suicide, as can be seen in Table 11.2. However, suicide statistics may be somewhat inaccurate. Countries vary in how they report suicides, and in most places it is probably underreported. In the United States, the coroner usually determines whether a death is reported as suicide. A coroner who is uncertain about the cause is more likely to label the death as due to natural causes. In

Table 11.2   Suicide Rates (per 100,000 People) in Selected Countries, 1974–1975

Hungary	38	Australia	12
Finland	25	Italy	5
Denmark	24	Israel	5
Austria	24	Ireland	4
Switzerland	23	Spain	4
West Germany	21	Costa Rica	4
Sweden	20	Greece	3
Japan	18	Mexico	2
France	16	Kuwait	1
United States	13	Philippines	1

Demographic Yearbook, 1976.

[5]Information on reported crimes and arrests comes from the *Uniform Crime Reports—1977,* which is published annually by the FBI.

[6]These figures on suicides come from *Demographic Yearbook* (a U.N. publication), and *Vital Statistics of the United States* (from the Department of Health, Education, and Welfare).

addition, relatives, motivated by personal or religious beliefs, may press for a "death by natural causes" decision from the coroner.

Suicides in America are more likely to be male, white, over forty-five, single, divorced, or widowed, and Protestant. Although men commit suicide more than women do, more women than men attempt suicide. This has led some to the conclusion that at least for women, suicide may often be an attention-getting device. Men more often use guns to commit suicide; women tend to use poison. Some occupational groups are high in suicide—military officers, policemen, psychiatrists. And, interestingly, suicide is a leading cause of death for young adults.

In the late nineteenth century Emile Durkheim studied suicide in Europe and described in detail three types of suicide: egoistic, altruistic, and anomic.[7] *Egoistic* suicide occurs when interpersonal relationships are secondary, distant, and not group oriented. In such situations, the individual lacks group attachments, and when personal problems appear, the individual in the absence of emotional support resorts to suicide. The high suicide rate of single people might be an example of egoistic suicide. *Altruistic* suicide, on the other hand, is the result of strong group attachments. The individual commits suicide to benefit the group and to follow group norms. Suicides of Japanese soldiers and airmen during World War II and the self-immolation of Buddhist monks in Vietnam are described as altruistic suicides. *Anomic* suicide occurs in situations in which norms are confused or are breaking down. Economic depressions or rapid social changes that lead to disequilibrium in society and a state of normlessness may result in anomic suicides.

Deviant Behavior and Criminal Behavior

A distinction should be made between deviant behavior and criminal behavior. As we have mentioned, deviant behavior, like beauty, is in the eye of the beholder. Behaviors are not naturally deviant; they are defined as deviant by groups. Similarly, reactions to deviation vary greatly. Some deviant behavior is ignored, some deviant behavior is tolerated, and some deviant behavior brings severely critical reactions by others. As behaviors fall further outside the range of what is defined as normal, societies feel that they must formally proscribe the behaviors. Rule makers decide that certain acts are a threat to the organization and structure of society and must therefore be prohibited. Laws are passed, and these forms of deviation become illegal or criminal if performed.

Conflict theorists tell us to be alert here and ask crucial questions. Who are the rule makers? Who passes the laws? The answer—middle- and upper-class representatives of the power structure. Who enforces the laws? Police, who, if they are not members of the middle class, are agents of and are working for the middle class. The theme continues for courts and prison systems. Conflict theorists suggest that we should not be surprised when arrest figures show that those without power and wealth commit most crime—the system is designed to work that way. According

[7]Emile Durkheim, *Suicide,* translated by John A. Spaulding and George Simpson (New York: Free Press, 1951).

to this view, the whole criminal justice system from law to prison is an instrument the ruling class uses to perpetuate existing patterns of power and privilege.[8]

Law violation is called **criminal behavior,** and there are several categories of crimes. More serious acts are called *felonies* (punished by a year or more in a state prison or by death). Less serious crimes are called *misdemeanors.* The FBI has developed a list of seven major crimes: homicide, rape, aggravated assault, robbery, burglary, larceny, and auto theft. Trends in crime are studied by noting the number of crimes reported to police throughout the country. Table 11.3 shows the number of reported major crimes in the United States in 1977.

Aside from the seven major crimes, a number of other acts are illegal—prostitution, gambling, fraud, embezzlement, arson, vandalism, traffic offenses, and so on. Some of the forms of deviant behavior previously discussed in this chapter may fall into criminal categories. If alcoholism means drunk driving, it becomes a crime. The sale, possession, and/or use of certain drugs becomes a crime.

One might assume that if an act is defined as criminal, there must be general agreement about it. Such a serious move by a society must mean that people are in accord with each other and that group differences and vested interests have been set aside. This, of course, is not necessarily so. One category of behaviors is called crime because it threatens the public order. There is general agreement that acts such as homicide, arson, robbery, and larceny threaten the public order. About other categories of crime, however, there may be less agreement. For example, one such category grew out of the concern, religious beliefs, and moral outrage of our Puritan ancestors, who felt that in certain areas of behavior, individuals must be protected from themselves. It is not so much that their behavior may be a threat to society as that their behavior may be a threat to themselves. Consequently, a number of acts, some of which we today call vices, were defined as crimes. These include gambling, prostitution, narcotics use, abortion, and a variety of sexual activities, including homosexuality. Opinions as to the "rightness" or "wrongness" of these acts vary from individual to individual and from group to group. In fact, however, there is a substantial demand to engage in many of these acts.

Table 11.3   Reported Crime in the United States, 1977

Crime	Number	Type
Murder	19,120	
Forcible rape	63,020	1,009,500 Violent (9%)
Robbery	404,850	
Aggravated assault	522,510	
Burglary	3,052,200	
Larceny-theft	5,905,700	9,926,300 Property (91%)
Motor vehicle theft	968,400	
Total	10,935,800	

Uniform Crime Reports, 1977.

[8]The conflict perspective starts, of course, with Marx. Today, the major spokesman is Richard Quinney. He has written a number of books including *Critique of Legal Order: Crime Control in Capitalist Society* (Boston: Little, Brown, 1974); and *Criminology,* 2d ed. (Boston: Little, Brown, 1979).

Gambling is legal in some states and is widely sought and available throughout the country even where not legal. Prostitution is legal in some areas (in all Nevada counties but two, for example). Many young people as well as some of their elders wonder at the current laws punishing marijuana use. Studies show that marijuana is widely used and is relatively easy to obtain. Laws in nearly all our states outlaw sodomy, the "infamous crimes against nature," and yet Kinsey reported that many of these "crimes," which involve various types of sexual behavior, have been relatively common practices. People wonder why homosexual acts between consenting adults in private are not legal if heterosexual acts under the same conditions are legal.

Edwin Schur has commented that since all parties involved in these actions (gambling, prostitution, abortion, etc.) are seeking them or at least consenting to them, these are "crimes without victims."[9] If there is no victim, Schur wonders whether anyone should be punished. He points out that when these activities are called crimes, they are forced underground to a certain extent and become more expensive to obtain. This leads to secondary crime—theft, for example, to obtain funds to support the primary crime, such as narcotics or abortion. So, although certain acts are defined as criminal by society, this does not mean that there is universal agreement as to their "wrongness."

Juvenile delinquency refers to young people (under twenty-one in some states, under eighteen in others) who commit criminal acts or who are wayward, disobedient, uncontrollable, truant, or runaways. Delinquency is a confusing concept. Young people *are* heavily involved in certain types of crimes, as can be seen in Table 11.4. At the same time, many young people are defined as juvenile delinquents for acts that are ignored if committed by adults (disobedience, running away). American law is such that we are very strict with juveniles. "Get ahold of the bad kids quick and change them so they won't grow up to worse activities." In fact, however, as we will see in the section on primary and secondary deviation, if the juvenile is thrown into a reform school with other more hardened delinquents, we almost guarantee the result we were trying to avoid. Most countries are more lenient than the United States in their treatment of juveniles.

Table 11.4   Arrests of Young People, 1977

	Percentage of Arrests that Were of People:	
	Under 15	Under 18
Robbery	8	32
Burglary	19	52
Larceny-theft	19	43
Motor vehicle theft	14	53
Arson	31	50
Vandalism	33	60

Uniform Crime Reports, 1977.

[9]In his book, *Crimes Without Victims,* Edwin Schur discusses abortion, narcotics use, and homosexuality as victimless crimes (Englewood Cliffs, N.J.: Prentice-Hall, 1965).

Our purpose throughout this chapter has been to demonstrate that deviation is basically a labeling process that involves group definitions and that may result in many different viewpoints concerning what is deviant and what is not. This same condition extends, unfortunately, to the realm of criminal and delinquent behavior as well.

Explanations for Deviant Behavior

If deviant behavior is the result of a labeling process by selected groups of people, explanations for individual acts of deviant behavior are of only passing interest— the emphasis is on the labeling or defining process rather than on the deviant behavior. Our time would be better spent attempting to understand how the labeling takes place, who does the labeling, and why. On the other hand, society feels threatened by the presence of crime and deviant behavior in their midst—it is a disease that must be eradicated. Concerned citizens demand explanations, and social scientists have responded with numerous studies that attempt to explain the deviant's behavior. The theories that have been developed are quite varied, as we may see by looking at some of the explanations for criminal behavior.[10]

In 1875, Lombroso stated that deviant behavior was inherited and that criminals were throwbacks (closer in the evolutionary chain) to apes. Lombroso came to this conclusion by taking a series of body measurements of institutionalized criminals and noncriminals and comparing these with measurements of primitive man. Subsequent investigators showed the inadequacy of his research and failed to find any support for his theories. Lombroso's claim to fame remains that he was one of the first to try to scientifically discover the causes of crime. Other studies of biological and inheritance factors in crime causation have focused on comparisons of the behavior of identical and fraternal twins, on physique and body type as causal factors, and more recently, on aberrant chromosome patterns among institutionalized violent offenders.

Generally, however, social scientists tend to discount the purely biological explanations for behavior. The psychologist looks within the individual at his personality and perceptions and emphasizes the importance of childhood experiences to explain later deviant behavior. The sociologist studies conditions in the social structure and the effects of group affiliations and orientations. Edwin Sutherland's theory of "differential association" is typical of many sociological theories in that it emphasizes that behavior, both normal and deviant, is learned in interaction with others. Sutherland felt that the behavior of the prostitute, the professional thief, and the white-collar criminal is learned through association and communication with people defining the behavior favorably, and in isolation of people defining it unfavorably. Other theories attempt to describe the conditions in which this learning takes place.

Another sociological approach suggests that certain elements in the social

[10]Most criminology texts go into causal explanations in great detail. See, for example, Walter Reckless, *The Crime Problem,* 5th ed. (New York: Appleton-Century-Crofts, 1973).

structure lead to crime and delinquency. Poverty, lack of legitimate opportunity to move up the social class ladder, racism, sexism, and other social conditions place tremendous pressures on people and may push some of them into delinquency and crime. Several of these approaches focus on class conflict and the higher arrest rates of lower-class people. The emphasis on structural conditions comes from people like Robert Merton, the gang theorists we mentioned in Chapter 5 (p. 141), and conflict theorists such as Marx and Quinney, discussed earlier in this chapter.

The important point, however, is that most sociological theories tend to look at deviant behavior in the same way that they look at nondeviant behavior. Both are forms of social behavior that are developed through the socialization process. These forms of behavior are understood by studying norms, roles, culture, groups, and other aspects of social organization. Deviant behavior is not seen as the strange and peculiar actions of sick people but merely another form of social behavior that can be understood by applying the basic concepts of sociology.

Primary and Secondary Deviation

In an approach to deviation that emphasizes society's *reaction* to behavior as the labeling approach does, the distinction between primary and secondary deviation is of central importance. **Primary deviation** is initial, often low-level, deviation that does not affect the individual's self-concept. People can rationalize primary deviant acts as being within the bounds of reasonable, acceptable, and normal behavior for people like them. It fits in with or does not seriously detract from the person's typical status and role. The doctor who splits fees, the person who drinks too much, and the eccentric college professor are all deviant to be sure, but it is primary deviation because it is not far beyond the boundaries of the conventional statuses and roles they occupy.

A process occurs whereby society reacts to continued primary deviation by expressing moral indignation, rejection, and penalties. **Secondary deviation** refers to deviation that represents a defense, attack, or adjustment to the problems created by the societal reaction to the primary deviation. The individual becomes labeled and stigmatized. The person begins to see himself or herself as others do, and the self-concept begins to change. A self-fulfilling prophecy is at work. It is not long before the clever lawyer who drinks a little too much becomes the drunk who occasionally practices law. As one's self-concept changes in secondary deviation, the person may become involved in a deviant subculture and gain further knowledge and skill regarding the behavior, including techniques for avoiding detection. The important factors in secondary deviation are the redefinition of self that follows society's reaction and the consequences of that redefinition for future behavior.[11]

---

[11]The idea of primary and secondary deviation was first developed by Edwin Lemert. See his *Human Deviance, Social Problems, & Social Control* (Englewood Cliffs, N.J.: Prentice-Hall, 1967), especially pp. 17–18 and 40–64. Also see the discussion in Clinard and Meier, *Sociology of Deviant Behavior,* pp. 75–76.

There is a paradoxical and important outcome of this sequence: The societal reaction has the intent of stopping primary deviation, but it may force one into secondary deviation. This in turn often leads to an *increase* in deviant involvement and behavior. Some examples: The basketball player fouls out of a couple of games. The local paper labels him a rough and aggressive player, he begins to see himself differently, and suddenly he fouls out of *every* game. The juvenile is picked up on a minor charge such as a runaway or curfew violation. She is locked up in a detention home and treated like the other delinquents. She learns from them, starts to see herself differently, and when she is released she is ready for a full-blown delinquent career.

Deviant Behavior in Perspective

Deviant behavior is often seen as a malignant element in society to be eradicated at all costs. To say that something is deviant is to imply that something is wrong and needs to be fixed. This is an incorrect view for several reasons. First, it is important to remember that deviant behavior is basically the product of people's definitions rather than something natural or inherent in an act. This allows us to shift our focus from the person's behavior to the question, "Why is his behavior being called deviant?" Second, Durkheim, Erikson, and others have pointed out that deviant behavior is not necessarily harmful to group life. In fact, it often plays an important part in keeping the social order intact. Deviant behavior enables groups to define boundaries—it preserves stability within the group by pointing out the contrast between what is inside the group and what is outside. Erikson suggests that without the battle between "normal" and "deviant," the community would lack a sense of identity and cohesion, a sense of what makes it a special place in the larger world.[12]

Finally, deviant behavior appears to be one of the processes involved in social change. Often, what is deviant today is accepted tomorrow and expected the next day. Maybe the people who seem to be listening to a different drummer just heard the beat before the rest of us. *Some* forms of deviant behavior represent an early adaptation to changing conditions. There are many examples of this: Deviant clothing styles of the past are the fashion of today. Yesterday's pornography is accepted literature today. Of course, not all of what we call deviant at present is destined to be the norm of tomorrow. Many types of behavior—for example, homicide, theft, incest—are more firmly fixed in deviant definitions. The point, however, is that deviant behavior does not necessarily represent the evil its title implies; often it serves necessary and important functions in society, including those of defining the group's boundaries and as a forerunner of social change.

[12]Kai Erikson deals with these ideas in detail in his *Wayward Puritans* (New York: John Wiley, 1966), Chapter 1, and in "Notes on the Sociology of Deviance," in *The Other Side,* edited by Howard S. Becker (New York: Free Press, 1964), especially pp. 9–15.

Social Control

Social control refers to the processes, planned or unplanned, by which people are made to conform to collective norms. A certain amount of conformity seems to be essential in all societies. Predictability and order are necessary to the social organization of group behavior. If people could act in complete isolation, possibly they could ignore the existence of any norms. However, it is almost impossible to imagine such a situation because people behave in groups, and other group members constantly place expectations on one's behavior. Individuality and nonconformity are highly valued; most of us want to be individualists. We should realize, however, that these words only have meaning when most people, most of the time, conform.

Social control may be provided in a variety of ways. We could, for example, hope that people will naturally conform; that conformity is in the nature of people, and it is inherent to conform. It seems, however, that conformity doesn't come naturally with birth but that people have to be *trained* to conform. Basic social control is taught through the socialization process. Shortly after the child is born, the family begins telling him or her what to do and what not to do, what is right and what is wrong. Sanctions or punishments are applied if the child misbehaves. Children who fail to conform are told, in effect, that mother and father won't love them or will beat them, depending on the family's view of proper child-rearing practices. Later, influences outside the family continue the process. Peers, teachers in the school system, the church, the mass media—all these have a profound effect on inculcating group and societal norms and encouraging conformity to group expectations. Finally, if all else fails, the society can pass laws to ensure conformity. Laws force people to conform and are a response to breakdown in other forms of social control. Again, sanctions are applied for failure. These sanctions may range from a fine to imprisonment to death.

Social control mechanisms vary depending on the type of group or society. In a primary group or small primitive society, rules are not written and social control is informal. Violators may be subjected to gossip or ridicule or possibly even ostracism; although these techniques do not have the dramatic effect of the FBI swooping down, they are surprisingly effective. In secondary groups and larger, urbanized societies, social control becomes more formal, and we have written laws, police, courts, prisons—an exceedingly complicated legal system to guarantee an acceptable degree of conformity.

Social control mechanisms also vary depending on the type of norm being violated. If the violated norm is a folkway regarded as of minor consequence to the group, informal and minor sanctions are called forth: whispering, giggling, or a little mild ridicule. If one of the mores of the group is being abused, however, more formal sanctions may be used.

Individual social control probably emerges from both internal and external sources. Internal constraints would be those aspects of the normative system that one internalizes through the socialization process. Internalized norms become the individual's conscience. External social control refers to the external mechanisms

The Reformed Mennonite Church imposed its "doctrine of avoidance" on Robert Bear of Carlisle, Pennsylvania. Commonly called shunning, this meant no one in the church including his family could speak or have anything to do with him. His wife and six children left him when the sanction was imposed. His parents died shortly after the church action and, according to Bear, "To the moment they died they looked at me with disgust. I was already burning in hell." Five years later in 1977 the punishment remained in effect.

There are about six beheadings a year in Jidda, Saudi Arabia. They take place on a public street and are well attended. A police squad car brings the victim, a Yemeni who has killed his sixteen-year-old wife. The Yemeni, chained and blindfolded, is guided to a piece of cardboard on the street, where he obediently drops to his knees. The black executioner, elegantly dressed in white with a black bandolier and sash, stands about three steps behind him with a polished, double-edged sword about 3½ feet long. A signal is given and the executioner's assistant jabs the kneeling Yemeni in the side with a sharp stick which causes his bowed neck to stiffen. The executioner is already moving and everything is soundless. He takes a few tiny ballet steps and then one long stride as the blade rises and drops through a perfect arc, severing the head in one majestic stroke. The head rolls forward, the neck spurts blood over the street, and the body topples backward. The assistant fetches the head and puts it on a stretcher, and sound returns. The crowd roars once in exclamation and disperses.

—rules and laws—applied by society. It would be fortunate if the two were in balance, but as we saw in the previous section on deviant behavior, this is frequently not the case. Take, for example, the boy whose little peers happen to be little hoods—his most important primary group is a delinquent gang. He internalizes a set of values and norms from them. He obeys the norms of the gang or he is ridiculed and ostracized. Yet in following gang social control he runs afoul of external societal social control, which in many cases makes opposing demands. To complete the dilemma, it is obvious that the social control system of the primary group, the gang, is much more important for one's behavior than is any external social control system. This type of gap occurs when the values of one segment of society are vastly different from the values of the rule makers of society.

Another type of gap or difference between internal and external social control occurs when people's attitudes, values, and norms change more rapidly than laws change. A cultural lag results. For example, there are sharp differences of opinion regarding whether to and how to enforce existing gambling and prostitution laws. Laws traditionally have been slow to change (and perhaps they should be, so as not to respond to every whim or alteration in public opinion). We might predict a pattern through which change in laws occurs: (1) attitudes change; (2) laws relating to the changed attitudes are not enforced; and (3) laws change. It is likely, however, that there is a large lapse of time between step 2 and step 3. Consequently, when attitudes change, laws tend to be kept on the books but just not enforced as vigorously as they might be. Law enforcement agencies and individual citizens often find themselves in a difficult position because of this situation. The marijuana laws in California—first strictly enforced with heavy penalties, then less enforced, now changing—are a good example of this sequence.

White-collar crime and organized crime provide examples of another type of conflict between society's laws and people's attitudes. The public favors and encourages prosecution of offenses such as burglary, assault, larceny, homicide, and sex offenses. They are indignant with the small-time thieves and quick to lock them up for their sins. On the other hand, white-collar crime is seldom punished. White-collar crime refers to the illegal acts committed by middle- and upper-class people during the course of their regular business activities, and includes such examples as the bank vice-president who embezzles funds, the physician who splits fees or performs unnecessary operations, the executive who cheats on his or her income tax, and the disk jockey who accepts payola.

Individual white-collar crime is only part of the picture. Corporations are where the action really is; they have developed sharp business practices, unethical dealings, and out-and-out crime to a fine art. The list is long and includes the following: price fixing (by computer, steel, and electrical companies); false advertising (drugs, food); collusion between government regulatory agencies and the companies they are supposed to be regulating; campaign payoffs in return for favors; bribery; cost overruns on defense contracts; land fraud, computer fraud; and on and on. Take one case: General Electric, Westinghouse, and some twenty other electrical companies got together and fixed prices on electrical equipment. Bids, supposed to be secret and competitive, were neither. The companies worked out ahead of time which company would bid lowest on a contract and what the other bids should be to make it look good. The resulting lowest bid was far higher than it should have been, and the companies made good money—in the neighborhood of $2 billion more than they should have in one seven-year period. But (surprise) they were caught. An outraged judge levied $2 million in fines (a drop in the bucket compared to the take) and sentenced seven men to thirty days in jail. See whether the average thief who steals a car or burglarizes a house gets off with thirty days. However, people were amazed at the "harshness" of the sentences in the great electrical conspiracy, for corporate criminals never go to jail, even for thirty days.

Criminologist Edwin Sutherland has maintained that more money is lost yearly through white-collar crime than through all other forms of crime combined, and that the damage to social relationships that results (no one can be trusted, everyone is on the take) is even more serious. Yet, as we said, the larceny or theft of the white-collar criminal is seldom punished, and even when it is, the penalties are slight compared with those for other crimes. Why? Well, the activity may have involved substantial skill and ingenuity and wasn't violent, so the public tends to identify with it or at least not object to it. Many times the victim (often a large organization or the public in general) is invisible or not easy to identify with. Often the culprit is a large corporation that has spent much money over the years to cultivate its image, and the public finds it difficult to believe that such an upstand-

---

A TOMBSTONE EPITAPH—GIRARD, PENNSYLVANIA, 1870

In memory of
Ellen Shannon
Aged 26 years
Who was fatally burned ·
March 21st 1870
by the explosion of a lamp
filled with "R. E. Danforth's
Non Explosive
Burning Fluid"

From *Folklore on the American Land* by Duncan Emrich (Boston: Little, Brown, 1972).

---

ing important company could be guilty of such dastardly deeds. And finally, the white-collar criminal is a "good" person—middle-class and respectable. So, the public prefers to look the other way.

Likewise, the activities of organized crime go largely unpunished, but the reasons for breakdown in social control in this case are more basic and easier to understand. Many people *want* what organized crime supplies: gambling, narcotics, tax-free cigarettes and alcohol, prostitution, and loan rackets. The conclusion is clear: The attitudes and values of society are reflected even more in punishment practices than they are in the written laws of society.

SUMMARY

The previous chapters in this section have dealt with social change, social disorganization, and collective behavior. In this chapter we return to the topic of norms, which was first discussed in Chapter 3. A norm is defined as the accepted or required behavior in a specific situation. Most behavior is predictable because it is in accordance with mutually understood norms. However, some behavior is contrary to generally accepted norms, and this is called deviant behavior. Societies attempt to restrict the amount of deviant behavior through social control measures. This chapter addressed itself to these concepts—deviation and social control.

Individual variation and individual differences are a basic part of the human condition. When differences from group norms reach a certain point, however, social differentiation becomes social deviation. Many sociologists believe that deviation is best understood as a *labeling* process. Behaviors and/or characteristics of individuals are deviant when they are defined that way by members of society. Deviation is neither a natural nor statistical phenomenon but is a product of group viewpoints and definitions.

Criminal and delinquent behavior are also seen as products of a defining or labeling process. If society is especially concerned about certain types of behavior, it may define these behaviors as not only deviant but criminal as well. Frequently there are differences of opinion about the "rightness" or "wrongness" of particular acts. Such differences are more likely to occur in large, complex societies in which a variety of viewpoints exist about what is deviant and what is normal. These variations in definitions make it possible that within a society, a given act may be viewed as criminal and deviant, as criminal but not deviant, as deviant but not criminal, or as "normal."

We briefly examined several categories of deviation—mental illness, mental deficiency, alcoholism, drug usage, and suicide—as well as some descriptions of and explanations for criminal and delinquent behavior. Finally, we discussed social control, which refers to the processes by which people are made to conform to collective norms. Social control mechanisms are practiced by all societies and include norms internalized through the socialization process as well as laws enforced by the police and courts of a society.

The first of the readings that follow describes two people who, for quite different reasons, are labeled deviants. The article, written by one of them, relates how they react to their condition, and how society reacts to them. Society is often placed in the peculiar and hypocritical position of condemning a behavior and actively seeking and patronizing it at the same time. Gambling, prostitution, and abortion in some places are among numerous examples of this situation. Businesses and professions develop to satisfy "deviant" needs; the second reading deals with one such profession, the professional party girl. Most forms of deviant behavior are learned behavior. Barbara Anderson in her article on wine drinking and alcoholism in France illustrates the importance of the socialization process and experiences in the cultural environment in producing a given type of behavior. The final reading is a short passage from *The Painted Bird,* which describes how a nonhuman society reacts to those who are different.

Reading 11.1

Two Delicate Conditions

ROBIN ZEHRING

People are labeled as deviants for a variety of reasons. As this article demonstrates, you don't have to be a criminal to be deviant; being different physically is perhaps an even faster way of obtaining the deviant label. Robin Zehring is a free-lance writer living in San Francisco.

One thing about a five-foot-eight-inch-and-obtusely-pregnant woman walking down the street with a considerably shorter, cerebral-palsied male escort on crutches: They'll get noticed, all right.

Noticed like The Pox.

From *California Living Magazine, San Francisco Sunday Examiner & Chronicle,* 11 March 1973. Reprinted by permission of the author.

I, being the pregnant person and Bernard being the shorter, rarely advance more than five City yards before we are not only noticed: we are avoided with a physiological energy so overwhelming that The Natural Order Of Life And Things falls shambled to the sidewalk. On account of our delicate physical conditions, I mean, one public pregnancy partnered by a crippled man and the world goes bananas.

Take, for instance, dogs. Dogs walk backwards, retreating at the mere sight of Bernard and me, misshapen beasts that we are. We've seen dogs forget they are moving and fall off the curb from just looking at us. Seen people fall off too. And trip over fire hydrants, parking meters, invisible trash or their imaginations. We've caused buses to bypass their stops, taxis to pause for red lights, cars to screech in unexpected halts at pedestrian crosswalks ("Lordy, can you imagine hitting one of *those*"). Children are hustled away from us ("Hey Mom whatsamatter with . . . "), adolescents cluster in giggling groups ("I wonder if they're like *married* or some-thin'?"). No adult will meet our eyes ("For Godssake, Martha, don't *stare!*"). But their sidelong glances at my swollen torso and Bernard's bent legs indicate Dr. Rubin has plenty more What You Always Wanted To Knows . . . to write about.

Granted, we do walk slowly. Bernard drags his feet to reach each stretch of his stronger crutch and my feet are fluid-retentive and heavy from prenatal pressure of The Occupant (my Unborne Babe, as I call It) and likewise, they drag too. So perhaps the odds of boggled phenomena are directly related to our slow rate of speed: If you walk slowly enough, you're bound to see a dog fall off the curb eventually, or a cow jump over the moon, maybe? But Bernard, who has twenty-six years of public experience being sidetracked as a subhuman, explains to me kindly that those things are just part of it all; in fact, the slower you go, the more willing are people and buses and dogs to accept your physical handicap. Because people like you are *supposed* to go slowly.

"A handicapped person is one thing," cracks Bernard, "But a handicapped person *in a hurry* . . . "

I see what he means. Trudging (slowly) up and down the hills of Powell Street one day, Bernard and I decide to 'run' for the next cable car. Traffic at Bush Street intersection backs up three blocks, not only because we delay it a bit by crossing, but also because astonished drivers in the first few rows can't believe their eyes as down the incline I gallop, full-tilt and waving. The Occupant does cartwheels. Bernard races close behind me, his steel leg braces half-sliding on the concrete. The cable car is already sailing when the gripman sees us, rolls his eyes heavenward, and grabs the brake handle like it's the Titanic anchor, pulling back for all he's worth. The brake snags on the downhill angle. Passengers climb all over themselves (not) to see if we make it, their eyes riveted to my jouncing tummy and Bernard's steel scuttle. Both breathless, we reach the car, Bernard tossing his crutches aboard and hiking himself up. I take a deep breath, conquer the steps and we're off. Gradually, Bush Street traffic resumes. Passengers, now timid with us at close range, study the floor. The gripman is perspiring. The Occupant somersaults. I giggle. Bernard guffaws. "Told you so!" he chortles. "Haw, Haw, Haw!"

I first met Bernard Maxon at The Noble Frankfurter on Powell Street when I was five months pregnant and feeling nauseous. He was at the next table, wolfing down two kosher hot dogs smothered in sauerkraut and mustard and onions, with a side order of potato salad and a hunk of Maria's Bavarian cheesecake waiting for dessert. It all looked enormously tasty and I couldn't help overhearing Bernard's vociferous manner of chewing which made it sound even tastier. I wanted to order six of everything. However, one occupational dilemma of a delicate condition such as mine is relishing the idea of copious food intake and then having The Occupant play soccer with it in my stomach. One learns to nibble Saltines and sip tea instead.

Bernard caught me watching him and listening to his chew. Sure, I had noticed the crutches propped against the chair next to his but I hadn't dwelled on them. I was more intrigued with his food. And yet, when Bernard noticed me noticing, I figured it was for the crutches. But he didn't. He was more interested in figuring me.

"Can't hack the hot dogs these days?" he asked, eyes twinkling behind hornrims.

I shook my head.

"Here, try one of these. I carry a spare." He rolled a pack of TUMS across my table. I blinked at them, dumbfounded. I'd never met anyone under fifty who carried spare TUMS around.

"Ulcer?" I wondered.

He began to answer with a gesture which accidentally followed through to the chair with the crutches. A clatter of aluminum banged to the floor. I started to rise.

"Hold it!" he ordered, "No bending over in your condition. It'll make you throw up." It was nice to meet a man who knew about being pregnant.

I sat as Bernard eased himself down to the floor, swept up both crutches and held them together like a canoe paddle, stiffening his body and pushing himself upwards to a standing position, much as a skier remounts with his poles. Then he sat down again and rearranged himself. The entire procedure was complete in about fifteen seconds. I was impressed.

"Pretty tricky," I said.

"That's nothing," said Bernard, "You should see me put on my socks."

I thought carefully for a moment. We had a lot in common.

"The same goes for my pantyhose."

We laughed hard together, knowing we each began the day by dressing on the floor.

In the months following, Bernard and I meet frequently for lunch. I learn to enjoy tea very much and forsake my Saltines for TUMS. We share our life stories and our hope and dream stories and our delicate condition stories which are remarkably similar and occasionally the same. Except that I, as a slightly handicapped person with a temporary condition, don't know the half of it compared to Bernard's life-time experience of prejudice, pain and abuse. Bernard Maxon's got the stiffest upper lip I've ever seen. Why he hasn't drunk himself into oblivion, jumped off the Bridge, or at least clobbered someone with his crutch is beyond me until he reminds:

"Considering that from the moment I was born three months premature and motionless, what have I got to lose?"

I instinctively fold my hands across the The Occupant's seven-month Mound and ponder.

What Bernard has got to lose is plenty.

Incidental losses like his balance (when Bernard sneezes hard, he falls down), his public rights to restaurant seating ("They always put me in the back so I won't upset the 'dining decorum' "), hotel reservations, rental privileges (Managers claim they're not insured), some shopping prerogatives (Antique dealers and car salesmen are rarely overjoyed when he comes clomping in; they discourage him from handling the Dresden or testing the gearshift). Also, lost privacy. A lot of people ask Bernard a lot of very personal questions. Also, lost sexual title ("Just once I'd like to be accused of rape."). And the loss of acceptance by his fellow humans as a healthy able-bodied person worthy of friendship, wisdom and strength. People constantly suggest to Bernard that he sit down—at a distance!

Some of the above also goes for being pregnant.

Major losses? Jobs. Bernard has a difficult time finding a good one, despite his six-and-a-half years of college credits, his high I.Q. ratings and physical maneuverability. He was once denied a volunteer job to help recently disabled veterans at Letterman Hospital on grounds that his presence might depress the patients.

"OK, so I'd be lousy at brain surgery or fashion modeling," chides Bernard. "But jobs in management, accounting and teaching are all available to people of my qualifications. Clerical jobs: I can type forty words a minute, with my left hand. But the minute I arrive for an interview, they tell me, 'We're not hiring.' One look at me and they suggest I try elsewhere, like on the street corner selling pencils."

Working the street is not Bernard's bag. He often ends up soliciting books or real estate or vacuum cleaners by phone, dialing the numbers with his typing hand. Telephone sales jobs endure about six weeks before something happens to the Company (bankruptcy, fraud, a quick self-export by the Boss) and the phone is disconnected. So is Bernard from his income, until the next State Disability check comes through. Which doesn't go very far in paying for food and rent and medical bills and custom-altered clothing and new shoes every month and a pair of socks a day and a college education.

So there's money to lose. Ignoring the doom of a butterless future, Bernard admits a weakness for lending whatever cash he does possess. He'll even go to such lengths as borrowing from someone else and re-lending it. And seldom see it again.

"It's true, I'm flattered if people tap me for loans," he says, "It's a rebellion on my part, all related to that crippled pauper image and peddling pencils. I don't think of myself as crippled, I don't wake up in the morning and feel it. I want to live and earn my money through normal channels, not through opportunities specifically for The Handicapped, not by dealing in money like that."

Sometimes, money like that deals him. It belongs to people who cannot dissimulate a physical handicap from the downtrodden of the world. No matter that Bernard is dressed from Bullock and Jones—"Only place I can get to alter my pants to a twenty-eight inch waist and a 23 inch inseam without laughing"—and his facial expression maintained with purpose and intent. He finds it necessary to avoid busy City streets around Christmas and Eastertime and on Sunday mornings when pedestrians feel particularly righteous. They press money in his hand or stuff it in his pocket before he can explain that he really doesn't want it. One time a man gave him a personal check.

Another time a lady handed him a huge tin of Almond Roca as he waited for a WALK light. "I had to put it inside my shirt to carry it. Three more blocks, it was chocolate almond soup!"

Once he unknowingly put his crutches down on the sidewalk, leaning forward to tie his shoelace. Got a five dollar bill doing that.

I told Bernard that so far, no one has assessed my delicate condition as pathetic or needy and handed me cash for it. Or Almond Roca either. Bernard advised me to try limping a little.

Most major of losses Bernard has got to lose is affection. Lost affection can be sad for anyone, but it's sadder when a person is excluded beforehand because of a physical handicap. Generally, people suppose that The Handicapped are probably as nice and charming and at least as deserving as anyone else—and all that—but most people don't want to get involved. And don't want their son or daughter marrying one. We are brought up to be kind on the subject. But closed.

The following advertisement that appeared in a local classified section points up reality's grim divide:

> WOMAN, slightly disabled, happy, gentle, sensitive, alive, would appreciate your friendship. Also used paperback books to read. Call or write . . .

As Bernard says, "If you don't advertise for it, you don't get it. In the meantime, you can always read about it."

Beginning with his premature birth Bernard has endured a holocaust of rejections by doctors, therapists, psychiatrists, faith healers, quacks, schoolmates, teachers, employers, relatives, strangers and the public at large. He doesn't talk about these times very often, apart from periodic shrugs and allusions.

But one day at lunch, Bernard cast his eyes downward at The Occupant's Full-Term Mountain and chuckled.

"Listen," he said, hand on my hand and suddenly serious. "Most people don't let me near their kids, afraid I might rub off on them or something. Do you think maybe I could hold yours once in a while?"

I told him, come time, The Occupant and I would be delighted.

Questions 11.1

1. Illustrate the terms "deviation" and "labeling" with examples from this reading.
2. Describe the reactions of people to deviants. If, instead of a cripple or pregnant woman, the object of attention were a criminal, movie star, or well-known politician, how would the reactions differ? Why or why not? Explain.
3. How did being defined as deviant affect the behavior of Robin and Bernard?
4. The reaction to deviants is the same regardless of the particular type of deviation being observed. Discuss.
5. Recall the definition of minority group and apply this concept to the people discussed in this article.

Reading 11.2

The Corporation Prostitute

ANONYMOUS

There are a number of different types of prostitutes: the streetwalker, the house girl, the high-class call girl. This article describes another type—the party girl, hostess, or date for the big business or corporation. She is recruited by the corporation, and her services are sought after and appreciated by the corporation's clients; and society defines her behavior as deviant and criminal although she is never punished. The author of this essay states, "This is an explanation of another field of prostitution that existed some twenty years ago, and even in this more sophisticated era, still does in all probability." The essay was written by a sociology student with a rather varied past.

"Public Relations Consultant" is to a corporation prostitute what "modeling" is to a call girl, but by whatever name, a whore is a whore. The demands are the same and whether he is chairman of the board or straight off the street, a John is a John.

Assuming that the basic equipment is in order, there are certain refinements that determine your place in the flesh market caste system. Whether or not it is harder work to be a streetwalker is a matter of personal definition, but if a girl has a taste for a classy couch, she should apply at _____. The fringe benefits are good (they had a mandatory health plan), and sometimes you could stumble into a unique retirement plan. It may be temporary, depending upon the vagaries of the market and the Baby's own fickleness—but diamonds are ALWAYS a girl's best friend. There are drawbacks as in everything else—no tenure, you can't collect unemployment, and nobody would believe your references. However, you can tell yourself you were a highclass hooker.

More care was taken in the selection of the women than was given to that of a new vice president. There were stringent requirements and the screening was intensive. Much depended upon the sponsor, which equated to letters of reference in a more legitimate endeavor. This sponsor observed the prospective employee and assessed her qualities sometimes for a period of weeks before the initial contact was made but once the recommendation was in, the girl had her security clearance.

The major prerequisite was that the girl must be a professional prostitute, either from a good house or working her own book. Call girls (even the expensive ones) and hustlers were considered too risky, for their operation involved too many people. They were also over-exposed. It didn't seem to matter if you had started in the streets, but to have improved your situation indicated a fastidiousness and the ambition to do your own thing, which, in turn, denoted a degree of intelligence. The requirements were heavier than have-douche-bag-will-travel. The Company wanted its personal, elite stable, financed by the unsuspecting stockholders at large, covered discreetly by the Auditing Department, administered and controlled in the best tradition of American Corporate efficiency. For this they were willing to pay good money.

Under no circumstances was a freebee considered. Anyone who played for fun and games and no profit was dangerous. They had no ethical standards and the disquieting possibility of emotionalism or involvement was present. Competent detachment is an occupational hazard, or blessing, for the professional. Too often a non-professional falls back on outraged virtue when the demands get rough. No matter how discreetly structured or fiscally disguised, the commodity was still sex and to the businessman with a sentimental conscience, something free smacks of adultery. Besides, he could probably make it with his wife's best friend, or give his secretary a whirl, so what's the big deal.

The girl should have had legitimate experience working with the public—receptionist, hostess, entertainer—that gave her a social poise which if not real was efficiently faked. She had to be aware of the world around her and not just the world of sex, to have read a book or two that wasn't pornographic, to carry on a reasonable conversation and pretend to listen intelligently.

Appearance was important, of course. The girl had to be more than just attractive. Size, shape, personality and disposition all differed, but there was one absolute —she could not look like a prostitute. Hair styles and dress could be modified or brought into line if all the other requirements were in order, but her whole bearing must be in keeping with the carefully constructed sexual fraud—courtesans, classy broads, Princess Grace selling her ass.

Age didn't seem to be a significant factor as long as the girl was over the age of consent. You could tell the older ones, they saved their money. Years of experience was not as important as the quality of experience for some women can turn tricks most of their working lives and end up hustling still for twelve-and-two. There were, however, common characteristics and foremost among them was a taste for the good life, a tough sense of independence, and a determination to be treated as a "lady" even peripherally.

Naturally, there was one other area—sexual expertise. As a professional the talent should have been taken for granted—how many pianists audition for their concerts? If this area was checked out, it was done secretly and never mentioned, but it would have made a great work incentive plan for the recruiter. In a house it was probably a "very important client" and from a book, a favor for your favorite mark.

All these qualities were essential when dealing with men who, because of their positions or their pretensions, will not tolerate a chippy. After genuflecting before the GNP, only the choicest harlots were offered by the high priests. Corporations pimp for the industrial complex and such a select clientele must be catered to, their egos stroked, their reputations protected and their fetishes fanned. Bidding for a factory site? Fly the city fathers on a party to Acapulco. Wooing a merger? Prod it with charm, grace and prowess. Pushing a political issue? Knifing a competitor? Collecting proxies? Oil leases, anyone?

The preliminaries over, the recommendation in and the surveillance completed, e subject was contacted by her sponsor, and if she was interested, an interview was arranged.

It took a really well-trained eye to find potential in me. I was still half-gamin, defiantly determined to escape the streets and refusing to recognize any handicaps I might have. I owe it all to a fighter instinct and my Uncle Harry, a Vaudeville violinist ("The Fiddlin' Coon") and when he died he left his violin up for grabs.

In my family, nothing should be a total waste. Since we were stuck with the instrument, mother managed lessons for me and I promptly fell in love with music. Another cherished family tradition is that if you have a talent you sell it, which made earning a living much easier for the girls than the boys. When I was 10 it was discovered that I could sing—so, why aren't you working? I started paying my way as a band vocalist which drew attention away from my talent as a violinist and its dubious commercial value. At 14 I was on my own, winging to support myself and the violin. Wilhelm Van Hoogstratton was conducting the Portland Symphony and accepted me as a member which gave me a glimpse of a totally new world. It was a schizophrenic existence . . . I could play Hindemith but was incapable of a grammatical conversation. A competent vocalist with poise on the stand, I didn't know there were different folks, and thought everybody slept in their slips. . . . I wore the brightest colors I could find and felt naked without a watch, bracelet, beads, earrings, AND an ankle-chain. Luckily, the Symphony wore uniforms. Having learned submission at a very early age, I also learned about this time to augment my income between music jobs.

By the time I was 20, I was in San Francisco with a child to support and a little black book I used when I needed something. I was running scared but hanging in there, reading books, learning to talk and all the nice, social graces were there, if pretentious. One night it seemed to have all paid off and without even knowing it, I was considered for the big time.

My sponsor was a prominent San Francisco Madam who never offered to hire me herself. I was singing in a Pine Street Club and she came in down the street from her house every once in a while to relax and to see if any of her girls were free-lancing. We became friendly and talked. I think what impressed her most was the way I handled a big-time pimp who wanted to take over my thing for me. Whatever her reasons she decided to be my sponsor.

I wore white gloves to my interview in an office with a view of the bay. He sat behind a mahogany desk and lit my cigarettes with a heavy, silver lighter. When the telephone rang he apologized graciously for the interruption, treating me more like an executive secretary than an executive's whore. I was to be paid every two weeks by mail and he took my social security number for the personnel department. I would be given a wardrobe allowance and there was a prepared list of the types of clothing that should be on hand. I was to move to a "good" address (I lived on Baker Street, just over from Fillmore). Inquiry was made very solicitously as to child care arrangements for I would be traveling a great deal.

My personal life was my own as long as it did not interfere with or threaten the Company; I was made to realize immediately that the company had a battery of lawyers and any attempts at extortion would be handled quickly and efficiently, and I was guaranteed to lose, particularly since the fact of the professionalism made me a loser to start with; he gave me the name of the doctor where I was to have a monthly examination; I would not be "on call" but would be given my assignments in a purely business-like manner and well in advance although there would be emergency calls occasionally as well as luncheon appointments. I was expected to be entertaining, listen attentively even to drunken trivia and to converse as intelligently as I could depending upon the client; however, at no time could I interject my personal affairs.

Under entertainment, the customer was always right with one exception— nothing bizarre and no S&M—if that was the kick, report it to the program director. The company would also not tolerate orgies—just lots of bread and no circuses. He told me my new company name, shook my hand, wished me good luck, courteously escorted me to the door and I never saw him again.

There was a brief training period which consisted of a dinner and some drinks with a half-hearted attempt at erudite conversation. This was to see if I could handle myself and by this time I was pretty confident of the silverware. The staff-members conducting this research were lower echelon and not at all impressed by the Courtesan Corps. They were bored and so was I. The men probably wanted to do more than go to dinner. The woman, I remember, got juiced and had to be sent home in a cab.

The first assignment was a chartered flight to Texas to entertain some board members who where conducting some high-level skullduggery. This was not a sexual scene, but it was probably felt that some women hanging around would disarm somebody. I was also thrilled over the first cruise, until I learned you weren't supposed to watch the water. The clients were politicians, military men, executives and even the young ones ran to pot-bellies. I was hostess several times for conferences and there were a lot of just dinner-dates, but other than these little bonuses it was mostly business as usual except the rhetoric was nicer. It was an organizational meat market although attractively displayed. I got a kick-back from the stores which implemented the clothing allowance, and all the head-waiters split with us but the more money I made the faster I spent it and what I didn't spend, I gave away. I became more and more resentful of the system that hired me because I was intelligent and they treated me with amused contempt because I was. Lay down or go down—it didn't matter that I knew Mozart.

There was something for everyone and our duties were many and varied ranging from the bizarre to the mundane. Sometimes, it took on all the aspects of a Grade-B movie. At informal conferences and board meetings, a few selected women would mix drinks, mingle during breaks, provide a light touch and be generally charming and genial as befits any hostess. Not all the men attending these meetings were to be granted our favors and when the meeting adjourned, those of us who were to be paired off would either be among the last to leave and then go with the client, or we would have discreetly withdrawn and be waiting for them in their hotel room—never ours. As for selection, we were either told beforehand or, as would often happen, some of the men would prefer the same woman and she was held in reserve for one. Sometimes this would provide an ironic domestic touch and occasionally led to bigger and better things for the woman when he decided he didn't want her passed around any longer. The men who were not anted privileges contented themselves with flirting, squeezing, pinching and propositioning. Under no circumstances could we accept the latter. Only the men designated were to be taken to bed and you couldn't make arrangements for later with another one. I don't know how the company would know, but they did know if you started branching off for yourself.

When the company was wooing business or providing favors on a large scale, it was a different situation. Then we partied. It would be a week-end, lavishly planned—a flight, or a cruise. We would be flown to Las Vegas for instance to meet a group from the East. The women were not assigned, but were up for grabs. We spent a lot of time at Carmel and at Tahoe and once in Mexico City. The scene sometimes reminded me of a Shriner's convention on a small scale. Even this set-up could be surprising, though. Once in Carmel we spent most of the night playing bridge.

For the individual date, you went alone either meeting him at a restaurant or picking him up at his hotel. It was dinner, a show or a round of the clubs and it could be up to that point a very pleasant situation. However, afterwards it often became sticky. On a single you uncovered some strange appetites and it took a lot of handling to let him know how far he was allowed to go. If this didn't work, we reported him and he was "black-listed." However, we also knew that the customer was always right and most of his fetishes were to be catered to.

It was always strange to me that on the parties, sex was almost a secondary thing. The emphasis seemed to be on just plain swinging—drinking, dancing, and a lot of boasting. But the act itself was brief and "normal." As a matter of fact, it seemed as if they never slept and we had to go as long as they did—it was rough on us non-drinkers, believe me.

Occasionally, we acted as tour guides. Using a company car, we would drive the client (and sometimes his wife) or a group of clients around San Francisco and the environs ending up with either a lunch or a dinner at one of the more famous (to the tourist) restaurants. I got awfully sick of the Top of the Mark and Fisherman's Wharf. Once I even acted as a baby sitter for a very important executive's children and took them to the Zoo and Funland at the Beach. Quite often we would be assigned to meet a man at the airport to save him the inconvenience of the limousine and the long, boring drive to the city.

One thing I haven't mentioned was the relationship between the women. Naturally, we all knew each other for we were together quite a bit. However, no friendships ever seemed to develop. We exchanged no personal information nor, to my knowledge, did we ever contact each other away from business. Also, during working hours we did not even discuss the Johns in the powder room. We mixed together beautifully while we were working but it was a mechanical thing and all our attention was to the men and why we were there—conversations were always general and remote.

We were utilized to some extent for the relaxation of the company executives or board members. If his stay was for a number of days, you were his exclusive property during that time. If he decided he wanted a change, you were notified by the office. And his relaxation meant mostly sex. I was hired once for a week to take care of an alcoholic executive whose family was too important to allow the company to fire him.

One night on a dinner date while we were still in the lounge a nightclub hustler tried to solicit my client. I watched her with what I hoped was the proper amount of amusement and doing my best lady bit I told her to make it. She looked at me in my Original and the furs and she laughed. "Bitch," she said, "You're 'hoe-in' just like me." What's more, I knew she was right, and at that moment it seemed I had to make up my mind what I was to be and more importantly, what I wanted to be. I was talented, for my music attested to that, but I had never really failed because I had never really tried. If I put a price on my body, for whatever reason, I couldn't really complain if somebody bought the merchandise. I wasn't even too good at that for I was using the John, he wasn't using me. That particular night was just a preliminary. If I was going to be a whore, then be an honest one. If I didn't want to be a whore, the answer was simple. Don't be one. Walk away from it and keep stepping.

I never went back. I don't know how they wrote me off in Payroll, but no one came after me either. I found an agent and my son and I went on the road with a group. I discovered I was not the best vocalist in the world and the knowledge didn't shatter me for I also discovered I wasn't the worst either and better than most. In 20 years I've made a million mistakes and an equal number of wrong turns, including a very bad marriage that stretched interminably for all the same reasons. I was still whoring, but it was respectable and legitimate. However, I accept the full responsibility. It begins to look as if I might be on my way to being a really classy broad.

Questions 11.2

1. Prostitution is a crime without a victim; if there is no victim, there should be no crime and, therefore, no punishment. Discuss.
2. "Prostitution is criminal but not deviant." Do you agree or disagree? Why? Discuss.
3. Where does society focus its attempts at social control—the prostitute, the John, or the corporation? Why? Where should it? Discuss.

Reading 11.3
How French Children Learn to Drink
BARBARA GALLATIN ANDERSON

The French consume more wine than any other people in the world. According to French government figures, thirty percent of France's men consume alcohol in amounts dangerous to their health, and fifteen percent of Frenchmen are alcoholics. Government campaigns against wine drinking have met with little success, however, because children are taught to

Published by permission of Transaction, Inc., from TRANSACTION, Vol. 5, No. 7. Copyright © 1968 by Transaction, Inc.

drink wine at an early age, and their behavior is reinforced later by a number of cultural beliefs. This article by anthropologist Barbara Anderson illustrates how deviant behavior, like normal behavior, is learned through the socialization process and how conflicting definitions of behavior (deviant versus normal) may exist side by side.

Visitors to France—even those with some knowledge of life in Mediterranean cultures—are often startled by the great amount of wine-drinking they find. Frenchmen everywhere drink with unflagging dedication and a quiet passion. For two years, my husband and I lived in the Seine-et-Oise village of Wissous, an area 10 miles from Paris. As anthropologists, we were struck by the tenacity with which villagers clung to their old drinking habits, specifically wine-drinking, despite considerable pressure from the government to abandon or at least cut down on their alcohol consumption. In particular, we were interested in finding out just how these drinking practices were transmitted to the village children.

Our two daughters, Andrea and Robin, then seven and two, were with us, and our son, Scott, was born there. We participated in the village life and, where possible, penetrated behind the scenes, gathering information about village customs. Of course, the questions we asked about children's drinking habits presented problems. The questions had to be very specific, yet apparently off the cuff. Eventually we incorporated them into a rather elaborate questionnaire on child care in general.

On the questionnaire, we asked people what every member of the household had eaten or drunk in the past 24 hours—at home or away from home. When feasible, we called at the villagers' homes during meal hours. Our interest was in what they had drunk, but we tried to give our questions no particular emphasis. We were as scrupulous in our attention to the kinds and quantities of foods they ate as we were in cataloging the beverages they drank. We administered these questionnaires and conducted follow-up interviews beginning in late February and ending in late April—a period of increasing warmth, which lowered the amount of drinking slightly. (To the villagers, cold weather is often a rationale for wine-drinking.)

Now, our interest lay specifically in the village's socially accepted drinking practices. For the French, this amounts to a study of wine-drinking. Our findings: Adult male villagers consumed approximately 1.58 quarts of wine per day. Women drank more than half a quart. The averages for children, however, could not be estimated—for reasons that will become clear later.

Our village was representative of France, where the total consumption of *pure* alcohol for the year 1955 (our study was done in 1957–59) averaged 23.78 quarts per person, or 32.1 for adults over 20. This average for adults was 16.9 quarts more than was consumed that same year by the world's second-largest wine-consuming country—Italy. The Danes drink only 3.17 quarts of pure alcohol per year. Americans drink 9.29 quarts.

According to the French government's figures, 15 percent of France's men are alcoholics, and 30 percent consume alcohol in amounts dangerous to their health.

The government's National Institute of Hygiene has said that very active manual workers should not drink over one liter (1.057 quarts) of wine per day. Yet many sedentary workers, who are advised not to drink more than half a liter per day, drink a whole liter—as much as the most active workers. Alcoholism, to the average Frenchman, is identified only with reeling drunkenness.

Children Encouraged to Drink

Now, how does this receptivity to wine-drinking take shape in the children of the village? In other words, how is wine-drinking enculturated?

First of all, in Wissous, a positive value is attached to wine. People view wine-drinking as an act of virility. Men and families cannot socialize without wine. For a host not to offer wine is at best impolite.

In addition, wine is thought to have nutritive value. One reason: Throughout the schools, the very active wine lobby distributes blotters that carry highly dubious statements. One such blotter states that a liter of wine (12 percent alcohol) has nutritive value equivalent to 850 grams of milk, 370 grams of bread, 585 grams of meat, or 5 eggs. The blotter has a drawing of a scale with a wine-bottle balancing these foods.

Wine is also believed to be necessary for working. While at work, a manual or farm worker must have wine at fairly regular intervals. The body can best endure prolonged muscular exertion, it is alleged, with the sustained, revitalizing support of wine. Strong men have a propensity for drink. It is nature's way—*"C'est comme ça."*

Finally, wine may not be purer than any other drink, but Frenchmen think it is. In fact, the alcohol in wine is widely believed to compensate for the unsanitary conditions under which it, and many other food products, are prepared.

These beliefs about wine are strongest among the peasants. The few upper-middle-class families of Wissous also link wine-drinking to vigor. But they are more likely to stress moderation, and they drink less wine than the peasants. The moderation of the upper-middle-class, however, does not appear to extend to *apéritifs* and *digestifs.* They drink considerably more of these than the other villagers do, at home and in cafés.

In contrast with the positive value placed on wine, the French place a negative value on Western Europe's two major *non*alcoholic drinks: water and milk. The Wissous village spring water, which flows from two central fountains, is potable, but little is drunk (except in coffee), especially by the men. The local attitude is that, although a certain amount of water-drinking is inevitable, water takes second place to almost any other beverage. As one of the subway signs posted by France's powerful lobby puts it, "Water is for frogs."

In its campaign against the wine lobby, the French government has recently turned to building the image of fruit juice. Government ads show popular sportsmen drinking fruit juice with apparent gusto. But the wine lobby is still far more successful than any other lobby in France at carrying its message to the people.

As for milk, a precept firmly adhered to by all classes is summed up in a popular 1947 book on child care: "Milk should never constitute the mealtime drink." This book also states that "the quantity of milk drunk in a day should not exceed half a liter, under risk of digestive troubles such as diarrhea." In this regard, the villagers run no risks. When children stop taking the bottle, and stop eating the *bouillies* (thin milk mushes) of babyhood, they rarely drink milk at all, except in *café au lait*, chocolate, or the milk-thinned vegetables called *purées*.

Of course, the fact that milk is unrefrigerated, especially in the villages, does nothing to increase its appeal. And though it is pasteurized, it is *not* homogenized. When poured, it goes clunk-clunk in uneven globs. And in warm weather, it has a strong, almost curdled flavor.

During the time we lived in Wissous, milk was delivered to the village in huge tin urns, and poured into bottles by the grocer. Unknown to him, I once followed him to the back of his shop and saw him slosh a dirty bottle around in a tub of cold water before filling it with milk.

A book on practical child-raising, known in the village since the early twenties, differs little in its warnings about milk, but acknowledges that children cannot be "bad off" if they drink milk almost exclusively for the first two years. I quote: "One can also give at mealtime a half-glass of water lightly reddened with wine, or some beer or cider very diluted with water." In general, the recent literature is more cautious. It suggests, as a more suitable time for introducing children to alcoholic beverages, four years of age rather than two.

Wine Introduced as "Reddened Water"

Here, then, is our major point: Wine-drinking begins while the child is still in near-infancy. And government efforts to show that wine hurts children run into a semantic trap. A child does not drink *wine:* he drinks "reddened water."

To the French, the consumption of wine in quantities of less than a fourth of a quart is equivalent to abstinence. The mother of a boy of 12 will tell you, though the boy may be sitting across from you with a glass of the diluted wine in his hand, that her son does not drink at all. By this, she means that his "reddened water" contains only a couple of soup-spoons of wine.

One day I bought refreshments for my daughter and her 11-year-old playmate at a cafe. The playmate ordered and drank a bottle of beer. It surprised me a little, because her mother had told me that the girl did not drink. But I am sure that, to the mother, her child's minimal and irregular intake did not constitute drinking.

If parents are drinking wine, beer, or cider, they give some—diluted with water —to their children. The younger ones sip beer or cider from a parent's glass. As they get older and more demanding, they are given small glasses of their own.

Children of lower-class homes drink more wine than children of middle-class homes, and they start drinking when they are younger. One mother even reported putting a drop or two of wine in a baby's bottle to "fortify" the milk. Generally, though, wine is first offered when the child is two or more, can hold his own glass quite safely in his hand, and can join the family at table.

In short, wine-drinking is already a habit before French children are old enough to reflect about it. If they do begin to assess their drinking practices, it is against a cultural backdrop where all the answers are value-loaded. Under the circumstances, it is hardly surprising that the campaigns in France against wine-drinking—led by teachers, social workers, and specialists in child welfare—have met with little success, and that in the past quarter-century the drinking patterns of French villagers, despite much social change and many social pressures, have hardly changed at all.

Questions 11.3

1. Make a case for each of these propositions: (a) drinking wine in France is deviant; (b) not drinking wine in France is deviant.
2. What social control techniques is the French government using to discourage wine drinking? Why aren't they working?
3. What kind of social control techniques would be most effective in this situation? Design a program that you think would work.

Reading 11.4

The Painted Bird

JERZY KOSINSKI

The point of much of the discussion in this chapter is that one way to study deviant behavior is to see it as a product of labeling some people by others. People are called deviant because of certain behaviors or characteristics they have—he is a cripple, she is pregnant, he is an ex-convict, she is a prostitute. People have a tendency, it seems, to find comfort and safety in similarity, and consequently, to seek out and call attention to the different among them. This common theme is behind not only definitions of deviant behavior but is the basis for discrimination, prejudice, stereotyping, and scapegoating as well.

This point has probably been made sufficiently well, but as a final illustration look at this amazing passage from the novel *The Painted Bird*, by Jerzy Kosinski. This book tells the story of a boy's wanderings through Poland during World War II. One of his friends is a young man named Lekh who traps birds for a living. Lekh has been having a passionate affair with a wild young woman of the forest who is called "stupid Ludmila."

Sometimes days passed and Stupid Ludmila did not appear in the forest. Lekh would become possessed by a silent rage. He would stare solemnly at the birds in the cages, mumbling something to himself. Finally, after prolonged scrutiny, he would choose the strongest bird, tie it to his wrist, and prepare stinking paints of different colors which he mixed together from the most varied components. When the colors satisfied him, Lekh would turn the bird over and paint its wings, head, and breast in rainbow hues until it became more dappled and vivid than a bouquet of wildflowers.

Then we would go into the thick of the forest. There Lekh took out the painted bird and ordered me to hold it in my hand and squeeze it lightly. The bird would begin to twitter and attract a flock of the same species which would fly nervously over our heads. Our prisoner, hearing them, strained toward them, warbling more loudly, its little heart, locked in its freshly painted breast, beating violently.

When a sufficient number of birds gathered above our heads, Lekh would give me a sign to release the prisoner. It would soar, happy and free, a spot of rainbow against the backdrops of clouds, and then plunge into the waiting brown flock. For an instant the birds were confounded. The painted bird circled from one end of the flock to the other, vainly trying to convince its kin that it was one of them. But, dazzled by its brilliant colors, they flew around it unconvinced. The painted bird would be forced farther and farther away as it zealously tried to enter the ranks of the flock. We saw soon afterwards how one bird after another would peel off in a fierce attack. Shortly the many-hued shape lost its place in the sky and dropped to the ground. These incidents happened often. When we finally found the painted birds they were usually dead. Lekh keenly examined the number of blows which the birds had received. Blood seeped through their colored wings, diluting the paint and soiling Lekh's hands.

Stupid Ludmila did not return. Lekh, sulking and glum, removed one bird after another from the cages, painted them in still gaudier colors, and released them into the air to be killed by their kin. One day he trapped a large raven, whose wings he painted red, the breast green, and the tail blue. When a flock of ravens appeared over our hut, Lekh freed the painted bird. As soon as it joined the flock a desperate battle began. The changeling was attacked from all sides. Black, red, green, blue feathers began to drop at our feet. The ravens ran amuck in the skies, and suddenly the painted raven plummeted to the fresh-plowed soil. It was still alive, opening its beak and vainly trying to move its wings. Its eyes had been pecked out, and fresh blood streamed over its painted feathers. It made yet another attempt to flutter up from the sticky earth, but its strength was gone.

Questions 11.4

1. The painted bird is attacked by the flock because it is different. How does human society "discolor" its own members?
2. The flock pecks the painted bird to death. How do people respond to "painted birds" in their midst?
3. Pick a type of behavior and outline how it becomes deviant. Explain reactions to it by using the metaphor of the "painted bird."

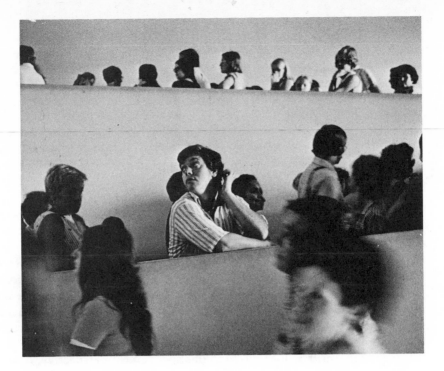

12 What Is Sociology?

Throughout this book, we have looked at the concepts of sociology in an attempt to give some idea of what sociology is. One gains an understanding of a discipline by becoming acquainted with the tools, techniques, and terms of that discipline. The concepts and the readings included in this book should give you some feeling for what sociology is all about.

Is it enough, however, merely to be familiar with the concepts of an endeavor? For example, a beginning understanding of the tools and techniques of the garage mechanic may be enlightening, but that understanding won't provide an individual with sufficient skill or experience to fix a car. It is possible that although we have covered a number of the important concepts that sociologists use, you may not be able to go out and solve the problems of the world or even to apply sociology in a meaningful manner. Of course this is only an introductory view of sociology. Additional courses should bring greater knowledge and facility in the use of sociological concepts. In addition, however, there are probably other aspects and characteristics of sociology, aside from its concepts, that would help bring a better understanding of what it is.

A Sociological Perspective

Members of a discipline develop a particular way of looking at the world. They share these views as individuals, although the similarity of their perspectives is most readily seen when a group of people from the same discipline are together. The same thing occurs among engineers, doctors, musicians, sociologists. Becoming a sociologist involves learning the meaning and use of a series of concepts and techniques and acquiring a body of knowledge. Going through this learning—a socialization process—provides one with a particular viewpoint. Members of a discipline share this viewpoint, and it affects the way they think, the way they talk, the way they behave.

There are a number of aspects to this sociological perspective. A major aspect is the tendency to see human behavior in the context of the group. To put it another way, sociologists understand people's behavior to be a product of their group affiliations. Consequently, in their studies, it is on these group affiliations that sociologists focus. For example, let's look at Joe Blow as some of his friends and colleagues might look at him. What stands out to his doctor is Joe's height, weight, pulse rate, blood pressure, and medical history. What his banker sees is his investment portfolio, cash reserves, and loan collateral. His minister may see him as a soul to be saved, a moral state to be improved. His professor may see him as a mind to be molded, a vessel to be filled with knowledge, or an intellect to be challenged. A sociologist looks at him and sees a white, middle-class, twenty-one-year-old man who is a member of the Democratic Party, the SLA, and the John Birch Society (odd . . .).

Sociologists typically are more interested in characteristics of categories and groups than in specific individuals. In Joe's case, the focus would probably be on the characteristics of middle-class whites, of twenty-one-year-old men, or of Democrats rather than on Joe as an individual. The sociologist usually studies numbers of people—groups, categories, societies—and their patterns of behavior —norms, roles, and institutions.

Other aspects of the sociological perspective are discussed by Peter Berger in his book *Invitation to Sociology*. Berger feels that there is a "sociological conscious-ness" having several facets.[1] A *debunking* tendency of sociologists is reflected in

---

[1]The discussion in the following paragraphs is drawn from Berger's Chapter 2, "Sociology as a Form of Consciousness." Peter L. Berger, *Invitation to Sociology* (Garden City, N.Y.: Doubleday, 1963).

their study of things taken for granted. Berger suggests that in analyzing the structure and institutions of societies, it is often necessary to "unmask the pretensions and the propaganda with which men cloak their actions with each other." There is a constant attempt, then, to find the underlying explanations for phenomena instead of just accepting the handy or traditional explanations that people readily give. For example, sociologists would view it as important to put common-sense explanations aside and determine what the real relationship is between narcotics legislation and drug usage, or between use of the death penalty and the homicide rate.

A part of sociology is devoted to the study of the *unrespectable.* Early sociologists were reformers and muckrakers. They believed that sociologists should intervene and attempt to ameliorate problem conditions to ensure social progress. This preoccupation with social problems and the unrespectable has abated somewhat today, but its influence in sociology is still strong. We see, for example, a variety of recent studies of underdogs, deviants, and outsiders. In addition to several studies of drug users and hippies, books have appeared dealing with shoplifters, pool players, bar behavior, behavior of race track gamblers, prison behavior, death and dying, and mental illness, to mention a few topics.[2]

This is not meant to imply that so-called respectable aspects of society are outside the scope of sociology. On the contrary, most sociological study is of this variety. In fact, there has been criticism of late that sociology has become too establishment, too interested in describing and supporting the *status quo,* and less than it should be, an agent for social change. Without getting involved in that debate, we could conclude that although much of sociology deals with the respectable, a prominent and growing segment of the discipline deals with the unrespectable, with problems and/or deviant aspects of society.

Berger suggests that sociologists tend to be *relativists* and *cosmopolitan* in their outlook. Sociologists are involved in studying patterns of human interaction in a variety of cultures under many different conditions. This type of study soon makes it apparent that behavior, ideas, and institutions are relative, relevant to specific cultures and specific locations. The general absence of universals in the social world demands that the outlook of the social scientist be cosmopolitan. It is unacceptable for social scientists to generalize from the situation immediately around them. They must take a world view, and this becomes part of their sociological consciousness.

The similarities in outlook that are shared by sociologists emerge, to a great

[2]A short list of books on "unrespectable" topics: Lewis Yablonsky, *The Hippie Trip* (New York: Pegasus, 1968); James T. Carey, *The College Drug Scene* (Englewood Cliffs, N.J.: Prentice-Hall, 1968); Mary Cameron, *The Booster and the Snitch* (New York: Free Press, 1964); Ned Polsky, *Hustlers, Beats, and Others* (Chicago: Aldine, 1967); Sherri Cavan, *Liquor License* (Chicago: Aldine, 1966); Marvin B. Scott, *The Racing Game* (Chicago: Aldine, 1968); David Ward and Gene Kassebaum, *Women's Prison* (Chicago: Aldine, 1965); Gresham Sykes, *The Society of Captives* (Princeton, N.J.: Princeton University Press, 1958); Barney Glaser and Anselm Strauss, *Awareness of Dying* and *Time for Dying* (Chicago: Aldine, 1965 and 1968); Thomas Scheff, *Being Mentally Ill* (Chicago: Aldine, 1966); Howard S. Becker, *Outsiders* (New York: Free Press, 1963); Howard S. Becker, ed., *The Other Side* (New York: Free Press, 1964).

extent, as a result of their training. There are, as well, many differences among sociologists. One area of difference is evident when we examine how sociologists look at sociology.

Sociological Perspectives of Sociology

The discipline of sociology encompasses certain themes or traditions. In combination, these traditions constitute a heritage from which all sociologists draw. A particular sociologist, however, will be influenced more strongly by one tradition or perspective than by others. Just as a doctor specializes in certain aspects of medicine and a lawyer concentrates in certain aspects of law, so the sociologist specializes in specific areas of sociology (race, social class, or deviant behavior, for example) and follows a particular theme or tradition that he or she feels to be most appropriate.

There has always been in sociology, as in other disciplines, a debate over what we are and what we should be doing. This is a continual self-analysis, which attracts the interest and attention of many sociologists. It seems appropriate to me to describe this as "sociological perspectives on sociology." It is an interesting debate and probably reflects the growing pains of an area of study that is still trying to define itself and its place in the world of knowledge.

As we mentioned in Chapter 1, science is often divided into *pure* and *applied* categories. Into which of these categories does sociology properly fall? Sociology is seen by some as a *pure* science in that its practitioners seek knowledge for knowledge's sake alone, without regard for the possible uses the knowledge may have. The Weberian model suggests that sociology is a science, not a vehicle for social action. In recent years, however, a growing number of sociologists have encouraged the development of an *applied* sociology. In a variety of ways, sociologists are putting their concepts and techniques to practical use. In general, these efforts involve attempts to deal with the problems of society or of individual segments of society: industry, education, labor, government, and the community. Applied sociology is often designed to encourage desired social change or to forestall undesired social change. Applied sociology has been referred to as *action sociology,* and those involved are sometimes called *social engineers.* Philip Hauser points out that with the proliferation of economic and social planning and the increase in welfare functions of government, the need for sociologists will continue to increase for the performance of both scientific and social engineering tasks.[3]

Some sociologists have a *scientific* perspective. For them, sociology is a social science, and they emphasize the procedures and techniques of science. Such sociologists see themselves as white-coated individuals who gain knowledge by applying scientific methods to social phenomena. They are objective, they are detached, they are free of any values or biases that might affect their work. They are, perhaps,

[3]Philip M. Hauser; "On Actionism in the Craft of Sociology," *Sociology Inquiry,* vol. 39, no. 2 (Spring 1969), pp. 139–147. For more on applied sociology, see Arthur Shostak, ed., *Sociology in Action* (Homewood, Ill.: Dorsey Press, 1966); and Alvin Gouldner and S. M. Miller, ed., *Applied Sociology* (New York: Free Press, 1965).

bundles of sensory neurons moving in space, observing and recording the facts of social interaction. Sociologists today are developing sophisticated mathematical models and statistical techniques and using ever larger computers to aid them in the scientific analysis of human behavior.[4]

The scientists I have just described are often called positivists. They adhere pretty much to the classical view of science as outlined in Chapter 1. Their role as scientists is based on the model that has worked so well for those in the physical and biological sciences, and its adoption by sociologists probably reflects the hope that our success may be as great as theirs. At the same time the positivistic model in sociology is criticized by some, and this debate over method has increased in recent years. The criticism has several origins. First, there is the criticism of science in general. There is concern that blind faith in, and uncritical acceptance of, science has led people to ignore the faults of science. Questions are raised about a series of ethical considerations: Shouldn't scientists be responsible for the possible harmful uses of their discoveries? Should scientists tamper with and manipulate people without their knowledge, or even *with* their knowledge? Whom do the scientists represent—themselves, science in general, society, or those people (government agencies, large organizations, private concerns) who are paying their research bills? Failure to receive satisfactory answers to these questions has led many to be disillusioned with science.[5]

A second form of criticism of the positivistic model is more specific to sociology. The complaint here is that the information we have, especially when gathered by questionnaires and interviews, is not valid, not accurate. This is a serious criticism. Derek Phillips states in his book *Knowledge From What?* that ninety percent of the data collected by sociologists is done by means of interviews and questionnaires. What sociologists have failed to take into account, he maintains, is that the questionnaire or interview situation is a *social* situation. The statements of the people being studied are affected by the questionnaire, by their response to the interviewer and the interviewer's characteristics (sex, age, race, social class, demeanor, etc.), by the nature of the interaction between the interviewer and interviewed, and by numerous other factors that have been left uncontrolled. The basic problem is that most sociological research is based on people's *reports* of their own behavior rather than on *actual observation* of their behavior. This is the issue of reactive versus nonreactive research, which we discussed in Chapter 1. Phillips suggests that sociologists should instead concentrate on participant observation and hidden observation techniques. Participant observation, as we mentioned earlier, involves the investigator joining or living with the subjects being studied. The researcher becomes part of the group. Studies of primitive tribes, delinquent gangs, large organizations (remember Elinor Langer's study of the telephone company, Reading 4.2), and class and ethnic structure of communities, as well as many other

[4]A thorough and interesting discussion of several sociological perspectives, including "abstracted empiricism," is included in C. Wright Mills' excellent book, *The Sociological Imagination* (New York: Oxford University Press, 1959).

[5]A number of works deal with these issues. See, for example, Gideon Sjoberg, ed., *Ethics, Politics, and Social Research* (Cambridge, Mass.: Schenkman, 1967); Ralph Beals, *Politics of Social Research* (Chicago: Aldine, 1968); Irving L. Horowitz, ed., *The Rise and Fall of Project Camelot* (Cambridge, Mass.: M.I.T. Press, 1967). There is a discussion of scientific ethics in most methodology texts.

topics, have been made with this technique. Participant observation allows study of some events that could not otherwise be studied, and may provide many insights that escape the more formal interview and questionnaire methods. Hidden observation refers to making use of records or traces left behind by people (checking the nose prints on the glass or the wear on the floor tile to determine the popularity of a museum exhibit) or by actually observing people without letting them know.[6] The key element in both participant and hidden observation is that we *watch* people's behavior rather than *ask* them about it. Concerns about the *accuracy* of what we are doing, then, has led to further disillusionment with some of the scientific aspects of sociology.

These problems, as well as other beliefs regarding the most appropriate path to knowledge, have led some sociologists to see the discipline not as science but as *social philosophy*. For them, sociologists are theorists, perhaps armchair philosophers who sit by the fire spinning grand generalizations about the nature of the universe. They frequently have remarkable insights about human behavior. However, from the scientist's viewpoint, the social philosopher's statements are often too general and abstract to be put to empirical test. Others see sociologists-as-social-philosophers as true scholars rather than mere scientific technicians—they are widely read, masters of many disciplines, and students may gather adoringly at their feet.

Some sociologists have a *humanistic* perspective. For them, the sociologist is interested in and concerned about human welfare, values, and conduct—he or she wants to improve the lot of people in general. An ultimate goal for the humanist is the self-realization and full development of the cultivated person. There may

[6]Derek Phillips, *Knowledge From What?* (Chicago: Rand McNally, 1971). Also see John Lofland, *Analyzing Social Settings* (Belmont, Calif.: Wadsworth, 1971), and Eugene Webb, Donald Campbell, Richard Schwartz, and Lee Sechrest, *Unobtrusive Measures: Nonreactive Research in the Social Sciences* (Chicago: Rand McNally, 1966).

occasionally be a tendency for the humanistic and scientific perspectives to be at odds with each other. The humanist is interested in bettering the condition of people and developing the individual to the fullest. The objective of science is the gaining of empirical knowledge about the world, without regard for the possible uses of such knowledge. Don Martindale suggests that humanism is a system of values describing "what ought to be" and modes of conduct designed to secure them; science is the value-free pursuit of knowledge, "of what is," renouncing all concern with what ought to be. It has also been suggested that the scientist is more interested in the *means*—gaining knowledge; the humanist, in the *ends*—improving the lot of people. The humanist may be seen as a moralist; the scientist is seen (usually by the humanist) as amoral, sometimes as immoral.[7]

Is sociology basically concerned with gathering empirical data about people's behavior in a scientific sense or with the study of those conditions that will enable individuals to realize their fullest potential in a humanistic sense? It is impossible to put all of sociology into one camp or the other. Most sociologists probably operate with a combination of scientific and humanistic viewpoints. Peter Berger expresses the view of many, however, when he argues that sociology must be used for humanity's sake. Social science, like other sciences, can be and sometimes is dehumanizing and even inhuman. It should not be. When sociologists pursue their task with insight, sensitivity, empathy, humility, and a desire to *understand* the human condition, rather than with a cold and humorless scientism, then indeed, the "sociological perspective helps illuminate man's social existence."[8]

Sociologists—What Are They and What Do They Do?

What is a sociologist? Is it anyone who says he or she is? Sometimes, but more precisely, a sociologist is a person who has a bachelor's, master's, or doctor's degree in sociology. In 1976, there were 28,000 bachelor's degress, 2,000 master's degrees, and 700 doctor's degrees awarded in sociology in the United States. Most professional sociologists have master's or doctor's degrees, and many students who receive bachelor's degrees in sociology go into other fields, so the exact number of sociologists practicing sociology for a living is hard to determine. The field's professional organization, the American Sociological Association, has about 15,000 members. However, this is not a precise count of all sociologists because there are some student members in the ASA and not all professional sociologists join the organization.

Sociologists communicate with each other in several ways. They form groups (how strange) such as the Midwestern Sociological Association and the Pacific Sociological Association. In addition, they publish journals (*American Sociological Review, American Journal of Sociology, Social Forces, Social Problems, Sociometry,* and many others) for which they write articles that describe recent efforts in theory and

---

[7]This discussion of humanistic and scientific thought follows from Don Martindale's analysis in his *Social Life and Cultural Change* (Princeton, N.J.: Van Nostrand, 1962), pp. 443–462.

[8]See Peter Berger's chapter, "Sociology as a Humanistic Discipline," in *Invitation to Sociology* (see footnote 1). Also see R. P. Cuzzort's discussion of Berger in Cuzzort's book, *Humanity and Modern Sociological Thought* (New York: Holt, Rinehart and Winston, 1969), Chapter 10.

research. The regional and national groups have yearly meetings at which papers are read, old friendships are renewed, little is accomplished, and a good time is had by all.

Most sociologists spend most of their time teaching. Opportunities for teaching sociology are found predominantly at the college and university level, but increasing numbers of high schools are adding sociology courses to their curricula. Some sociology courses, especially at the high school level, have more of a practical, how-to-do-it focus. These courses might deal with dating, marriage, senior problems, or personal adjustment.

Many sociologists are involved in research, either full time or in combination with their teaching. Full-time researchers may run their own research agencies, but more often they work for state or federal agencies. They may, for example, be responsible for collecting and analyzing population and census data. They may collect police arrest statistics and analyze and combine these into crime reports. Sociologists, especially at the larger universities, are about equally involved in research and teaching. Often they seek grants to support their research, and this in itself has become big business. Sociologists, like other academicians, are increasingly being criticized for spending more time with their research than with their students. Perhaps this criticism is well founded, but the situation has been created at least in part by the promotion and salary structure of institutions, which rewards professors more for their research and publications than it does for their teaching.

In the 1970s, job markets began changing for sociologists. Up to that time it had not been difficult to obtain a college teaching job. However, an oversupply of people with doctorates in sociology (and social science generally) developed in the 1970s. About the same time, student enrollment in sociology, which had increased rapidly in the 1960s, began leveling off in many parts of the country, and this meant fewer teaching jobs. The consequence has been that sociologists have been moving in greater numbers into applied fields. Sociologists work in a number of capacities for a variety of private, state, and federal agencies. Criminologists are hired by institutions (prisons, reformatories) and by departments of correction. Population experts are valuable in a policy-making capacity for a number of agencies. Sociologists act as consultants to cities for recreation programs, city planning, urban renewal, mass transit, etc. The services of specialists in marriage and the family are used by schools, churches, and social agencies, and some sociologists are involved in private marriage counseling.

Sociology and You

What good has this time spent in sociology done you? For one thing, with any luck at all you are three or four units closer to that piece of paper that you came to college to collect. Maybe that is enough justification, but possibly something more has occurred. Admittedly it is hard to measure what might have happened. If the subject were typing and you had progressed from two words a minute to eighty, there would be tangible evidence of success. Since the subject is sociology, if you went out and solved eight social problems during summer vacation, that might prove that the course had taught something. The problem is, however, that we are not teaching a skill or a technique but a viewpoint. And it is sometimes difficult to measure the immediate usefulness of a new viewpoint or a new way of looking at things.

After a semester of introductory sociology, you will probably know more about the world you live in. You will certainly know more facts about that world —mainly because you will have stayed up until all hours several nights during the semester frantically trying to sponge up facts for the next day's test. But principally, it seems to me that what you should have discovered from the course is a way of looking at the world and at yourself. As C. Wright Mills suggested in *The Sociological Imagination,* the study of sociology may provide you with a self-consciousness. You have a means for evaluating yourself as more than an isolated individual in a sea of humanity. The study of sociology may help you place yourself and history in perspective. You may more accurately identify and evaluate the factors that affect your behavior and the behavior of others. You may become more critical and evaluative of aspects of the world that heretofore you took for granted.

"Who am I?" and "How did I get this way?" are questions that are difficult to answer to anyone's satisfaction. Perhaps a sociological viewpoint will help deal with these questions; perhaps it won't. If the sociological viewpoint only helps to make you more aware of your social environment and some of the forces at work there, it has been worthwhile, for this will provide you with a greater understanding of and compassion for others.

Glossary

Acculturation The process of assimilating, blending in, and taking on the characteristics of another culture.

Achieved statuses Positions in society that are earned or achieved in some way.

Aggregate A number of people clustered together in one place.

Amalgamation Refers to biological (rather than cultural) mixing.

Annihilation Elimination of one group by another.

Anomie A state of normlessness; a condition in which the norms and rules governing people's aspirations and moral conduct have disintegrated.

Anticipatory socialization Occurs when a person adopts the values, behavior, or viewpoints of a group he or she would like to, but does not yet, belong to.

Ascribed statuses Positions automatically conferred on individuals through no choice of their own; statuses one is born with.

Assimilation Mixing and merging of unlike cultures so that the two groups come to have a common culture.

Bureaucracy (formal organization) An organization in which the activities of some people are systematically planned by other people in order to achieve some special purpose; usually involves such characteristics as division of labor, hierarchy of authority, system of rules, impersonality, and technical efficiency.

Category A number of people who have a particular characteristic in common.

Centralization The tendency of people to gather around some central or pivotal point in a city.

Charisma A quality in an individual that sets one apart from others—the person is viewed as superhuman and capable of exceptional acts.

Charismatic retinue A type of organization made up of followers or disciples of a charismatic leader.

Church A large and highly organized religious organization that represents and supports the *status quo,* is respectable, and in which membership is automatic; one is born into a church.

Closed group A group into which it is difficult if not impossible to gain membership.

Collective behavior Spontaneous, unstructured, and unstable group behavior.

Compound family The family resulting from polygamy; marriages involving multiple spouses—several wives and/or husbands at the same time.

Conflict theory A sociological theory that holds that the most appropriate way to understand society is to focus on the consequences of the conflict, competition, and discord that are common in social interaction.

Conjugal family Family in which members are related by marital ties.

Consanguine family Family in which members are related by blood ties.

Contraculture Similar to subculture, but with the idea of opposition to or conflict with the norms and values of the dominant culture. Some customs and norms of the subculture differ from those of the dominant culture; customs and norms of the contraculture conflict with those of the dominant culture.

Criminal behavior Behavior prohibited by law and subject to formal punishment.

Crowd A temporary collection of people in close physical contact reacting together to a common stimulus.

Cult A religious organization that is a small, short-lived, often local group, that is frequently built around a dominant leader. The cult is smaller, less organized, and more transitory than the sect.

Cultural lag Phenomenon that occurs when related segments of society change at different rates.

Cultural pluralism A pattern of interaction in which unlike cultures maintain their own identity and yet interact with each other relatively peacefully.

Cultural relativism Opposite of ethnocentrism: suggests that each culture be judged from its own viewpoint without imposing outside standards of judgment.

Culture The complex set of learned and shared beliefs, customs, skills, habits, traditions, and knowledge common to the members of a society; the social heritage of a society.

Decentralization The tendency of people to move outward and away from the center of the city.

Definition of the situation The suggestion, first offered by W. I. Thomas, that reality is socially structured, with the result that people respond more to the meaning a situation has for them than to the objective features of that situation.

Demographic transition The movement of a population from high birth and death rates to high birth and low death rates (and rapid population growth) to low birth and death rates.

Demography The study of human population, its distribution, composition, and change.

Denomination A religious organization that has less universality than the church or the ecclesia and appeals to a smaller category of people—a racial, ethnic, or social-class grouping that is conventional and respectable.

Dependent variable The "effect"; that quantity or aspect of the study whose change the researcher wants to understand.

Deviant behavior Behavior contrary to generally accepted norms; limits are often established by custom or public opinion, sometimes by law.

Diffusion The spread of objects or ideas from one society to another or from one group to another within the same society, resulting in changes in society.

Disaster A situation in which there is a basic disruption of the social context within which individuals and groups function; a radical departure from the pattern of normal expectations.

Discrimination Actual behavior resulting in unfavorable and unequal treatment of individuals or groups.

Ego In Freud's view, the acting self, the mediator between the id and superego.

Empiricism Knowledge gained through experience and sense observation.

Endogamy Marriage within a certain group.

Ethnicity Refers to people bound together by cultural ties.

Ethnocentrism A type of prejudice that maintains that one's own culture's ways are right and other cultures' ways, if different, are wrong.

Exogamy Marriage outside a certain group.

Experiment Type of research in which the researcher introduces a stimulus to a subject or group and then observes the response; the researcher manipulates the independent variable (exercise, for example) and watches for change in the dependent variable (heart disease, for example).

Expulsion Removal of a group from the territory in which it resides.

Extended family More than two generations of the same family living together in close association or under the same roof.

Fads The relatively short-term obsessions that members of a society or members of specific groups have toward specific behaviors or objects.

Family of orientation The family one is born into.

Family of procreation The family of which one is a parent.

Fashions Temporary attachments to specific behaviors, styles, or objects; similar to fads but more widespread and of longer duration.

Feudal administration A type of organization that is separate from but responsible to a parent organization; it has local autonomy to act in terms of its own interests.

Folkways Norms that are less obligatory than mores, the "shoulds" of society; sanctions for violation are mild.

Functional analysis A sociological theory that focuses on the structures that emerge in society and the functions that these structures perform in the operation of society as a whole.

Gemeinschaft Primary, closely-knit society in which relationships are personal and informal and there is a commitment to or identification with the community.

Generalized other The sum of the viewpoints and expectations of the social group or community to which an individual belongs.

Gesellschaft Secondary society based on contractual arrangements, bargaining, a well-developed division of labor, and on rational thought rather than emotion.

Group A number of people who have shared or patterned interaction and who feel bound together by a "consciousness of kind" or a "we" feeling.

Horizontal groups Groups whose members come predominantly from one social-class level, such as associations of doctors or carpenters.

Horizontal social mobility Movement from one occupation to another within the same social class; also used to refer to spatial or geographical mobility.

Human ecology The adaptation of people to their physical environment, their location in space.

Hypothesis A testable statement or proposition used to guide an investigation.

Id In Freud's view, the primitive part of the personality made up of inborn, instinctual, antisocial drives.

Ideal norms How a person should behave in a particular situation.

Idealistic culture Sorokin's term describing a culture midway between the sensate and ideational, which emphasizes logic and rationality.

Ideational culture Sorokin's term describing a culture that emphasizes feelings and emotions and is subjective, expressive, and religious.

Independent variable The "cause"; that quantity or aspect of the study that seems to produce change in another variable.

In-groups Groups the individual identifies with and feels comfortable with.

Interaction process analysis (IPA) A technique for group study in which interaction between group members is broken down into small parts or acts. The acts are then classified into a set of predetermined categories (shows agreement, gives information, asks for opinion, etc.).

Invasion The penetration of one group or function into an area dominated by another group or function.

Invention Change introduced through the creation of a new object or idea.

Involuntary groups Groups in which membership is automatic and the participant has no choice regarding joining, such as one's family or the army platoon one is drafted into.

Labeling The public stamping, typing, or categorizing of a person as deviant.

Looking-glass self Attitudes toward self derived from one's interpretations of how others are evaluating self.

Marginal person A person who is caught between two antagonistic cultures; a product of both but a true member of neither.

Mass hysteria A type of collective behavior in which a particular behavior, fear, or belief sweeps through a large number of people such as a crowd, a city, or a nation.

Material culture The real, tangible things that a society creates and uses: screwdriver, house, classroom, supersonic jet, computer.

Matriarchal society Society in which decisions are made by females.

Mean The sum of all the items in a series divided by the number of items; often referred to as the "average."

Median The middle case in a series that has been ranked or ordered by size.

Milling The excited, restless, physical movement of the people in a crowd through which communication occurs leading to a definition of the situation and possible collective action.

Minority status People treated as lower in social ranking and subject to domination by other segments of the population.

Mob A focused, acting crowd, emotionally aroused, intent on taking aggressive action.

Modern bureaucracy In Weber's view, a type of large organization in which specialization, a system of rules, formality, and a hierarchy of authority are highly developed.

Modern professional organization A type of large organization in which responsibility is decentralized; less bureaucratic in Weber's sense than the modern bureaucracy.

Monogamy Marriage with one person at a time.

Mores Obligatory norms, the "musts" of society; sanctions are harsh if these are violated.

Mysticism Information or knowledge gained by mystical means: intuition, revelation, inspiration, magic, visions, spells; tends to be private knowledge experienced only by the mystic.

Nativism The attempt to improve a people's existence by eliminating all foreign persons, objects, and customs.

Nonmaterial culture The abstract creations of a society such as customs, laws, ideas, values, beliefs.

Nonreactive research Research in which records, physical traces, and signs left by people are studied; observation of subjects without direct intrusion; subject is not aware of being studied. (Compare with *reactive research.*)

Norms The accepted or required behavior for a person in a particular situation.

Nuclear family A married couple and their children.

Open group A group that is easy to gain membership to.

Out-groups Groups the individual does not identify with, does not feel comfortable with, and sees as different from self.

Panic Nonadaptive or nonrational flight resulting from extreme fear and loss of self-control.

Participant observation Research in which the researcher is or appears to be a participant in the activity or group that is being studied.

Patriarchal society Society in which decisions are made by males.

Peer group Consists of people of relatively the same age, interests, and social position with whom one has reasonably close association and contact.

Permanent group A group which has durability, constancy, and a long life span, such as a family.

Personality The sum total of the physical, mental, emotional, social, and behavioral characteristics of an individual.

Polyandry A form of polygamy in which one woman has several husbands at a time.

Polygamy Plural marriage; the practice of having more than one husband or wife at a time.

Polygyny A form of polygamy in which one man has several wives at a time.

Prejudice Favorable or unfavorable attitudes toward a person or group, not based on actual experience.

Primary deviation Beginning, often minor acts of deviant behavior, which do not affect the individual's self-concept—the individual does not see himself or herself as a deviant. (Compare with *secondary deviation.*)

Primary group A group in which contacts between members are intimate, personal, and face to face.

Primary socialization The first socialization an individual undergoes in childhood; one must undergo this to become a member of society; it ends with the establishment of the generalized other.

Propaganda Attempts to influence and change the public's viewpoint on an issue.

Public A number of people who have an interest in, and difference of opinion about, a common issue.

Public opinion The opinions (ideas, beliefs) held by a public on a given issue.

Race People related by common descent or heredity; usually identified by hereditary physical features.

Random sample A sample of subjects in which every element in the total population being studied has an equal chance of being selected; the small sample of subjects is then theoretically representative of the larger population from which it was selected.

Rationalism Knowledge gained through reason and logic.

Reactive research Research in which subjects react or respond to a questionnaire or an interviewer. (Compare with *nonreactive research.*)

Reference groups Groups that serve as models for our behavior, groups whose perspectives we assume and mold our behavior after.

Reform movement A movement that seeks modification in certain aspects of society.

Resocialization A process in which major modifications or reconstructions are made of a person's patterns of behavior, personality, and self-concept.

Revolutionary movement A movement that seeks a complete change in the social order.

Riot A situation in which mob behavior becomes increasingly widespread and destructive.

Role The behavior of one who occupies a particular status or position in society.

Role conflict Conflict that occurs when a person occupies several statuses or positions that have contradictory role requirements.

Role requirements Norms specifying the expected behavior of persons holding a particular position in society.

Role strain Strain that occurs when there are differing and conflicting expectations regarding one's status or position.

Rumor Unconfirmed, although not necessarily false, person-to-person communication.

Sample A selection of a few from a larger universe. The sample may or may not be representative of the whole depending on how it is selected.

Sanction The punishment one receives for violation of a norm (or the reward granted for compliance with norms).

Secondary deviation Deviant acts that represent a defense, attack, or adjustment to the problems created by reactions to primary deviation; the self-concept changes so that the individual begins to see and define self as deviant. (Compare with *primary deviation.*)

Secondary group Group in which contacts between members are more impersonal than in a primary group; interaction is more superficial and probably based on utilitarian goals.

Secondary socialization Takes over where primary socialization leaves off; involves internalizing knowledge of new areas and new sectors of life, of special skills and techniques.

Sect Small religious organization that is less organized than the church, in which membership is voluntary. Members of sects usually show greater depth and fervor in their religious commitment than members of churches.

Segregation (1) Group conflict context: The setting apart of one group. (2) Ecological context: The clustering together of similar people.

Self One's awareness of and ideas and attitudes about one's own personal and social identity.

Self-fulfilling prophecy Occurs when a false definition of a situation evokes a new behavior that makes the originally false conception come true.

Sensate culture Sorokin's term describing a culture that emphasizes the senses and is objective, scientific, materialistic, profane, and instrumental.

Sex ratio Number of males per 100 females.

Significant others People (mother, father, older brother, etc.) whose viewpoints and expectations the individual considers particularly important.

Social change Significant alterations in the social relationships and cultural ideas of a society.

Social control The processes, planned or unplanned, by which people are made to conform to collective norms.

Social disorganization The condition resulting when norms and roles break down and customary ways of behaving no longer operate.

Social institutions Organized systems of social relationships that embody some common values and procedures and meet some basic needs of society.

Social interaction The process of being aware of others when we act, of modifying our behavior in accordance with others' responses.

Socialization The social process whereby one learns the expectations, habits, skills, values, beliefs, and other requirements necessary for effective participation in social groups.

Social movement A group of people acting with some continuity to promote or to resist a change in their society or group.

Social organization The social fabric of society; the integrated set of norms, roles, cultural values, and beliefs through which people interact with each other, individually and in groups.

Social stratification The division of people in society into layers or ranks. The source of the ranking may be one or a combination of factors: wealth, power, prestige, race, sex, age, religion, and so on.

Social structure The network of norms, roles, statuses, groups, and institutions through which people relate to each other in society.

Society A number of people living in a specific area who are relatively organized, self-sufficient and independent, and who share a common culture.

Sociobiology The systematic study of the biological basis of social behavior in all kinds of organisms, including man.

Sociometry A technique for group study in which group members are asked to designate the person or persons in the group whom they "like most," "would most like to work with," "would like expelled from the group," and so on. The resulting responses for all members of the group are then plotted in a figure called a sociogram, which shows the patterns and directions of interaction in the group.

Statistical norms How a person actually behaves in a particular situation.

Status A position in society or in a group.

Status inconsistency The factors that determine an individual's rank in society are not consistent with each other—for example, a college-educated carpenter, or a black court justice.

Stereotyping Using a simplified and standardized image or label to describe a group or category of people.

Subcultures Groups or segments of society that share many of the characteristics of the dominant culture, but that have some of their own specific customs or ways that tend to separate them from the rest of society.

Succession The complete displacement or removal of an established group; the end product of invasion.

Superego In Freud's view, that part of the personality made up of an internalized set of rules and regulations forming the conscience.

Survey research Research that involves the collection of information from subjects through use of questionnaires or interviews; may be descriptive or causal-explanatory.

Symbolic interaction A sociological theory that focuses on the *process* of person-to-person interaction, on how people come to develop viewpoints about themselves and others, and on forms of interpersonal communication.

Temporary group A group that is brought together to perform a single short-term task and that disbands at the task's conclusion.

Vertical group A group whose members come from a variety of social classes.

Vertical social mobility Movement up or down the social class ladder.

Voluntary groups Groups that have open membership; people may join or not as they wish.

Annotated Bibliography

If you would like to delve deeper into the subjects we have discussed in this book, let me suggest the following sources, some of which have been cited in footnotes. Most are available in paperback.

1: Introduction: Knowledge, Science, and Sociology

Bronowski, Jacob. *The Ascent of Man* (Boston: Little, Brown, 1973). Very readable and beautifully illustrated history of science and civilization developed from Bronowski's highly acclaimed television series.

Bronowski, Jacob. *The Common Sense of Science* (New York: Random House, 1959). A short, interesting history of science.

Brown, Robert. *Explanation in Social Science* (Chicago: Aldine, 1963). A detailed, systematic analysis of how social science research is done.

Chase, Stuart. *The Proper Study of Mankind* (New York: Harper & Row, 1956). An analysis of social science: what it attempts to do, its methods of inquiry, and the characteristics of individual social science disciplines.

Conant, James. *On Understanding Science* (New York: New American Library-Mentor, 1947). Another short, interesting history of several great scientists and how they solved their problems.

Kuhn, Thomas. *The Structure of Scientific Revolutions*, 2d ed. (Chicago: University of Chicago Press, 1970). Kuhn describes the development of scientific knowledge in terms of revolutions between competing paradigms, or viewpoints.

McCain, Garvin, and Erwin Segal. *The Game of Science*, 2d ed. (Monterey, Calif.: Brooks/Cole, 1973). A very readable description of the characteristics of science and of scientists.

Ravetz, Jerome. *Scientific Knowledge and Its Social Problems* (New York: Oxford University Press, 1971). A thorough evaluation and critique of the scientific establishment.

Sklair, Leslie. *Organized Knowledge* (Bungay, England: Chaucer Press, 1973). Sklair deals with the question of social responsibility in scientific endeavor. He demonstrates that science is the most important basis on which knowledge is organized in the modern world, and he examines the political consequences of science and technology for societies.

Watson, J. D. *The Double Helix* (New York: Signet, 1967). A fascinating account of competition and cooperation among scientists and the process of scientific discovery.

Numerous short books dealing with social science research methodology are available. For example, see:

Labovitz, Sanford, and Robert Hagedorn. *Introduction to Social Research* (New York: McGraw-Hill, 1971).

Lofland, John. *Analyzing Social Settings* (Belmont, Calif.: Wadsworth, 1971). Description of field or qualitative research with many examples.

Wallace, Walter. *The Logic of Science in Sociology* (Chicago: Aldine, 1971).

Webb, Eugene, Donald Campbell, Richard Schwartz, and Lee Sechrest. *Unobtrusive Measures: Nonreactive Research in the Social Sciences* (Chicago: Rand McNally, 1966). *The* sourcebook for nonreactive research—provides a rationale for this type of research as well as many examples of nonreactive studies.

The following two books focus on specific sociological research efforts. A number of projects are described. We see the problems sociologists study, the methods they use, the answers they find, and the mistakes they make.

Hammond, Phillip, ed. *Sociologists at Work* (New York: Doubleday, 1967).

Madge, John. *The Origins of Scientific Sociology* (New York: Free Press, 1962).

2: Socialization and Self

Aronson, Elliot. *The Social Animal,* 2d ed. (San Francisco: Freeman, 1976). This interesting and well-written book outlines the ideas and theories of the field of social psychology. Aronson defines the field and discusses such topics as conformity, self, and sensitivity-training groups.

Berger, Peter L., and Thomas Luckmann. *The Social Construction of Reality* (Garden City, N.Y.: Doubleday, 1966). This short but influential book covers primary and secondary socialization, social interaction, and society as objective and subjective reality.

Brownfield, Charles. *The Brain Benders* (New York: Exposition Press, 1972). A study of the effects of isolation and sensory deprivation. Includes descriptions of brainwashing in China and Korea as well as in laboratory experiments.

Des Pres, Terrence. *The Survivor* (New York: Pocket Books, 1977). This is an anatomy of life in the death camps—an account of how people survive in the worst of all possible worlds. It deals with the problem of staying alive *and* staying human.

Elkin, Frederick. *The Child and Society* (New York: Random House, 1960). Elkin defines socialization, describes its processes and agencies, and analyzes socialization in subcultural patterns and in later life.

Erikson, Erik. *Childhood and Society,* 2d ed. (New York: Norton, 1963). A study of the social significance of childhood by one of the leading figures in the field of psychoanalysis and human development.

Goffman, Erving. *The Presentation of Self in Everyday Life* (Garden City, N.Y.: Doubleday, 1959). A very readable, interesting analysis of the self. Goffman uses the language of the theater to describe how we present ourselves to others and attempt to manipulate the impressions others have of us.

Goffman, Erving. *Stigma* (Englewood Cliffs, N.J.: Prentice-Hall, 1963). Goffman deals with the physically deformed, the ex-mental patient, the drug addict, the prostitute; he analyzes the stigmatized individual's feelings about himself or herself, and his or her relationship to others and management of the self-image.

Socialization and development of self can be observed in many biographical and autobiographical works. For example, see:

Dayan, Ruth, and Helga Dudman. *And Perhaps . . . The Story of Ruth Dayan* (New York: Harcourt Brace Jovanovich, 1973).
Frank, Anne. *Anne Frank: The Diary of a Young Girl* (New York: Pocket Books, 1967).
Gibson, William. *Miracle Worker* (New York: Knopf, 1957).
Keller, Helen. *The Story of My Life* (New York: Dell, 1961).
Lindbergh, Anne Morrow. *Bring Me a Unicorn* (New York: Harcourt Brace Jovanovich and New American Library, 1971).
Malcolm X, and Alex Haley. *The Autobiography of Malcolm X* (New York: Grove Press, 1966).
Mead, Margaret. *Blackberry Winter* (New York: Morrow, 1972).
Shainberg, Lawrence. *Brain Surgeon* (New York: Lippincott, 1979).

See also descriptions of socialization into occupations. The following come to mind:

Greenwald, Harold. *The Elegant Prostitute* (New York: Ballantine, 1970).
Letkemann, Peter. *Crime as Work* (Englewood Cliffs, N.J.: Prentice-Hall, 1973).
Millman, Marcia. *The Unkindest Cut: Life in the Backrooms of Medicine* (New York: Morrow, 1977).
Niederhoffer, Arthur. *Behind the Shield* (Garden City, N.Y.: Doubleday, 1967).
Smith, Dennis. *Report from Engine Co. 82* (New York: Pocket Books, 1972).

3: Norms, Roles, Culture

There are numerous anthropological studies of exotic primitive and contemporary cultures. Old standbys:

Benedict, Ruth. *Patterns of Culture* (Boston: Houghton Mifflin, 1934).
Mead, Margaret. *Sex and Temperament* (New York: Morrow, 1935).
Riesman, D., N. Glazer, and R. Denney. *The Lonely Crowd* (Garden City, N.Y.: Doubleday, 1953). A study of changing American character that put the terms "inner-directed," "other-directed," and "tradition-directed" into the English vocabulary.
Ruesch, Hans. *Top of the World* (New York: Pocket Books, 1951). A novel, closely based on fact, that details the fascinating and unusual culture of the Eskimo.

A number of novelists have offered us a glimpse of cultures of the future:

Heinlein, R. A. *Stranger in a Strange Land* (New York: Medallion, 1968).
Huxley, Aldous. *Brave New World* (New York: Harper & Row, 1969).
Orwell, George. *1984* (New York: New American Library, 1971).
Skinner, B. F. *Walden Two* (New York: Macmillan, 1969).

4: Groups

Blau, Peter, and Marshall Meyer. *Bureaucracy in Modern Society,* 2d ed. (New York: Random House, 1971). An analysis of what sociologists know about large formal organizations in theory and in practice.
Crosbie, Paul V. *Interaction in Small Groups* (New York: Macmillan, 1975). A series of readings that describe a number of interesting research studies dealing with various aspects of small group research.

Perrow, Charles. *Organizational Analysis: A Sociological View* (Monterey, Calif.: Brooks/ Cole, 1970). An analysis of formal organizations covering such topics as contrasting levels of bureaucratization, the structure and functioning of organizations, the nature of organizational goals and the strategies used to achieve them.

Whyte, William H., Jr. *The Organization Man* (Garden City, N.Y.: Doubleday, 1956). This classic work describes the new life style of Americans—life under the protection of a big organization. According to Whyte, modern Americans find jobs in large organizations that promise security and a high standard of living; in doing so, they give up the hopes and ambitions that dominated earlier generations of Americans.

There are several short texts that summarize the research and theoretical knowledge available concerning small groups:

Mills, Theodore. *The Sociology of Small Groups* (Englewood Cliffs, N.J.: Prentice-Hall, 1967).

Olmsted, Michel, and Paul Hare. *The Small Group,* 2d ed. (New York: Random House, 1978).

Shepard, Clovis. *Small Groups* (San Francisco: Chandler, 1964).

A number of short texts summarize the research and theoretical knowledge available concerning large organizations:

Drabek, Thomas, and Eugene Haas. *Understanding Complex Organizations* (Dubuque, Iowa: Wm. C. Brown, 1974).

Etzioni, Amitai. *Modern Organizations* (Englewood Cliffs, N.J.: Prentice-Hall, 1964).

Whisler, Thomas. *Information Technology and Organizational Change* (Belmont, Calif.: Wadsworth, 1970).

Descriptions of small and primary group interaction appear in numerous works. For example, see:

Liebow, Elliot. *Tally's Corner* (Boston: Little, Brown, 1967).

Whyte, William F. *Street Corner Society* (Chicago: University of Chicago Press, 1943).

Several books satirize aspects of large bureaucratic organizations:

Parkinson, C. Northcote. *Parkinson's Law* (New York: Ballantine, 1964).

Peter, L. J., and R. Hull. *The Peter Principle* (New York: Bantam, 1970).

5: Social Differentiation: Social Class

Coleman, Richard, and Lee Rainwater. *Social Standing in America: New Dimensions of Class* (New York: Basic Books, 1978). A comprehensive study of social class in America. It assesses the importance of income and education and describes a seven-class view of stratification in the United States.

Lipset, Seymour Martin, and Reinhard Bendix. *Social Mobility in Industrial Society* (Berkeley, Calif.: University of California Press, 1966). Lipset and Bendix compare rates of social mobility in the United States with rates in other industrialized countries and clearly challenge the view that the United States is the most fluid and mobile society in the world.

Mayer, Kurt, and Walter Buckley. *Class and Society,* 3d ed. (New York: Random House, 1970). A short basic text covering the central issues in social stratification.

Reissman, Leonard. *Inequality in American Society* (Glenview, Ill.: Scott, Foresman, 1973).

Reissman discusses equality as a positive goal, some problems with equality, and the future of inequality. He discusses stratification produced by racial and economic differences.

Schnore, Leo F. *Class and Race in Cities and Suburbs* (Chicago: Markham, 1972). A short statistical study comparing the characteristics of city and suburban populations.

Shostak, Arthur. *Blue-Collar Life* (New York: Random House, 1969). An exhaustive study of the blue-collar or working class in America.

As mentioned in Chapter 5, there is an interesting series of books that explore the nature of power and influence in the United States. Among these are:

Domhoff, C. William. *The Higher Circles* (New York: Random House, 1970).

Domhoff, C. William. *Who Rules America* (Englewood Cliffs, N.J.: Prentice-Hall, 1967).

Keller, Suzanne. *Beyond the Ruling Class: Strategic Elites in Modern Society* (New York: Random House, 1963).

Mills, C. Wright. *The Power Elite* (New York: Oxford University Press, 1959).

Rose, Arnold. *The Power Structure* (New York: Oxford University Press, 1967).

There are a number of studies of the stratification in specific communities. For example, see:

Baltzell, E. Digby. *Philadelphia Gentlemen* (New York: Free Press, 1958).

Hollingshead, August. *Elmtown's Youth* (New York: Wiley, 1949).

Hunter, Floyd. *Community Power Structure* (Chapel Hill, N.C.: University of North Carolina Press, 1953).

Seeley, J. R., R. A. Sim, and E. W. Loosley. *Crestwood Heights* (New York: Wiley, 1963).

Warner, W. Lloyd, and Paul Lunt. *The Social Life of a Modern Community* (New Haven, Conn.: Yale University Press, 1941).

For further study of poverty and the welfare system in America, see:

Caplovitz, David. *The Poor Pay More* (New York: Free Press, 1963).

Harrington, Michael. *The Other America* (Baltimore: Penguin, 1962).

Ryan, William. *Blaming the Victim,* rev. ed. (New York: Random House, 1976).

Skolnick, Jerome, and Elliott Currie. *Crisis in American Institutions,* 3d ed. (Boston, Mass.: Little, Brown, 1976).

Turner, Jonathan, and Charles Starnes. *Inequality: Privilege & Poverty in America* (Pacific Palisades, Calif.: Goodyear, 1976).

Many novels use social class characteristics and life styles as a basic theme:

Marquand, John P. *Point of No Return* (New York: Little, Brown, 1949).

O'Hara, John, almost any work.

Schulberg, Budd. *What Makes Sammy Run?* (New York: Modern Library, 1952).

Wilson, Sloan. *Man in the Grey Flannel Suit* (New York: Simon & Schuster, 1955).

6: Social Differentiation: Race, Ethnicity, Sex, Age

Blau, Zena Smith. *Old Age in a Changing Society* (New York: New Viewpoints, 1973). A detailed analysis of the problems facing older people in a postindustrial society.

Brown, Claude. *Manchild in the Promised Land* (New York: Signet, 1966). An autobiography by a black who made it out of the slums of Harlem. Brown provides an insider's view of the black ghetto that is both brutal and humorous.

Brown, Dee. *Bury My Heart at Wounded Knee* (New York: Bantam/Holt, 1971). Describes how the American Indian was sacrificed to the doctrine of Manifest Destiny—the idea that whites are the dominant race and therefore destined to rule all of America.

De La Garza, Rudolph, Anthony Kruszewski, and Tomas Arciniega. *Chicanos and Native Americans: The Territorial Minorities* (Englewood Cliffs, N.J.: Prentice-Hall, 1973). A series of readings that examine the diverse social, educational, and governmental problems that affect Chicanos and Native Americans. The authors outline steps that can be taken to avoid continued confrontations and strife.

Frazier, E. Franklin. *Black Bourgeoisie* (New York: Free Press, 1957). An analysis of the frustrations and insecurities of a new middle class—American blacks.

Gans, Herbert J. *The Urban Villagers* (New York: Free Press, 1962). A participant observation study of Italian-Americans in Boston's West End.

Greer, Germaine. *The Female Eunuch* (New York: McGraw-Hill/Bantam, 1971). Greer's central thesis is that as wives, employees, mothers, and lovers, women are still body and soul in bondage to men and are deformed by them—made into eunuchs.

Knowles, Louis, and Kenneth Prewitt, eds. *Institutional Racism in American* (Englewood Cliffs, N.J.: Prentice-Hall, 1969). This book reveals how numerous institutions under white control deny blacks a relevant education, a voice in the political process, the right of economic self-determination, just treatment under the law, and decent health care.

Liebow, Elliot. *Tally's Corner* (Boston: Little, Brown, 1967). A participant observation study of lower-class black streetcorner men in Washington, D.C.

Millett, Kate. *Sexual Politics* (Garden City, N.Y.: Doubleday, 1970). Millett argues that the relationship between the sexes is and always has been a political one—a continuing power struggle in which women are sometimes idolized, other times patronized, always exploited.

Nava, Julian. *Viva La Raza!* (New York: Van Nostrand, 1973). An anthology designed to acquaint readers with the history and cultural past of the Mexican-American.

Rowbotham, Sheila. *Women, Resistance & Revolution* (New York: Random House, 1972). Rowbotham, a social historian, explores the relationship between feminism and social revolution and the varied historical forms that the attempt to change the position of women has taken in the West and in revolutionary countries such as China, the U.S.S.R., Cuba, Algeria, and Vietnam.

Silberman, Charles E. *Crisis in Black and White* (New York: Vintage, 1964). Highly acclaimed book that examines the situation of blacks in America. Silberman disputes the theories of some of the "authorities" and gives special attention to the problem of identification that confronts blacks.

Stoll, Clarice Stasz. *Female and Male* (Dubuque, Iowa: Wm. C. Brown, 1974). A study of sex roles, sexism in America and in social science, and the politics of gender. Discusses the process of socialization into female and male roles and the consequences.

Tavris, Carole, and Carole Offir. *The Longest War: Sex Differences in Perspective* (New York: Harcourt Brace Jovanovich, 1977). A detailed analysis of sex differences—evidence and explanations for them from a variety of theoretical perspectives.

Van Der Slik, Jack, ed. *Black Conflict with White America* (Columbus, Ohio: Merrill, 1970). Articles deal with competition, co-optation, confrontation, combat, and the future.

7: Institutions

The following books deal with various aspects of the institution of the family:

Billingsley, Andrew. *Black Families in White America* (Englewood Cliffs, N.J.: Prentice-Hall, 1968). An analysis of the history, structure, aspirations, and problems of black families in a white-controlled society.

Cuber, John F., and Peggy B. Harroff. *Sex and the Significant Americans* (Baltimore: Penguin, 1965). The authors describe five categories of marital adjustment that they discovered when they interviewed 437 upper-middle-class men and women.

Delora, Joann S., and Jack Delora, eds. *Intimate Life Styles: Marriage and Its Alternatives* (Pacific Palisades, Calif.: Goodyear, 1972). The articles in this book analyze traditional forms of courtship and marriage in the United States along with emerging patterns of interaction involving intimacy and sex. Predictions are made regarding forms that sexual and erotic behavior will take in the future.

Goode, William J. *The Family* (Englewood Cliffs, N.J.: Prentice-Hall, 1964). A theoretical treatment of the family, dealing with mate selection, illegitimacy, family roles, and divorce.

Gordon, Michael, ed. *The Nuclear Family in Crisis: The Search for an Alternative* (New York: Harper & Row, 1972). The articles in this book deal with the family in the kibbutz, the family in socialist and welfare nations, and the current communal movement and group marriage.

Spiro, Melford E. *Children of the Kibbutz* (New York: Schocken Books, 1965). A study of child training and personality on an Israeli kibbutz, where children are raised by the community.

The following books deal with aspects of the institution of religion:

Berger, Peter. *A Rumor of Angels* (New York: Doubleday, 1970). Sociologist Berger attempts to deal with the question of whether theological thinking is possible at all today, and, if it is, in what way.

Greeley, Andrew M. *The Denominational Society* (Glenview, Ill.: Scott, Foresman, 1972). A thorough study of religion in the United States with a good sprinkling of statistical data. Deals with traditional topics such as the nature, origins, and functions of religion and the characteristics of religious organizations. Also covers religion as an ethnic phenomenon, diversity within unity, the secularization myth, prejudice and conflict, and predictions for the future.

Hadden, Jeffrey K. *The Gathering Storm in the Churches* (New York: Doubleday, 1970). Hadden describes the growing conflict between the clergy and the laiety that threatens the traditional role and influence of the church in a modern secular world.

Heenan, Edward, ed. *Mystery, Magic, and Miracle: Religion in a Post-Aquarian Age* (Englewood Cliffs, N.J.: Prentice-Hall, 1973). A chronicle of the varieties of religious experience in the 1970s from the "cabalistic cult of Satanism to the fusion of religion and rock music, from the Americanization of Eastern mysticism to the exuberant exhortations of the Jesus freaks." Heenan analyzes the future of this modern religious revival by means of the elements of mystery, magic, and miracle.

Herberg, Will. *Protestant-Catholic-Jew* (New York: Doubleday, 1960). An interesting analysis of the religions of America.

McNamara, Patrick H., ed. *Religion American Style* (New York: Harper & Row, 1974). A recent book of readings that discuss the role of religion in society, religious organizations, religion and social conflict, and religion and social change.

8: Population and Ecology

Brown, Harrison, and Edward Hutchings, Jr., eds. *Are Our Descendants Doomed?* (New York: Viking, 1972). This collection of papers resulted from a conference at Cal Tech and deals with the problems of rapid population growth, the distribution of human population, technological change, economic development, the environment, and the individual desires of human beings.

Ehrlich, Paul. *The Population Bomb* (New York: Ballantine, 1968). Biologist Ehrlich describes the crisis of overpopulation that faces us and evaluates our prospects of surviving it.

Petersen, William. *The Politics of Population* (Garden City, N.Y.: Anchor Books, 1964). A series of essays by a population expert on how population relates to social policy, especially in such fields as social welfare, urban planning, and international migration. Also examines the theories of Malthus, Marx, and Keynes.

Pohlman, Edward, ed. *Population: A Clash of Prophets* (New York: Mentor, 1973). Readings —mostly from popular sources—on the population question. Includes a section on Third World reactions to population issues.

Robertson, James and Carolyn. *The Small Towns Book* (Garden City, N.Y.: Anchor Books, 1978). Describes the migration of Americans back to small towns, the resulting pressures on small towns, and how a few small towns have attempted to confront these pressures.

Scientific American, September 1974. The whole issue is devoted to population.

Stanford, Quentin H., ed. *The World's Population* (New York: Oxford University Press, 1972). A text that provides world population data, considers the roots of the population crisis, and discusses solutions.

Vidich, Arthur, and Joseph Bensman. *Small Town in Mass Society* (Garden City, N.Y.: Doubleday, 1958). A study of a small rural community striving to maintain its own identity in a mass society.

Warner, Sam Bass, Jr. *The Urban Wilderness* (New York: Harper & Row, 1972). An interesting book describing the historical development of the American city.

Weber, Max. *The City* (New York: Free Press, 1958). A classic sociological analysis of the development of cities in Western civilization.

Wrong, Dennis. *Population and Society,* 2d ed. (New York: Random House, 1961). A short basic text dealing with population concepts and variables.

A number of books analyze the problems of the city: urban sprawl, urban renewal, race and class conflict, municipal services, overcrowding, ugliness, mass transit, and so on. The following are among the best:

Banfield, Edward. *The Unheavenly City* (Boston: Little, Brown, 1970).

Banfield, Edward. *The Unheavenly City Revisited* (Boston: Little, Brown 1974).

Breines, Simon, and William J. Dean. *The Pedestrian Revolution* (New York: Random House, 1974).

Downs, Anthony. *Urban Problems and Prospects* (Chicago: Markham, 1970).

Gabree, John, ed. *Surviving the City* (New York: Ballantine, 1973).

Gordon, Mitchell. *Sick Cities* (Baltimore: Penguin, 1963).

Haar, Charles M., ed. *The End of Innocence: A Suburban Reader* (Glenview, Ill.: Scott, Foresman, 1972).

Jacobs, Jane. *The Death and Life of Great American Cities* (New York: Vintage, 1961).

Starr, Roger. *Urban Choices* (Baltimore: Penguin, 1966).

9: Social Change and Social Disorganization

Gusfield, Joseph R., ed. *Protest, Reform, and Revolt: A Reader in Social Movements* (New York: Wiley, 1970). An excellent sourcebook on all aspects of social movements.

Hoffer, Eric. *The True Believer* (New York: Harper & Row, 1951). The most famous of Hoffer's books deals with mass movements from the viewpoint of the true believer, the man compelled to join a cause, any cause.

Hoffer, Eric. *The Ordeal of Change* (New York: Harper & Row, 1964). An interesting if somewhat one-sided analysis of the causes and consequences of social change by the longshoreman-philosopher.

King, C. Wendell. *Social Movements in the United States* (New York: Random House, 1956). A short but thorough analysis of social movements, including their relationships to mass society, their careers, growth factors, and purposes and consequences.

Lauer, Robert H. *Perspectives on Social Change* (Boston: Allyn and Bacon, 1973). A comprehensive look at questions of youth and change, violence and change, and strategies for effecting change. Lauer discusses the various theories of social change as well as mechanisms and patterns of change.

Moore, Wilbert E. *Social Change* (Englewood Cliffs, N.J.: Prentice-Hall, 1963). A short but comprehensive sociological analysis of social change.

Roberts, Ron, and Robert Kloss. *Social Movements*, 2d ed. (St. Louis, Mo.: Mosby, 1979). A text on social movements.

Slater, Philip. *The Pursuit of Loneliness* (Boston: Beacon Press, 1970). Slater focuses on our subservience to technology and the disastrous effect this attitude is having on the quality of life in the United States. He suggests some ways that American society might be changed to avoid even further alienation and disaffection.

Toffler, Alvin. *Future Shock* (New York: Random House/Bantam, 1970). Toffler discusses the social and psychological implications of the technological revolution—the problems of people and groups who are overwhelmed by change in the emerging superindustrial world.

Books making projections about social change of the future include:

McGee, Reece. *Social Disorganization in America* (San Francisco: Chandler, 1962). McGee analyzes the disorganized individual, the disorganized group, the disorganized organization, and the disorganized society. He sees social disorganization as arising from two conditions: group conflict and anomie. He also provides an excellent short summary of Meadian social psychology.

Phillips, Bernard S. *Worlds of the Future* (Columbus, Ohio: Merrill, 1972).

10: Collective Behavior

Berk, Richard A. *Collective Behavior* (Dubuque, Iowa: Wm. C. Brown, 1974). A short and concise overview of the sociology of collective behavior. Attention is given to methodological issues, outdated theories, and recent developments in theory and research.

Cantril, Hadley. *The Invasion from Mars* (New York: Harper & Row, 1940). A study of the collective behavior, rumor, mass communication, and panic that resulted from Orson Welles' 1938 radio dramatization of *The War of the Worlds.*

Chaplin, J. P. *Rumor, Fear and the Madness of Crowds* (New York: Ballantine, 1959). Chaplin describes in detail eleven instances of mass collective behavior, including examples of mass hysteria, rumor, crowd, mob, and riot behavior. The cases range from the death of Valentino to Martians in New Jersey, from flying saucers to high treason in the State Department.

Evans, Robert R., ed. *Readings in Collective Behavior*, 2d ed. (Chicago: Rand McNally, 1975). These readings describe a number of collective behavior research projects on such topics as disaster research, analyses of protests, and the testing of selected theories.

Hersey, John. *Hiroshima* (New York: Bantam, 1959). A journalistic account of the dropping of an atomic bomb. A fascinating and horrifying description of the process and aftermath of a disaster.

Report of the National Advisory Commission on Civil Disorders (New York: Bantam, 1968). The report of the Kerner Commission provides a comprehensive analysis of the riots that occurred in the United States during the summer of 1967.

Schultz, Duane. *Panic Behavior* (New York: Random House, 1964). A comprehensive analysis of panic, including a discussion of a number of theories of panic behavior in relation to actual disaster situations.

Skolnick, Jerome. *The Politics of Protest* (New York: Ballantine, 1969). The last chapter of this report of the National Commission on the Causes and Prevention of Violence provides an excellent short analysis of collective behavior concepts.

11: Deviation and Social Control

Becker, Howard S., ed. *The Other Side* (New York: Free Press, 1964). A series of essays by authors who, like Becker, use the labeling perspective to explain deviant behavior. The essays, which deal with a variety of types of deviant behavior, generally follow the proposition that deviance is a product of group definitions, not a product of something inherent in the act itself.

Clark, Ramsey. *Crime in America* (New York: Pocket Books, 1970). Straightforward and easy-to-read observations on the nature, causes, prevention, and control of crime in America by the former attorney general.

Erikson, Kai. *Wayward Puritans* (New York: Wiley, 1966). Erikson applies current theories of deviant behavior to the seventeenth-century Puritans of Massachusetts Bay. Using historical documents, he illustrates how deviant behavior served to define social boundaries and to help keep the social order intact. Crime statistics are analyzed to demonstrate that, even for the Puritans, the number of deviant offenders a community can afford to recognize is likely to remain fairly stable over time.

McCaghy, Charles H. *Deviant Behavior* (New York: Macmillan, 1976). A text covering the various theories of deviant behavior, personal and property crime, white-collar crime by individuals and by organizations, drug use, mental disorders, and sexual deviance.

Reiman, Jeffrey. *The Rich Get Richer and the Poor Get Prison* (New York: Wiley, 1979). The American criminal justice system has failed according to Reiman because of the system's economic bias. Its failure will persist because the wealthy and powerful want it to. The author also examines the dangers of "noncriminal" acts, ignored by the criminal justice system.

Rubington, Earl, and Martin Weinberg. *Deviance: The Interactionist Perspective,* 3d ed. (New York: Macmillan, 1978). Readings on the interactionist or labeling perspective with sections on the social deviant, the public regulation of deviance, deviant subcultures, and deviant identity.

The following selections present good analyses of social control agencies, such as the police and prison systems:

Niederhoffer, Arthur. *Behind the Shield* (Garden City, N.Y.: Doubleday, 1967). Niederhoffer, a former member of the New York City police, describes the profession. He calls special attention to some attitudes—authoritarianism and cynicism—that police officers develop.

Sykes, Gresham M. *The Society of Captives* (New York: Atheneum, 1958). A short but thorough analysis of an American maximum-security prison.

Wambaugh, Joseph. *The New Centurions* (Boston: Little, Brown, 1970). An interesting novel on police work during the time of the Watts riots, written by a Los Angeles police officer.

Wilson, James Q. *Varieties of Police Behavior* (New York: Atheneum, 1970). Wilson studies communities in the United States, identifies the major problems that police agencies face, and describes three styles of police behavior that seem to emerge.

There are numerous good analyses of specific types of criminal and deviant behavior:

Cressey, Donald. *Other People's Money* (Belmont, Calif.: Wadsworth, 1971).

Greenwald, Harold. *The Elegant Prostitute* (New York: Ballantine, 1970).

Ianni, Francis. *A Family Business* (New York: Mentor, 1972).

Jackson, Bruce. *Outside the Law: A Thief's Primer* (New Brunswick, N.J.: Transaction Books, 1972).

Maas, Peter. *The Valachi Papers* (New York: Bantam, 1968).

Maris, Ronald. *Social Forces in Urban Suicide* (Homewood, Ill.: Dorsey, 1969).

Sutherland, Edwin. *White Collar Crime* (New York: Holt, 1949).

Talese, Gay. *Honor Thy Father* (Greenwich, Conn.: Fawcett-Crest, 1971).

Thompson, Hunter. *Hell's Angels* (New York: Ballantine, 1966).

Wallace, Samuel. *Skid Row as a Way of Life* (New York: Harper & Row, 1965).

12: What Is Sociology?

Berger, Peter L. *Invitation to Sociology* (Garden City, N.Y.: Doubleday, 1963). For Berger, sociology is a form of consciousness. This consciousness determines how sociologists behave and how they see the world. In describing what sociology is, Berger's focus is the humanistic perspective.

Cuzzort, R. P., and E. W. King. *Humanity and Modern Social Thought,* 2d ed. (Hinsdale, Ill.: Dryden Press, 1976). An interesting discussion of the major works of fifteen social scientists who have contributed to social thought and the discipline of sociology, including Durkheim, Weber, Marx, Freud, Mills, Becker, Merton, and Goffman.

Mills, C. Wright. *The Sociological Imagination* (New York: Grove Press, 1961). Mills provides a searching critique and analysis of what sociology is and what it should be. He challenges the approaches represented by "grand theorists" and "abstracted empiricists" and describes the perspective and approach that he feels best embodies the sociological imagination.

The following two books are collections of essays that evaluate and criticize sociology from a variety of viewpoints:

Douglas, Jack, ed. *The Relevance of Sociology* (New York: Appleton-Century-Crofts, 1970).

Reynolds, Larry, and Janice Reynolds, eds. *The Sociology of Sociology* (New York: McKay, 1970).

It is often helpful to look at the journals of a discipline to get further insight into its nature. Sociology journals include the *American Journal of Sociology,* the *American Sociological Review, Social Forces, Social Problems,* and *Sociometry.* But look especially at *The American Sociologist,* which tends to give an internal view, showing a sociology of sociology.

Index